Philosophy: The Big Questions

Philosophy: The Big Questions

Series Editor: James P. Sterba, University of Notre Dame, Indiana

Designed to elicit a philosophical response in the mind of the student, this distinctive series of anthologies provides essential classical and contemporary readings that serve to make the central questions of philosophy come alive for today's students. It presents complete coverage of the Anglo-American tradition of philosophy as well as the kinds of questions and challenges that it confronts today, both from other cultural traditions and from theoretical movements such as feminism and postmodernism.

Aesthetics: The Big Questions
Edited by Carolyn Korsmeyer

Epistemology: The Big Questions
Edited by Linda Martín Alcoff

Ethics: The Big Questions
Edited by James P. Sterba

Metaphysics: The Big Questions
Edited by Peter van Inwagen and Dean W. Zimmerman

Philosophy of Language: The Big Questions
Edited by Andrea Nye

Philosophy of Religion: The Big Questions
Edited by Eleonore Stump and Michael J. Murray

Race, Class, Gender, and Sexuality: The Big Questions
Edited by Naomi Zack, Laurie Shrage, and Crispin Sartwell

Philosophy: The Big Questions
Edited by Ruth J. Sample, Charles W. Mills, and James P. Sterba

PHILOSOPHY:

The Big Questions

EDITED BY RUTH J. SAMPLE, CHARLES W. MILLS,
AND JAMES P. STERBA

Blackwell
Publishing

Editorial material and organization © 2004 by Blackwell Publishing Ltd

BLACKWELL PUBLISHING
350 Main Street, Malden, MA 02148-5020, USA
9600 Garsington Road, Oxford OX4 2DQ, UK
550 Swanston Street, Carlton, Victoria 3053, Australia

First published 2004 by Blackwell Publishing Ltd

2   2006

Library of Congress Cataloging-in-Publication Data

Philosophy : the big questions / edited by Ruth J. Sample, Charles W. Mills, and James P. Sterba.
        p.   cm. — (Philosophy, the big questions)
Includes bibliographical references and index.
    ISBN 1-4051-0828-2 (alk. paper) — ISBN 1-4051-0827-4 (pbk. : alk. paper)
    1. Philosophy—Introductions.   I. Sample, Ruth J., 1964–   II. Mills, Charles W. (Charles Wade)   III. Sterba, James P.   IV. Series.

    B21.P57 2004
    100—dc21

                                            2003011348

ISBN-13: 978-1-4051-0828-7 (alk. paper) — ISBN-13: 978-1-4051-0828-0 (pbk. : alk. paper)

A catalogue record for this title is available from the British Library.

Set in 9.5 on 12 pt Galliard
by SNP Best-set Typesetter Ltd., Hong Kong
Printed and bound in the United Kingdom
by TJ International, Padstow, Cornwall

The publisher's policy is to use permanent paper from mills that operate a sustainable forestry policy, and which has been manufactured from pulp processed using acid-free and elementary chlorine-free practices. Furthermore, the publisher ensures that the text paper and cover board used have met acceptable environmental accreditation standards.

For further information on
Blackwell Publishing, visit our website:
http://www.blackwellpublishing.com

CONTENTS

Preface   ix

Acknowledgments   xi

PART ONE   WHAT CAN WE KNOW?   1

Introduction   3

1   From *Meditations on First Philosophy*   6
RENÉ DESCARTES

2   From *An Enquiry Concerning Human Understanding*   34
DAVID HUME

3   Cartesian Skepticism and Inference to the Best Explanation   64
JONATHAN VOGEL

4   From *Science as Social Knowledge*   71
HELEN LONGINO

5   The 'Maleness' of Reason   78
GENEVIEVE LLOYD

6   The Ethics of Belief   83
WILLIAM CLIFFORD

7   It is Wrong, Everywhere, Always, and for Anyone,
to Believe Anything upon Insufficient Evidence   87
PETER VAN INWAGEN

Epistemology: Suggestions for Further Reading   99

PART TWO   WHAT CAN WE KNOW ABOUT THE NATURE AND EXISTENCE OF GOD?   101

Introduction   103

8   From *Proslogium*   106
ST. ANSELM

9   In Behalf of the Fool: An Answer to the Argument of Anselm
in the *Proslogium*   107
GAUNILO

10   The Ontological Argument   111
WILLIAM L. ROWE

11   The Cosmological Argument   123
     WILLIAM L. ROWE

12   From *Dialogues Concerning Natural Religion*   133
     DAVID HUME

13   The Argument from Design   141
     R. G. SWINBURNE

14   The Wager   151
     BLAISE PASCAL

15   The Recombinant DNA Debate: A Difficulty for Pascalian-Style Wagering   154
     STEPHEN P. STICH

16   A Central Theistic Argument   155
     GEORGE SCHLESINGER

17   Evil and Omnipotence   167
     J. L. MACKIE

18   The Problem of Evil   176
     ELEONORE STUMP

19   Male-Chauvinist Religion   190
     DEBORAH MATHIEU

20   Divine Racism: A Philosophical and Theological Analysis   201
     WILLIAM R. JONES

Religion: Suggestions for Further Reading   212

PART THREE   ARE WE EVER FREE?

                                                                                  213

Introduction   215

21   From *The System of Nature*   218
     PAUL HOLBACH

22   Freedom and Necessity   225
     A. J. AYER

23   Human Freedom and the Self   231
     RODERICK M. CHISHOLM

24   Alternate Possibilities and Moral Responsibility   239
     HARRY G. FRANKFURT

25   How to Complete the Compatibilist Account of Free Action   246
     JAMES P. STERBA AND JANET A. KOURANY

26   Living without Free Will: The Case for Hard Incompatibilism   257
     DERK PEREBOOM

27   Metaethics, Metaphilosophy, and Free Will Subjectivism   267
     RICHARD DOUBLE

Freedom and Determinism: Suggestions for Further Reading   276

PART FOUR DOES OUR EXISTENCE HAVE A MEANING OR PURPOSE?

277

Introduction 279
28 From *My Confession* 281
    LEO TOLSTOY
29 The Absurdity of Life without God 288
    WILLIAM LANE CRAIG
30 On the Vanity of Existence 302
    ARTHUR SCHOPENHAUER
31 An Absurd Reasoning 305
    ALBERT CAMUS
32 Existentialism Is a Humanism 313
    JEAN-PAUL SARTRE
33 The Absurd 322
    THOMAS NAGEL
34 What Makes Life Worth Living? 330
    OWEN FLANAGAN
35 The Meaning of Life 337
    JOHN KEKES
36 Tolstoi and the Meaning of Life 353
    ANTHONY FLEW
The Meaning of Life: Suggestions for Further Reading 361

PART FIVE HOW SHOULD WE LIVE?

363

Introduction 365
37 Morality as Good in Itself 367
    PLATO
38 The Problem of Rationality: Is Morality Rationally Required? 374
    JAMES P. STERBA
39 From *Utilitarianism* 383
    JOHN STUART MILL
40 Fundamental Principles of the Metaphysic of Morals 399
    IMMANUEL KANT
41 From *Two Treatises of Government* 414
    JOHN LOCKE
42 From *A Theory of Justice* 421
    JOHN RAWLS
43 Distributive Justice 445
    ROBERT NOZICK
44 Gender Inequality and Cultural Difference 455
    SUSAN MOLLER OKIN
45 Race/Gender and the Ethics of Difference 470
    JANE FLAX
46 A Response to Jane Flax 478
    SUSAN MOLLER OKIN

CONTENTS

47 Equality, Discrimination and Preferential Treatment   482
    BERNARD R. BOXILL
48 All Animals Are Equal . . .   490
    PETER SINGER
49 The Ethics of Respect for Nature   505
    PAUL W. TAYLOR

Ethics: Suggestions for Further Reading   519

Index   520

PREFACE

Philosophers attempt to understand the basic structure of reality. Questions about the nature of reality are Big Questions. Clearly, adequately answering them is a massive undertaking, and few people will pretend to have succeeded. Nonetheless, many have found it worthwhile and even exhilarating to try. As professors of philosophy we have made the challenges of philosophy our life's work, and part of that work has been to keep the love of philosophical inquiry alive in our students. We hope this collection contributes to that end.

This volume contains a selection of philosophical readings from the Western tradition. Readers may be surprised to discover just how many Big Questions there are. We group them into five major topics. First, there are questions about the nature and scope of human knowledge. How much, if anything, can we really know about reality, and what is knowledge itself? What kinds of beliefs are we warranted in accepting? Second, there are questions pertaining to religious reality and experience. Is there a God, and if so, what is God's nature? Why is there evil when God is supposed to be morally perfect? Third, philosophers want to know whether human agency is as free as it often appears to be. Do human beings really freely choose to do what they do, or is free will an illusion? If there is no free will, does that mean that we are not responsible for the things we appear to choose to do? Fourth, nearly everyone has wondered whether life is meaningless. Does life have a meaning, or is the whole thing pointless? What, if anything, could make a life meaningful? Fifth, and for many people most importantly, what is the nature of right conduct and the good life for us? Are humans the only members of the moral domain, or should animals, other creatures, and even the environment itself have moral standing? How would a just society be organized?

Such questions do not exhaust the range of philosophical inquiry; nor do they plumb its depths. We do not address non-Western philosophical writing, which has a very different character. We have omitted many important philosophical works that would be too challenging for beginners or rely on a complex and unfamiliar vocabulary. We have tried to include a range of readings that is broader than many contemporary texts, which often neglect the influence of the existentialists, feminists, and multiculturalists. At the same time, the readings we present here are clear and accessible, even though they are challenging. No previous experience with philosophy is necessary to appreciate them.

Philosophers live in the domain of giving and asking for reasons. It is important to master the views of the philosophers that we discuss. Yet it is equally important to respond to those views with reasons for agreeing or disagreeing. Any good first course in philosophy will require students to do some of both. We find both of these aspects of philosophizing fascinating, engaging, and intellectually satisfying. We hope that our readers will too.

We would like to thank our students, who inspire us to ask these timeless Big Questions and make them new again. We are indebted to our very capable and tireless research assistants Erica Brown and Kim Jarvis. We are grateful as well for financial support provided by Marilyn Hoskin, Dean of Liberal Arts, who authorized a generous gift from the Alumni Fund of the University of New Hampshire, as well as for funding provided by the Philosophy Department. Jeff Dean at Blackwell Publishing provided us with valuable guidance and editorial assistance. Finally, Ruth Sample would like to express her personal indebtedness to her colleagues in the Philosophy Department, to Dean Rubine, Margaret Love Denman, and to Cathy Frierson for the encouragement, support, and advice that helped this project to fruition.

RUTH J. SAMPLE
CHARLES W. MILLS
JAMES P. STERBA

ACKNOWLEDGMENTS

The editors and publisher gratefully acknowledge the permission granted to reproduce the copyright material in this book:

1. René Descartes, from *Meditations on First Philosophy*, revised edn, edited and translated by John Cottingham (Cambridge: Cambridge University Press, 1986), pp. 9–36 and 50–62. Reprinted with the permission of Cambridge University Press.
2. David Hume, *An Enquiry Concerning Human Understanding*, Sections II–VII. Public domain. First published in 1748.
3. Jonathan Vogel, "Cartesian Skepticism and Inference to the Best Explanation," *The Journal of Philosophy*, 87 (November 1990), pp. 658–66. Reprinted with permission of The Journal of Philosophy and Jonathan Vogel.
4. Helen Longino, from *Science as Social Knowledge* (Princeton, NJ: Princeton University Press, 1990), pp. 4–12. © 1990 by Princeton University Press.
5. Genevieve Lloyd, "The 'Maleness' of Reason," from *The Man of Reason* (University of Minnesota Press, 1984), pp. 103–10. Reprinted with permission.
6. W. K. Clifford, "The Ethics of Belief," from *Lectures and Essays* (New York: Macmillan, 1901), pp. 163–76.
7. Peter van Inwagen, "It Is Wrong, Everywhere, Always, and for Anyone, to Believe Anything upon Insufficient Evidence," from Jeff Jordan and Daniel Howard-Snyder (eds.), *Faith, Freedom and Rationality: Philosophy of Religion Today.* (Lanham, MD: Rowman & Littlefield, 1996), pp. 137–53. Reprinted with permission.
8. St. Anselm, *Proslogium*, chapters II and II, from "Proslogium," in *St. Anselm: Basic Writings*, 2nd edn, translated by S. N. Deane (Chicago: Open Court, 1962), pp. 53–5. Reprinted by permission of Open Court Publishing Company, a division of Carus Publishing Company, Peru, IL, © 1962 by Open Court Publishing Company.
9. Gaunilo, "In Behalf of the Fool: An Answer to the Argument of Anselm in the Proslogium," from *St. Anselm: Basic Writings*, 2nd edn, translated by S. N. Deane. (Chicago: Open Court, 1962), pp. 303–11. Reprinted by permission of Open Court Publishing Company, a division of Carus Publishing Company, Peru, IL, © 1962 by Open Court Publishing Company.
10. William L. Rowe, "The Ontological Argument," from Joel Feinberg (ed.), *Reason and Responsibility: Readings in Some Basic Problems of Philosophy*, 8th edn (Belmont, CA: Wadsworth, 1993), pp. 8–17. © 1974 by William L. Rowe. Reprinted with

permission. This essay was originally commissioned expressly for the third edition of the Wadsworth anthology.

11. William L. Rowe, "The Cosmological Argument," from *Philosophy of Religion: An Introduction*, 1st edn (Belmont, CA: Wadsworth, 1978), pp. 16–29. © 1978. Reprinted with permission of Wadsworth, an imprint of the Wadsworth Group, a division of Thomson Learning.

12. David Hume, extracts from *Dialogues Concerning Natural Religion*, Parts II and V. Public domain. First published in 1779.

13. R. G. Swinburne, "The Argument from Design," *Philosophy*, 43 (July 1968), pp. 199–212. © 1968 by Royal Institute of Philosophy. Reprinted with the permission of Cambridge University Press.

14. Blaise Pascal, "The Wager," from *Pensées and Other Writings*, translated by Honor Levi, with an introduction and notes by Anthony Levi, World's Classics (Oxford: Oxford University Press, 1995), pp. 153–6. Translation © 1995 by Honor Levi Reprinted by permission of Oxford University Press.

15. Stephen P. Stich, from "The Recombinant DNA Debate: A Difficulty for Pascalian-Style Wagering," *Philosophy and Public Affairs*, 7/3 (1978), pp. 189–91. © 1978 by Princeton University Press. Reprinted by permission.

16. George Schlesinger, "A Central Theistic Argument," from Jeff Jordan (ed.), *Gambling on God: Essays on Pascal's Wager* (Lanham, MD: Rowman & Littlefield, 1994), pp. 83–99. Reprinted with permission.

17. J. L. Mackie, "Evil and Omnipotence," *Mind*, NS 64 (April 1955), pp. 200–12. Reprinted by permission of Oxford University Press.

18. Eleonore Stump, from "The Problem of Evil," *Faith and Philosophy*, 2/4 (1985), pp. 392–5, 397–8, 406–15, and 417–18. Reprinted with permission.

19. Deborah Mathieu, "Male-Chauvinist Religion," from Joel Feinberg and Russ Shafer-Landau (eds), *Reason and Responsibility*, 11th edn (Belmont, CA: Wadsworth, 2002), pp. 80–9. Reprinted with permission.

20. William R. Jones, from *Is God a White Racist? A Preamble to Black Theology* (Garden City, NY: Anchor Press/Doubleday, 1973), pp. 3–23 and 77–8.

21. Paul Holbach, extracts from *The System of Nature: Laws of the Moral and Physical World*, translated by H. D. Robinson (Boston, MA: J. P. Mendum, 1889), chapter XI.

22. A. J. Ayer, "Freedom and Necessity," from *Philosophical Essays* (London: Macmillan and New York: St. Martin's Press, 1954), pp. 271–84. Reprinted with permission of Bedford/St. Martin's.

23. Roderick M. Chisholm, "Human Freedom and the Self," from John Bricke (ed.), *Freedom and Morality: The Lindley Lectures* (Lawrence: University of Kansas, 1976), pp. 23–35. Reprinted with permission. This essay was originally delivered as an E. H. Lindley Lecture at the University of Kansas in 1964.

24. Harry G. Frankfurt, "Alternate Possibilities and Moral Responsibility," *The Journal of Philosophy*, 66/23 (December 4, 1969), pp. 829–39. Reprinted with permission of The Journal of Philosophy and Harry Frankfurt.

25. James P. Sterba and Janet A. Kourany, "How to Complete the Compatibilist Account of Free Action," *Philosophy and Phenomenological Research*, 41/4 (1981), pp. 508–23. Reprinted with permission.

26. Derk Pereboom, "Living Without Free Will: The Case for Hard Incompatibilism," from Robert Kane (ed.), *Oxford Handbook of Free Will* (Oxford: Oxford University

Press, 2002), pp. 477–88. © 2001 by Robert Kane. Used by permission of Oxford University Press, Inc.

27. Richard Double, "Metaethics, Metaphilosophy, and Free Will Subjectivism," from Robert Kane (ed.), *Oxford Handbook of Free Will* (Oxford: Oxford University Press, 2002), pp. 507–16 and 525. © 2001 by Robert Kane. Used by permission of Oxford University Press, Inc.

28. Leo Tolstoy, from *My Confession*, translated by Leo Wierner (London: J. M. Dent, 1905), pp. 11–20.

29. William Lane Craig, "The Absurdity of Life Without God," from *Reasonable Faith: Christian Truth and Apologetics* (Wheaton, ILL: Crossway Books), pp. 57–75. © 1984. Used by permission of Good News Publishers/Crossway Books, Wheaton, Illinois 60187, www.crosswaybooks.org.

30. Arthur Schopenhauer, "On the Vanity of Existence," from *Essays and Aphorisms*, translated by R. J. Hollingdale (Penguin, 1970). Translation © 1970 by R. J. Hollingdale. Reproduced by permission of Penguin Books Ltd.

31. Albert Camus, from *The Myth of Sisyphus and Other Essays*, translated by Justin O'Brien (New York: Alfred A. Knopf, 1955), pp. 3–9, 12–16, 21, 28–30, and 51–5. © 1955 by Alfred A. Knopf, a division of Random House Inc. Used by permission.

32. Jean-Paul Sartre, extracts from *Existentialism*, translated by Bernard Frechtman (New York: Philosophical Library, 1947), pp. 11–38 and 59–61. © 1947 by The Philosophical Library Inc.

33. Thomas Nagel, "The Absurd," *The Journal of Philosophy*, 68 (1971), pp. 716–27. Reprinted with permission of The Journal of Philosophy and Thomas Nagel.

34. Owen Flanagan, "What Makes Life Worth Living?", from *Self Expressions: Mind, Morals, and the Meaning of Life* (Oxford: Oxford University Press, 1996), pp. 3–11. © 1996 by Oxford University Press Inc. Used by permission of Oxford University Press Inc.

35. John Kekes, "The Meaning of Life," *Midwest Studies in Philosophy*, 24 (2000), pp. 17–34. Reprinted with permission.

36. Antony Flew, "Tolstoi and the Meaning of Life," *Ethics*, 73 (1963), pp. 110–18. Reprinted by permission of the University of Chicago Press.

37. Plato, "Morality as Good in Itself," from *The Republic*, Book II. Public domain.

38. James P. Sterba, from *Three Challenges to Ethics: Environmentalism, Feminism, and Multiculturalism* (New York: Oxford University Press, 2001), pp. 5–19. © 2001 by Oxford University Press Inc. Used by permission of Oxford University Press Inc.

39. John Stuart Mill, extracts from chapters I, II, and IV of *Utilitarianism*. First published in 1863. Public domain.

40. Immanuel Kant, "Fundamental Principles of the Metaphysic of Morals," from *Kant's Critique of Practical Reason and Other Works on the Theory of Ethics*, 6th edn, translated by Thomas Kingsmill Abbott (London: Longman, 1909), pp. 9–22 and 29–59.

41. John Locke, from *Two Treatises of Government*, Part II, sections 4, 6, 7, 10, 25–38, and 51. First published in 1690. Public domain.

42. John Rawls, from *A Theory of Justice* (Cambridge, MA: The Belknap Press of Harvard University Press, 1971), pp. 3–22, 60–5, 150–6, 251–7, and 302–3. © 1971, 1999 by the President and Fellows of Harvard College. Reprinted by permission of the publisher.

43. Robert Nozick, "Distributive Justice," from *Anarchy, State, and Utopia* (New York: Basic Books, 1974), pp. 149–64. © 1974 by Basic Books Inc. Reprinted by permission of Basic Books, a member of Perseus Books, L.L.C.

44. Susan Moller Okin, "Gender Inequality and Cultural Difference," *Political Theory*, 22/1 (February 1994), pp. 5–24. Reprinted by permission of Sage Publications.

45. Jane Flax, "Race/Gender and the Ethics of Difference," *Political Theory*, 23/3 (August 1995), pp. 500–10. Reprinted by permission of Sage Publications.

46. Susan Moller Okin, "A Response to Jane Flax," *Political Theory*, 23/3 (August 1995), pp. 511–16. Reprinted by permission of Sage Publications.

47. Bernard R. Boxill, "Equality, Discrimination and Preferential Treatment," from Peter Singer (ed.), *A Companion to Ethics* (Oxford: Blackwell, 1991), pp. 333–42. Reprinted with permission.

48. Peter Singer, "All Animals Are Equal . . .", from *Animal Liberation*, 2nd edn (New York: New York Review, 1990), pp. 1–23. © 1990 by Peter Singer.

49. Paul W. Taylor, "The Ethics of Respect for Nature," *Environmental Ethics*, 3:3 (1981), pp. 197–218.

Every effort has been made to trace copyright holders and to obtain their permission for the use of copyright material. The publisher apologizes for any errors or omissions in the above list and would be grateful if notified of any corrections that should be incorporated in future reprints or editions of this book.

PART ONE

WHAT CAN WE KNOW?

Introduction

1 From *Meditations on First Philosophy*
 RENÉ DESCARTES

2 From *An Enquiry Concerning Human Understanding*
 DAVID HUME

3 Cartesian Skepticism and Inference to the Best Explanation
 JONATHAN VOGEL

4 From *Science as Social Knowledge*
 HELEN LONGINO

5 The 'Maleness' of Reason
 GENEVIEVE LLOYD

6 The Ethics of Belief
 WILLIAM CLIFFORD

7 It is Wrong, Everywhere, Always, and for Anyone, to Believe
 Anything upon Insufficient Evidence
 PETER VAN INWAGEN

Epistemology: Suggestions for Further Reading

Introduction

We have all had the experience of thinking that we knew something, and later discovering – perhaps to our shock – that what we thought we knew was actually false, so that though we believed it, we didn't actually *know* it after all. Reflecting on such mistakes, and wondering why we got it wrong, may lead us to ask deeper questions: what is the difference between knowledge and belief? what are the sources of our knowledge? when are we justified in believing something? when are we justified in claiming that we actually know something? and what in general constitutes good cognitive practice?

Epistemology is that branch of philosophy concerned with the issue of knowledge. It does not deal with *particular* branches of knowledge (history, physics, geology, etc.) but with the concept of knowledge in *general*, knowledge in the abstract, and its distinctive characteristics. Epistemology tries to set out the norms for determining justified and unjustified claims to knowledge. It also considers the famous and disconcerting challenge which puts into question the very assumption that we can know, or have good reasons for believing, anything: skepticism. We probably all take for granted that most, or at least a large proportion, of our beliefs deserve to be called knowledge. But skepticism forces us to reflect on what basis we have for making this casual assumption. Can we even say with certainty that what we take to be the physical world around us exists?

These questions have all been couched in general terms, with no reference being made to the particular kinds of knowers involved (e.g., male/female, white/nonwhite). But in recent years, with the entry into philosophy of more members of historically underrepresented groups, such as women and people of color, some critics of mainstream epistemology have argued that the gender and/or race of the knower is relevant to answering at least some of the above questions. In the readings we have selected for this section, then, we have aimed at the inclusion both of traditional and more unconventional material.

René Descartes' *Meditations* is standardly seen as the foundational text of modern epistemology, since though philosophers had always raised questions about knowledge, he put them into a distinctively modern framework. Descartes sets the stage for contemporary discussions by asking how many of our beliefs are actually well founded. In a famous philosophical analogy, he likens our belief-set to a building resting on a foundation. Obviously it would take for ever to examine every single belief we have, but if some are more basic than others – the foundation on which the building is erected – then by subjecting them to skeptical doubt, we can determine which are well supported and which should be discarded. With this cognitive operation completed, we can then reconstruct the edifice of our beliefs on a reliable, because indubitable, foundation. In the process of testing his beliefs, Descartes came up with another famous image that has haunted philosophy ever since: the possibility that a "malicious demon" is systematically deceiving us with false perceptions. Today, of course, it appears in the updated form of science-fiction scenarios, for example that we are really brains in a vat being electronically fed a simulated world that we wrongly take for reality.

Having discarded all his beliefs except his indubitable conviction that he exists – since even if you doubt your own existence, the very fact of doubting proves it – Descartes then rebuilt everything with the help of a proof that God exists, and would not let him be deceived. But later generations of philosophers have found his proof, and this "solution," deeply unsatisfactory and question-begging: an epistemological *deus ex machina*. David Hume demonstrates what happens if you begin with the Cartesian predicament, but dispense with a convenient deity to make everything come out all right in the end. He claims, in the empiricist tradition, that all we actually have access to are sense-impressions and ideas derived from them, and that though, through constant association, we *infer* a physical world linked by causal connections independent of us, we cannot actually prove its existence, so this inference is unwarranted. Skepticism of some kind, then, seems to be the only justified conclusion, though Hume readily agreed that this conclusion did not have much practical import for everyday life. In the next reading in this section, however, Jonathan Vogel seeks to deny the skeptic even this theoretical victory. He argues that, though superficially it might seem that the underdetermination of theory by evidence makes skepticism just as viable a cognitive approach as any other, once we actually do a comparison of alternatives, we will realize that commonsense is actually superior. Invoking the epistemic principle of inference to the best explanation, Vogel suggests that, by comparing the commonsense view that the world exists with the science-fiction hypothesis that the "world" is really a computer-generated simulacrum (an example of the updated Cartesian demon), we will see that, on grounds of simplicity, the real-world hypothesis is clearly preferable.

The next two articles explore the social dimension of epistemology, both in general and with specific respect to group differentiation. What has come to be called "standpoint theory" argues that those socially *disadvantaged* by a system of oppression will be cognitively *advantaged* in seeing its real character. The socially privileged (rich as against poor, men as against women, whites as against nonwhites) will not experience the oppressions of class, gender, and race directly, and will have a vested group interest in not admitting their privilege. So the claim is that the view from the bottom will tend (emphasis on "tend") in crucial respects to be more accurate than the view from the top. Insofar as scientific research has often been complicit with structures of social privilege, producing theories justifying the status quo that were later discredited (e.g., Social Darwinism, pseudo-scientific sexist and racist theories), the broader question is also raised of whether and how scientific objectivity is possible given these social realities.

In her selection on how to achieve good scientific practice, Helen Longino compares three main positions on the relation between constitutive values (internal methodological scientific ideals) and contextual values (external socio-cultural norms), and argues that they are all three problematic. She concludes that the unavoidably social character of the development of knowledge carries both risks and the benefit of safeguards, whose complex interrelations cannot be reduced to simple formulas, but need to be thought out in detail. Focusing on gender, Genevieve Lloyd looks at the role of metaphors in shaping our cognition. Since the terms "male" and "female" have acquired powerful symbolic associations from thousands of years of gender differentiation and subordination, and since reason has traditionally been represented as *male*, epistemological inquiry here involves a reflexive self-examination: looking at reason with possibly contaminated tools that themselves stand in need of critical scrutiny. Indeed, Lloyd argues that some of the metaphors Descartes uses have a gendered dimension.

Finally, the last two readings, by W. K. Clifford and Peter van Inwagen, take opposing stands on the issue of what justifies belief. By analogy with the concept of a virtuous moral agent, some epistemologists have argued that it also makes sense to speak of *epis-*

temic virtue. A virtuous cognizing agent should follow certain rules in deciding what to believe, and how strongly to believe it. Clifford outlines the very strong position that we should never believe anything on insufficient evidence. (This would be an epistemic vice.) On first hearing, such an injunction may not sound particularly demanding, but imagine applying it to *all* our beliefs. Would carrying out such a program really be feasible, if it were to be applied wholesale? In his critique of Clifford, van Inwagen argues that, though Clifford does not come right out and say it, his target is really *religious* belief. So unless we think that theism should be held to a different, more demanding epistemic standard, a legitimate test for the viability of his recommendation would just be to imagine its being generally implemented. And if we carry out this thought experiment, van Inwagen suggests, we will quickly realize that the consistent application of Clifford's principle would make us all skeptics, who should not believe anything.

1 From *Meditations on First Philosophy**

René Descartes

Synopsis of the Following Six Meditations

In the First Meditation reasons are provided which give us possible grounds for doubt about all things, especially material things, so long as we have no foundations for the sciences other than those which we have had up till now. Although the usefulness of such extensive doubt is not apparent at first sight, its greatest benefit lies in freeing us from all our preconceived opinions, and providing the easiest route by which the mind may be led away from the senses. The eventual result of this doubt is to make it impossible for us to have any further doubts about what we subsequently discover to be true.

In the Second Meditation, the mind uses its own freedom and supposes the non-existence of all the things about whose existence it can have even the slightest doubt; and in so doing the mind notices that it is impossible that it should not itself exist during this time. This exercise is also of the greatest benefit, since it enables the mind to distinguish without difficulty what belongs to itself, i.e. to an intellectual nature, from what belongs to the body. But since some people may perhaps expect arguments for the immortality of the soul in this section, I think they should be warned here and now that I have tried not to put down anything which I could not precisely demonstrate. Hence the only order which I could follow was that normally employed by geometers, namely to set out all the premises on which a desired proposition depends, before drawing any conclusions about it. Now the first and most important prerequisite for knowledge of the immortality of the soul is for us to form a concept of the soul which is as clear as possible and is also quite distinct from every concept of body; and that is just what has been done in this section. A further requirement is that we should know that everything that we clearly and distinctly understand is true in a way which corresponds exactly to our understanding of it; but it was not possible to prove this before the Fourth Meditation. In addition we need to have a distinct concept of corporeal nature, and this is developed partly in the Second Meditation itself, and partly in the Fifth and Sixth Meditations. The inference to be drawn from these results is that all the things that we clearly and distinctly conceive of as different substances (as we do in the case of mind and body) are in fact substances which are really distinct one from the other; and this conclusion is drawn in the Sixth Meditation. This conclusion is confirmed in the same Meditation by the fact that we cannot understand a body except as being divisible, while by contrast we cannot understand a mind except as being indivisible. For we cannot conceive of half of a mind, while we can always conceive of half of a body, however small; and this leads us to recognize that the natures of mind and body are not only different, but in some way opposite. But I have not pursued this topic any further in this book, first because these arguments are enough to show that the decay of the body does not imply the destruction of the mind, and are hence

* From René Descartes, *Meditations on First Philosophy*, revised edition, edited and translated by John Cottingham (Cambridge: Cambridge University Press, 1986), pp. 9–36 and 50–62. Reprinted with the permission of Cambridge University Press.

enough to give mortals the hope of an after-life, and secondly because the premises which lead to the conclusion that the soul is immortal depend on an account of the whole of physics. This is required for two reasons. First, we need to know that absolutely all substances, or things which must be created by God in order to exist, are by their nature incorruptible and cannot ever cease to exist unless they are reduced to nothingness by God's denying his concurrence[1] to them. Secondly, we need to recognize that body, taken in the general sense, is a substance, so that it too never perishes. But the human body, in so far as it differs from other bodies, is simply made up of a certain configuration of limbs and other accidents[2] of this sort; whereas the human mind is not made up of any accidents in this way, but is a pure substance. For even if all the accidents of the mind change, so that it has different objects of the understanding and different desires and sensations, it does not on that account become a different mind; whereas a human body loses its identity merely as a result of a change in the shape of some of its parts. And it follows from this that while the body can very easily perish, the mind[3] is immortal by its very nature.

In the Third Meditation I have explained quite fully enough, I think, my principal argument for proving the existence of God. But in order to draw my readers' minds away from the senses as far as possible, I was not willing to use any comparison taken from bodily things. So it may be that many obscurities remain; but I hope they will be completely removed later, in my Replies to the Objections. One such problem, among others, is how the idea of a supremely perfect being, which is in us, possesses so much objective[4] reality that it can come only from a cause which is supremely perfect. In the Replies this is illustrated by the comparison of a very perfect machine, the idea of which is in the mind of some engineer. Just as the objective intricacy belonging to the idea must have some cause, namely the scientific knowledge of the engineer, or of someone else who passed the idea on to him, so the idea of God which is in us must have God himself as its cause.

In the Fourth Meditation it is proved that everything that we clearly and distinctly perceive is true, and I also explain what the nature of falsity consists in. These results need to be known both in order to confirm what has gone before and also to make intelligible what is to come later. (But here it should be noted in passing that I do not deal at all with sin, i.e. the error which is committed in pursuing good and evil but only with the error that occurs in distinguishing truth from falsehood. And there is no discussion of matters pertaining to faith or the conduct of life, but simply of speculative truths which are known solely by means of the natural light.)[5]

In the Fifth Meditation, besides an account of corporeal nature taken in general, there is a new argument demonstrating the existence of God. Again, several difficulties may arise here, but these are resolved later in the Replies to the Objections. Finally I explain the sense in which it is true that the certainty even of geometrical demonstrations depends on the knowledge of God.

Lastly, in the Sixth Meditation, the intellect is distinguished from the imagination; the criteria for this distinction are explained; the mind is proved to be really distinct from the body, but is shown, notwithstanding, to be so closely joined to it that the mind and the body make up a kind of unit; there is a survey of all the errors which commonly come from the senses, and an explanation of how they may be avoided; and, lastly, there is a presentation of all the arguments which enable the existence of material things to be inferred. The great benefit of these arguments is not, in my view, that they prove what they establish – namely that there really is a world, and that human beings have bodies and so on – since no sane person has ever seriously doubted these things. The point is that in considering these arguments we come to realize that they are not as solid or as transparent as the arguments which lead us to knowledge of our own minds and of God, so that the latter are the most certain and evident of all possible objects of knowledge for the human intellect. Indeed this is the one thing that I set myself to prove in these Meditations. And for that reason I will not now go over the various other issues in the book which are dealt with as they come up.

Meditations on First Philosophy

in which are demonstrated the existence of God and the distinction between the human soul and the body

First meditation
What can be called into doubt

Some years ago I was struck by the large number of falsehoods that I had accepted as true in my childhood, and by the highly doubtful nature of the whole edifice that I had subsequently based on them. I realized that it was necessary, once in the course of my life, to demolish everything completely and start again right from the foundations if I wanted to establish anything at all in the sciences that was stable and likely to last. But the task looked an enormous one, and I began to wait until I should reach a mature enough age to ensure that no subsequent time of life would be more suitable for tackling such inquiries. This led me to put the project off for so long that I would now be to blame if by pondering over it any further I wasted the time still left for carrying it out. So today I have expressly rid my mind of all worries and arranged for myself a clear stretch of free time. I am here quite alone, and at last I will devote myself sincerely and without reservation to the general demolition of my opinions.

But to accomplish this, it will not be necessary for me to show that all my opinions are false, which is something I could perhaps never manage. Reason now leads me to think that I should hold back my assent from opinions which are not completely certain and indubitable just as carefully as I do from those which are patently false. So, for the purpose of rejecting all my opinions, it will be enough if I find in each of them at least some reason for doubt. And to do this I will not need to run through them all individ-ually, which would be an endless task. Once the foundations of a building are under-mined, anything built on them collapses of its own accord; so I will go straight for the basic principles on which all my former beliefs rested.

Whatever I have up till now accepted as most true I have acquired either from the senses or through the senses. But from time to time I have found that the senses deceive, and it is prudent never to trust completely those who have deceived us even once.

Yet although the senses occasionally deceive us with respect to objects which are very small or in the distance, there are many other beliefs about which doubt is quite impossible, even though they are derived from the senses – for example, that I am here, sitting by the fire, wearing a winter dressing-gown, holding this piece of paper in my hands, and so on. Again, how could it be denied that these hands or this whole body are mine? Unless perhaps I were to liken myself to madmen, whose brains are so damaged by the persistent vapours of melancholia that they firmly maintain they are kings when they are paupers, or say they are dressed in purple when they are naked, or that their heads are made of earthenware, or that they are pumpkins, or made of glass. But such people are insane, and I would be thought equally mad if I took anything from them as a model for myself.

A brilliant piece of reasoning! As if I were not a man who sleeps at night, and regularly has all the same experiences[6] while asleep as madmen do when awake – indeed sometimes even more improbable ones. How often, asleep at night, am I convinced of just such familiar events – that I am here in my dressing-gown, sitting by the fire – when in fact I am lying undressed in bed! Yet at the moment my eyes are certainly wide awake when I look at this piece of paper; I shake my head and it is not asleep; as I stretch out and feel my hand I do so deliberately, and I know what I am doing. All this would not happen with such distinctness to someone asleep. Indeed! As if I did not remember other occasions when I have been tricked by exactly similar thoughts while asleep! As I think about this more carefully, I see plainly that there are never any sure signs by means of which being awake can be distinguished from being asleep. The result is that I begin to feel dazed, and this very feeling only reinforces the notion that I may be asleep.

Suppose then that I am dreaming, and that these particulars – that my eyes are open, that I am moving my head and stretching out my hands – are not true. Perhaps, indeed, I do not even have such hands or such a body at all. Nonetheless, it must surely be admitted that the visions which come in sleep are like paintings, which must have been fashioned in the likeness of things that are real, and hence that at least these general kinds of things – eyes, head, hands and the body as a whole – are things which are not imaginary but are real and exist. For even when painters try to create sirens and satyrs with the most extraordinary bodies, they cannot give them natures which are new in all respects; they simply jumble up the limbs of different animals. Or if perhaps they manage to think up something so new that nothing remotely similar has ever been seen before – something which is therefore completely fictitious and unreal – at least the colours used in the composition must be real. By similar reasoning, although these general kinds of things – eyes, head, hands and so on – could be imaginary, it must at least be admitted that certain other even simpler and more universal things are real. These are as it were the real colours from which we form all the images of things, whether true or false, that occur in our thought.

This class appears to include corporeal nature in general, and its extension; the shape of extended things; the quantity, or size and number of these things; the place in which they may exist, the time through which they may endure,[7] and so on.

So a reasonable conclusion from this might be that physics, astronomy, medicine, and all other disciplines which depend on the study of composite things, are doubtful; while arithmetic, geometry and other subjects of this kind, which deal only with the simplest and most general things, regardless of whether they really exist in nature or not, contain something certain and indubitable. For whether I am awake or asleep, two and three added together are five, and a square has no more than four sides. It seems impossible that such transparent truths should incur any suspicion of being false.

And yet firmly rooted in my mind is the long-standing opinion that there is an omnipotent God who made me the kind of creature that I am. How do I know that he has not brought it about that there is no earth, no sky, no extended thing, no shape, no size, no place, while at the same time ensuring that all these things appear to me to exist just as they do now? What is more, since I sometimes believe that others go astray in cases where they think they have the most perfect knowledge, may I not similarly go wrong every time I add two and three or count the sides of a square, or in some even simpler matter, if that is imaginable? But perhaps God would not have allowed me to be deceived in this way, since he is said to be supremely good. But if it were inconsistent with his goodness to have created me such that I am deceived all the time, it would seem equally foreign to his goodness to allow me to be deceived even occasionally; yet this last assertion cannot be made.[8]

Perhaps there may be some who would prefer to deny the existence of so powerful a God rather than believe that everything else is uncertain. Let us not argue with them, but grant them that everything said about God is a fiction. According to their supposition, then, I have arrived at my present state by fate or chance or a continuous chain of events, or by some other means; yet since deception and error seem to be imperfections, the less powerful they make my original cause, the more likely it is that I am so imperfect as to be deceived all the time. I have no answer to these arguments, but am finally compelled to admit that there is not one of my former beliefs about which a doubt may not properly be raised; and this is not a flippant or ill-considered conclusion, but is based on powerful and well thought-out reasons. So in future I must withhold my assent from these former beliefs just as carefully as I would from obvious falsehoods, if I want to discover any certainty.[9]

But it is not enough merely to have noticed this; I must make an effort to remember it. My habitual opinions keep coming back, and, despite my wishes, they capture my belief, which is as it were bound over to them as a result of long occupation and the law of custom. I shall never get out of the habit of confidently assenting to these opinions, so long as I suppose them to be what in fact they are, namely highly probable opinions – opinions which, despite the fact that they are in a sense doubtful, as has just been shown, it is still much more reasonable to believe than to deny. In view of this, I think it will be a good plan to turn my will in completely the opposite direction and deceive myself, by pretending for a time that these former opinions are utterly false and imaginary. I shall do this until the weight of preconceived opinion is counter-balanced and the distorting influence of habit no longer prevents my judgement from perceiving things correctly. In the meantime, I know that no danger or error will result from my plan, and that I cannot possibly go too far in my distrustful attitude. This is because the task now in hand does not involve action but merely the acquisition of knowledge.

I will suppose therefore that not God, who is supremely good and the source of truth, but rather some malicious demon of the utmost power and cunning has employed all his energies in order to deceive me. I shall think that the sky, the air, the earth, colours, shapes, sounds and all external things are merely the delusions of dreams which he has devised to ensnare my judgement. I shall consider myself as not having hands or eyes, or flesh, or blood or senses, but as falsely believing that I have all these things. I shall stubbornly and firmly persist in this meditation; and, even if it is not in my power to know any truth, I shall at least do what is in my power,[10] that is, resolutely guard against assenting to any falsehoods, so that the deceiver, however powerful and cunning he may be, will be unable to impose on me in the slightest degree. But this is an arduous undertaking, and a kind of laziness brings me back to normal life. I am like a prisoner who is enjoying an imaginary freedom while asleep; as he begins to suspect that he is asleep, he dreads being woken up, and goes along with the pleasant illusion as long as he can. In the same way, I happily slide back into my old opinions and dread being shaken out of them, for fear that my peaceful sleep may be followed by hard labour when I wake, and that I shall have to toil not in the light, but amid the inextricable darkness of the problems I have now raised.

Second meditation
The nature of the human mind, and how it is better known than the body

So serious are the doubts into which I have been thrown as a result of yesterday's meditation that I can neither put them out of my mind nor see any way of resolving them.
It feels as if I have fallen unexpectedly into a deep whirlpool which tumbles me around
so that I can neither stand on the bottom nor swim up to the top. Nevertheless I will
make an effort and once more attempt the same path which I started on yesterday. Anything which admits of the slightest doubt I will set aside just as if I had found it to be
wholly false; and I will proceed in this way until I recognize something certain, or, if
nothing else, until I at least recognize for certain that there is no certainty. Archimedes
used to demand just one firm and immovable point in order to shift the entire earth; so
I too can hope for great things if I manage to find just one thing, however slight, that is
certain and unshakeable.

I will suppose then, that everything I see is spurious. I will believe that my memory
tells me lies, and that none of the things that it reports ever happened. I have no senses.
Body, shape, extension, movement and place are chimeras. So what remains true? Perhaps
just the one fact that nothing is certain.

Yet apart from everything I have just listed, how do I know that there is not something else which does not allow even the slightest occasion for doubt? Is there not a God,
or whatever I may call him, who puts into me[11] the thoughts I am now having? But why
do I think this, since I myself may perhaps be the author of these thoughts? In that case
am not I, at least, something? But I have just said that I have no senses and no body.
This is the sticking point: what follows from this? Am I not so bound up with a body
and with senses that I cannot exist without them? But I have convinced myself that there
is absolutely nothing in the world, no sky, no earth, no minds, no bodies. Does it now
follow that I too do not exist? No: if I convinced myself of something[12] then I certainly
existed. But there is a deceiver of supreme power and cunning who is deliberately and
constantly deceiving me. In that case I too undoubtedly exist, if he is deceiving me; and
let him deceive me as much as he can, he will never bring it about that I am nothing so
long as I think that I am something. So after considering everything very thoroughly, I
must finally conclude that this proposition, *I am, I exist*, is necessarily true whenever it
is put forward by me or conceived in my mind.

But I do not yet have a sufficient understanding of what this 'I' is, that now necessarily exists. So I must be on my guard against carelessly taking something else to be
this 'I', and so making a mistake in the very item of knowledge that I maintain is the
most certain and evident of all. I will therefore go back and meditate on what I originally believed myself to be, before I embarked on this present train of thought. I will
then subtract anything capable of being weakened, even minimally, by the arguments now
introduced, so that what is left at the end may be exactly and only what is certain and
unshakeable.

What then did I formerly think I was? A man. But what is a man? Shall I say 'a rational
animal'? No; for then I should have to inquire what an animal is, what rationality is, and
in this way one question would lead me down the slope to other harder ones, and I do
not now have the time to waste on subtleties of this kind. Instead I propose to concentrate on what came into my thoughts spontaneously and quite naturally whenever I used
to consider what I was. Well, the first thought to come to mind was that I had a face,
hands, arms and the whole mechanical structure of limbs which can be seen in a corpse,

and which I called the body. The next thought was that I was nourished, that I moved about, and that I engaged in sense-perception and thinking; and these actions I attributed to the soul. But as to the nature of this soul, either I did not think about this or else I imagined it to be something tenuous, like a wind or fire or ether, which permeated my more solid parts. As to the body, however, I had no doubts about it, but thought I knew its nature distinctly. If I had tried to describe the mental conception I had of it, I would have expressed it as follows: by a body I understand whatever has a determinable shape and a definable location and can occupy a space in such a way as to exclude any other body; it can be perceived by touch, sight, hearing, taste or smell, and can be moved in various ways, not by itself but by whatever else comes into contact with it. For, according to my judgement, the power of self-movement, like the power of sensation or of thought, was quite foreign to the nature of a body; indeed, it was a source of wonder to me that certain bodies were found to contain faculties of this kind.

But what shall I now say that I am, when I am supposing that there is some supremely powerful and, if it is permissible to say so, malicious deceiver, who is deliberately trying to trick me in every way he can? Can I now assert that I possess even the most insignificant of all the attributes which I have just said belong to the nature of a body? I scrutinize them, think about them, go over them again, but nothing suggests itself; it is tiresome and pointless to go through the list once more. But what about the attributes I assigned to the soul? Nutrition or movement? Since now I do not have a body, these are mere fabrications. Sense-perception? This surely does not occur without a body, and besides, when asleep I have appeared to perceive through the senses many things which I afterwards realized I did not perceive through the senses at all. Thinking? At last I have discovered it – thought; this alone is inseparable from me. I am, I exist – that is certain. But for how long? For as long as I am thinking. For it could be that were I totally to cease from thinking, I should totally cease to exist. At present I am not admitting anything except what is necessarily true. I am, then, in the strict sense only a thing that thinks;[13] that is, I am a mind, or intelligence, or intellect, or reason – words whose meaning I have been ignorant of until now. But for all that I am a thing which is real and which truly exists. But what kind of a thing? As I have just said – a thinking thing.

What else am I? I will use my imagination.[14] I am not that structure of limbs which is called a human body. I am not even some thin vapour which permeates the limbs – a wind, fire, air, breath, or whatever I depict in my imagination; for these are things which I have supposed to be nothing. Let this supposition stand;[15] for all that I am still something. And yet may it not perhaps be the case that these very things which I am supposing to be nothing, because they are unknown to me, are in reality identical with the 'I' of which I am aware? I do not know, and for the moment I shall not argue the point, since I can make judgements only about things which are known to me. I know that I exist; the question is, what is this 'I' that I know? If the 'I' is understood strictly as we have been taking it, then it is quite certain that knowledge of it does not depend on things of whose existence I am as yet unaware; so it cannot depend on any of the things which I invent in my imagination. And this very word 'invent' shows me my mistake. It would indeed be a case of fictitious invention if I used my imagination to establish that I was something or other; for imagining is simply contemplating the shape or image of a corporeal thing. Yet now I know for certain both that I exist and at the same time that all such images and, in general, everything relating to the nature of body, could be mere dreams ⟨and chimeras⟩. Once this point has been grasped, to say 'I will use my imagination to get to know more distinctly what I am' would seem to be as silly as saying 'I am now awake, and see some truth; but since my vision is not yet clear enough, I will deliberately fall asleep so that my dreams may provide a truer and clearer representation.' I thus realize that none of the things that the imagination enables me to grasp is at all relevant to this knowledge of myself which I possess, and that the mind must therefore be most carefully diverted from such things[16] if it is to perceive its own nature as distinctly as possible.

But what then am I? A thing that thinks. What is that? A thing that doubts, understands, affirms, denies, is willing, is unwilling, and also imagines and has sensory perceptions.

This is a considerable list, if everything on it belongs to me. But does it? Is it not one and the same 'I' who is now doubting almost everything, who nonetheless understands some things, who affirms that this one thing is true, denies everything else, desires to know more, is unwilling to be deceived, imagines many things even involuntarily, and is aware of many things which apparently come from the senses? Are not all these things just as true as the fact that I exist, even if I am asleep all the time, and even if he who created me is doing all he can to deceive me? Which of all these activities is distinct from my thinking? Which of them can be said to be separate from myself? The fact that it is I who am doubting and understanding and willing is so evident that I see no way of making it any clearer. But it is also the case that the 'I' who imagines is the same 'I'. For even if, as I have supposed, none of the objects of imagination are real, the power of imagination is something which really exists and is part of my thinking. Lastly, it is also the same 'I' who has sensory perceptions, or is aware of bodily things as it were through the senses. For example, I am now seeing light, hearing a noise, feeling heat. But I am asleep, so all this is false. Yet I certainly *seem* to see, to hear, and to be warmed. This cannot be false; what is called 'having a sensory perception' is strictly just this, and in this restricted sense of the term it is simply thinking.

From all this I am beginning to have a rather better understanding of what I am. But it still appears – and I cannot stop thinking this – that the corporeal things of which images are formed in my thought, and which the senses investigate, are known with much more distinctness than this puzzling 'I' which cannot be pictured in the imagination. And yet it is surely surprising that I should have a more distinct grasp of things which I realize are doubtful, unknown and foreign to me, than I have of that which is true and known – my own self. But I see what it is: my mind enjoys wandering off and will not yet submit to being restrained within the bounds of truth. Very well then; just this once let us give it a completely free rein, so that after a while, when it is time to tighten the reins, it may more readily submit to being curbed.

Let us consider the things which people commonly think they understand most distinctly of all; that is, the bodies which we touch and see. I do not mean bodies in general – for general perceptions are apt to be somewhat more confused – but one particular body. Let us take, for example, this piece of wax. It has just been taken from the honeycomb; it has not yet quite lost the taste of the honey; it retains some of the scent of the flowers from which it was gathered; its colour, shape and size are plain to see; it is hard, cold and can be handled without difficulty; if you rap it with your knuckle it makes a sound. In short, it has everything which appears necessary to enable a body to be known as distinctly as possible. But even as I speak, I put the wax by the fire, and look: the residual taste is eliminated, the smell goes away, the colour changes, the shape is lost, the size increases; it becomes liquid and hot; you can hardly touch it, and if you strike it, it no longer makes a sound. But does the same wax remain? It must be admitted that it does; no one denies it, no one thinks otherwise. So what was it in the wax that

I understood with such distinctness? Evidently none of the features which I arrived at by means of the senses; for whatever came under taste, smell, sight, touch or hearing has now altered – yet the wax remains.

Perhaps the answer lies in the thought which now comes to my mind; namely, the wax was not after all the sweetness of the honey, or the fragrance of the flowers, or the whiteness, or the shape, or the sound, but was rather a body which presented itself to me in these various forms a little while ago, but which now exhibits different ones. But what exactly is it that I am now imagining? Let us concentrate, take away everything which does not belong to the wax, and see what is left: merely something extended, flexible and changeable. But what is meant here by 'flexible' and 'changeable'? Is it what I picture in my imagination: that this piece of wax is capable of changing from a round shape to a square shape, or from a square shape to a triangular shape? Not at all; for I can grasp that the wax is capable of countless changes of this kind, yet I am unable to run through this immeasurable number of changes in my imagination, from which it follows that it is not the faculty of imagination that gives me my grasp of the wax as flexible and changeable. And what is meant by 'extended'? Is the extension of the wax also unknown? For it increases if the wax melts, increases again if it boils, and is greater still if the heat is increased. I would not be making a correct judgement about the nature of wax unless I believed it capable of being extended in many more different ways than I will ever encompass in my imagination. I must therefore admit that the nature of this piece of wax is in no way revealed by my imagination, but is perceived by the mind alone. (I am speaking of this particular piece of wax; the point is even clearer with regard to wax in general.) But what is this wax which is perceived by the mind alone?[17] It is of course the same wax which I see, which I touch, which I picture in my imagination, in short the same wax which I thought it to be from the start. And yet, and here is the point, the perception I have of it[18] is a case not of vision or touch or imagination – nor has it ever been, despite previous appearances – but of purely mental scrutiny; and this can be imperfect and confused, as it was before, or clear and distinct as it is now, depending on how carefully I concentrate on what the wax consists in.

But as I reach this conclusion I am amazed at how ⟨weak and⟩ prone to error my mind is. For although I am thinking about these matters within myself, silently and without speaking, nonetheless the actual words bring me up short, and I am almost tricked by ordinary ways of talking. We say that we see the wax itself, if it is there before us, not that we judge it to be there from its colour or shape; and this might lead me to conclude without more ado that knowledge of the wax comes from what the eye sees, and not from the scrutiny of the mind alone. But then if I look out of the window and see men crossing the square, as I just happen to have done, I normally say that I see the men themselves, just as I say that I see the wax. Yet do I see any more than hats and coats which could conceal automatons? I *judge* that they are men. And so something which I thought I was seeing with my eyes is in fact grasped solely by the faculty of judgement which is in my mind.

However, one who wants to achieve knowledge above the ordinary level should feel ashamed at having taken ordinary ways of talking as a basis for doubt. So let us proceed, and consider on which occasion my perception of the nature of the wax was more perfect and evident. Was it when I first looked at it, and believed I knew it by my external senses, or at least by what they call the 'common' sense[19] – that is, the power of imagination? Or is my knowledge more perfect now, after a more careful investigation of the nature of the wax and of the means by which it is known? Any doubt on this issue would clearly be foolish; for what distinctness was there in my earlier perception? Was there anything in it which an animal could not possess? But when I distinguish the wax from its outward forms – take the clothes off, as it were, and consider it naked – then although my judgement may still contain errors, at least my perception now requires a human mind.

But what am I to say about this mind, or about myself? (So far, remember, I am not admitting that there is anything else in me except a mind.) What, I ask, is this 'I' which seems to perceive the wax so distinctly? Surely my awareness of my own self is not merely much truer and more certain than my awareness of the wax, but also much more distinct and evident. For if I judge that the wax exists from the fact that I see it, clearly this same fact entails much more evidently that I myself also exist. It is possible that what I see is not really the wax; it is possible that I do not even have eyes with which to see anything. But when I see, or think I see (I am not here distinguishing the two), it is simply not possible that I who am now thinking am not something. By the same token, if I judge that the wax exists from the fact that I touch it, the same result follows, namely that I exist. If I judge that it exists from the fact that I imagine it, or for any other reason, exactly the same thing follows. And the result that I have grasped in the case of the wax may be applied to everything else located outside me. Moreover, if my perception of the wax seemed more distinct[20] after it was established not just by sight or touch but by many other considerations, it must be admitted that I now know myself even more distinctly. This is because every consideration whatsoever which contributes to my perception of the wax, or of any other body, cannot but establish even more effectively the nature of my own mind. But besides this, there is so much else in the mind itself which can serve to make my knowledge of it more distinct, that it scarcely seems worth going through the contributions made by considering bodily things.

I see that without any effort I have now finally got back to where I wanted. I now know that even bodies are not strictly perceived by the senses or the faculty of imagination but by the intellect alone, and that this perception derives not from their being touched or seen but from their being understood; and in view of this I know plainly that I can achieve an easier and more evident perception of my own mind than of anything else. But since the habit of holding on to old opinions cannot be set aside so quickly, I should like to stop here and meditate for some time on this new knowledge I have gained, so as to fix it more deeply in my memory.

Third meditation
The existence of God

I will now shut my eyes, stop my ears, and withdraw all my senses. I will eliminate from my thoughts all images of bodily things, or rather, since this is hardly possible, I will regard all such images as vacuous, false and worthless. I will converse with myself and scrutinize myself more deeply; and in this way I will attempt to achieve, little by little, a more intimate knowledge of myself. I am a thing that thinks: that is, a thing that doubts, affirms, denies, understands a few things, is ignorant of many things,[21] is willing, is unwilling, and also which imagines and has sensory perceptions; for as I have noted before, even though the objects of my sensory experience and imagination may have no existence outside me, nonetheless the modes of thinking which I refer to as cases of sensory perception and imagination, in so far as they are simply modes of thinking, do exist within me – of that I am certain.

In this brief list I have gone through everything I truly know, or at least everything I have so far discovered that I know. Now I will cast around more carefully to see whether there may be other things within me which I have not yet noticed. I am certain that I am a thinking thing. Do I not therefore also know what is required for my being certain about anything? In this first item of knowledge there is simply a clear and distinct perception of what I am asserting; this would not be enough to make me certain of the truth of the matter if it could ever turn out that something which I perceived with such clarity and distinctness was false. So I now seem to be able to lay it down as a general rule that whatever I perceive very clearly and distinctly is true.[22]

Yet I previously accepted as wholly certain and evident many things which I afterwards realized were doubtful. What were these? The earth, sky, stars, and everything else that I apprehended with the senses. But what was it about them that I perceived clearly? Just that the ideas, or thoughts, of such things appeared before my mind. Yet even now I am not denying that these ideas occur within me. But there was something else which I used to assert, and which through habitual belief I thought I perceived clearly, although I did not in fact do so. This was that there were things outside me which were the sources of my ideas and which resembled them in all respects. Here was my mistake; or at any rate, if my judgement was true, it was not thanks to the strength of my perception.[23]

But what about when I was considering something very simple and straightforward in arithmetic or geometry, for example that two and three added together make five, and so on? Did I not see at least these things clearly enough to affirm their truth? Indeed, the only reason for my later judgement that they were open to doubt was that it occurred to me that perhaps some God could have given me a nature such that I was deceived even in matters which seemed most evident. And whenever my preconceived belief in the supreme power of God comes to mind, I cannot but admit that it would be easy for him, if he so desired, to bring it about that I go wrong even in those matters which I think I see utterly clearly with my mind's eye. Yet when I turn to the things themselves which I think I perceive very clearly, I am so convinced by them that I spontaneously declare: let whoever can do so deceive me, he will never bring it about that I am nothing, so long as I continue to think I am something; or make it true at some future time that I have never existed, since it is now true that I exist; or bring it about that two and three added together are more or less than five, or anything of this kind in which I see a manifest contradiction. And since I have no cause to think that there is a deceiving God, and I do not yet even know for sure whether there is a God at all, any reason for doubt which depends simply on this supposition is a very slight and, so to speak, metaphysical one. But in order to remove even this slight reason for doubt, as soon as the opportunity arises I must examine whether there is a God, and, if there is, whether he can be a deceiver. For if I do not know this, it seems that I can never be quite certain about anything else.

First, however, considerations of order appear to dictate that I now classify my thoughts into definite kinds,[24] and ask which of them can properly be said to be the bearers of truth and falsity. Some of my thoughts are as it were the images of things, and it is only in these cases that the term 'idea' is strictly appropriate – for example, when I think of a man, or a chimera, or the sky, or an angel, or God. Other thoughts have various additional forms: thus when I will, or am afraid, or affirm, or deny, there is always a particular thing which I take as the object of my thought, but my thought includes something more than the likeness of that thing. Some thoughts in this category are called volitions or emotions, while others are called judgements.

Now as far as ideas are concerned, provided they are considered solely in themselves and I do not refer them to anything else, they cannot strictly speaking be false; for whether it is a goat or a chimera that I am imagining, it is just as true that I imagine the former as the latter. As for the will and the emotions, here too one need not worry about falsity; for even if the things which I may desire are wicked or even non-existent, that does not make it any less true that I desire them. Thus the only remaining thoughts where I must be on my guard against making a mistake are judgements. And the chief and most common mistake which is to be found here consists in my judging that the ideas which are in me resemble, or conform to, things located outside me. Of course, if I considered just the ideas themselves simply as modes of my thought, without referring them to anything else, they could scarcely give me any material for error.

Among my ideas, some appear to be innate, some to be adventitious,[25] and others to have been invented by me. My understanding of what a thing is, what truth is, and what thought is, seems to derive simply from my own nature. But my hearing a noise, as I do now, or seeing the sun, or feeling the fire, comes from things which are located outside me, or so I have hitherto judged. Lastly, sirens, hippogriffs and the like are my own invention. But perhaps all my ideas may be thought of as adventitious, or they may all be innate, or all made up; for as yet I have not clearly perceived their true origin.

But the chief question at this point concerns the ideas which I take to be derived from things existing outside me: what is my reason for thinking that they resemble these things? Nature has apparently taught me to think this. But in addition I know by experience that these ideas do not depend on my will, and hence that they do not depend simply on me. Frequently I notice them even when I do not want to: now, for example, I feel the heat whether I want to or not, and this is why I think that this sensation or idea of heat comes to me from something other than myself, namely the heat of the fire by which I am sitting. And the most obvious judgement for me to make is that the thing in question transmits to me its own likeness rather than something else.

I will now see if these arguments are strong enough. When I say 'Nature taught me to think this', all I mean is that a spontaneous impulse leads me to believe it, not that its truth has been revealed to me by some natural light. There is a big difference here. Whatever is revealed to me by the natural light – for example that from the fact that I am doubting it follows that I exist, and so on – cannot in any way be open to doubt. This is because there cannot be another faculty[26] both as trustworthy as the natural light and also capable of showing me that such things are not true. But as for my natural impulses, I have often judged in the past that they were pushing me in the wrong direction when it was a question of choosing the good, and I do not see why I should place any greater confidence in them in other matters.[27]

Then again, although these ideas do not depend on my will, it does not follow that they must come from things located outside me. Just as the impulses which I was speaking of a moment ago seem opposed to my will even though they are within me, so there may be some other faculty not yet fully known to me, which produces these ideas without any assistance from external things; this is, after all, just how I have always thought ideas are produced in me when I am dreaming.

And finally, even if these ideas did come from things other than myself, it would not follow that they must resemble those things. Indeed, I think I have often discovered a great disparity ⟨between an object and its idea⟩ in many cases. For example, there are two different ideas of the sun which I find within me. One of them, which is acquired as it were from the senses and which is a prime example of an idea which I reckon to come from an external source, makes the sun appear very small. The other idea is based on astronomical reasoning, that is, it is derived from certain notions which are innate in me (or else it is constructed by me in some other way), and this idea shows the sun to be several times larger than the earth. Obviously both these ideas cannot resemble the sun which exists outside me; and reason persuades me that the idea which seems to have emanated most directly from the sun itself has in fact no resemblance to it at all.

All these considerations are enough to establish that it is not reliable judgement but merely some blind impulse that has made me believe up till now that there exist things distinct from myself which transmit to me ideas or images of themselves through the sense organs or in some other way.

But it now occurs to me that there is another way of investigating whether some of the things of which I possess ideas exist outside me. In so far as the ideas are ⟨considered⟩ simply ⟨as⟩ modes of thought, there is no recognizable inequality among them: they all appear to come from within me in the same fashion. But in so far as different ideas ⟨are considered as images which⟩ represent different things, it is clear that they differ widely. Undoubtedly, the ideas which represent substances to me amount to something more and, so to speak, contain within themselves more objective[28] reality than the ideas which merely represent modes or accidents. Again, the idea that gives me my understanding of a supreme God, eternal, infinite, ⟨immutable,⟩ omniscient, omnipotent and the creator of all things that exist apart from him, certainly has in it more objective reality than the ideas that represent finite substances.

Now it is manifest by the natural light that there must be at least as much ⟨reality⟩ in the efficient and total cause as in the effect of that cause. For where, I ask, could the effect get its reality from, if not from the cause? And how could the cause give it to the effect unless it possessed it? It follows from this both that something cannot arise from nothing, and also that what is more perfect – that is, contains in itself more reality – cannot arise from what is less perfect. And this is transparently true not only in the case of effects which possess ⟨what the philosophers call⟩ actual or formal reality, but also in the case of ideas, where one is considering only ⟨what they call⟩ objective reality. A stone, for example, which previously did not exist, cannot begin to exist unless it is produced by something which contains, either formally or eminently everything to be found in the stone;[29] similarly, heat cannot be produced in an object which was not previously hot, except by something of at least the same order ⟨degree or kind⟩ of perfection as heat, and so on. But it is also true that the *idea* of heat, or of a stone, cannot exist in me unless it is put there by some cause which contains at least as much reality as I conceive to be in the heat or in the stone. For although this cause does not transfer any of its actual or formal reality to my idea, it should not on that account be supposed that it must be less real.[30] The nature of an idea is such that of itself it requires no formal reality except what it derives from my thought, of which it is a mode.[31] But in order for a given idea to contain such and such objective reality, it must surely derive it from some cause which contains at least as much formal reality as there is objective reality in the idea. For if we suppose that an idea contains something which was not in its cause, it must have got this from nothing; yet the mode of being by which a thing exists objectively ⟨or representatively⟩ in the intellect by way of an idea, imperfect though it may be, is certainly not nothing, and so it cannot come from nothing.

And although the reality which I am considering in my ideas is merely objective reality, I must not on that account suppose that the same reality need not exist formally in the causes of my ideas, but that it is enough for it to be present in them objectively. For just as the objective mode of being belongs to ideas by their very nature, so the formal mode of being belongs to the causes of ideas – or at least the first and most important ones – by *their* very nature. And although one idea may perhaps originate from another, there cannot be an infinite regress here; eventually one must reach a primary idea, the cause of which will be like an archetype which contains formally ⟨and in fact⟩ all the reality ⟨or perfection⟩ which is present only objectively ⟨or representatively⟩ in the idea. So it is clear to me, by the natural light, that the ideas in me are like ⟨pictures, or⟩ images which can easily fall short of the perfection of the things from which they are taken, but which cannot contain anything greater or more perfect.

The longer and more carefully I examine all these points, the more clearly and distinctly I recognize their truth. But what is my conclusion to be? If the objective reality of any of my ideas turns out to be so great that I am sure the same reality does not reside in me, either formally or eminently, and hence that I myself cannot be its cause, it will necessarily follow that I am not alone in the world, but that some other thing which is the cause of this idea also exists. But if no such idea is to be found in me, I shall have no argument to convince me of the existence of anything apart from myself. For despite a most careful and comprehensive survey, this is the only argument I have so far been able to find.

Among my ideas, apart from the idea which gives me a representation of myself, which cannot present any difficulty in this context, there are ideas which variously represent God, corporeal and inanimate things, angels, animals and finally other men like myself.

As far as concerns the ideas which represent other men, or animals, or angels, I have no difficulty in understanding that they could be put together from the ideas I have of myself, of corporeal things and of God, even if the world contained no men besides me, no animals and no angels.

As to my ideas of corporeal things, I can see nothing in them which is so great ⟨or excellent⟩ as to make it seem impossible that it originated in myself. For if I scrutinize them thoroughly and examine them one by one, in the way in which I examined the idea of the wax yesterday, I notice that the things which I perceive clearly and distinctly in them are very few in number. The list comprises size, or extension in length, breadth and depth; shape, which is a function of the boundaries of this extension; position, which is a relation between various items possessing shape; and motion, or change in position; to these may be added substance, duration and number. But as for all the rest, including light and colours, sounds, smells, tastes, heat and cold and the other tactile qualities, I think of these only in a very confused and obscure way, to the extent that I do not even know whether they are true or false, that is, whether the ideas I have of them are ideas of real things or of non-things.[32] For although, as I have noted before, falsity in the strict sense, or formal falsity, can occur only in judgements, there is another kind of falsity, material falsity, which occurs in ideas, when they represent non-things as things. For example, the ideas which I have of heat and cold contain so little clarity and distinctness that they do not enable me to tell whether cold is merely the absence of heat or vice versa, or whether both of them are real qualities, or neither is. And since there can be no ideas which are not as it were of things,[33] if it is true that cold is nothing but the absence of heat, the idea which represents it to me as something real and positive deserves to be called false; and the same goes for other ideas of this kind.

Such ideas obviously do not require me to posit a source distinct from myself. For on the one hand, if they are false, that is, represent non-things, I know by the natural light that they arise from nothing – that is, they are in me only because of a deficiency and lack of perfection in my nature. If on the other hand they are true, then since the reality which they represent is so extremely slight that I cannot even distinguish it from a non-thing, I do not see why they cannot originate from myself.

With regard to the clear and distinct elements in my ideas of corporeal things, it appears that I could have borrowed some of these from my idea of myself, namely substance, duration, number and anything else of this kind. For example, I think that a stone is a substance, or is a thing capable of existing independently, and I also think that I am a substance. Admittedly I conceive of myself as a thing that thinks and is not extended, whereas I conceive of the stone as a thing that is extended and does not think, so that the two conceptions differ enormously; but they seem to agree with respect to the classification 'substance'.[34] Again, I perceive that I now exist, and remember that I have existed for some time; moreover, I have various thoughts which I can count; it is in these ways that I acquire the ideas of duration and number which I can then transfer to other things. As for all the other elements which make up the ideas of corporeal things, namely extension, shape, position and movement, these are not formally contained in me, since I am nothing but a thinking thing; but since they are merely modes of a substance,[35] and I am a substance, it seems possible that they are contained in me eminently.

So there remains only the idea of God; and I must consider whether there is anything in the idea which could not have originated in myself. By the word 'God' I understand a substance that is infinite, ⟨eternal, immutable,⟩ independent, supremely intelligent, supremely powerful, and which created both myself and everything else (if anything else there be) that exists. All these attributes are such that, the more carefully I concentrate on them, the less possible it seems that they[36] could have originated from me alone. So from what has been said it must be concluded that God necessarily exists.

It is true that I have the idea of substance in me in virtue of the fact that I am a substance; but this would not account for my having the idea of an infinite substance, when I am finite, unless this idea proceeded from some substance which really was infinite.

And I must not think that, just as my conceptions of rest and darkness are arrived at by negating movement and light, so my perception of the infinite is arrived at not by means of a true idea but merely by negating the finite. On the contrary, I clearly understand that there is more reality in an infinite substance than in a finite one, and hence that my perception of the infinite, that is God, is in some way prior to my perception of the finite, that is myself. For how could I understand that I doubted or desired – that is, lacked something – and that I was not wholly perfect, unless there were in me some idea of a more perfect being which enabled me to recognize my own defects by comparison?

Nor can it be said that this idea of God is perhaps materially false and so could have come from nothing,[37] which is what I observed just a moment ago in the case of the ideas of heat and cold, and so on. On the contrary, it is utterly clear and distinct, and contains in itself more objective reality than any other idea; hence there is no idea which is in itself truer or less liable to be suspected of falsehood. This idea of a supremely perfect and infinite being is, I say, true in the highest degree; for although perhaps one may imagine that such a being does not exist, it cannot be supposed that the idea of such a being represents something unreal, as I said with regard to the idea of cold. The idea is, moreover, utterly clear and distinct; for whatever I clearly and distinctly perceive as being real and true, and implying any perfection, is wholly contained in it. It does not matter that I do not grasp the infinite, or that there are countless additional attributes of God which I cannot in any way grasp, and perhaps cannot even reach in my thought; for it is in the nature of the infinite not to be grasped by a finite being like myself. It is enough that I understand[38] the infinite, and that I judge that all the attributes which I clearly perceive and know to imply some perfection – and perhaps countless others of which I am ignorant – are present in God either formally or eminently. This is enough to make the idea that I have of God the truest and most clear and distinct of all my ideas.

But perhaps I am something greater than I myself understand, and all the perfections which I attribute to God are somehow in me potentially, though not yet emerging or actualized. For I am now experiencing a gradual increase in my knowledge, and I see nothing to prevent its increasing more and more to infinity. Further, I see no reason why I should not be able to use this increased knowledge to acquire all the other perfections of God. And finally, if the potentiality for these perfections is already within me, why should not this be enough to generate the idea of such perfections?

But all this is impossible. First, though it is true that there is a gradual increase in my knowledge, and that I have many potentialities which are not yet actual, this is all quite irrelevant to the idea of God, which contains absolutely nothing that is potential;[39] indeed, this gradual increase in knowledge is itself the surest sign of imperfection. What is more, even if my knowledge always increases more and more, I recognize that it will never actually be infinite, since it will never reach the point where it is not capable of a further increase; God, on the other hand, I take to be actually infinite, so that nothing can be added to his perfection. And finally, I perceive that the objective being of an idea cannot be produced merely by potential being, which strictly speaking is nothing, but only by actual or formal being.

If one concentrates carefully, all this is quite evident by the natural light. But when I relax my concentration, and my mental vision is blinded by the images of things perceived by the senses, it is not so easy for me to remember why the idea of a being more perfect than myself must necessarily proceed from some being which is in reality more perfect. I should therefore like to go further and inquire whether I myself, who have this idea, could exist if no such being existed.

From whom, in that case, would I derive my existence? From myself presumably, or from my parents, or from some other beings less perfect than God; for nothing more perfect than God, or even as perfect, can be thought of or imagined.

Yet if I derived my existence from myself,[40] then I should neither doubt nor want, nor lack anything at all; for I should have given myself all the perfections of which I have any idea, and thus I should myself be God. I must not suppose that the items I lack would be more difficult to acquire than those I now have. On the contrary, it is clear that, since I am a thinking thing or substance, it would have been far more difficult for me to emerge out of nothing than merely to acquire knowledge of the many things of which I am ignorant – such knowledge being merely an accident of that substance. And if I had derived my existence from myself, which is a greater achievement, I should certainly not have denied myself the knowledge in question, which is something much easier to acquire, or indeed any of the attributes which I perceive to be contained in the idea of God; for none of them seem any harder to achieve. And if any of them were harder to achieve, they would certainly appear so to me, if I had indeed got all my other attributes from myself, since I should experience a limitation of my power in this respect.

I do not escape the force of these arguments by supposing that I have always existed as I do now, as if it followed from this that there was no need to look for any author of my existence. For a lifespan can be divided into countless parts, each completely independent of the others, so that it does not follow from the fact that I existed a little while ago that I must exist now, unless there is some cause which as it were creates me afresh at this moment – that is, which preserves me. For it is quite clear to anyone who atten-tively considers the nature of time that the same power and action are needed to preserve anything at each individual moment of its duration as would be required to create that thing anew if it were not yet in existence. Hence the distinction between preservation and creation is only a conceptual one,[41] and this is one of the things that are evident by the natural light.

I must therefore now ask myself whether I possess some power enabling me to bring it about that I who now exist will still exist a little while from now. For since I am nothing but a thinking thing – or at least since I am now concerned only and precisely with that part of me which is a thinking thing – if there were such a power in me, I should undoubt-edly be aware of it. But I experience no such power, and this very fact makes me recog-nize most clearly that I depend on some being distinct from myself.

But perhaps this being is not God, and perhaps I was produced either by my parents or by other causes less perfect than God. No; for as I have said before, it is quite clear that there must be at least as much in the cause as in the effect.[42] And therefore what-ever kind of cause is eventually proposed, since I am a thinking thing and have within me some idea of God, it must be admitted that what caused me is itself a thinking thing and possesses the idea of all the perfections which I attribute to God. In respect of this cause one may again inquire whether it derives its existence from itself or from another cause. If from itself, then it is clear from what has been said that it is itself God, since if it has the power of existing through its own might,[43] then undoubtedly it also has the power of actually possessing all the perfections of which it has an idea – that is, all the perfec-tions which I conceive to be in God. If, on the other hand, it derives its existence from another cause, then the same question may be repeated concerning this further cause, namely whether it derives its existence from itself or from another cause, until eventually the ultimate cause is reached, and this will be God.

It is clear enough that an infinite regress is impossible here, especially since I am dealing not just with the cause that produced me in the past, but also and most importantly with the cause that preserves me at the present moment.

Nor can it be supposed that several partial causes contributed to my creation, or that I received the idea of one of the perfections which I attribute to God from one cause and the idea of another from another – the supposition here being that all the perfections are to be found somewhere in the universe but not joined together in a single being, God. On the contrary, the unity, the simplicity, or the inseparability of all the attributes of God is one of the most important of the perfections which I understand him to have. And surely the idea of the unity of all his perfections could not have been placed in me by any cause which did not also provide me with the ideas of the other perfections; for no cause could have made me understand the interconnection and inseparability of the perfections without at the same time making me recognize what they were.

Lastly, as regards my parents, even if everything I have ever believed about them is true, it is certainly not they who preserve me; and in so far as I am a thinking thing, they did not even make me; they merely placed certain dispositions in the matter which I have always regarded as containing me, or rather my mind, for that is all I now take myself to be. So there can be no difficulty regarding my parents in this context. Altogether then, it must be concluded that the mere fact that I exist and have within me an idea of a most perfect being, that is, God, provides a very clear proof that God indeed exists.

It only remains for me to examine how I received this idea from God. For I did not acquire it from the senses; it has never come to me unexpectedly, as usually happens with the ideas of things that are perceivable by the senses, when these things present themselves to the external sense organs – or seem to do so. And it was not invented by me either; for I am plainly unable either to take away anything from it or to add anything to it. The only remaining alternative is that it is innate in me, just as the idea of myself is innate in me.

And indeed it is no surprise that God, in creating me, should have placed this idea in me to be, as it were, the mark of the craftsman stamped on his work – not that the mark need be anything distinct from the work itself. But the mere fact that God created me is a very strong basis for believing that I am somehow made in his image and likeness, and that I perceive that likeness, which includes the idea of God, by the same faculty which enables me to perceive myself. That is, when I turn my mind's eye upon myself, I understand that I am a thing which is incomplete and dependent on another and which aspires without limit to ever greater and better things; but I also understand at the same time that he on whom I depend has within him all those greater things, not just indefinitely and potentially but actually and infinitely, and hence that he is God. The whole force of the argument lies in this: I recognize that it would be impossible for me to exist with the kind of nature I have – that is, having within me the idea of God – were it not the case that God really existed. By 'God' I mean the very being the idea of whom is within me, that is, the possessor of all the perfections which I cannot grasp, but can somehow reach in my thought, who is subject to no defects whatsoever.[44] It is clear enough from this that he cannot be a deceiver, since it is manifest by the natural light that all fraud and deception depend on some defect.

But before examining this point more carefully and investigating other truths which may be derived from it, I should like to pause here and spend some time in the contemplation of God; to reflect on his attributes, and to gaze with wonder and adoration on the beauty of this immense light, so far as the eye of my darkened intellect can bear it. For just as we believe through faith that the supreme happiness of the next life consists solely in the contemplation of the divine majesty, so experience tells us that this same contemplation, albeit much less perfect, enables us to know the greatest joy of which we are capable in this life. . . .

Sixth Meditation
The existence of material things, and the real distinction
between mind and body[45]

It remains for me to examine whether material things exist. And at least I now know they are capable of existing, in so far as they are the subject-matter of pure mathematics, since I perceive them clearly and distinctly. For there is no doubt that God is capable of creating everything that I am capable of perceiving in this manner; and I have never judged that something could not be made by him except on the grounds that there would be a contradiction in my perceiving it distinctly. The conclusion that material things exist is also suggested by the faculty of imagination, which I am aware of using when I turn my mind to material things. For when I give more attentive consideration to what imagination is, it seems to be nothing else but an application of the cognitive faculty to a body which is intimately present to it, and which therefore exists.

To make this clear, I will first examine the difference between imagination and pure understanding. When I imagine a triangle, for example, I do not merely understand that it is a figure bounded by three lines, but at the same time I also see the three lines with my mind's eye as if they were present before me; and this is what I call imagining. But if I want to think of a chiliagon, although I understand that it is a figure consisting of a thousand sides just as well as I understand the triangle to be a three-sided figure, I do not in the same way imagine the thousand sides or see them as if they were present before me. It is true that since I am in the habit of imagining something whenever I think of a corporeal thing, I may construct in my mind a confused representation of some figure; but it is clear that this is not a chiliagon. For it differs in no way from the representation I should form if I were thinking of a myriagon, or any figure with very many sides. Moreover, such a representation is useless for recognizing the properties which distinguish a chiliagon from other polygons. But suppose I am dealing with a pentagon: I can of course understand the figure of a pentagon, just as I can the figure of a chiliagon, without the help of the imagination; but I can also imagine a pentagon, by applying my mind's eye to its five sides and the area contained within them. And in doing this I notice quite clearly that imagination requires a peculiar effort of mind which is not required for understanding; this additional effort of mind clearly shows the difference between imagination and pure understanding.

Besides this, I consider that this power of imagining which is in me, differing as it does from the power of understanding, is not a necessary constituent of my own essence, that is, of the essence of my mind. For if I lacked it, I should undoubtedly remain the same individual as I now am; from which it seems to follow that it depends on something distinct from myself. And I can easily understand that, if there does exist some body to which the mind is so joined that it can apply itself to contemplate it, as it were, whenever it pleases, then it may possibly be this very body that enables me to imagine corporeal things. So the difference between this mode of thinking and pure understanding may simply be this: when the mind understands, it in some way turns towards itself and inspects one of the ideas which are within it; but when it imagines, it turns towards the body and looks at something in the body which conforms to an idea understood by the mind or perceived by the senses. I can, as I say, easily understand that this is how imagination comes about, if the body exists; and since there is no other equally suitable way of explaining imagination that comes to mind, I can make a probable conjecture that the body exists. But this is only a probability; and despite a careful and comprehensive investigation, I do not yet see how the distinct idea of corporeal nature which I find in my imagination can provide any basis for a necessary inference that some body exists.

But besides that corporeal nature which is the subject-matter of pure mathematics, there is much else that I habitually imagine, such as colours, sounds, tastes, pain and so on – though not so distinctly. Now I perceive these things much better by means of the senses, which is how, with the assistance of memory, they appear to have reached the imagination. So in order to deal with them more fully, I must pay equal attention to the senses, and see whether the things which are perceived by means of that mode of thinking which I call 'sensory perception' provide me with any sure argument for the existence of corporeal things.

To begin with, I will go back over all the things which I previously took to be perceived by the senses, and reckoned to be true; and I will go over my reasons for thinking this. Next, I will set out my reasons for subsequently calling these things into doubt. And finally I will consider what I should now believe about them.

First of all then, I perceived by my senses that I had a head, hands, feet and other limbs making up the body which I regarded as part of myself, or perhaps even as my whole self. I also perceived by my senses that this body was situated among many other bodies which could affect it in various favourable or unfavourable ways; and I gauged the favourable effects by a sensation of pleasure, and the unfavourable ones by a sensation of pain. In addition to pain and pleasure, I also had sensations within me of hunger, thirst, and other such appetites, and also of physical propensities towards cheerfulness, sadness, anger and similar emotions. And outside me, besides the extension, shapes and movements of bodies, I also had sensations of their hardness and heat, and of the other tactile qualities. In addition, I had sensations of light, colours, smells, tastes and sounds, the variety of which enabled me to distinguish the sky, the earth, the seas, and all other bodies, one from another. Considering the ideas of all these qualities which presented themselves to my thought, although the ideas were, strictly speaking, the only immediate objects of my sensory awareness, it was not unreasonable for me to think that the items which I was perceiving through the senses were things quite distinct from my thought, namely bodies which produced the ideas. For my experience was that these ideas came to me quite without my consent, so that I could not have sensory awareness of any object, even if I wanted to, unless it was present to my sense organs; and I could not avoid having sensory awareness of it when it was present. And since the ideas perceived by the senses were much more lively and vivid and even, in their own way, more distinct than any of those which I deliberately formed through meditating or which I found impressed on my memory, it seemed impossible that they should have come from within me; so the only alternative was that they came from other things. Since the sole source of my knowledge of these things was the ideas themselves, the supposition that the things resembled the ideas was bound to occur to me. In addition, I remembered that the use of my senses had come first, while the use of my reason came only later; and I saw that the ideas which I formed myself were less vivid than those which I perceived with the senses and were, for the most part, made up of elements of sensory ideas. In this way I easily convinced myself that I had nothing at all in the intellect which I had not previously had in sensation. As for the body which by some special right I called 'mine', my belief that this body, more than any other, belonged to me had some justification. For I could never be separated from it, as I could from other bodies; and I felt all my appetites and emotions in, and on account of, this body; and finally, I was aware of pain and pleasurable ticklings in parts of this body, but not in other bodies external to it. But why should that curious sensation of pain give rise to a particular distress of mind; or why should a certain kind of delight follow on a tickling sensation? Again, why should that curious tugging in the stomach which I call hunger tell me that I should eat, or a dryness of the throat tell me to drink, and so on? I was not able to give any explanation of all this, except that nature taught me so. For there is absolutely no connection (at least that I can understand) between the tugging sensation and the decision to take food, or between the sensation of something causing pain and the mental apprehension of distress that arises from that sensation. These and other judgements that I made concerning sensory objects, I was apparently taught to make by nature; for I had already made up my mind that this was how things were, before working out any arguments to prove it.

Later on, however, I had many experiences which gradually undermined all the faith I had had in the senses. Sometimes towers which had looked round from a distance appeared square from close up; and enormous statues standing on their pediments did not seem large when observed from the ground. In these and countless other such cases, I found that the judgements of the external senses were mistaken. And this applied not just to the external senses but to the internal senses as well. For what can be more internal than pain? And yet I had heard that those who had had a leg or an arm amputated sometimes still seemed to feel pain intermittently in the missing part of the body. So even in my own case it was apparently not quite certain that a particular limb was hurting, even if I felt pain in it. To these reasons for doubting, I recently added two very general ones.[46] The first was that every sensory experience I have ever thought I was having while awake I can also think of myself as sometimes having while asleep; and since I do not believe that what I seem to perceive in sleep comes from things located outside me, I did not see why I should be any more inclined to believe this of what I think I perceive while awake. The second reason for doubt was that since I did not know the author of my being (or at least was pretending not to), I saw nothing to rule out the possibility that my natural constitution made me prone to error even in matters which seemed to me most true. As for the reasons for my previous confident belief in the truth of the things perceived by the senses, I had no trouble in refuting them. For since I apparently had natural impulses towards many things which reason told me to avoid, I reckoned that a great deal of confidence should not be placed in what I was taught by nature. And despite the fact that the perceptions of the senses were not dependent on my will, I did not think that I should on that account infer that they proceeded from things distinct from myself, since I might perhaps have a faculty not yet known to me which produced them.[47]

But now, when I am beginning to achieve a better knowledge of myself and the author of my being, although I do not think I should heedlessly accept everything I seem to have acquired from the senses, neither do I think that everything should be called into doubt.

First, I know that everything which I clearly and distinctly understand is capable of being created by God so as to correspond exactly with my understanding of it. Hence the fact that I can clearly and distinctly understand one thing apart from another is enough to make me certain that the two things are distinct, since they are capable of being separated, at least by God. The question of what kind of power is required to bring about such a separation does not affect the judgement that the two things are distinct. Thus, simply by knowing that I exist and seeing at the same time that absolutely nothing else belongs to my nature or essence except that I am a thinking thing, I can infer correctly that my essence consists solely in the fact that I am a thinking thing. It is true that I may have (or, to anticipate, that I certainly have) a body that is very closely joined to me. But nevertheless, on the one hand I have a clear and distinct idea of myself, in so far as I am simply a thinking, non-extended thing; and on the other hand I have a distinct idea of body,[48] in so far as this is simply an extended, non-thinking thing. And accordingly, it is certain that I[49] am really distinct from my body, and can exist without it.

Besides this, I find in myself faculties for certain special modes of thinking,[50] namely imagination and sensory perception. Now I can clearly and distinctly understand myself as a whole without these faculties; but I cannot, conversely, understand these faculties without me, that is, without an intellectual substance to inhere in. This is because there is an intellectual act included in their essential definition; and hence I perceive that the distinction between them and myself corresponds to the distinction between the modes of a thing and the thing itself.[51] Of course I also recognize that there are other faculties (like those of changing position, of taking on various shapes, and so on) which, like sensory perception and imagination, cannot be understood apart from some substance for them to inhere in, and hence cannot exist without it. But it is clear that these other faculties, if they exist, must be in a corporeal or extended substance and not an intellectual one; for the clear and distinct conception of them includes extension, but does not include any intellectual act whatsoever. Now there is in me a passive faculty of sensory perception, that is, a faculty for receiving and recognizing the ideas of sensible objects; but I could not make use of it unless there was also an active faculty, either in me or in something else, which produced or brought about these ideas. But this faculty cannot be in me, since clearly it presupposes no intellectual act on my part,[52] and the ideas in question are produced without my cooperation and often even against my will. So the only alternative is that it is in another substance distinct from me – a substance which contains either formally or eminently all the reality which exists objectively[53] in the ideas produced by this faculty (as I have just noted). This substance is either a body, that is, a corporeal nature, in which case it will contain formally ⟨and in fact⟩ everything which is to be found objectively ⟨or representatively⟩ in the ideas; or else it is God, or some creature more noble than a body, in which case it will contain eminently whatever is to be found in the ideas. But since God is not a deceiver, it is quite clear that he does not transmit the ideas to me either directly from himself, or indirectly, via some creature which contains the objective reality of the ideas not formally but only eminently. For God has given me no faculty at all for recognizing any such source for these ideas; on the contrary, he has given me a great propensity to believe that they are produced by corporeal things. So I do not see how God could be understood to be anything but a deceiver if the ideas were transmitted from a source other than corporeal things. It follows that corporeal things exist. They may not all exist in a way that exactly corresponds with my sensory grasp of them, for in many cases the grasp of the senses is very obscure and confused. But at least they possess all the properties which I clearly and distinctly understand, that is, all those which, viewed in general terms, are comprised within the subject-matter of pure mathematics.

What of the other aspects of corporeal things which are either particular (for example that the sun is of such and such a size or shape), or less clearly understood, such as light or sound or pain, and so on? Despite the high degree of doubt and uncertainty involved here, the very fact that God is not a deceiver, and the consequent impossibility of there being any falsity in my opinions which cannot be corrected by some other faculty supplied by God, offers me a sure hope that I can attain the truth even in these matters. Indeed, there is no doubt that everything that I am taught by nature contains some truth. For if nature is considered in its general aspect, then I understand by the term nothing other than God himself, or the ordered system of created things established by God. And by my own nature in particular I understand nothing other than the totality of things bestowed on me by God.

There is nothing that my own nature teaches me more vividly than that I have a body, and that when I feel pain there is something wrong with the body, and that when I am hungry or thirsty the body needs food and drink, and so on. So I should not doubt that there is some truth in this.

Nature also teaches me, by these sensations of pain, hunger, thirst and so on, that I am not merely present in my body as a sailor is present in a ship,[54] but that I am very closely joined and, as it were, intermingled with it, so that I and the body form a unit. If this were not so, I, who am nothing but a thinking thing, would not feel pain when the body was hurt, but would perceive the damage purely by the intellect, just as a sailor perceives by sight if anything in his ship is broken. Similarly, when the body needed food or drink, I should have an explicit understanding of the fact, instead of having confused sensations of hunger and thirst. For these sensations of hunger, thirst, pain and so on are nothing but confused modes of thinking which arise from the union and, as it were, intermingling of the mind with the body.

I am also taught by nature that various other bodies exist in the vicinity of my body, and that some of these are to be sought out and others avoided. And from the fact that I perceive by my senses a great variety of colours, sounds, smells and tastes, as well as differences in heat, hardness and the like, I am correct in inferring that the bodies which are the source of these various sensory perceptions possess differences corresponding to them, though perhaps not resembling them. Also, the fact that some of the perceptions are agreeable to me while others are disagreeable makes it quite certain that my body, or rather my whole self, in so far as I am a combination of body and mind, can be affected by the various beneficial or harmful bodies which surround it.

There are, however, many other things which I may appear to have been taught by nature, but which in reality I acquired not from nature but from a habit of making ill-considered judgements; and it is therefore quite possible that these are false. Cases in point are the belief that any space in which nothing is occurring to stimulate my senses must be empty; or that the heat in a body is something exactly resembling the idea of heat which is in me; or that when a body is white or green, the selfsame whiteness or greenness which I perceive through my senses is present in the body; or that in a body which is bitter or sweet there is the selfsame taste which I experience, and so on; or, finally, that stars and towers and other distant bodies have the same size and shape which they present to my senses, and other examples of this kind. But to make sure that my perceptions in this matter are sufficiently distinct, I must more accurately define exactly what I mean when I say that I am taught something by nature. In this context I am taking nature to be something more limited than the totality of things bestowed on me by God. For this includes many things that belong to the mind alone – for example my perception that what is done cannot be undone, and all other things that are known by the natural light;[55] but at this stage I am not speaking of these matters. It also includes much that relates to the body alone, like the tendency to move in a downward direction, and so on; but I am not speaking of these matters either. My sole concern here is with what God has bestowed on me as a combination of mind and body. My nature, then, in this limited sense, does indeed teach me to avoid what induces a feeling of pain and to seek out what induces feelings of pleasure, and so on. But it does not appear to teach us to draw any conclusions from these sensory perceptions about things located outside us without waiting until the intellect has examined[56] the matter. For knowledge of the truth about such things seems to belong to the mind alone, not to the combination of mind and body. Hence, although a star has no greater effect on my eye than the flame of a small light, that does not mean that there is any real or positive inclination in me to believe that the star is no bigger than the light; I have simply made this judgement from childhood onwards without any rational basis. Similarly, although I feel heat when I go near a fire and feel pain when I go too near, there is no convincing argument for supposing that there is something in the fire which resembles the heat, any more than for supposing that there is something which resembles the pain. There is simply reason to suppose that there is something in the fire, whatever it may eventually turn out to be, which produces in us the feelings of heat or pain. And likewise, even though there is nothing in any given space that stimulates the senses, it does not follow that there is no body there. In these cases and many others I see that I have been in the habit of misusing the order of nature. For the proper purpose of the sensory perception given me by nature is simply to inform the mind of what is beneficial or harmful for the composite of which the mind is a part; and to this extent they are sufficiently clear and distinct. But I misuse them by treating them as reliable touchstones for immediate judgements about the essential nature of the bodies located outside us; yet this is an area where they provide only very obscure information.

I have already looked in sufficient detail at how, notwithstanding the goodness of God, it may happen that my judgements are false. But a further problem now comes to mind regarding those very things which nature presents to me as objects which I should seek out or avoid, and also regarding the internal sensations, where I seem to have detected errors[57] – e.g. when someone is tricked by the pleasant taste of some food into eating the poison concealed inside it. Yet in this case, what the man's nature urges him to go for is simply what is responsible for the pleasant taste, and not the poison, which his nature knows nothing about. The only inference that can be drawn from this is that his nature is not omniscient. And this is not surprising, since man is a limited thing, and so it is only fitting that his perfection should be limited.

And yet it is not unusual for us to go wrong even in cases where nature does urge us towards something. Those who are ill, for example, may desire food or drink that will shortly afterwards turn out to be bad for them. Perhaps it may be said that they go wrong because their nature is disordered, but this does not remove the difficulty. A sick man is no less one of God's creatures than a healthy one, and it seems no less a contradiction to suppose that he has received from God a nature which deceives him. Yet a clock constructed with wheels and weights observes all the laws of its nature just as closely when it is badly made and tells the wrong time as when it completely fulfils the wishes of the clockmaker. In the same way, I might consider the body of a man as a kind of machine equipped with and made up of bones, nerves, muscles, veins, blood and skin in such a way that, even if there were no mind in it, it would still perform all the same movements as it now does in those cases where movement is not under the control of the will or, consequently, of the mind.[58] I can easily see that if such a body suffers from dropsy, for example, and is affected by the dryness of the throat which normally produces in the mind the sensation of thirst, the resulting condition of the nerves and other parts will dispose the body to take a drink, with the result that the disease will be aggravated. Yet this is just as natural as the body's being stimulated by a similar dryness of the throat to take a drink when there is no such illness and the drink is beneficial. Admittedly, when I consider the purpose of the clock, I may say that it is departing from its nature when it does not tell the right time; and similarly when I consider the mechanism of the human body, I may think that, in relation to the movements which normally occur in it, it too is deviating from its nature if the throat is dry at a time when drinking is not beneficial to its continued health. But I am well aware that 'nature' as I have just used it has a very different significance from 'nature' in the other sense. As I have just used it, 'nature' is simply a label which depends on my thought; it is quite extraneous to the things to which it is applied, and depends simply on my comparison between the idea of a sick man and a badly-made clock, and the idea of a healthy man and a well-made clock. But by 'nature' in the other sense I understand something which is really to be found in the things themselves; in this sense, therefore, the term contains something of the truth.

When we say, then, with respect to the body suffering from dropsy, that it has a disordered nature because it has a dry throat and yet does not need drink, the term 'nature' is here used merely as an extraneous label. However, with respect to the composite, that is, the mind united with this body, what is involved is not a mere label, but a true error of nature, namely that it is thirsty at a time when drink is going to cause it harm. It thus remains to inquire how it is that the goodness of God does not prevent nature, in this sense, from deceiving us.

The first observation I make at this point is that there is a great difference between the mind and the body, inasmuch as the body is by its very nature always divisible, while the mind is utterly indivisible. For when I consider the mind, or myself in so far as I am merely a thinking thing, I am unable to distinguish any parts within myself; I understand myself to be something quite single and complete. Although the whole mind seems to be united to the whole body, I recognize that if a foot or arm or any other part of the body is cut off, nothing has thereby been taken away from the mind. As for the faculties of willing, of understanding, of sensory perception and so on, these cannot be termed parts of the mind, since it is one and the same mind that wills, and understands and has sensory perceptions. By contrast, there is no corporeal or extended thing that I can think of which in my thought I cannot easily divide into parts; and this very fact makes me understand that it is divisible. This one argument would be enough to show me that the mind is completely different from the body, even if I did not already know as much from other considerations.

My next observation is that the mind is not immediately affected by all parts of the body, but only by the brain, or perhaps just by one small part of the brain, namely the part which is said to contain the 'common' sense.[59] Every time this part of the brain is in a given state, it presents the same signals to the mind, even though the other parts of the body may be in a different condition at the time. This is established by countless observations, which there is no need to review here.

I observe, in addition, that the nature of the body is such that whenever any part of it is moved by another part which is some distance away, it can always be moved in the same fashion by any of the parts which lie in between, even if the more distant part does nothing. For example, in a cord ABCD, if one end D is pulled so that the other end A moves, the exact same movement could have been brought about if one of the intermediate points B or C had been pulled, and D had not moved at all. In similar fashion, when I feel a pain in my foot, physiology tells me that this happens by means of nerves distributed throughout the foot, and that these nerves are like cords which go from the foot right up to the brain. When the nerves are pulled in the foot, they in turn pull on inner parts of the brain to which they are attached, and produce a certain motion in them; and nature has laid it down that this motion should produce in the mind a sensation of pain, as occurring in the foot. But since these nerves, in passing from the foot to the brain, must pass through the calf, the thigh, the lumbar region, the back and the neck, it can happen that, even if it is not the part in the foot but one of the intermediate parts which is being pulled, the same motion will occur in the brain as occurs when the foot is hurt, and so it will necessarily come about that the mind feels the same sensation of pain. And we must suppose the same thing happens with regard to any other sensation.

My final observation is that any given movement occurring in the part of the brain that immediately affects the mind produces just one corresponding sensation; and hence the best system that could be devised is that it should produce the one sensation which, of all possible sensations, is most especially and most frequently conducive to the preservation of the healthy man. And experience shows that the sensations which nature has given us are all of this kind; and so there is absolutely nothing to be found in them that does not bear witness to the power and goodness of God. For example, when the nerves in the foot are set in motion in a violent and unusual manner, this motion, by way of the spinal cord, reaches the inner parts of the brain, and there gives the mind its signal for having a certain sensation, namely the sensation of a pain as occurring in the foot. This stimulates the mind to do its best to get rid of the cause of the pain, which it takes to be harmful to the foot. It is true that God could have made the nature of man such that this particular motion in the brain indicated something else to the mind; it might, for example, have made the mind aware of the actual motion occurring in the brain, or in the foot, or in any of the intermediate regions; or it might have indicated something else entirely. But there is nothing else which would have been so conducive to the continued well-being of the body. In the same way, when we need drink, there arises a certain dryness in the throat; this sets in motion the nerves of the throat, which in turn move the inner parts of the brain. This motion produces in the mind a sensation of thirst, because the most useful thing for us to know about the whole business is that we need drink in order to stay healthy. And so it is in the other cases.

It is quite clear from all this that, notwithstanding the immense goodness of God, the nature of man as a combination of mind and body is such that it is bound to mislead him from time to time. For there may be some occurrence, not in the foot but in one of the other areas through which the nerves travel in their route from the foot to the brain, or even in the brain itself; and if this cause produces the same motion which is generally produced by injury to the foot, then pain will be felt as if it were in the foot. This deception of the senses is natural, because a given motion in the brain must always produce the same sensation in the mind; and the origin of the motion in question is much more often going to be something which is hurting the foot, rather than something existing elsewhere. So it is reasonable that this motion should always indicate to the mind a pain in the foot rather than in any other part of the body. Again, dryness of the throat may sometimes arise not, as it normally does, from the fact that a drink is necessary to the health of the body, but from some quite opposite cause, as happens in the case of the man with dropsy. Yet it is much better that it should mislead on this occasion than that it should always mislead when the body is in good health. And the same goes for the other cases.

This consideration is the greatest help to me, not only for noticing all the errors to which my nature is liable, but also for enabling me to correct or avoid them without difficulty. For I know that in matters regarding the well-being of the body, all my senses report the truth much more frequently than not. Also, I can almost always make use of more than one sense to investigate the same thing; and in addition, I can use both my memory, which connects present experiences with preceding ones, and my intellect, which has by now examined all the causes of error. Accordingly, I should not have any further fears about the falsity of what my senses tell me every day; on the contrary, the exaggerated doubts of the last few days should be dismissed as laughable. This applies especially to the principal reason for doubt, namely my inability to distinguish between being asleep and being awake. For I now notice that there is a vast difference between the two, in that dreams are never linked by memory with all the other actions of life as waking experiences are. If, while I am awake, anyone were suddenly to appear to me and then disappear immediately, as happens in sleep, so that I could not see where he had come from or where he had gone to, it would not be unreasonable for me to judge that he was a ghost, or a vision created in my brain,[60] rather than a real man. But when I distinctly see where things come from and where and when they come to me, and when I can connect my perceptions of them with the whole of the rest of my life without a break, then I am quite certain that when I encounter these things I am not asleep but awake. And I ought not to have even the slightest doubt of their reality if, after calling upon all the senses as well as my memory and my intellect in order to check them, I receive no conflicting reports from any of these sources. For from the fact that God is not a deceiver it follows that in cases like these I am completely free from error. But since the pressure of things to be done does not always allow us to stop and make such a meticulous check, it must be admitted that in this human life we are often liable to make mistakes about particular things, and we must acknowledge the weakness of our nature.

Notes

1 The continuous divine action necessary to maintain things in existence.
2 Descartes here uses this scholastic term to refer to those features of a thing which may alter, e.g. the particular size, shape etc. of a body, or the particular thoughts, desires etc. of a mind.
3 '... or the soul of man, for I make no distinction between them' (added in French version).
4 For Descartes' use of this term, see Med. III, below.
5 Descartes added this passage on the advice of Arnauld (cf AT VII 215 CSM II 151). He told Mersenne 'please put the words in brackets so that it can be seen that they have been added' (letter of 18 March 1641).
6 '... and in my dreams regularly represent to myself the same things' (French version).
7 '... the place where they are, the time which measures their duration' (French version).
8 '... yet I cannot doubt that he does allow this' (French version).
9 '... in the sciences' (added in French version).
10 '... nevertheless it is in my power to suspend my judgement' (French version).
11 '... puts into my mind' (French version).
12 '... or thought anything at all' (French version).
13 The word 'only' is most naturally taken as going with 'a thing that thinks', and this interpretation is followed in the French version. When discussing this passage with Gassendi, however, Descartes suggests that he meant the 'only' to govern 'in the strict sense'; cf AT IXA 215; CSM II 276.
14 '... to see if I am not something more' (added in French version).
15 Lat. *maneat* ('let it stand'), first edition. The second edition has the indicative *manet*: 'The proposition still stands, *viz*, that I am nonetheless something.' The French version reads: 'without changing this supposition, I find that I am still certain that I am something'.
16 '... from this manner of conceiving things' (French version).
17 '... which can be conceived only by the understanding or the mind' (French version).
18 '... or rather the act whereby it is perceived' (added in French version).
19 See note 59 below.
20 The French version has 'more clear and distinct' and, at the end of this sentence, 'more evidently, distinctly and clearly'.
21 The French version here inserts 'loves, hates'.
22 '... all the things which we conceive very clearly and very distinctly are true' (French version).
23 '... it was not because of any knowledge I possessed' (French version).
24 The opening of this sentence is greatly expanded in the French version: 'In order that I may have the opportunity of examining this without interrupting the order of meditating which I have decided upon, which is to start only from those notions which I find first of all in my mind and pass gradually to those which I may find later on, I must here divide my thoughts ...'
25 '... foreign to me and coming from outside' (French version).
26 '... or power for distinguishing truth from falsehood' (French version).
27 '... concerning truth and falsehood' (French version).
28 '... i.e. participate by representation in a higher degree of being or perfection' (added in French version). According to the scholastic distinction invoked in the paragraphs that follow, the

'formal' reality of anything is its own intrinsic reality, while the 'objective' reality of an idea is a function of its representational content. Thus if an idea *A* represents some object *X* which is *F*, then *F*-ness will be contained 'formally' in *X* but 'objectively' in *A*.

29 '. . . i.e. it will contain in itself the same things as are in the stone or other more excellent things' (added in French version). In scholastic terminology, to possess a property 'formally' is to possess it literally, in accordance with its definition; to possess it 'eminently' is to possess it in some higher form.

30 '. . . that this cause must be less real' (French version).

31 '. . . i.e. a manner or way of thinking' (added in French version).

32 '. . . chimerical things which cannot exist' (French version).

33 'And since ideas, being like images, must in each case appear to us to represent something' (French version).

34 '. . . in so far as they represent substances' (French version).

35 '. . . and as it were the garments under which corporeal substance appears to us' (French version).

36 '. . . that the idea I have of them' (French version).

37 '. . . i.e. could be in me in virtue of my imperfection' (added in French version).

38 According to Descartes one can know or understand something without fully grasping it 'just as we can touch a mountain but not put our arms around it. To grasp something is to embrace it in one's thought; to know something, it suffices to touch it with one's thought' (letter to Mersenne, 26 May 1630).

39 '. . . but only what is actual and real' (added in French version).

40 '. . . and were independent of every other being' (added in French version).

41 Cf. *Principles*, Part I, art. 62: AT VIII 30; CSM 1214.

42 '. . . at least as much reality in the cause as in its effect' (French version).

43 Lat. *per se*; literally 'through itself'.

44 '. . . and has not one of the things which indicate some imperfection' (added in French version).

45 '. . . between the soul and body of a man' (French version).

46 Cf. Med. I, above pp. 9–10.

47 Cf. Med. III, above p. 17.

48 The Latin term *corpus* as used here by Descartes is ambiguous as between 'body' (i.e. corporeal matter in general) and 'the body' (i.e. this particular body of mine). The French version preserves the ambiguity.

49 '. . . that is, my soul, by which I am what I am' (added in French version).

50 '. . . certain modes of thinking which are quite special and distinct from me' (French version).

51 '. . . between the shapes, movements and other modes or accidents of a body and the body which supports them' (French version).

52 '. . . cannot be in me in so far as I am merely a thinking thing, since it does not presuppose any thought on my part' (French version).

53 For the terms 'formally', 'eminently' and 'objectively', see notes 28–31 above.

54 '. . . as a pilot in his ship' (French version).

55 '. . . without any help from the body' (added in French version).

56 '. . . carefully and maturely examined' (French version).

57 '. . . and thus seem to have been directly deceived by my nature' (added in French version).

58 '. . . but occurs merely as a result of the disposition of the organs' (French version).

59 The supposed faculty which integrates the data from the five specialized senses (the notion goes back ultimately to Aristotle). 'The seat of the common sense must be very mobile, to receive all the impressions coming from the senses, but must be moveable only by the spirits which transmit these impressions. Only the *conarion* [pineal gland] fits these conditions' (letter to Mersenne, 21 April 1641).

60 '. . . like those that are formed in the brain when I sleep' (added in French version).

2 From *An Enquiry Concerning Human Understanding**

David Hume

Section II
Of the Origin of Ideas

Every one will readily allow, that there is a considerable difference between the perceptions of the mind, when a man feels the pain of excessive heat, or the pleasure of moderate warmth, and when he afterwards recalls to his memory this sensation, or anticipates it by his imagination. These faculties may mimic or copy the perceptions of the senses; but they never can entirely reach the force and vivacity of the original sentiment. The utmost we say of them, even when they operate with greatest vigour, is, that they represent their object in so lively a manner, that we could *almost* say we feel or see it: But, except the mind be disordered by disease or madness, they never can arrive at such a pitch of vivacity, as to render these perceptions altogether undistinguishable. All the colours of poetry, however splendid, can never paint natural objects in such a manner as to make the description be taken for a real landskip. The most lively thought is still inferior to the dullest sensation.

We may observe a like distinction to run though all the other perceptions of the mind. A man in a fit of anger, is actuated in a very different manner from one who only thinks of that emotion. If you tell me, that any person is in love, I easily understand your meaning, and form a just conception of his situation; but never can mistake that conception for the real disorders and agitations of the passion. When we reflect on our past sentiments and affections, our thought is a faithful mirror, and copies its objects truly; but the colours which it employs are faint and dull, in comparison of those in which our original perceptions were clothed. It requires no nice discernment or metaphysical head to mark the distinction between them.

Here therefore we may divide all the perceptions of the mind into two classes or species, which are distinguished by their different degrees of force and vivacity. The less forcible and lively are commonly denominated THOUGHTS or IDEAS. The other species want a name in our language, and in most others; I suppose, because it was not requisite for any, but philosophical purposes, to rank them under a general term or appellation. Let us, therefore, use a little freedom, and call them IMPRESSIONS; employing that word in a sense somewhat different from the usual. By the term *impression*, then, I mean all our more lively perceptions, when we hear, or see, or feel, or love, or hate, or desire, or will. And impressions are distinguished from ideas, which are the less lively perceptions, of which we are conscious, when we reflect on any of those sensations or movements above mentioned.

Nothing, at first view, may seem more unbounded than the thought of man, which not only escapes all human power and authority, but is not even restrained within the

* From David Hume, *An Enquiry Concerning Human Understanding*, Sections II–VII. Public domain. First published in 1748.

limits of nature and reality. To form monsters, and join incongruous shapes and appearances, costs the imagination no more trouble than to conceive the most natural and familiar objects. And while the body is confined to one planet, along which it creeps with pain and difficulty; the thought can in an instant transport us into the most distant regions of the universe; or even beyond the universe, into the unbounded chaos, where nature is supposed to lie in total confusion. What never was seen, or heard of, may yet be conceived; nor is any thing beyond the power of thought, except what implies an absolute contradiction.

But though our thought seems to possess this unbounded liberty, we shall find, upon a nearer examination, that it is really confined within very narrow limits, and that all this creative power of the mind amounts to no more than the faculty of compounding, transposing, augmenting, or diminishing the materials afforded us by the senses and experience. When we think of a golden mountain, we only join two consistent ideas, *gold*, and *mountain*, with which we were formerly acquainted. A virtuous horse we can conceive; because, from our own feeling, we can conceive virtue; and this we may unite to the figure and shape of a horse, which is an animal familiar to us. In short, all the materials of thinking are derived either from our outward or inward sentiment: The mixture and composition of these belongs alone to the mind and will. Or, to express myself in philosophical language, all our ideas or more feeble perceptions are copies of our impressions or more lively ones.

To prove this, the two following arguments will, I hope, be sufficient. First, when we analyse our thoughts or ideas, however compounded or sublime, we always find, that they resolve themselves into such simple ideas as were copied from a precedent feeling or sentiment. Even those ideas, which, at first view, seem the most wide of this origin, are found, upon a nearer scrutiny, to be derived from it. The idea of God, as meaning an infinitely intelligent, wise, and good Being, arises from reflecting on the operations of our own mind, and augmenting, without limit, those qualities of goodness and wisdom. We may prosecute this enquiry to what length we please; where we shall always find, that every idea which we examine is copied from a similar impression. Those who would assert, that this position is not universally true nor without exception, have only one, and that an easy method of refuting it; by producing that idea, which, in their opinion, is not derived from this source. It will then be incumbent on us, if we would maintain our doctrine, to produce the impression or lively perception, which corresponds to it.

Secondly. If it happen, from a defect of the organ, that a man is not susceptible of any species of sensation, we always find, that he is as little susceptible of the correspondent ideas. A blind man can form no notion of colours; a deaf man of sounds. Restore either of them that sense, in which he is deficient; by opening this new inlet for his sensations, you also open an inlet for the ideas; and he finds no difficulty in conceiving these objects. The case is the same, if the object, proper for exciting any sensation, has never been applied to the organ. A LAPLANDER or NEGRO has no notion of the relish of wine. And though there are few or no instances of a like deficiency in the mind, where a person has never felt or is wholly incapable of a sentiment or passion, that belongs to his species; yet we find the same observation to take place in a less degree. A man of mild manners can form no idea of inveterate revenge or cruelty; nor can a selfish heart easily conceive the heights of friendship and generosity. It is readily allowed, that other beings may possess many senses of which we can have no conception; because the ideas of them have never been introduced to us, in the only manner, by which an idea can have access to the mind, to wit, by the actual feeling and sensation.

There is, however, one contradictory phenomenon, which may prove, that it is not absolutely impossible for ideas to arise, independent of their correspondent impressions. I believe it will readily be allowed, that the several distinct ideas of colour, which enter by the eye, or those of sound, which are conveyed by the ear, are really different from each other; though, at the same time, resembling. Now if this be true of different colours, it must be no less so of the different shades of the same colour; and each shade produces a distinct idea, independent of the rest. For if this should be denied, it is possible, by the continual gradation of shades, to run a colour insensibly into what is most remote from it; and if you will not allow any of the means to be different, you cannot, without absurdity, deny the extremes to be the same. Suppose, therefore, a person to have enjoyed his sight for thirty years, and to have become perfectly acquainted with colours of all kinds, except one particular shade of blue, for instance, which it never has been his fortune to meet with. Let all the different shades of that colour, except that single one, be placed before him, descending gradually from the deepest to the lightest; it is plain, that he will perceive a blank, where that shade is wanting, and will be sensible, that there is a greater distance in that place between the contiguous colours than in any other. Now I ask, whether it be possible for him, from his own imagination, to supply this deficiency, and raise up to himself the idea of that particular shade, though it had never been conveyed to him by his senses? I believe there are few but will be of opinion that he can: And this may serve as a proof, that the simple ideas are not always, in every instance, derived from the correspondent impressions; though this instance is so singular, that it is scarcely worth our observing, and does not merit, that for it alone we should alter our general maxim.

Here, therefore, is a proposition, which not only seems, in itself, simple and intelligible; but, if a proper use were made of it, might render every dispute equally intelligible, and banish all that jargon, which has so long taken possession of metaphysical reasonings, and drawn disgrace upon them. All ideas, especially abstract ones, are naturally faint and obscure: The mind has but a slender hold of them: They are apt to be confounded with other resembling ideas; and when we have often employed any term, though without a distinct meaning, we are apt to imagine it has a determinate idea, annexed to it. On the contrary, all impressions, that is, all sensations, either outward or inward, are strong and vivid: The limits between them are more exactly determined: Nor is it easy to fall into any error or mistake with regard to them. When we entertain, therefore, any suspicion, that a philosophical term is employed without any meaning or idea (as is but too frequent), we need but enquire, *from what impression is that supposed idea derived?* And if it be impossible to assign any, this will serve to confirm our suspicion. By bringing ideas into so clear a light, we may reasonably hope to remove all dispute, which may arise, concerning their nature and reality.[1]

Section III
Of the Association of Ideas

It is evident, that there is a principle of connexion between the different thoughts or ideas of the mind, and that, in their appearance to the memory or imagination, they introduce each other with a certain degree of method and regularity. In our more serious thinking or discourse, this is so observable, that any particular thought, which breaks in upon the regular tract or chain of ideas, is immediately remarked and rejected. And even in our wildest and most wandering reveries, nay in our very dreams, we shall find, if we reflect, that the imagination ran not altogether at adventures, but that there was still a connexion upheld among the different ideas, which succeeded each other. Were the loosest and freest conversation to be transcribed, there would immediately be observed something, which connected it in all its transitions. Or where this is wanting, the person, who broke the thread of discourse, might still inform you, that there had secretly revolved in his mind a succession of thought, which had gradually led him from the subject of conversation. Among different languages, even where we cannot suspect the least connexion or communication, it is found, that the words, expressive of ideas, the most compounded, do yet nearly correspond to each other: A certain proof, that the simple ideas, comprehended in the compound ones, were bound together by some universal principle, which had an equal influence on all mankind.

Though it be too obvious to escape observation, that different ideas are connected together; I do not find, that any philosopher has attempted to enumerate or class all the principles of association; a subject, however, that seems worthy of curiosity. To me, there appear to be only three principles of connexion among ideas, namely, *Resemblance, Contiguity* in time or place, and *Cause* or *Effect*.

That these principles serve to connect ideas will not, I believe, be much doubted. A picture naturally leads our thoughts to the original:[2] The mention of one apartment in a building naturally introduces an enquiry or discourse concerning the others:[3] And if we think of a wound, we can scarcely forbear reflecting on the pain which follows it.[4] But that this enumeration is complete, and that there are no other principles of association, except these, may be difficult to prove to the satisfaction of the reader, or even to a man's own satisfaction. All we can do, in such cases, is to run over several instances, and examine carefully the principle, which binds the different thoughts to each other, never stopping till we render the principle as general as possible.[5] The more instances we examine, and the more care we employ, the more assurance shall we acquire, that the enumeration, which we form from the whole, is complete and entire.

Section IV
Sceptical Doubts Concerning the Operations of the Understanding

Part I

All the objects of human reason or enquiry may naturally be divided into two kinds, to wit, *Relations of Ideas*, and *Matters of Fact*. Of the first kind are the sciences of Geometry, Algebra, and Arithmetic; and in short, every affirmation, which is either intuitively or demonstratively certain. *That the square of the hypothenuse is equal to the square of the two sides*, is a proposition, which expresses a relation between these figures. *That three times five is equal to the half of thirty*, expresses a relation between these numbers. Propositions of this kind are discoverable by the mere operation of thought, without dependence on what is any where existent in the universe. Though there never were a circle or triangle in nature, the truths, demonstrated by EUCLID, would for ever retain their certainty and evidence.

Matters of fact, which are the second objects of human reason, are not ascertained in the same manner; nor is our evidence of their truth, however great, of a like nature with the foregoing. The contrary of every matter of fact is still possible; because it can never imply a contradiction, and is conceived by the mind with the same facility and distinctness, as if ever so conformable to reality. *That the sun will not rise to-morrow* is no less intelligible a proposition, and implies no more contradiction, than the affirmation, *that it will rise*. We should in vain, therefore, attempt to demonstrate its falsehood. Were it demonstratively false, it would imply a contradiction, and could never be distinctly conceived by the mind.

It may, therefore, be a subject worthy of curiosity, to enquire what is the nature of that evidence, which assures us of any real existence and matter of fact, beyond the present testimony of our senses, or the records of our memory. This part of philosophy, it is observable, has been little cultivated, either by the ancients or moderns; and therefore our doubts and errors, in the prosecution of so important an enquiry, may be the more excusable; while we march through such difficult paths, without any guide or direction. They may even prove useful, by exciting curiosity, and destroying that implicit faith and security, which is the bane of all reasoning and free enquiry. The discovery of defects in the common philosophy, if any such there be, will not, I presume, be a discouragement, but rather an incitement, as is usual, to attempt something more full and satisfactory, than has yet been proposed to the public.

All reasonings concerning matter of fact seem to be founded on the relation of *Cause and Effect*. By means of that relation alone we can go beyond the evidence of our memory and senses. If you were to ask a man, why he believes any matter of fact, which is absent; for instance, that his friend is in the country, or in FRANCE; he would give you a reason; and this reason would be some other fact; as a letter received from him, or the knowledge of his former resolutions and promises. A man, finding a watch or any other machine in a desert island, would conclude, that there had once been men in that island. All our reasonings concerning fact are of the same nature. And here it is constantly supposed, that there is a connexion between the present fact and that which is inferred from it. Were there nothing to bind them together, the inference would be entirely precarious. The hearing of an articulate voice and rational discourse in the dark assures us of the presence of some person: Why? because these are the effects of the human make and fabric, and closely connected with it. If we anatomize all the other reasonings of this nature, we shall find, that they are founded on the relation of cause and effect, and that this relation is either near or remote, direct or collateral. Heat and light are collateral effects of fire, and the one effect may justly be inferred from the other.

If we would satisfy ourselves, therefore, concerning the nature of that evidence, which assures us of matters of fact, we must enquire how we arrive at the knowledge of cause and effect.

I shall venture to affirm, as a general proposition, which admits of no exception, that the knowledge of this relation is not, in any instance, attained by reasonings *a priori*; but arises entirely from experience, when we find, that any particular objects are constantly conjoined with each other. Let an object be presented to a man of ever so strong natural reason and abilities; if that object be entirely new to him, he will not be able, by the most accurate examination of its sensible qualities, to discover any of its causes or effects. ADAM, though his rational faculties be supposed, at the very first, entirely perfect, could not have inferred from the fluidity, and transparency of water, that it would suffocate him, or from the light and warmth of fire, that it would consume him. No object ever discovers, by the qualities which appear to the senses, either the causes which produced it, or the effects which will arise from it; nor can our reason, unassisted by experience, ever draw any inference concerning real existence and matter of fact.

This proposition, *that causes and effects are discoverable, not by reason, but by experience*, will readily be admitted with regard to such objects, as we remember to have once been altogether unknown to us; since we must be conscious of the utter inability, which we then lay under, of foretelling, what would arise from them. Present two smooth pieces of marble to a man, who has no tincture of natural philosophy; he will never discover, that they will adhere together, in such a manner as to require great force to separate them in a direct line, while they make so small a resistance to a lateral pressure. Such events, as bear little analogy to the common course of nature, are also readily confessed to be known only by experience; nor does any man imagine that the explosion of gunpowder, or the attraction of a loadstone, could ever be discovered by arguments *a priori*. In like manner, when an effect is supposed to depend upon an intricate machinery or secret structure of parts, we make no difficulty in attributing all our knowledge of it to experience. Who will assert, that he can give the ultimate reason, why milk or bread is proper nourishment for a man, not for a lion or a tiger?

But the same truth may not appear, at first sight, to have the same evidence with regard to events, which have become familiar to us from our first appearance in the world, which bear a close analogy to the whole course of nature, and which are supposed to depend on the simple qualities of objects, without any secret structure of parts. We are apt to imagine, that we could discover these effects by the mere operation of our reason, without experience. We fancy, that were we brought, on a sudden, into this world, we could at first have inferred, that one Billiard-ball would communicate motion to another upon impulse; and that we needed not to have waited for the event, in order to pronounce with certainty concerning it. Such is the influence of custom, that, where it is strongest, it not only covers our natural ignorance, but even conceals itself, and seems not to take place, merely because it is found in the highest degree.

But to convince us, that all the laws of nature, and all the operations of bodies without exception, are known only by experience, the following reflections may, perhaps, suffice. Were any object presented to us, and were we required to pronounce concerning the effect, which will result from it, without consulting past observation; after what manner, I beseech you, must the mind proceed in this operation? It must invent or imagine some event, which it ascribes to the object as its effect; and it is plain that this invention must be entirely arbitrary. The mind can never possibly find the effect in the supposed cause, by the most accurate scrutiny and examination. For the effect is totally different from the cause, and consequently can never be discovered in it. Motion in the second Billiard-ball is a quite distinct event from motion in the first; nor is there any thing in the one to suggest the smallest hint of the other. A stone or piece of metal raised into the air, and left without any support, immediately falls: But to consider the matter *a priori*, is there any thing we discover in this situation, which can beget the idea of a downward, rather than an upward, or any other motion, in the stone or metal?

And as the first imagination or invention of a particular effect, in all natural operations, is arbitrary, where we consult not experience; so must we also esteem the supposed tie or connexion between the cause and effect, which binds them together, and renders it impossible, that any other defect could result from the operation of that cause. When I see, for instance, a Billiard-ball moving in a straight line towards another; even suppose motion in the second ball should by accident be suggested to me, as the result of their contact or impulse; may I not conceive, that a hundred different events might as well follow from that cause? May not both these balls remain at absolute rest? May not the first ball return in a straight line, or leap off from the second in any line or direction? All these suppositions are consistent and conceivable. Why then should we give the preference to one, which is no more consistent or conceivable than the rest? All our reasonings *a priori* will never be able to show us any foundation for this preference.

In a word, then, every effect is a distinct event from its cause. It could not, therefore, be discovered in the cause, and the first invention or conception of it, *a priori*, must be entirely arbitrary. And even after it is suggested, the conjunction of it with the cause must appear equally arbitrary; since there are always many other effects, which, to reason, must seem fully as consistent and natural. In vain, therefore, should we pretend to determine any single event, or infer any cause or effect, without the assistance of observation and experience.

Hence we may discover the reason, why no philosopher, who is rational and modest, has ever pretended to assign the ultimate cause of any natural operation, or to show distinctly the action of that power, which produces any single effect in the universe. It is confessed, that the utmost effort of human reason is, to reduce the principles, productive of natural phenomena, to a greater simplicity, and to resolve the many particular effects into a few general causes, by means of reasonings from analogy, experience, and observation. But as to the causes of these general causes, we should in vain attempt their discovery; nor shall we ever be able to satisfy ourselves, by any particular explication of them. These ultimate springs and principles are totally shut up from human curiosity and enquiry. Elasticity, gravity, cohesion of parts, communication of motion by impulse; these are probably the ultimate causes and principles which we shall ever discover in nature; and we may esteem ourselves sufficiently happy, if, by accurate enquiry and reasoning, we can trace up the particular phenomena to, or near to, these general principles. The most perfect philosophy of the natural kind only staves off our ignorance a little longer: As perhaps the most perfect philosophy of the moral or metaphysical kind serves only to discover larger portions of it. Thus the observation of human blindness and weakness is the result of all philosophy, and meets us, at every turn, in spite of our endeavours to elude or avoid it.

Nor is geometry, when taken into the assistance of natural philosophy, ever able to remedy this effect, or lead us into the knowledge of ultimate causes, by all that accuracy of reasoning, for which it is so justly celebrated. Every part of mixed mathematics proceeds upon the supposition, that certain laws are established by nature in her operations; and abstract reasonings are employed, either to assist experience in the discovery of these laws, or to determine their influence in particular instances, where it depends upon any precise degree of distance and quantity. Thus, it is a law of motion, discovered by experience, that the moment or force of any body in motion is in the compound ratio or proportion of its solid contents and its velocity; and consequently, that a small force may remove the greatest obstacle or raise the greatest weight, if, by any contrivance or machinery, we can increase the velocity of that force, so as to make it an overmatch for its antagonist. Geometry assists us in the application of this law, by giving us the just dimensions of all the parts and figures, which can enter into any species of machine; but still the discovery of the law itself is owing merely to experience, and all the abstract reasonings in the world could never lead us one step towards the knowledge of it. When we reason *a priori*, and consider merely any object or cause, as it appears to the mind, independent of all observation, it never could suggest to us the notion of any distinct object, such as its effect; much less, show us the inseparable and inviolable connection between them. A man must be very sagacious, who could discover by reasoning, that crystal is the effect of heat, and ice of cold, without being previously acquainted with the operation of these qualities.

Part II

But we have not, yet, attained any tolerable satisfaction with regard to the question first proposed. Each solution still gives rise to a new question as difficult as the foregoing, and leads us on to farther enquiries. When it is asked, *What is the nature of all our reasonings concerning matter of fact?* the proper answer seems to be, that they are founded on the relation of cause and effect. When again it is asked, *What is the foundation of all our reasonings and conclusions concerning that relation?* it may be replied in one word, EXPERIENCE. But if we still carry on our sifting humour, and ask, *What is the foundation of all conclusions from experience?* this implies a new question, which may be of more difficult solution and explication. Philosophers, that give themselves airs of superior wisdom and sufficiency, have a hard task, when they encounter persons of inquisitive dispositions, who push them from every corner, to which they retreat, and who are sure at last to bring them to some dangerous dilemma. The best expedient to prevent this confusion, is to be modest in our pretensions; and even to discover the difficulty ourselves before it is objected to us. By this means, we may make a kind of merit of our very ignorance.

I shall content myself, in this section, with an easy task, and shall pretend only to give a negative answer to the question here proposed. I say then, that, even after we have experience of the operations of cause and effect, our conclusions from that experience are *not* founded on reasoning, or any process of the understanding. This answer we must endeavour, both to explain and to defend.

It must certainly be allowed, that nature has kept us at a great distance from all her secrets, and has afforded us only the knowledge of a few superficial qualities of objects; while she conceals from us those powers and principles, on which the influence of these objects entirely depends. Our senses inform us of the colour, weight, and consistence of bread; but neither sense nor reason can ever inform us of those qualities, which fit it for the nourishment and support of a human body. Sight or feeling conveys an idea of the actual motion of bodies; but as to that wonderful force or power, which would carry on a moving body for ever in a continued change of place, and which bodies never lose but by communicating it to others; of this we cannot form the most distant conception. But notwithstanding this ignorance of natural powers[6] and principles, we always presume, when we see like sensible qualities, that they have like secret powers, and expect, that effects, similar to those which we have experienced, will follow from them. If a body of like colour and consistence with that bread, which we have formerly eat, be presented to us, we make no scruple of repeating the experiment, and foresee, with certainty, like nourishment and support. Now this is a process of the mind or thought, of which I would willingly know the foundation. It is allowed on all hands, that there is no known connexion between the sensible qualities and the secret powers; and consequently, that the mind is not led to form such a conclusion concerning their constant and regular conjunction, by any thing which it knows of their nature. As to past *Experience*, it can be allowed to give *direct* and *certain* information of those precise objects only, and that precise period of time, which fell under its cognizance: But why this experience should be extended to future times, and to other objects, which for aught we know, may be only in appearance similar; this is the main question on which I would insist. The bread, which

I formerly eat, nourished me; that is, a body of such sensible qualities, was, at that time, endued with such secret powers: But does it follow, that other bread must also nourish me at another time, and that like sensible qualities must always be attended with like secret powers? The consequence seems nowise necessary. At least, it must be acknowledged, that there is here a consequence drawn by the mind; that there is a certain step taken; a process of thought, and an inference, which wants to be explained. These two propositions are far from being the same, *I have found that such an object has always been attended with such an effect,* and *I foresee, that other objects, which are, in appearance, similar, will be attended with similar effects.* I shall allow, if you please, that the one proposition may justly be inferred from the other: I know in fact, that it always is inferred. But if you insist, that the inference is made by a chain of reasoning, I desire you to produce that reasoning. The connexion between these propositions is not intuitive. There is required a medium, which may enable the mind to draw such an inference, if indeed it be drawn by reasoning and argument. What that medium is, I must confess, passes my comprehension; and it is incumbent on those to produce it, who assert, that it really exists, and is the origin of all our conclusions concerning matter of fact.

This negative argument must certainly, in process of time, become altogether convincing, if many penetrating and able philosophers shall turn their enquiries this way; and no one be ever able to discover any connecting proposition or intermediate step, which supports the understanding in this conclusion. But as the question is yet new, every reader may not trust so far to his own penetration, as to conclude, because an argument escapes his enquiry, that therefore it does not really exist. For this reason it may be requisite to venture upon a more difficult task; and enumerating all the branches of human knowledge, endeavour to show, that none of them can afford such an argument.

All reasonings may be divided into two kinds, namely demonstrative reasoning, or that concerning relations of ideas, and moral reasoning, or that concerning matter of fact and existence. That there are no demonstrative arguments in the case, seems evident; since it implies no contradiction, that the course of nature may change, and that an object, seemingly like those which we have experienced, may be attended with different or contrary effects. May I not clearly and distinctly conceive, that a body, falling from the clouds, and which, in all other respects, resembles snow, has yet the taste of salt or feeling of fire? Is there any more intelligible proposition than to affirm, that all the trees will flourish in DECEMBER and JANUARY, and decay in MAY and JUNE? Now whatever is intelligible, and can be distinctly conceived, implies no contradiction, and can never be proved false by any demonstrative argument or abstract reasoning *a priori.*

If we be, therefore, engaged by arguments to put trust in past experience, and make it the standard of our future judgment, these arguments must be probable only, or such as regard matter of fact and real existence, according to the division above mentioned. But that there is no argument of this kind, must appear, if our explication of that species of reasoning be admitted as solid and satisfactory. We have said, that all arguments concerning existence are founded on the relation of cause and effect; that our knowledge of that relation is derived entirely from experience; and that all our experimental conclusions proceed upon the supposition, that the future will be conformable to the past. To endeavour, therefore, the proof of this last supposition by probable arguments, or arguments regarding existence, must be evidently going in a circle, and taking that for granted, which is the very point in question.

In reality, all arguments from experience are founded on the similarity, which we discover among natural objects, and by which we are induced to expect effects similar to those, which we have found to follow from such objects. And though none but a fool or madman will ever pretend to dispute the authority of experience, or to reject that great guide of human life; it may surely be allowed a philosopher to have so much curiosity at least, as to examine the principle of human nature, which gives this mighty authority to experience, and makes us draw advantage from that similarity, which nature has placed among different objects. From causes, which appear *similar*, we expect similar effects. This is the sum of all our experimental conclusions. Now it seems evident, that, if this conclusion were formed by reason, it would be as perfect at first, and upon one instance, as after ever so long a course of experience. But the case is far otherwise. Nothing so like as eggs; yet no one, on account of this appearing similarity, expects the same taste and relish in all of them. It is only after a long course of uniform experiments in any kind, that we attain a firm reliance and security with regard to a particular event. Now where is that process of reasoning, which, from one instance, draws a conclusion, so different from that which it infers from a hundred instances, that are nowise different from that single one? This question I propose as much for the sake of information, as with an intention of raising difficulties. I cannot find, I cannot imagine any such reasoning. But I keep my mind still open to instruction; if any one will vouchsafe to bestow it on me.

Should it be said, that, from a number of uniform experiments, we *infer* a connexion between the sensible qualities and the secret powers; this, I must confess, seems the same difficulty, couched in different terms. The question still recurs, on what process of argument this *inference* is founded? Where is the medium, the interposing ideas, which join propositions so very wide of each other? It is confessed, that the colour, consistence, and other sensible qualities of bread appear not, of themselves, to have any connexion with the secret powers of nourishment and support. For otherwise we could infer these secret powers from the first appearance of these sensible qualities, without the aid of experience; contrary to the sentiment of all philosophers, and contrary to plain matter of fact. Here then is our natural state of ignorance with regard to the powers and influence of all objects. How is this remedied by experience? It only shows us a number of uniform effects, resulting from certain objects, and teaches us, that those particular objects, at that particular time, were endowed with such powers and forces. When a new object, endowed with similar sensible qualities, is produced, we expect similar powers and forces, and look for a like effect. From a body of like colour and consistence with bread, we expect like nourishment and support. But this surely is a step or progress of the mind, which wants to be explained. When a man says, *I have found, in all past instances, such sensible qualities conjoined with such secret powers:* And when he says, *similar sensible qualities will always be conjoined with similar secret powers;* he is not guilty of a tautology, nor are these propositions in any respect the same. You say that the one proposition is an inference from the other. But you must confess that the inference is not intuitive; neither is it demonstrative: Of what nature is it then? To say it is experimental, is begging the question. For all inferences from experience suppose, as their foundation, that the future will resemble the past, and that similar powers will be conjoined with similar sensible qualities. If there be any suspicion, that the course of nature may change, and that the past may be no rule for the future, all experience becomes useless, and can give rise to no inference or conclusion. It is impossible, therefore, that any arguments from experience can prove this resemblance of the past to the future; since all these arguments are founded on the supposition of that resemblance. Let the course of things be allowed hitherto ever so regular; that alone, without some new argument or inference, proves not, that, for the future, it will continue so. In vain do you pretend to have learned the nature of bodies from your past experience. Their secret nature, and consequently, all their effects and influence, may change, without any change in their sensible qualities. This happens sometimes, and with regard to some objects: Why may it not happen always, and with regard to all objects? What logic, what process of argument secures you against this supposition? My practice, you say, refutes my doubts. But you mistake the purport of my question. As an agent, I am quite satisfied in the point; but as a philosopher, who has some share of curiosity, I will not say scepticism, I want to learn the foundation of this inference. No reading, no enquiry has yet been able to remove my difficulty, or give me satisfaction in a matter of such importance. Can I do better than propose the difficulty to the public, even though, perhaps, I have small hopes of obtaining a solution? We shall at least, by this means, be sensible of our ignorance, if we do not augment our knowledge.

I must confess, that a man is guilty of unpardonable arrogance, who concludes, because an argument has escaped his own investigation, that therefore it does not really exist. I must also confess, that, though all the learned, for several ages, should have employed themselves in fruitless search upon any subject, it may still, perhaps, be rash to conclude positively, that the subject must, therefore, pass all human comprehension. Even though we examine all the sources of our knowledge, and conclude them unfit for such a subject, there may still remain a suspicion, that the enumeration is not complete, or the examination not accurate. But with regard to the present subject, there are some considerations, which seem to remove all this accusation of arrogance or suspicion of mistake.

It is certain, that the most ignorant and stupid peasants, nay infants, nay even brute beasts, improve by experience, and learn the qualities of natural objects, by observing the effects, which result from them. When a child has felt the sensation of pain from touching the flame of a candle, he will be careful not to put his hand near any candle; but will expect a similar effect from a cause, which is similar in its sensible qualities and appearance. If you assert, therefore, that the understanding of the child is led into this conclusion by any process of argument or ratiocination, I may justly require you to produce that argument; nor have you any pretence to refuse so equitable a demand. You cannot say, that the argument is abstruse, and may possibly escape your enquiry; since you confess, that it is obvious to the capacity of a mere infant. If you hesitate, therefore, a moment, or if, after reflection, you produce any intricate or profound argument, you, in a manner, give up the question, and confess, that it is not reasoning which engages us to suppose the past resembling the future, and to expect similar effects from causes, which are, to appearance, similar. This is the proposition which I intended to enforce in the present section. If I be right, I pretend not to have made any mighty discovery. And if I be wrong, I must acknowledge myself to be indeed a very backward scholar; since I cannot now discover an argument, which, it seems, was perfectly familiar to me, long before I was out of my cradle.

Section V
Sceptical Solution of these Doubts

Part I

The passion for philosophy, like that for religion, seems liable to this inconvenience, that, though it aims at the correction of our manners, and extirpation of our vices, it may only serve, by imprudent management, to foster a predominant inclination, and push the mind, with more determined resolution, towards that side, which already *draws* too much, by the biass and propensity of the natural temper. It is certain, that, while we aspire to the magnanimous firmness of the philosophic sage, and endeavour to confine our pleasures altogether within our own minds, we may, at last, render our philosophy like that of EPICTETUS, and other *Stoics*, only a more refined system of selfishness, and reason ourselves out of all virtue, as well as social enjoyment. While we study with attention the vanity of human life, and turn all our thoughts towards the empty and transitory nature of riches and honours, we are, perhaps, all the while, flattering our natural indolence, which, hating the bustle of the world, and drudgery of business, seeks a pretence of reason, to give itself a full and uncontrolled indulgence. There is, however, one species of philosophy, which seems little liable to this inconvenience, and that because it strikes in with no disorderly passion of the human mind, nor can mingle itself with any natural affection or propensity; and that is the ACADEMIC or SCEPTICAL philosophy. The academics always talk of doubt and suspense of judgment, of danger in hasty determinations, of confining to very narrow bounds the enquiries of the understanding, and of renouncing all speculations which lie not within the limits of common life and practice. Nothing, therefore, can be more contrary than such a philosophy to the supine indolence of the mind, its rash arrogance, its lofty pretensions, and its superstitious credulity. Every passion is mortified by it, except the love of truth; and that passion never is, nor can be carried to too high a degree. It is surprising, therefore, that this philosophy, which, in almost every instance, must be harmless and innocent, should be the subject of so much groundless reproach and obloquy. But, perhaps, the very circumstance, which renders it so innocent, is what chiefly exposes it to the public hatred and resentment. By flattering no irregular passion, it gains few partizans: By opposing so many vices and follies, it raises to itself abundance of enemies, who stigmatize it as libertine, profane, and irreligious.

Nor need we fear, that this philosophy, while it endeavours to limit our enquiries to common life, should ever undermine the reasonings of common life, and carry its doubts so far as to destroy all action, as well as speculation. Nature will always maintain her rights, and prevail in the end over any abstract reasoning whatsoever. Though we should conclude, for instance, as in the foregoing section, that, in all reasonings from experience, there is a step taken by the mind, which is not supported by any argument or process of the understanding; there is no danger, that these reasonings, on which almost all knowledge depends, will ever be affected by such a discovery. If the mind be not engaged by argument to make this step, it must be induced by some other principle of equal weight and authority; and that principle will preserve its influence as long as human nature remains the same. What that principle is, may well be worth the pains of enquiry.

Suppose a person, though endowed with the strongest faculties of reason and reflection, to be brought on a sudden into this world; he would, indeed, immediately observe a continual succession of objects, and one event following another; but he would not be able to discover any thing farther. He would not, at first, by any reasoning, be able to reach the idea of cause and effect; since the particular powers, by which all natural operations are performed, never appear to the senses; nor is it reasonable to conclude, merely because one event, in one instance, precedes another, that therefore the one is the cause, the other the effect. Their conjunction may be arbitrary and casual. There may be no reason to infer the existence of one from the appearance of the other. And in a word, such a person, without more experience, could never employ his conjecture or reasoning concerning any matter of fact, or be assured of any thing beyond what was immediately present to his memory and senses.

Suppose again, that he has acquired more experience, and has lived so long in the world as to have observed similar objects or events to be constantly conjoined together; what is the consequence of this experience? He immediately infers the existence of one object from the appearance of the other. Yet he has not, by all his experience, acquired any idea or knowledge of the secret power, by which the one object produces the other; nor is it, by any process of reasoning, he is engaged to draw this inference. But still he finds himself determined to draw it: And though he should be convinced, that his understanding has no part in the operation, he would nevertheless continue in the same course of thinking. There is some other principle, which determines him to form such a conclusion.

This principle is CUSTOM or HABIT. For wherever the repetition of any particular act or operation produces a propensity to renew the same act or operation, without being impelled by any reasoning or process of the understanding; we always say, that this propensity is the effect of *Custom*. By employing that word, we pretend not to have given the ultimate reason of such a propensity. We only point out a principle of human nature, which is universally acknowledged, and which is well known by its effects. Perhaps, we can push our enquiries no farther, or pretend to give the cause of this cause; but must rest contented with it as the ultimate principle, which we can assign, of all our conclusions from experience. It is sufficient satisfaction, that we can go so far; without repining at the narrowness of our faculties, because they will carry us no farther. And it is certain we here advance a very intelligible proposition at least, if not a true one, when we assert, that, after the constant conjunction of two objects, heat and flame, for instance, weight and solidity, we are determined by custom alone to expect the one from the appearance of the other. This hypothesis seems even the only one, which explains the difficulty, why we draw, from a thousand instances, an inference, which we are not able to draw from one instance, that is, in no respect, different from them. Reason is incapable of any such variation. The conclusions, which it draws from considering one circle, are the same which it would form upon surveying all the circles in the universe. But no man, having seen only one body move after being impelled by another, could infer, that every other body will move after a like impulse. All inferences from experience, therefore, are effects of custom, not of reasoning.[7]

Custom, then, is the great guide of human life. It is that principle alone, which renders our experience useful to us, and makes us expect, for the future, a similar train of events with those which have appeared in the past. Without the influence of custom, we should be entirely ignorant of every matter of fact, beyond what is immediately present to the memory and senses. We should never know how to adjust means to ends, or to employ our natural powers in the production of any effect. There would be an end at once of all action, as well as of the chief part of speculation.

But here it may be proper to remark, that though our conclusions from experience carry us beyond our memory and senses, and assure us of matters of fact, which happened in the most distant places and most remote ages; yet some fact must always be present to the senses or memory, from which we may first proceed in drawing these conclusions. A man, who should find in a desert country the remains of pompous buildings, would conclude, that the country had, in ancient times, been cultivated by civilized inhabitants; but did nothing of this nature occur to him, he could never form such an inference. We learn the events of former ages from history; but then we must peruse the volumes, in which this instruction is contained, and thence carry up our inferences from one testimony to another, till we arrive at the eye-witnesses and spectators of these distant events. In a word, if we proceed not upon some fact, present to the memory or senses, our reasonings would be merely hypothetical; and however the particular links might be connected with each other, the whole chain of inferences would have nothing to support it, nor could we ever, by its means, arrive at the knowledge of any real existence. If I ask, why you believe any particular matter of fact, which you relate, you must tell me some reason; and this reason will be some other fact, connected with it. But as you cannot proceed after this manner, *in infinitum,* you must at last terminate in some fact, which is present to your memory or senses; or must allow that your belief is entirely without foundation.

What then is the conclusion of the whole matter? A simple one; though, it must be confessed, pretty remote from the common theories of philosophy. All belief of matter of fact or real existence is derived merely from some object, present to the memory or senses, and a customary conjunction between that and some other object. Or in other words; having found, in many instances, that any two kinds of objects, flame and heat, snow and cold, have always been conjoined together; if flame or snow be presented anew to the senses, the mind is carried by custom to expect heat or cold, and to *believe,* that such a quality does exist, and will discover itself upon a nearer approach. This belief is the necessary result of placing the mind in such circumstances. It is an operation of the soul, when we are so situated, as unavoidable as to feel the passion of love, when we receive benefits; or hatred, when we meet with injuries. All these operations are a species of natural instincts, which no reasoning or process of the thought and understanding is able, either to produce, or to prevent.

At this point, it would be very allowable for us to stop our philosophical researches. In most questions, we can never make a single step farther; and in all questions, we must terminate here at last, after our most restless and curious enquiries. But still our curiosity will be pardonable, perhaps commendable, if it carry us on to still farther researches, and make us examine more accurately the nature of this *belief,* and of the *customary conjunction,* whence it is derived. By this means we may meet with some explications and analogies, that will give satisfaction; at least to such as love the abstract sciences, and can be entertained with speculations, which, however accurate, may still retain a degree of doubt and uncertainty. As to readers of a different taste; the remaining part of this section is not calculated for them, and the following enquiries may well be understood, though it be neglected.

Part II

Nothing is more free than the imagination of man; and though it cannot exceed that original stock of ideas, furnished by the internal and external senses, it has unlimited power of mixing, compounding, separating, and dividing these ideas, in all the varieties of fiction and vision. It can feign a train of events, with all the appearance of reality, ascribe to them a particular time and place, conceive them as existent, and paint them out to itself with every circumstance, that belongs to any historical fact, which it believes with the greatest certainty. Wherein, therefore, consists the difference between such a fiction and belief? It lies not merely in any peculiar idea, which is annexed to such a conception as commands our assent, and which is wanting to every known fiction. For as the mind has authority over all its ideas, it could voluntarily annex this particular idea to any fiction, and consequently be able to believe whatever it pleases; contrary to what we find by daily experience. We can, in our conception, join the head of a man to the body of a horse; but it is not in our power to believe, that such an animal has ever really existed.

It follows, therefore, that the difference between *fiction* and *belief* lies in some sentiment or feeling, which is annexed to the latter, not to the former, and which depends not on the will, nor can be commanded at pleasure. It must be excited by nature, like all other sentiments; and must arise from the particular situation, in which the mind is placed at any particular juncture. Whenever any object is presented to the memory or senses, it immediately, by the force of custom, carries the imagination to conceive that object, which is usually conjoined to it; and this conception is attended with a feeling or sentiment, different from the loose reveries of the fancy. In this consists the whole nature of belief. For as there is no matter of fact which we believe so firmly, that we cannot conceive the contrary, there would be no difference between the conception assented to, and that which is rejected, were it not for some sentiment, which distinguishes the one from the other. If I see a billiard-ball moving towards another, on a smooth table, I can easily conceive it to stop upon contact. This conception implies no contradiction; but still it feels very differently from that conception, by which I represent to myself the impulse, and the communication of motion from one ball to another.

Were we to attempt a *definition* of this sentiment, we should, perhaps, find it a very difficult, if not an impossible task; in the same manner as if we should endeavour to define the feeling of cold or passion of anger, to a creature who never had any experience of these sentiments. BELIEF is the true and proper name of this feeling; and no one is ever at a loss to know the meaning of that term; because every man is every moment conscious of the sentiment represented by it. It may not, however, be improper to attempt a *description* of this sentiment; in hopes we may, by that means, arrive at some analogies, which may afford a more perfect explication of it. I say then, that belief is nothing but a more vivid, lively, forcible, firm, steady conception of an object, than what the imagination alone is ever able to attain. This variety of terms, which may seem so unphilosophical, is intended only to express that act of the mind, which renders realities, or what is taken for such, more present to us than fictions, causes them to weigh more in the thought, and gives them a superior influence on the passions and imagination. Provided we agree about the thing, it is needless to dispute about the terms. The imagination has the command over all its ideas, and can join and mix and vary them, in all the ways possible. It may conceive fictitious objects with all the circumstances of place and time. It may set them, in a manner, before our eyes, in their true colours, just as they might have existed. But as it is impossible, that this faculty of imagination can ever, of itself, reach belief, it is evident, that belief consists not in the peculiar nature or order of ideas, but in the *manner* of their conception, and in their *feeling* to the mind. I confess, that it is impossible perfectly to explain this feeling or manner of conception. We may make use of words, which express something near it. But its true and proper name, as we observed before, is *belief*; which is a term, that every one sufficiently understands in common life. And in philosophy, we can go no farther than assert, that *belief* is something felt by the mind, which distinguishes the ideas of the judgment from the fictions of the imagination. It gives them more weight and influence; makes them appear of greater importance; enforces them in the mind; and renders them the governing principle of our actions. I hear at present, for instance, a person's voice, with whom I am acquainted; and the sound comes as from the next room. This impression of my senses immediately conveys my thought to the person, together with all the surrounding objects. I paint them out to myself as existing at present, with the same qualities and relations, of which I formerly knew them possessed. These ideas take faster hold of my mind, than ideas of an enchanted castle. They are very different to the feeling, and have a much greater influence of every kind, either to give pleasure or pain, joy or sorrow.

Let us, then, take in the whole compass of this doctrine, and allow, that the sentiment of belief is nothing but a conception more intense and steady than what attends the mere fictions of the imagination, and that this *manner* of conception arises from a customary conjunction of the object with something present to the memory or senses: I believe that it will not be difficult, upon these suppositions, to find other operations of the mind analogous to it, and to trace up these phenomena to principles still more general.

We have already observed, that nature has established connexions among particular ideas, and that no sooner one idea occurs to our thoughts than it introduces its correlative, and carries our attention towards it, by a gentle and insensible movement. These principles of connexion or association we have reduced to three, namely, *Resemblance, Contiguity*, and *Causation*; which are the only bonds, that unite our thoughts together, and beget that regular train of reflection or discourse, which, in a greater or less degree, takes place among all mankind. Now here arises a question, on which the solution of the present difficulty will depend. Does it happen, in all these relations, that, when one of the objects is presented to the senses or memory, the mind is not only carried to the conception of the correlative, but reaches a steadier and stronger conception of it than what otherwise it would have been able to attain? This seems to be the case with that belief, which arises from the relation of cause and effect. And if the case be the same with the other relations or principles of association, this may be established as a general law, which takes place in all the operations of the mind.

We may, therefore, observe, as the first experiment to our present purpose, that, upon the appearance of the picture of an absent friend, our idea of him is evidently enlivened by the *resemblance*, and that every passion, which that idea occasions, whether of joy or sorrow, acquires new force and vigour. In producing this effect, there concur both a relation and a present impression. Where the picture bears him no resemblance, at least was not intended for him, it never so much as conveys our thought to him: And where it is absent, as well as the person; though the mind may pass from the thought of the one to that of the other; it feels its idea to be rather weakened than enlivened by that transition. We take a pleasure in viewing the picture of a friend, when it is set before us; but when it is removed, rather choose to consider him directly, than by reflection in an image, which is equally distant and obscure.

The ceremonies of the ROMAN CATHOLIC religion may be considered as instances of the same nature. The devotees of that superstition usually plead in excuse for the mummeries, with which they are upbraided, that they feel the good effect of those external motions, and postures, and actions, in enlivening their devotion and quickening their fervour, which otherwise would decay, if directed entirely to distant and immaterial objects. We shadow out the objects of our faith, say they, in sensible types and images, and render them more present to us by the immediate presence of these types, than it is possible for us to do, merely by an intellectual view and contemplation. Sensible objects have always a greater influence on the fancy than any other; and this influence they readily convey to those ideas, to which they are related, and which they resemble. I shall only infer from these practices, and this reasoning, that the effect of resemblance in enlivening the ideas is very common; and as in every case a resemblance and a present impression must concur, we are abundantly supplied with experiments to prove the reality of the foregoing principle.

We may add force to these experiments by others of a different kind, in considering the effects of *contiguity* as well as of *resemblance*. It is certain, that distance diminishes the force of every idea, and that, upon our approach to any object; though it does not discover itself to our senses; it operates upon the mind with an influence, which imitates an immediate impression. The thinking on any object readily transports the mind to what is contiguous; but it is only the actual presence of an object, that transports it with a superior vivacity. When I am a few miles from home, whatever relates to it touches me more nearly than when I am two hundred leagues distant; though even at that distance the reflecting on any thing in the neighbourhood of my friends or family naturally produces an idea of them. But as in this latter case, both the objects of the mind are ideas; notwithstanding there is an easy transition between them; that transition alone is not able to give a superior vivacity to any of the ideas, for want of some immediate impression.[8]

No one can doubt but causation has the same influence as the other two relations of resemblance and contiguity. Superstitious people are fond of the relics of saints and holy men, for the same reason, that they seek after types or images, in order to enliven their devotion, and give them a more intimate and strong conception of those exemplary lives, which they desire to imitate. Now it is evident, that one of the best relics, which a devotee could procure, would be the handiwork of a saint; and if his clothes and furniture are ever to be considered in this light, it is because they were once at his disposal, and were moved and affected by him; in which respect they are to be considered as imperfect effects, and as connected with him by a shorter chain of consequences than any of those, by which we learn the reality of his existence.

Suppose, that the son of a friend, who had been long dead or absent, were presented to us; it is evident, that this object would instantly revive its correlative idea, and recall to our thoughts all past intimacies and familiarities, in more lively colours than they would otherwise have appeared to us. This is another phenomenon, which seems to prove the principle above-mentioned.

We may observe, that, in these phenomena, the belief of the correlative object is always presupposed; without which the relation could have no effect. The influence of the picture supposes, that we *believe* our friend to have once existed. Contiguity to home can never excite our ideas of home, unless we *believe* that it really exists. Now I assert, that this belief, where it reaches beyond the memory or senses, is of a similar nature, and arises from similar causes, with the transition of thought and vivacity of conception here explained. When I throw a piece of dry wood into a fire, my mind is immediately carried to conceive, that it augments, not extinguishes the flame. This transition of thought from the cause to the effect proceeds not from reason. It derives its origin altogether from custom and experience. And as it first begins from an object, present to the senses, it renders the idea or conception of flame more strong and lively than any loose, floating reverie of the imagination. That idea arises immediately. The thought moves instantly towards it, and conveys to it all that force of conception, which is derived from the impression present to the senses. When a sword is levelled at my breast, does not the idea of wound and pain strike me more strongly, than when a glass of wine is presented to me, even though by accident this idea should occur after the appearance of the latter object? But what is there in this whole matter to cause such a strong conception, except only a present object and a customary transition to the idea of another object, which we have been accustomed to conjoin with the former? This is the whole operation of the mind, in all our conclusions concerning matter of fact and existence; and it is a satisfaction to find some analogies, by which it may be explained. The transition from a present object does in all cases give strength and solidity to the related idea.

Here, then, is a kind of pre-established harmony between the course of nature and the succession of our ideas; and though the powers and forces, by which the former is governed, be wholly unknown to us; yet our thoughts and conceptions have still, we find, gone on in the same train with the other works of nature. Custom is that principle, by which this correspondence has been effected; so necessary to the subsistence of our species, and the regulation of our conduct, in every circumstance and occurrence of human life. Had not the presence of an object instantly excited the idea of those objects, commonly conjoined with it, all our knowledge must have been limited to the narrow sphere of our memory and senses; and we should never have been able to adjust means to ends, or employ our natural powers, either to the producing of good, or avoiding of evil. Those, who delight in the discovery and contemplation of *final causes*, have here ample subject to employ their wonder and admiration.

I shall add, for a further confirmation of the foregoing theory, that, as this operation of the mind, by which we infer like effects from like causes, and *vice versa*, is so essential to the subsistence of all human creatures, it is not probable, that it could be trusted to the fallacious deductions of our reason, which is slow in its operations; appears not, in any degree, during the first years of infancy; and at best is, in every age and period of human life, extremely liable to error and mistake. It is more conformable to the ordinary wisdom of nature to secure so necessary an act of the mind, by some instinct or mechanical tendency, which may be infallible in its operations, may discover itself at the first appearance of life and thought, and may be independent of all the laboured deductions of the understanding. As nature has taught us the use of our limbs, without giving us the knowledge of the muscles and nerves, by which they are actuated; so has she implanted in us an instinct, which carries forward the thought in a correspondent course to that which she has established among external objects; though we are ignorant of those powers and forces, on which this regular course and succession of objects totally depends.

Section VI
Of Probability[9]

Though there be no such thing as *Chance* in the world; our ignorance of the real cause of any event has the same influence on the understanding, and begets a like species of belief or opinion.

There is certainly a probability, which arises from a superiority of chances on any side; and according as this superiority increases, and surpasses the opposite chances, the probability receives a proportionable increase, and begets still a higher degree of belief or assent to that side, in which we discover the superiority. If a die were marked with one figure or number of spots on four sides, and with another figure or number of spots on the two remaining sides, it would be more probable, that the former would turn up than the latter; though, if it had a thousand sides marked in the same manner, and only one side different, the probability would be much higher, and our belief or expectation of the event more steady and secure. This process of the thought or reasoning may seem trivial and obvious; but to those who consider it more narrowly, it may, perhaps, afford matter for curious speculation.

It seems evident, that, when the mind look forward to discover the event, which may result from the throw of such a die, it considers the turning up of each particular side as alike probable; and this is the very nature of chance, to render all the particular events, comprehended in it, entirely equal. But finding a greater number of sides concur in the one event than in the other, the mind is carried more frequently to that event, and meets it oftener, in revolving the various possibilities or chances, on which the ultimate result depends. This concurrence of several views in one particular event begets immediately, by an inexplicable contrivance of nature, the sentiment of belief, and gives that event the advantage over its antagonist, which is supported by a smaller number of views, and recurs less frequently to the mind. If we allow, that belief is nothing but a firmer and stronger conception of an object than what attends the mere fictions of the imagination, this operation may, perhaps, in some measure, be accounted for. The concurrence of these several views or glimpses imprints the idea more strongly on the imagination; gives it superior force and vigour; renders its influence on the passions and affections more sensible; and in a word, begets that reliance or security, which constitutes the nature of belief and opinion.

The case is the same with the probability of causes, as with that of chance. There are some causes, which are entirely uniform and constant in producing a particular effect; and no instance has ever yet been found of any failure or irregularity in their operation. Fire has always burned, and water suffocated every human creature: The production of motion by impulse and gravity is an universal law, which has hitherto admitted of no exception. But there are other causes, which have been found more irregular and uncertain; nor has rhubarb always proved a purge, or opium a soporific to every one, who has taken these medicines. It is true, when any cause fails of producing its usual effect, philosophers ascribe not this to any irregularity in nature; but suppose, that some secret causes, in the particular structure of parts, have prevented the operation. Our reasonings, however, and conclusions concerning the event are the same as if this principle had no place. Being determined by custom to transfer the past to the future, in all our inferences; where the past has been entirely regular and uniform, we expect the event with the greatest assurance, and leave no room for any contrary supposition. But where different effects have been found to follow from causes, which are to *appearance* exactly similar, all these various effects must occur to the mind in transferring the past to the future, and enter into our consideration, when we determine the probability of the event. Though we give the preference to that which has been found most usual, and believe that this effect will exist, we must not overlook the other effects, but must assign to each of them a particular weight and authority, in proportion as we have found it to be more or less frequent. It is more probable, in almost every country of EUROPE, that there will be frost sometime in JANUARY, than that the weather will continue open throughout that whole month; though this probability varies according to the different climates, and approaches to a certainty in the more northern kingdoms. Here then it seems evident, that, when we transfer the past to the future, in order to determine the effect, which will result from any cause, we transfer all the different events, in the same proportion as they have appeared in the past, and conceive one to have existed a hundred times, for instance, another ten times, and another once. As a great number of views do here concur in one event, they fortify and confirm it to the imagination, beget that sentiment which we call *belief,* and give its object the preference above the contrary event, which is not supported by an equal number of experiments, and recurs not so frequently to the thought in transferring the past to the future. Let any one try to account for this operation of the mind upon any of the received systems of philosophy, and he will be sensible of the difficulty. For my part, I shall think it sufficient, if the present hints excite the curiosity of philosophers, and make them sensible how defective all common theories are in treating of such curious and such sublime subjects.

Section VII
Of the Idea of Necessary Connexion

Part I

The great advantage of the mathematical sciences above the moral consists in this, that the ideas of the former, being sensible, are always clear and determinate, the smallest distinction between them is immediately perceptible, and the same terms are still expressive of the same ideas, without ambiguity or variation. An oval is never mistaken for a circle, nor an hyperbola for an ellipsis. The isosceles and scalenum are distinguished by boundaries more exact than vice and virtue, right and wrong. If any term be defined in geometry, the mind readily, of itself, substitutes, on all occasions, the definition for the term defined: Or even when no definition is employed, the object itself may be presented to the senses, and by that means be steadily and clearly apprehended. But the finer sentiments of the mind, the operations of the understanding, the various agitations of the passions, though really in themselves distinct, easily escape us, when surveyed by reflection; nor is it in our power to recall the original object, as often as we have occasion to contemplate it. Ambiguity, by this means, is gradually introduced into our reasonings: Similar objects are readily taken to be the same: And the conclusion becomes at last very wide of the premises.

One may safely, however, affirm, that, if we consider these sciences in a proper light, their advantages and disadvantages nearly compensate each other, and reduce both of them to a state of equality. If the mind, with greater facility, retains the ideas of geometry clear and determinate, it must carry on a much longer and more intricate chain of reasoning, and compare ideas much wider of each other, in order to reach the abstruser truths of that science. And if moral ideas are apt, without extreme care, to fall into obscurity and confusion, the inferences are always much shorter in these disquisitions, and the intermediate steps, which lead to the conclusion, much fewer than in the sciences which treat of quantity and number. In reality, there is scarcely a proposition in EUCLID so simple, as not to consist of more parts, than are to be found in any moral reasoning which runs not into chimera and conceit. Where we trace the principles of the human mind through a few steps, we may be very well satisfied with our progress; considering how soon nature throws a bar to all our enquiries concerning causes, and reduces us to an acknowledgment of our ignorance. The chief obstacle, therefore, to our improvement in the moral or metaphysical sciences is the obscurity of the ideas, and ambiguity of the terms. The principal difficulty in the mathematics is the length of inferences and compass of thought, requisite to the forming of any conclusion. And, perhaps, our progress in natural philosophy is chiefly retarded by the want of proper experiments and phenomena, which are often discovered by chance, and cannot always be found, when requisite, even by the most diligent and prudent enquiry. As moral philosophy seems hitherto to have received less improvement than either geometry or physics, we may conclude, that, if there be any difference in this respect among these sciences, the difficulties, which obstruct the progress of the former, require superior care and capacity to be surmounted.

There are no ideas, which occur in metaphysics, more obscure and uncertain, than those of *power, force, energy,* or *necessary connexion,* of which it is every moment necessary for us to treat in all our disquisitions. We shall, therefore, endeavour, in this section, to fix, if possible, the precise meaning of these terms, and thereby remove some part of that obscurity, which is so much complained of in this species of philosophy.

It seems a proposition, which will not admit of much dispute, that all our ideas are nothing but copies of our impressions, or, in other words, that it is impossible for us to *think* of any thing, which we have not antecedently *felt,* either by our external or internal senses. I have endeavoured[10] to explain and prove this proposition, and have expressed my hopes, that, by a proper application of it, men may reach a greater clearness and precision in philosophical reasonings, than what they have hitherto been able to attain. Complex ideas may, perhaps, be well known by definition, which is nothing but an enumeration of those parts or simple ideas, that compose them. But when we have pushed up definitions to the most simple ideas, and find still some ambiguity and obscurity; what resource are we then possessed of? By what invention can we throw light upon these ideas, and render them altogether precise and determinate to our intellectual view? Produce the impressions or original sentiments, from which the ideas are copied. These impressions are all strong and sensible. They admit not of ambiguity. They are not only placed in a full light themselves, but may throw light on their correspondent ideas, which lie in obscurity. And by this means, we may, perhaps, attain a new microscope or species of optics, by which, in the moral sciences, the most minute, and most simple ideas may be so enlarged as to fall readily under our apprehension, and be equally known with the grossest and most sensible ideas, that can be the object of our enquiry.

To be fully acquainted, therefore, with the idea of power or necessary connexion, let us examine its impression; and in order to find the impression with greater certainty, let us search for it in all the sources, from which it may possibly be derived.

When we look about us towards external objects, and consider the operation of causes, we are never able, in a single instance, to discover any power or necessary connexion; any quality, which binds the effect to the cause, and renders the one an infallible consequence of the other. We only find, that the one does actually, in fact, follow the other. The impulse of one billiard-ball is attended with motion in the second. This is the whole that appears to the *outward* senses. The mind feels no sentiment or *inward* impression from this succession of objects: Consequently, there is not, in any single, particular instance of cause and effect, any thing which can suggest the idea of power or necessary connexion.

From the first appearance of an object, we never can conjecture what effect will result from it. But were the power or energy of any cause discoverable by the mind, we could foresee the effect, even without experience; and might, at first, pronounce with certainty concerning it, by the mere dint of thought and reasoning.

In reality, there is no part of matter, that does ever, by its sensible qualities, discover any power or energy, or give us ground to imagine, that it could produce any thing, or be followed by any other object, which we could denominate its effect. Solidity, extension, motion; these qualities are all complete in themselves, and never point out any other event which may result from them. The scenes of the universe are continually shifting, and one object follows another in an uninterrupted succession; but the power or force, which actuates the whole machine, is entirely concealed from us, and never discovers itself in any of the sensible qualities of body. We know, that, in fact, heat is a constant attendant of flame; but what is the connexion between them, we have no room so much as to conjecture or imagine. It is impossible, therefore, that the idea of power can be derived from the contemplation of bodies, in single instances of their operation; because no bodies ever discover any power, which can be the original of this idea.[11]

Since, therefore, external objects as they appear to the senses, give us no idea of power or necessary connexion, by their operation in particular instances, let us see, whether this idea be derived from reflection on the operations of our own minds, and be copied from any internal impression. It may be said, that we are every moment conscious of internal power; while we feel, that, by the simple command of our will, we can move the organs of our body, or direct the faculties of our mind. An act of volition produces motion in our limbs, or raises a new idea in our imagination. This influence of the will we know by consciousness. Hence we acquire the idea of power or energy; and are certain, that we ourselves and all other intelligent beings are possessed of power. This idea, then, is an idea of reflection, since it arises from reflecting on the operations of our own mind, and on the command which is exercised by will, both over the organs of the body and faculties of the soul.

We shall proceed to examine this pretension; and first with regard to the influence of volition over the organs of the body. This influence, we may observe, is a fact, which, like all other natural events, can be known only by experience, and can never be foreseen from any apparent energy or power in the cause, which connects it with the effect, and renders the one an infallible consequence of the other. The motion of our body follows upon the command of our will. Of this we are every moment conscious. But the means, by which this is effected; the energy, by which the will performs so extraordinary an operation; of this we are so far from being immediately conscious, that it must for ever escape our most diligent enquiry.

For *first*, is there any principle in all nature more mysterious than the union of soul with body; by which a supposed spiritual substance acquires such an influence over a material one, that the most refined thought is able to actuate the grossest matter? Were we empowered, by a secret wish, to remove mountains, or control the planets in their orbit; this extensive authority would not be more extraordinary, nor more beyond our comprehension. But if by consciousness we perceived any power or energy in the will, we must know this power; we must know its connexion with the effect; we must know the secret union of soul and body, and the nature of both these substances; by which the one is able to operate, in so many instances, upon the other.

Secondly, We are not able to move all the organs of the body with a like authority; though we cannot assign any reason besides experience, for so remarkable a difference between one and the other. Why has the will an influence over the tongue and fingers, not over the heart or liver? This question would never embarrass us, were we conscious of a power in the former case, not in the latter. We should then perceive, independent of experience, why the authority of will over the organs of the body is circumscribed within such particular limits. Being in that case fully acquainted with the power or force, by which it operates, we should also know, why its influence reaches precisely to such boundaries, and no farther.

A man, suddenly struck with a palsy in the leg or arm, or who had newly lost those members, frequently endeavours, at first, to move them, and employ them in their usual offices. Here he is as much conscious of power to command such limbs, as a man in perfect health is conscious of power to actuate any member which remains in its natural state and condition. But consciousness never deceives. Consequently, neither in the one case nor in the other, are we ever conscious of any power. We learn the influence of our will from experience alone. And experience only teaches us, how one event constantly follows another; without instructing us in the secret connexion, which binds them together, and renders them inseparable.

Thirdly, We learn from anatomy, that the immediate object of power in voluntary motion, is not the member itself which is moved, but certain muscles, and nerves, and animal spirits, and, perhaps, something still more minute and more unknown, through which the motion is successively propagated, ere it reach the member itself whose motion is the immediate object of volition. Can there be a more certain proof, that the power, by which this whole operation is performed, so far from being directly and fully known by an inward sentiment or consciousness, is, to the last degree, mysterious and unintelligible? Here the mind wills a certain event: Immediately another event, unknown to ourselves, and totally different from the one intended, is produced: This event produces another, equally unknown: Till at last, through a long succession, the desired event is produced. But if the original power were felt, it must be known: Were it known, its effect must also be known; since all power is relative to its effect. And *vice versa*, if the effect be not known, the power cannot be known nor felt. How indeed can we be conscious of a power to move our limbs, when we have no such power; but only that to move certain animal spirits, which, though they produce at last the motion of our limbs, yet operate in such a manner as is wholly beyond our comprehension?

We may, therefore, conclude from the whole, I hope, without any temerity, though with assurance; that our idea of power is not copied from any sentiment or consciousness of power within ourselves, when we give rise to animal motion, or apply our limbs to their proper use and office. That their motion follows the command of the will is a matter of common experience, like other natural events: But the power or energy by which this is effected, like that in other natural events, is unknown and inconceivable.[12]

Shall we then assert, that we are conscious of a power or energy in our own minds, when, by an act or command of our will, we raise up a new idea, fix the mind to the contemplation of it, turn it on all sides, and at last dismiss it for some other idea, when we think that we have surveyed it with sufficient accuracy? I believe the same arguments will prove, that even this command of the will gives us no real idea of force or energy.

First, It must be allowed, that, when we know a power, we know that very circumstance in the cause, by which it is enabled to produce the effect: For these are supposed to be synonymous. We must, therefore, know both the cause and effect, and the relation between them. But do we pretend to be acquainted with the nature of the human soul and the nature of an idea, or the aptitude of the one to produce the other? This is a real creation; a production of something out of nothing: Which implies a power so great, that it may seem, at first sight, beyond the reach of any being, less than infinite. At least it must be owned, that such a power is not felt, nor known, nor even conceivable by the mind. We only feel the event, namely, the existence of an idea, consequent to a command of the will: But the manner, in which this operation is performed; the power, by which it is produced; is entirely beyond our comprehension.

Secondly, The command of the mind over itself is limited, as well as its command over the body; and these limits are not known by reason, or any acquaintance with the nature of cause and effect; but only by experience and observation, as in all other natural events and in the operation of external objects. Our authority over our sentiments and passions is much weaker than that over our ideas; and even the latter authority is circumscribed within very narrow boundaries. Will any one pretend to assign the ultimate reason of these boundaries, or show why the power is deficient in one case not in another.

Thirdly, This self-command is very different at different times. A man in health possesses more of it, than one languishing with sickness. We are more master of our thoughts in the morning than in the evening: Fasting, than after a full meal. Can we give any reason for these variations, except experience? Where then is the power, of which we pretend to be conscious? Is there not here, either in a spiritual or material substance, or both, some secret mechanism or structure of parts, upon which the effect depends, and which, being entirely unknown to us, renders the power or energy of the will equally unknown and incomprehensible?

Volition is surely an act of the mind, with which we are sufficiently acquainted. Reflect upon it. Consider it on all sides. Do you find anything in it like this creative power, by which it raises from nothing a new idea, and with a kind of FIAT, imitates the omnipotence of its Maker, if I may be allowed so to speak, who called forth into existence all the various scenes of nature? So far from being conscious of this energy in the will, it requires as certain experience, as that of which we are possessed, to convince us, that such extraordinary effects do ever result from a simple act of volition.

The generality of mankind never find any difficulty in accounting for the more common and familiar operations of nature; such as the descent of heavy bodies, the growth of plants, the generation of animals, or the nourishment of bodies by food: But suppose, that, in all these cases, they perceive the very force or energy of the cause, by which it is connected with its effect, and is for ever infallible in its operation. They acquire, by long habit, such a turn of mind, that, upon the appearance of the cause, they immediately expect with assurance its usual attendant, and hardly conceive it possible, that any other event could result from it. It is only on the discovery of extraordinary phenomena, such as earthquakes, pestilence, and prodigies of any kind, that they find themselves at a loss to assign a proper cause, and to explain the manner, in which the effect is produced by it. It is usual for men, in such difficulties, to have resource to some invisible intelligent principle,[13] as the immediate cause of that event, which surprises them, and which they think, cannot be accounted for from the common powers of nature. But philosophers, who carry their scrutiny a little farther, immediately perceive, that, even in the most familiar events, the energy of the cause is as unintelligible as in the most unusual, and that we only learn by experience the frequent CONJUNCTION of objects, without being ever able to comprehend any thing like CONNEXION between them. Here then, many philosophers think themselves obliged by reason to have recourse, on all occasions, to the same principle, which the vulgar never appeal to but in cases, that appear miraculous and supernatural. They acknowledge mind and intelligence to be, not only the ultimate and original cause of all things, but the immediate and sole cause of every event, which appears in nature. They pretend, that those objects, which are commonly denominated *causes*, are in reality nothing but *occasions*; and that the true and direct principle of every effect is not any power or force in nature, but a volition of the Supreme Being, who wills, that such particular objects should, for ever, be conjoined with each other. Instead of saying, that one billiard-ball moves another, by a force, which it has derived from the author of nature; it is the Deity himself, they say, who, by a particular volition, moves the second ball, being determined to this operation by the impulse of the first ball; in consequence of those general laws, which he has laid down to himself in the government of the universe. But philosophers advancing still in their enquiries, discover, that, as we are totally ignorant of that power, on which depends the mutual operation of bodies, we are no less ignorant of that power, on which depends the operation of mind on body, or of body on mind; nor are we able, either from our senses or consciousness, to assign the ultimate principle in one case, more than in the other. The same ignorance, therefore, reduces them to the same conclusion. They assert, that the Deity is the immediate cause of the union between soul and body; and that they are not the organs of sense, which, being agitated by external objects, produce sensations in the mind; but that it is a particular volition of our omnipotent Maker, which excites such a sensation, in consequence of such a motion in the organ. In like manner, it is not any energy in the will, that produces local motion in our members: It is God himself, who is pleased to second our will, in itself impotent, and to command that motion, which we erroneously attribute to our own power and efficacy. Nor do philosophers stop at this conclusion. They sometimes extend the same inference to the mind itself, in its internal operations. Our mental vision or conception of ideas is nothing but a revelation made to us by our Maker. When we voluntarily turn our thoughts to any object, and raise up its image in the fancy; it is not the will which creates that idea: It is the universal Creator, who discovers it to the mind, and renders it present to us.

Thus, according to these philosophers, every thing is full of God. Not content with the principle, that nothing exists but by his will, that nothing possesses any power but by his concession: They rob nature, and all created beings, of every power, in order to render their dependence on the Deity still more sensible and immediate. They consider not, that, by this theory, they diminish, instead of magnifying, the grandeur of those attributes, which they affect so much to celebrate. It argues surely more power in the Deity to delegate a certain degree of power to inferior creatures, than to produce every thing by his own immediate volition. It argues more wisdom to contrive at first the fabric of the world with such perfect foresight, that, of itself, and by its proper operation, it may serve all the purposes of providence, than if the great Creator were obliged every moment to adjust its parts, and animate by his breath all the wheels of that stupendous machine.

But if we would have a more philosophical confutation of this theory, perhaps the two following reflections may suffice.

First, It seems to me, that this theory of the universal energy and operation of the Supreme Being, is too bold ever to carry conviction with it to a man, sufficiently apprized of the weakness of human reason, and the narrow limits, to which it is confined in all its operations. Though the chain of arguments, which conduct to it, were ever so logical, there must arise a strong suspicion, if not an absolute assurance, that it has carried us quite beyond the reach of our faculties, when it leads to conclusions so extraordinary, and so remote from common life and experience. We are got into fairy land, long ere we have reached the last steps of our theory; and *there* we have no reason to trust our common methods of argument, or to think that our usual analogies and probabilities have any authority. Our line is too short to fathom such immense abysses. And however we may flatter ourselves, that we are guided, in every step which we take, by a kind of verisimilitude and experience; we may be assured, that this fancied experience has no authority, when we thus apply it to subjects, that lie entirely out of the sphere of experience. But on this we shall have occasion to touch afterwards.[14]

Secondly, I cannot perceive any force in the arguments, on which this theory is founded. We are ignorant, it is true, of the manner in which bodies operate on each other: Their force or energy is entirely incomprehensible: But are we not equally ignorant of the manner or force by which a mind, even the supreme mind, operates either on itself or on body? Whence, I beseech you, do we acquire any idea of it? We have no sentiment or consciousness of this power in ourselves. We have no idea of the Supreme Being but what we learn from reflection on our own faculties. Were our ignorance, therefore, a good reason for rejecting any thing, we should be led into that principle of denying all energy in the Supreme Being as much as in the grossest matter. We surely comprehend as little the operations of one as of the other. Is it more difficult to conceive, that motion may arise from impulse, than that it may arise from volition? All we know is our profound ignorance in both cases.[15]

Part II

But to hasten to a conclusion of this argument, which is already drawn out to too great a length: We have sought in vain for an idea of power or necessary connexion, in all the sources from which we could suppose it to be derived. It appears, that, in single instances of the operation of bodies, we never can, by our utmost scrutiny, discover any thing but one event following another; without being able to comprehend any force or power, by which the cause operates, or any connexion between it and its supposed effect. The same difficulty occurs in contemplating the operations of mind on body; where we observe the motion of the latter to follow upon the volition of the former; but are not able to observe or conceive the tie, which binds together the motion and volition, or the energy by which the mind produces this effect. The authority of the will over its own faculties and ideas is not a whit more comprehensible: So that, upon the whole, there appears not, through-out all nature, any one instance of connexion, which is conceivable by us. All events seem entirely loose and separate. One event follows another; but we never can observe any tie between them. They seem *conjoined*, but never *connected*. And as we can have no idea of any thing, which never appeared to our outward sense or inward sentiment, the neces-sary conclusion *seems* to be, that we have no idea of connexion or power at all, and that these words are absolutely without any meaning, when employed either in philosophical reasonings, or common life.

But there still remains one method of avoiding this conclusion, and one source which we have not yet examined. When any natural object or event is presented, it is impos-sible for us, by any sagacity or penetration, to discover, or even conjecture, without ex-perience, what event will result from it, or to carry our foresight beyond that object, which is immediately present to the memory and senses. Even after one instance or experi-ment, where we have observed a particular event to follow upon another, we are not entitled to form a general rule, or foretell what will happen in like cases; it being justly esteemed an unpardonable temerity to judge of the whole course of nature from one single experiment, however accurate or certain. But when one particular species of event has always, in all instances, been conjoined with another, we make no longer any scruple of foretelling one upon the appearance of the other, and of employing that reasoning, which can alone assure us of any matter of fact or existence. We then call the one object, *Cause*; the other, *Effect*. We suppose, that there is some connexion between them; some power in the one, by which it infallibly produces the other, and operates with the great-est certainty and strongest necessity.

It appears, then, that this idea of a necessary connexion among events arises from a number of similar instances, which occur, of the constant conjunction of these events; nor can that idea ever be suggested by any one of these instances, surveyed in all pos-sible lights and positions. But there is nothing in a number of instances, different from every single instance, which is supposed to be exactly similar; except only, that after a repetition of similar instances, the mind is carried by habit, upon the appearance of one event, to expect its usual attendant, and to believe, that it will exist. This connexion, therefore, which we *feel* in the mind, this customary transition of the imagination from one object to its usual attendant, is the sentiment or impression, from which we form the idea of power or necessary connexion. Nothing farther is in the case. Contemplate the subject on all sides; you will never find any other origin of that idea. This is the sole difference between one instance, from which we can never receive the idea of connexion, and a number of similar instances, by which it is suggested. The first time a man saw the communication of motion by impulse, as by the shock of two billiard-balls, he could not pronounce that the one event was *connected*: but only that it was *conjoined* with the other. After he has observed several instances of this nature, he then pronounces them to be *connected*. What alteration has happened to give rise to this new idea of *connexion*? Nothing but that he now *feels* these events to be *connected* in his imagination, and can readily foretell the existence of one from the appearance of the other. When we say, therefore, that one object is connected with another, we mean only, that they have acquired a connexion in our thought, and give rise to this inference, by which they become proofs of each other's existence: A conclusion, which is somewhat extraordinary; but which seems founded on sufficient evidence. Nor will its evidence be weakened by any general diffidence of the understanding, or sceptical suspicion concerning every conclusion, which is new and extraordinary. No conclusions can be more agreeable to scepticism than such as make discoveries concerning the weakness and narrow limits of human reason and capacity.

And what stronger instance can be produced of the surprising ignorance and weakness of the understanding, than the present? For surely, if there be any relation among objects, which it imports to us to know perfectly, it is that of cause and effect. On this are founded all our reasonings concerning matter of fact or existence. By means of it alone we attain any assurance concerning objects, which are removed from the present testimony of our memory and senses. The only immediate utility of all sciences, is to teach us, how to control and regulate future events by their causes. Our thoughts and enquiries are, therefore, every moment, employed about this relation: Yet so imperfect are the ideas which we form concerning it, that it is impossible to give any just definition of cause, except what is drawn from something extraneous and foreign to it. Similar objects are always conjoined with similar. Of this we have experience. Suitably to this experience, therefore, we may define a cause to be *an object, followed by another, and where all the objects, similar to the first, are followed by objects similar to the second.* Or in other words, *where, if the first object had not been, the second never had existed.* The appearance of a cause always conveys the mind, by a customary transition, to the idea of the effect. Of this also we have experience. We may, therefore, suitably to this experience, form another definition of cause; and call it, *an object followed by another, and whose appearance always conveys the thought to that other.* But though both these definitions be drawn from circumstances foreign to the cause, we cannot remedy this inconvenience, or attain any more perfect definition, which may point out that circumstance in the cause, which gives it a connexion with its effect. We have no idea of this connexion; nor even any distinct notion what it is we desire to know, when we endeavour at a conception of it. We say, for instance, that the vibration of this string is the cause of this particular sound. But what do we mean by that affirmation? We either mean, *that this vibration is followed by this sound, and that all similar vibrations have been followed by similar sounds:* Or, *that this vibration is followed by this sound, and that upon the appearance of one, the mind anticipates the senses, and forms immediately an idea of the other.* We may consider the relation of cause and effect in either of these two lights; but beyond these, we have no idea of it.[16]

To recapitulate, therefore, the reasonings of this section: Every idea is copied from some preceding impression or sentiment; and where we cannot find any impression, we may be certain that there is no idea. In all single instances of the operation of bodies or minds, there is nothing that produces any impression, nor consequently can suggest any idea, of power or necessary connexion. But when many uniform instances appear, and the same object is always followed by the same event; we then begin to entertain the notion of cause and connexion. We then *feel* a new sentiment or impression, to wit, a customary connexion in the thought or imagination between one object and its usual attendant; and this sentiment is the original of that idea which we seek for. For as this idea arises from a number of similar instances, and not from any single instance; it must arise from that circumstance, in which the number of instances differ from every individual instance. But this customary connexion or transition of the imagination is the only circumstance, in which they differ. In every other particular they are alike. The first instance which we saw of motion, communicated by the shock of two billiard-balls (to return to this obvious illustration) is exactly similar to any instance that may, at present, occur to us; except only, that we could not, at first, *infer* one event from the other; which we are enabled to do at present, after so long a course of uniform experience. I know not, whether the reader will readily apprehend this reasoning. I am afraid, that, should I multiply words about it, or throw it into a greater variety of lights, it would only become more obscure and intricate. In all abstract reasonings, there is one point of view, which, if we can happily hit, we shall go farther towards illustrating the subject, than by all the eloquence and copious expression in the world. This point of view we should endeavour to reach, and reserve the flowers of rhetoric for subjects which are more adapted to them.

Notes

1 It is probable that no more was meant by those, who denied innate ideas, than that all ideas were copies of our impressions; though it must be confessed, that the terms, which they employed, were not chosen with such caution, nor so exactly defined, as to prevent all mistakes about their doctrine. For what is meant by *innate*? If innate be equivalent to natural, then all the perceptions and ideas of the mind must be allowed to be innate or natural, in whatever sense we take the latter word, whether in opposition to what is uncommon, artificial, or miraculous. If by innate be meant, contemporary to our birth, the dispute seems to be frivolous; nor is it worth while to enquire at what time thinking begins, whether before, at, or after our birth. Again, the word *idea*, seems to be commonly taken in a very loose sense, by *Locke* and others: as standing for any of our perceptions, our sensations and passions, as well as thoughts. Now in this sense, I should desire to know, what can be meant by asserting, that self-love, or resentment of injuries, or the passion between the sexes is not innate?

But admitting these terms, *impressions* and *ideas*, in the sense above explained, and understanding by *innate*, what is original or copied from no precedent perception, then may we assert, that all our impressions are innate, and our ideas not innate.

To be ingenuous, I must own it to be my opinion, that Locke was betrayed into this question by the schoolmen, who, making use of undefined terms, draw out their disputes to a tedious length, without ever touching the point in question. A like ambiguity and circumlocution seem to run through that philosopher's reasonings on this as well as most other subjects.

2 Resemblance.
3 Contiguity.

4 Cause and Effect.

5 For instance, Contrast or Contrariety is also a connexion among Ideas: But it may, perhaps, be considered as a mixture of *Causation* and *Resemblance*. Where two objects are contrary, the one destroys the other; that is, the cause of its annihilation, and the idea of the annihilation of an object, implies the idea of its former existence.

6 The word, Power, is here used in a loose and popular sense. The more accurate explication of it would give additional evidence to this argument. See Sect. VII.

7 Nothing is more usual than for writers, even on *moral, political,* or *physical* subjects, to distinguish between *reason* and *experience,* and to suppose, that these species of argumentation are entirely different from each other. The former are taken for the mere result of our intellectual faculties, which, by considering *a priori* the nature of things, and examining the effects, that must follow from their operation, establish particular principles of science and philosophy. The latter are supposed to be derived entirely from sense and observation, by which we learn what has actually resulted from the operation of particular objects, and are thence able to infer, what will, for the future, result from them. Thus, for instance, the limitations and restraints of civil government, and a legal constitution, may be defended, either from *reason,* which reflecting on the great frailty and corruption of human nature, teaches, that no man can safely be trusted with unlimited authority; or from *experience* and history, which inform us of the enormous abuses, that ambition, in every age and country, has been found to make of so imprudent a confidence.

The same distinction between reason and experience is maintained in all our deliberations concerning the conduct of life; while the experienced statesman, general, physician, or merchant is trusted and followed; and the unpractised novice, with whatever natural talents endowed, neglected and despised. Though it be allowed, that reason may form very plausible conjectures with regard to the consequences of such a particular conduct in such particular circumstances; it is still supposed imperfect, without the assistance of experience, which is alone able to give stability and certainty to the maxims, derived from study and reflection.

But notwithstanding that this distinction be thus universally received, both in the active and speculative scenes of life, I shall not scruple to pronounce, that it is, at bottom, erroneous, at least, superficial.

If we examine those arguments which, in any of the sciences above-mentioned, are supposed to be the mere effects of reasoning and reflection, they will be found to terminate, at last, in some general principle or conclusion, for which we can assign no reason but observation and experience. The only difference between them and those maxims, which are vulgarly esteemed the result of pure experience, is, that the former cannot be established without some process of thought, and some reflection on what we have observed, in order to distinguish its circumstances, and trace its consequences: Whereas in the latter, the experienced event is exactly and fully similar to that which we infer as the result of any particular situation. The history of a TIBERIUS or a NERO makes us dread a like tyranny, were our monarchs freed from the restraints of laws and senates: But the observation of any fraud or cruelty in private life is sufficient, with the aid of a little thought, to give us the same apprehension; while it serves as an instance of the general corruption of human nature, and shows us the danger which we must incur by reposing an entire confidence in mankind. In both cases, it is experience which is ultimately the foundation of our inference and conclusion.

There is no man so young and unexperienced, as not to have formed, from observation, many general and just maxims concerning human affairs and the conduct of life; but it must be confessed, that, when a man comes to put these in practice, he will be extremely liable to error, till time and farther experience both enlarge these maxims, and teach him their proper use and application. In every situation or incident, there are many particular and seemingly minute circumstances, which the man of greatest talents is, at first, apt to overlook, though on them the justness of his conclusions, and consequently the prudence of his conduct, entirely depend. Not to mention, that, to a young beginner, the general observations and maxims occur not always on the proper occasions, nor can be immediately applied with due calmness and distinction. The truth is, an unexperienced reasoner could be no reasoner at all, were he absolutely unexperienced; and when we assign that character to any one, we mean it only in a comparative sense, and suppose him possessed of experience, in a smaller and more imperfect degree.

8 'Naturane nobis, inquit, datum dicam, an errore quodam, ut, cum ea loca videamus, in quibus memoria dignos viros accepimus multum esse versatos, magis moveamur, quam siquando eorum ipsorum aut facta audiamus aut scriptum aliquod legamus? Velut ego nunc moveor. Venit enim mihi PLATONIS in mentem, quem accepimus primum hic disputare solitum: Cujus etiam illi hortuli propinqui non memoriam solum mihi afferunt, sed ipsum videntur in conspectu meo hic ponere. Hic SPEUSIPPUS, hic XENOCRATES, hic ejus auditor POLEMO; cujus ipsa illa sessio fuit, quam videamus. Equidem etiam curiam nostram HOSTILIAM dico, non hanc novam, quae mihi minor esse videtur postquam est major, solebam intuens, SCIPIONEM, CATONEM, LAELIUM, nostrum vero in primis avum cogitare. Tanta vis admonitionis est in locis; ut non sine causa ex his memoriae deducta sit disciplina.' CICERO *de Finibus.* Lib. v.2.

9 Mr. Locke divides all arguments into demonstrative and probable. In this view, we must say, that it is only probable all men must die, or that the sun will rise to-morrow. But to conform our language more to common use, we ought to divide arguments into *demonstrations, proofs,* and *probabilities.* By proofs meaning such arguments from experience as leave no room for doubt or opposition.

10 Section II.

11 Mr. Locke, in his chapter of power, says, that, finding from experience, that there are several new productions in matter, and concluding that there must somewhere be a power capable of producing them, we arrive at last by this reasoning at the idea of power. But no reasoning can ever give us a new, original, simple idea; as this philosopher himself confesses. This, therefore, can never be the origin of that idea.

12 It may be pretended, that the resistance which we meet with in bodies, obliging us frequently to exert our force, and call up all our power, this gives us the idea of force and power. It is this *nisus* or strong endeavour, of which we are conscious, that is the original impression from which this idea is copied. But, first, we attribute power to a vast number of objects, where we never can suppose this resistance or exertion of force to take place; to the Supreme Being, who never meets with any resistance; to the mind in its command over its ideas and limbs, in common thinking and motion, where the effect follows immediately upon the will, without any exertion or summoning up of force; to inanimate matter, which is not capable of this sentiment. *Secondly,* This sentiment of an endeavour to overcome resistance has no known connexion with any event: What follows it, we know by experience; but could not know it *a priori.* It must, however, be confessed, that the animal *nisus,* which we experience, though it can afford no accurate precise idea of power, enters very much into that vulgar, inaccurate idea, which is formed of it.

13 Θεὺς ἀπὸ μηχανῆς.

14 Section XII.

15 I need not examine at length the *vis inertiae* which is so much talked of in the new philosophy, and which is ascribed to matter. We find by experience, that a body at rest or in motion continues for ever in its present state, till put from it by some new cause: And that a body impelled takes as much motion from the impelling body as it acquires itself. These are facts. When we call this a *vis inertiae,* we only mark these facts, without pretending to have any idea of the inert power; in the same manner as, when we talk of gravity, we mean certain effects without comprehending that active power. It was never the meaning of SIR ISAAC NEWTON to rob second causes of all force or energy; though some of his followers have endeavoured to establish that theory upon his authority. On the contrary, that great philosopher had recourse to an ethereal active fluid to explain his universal attraction; though he was so cautious and modest as to allow, that it was a mere hypothesis, not to be insisted on, without more

experiments. I must confess, that there is something in the fate of opinions a little extraordinary. DES CARTES insinuated that doctrine of the universal and sole efficacy of the Deity, without insisting on it. MALEBRANCHE and other CARTESIANS made it the foundation of all their philosophy. It had, however, no authority in ENGLAND. LOCKE, CLARKE [Samuel Clarke (1675–1729)], and, CUDWORTH [Ralph Cudworth (1617–1688)], never so much as take notice of it, but suppose all along, that matter has a real, though subordinate and derived power. By what means has it become so prevalent among our modern metaphysicians?

16 According to these explications and definitions, the idea of *power* is relative as much as that of *cause*; and both have a reference to an effect, or some other event constantly conjoined with the former. When we consider the *unknown* circumstance of an object, by which the degree or quantity of its effect is fixed and determined, we call that its power: And accordingly, it is allowed by all philosophers, that the effect is the measure of the power. But if they had any idea of power, as it is in itself, why could not they measure it in itself? The dispute whether the force of a body in motion be as its velocity, or the square of its velocity; this dispute, I say, needed not be decided by comparing its effects in equal or unequal times; but by a direct mensuration and comparison.

As to the frequent use of the words, Force, Power, Energy, &c. which every where occur in common conversation, as well as in philosophy; that is no proof, that we are acquainted, in any instance, with the connecting principle between cause and effect, or can account ultimately for the production of one thing by another. These words, as commonly used, have very loose meanings annexed to them; and their ideas are very uncertain and confused. No animal can put external bodies in motion without the sentiment of a *nisus* or endeavour; and every animal has a sentiment or feeling from the stroke or blow of an external object, that is in motion. These sensations, which are merely animal, and from which we can *a priori* draw no inference, we are apt to transfer to inanimate objects, and to suppose, that they have some such feelings, whenever they transfer or receive motion. With regard to energies, which are exerted, without our annexing to them any idea of communicated motion, we consider only the constant experienced conjunction of the events; and as we *feel* a customary connexion between the ideas, we transfer that feeling to the objects; as nothing is more usual than to apply to external bodies every internal sensation, which they occasion.

---

3   Cartesian Skepticism and Inference to the Best Explanation*

Jonathan Vogel

The problem of skepticism about the external world, or Cartesian skepticism, has its roots in the underdetermination of theory by evidence. We each adopt a body of common-sense beliefs about the world which answers to our sensory experience. In principle, however, the beliefs we base on that experience are subject to underdetermination, and we can devise radical alternatives to the common-sense account. Such alternatives take

* From *The Journal of Philosophy*, 87 (November 1990), pp. 658–66. Reprinted with permission of The Journal of Philosophy and Jonathan Vogel.

the form of skeptical hypotheses, like Descartes's fiction that his experiences are caused by an evil demon.

Certainly, when the choice arises, we hold to the common-sense view, and reject its skeptical competitors.[1] But what (epistemic) reasons can we have for doing so? In cases of underdetermination generally, principles of inference to the best explanation can license the choice of one theory over others. Accordingly, we would be justified in preferring the common-sense account to skeptical hypotheses, if the common-sense account provides better explanations of why our experience is the way it is.[2] My purpose here is to inquire into the explanatory advantages of the common-sense view, and to develop a response to skepticism along the lines just indicated.[3]

One obstacle to carrying out this project is that the standards by which explanations are evaluated are themselves difficult to identify and to make precise. In what follows, I shall be making some controversial assumptions about explanatory goodness, and I shall have to rely on largely unanalyzed notions of simplicity, ad-hoc-ness, and the like. To be explicit, I shall presuppose:

(a) Ad hoc explanations should be avoided, i.e., very roughly, if A is offered as an explanation of B, A ought not to be isolated from other explanations and data (it ought to be independently testable, it must figure in the explanation of something other than B, etc.).

(b) Other things being equal, a simpler explanation is superior to a more complicated one.

(c) Where explanation is concerned, more is better, if you get something for it. In particular, it is desirable to be able to give higher-level explanations of lower-level ones.

Another methodological point requires some comment. In comparing skeptical hypotheses with our everyday account of the world, I shall exclude from the latter any advanced scientific beliefs. To be sure, science adds great power and coherence to our explanations of phenomena, and one might argue that no explanatory scheme the skeptic devises could seriously compete with our best scientific theories. But it seems implausible that, without such theories, we would lack adequate grounds for rejecting skeptical hypotheses. Accordingly, I shall try to show that even a scientifically unsophisticated common-sense view of the world provides more adequate explanations than its skeptical competitors.

I

Our beliefs about the external world serve an explanatory function. A person's sensory experience exhibits patterns and regularities at many levels, and our common-sense beliefs account for these in ways that seem to be coherent and economical. I shall call the body of these beliefs the *real-world hypothesis* (RWH).[4]

The skeptic points out that there are alternative explanations of how a person's sensory experience arises. In principle, a great many ways of formulating and developing these counterhypotheses are open to the skeptic – for example, through various stories about evil demons and brains in vats. But elaborate (not to mention crazy) fantasies of deception may be only tenuously connected to the content of one's experiences and may lack cohesiveness. For instance, suppose that you seem to see some snow falling, and the skeptic suggests that this experience is being foisted on you by a demon. Then, to explain why the demon makes you have snow experience (rather than experience of some other kind), the skeptic tells you that there is a second demon that has put the first one up to it. Clearly, we are not getting anywhere; positing a second demon that directs the first on this occasion (and does only that) is explanatorily idle or ad hoc. The skeptic could try to escape such a result by refusing to say in any detail how your experiences come about. A hypothesis in this vein might specify only that your experiences are all caused by some deceptive spirit, and no more. The cure is as bad as the disease, however: the skeptic will succeed in avoiding ad hoc higher-level posits only by foregoing higher-level explanations altogether.

The RWH, by contrast, gives us a rich and well-integrated explanatory apparatus. We not only posit objects that cause our experiences, we are also able to explain why and how these objects behave as they do. If the explanations provided by a skeptical counterhypothesis are either ad hoc or impoverished in comparison with those of the RWH, then we have good grounds for preferring the latter to the former. According to the skeptic, we fail to know things because the RWH is faced with competitors that we have no reason to reject. But we have just seen that not any competitor will do. The skeptic's position will be empty unless he can provide us with reason to think that a *satisfactory* competitor exists (in particular, a sufficiently rich competitor that is not unduly burdened with ad hoc explanatory posits).

The lesson here is that the skeptic needs to frame an alternative that matches the RWH very closely. If a skeptical hypothesis can be made sufficiently similar in relevant respects to the RWH, then, one might expect, that skeptical hypothesis will match the RWH in explanatory adequacy. To the extent that explanatory virtues like coherence, depth, and simplicity are matters of theoretical structure, a skeptical hypothesis that is isomorphic to the RWH will explain things just as well as the RWH does. An improved skeptical hypothesis of this sort has to satisfy two principal constraints: (i) it should invoke items corresponding to the elements of the RWH; (ii) it should also posit, as holding of these items, a pattern of properties, relations, and explanatory generalizations mirroring those of the RWH.

As an example of how this would work, suppose you seem to see the wind blowing a piece of paper off your desk. According to the RWH, your visual impressions of the paper flying off your desk are caused by the paper. Similarly, your tactile sensations of the wind are caused by a real movement of air against your skin. And, finally, the wind stands in a relation of cause and effect to the movement of the paper. The skeptic's procedure will be to extract the explanatory skeleton or core from the RWH – that there are *some* entities bearing *some* properties that are related in ways exactly analogous to those specified by the RWH – and then to add that the entities and their properties are somehow different from the ones mentioned in the RWH.[5]

Thus, a skeptical hypothesis might present the following alternative explanation of your experiences. All that there is to the world is your brain in a vat, and a computer that is connected to your brain. Your tactile experiences are caused by the realization of a computer program that simulates wind, and your visual impressions are caused by the realization of another program that simulates a paper blowing off a desk. Also, the skeptical hypothesis can specify that the first routine calls the second, so that (as in the RWH) the cause of the wind experience would be the cause of the paper-blowing experience. This way of reconstructing the explanatory structure of a small fragment of the RWH might be extended to apply to all the entities and explanatory connections posited by the RWH. The result would be a skeptical hypothesis that was completely isomorphic to the RWH, with portions of the computer disk supposed to occupy the explanatory roles we normally assign to familiar objects.[6] I shall be calling this the *computer skeptical hypothesis* (CSH).

Of course, the CSH is an outlandish suggestion, and we are confident that it is false. Yet, in reflecting on this situation philosophically, it is possible to misread what has gone wrong. One proposal is that skeptical hypotheses are invariably burdened with more unexplained explainers than is the RWH.[7] The CSH will lack answers to questions like "Why does the computer operate the way it does?" or "Where did the computer come from in the first place?" But it is not at all clear that the RWH does any better in the face of analogous demands. Both the CSH and the RWH invoke ultimate regularities that are not themselves explained, and neither can account for the existence of the physical world as such. Generally, since the RWH and the CSH are meant to have the same structure, anywhere the RWH can explain a lower-level phenomenon by a higher-level regularity, the CSH should be able to do the same. The CSH will have unexplained explainers only insofar as the RWH has them also.

Another suggestion that enjoys some currency is that the RWH is, in a very straightforward way, simpler than the CSH, and hence to be preferred. The idea here is that there would be a one-one mapping from the objects posited by the RWH to their stand-ins in the computer's memory, where these are treated as discrete individuals. There are, though, items required (at least tacitly) by the CSH which escape this mapping, e.g., the computer's central processing unit and perhaps the brain in the vat itself. So, the argument runs, the CSH is committed to the existence of more items than the RWH, and is to be preferred on that account.

This line of thought is problematic in several respects. First, one could just as well argue that the CSH is simpler than the RWH, on the grounds that the CSH posits only two objects (the computer and one's brain), whereas the RWH is committed to the existence of a great many more things. Moreover, it is far from clear that, all by itself, positing fewer entities is a theoretical virtue.[8] And finally, if need be, the CSH could be revised to eliminate the role of the central processing unit altogether. The skeptic could suppose that the elements of the computer memory act directly on each other, and on the seat of consciousness, in causal patterns that mirror those of the RWH.

Now, as will emerge shortly, I think there is something right about the claims that the CSH is less coherent and less simple than the RWH. But if explanatory coherence and simplicity are treated solely in structural terms, it should not be surprising that these claims do not go through. After all, the causal-explanatory structures invoked by the RWH and the CSH are identical; the two differ only as to what entities bear the specified causal relations to one another.

The rejoinders just considered miss something important about the motivations behind the skeptic's argument. At root, the skeptic questions our ability to read off the "real" or intrinsic character of things from those things' causal behavior. This challenge emerges in its simplest form with the initial thought that one's experience of any familiar object might be caused by something other than that object (e.g., an evil demon). The point is that the known effect – namely, your experience – does not fix the character of its cause.[9]

On the face of it, the requirement that a skeptical hypothesis must have a more fully articulated structure – one that matches the RWH in various ways – seems insufficient to meet this problem. For, if we assume that causal relations are contingent and that there is in principle no obstacle to our positing whatever causal relations we like, what reason could there be why one set of entities is better suited than another to occupy the positions within the structure of the RWH itself? It would appear that, in principle, there should be skeptical hypotheses that will explain the contents of one's experience just as well as the RWH. The choice between such hypotheses and the RWH will then be arbitrary, giving the skeptic what he needs.

II

To appreciate the superiority of the RWH over its skeptical competitors, we need to take into account the content, as well as the form, of the explanations the RWH provides. In particular, our ordinary view of things involves beliefs in the existence of objects with familiar spatial characteristics (e.g., we believe that there are bricks that are oblong and oranges that are round). The ascription of specific spatial properties to objects does explanatory work within the RWH (e.g., accounting for why oranges roll easily and bricks do not). Since the CSH posits objects with altogether different spatial characteristics – we are assuming that its objects are just portions of a computer disk – the CSH will have to account for the relevant phenomena in some other fashion. But by bringing in these additional explanations (whatever they may be), the CSH runs the risk of taking on a more elaborate explanatory apparatus than the RWH. To put the point I am trying to make more directly: niceties aside, the fact that something is spherical explains why it behaves like a sphere (in its interactions with us and with other things). If something that *is not* a sphere behaves like one, this will call for a more extended explanation.

This intuitive claim is bound to raise some philosophical qualms. Why must the fact that the CSH invokes *different* configurations of matter in its explanations mean that CSH has to be *more complicated* than the RWH? Again, setting niceties aside, why is the skeptic not free to stipulate that, in his account, it is certain magnetic patterns on a disk, not spheres, which behave like spheres (at least in terms of the experiences they bring about, directly and indirectly)?

Let us see just what would be involved in maintaining an explanatory parity between the CSH and RWH. To fix ideas, suppose that, according to the RWH, there is a hyacinth beside your doorway. For each RWH object, there has to be a CSH counterpart, which we can imagine to be the piece of the computer disk which stores the information about the object to be simulated. So, the CSH would have it that there is a piece of the disk holding a file about a hyacinth beside your door, specifically. Moreover, wherever the RWH assigns a certain property to the hyacinth, the CSH must ascribe a corresponding, but different property to the hyacinth's CSH analog. According to the RWH, the hyacinth has a particular location, namely, that of being beside your door. The hyacinth counterpart will have some parallel feature, which we might call a "pseudo location." The pseudo location of the hyacinth counterpart is just that physical property in virtue of which the counterpart simulates being located near your door. In general, what the RWH explains by reference to genuine locations, the CSH will explain in terms of these pseudo locations.

Since we make reference to the locations of objects in giving various everyday explanations, location properties are part of the explanatory apparatus of the RWH. Now, we find that the (genuine) locations ascribed to any two objects at a time are invariably different. We do not need any empirical law or regularity to explain this; it is a necessary truth pertaining to the nature of physical objects that there cannot be two such objects at the same place at the same time.[10]

The explanatory structure of the CSH is meant to duplicate that of the RWH. Since the CSH is isomorphic to the RWH, and the RWH always ascribes different locations to the objects it posits, the CSH will invariably ascribe different pseudo locations to things it posits. This calls for an explanation, if possible. At this point, however, the CSH faces a loss in either simplicity or explanatory power. To make the issue more concrete, imagine that the way things work in the CSH computer is that each object's pseudo location is the physical realization of having coordinates (x, y, z) written in its file.[11] There will have to be some explicit principle within the CSH that no two objects are to be assigned the same pseudo location, i.e., that no two objects are to have the same coordinates written in their files. Otherwise, the fact that no two objects have the same pseudo location remains unexplained. Of course, the CSH would include within it the necessary truth that two physical objects cannot occupy the same *genuine* location in space, but this is of no help to the CSH in explaining why two of its objects cannot have the same *pseudo* location. To achieve this, it would appear that the CSH has to add an extra empirical regularity, to which no regularity in the RWH corresponds. Such an addition will make the CSH inferior to the RWH on simplicity grounds, however.

The skeptic could escape this outcome if it could be guaranteed by some other necessary truth that different CSH objects will have different pseudo locations. In other words, the pseudo location of a CSH object would have to be encoded by some physical property P (other than that of having some specified location), such that it is impossible for two physical objects to have P at the same time. But it seems to me that there are no such physical properties. After all, if a given physical object with whatever properties exists at one place, it appears perfectly possible for there to be an absolutely similar object elsewhere, instantiating all the same properties at the same time – except location.[12]

Actually, the problem facing the skeptic is a general one, independent of the fact that CSH itself invokes physical objects (i.e., bits of computer disk) in its explanations. Suppose that the skeptic offers instead a quasi-Leibnizian hypothesis, according to which the world consists solely of minds and their properties. These minds and their states are supposed to act in ways that mirror the behavior of everyday things as specified by the RWH. Each mind that stands in for a RWH object must have a property corresponding to the genuine location the RWH ascribes to its object; this pseudo location will be a (partial) mental state. The question arises again as to why these pseudo locations are invariably different from one mind to another. Presumably (*pace* Leibniz), it is possible for two different minds to think exactly the same thing at the same time, so no necessary truth prevents them from having the same pseudo location. Once again, such an occurrence would have to be ruled out by some kind of extra "exclusion principle," for which no counterpart exists in the RWH.

I claimed earlier that our normal ascription of spatial properties to things does real explanatory work; furthermore, it seems plausible that you incur an added explanatory burden if you suppose that something lacking a particular spatial property still behaves as though it had it. What I have been saying about locations and pseudo locations makes this same point on a more abstract level. In skeptical hypotheses, some other property (e.g., a magnetic property or a mental property) is supposed to substitute for the spatial property of being located at particular place. As we have seen, further explanation is then needed to establish why these properties, which are not genuine location properties, behave as though they were. It seems that this sort of difficulty will attach to skeptical hypotheses generally, giving us good reasons to reject them.[13]

III

I have presented some antiskeptical arguments based on explanatory considerations. But surely there is a world of familiar objects about us, and we have known that all along. So what, then, is the point of giving these arguments in the first place? This question deserves an extended response, but for now a very brief answer will have to do. I take it that the specious character of the explanations the skeptic offers is immediately apparent – they come across as contrived or unduly indirect – and this is a reason why we reject skepticism as a doctrine. Realizing that skeptical hypotheses are defective, however, is not the same thing as spelling out precisely what their defects are. To do this requires philosophical work – work of the sort I have undertaken here.

Notes

1 Some philosophers, especially followers of Ludwig Wittgenstein, would deny that skeptical hypotheses can genuinely compete for acceptance with the body of our common-sense beliefs. See, for example, Stanley Cavell, *The Claim of Reason* (New York: Oxford, 1979), pp. 218–20.

2 This approach to skepticism has been advocated by Michael Slote, Frank Jackson, Jonathan Bennett, James Cornman, J. L. Mackie, and Alan Goldman, among others.

3 On certain views about skepticism and about inference to the best explanation, this approach to skepticism will seem ill-conceived. One might hold that it is simply constitutive of rationality to reject skeptical hypotheses out of hand; thus, it is unnecessary to enter into the relative explanatory merits of the common-sense view and its skeptical alternatives. From another point of view, the explanatory advantages of the common-sense view could never give us a reason to accept it as *true*, rather than as merely handy or to our taste. The issues that arise here are important, and they must be addressed at some point by anyone who bases an answer to skepticism on explanatory considerations. These very general objections will be moot, however, if the appeal to explanatory considerations does not even succeed on its own terms. Whether it does so is my present concern.

4 This way of putting things may seem unfortunate to those who reject the representative theory of perception. But the point could be recast as follows: we have a set of beliefs about the world, i.e., the RWH. Our having those beliefs admits of alternative explanations, including skeptical explanations and the RWH itself. The tenability of skepticism turns on whether the truth of the RWH provides a better explanation than do skeptical hypotheses of why we believe the RWH in the first place.

5 Basically, this amounts to something like forming the Ramsey sentence of the RWH and adding to it further specifications that, in each case, the object or property denoted by the bound variables is something other than the one posited by the RWH. The RWH itself can be construed as the "Ramsey sentence" plus the stipulation that the objects and properties called for by the "Ramsey sentence" are indeed the familiar ones. See here Grover Maxwell, "Theories, Perception, and Structural Realism," in R. Colodny, ed., *The Nature and Function of Scientific Thought* (Pittsburgh: University Press, 1970) and for some needed refinements, David Lewis, "How to Define Theoretical Terms," *Philosophical Papers*, vol. I (New York: Oxford, 1983). The possibility of framing skeptical hypotheses with the same structure as the RWH is noted by Lawrence Sklar in his "Saving the Noumena," *Philosophy and Spacetime Physics* (Berkeley: California UP, 1985), pp. 59–60.

6 We need not suppose that the computer itself was built or programed by anyone. Rather, this hypothesis is to be understood simply as a description of an alternative way the (physical) world might be.

7 A claim of this sort is made by Alan Goldman, although it is directed at a fantastical skeptical story that postulates experimenters with deceptive motives. See Goldman, *Empirical Knowledge* (Berkeley: California UP, 1989), p. 212.

8 It could be objected that what matters for explanatory adequacy is not economy with respect to the number of individuals posited, but rather in the number of different kinds invoked. But this does not appear to help – the skeptic can get by with just a few kinds of things (brain, vat, computer) while the RWH might be said to invoke these and many more.

9 This was the way Kant understood the situation. The skeptic, he says, "assumed that the only immediate experience is inner experience and that from it we can only *infer* outer things – and this, moreover, only in an untrustworthy manner, as in all cases where we are inferring from given effects to determinate causes"; *The Critique of Pure Reason*, N. K. Smith, trans. (New York: St. Martin's, 1965), p. 245.

10 For a discussion of this principle, see Denis Robinson, "Re-identifying Matter," *The Philosophical Review*, XCI (1982): 317–41; on the role of necessary truths in explanations, see Clark Glymour, "Explanation and Realism," in J. Leplin, ed., *Scientific Realism* (Berkeley: California UP, 1984), esp. pp. 184–6.

11 For purposes of exposition, I am pretending that an object is located at a point rather than a region.

12 Of course, there are characterizations like "the only building taller than 110 stories" or "identical to Socrates", which are satisfied by at most one object at a time. If these expressions involve reference to properties, they are properties of a different type than those with which I am concerned here.

13 One might try to frame a skeptical hypothesis that avoids this difficulty by assigning to objects different locations (and spatial properties generally) in place of those specified by the RWH. Formulated this way, our problem becomes one of choosing a particular geometry of the world from among those logically compatible with the empirical data, and one might continue to defend the choice of the RWH by appeal to explanatory considerations. See here Lawrence Sklar, *Space, Time, and Spacetime* (Berkeley: California UP, 1977), pp. 91–101, although Sklar himself is highly critical of such uses of inference to the best explanation. Sklar has a valuable discussion of the affinities between Cartesian skepticism and problems in the epistemology of geometry.

4 From *Science as Social Knowledge**

Helen Longino

Constitutive and Contextual Values

It is, of course, nonsense to assert the value-freedom of natural science. Scientific practice is governed by norms and values generated from an understanding of the goals of

* From Helen Longino, *Science as Social Knowledge* (Princeton, NJ: Princeton University Press, 1990), pp. 4–12, © 1990 by Princeton University Press.

scientific inquiry. If we take the goal of scientific activity to be the production of explanations of the natural world, then these governing values and constraints are generated from an understanding of what counts as a good explanation, for example, the satisfaction of such criteria as truth, accuracy, simplicity, predictability, and breadth. These criteria are not always equally satisfiable and, as I shall suggest, are appropriate to different conceptions of what counts as a good explanation. Nevertheless, they clearly constitute values by which to judge competing explanations and from which norms and constraints governing scientific practice in particular fields (for example, the requirement for repeatability of experiments) can be generated.

Independence from these sorts of values, of course, is not what is meant by those debating the value freedom of science. The question is, rather, the extent to which science is free of personal, social, and cultural values, that is, independent of group or individual subjective preferences regarding what ought to be (or regarding what, among the things that are, is best). For the sake of clarity I will call the values generated from an understanding of the goals of science *constitutive* values to indicate that they are the source of the rules determining what constitutes acceptable scientific practice or scientific method. The personal, social, and cultural values, those group or individual preferences about what ought to be, I will call *contextual* values to indicate that they belong to the social and cultural environment in which science is done.[1] The traditional interpretation of the value freedom of modern natural science amounts to a claim that its constitutive and contextual features are clearly distinct from and independent of one another. Can this distinction, as commonly conceived, be maintained?

The issue of the independence of science and values (or constitutive and contextual values) can be reformulated as two questions. One question concerns the relevance of scientific theories (and methods) to contextual values: To what extent do or should scientific theories shape moral and social values? The other concerns the impact of contextual values upon scientific theories and methods: To what extent do social and moral values shape scientific theories? The first, then, has to do with the autonomy of questions of personal, social, and cultural values from the revelations, discoveries, and inventions of scientific inquiry. Does, for instance, the assertion that a certain form of behavior (for example, aggressive war) is an adaptation, sculpted into human nature by the chisel of natural selection, have any relevance to ethical judgments? This question and its cognates have been much discussed in the contemporary uproar about sociobiology. I shall pursue the question of the relevance of scientific theory to moral and political values as a consequence, instead, of the second question. This question concerns the autonomy of the content and practices of the sciences from personal, social, and cultural preferences regarding what ought to be and what, among the things that are, is best. I will argue not only that scientific practices and content on the one hand and social needs and values on the other are in dynamic interaction but that the logical and cognitive structures of scientific inquiry require such interaction.

When we ask whether the content of science is free from contextual values we are asking about the integrity and autonomy of scientific inquiry. These concepts can be understood both morally and logically or epistemologically. Thus scientists sometimes become defensive when asked to comment on the relation between science and values because they think their moral integrity is being challenged. Or they dismiss cases of value influence as "bad" science, practiced only by the corrupt or inept. But what does the attribution of epistemological integrity and autonomy to scientific inquiry mean in the first place?

Autonomy and integrity are separable attributes, and I shall consider them in sequence. In its most extreme form the attribution of *autonomy* is a claim that scientific inquiry proceeds undisturbed and unaffected by the values and interests of its social and cultural context, that it is propelled instead by its own internally generated momentum. In one sense this seems clearly false.

The dependence of most current science on corporate and/or government funding makes the conduct of science highly vulnerable to its funding sources. The questions to which the methods of scientific inquiry will be applied are at least partly a function of the values of its supporting context. That the questions also bear a logical relationship to prior research does not rule out their social determination. Consider, for instance, the commercialization of genetic engineering. The techniques of isolating and recombining selected bits of DNA molecules to effect the production of desired substances depend critically on the discovery of the structure of the DNA molecule in the 1950s and on the work that has been done since correlating segments of that molecule with phenotypic expressions of genetic information. There is a great deal of concern now that the commercial possibilities involved in the bacterial production of antibodies, growth and other hormones, et cetera, will incline biomedical research even further toward the search for cures of disease and away from the search for understanding of the causes of disease. This provides a simple and clear example of the interaction of internal and external factors in the development of inquiry. Studies of funding patterns and research pursued in other areas of inquiry reveal similar interactions.

This kind of palpable influence exerted by the social and cultural context on the directions of scientific development has led many observer-critics of science to reject the value freedom of science. Defenders of the idea that science is value-free can argue, however, that cases such as these show that science is not autonomous in the extreme sense but can also point out that the alleged science/value interactions are superficial ones. These sorts of considerations, the defender might continue, go nowhere towards showing that the internal, real practice of science is affected by contextual values. The thesis that the internal practices of science – observation and experiment, theory construction, inference – are not influenced by contextual values is what I call the thesis of the *integrity* of science. Contemporary criticisms of research in the biology of behavior and cognition pose a more severe challenge to the thesis of integrity, for they address not just how the context influences the questions thought worth asking but the answers given to those questions.

Societies in which one race or sex (or one race-sex combination, for example, white males) is dominant generally distribute their resources disproportionately, the greater share of benefits going to the dominant group. This distribution is usually justified on the basis of presumed inherent differences between the dominant and subordinated groups. Aristotle told us how women and slaves were inferior to free-born Athenian males. George Gilder and Michael Levin tell us how women are unsuited to the rigors of public life. Theories about the genetic basis of racial differences in I.Q. test performance and theories about the hormonal basis of gender differences are not propounded and contested in a vacuum. They are debated in a context informed about social inequality but divided about its nature and legitimacy.

To the extent that research on the biological basis of various socially significant differences is taken seriously as science, it is presumed to offer accurate and "unbiased" descriptions of what is the case – descriptions or theories that are not themselves in any part a product of cultural values or assumptions. This is what the thesis of the integrity of science claims and what the critics of this research deny. An account of evidence and reasoning in science ought, among other things, to give us a standard by which we can ascertain the degree to which these currently contested theories of cognition and behavior are or could be developed and supported independently of cultural values. This demand, it seems to me, encompasses two of the most pressing questions a contemporary methodologist of science must address – the questions of whether and to what extent a value-free or autonomous science is methodologically possible. These questions challenge traditional conceptions of rationality and objectivity. Answers to these questions would help us to assess the real relevance to cultural ideals and social policy of research with apparent social consequences. They would also prompt us to reexamine the ideas of "good science" and "bad science" and the assumption that value-laden or ideologically informed science is always bad science.

Debates about Science and Social Values

While most philosophers of science have ignored these questions, other theorists have either explicitly or by implication filled the void left by our silence. Several positions on the relation between science and values can be distinguished. One approach argues that to the extent that contextual values can be shown to influence reasoning, they are shown to have produced bad reasoning. This is the approach most scientists seem, by implication, to favor and to which many philosophers are committed in virtue of their analyses of reasoning and validation in the sciences. Another approach, the social constructionist tendency in sociology and history of science, argues that the processes by which scientific knowledge is built are social and hence ideological and interest-laden. A third, characteristic of many scientists who oppose some particular theory such as human sociobiology because of its social implications, tries to have it both ways. These critics state that science is value-laden and inevitably reflects the values of scientists and their society. Simultaneously they wish to claim that some specific (objectionable) scientific claim is also incorrect. To set my own inquiry in perspective, I shall briefly sketch out these approaches.

A recent article by Robert Richardson exemplifies the first form of response.[2] Richardson is sympathetic to the criticisms of science as value-laden and attempts, in his article, to articulate the proper role of "ideology critique" in the sciences. He is one of the very few philosophers of science to have addressed these questions and to have brought them to the attention of the professional philosophical community. While his attention is a welcome exception to the rule, ironically the particular analysis he develops ultimately supports the view that social values are associated with bad science.[3]

The specific target of Richardson's argument is the supposition that demonstrating the ideological bias of a scientific explanation is sufficient reason to reject it. Some of the early rejections of human sociobiology as racist and sexist are examples of this supposition in practice. Richardson argues instead that to reject a theory or hypothesis one must show that it is false or not warranted. Showing that it is ideologically incorrect is not sufficient. To make his point he reviews a number of cases – some notorious, others less so – in which racist, individualist, or sexist ideology plays a role. In each instance he elegantly demonstrates that the offending hypotheses are inadequately warranted. The role of ideology in these cases is to blind the proponents of the hypotheses to the fact that their warrants are inadequate. The role of ideology critique is to explain why their proponents cling to inadequately warranted hypotheses. Thus, Richardson seems to be saying that, properly followed, the methods of inquiry sanctioned by the constitutive values of science weed out the influence of subjective preferences. This thesis can be called the thesis of the integrity of science.

One striking feature of Richardson's examples is that the hypotheses in question are unwarranted with respect to the field or discipline or theory within which they are propounded: they violate or ignore methodological constraints accepted by workers in the field, including the individuals whose work he is criticizing. For instance, claims by the sociobiologists Richard Dawkins and John Maynard Smith that phenomena such as certain forms of sexual or parental behavior or the apparent self-limitations on animal violence represent adaptations or "evolutionarily stable strategies" fail to demonstrate that there was variation from which the alleged adaptation could have been selected. But a trait is an adaptation or "evolutionarily stable strategy" only if there was such variation. The analyses of the particular cases are compelling for each case, but Richardson seems to assume that all cases will be like the ones he discusses. His analysis will not, however, apply to those cases where the warrants themselves – that is, the methodological procedures or framing assumptions accepted within a field – are ideologically driven or value-laden. Moreover, the implication of Richardson's essay is that "ideology critique" has no role to play in discussions of "good science." But the scientist who is trying to do different science and to escape the ideology perceived in her or his field wishes to dissect its role in theories, not in order to show them wrong but to find the places where an alternative set of values might yield a different set of hypotheses. Richardson is persuasive about the particular examples he analyzes but does not support the claim that all cases of ideologically laden science are analogous to those.

The social constructionist approach urges us to abandon our obsession with truth and representation. The phrase "social constructionist" is used to refer to analytic programs in history and sociology of science that take scientific theories and hypotheses to be products of their political, economic, and cultural milieu. These programs employ a wide range of epistemological views, but their proponents are unanimous in rejecting the idea that science is objective or that it gives us an unbiased view of the real world. Social constructionism comes in two forms. The more modest form of the social constructionist thesis holds only that social interests influence the choice of research areas and problems. This is consistent with Richardson's view of the relation of science and values. Thus, defenders of the value neutrality of science can respond to the modest form of the thesis by pointing out that while such examples as the influence of governmental funding and commercial applicability on research show that science is not autonomous they do not have a bearing on the thesis of the integrity of science. Such defenders can invoke the distinction between discovery and justification and argue that as long as values are shown only to influence the discovery process, they have not been shown to undermine claims to objectivity in the justification process. And if values have influenced individual's justification procedures, then so much the worse for those individuals. The objectivity of science, conceived as a set of rules and procedures for distinguishing true from false accounts of nature, is not undermined by arguments establishing modest forms of social constructionism.

The so-called "strong program in sociology of science" associated with the University of Edinburgh scholars Barry Barnes and David Bloor holds that social interests are more deeply involved in scientific practice.[4] The strong program questions not merely the autonomy but the epistemological integrity of science. Barnes and Bloor have argued that social interests determine the *acceptance* of hypotheses in the sciences. They argue (1) that there is no transcendent or context independent criterion of rational justification that renders some beliefs (hypotheses) more credible than others and (2) that the explanation why a given set of beliefs is found in a given context depends on features of the context and not on intrinsic properties of the beliefs. Bloor extends Durkheim's thesis that "the classification of things reproduces the classification of men" to the sciences. Other social constructionists argue similarly that all outcomes in the sciences are negotiated and that social interests are involved in the negotiation of technical outcomes, such as the description of experimental results, as much as of political outcomes, such as who will head a research group.[5]

Feminist scholars, too, have rejected the idea of the value neutrality of the sciences. Donna Haraway, in a series of studies of twentieth-century primatology, has concentrated on the ways socio-political-economic ideology constructs the subject matter of that discipline. She shows how the basic concepts and forms of knowledge are subtly transformed in response to changing political agenda. For Haraway science is a series of political discourses and must be read as such. Scientist turned historian Evelyn Fox Keller has argued that the language of mainstream science is permeated by an ideology of domination created in the very processes of personal psychological development and individuation characteristic of modern European and North American societies.[6]

Proponents of the integrity of science thesis can respond to the strong form of the social constructionist program in either of two ways, depending on what kind of argument is used. To the extent that the argument rests on case histories, they can respond (1) that it fails to show that all science is interest-shaped or value-laden and (2) that the cases on which it rests are instances of "bad science," just the sort of thing that scientific methods, properly followed, are designed to eliminate. To the extent that the argument rests on philosophical arguments, it is only as strong as those arguments. For example, many social constructionists cite Kuhn's *Structure of Scientific Revolutions* as the philosophical basis of their work.[7] Kuhn's views, however, have been subjected to searching philosophical criticism. In neither case does the demonstration of social influence require the proponents of value-free science to alter their views.

Finally, some critiques of research programs with racist or sexist implications seem to combine the assumptions of a Richardsonian and a social constructionist approach. They argue that racist or sexist research is the inevitable product of a scientific community that excludes women of any background and members, male and female, of certain ethnic or racial groups. Citing Kuhn, they argue that all observation is theory-laden and that, hence, the observations of a racist or sexist scientific community will be laden with racism and sexism. At the same time these critics tackle particular research programs, such as the I.Q. research or human sociobiology, and show that these programs are methodologically flawed. Politically and polemically this approach can seem attractive as it suggests that if we want good – that is, methodologically respectable – research, we should put an end to exclusionary practices in science education and hiring. To eliminate the bad science more quickly, we should even engage in affirmative action to change the racial and sexual composition of the scientific work force.

Philosophically, however, this attempt to have it both ways is unsatisfactory. As Donna Haraway observed in a review of several collections of essays on sociobiology and hereditarianism, to simultaneously adopt an analysis of observation in science as theory- or paradigm-determined while asserting the incontrovertible existence of any fact is to embrace paradox.[8] Underlying her critique is the idea that if observation is theory-determined, then we can have no confidence that what appears to be a fact in the context of one theory will remain so in the next. Indeed, if sexist and racist science is bad science that ignores the facts or fails to treat them properly, this implies that there is a good or better methodology that will steer us away from biased conclusions. On the other hand, if sexist science is science as usual, then the best methodology in the world will not prevent us from attaining those conclusions unless we change paradigms. Is the scientific critic faced with a choice between critiquing methodologically incompetent science (but saying nothing more general about the relation between science and society) and critiquing science in general (but saying nothing in particular about politically pernicious science)? I will argue that this is a false dilemma. To see that this is so, however, requires a certain amount of philosophical groundwork.

The view that science is a social product is at least as old as Marxism. Marxists argued that the knowledge and culture of a society were ultimately determined by the relations of production. Part of what is at issue here is how to make good on that claim. According to Marxists, the knowledge and culture of a class society reflect the interests of its ruling class. A more objective and transformative knowledge can only be found or produced through another perspective – for Marxists, the perspective of wage laborers, or the proletariat. Feminist theorists have given this view a new form.[9] Knowledge in a male dominant society reflects the experience and interests of men. A more objective and transformative knowledge is therefore to be found in the perspective of women. Both forms of standpoint theory share the same weakness. Since neither wage laborers nor women share a common perspective, it becomes necessary to identify a subclass within each of those classes whose perspective does form an appropriate standpoint. However, the theory one is attempting to vindicate by a standpoint methodology is required to identify this subclass, thus making the procedure circular.

Are there criteria or standards of truth and rationality that can be articulated independently of social and political interests? I will argue that there are standards of rational acceptability that are independent of particular interests and values but that satisfaction of these standards by a theory or hypothesis does not guarantee that the theory or hypothesis in question is value- or interest-free. This argument involves a point similar to a different sort of feminist (and Marxist) claim. Feminist theorists have drawn our attention to the pervasiveness of interdependence in human societies – at its most obvious this claim is simply the observation that the public activities of production, commerce, and governance require the material support provided in the domestic realm to those carrying out those public activities. Individuals do not act alone but require others both for the execution and for the significance of their actions. Similarly, I will argue, the development of knowledge is a necessarily social rather than individual activity, and it is the social character of scientific knowledge that both protects it from and renders it vulnerable to social and political interests and values. The argument that develops this thesis is, therefore, simultaneously an account of what it means to say that science is socially constructed.

Notes

1   I introduce this distinction in Longino (1983).
2   Richardson (1984).
3   Richardson does distinguish between value-laden and value-loaded science and states that all science is value-laden. He does not, however, explain what value-laden science might be in

distinction from value-loaded science. Thus, his analysis invites being indiscriminately applied to all cases of contextual values in the sciences.

4 See, for example, the essays in Hubbard and Lowe, eds. (1979); Hubbard, Henifin, and Fried, eds. (1979); Ann Arbor Science for the People Collective (1977).
5 Haraway (1981).
6 Barnes and Bloor (1982); Bloor (1982); and Barnes and Edge, eds. (1982).
7 See, for example, Knorr-Cetina and Mulkay, eds. (1983), pp. 1–18.
8 See the introduction to Barnes and Edge, eds. (1982), pp. 1–12.
9 See Hartsock (1983) and Jaggar (1985) for two different ways of developing feminist standpoint theory.

References

Ann Arbor Science for the People Collective 1977. *Biology as a Social Weapon*. Minneapolis, MN: Burgess Publishing Co.

Barnes, Barry, and David Bloor. 1982. "Relativism, Rationalism and the Sociology of Knowledge." In *Rationality and Relativism*, ed. Martin Hollis and Steven Lukes, pp. 21–47. Cambridge, MA: MIT Press.

Barnes, Barry and David Edge, eds. 1982. *Science in Context*. Cambridge, MA: MIT Press.

Bloor, David. 1982. "Durkheim and Mauss Revisited: Classification and the Sociology of Knowledge." *Studies in History and Philosophy of Science* 13: 267–97.

Haraway, Donna. "In the Beginning Was the Word: The Genesis of Biological Theory." *Signs: Journal of Women in Culture and Society* 6(3): 469–82.

Hubbard, Ruth and Marian Lowe, eds. 1979. *Genes and Gender II*. New York: Gordian Press.

Hubbard, Ruth, Mary Sue Henifin, and Barbara Fried, eds. 1979. *Women Look at Biology Looking at Women*. Cambridge, MA: Schenkman Publishing.

Knorr-Cetina, Karin and Michael Mulkay, eds. 1983. *Science Observed*. London: Sage Publications.

Longino, Helen E. 1983. "Beyond 'Bad Science': Skeptical Reflections on the Value Freedom of Scientific Inquiry." *Science, Technology, and Human Values* 8(1): 7–17.

Richardson Robert C. 1984. "Biology and Ideology: The Interpenetration of Science and Values." *Philosophy of Science* 51(2): 396–420.

5 The 'Maleness' of Reason*

Genevieve Lloyd

What exactly does the 'maleness' of Reason amount to? It is clear that what we have in the history of philosophical thought is no mere succession of surface misogynist attitudes, which can now be shed, while leaving intact the deeper structures of our ideals of Reason. There is more at stake than the fact that past philosophers believed there to be flaws in female character. Many of them did indeed believe that women are less rational than

* From Genevieve Lloyd, *The Man of Reason* (University of Minnesota Press, 1984), pp. 103–10. Reprinted with permission.

men; and they have formulated their ideals of rationality with male paradigms in mind. But the maleness of Reason goes deeper than this. Our ideas and ideals of maleness and femaleness have been formed within structures of dominance – of superiority and inferiority, 'norms' and 'difference', 'positive' and 'negative', the 'essential' and the 'complementary'. And the male–female distinction itself has operated not as a straightforwardly descriptive principle of classification, but as an expression of values. The equation of maleness with superiority goes back at least as far as the Pythagoreans. What is valued – whether it be odd as against even numbers, 'aggressive' as against 'nurturing' skills and capacities, or Reason as against emotion – has been readily identified with maleness. Within the context of this association of maleness with preferred traits, it is not just incidental to the feminine that female traits have been construed as inferior – or, more subtly, as 'complementary' – to male norms of human excellence. Rationality has been conceived as transcendence of the feminine; and the 'feminine' itself has been partly constituted by its occurrence within this structure.

It is a natural response to the discovery of unfair discrimination to affirm the positive value of what has been downgraded. But with the kind of bias we are confronting here the situation is complicated by the fact that femininity, as we have it, has been partly formed by relation to, and differentiation from, a male norm. We may, for example, want to insist against past philosophers that the sexes are equal in possession of Reason; and that women must now be admitted to full participation in its cultural manifestations. But, in the case of de Beauvoir's feminist appropriation of the ideal of transcendence, this approach is fraught with difficulty. Women cannot easily be accommodated into a cultural ideal which has defined itself in opposition to the feminine. To affirm women's equal possession of rational traits, and their right of access to the public spaces within which they are cultivated and manifested, is politically important. But it does not get to the heart of the conceptual complexities of gender difference. And in repudiating one kind of exclusion, de Beauvoir's mode of response can help reinforce another. For it seems implicitly to accept the downgrading of the excluded character traits traditionally associated with femininity, and to endorse the assumption that the only human excellences and virtues which deserve to be taken seriously are those exemplified in the range of activities and concerns that have been associated with maleness.

However, alternative responses are no less beset by conceptual complexities. For example, it may seem easy to affirm the value and strengths of distinctively 'feminine' traits without subscribing to any covertly assumed 'norm' – to have, as it were, a genuine version of Rousseau's idea that the female mind is equal, but different. But extricating concepts of femininity from the intellectual structures within which our understanding of sexual difference has been formed is more difficult than it seems. The idea that women have their own distinctive kind of intellectual or moral character has itself been partly formed within the philosophical tradition to which it may now appear to be a reaction. Unless the structural features of our concepts of gender are understood, any emphasis on a supposedly distinctive style of thought or morality is liable to be caught up in a deeper, older structure of male norms and female complementation. The affirmation of the value and importance of 'the feminine' cannot of itself be expected to shake the underlying normative structures, for, ironically, it will occur in a space already prepared for it by the intellectual tradition it seeks to reject.

Thus it is an understandable reaction to the polarizations of Kantian ethics to want to stress the moral value of 'feminine' concerns with the personal and particular, as against the universal and impartial; or the warmth of feeling as against the chillingly abstract character of Reason. But it is important to be aware that the 'exclusion' of the feminine has not been a straightforward repudiation. Subtle accommodations have been incorporated into the social organization of sexual division – based on, or rationalized by, philosophical thought – which allow 'feminine' traits and activities to be both preserved and downgraded. There has been no lack of male affirmation of the importance and attractiveness of 'feminine' traits – in women – or of gallant acknowledgement of the impoverishment of male Reason. Making good the lacks in male consciousness, providing it with a necessary complementation by the 'feminine', is a large part of what the suppression, and the correlative constitution, of 'womankind' has been all about. An affirmation of the strengths of female 'difference' which is unaware of this may be doomed to repeat some of the sadder subplots in the history of western thought.

The content of femininity, as we have it, no less than its subordinate status, has been formed within an intellectual tradition. What has happened has been not a simple exclusion of women, but a constitution of femininity through that exclusion. It is remarkable that Hegel, the notorious exponent of the 'nether world' of femininity, should have had such insight into the conceptual complexities of sexual difference. Hegel's diagnosis of 'womankind' . . . occurs in a wider framework, which endorses the relegation of women to the private domain. But his understanding of the complexity, and the pathos, of gender difference in some ways transcends that. He saw that life in the nether world has conditioned the modes of female consciousness; that the distinctively 'feminine' is not a brute fact, but a structure largely constituted through suppression. To agree with this is not to deny that the 'feminine' has its own strengths and virtues. In the current climate of critical reflection on ideals of Reason, some of the strengths of female 'difference' can be seen as deriving from their very exclusion from 'male' thought-styles. To have been largely excluded from the dominant, and supposedly more 'advanced', forms of abstract thought or moral consciousness can be seen as a source of strength when their defects and impoverishment become apparent. But such strengths must be seen in relation to structural features of gender difference. They are strengths that derive from exclusion; and the merits of such 'minority consciousness' depend on avoiding asserting it as a rival norm.[1]

Attempting to identify or affirm anything distinctively 'feminine' has its hazards in a context of actual inequality. If the full range of human activities – both the nurturing tasks traditionally associated with the private domain and the activities which have hitherto occupied public space – were freely available to all, the exploration of sexual difference would be less fraught with the dangers of perpetuating norms and stereotypes which have mutilated men and women alike. But the task of exposing and criticizing the maleness of ideals of Reason need not wait upon the realization of such hopes; it may indeed be an important contribution to their realization.

The denigration of the 'feminine' is to feminists, understandably, the most salient aspect of the maleness of the philosophical tradition. But the issue is important for men, too. The lives of women incorporate the impoverishing restraints of Reason's transcended 'nether world'. But maleness, as we have inherited it, enacts, no less, the impoverishment and vulnerability of 'public' Reason. Understanding the contribution of past thought to 'male' and 'female' consciousness, as we now have them, can help make available a diversity of intellectual styles and characters to men and women alike. It need not involve a denial of all difference. Contemporary consciousness, male or female, reflects past philosophical ideals as well as past differences in the social organization of the lives of men and women. Such differences do not have to be taken as norms; and understanding them can be a source of richness and diversity in a human life whose full range of possibilities and experience is freely accessible to both men and women.

Can anything be salvaged of the ideal of a Reason which knows no sex? Much of past exultation in that ideal can be seen as a self-deceiving failure to acknowledge the differences between male and female minds, produced and played out in a social context of real inequalities. But it can also be seen as embodying a hope for the future. A similar ambiguity characterizes Hegel's own famous expression of faith in Reason, summed up in his slogan that the real is the rational and the rational the real. This has, not surprisingly, been seen by many as a dubious rationalization of the status quo. But it can also be taken as the expression of an ideal – as an affirmation of faith that the irrational will not prevail. Such a faith may well appear naive; but that does not mean it is bad faith. The confident affirmation that Reason 'knows no sex' may likewise be taking for reality something which, if valid at all, is so only as an ideal. Ideal equalities, here as elsewhere, can conceal actual inequalities. Notwithstanding many philosophers' hopes and aspirations to the contrary, our ideals of Reason are in fact male; and if there is a Reason genuinely common to all, it is something to be achieved in the future, not celebrated in the present. Past ideals of Reason, far from transcending sexual difference, have helped to constitute it. That ideas of maleness have developed under the guise of supposedly neutral ideals of Reason has been to the disadvantage of women and men alike.

Philosophers have defined their activity in terms of the pursuit of Reason, free of the conditioning effects of historical circumstance and social structures. But despite its professed transcendence of such contingencies, Philosophy has been deeply affected by, as well as deeply affecting, the social organization of sexual difference. The full dimensions of the maleness of Philosophy's past are only now becoming visible. Despite its aspirations to timeless truth, the History of Philosophy reflects the characteristic preoccupations and self-perceptions of the kinds of people who have at any time had access to the activity. Philosophers have at different periods been churchmen, men of letters, university professors. But there is one thing they have had in common throughout the history of the activity: they have been predominantly male; and the absence of women from the philosophical tradition has meant that the conceptualization of Reason has been done exclusively by men. It is not surprising that the results should reflect their sense of Philosophy as a male activity. There have of course been female philosophers throughout the western tradition. But, like Philo's or Augustine's women of Reason, they have been philosophers despite, rather than because of, their femaleness; there has been no input of femaleness into the formation of ideals of Reason.

As women begin to develop a presence in Philosophy, it is only to be expected that the maleness of Philosophy's past, and with it the maleness of ideals of Reason, should begin to come into focus; and that this should be accompanied by a sense of antagonism between feminism and Philosophy. We have seen that Philosophy has powerfully contributed to the exclusion of the feminine from cultural ideals, in ways that cannot be dismissed as minor aberrations of the philosophical imagination. But it is important that the tensions between feminism and Philosophy should not be misconstrued. The exclusion of the feminine has not resulted from a conspiracy by male philosophers. We have seen that in some cases it happened despite the conscious intent of the authors. Where it does appear explicitly in the texts, it is usually incidental to their main purposes; and often it emerges only in the conjunction of the text with surrounding social structures – a configuration which often is visible only in retrospect.

Feminist unease about ideals of Reason is sometimes expressed as a repudiation of allegedly male principles of rational thought. Such formulations of the point make it all too easy for professional philosophers to dismiss as confused all talk of the maleness of Reason. As I pointed out at the beginning, contemporary philosophical preoccupation with the requirements of rational belief, the objectivity of truth and the procedures of rational argument, can make it difficult for them to see the import of criticisms of broader cultural ideals associated with Reason. The claim that Reason is male need not at all involve sexual relativism about truth, or any suggestion that principles of logical thought valid for men do not hold also for female reasoners.

Philosophers can take seriously feminist dissatisfaction with the maleness of Reason without repudiating either Reason or Philosophy. Such criticisms of ideals of Reason can in fact be seen as continuous with a very old strand in the western philosophical tradition; it has been centrally concerned with bringing to reflective awareness the deeper structures of inherited ideals of Reason. Philosophy has defined ideals of Reason through exclusions of the feminine. But it also contains within it the resources for critical reflection on those ideals and on its own aspirations. Fortunately, Philosophy is not necessarily what it has in the past proudly claimed to be – a timeless rational representation of the real, free of the conditioning effects of history.

To study the History of Philosophy can be of itself to engage in a form of cultural critique. Few today share Hegel's vision of the History of Philosophy as the steady path of Reason's progress through human history. But it does reveal a succession of ways of construing Reason which have, for better or worse, had a formative influence on cultural ideals, and which still surface in contemporary consciousness. I have tried to bring out how these views of Reason have been connected with the male–female distinction. In doing so, I have of course often highlighted points which were not salient in the philosophers' own perceptions of what they were about. Bringing the male–female distinction to the centre of consideration of texts in this way may seem to misrepresent the History of Philosophy. But philosophers, when they tell the story of Philosophy's past, have always done so from the perspective of their own preoccupations, shared with their non-philosopher contemporaries – pressing questions which were not central to the philosophers they were explicating.

To highlight the male–female distinction in relation to philosophical texts is not to distort the History of Philosophy. It does, however, involve taking seriously the temporal distance that separates us from past thinkers. Taking temporal distance seriously demands also of course that we keep firmly in view what the thinkers themselves saw as central to their projects. This exercise involves a constant tension between the need to confront past ideals with perspectives drawn from the present and, on the other hand, an equally strong demand to present fairly what the authors took themselves to be doing. A constructive resolution of the tensions between contemporary feminism and past Philosophy requires that we do justice to both demands.

Note

1 The phrase 'minority consciousness' is from G. Deleuze, 'Philosophie et minorité', *Critique*, 369 (1978), 154–5.

6   The Ethics of Belief*

William Clifford

The Duty of Inquiry

A shipowner was about to send to sea an emigrant ship. He knew that she was old, and not over-well built at the first; that she had seen many seas and climes, and often had needed repairs. Doubts had been suggested to him that possibly she was not seaworthy. These doubts preyed upon his mind and made him unhappy; he thought that perhaps he ought to have her thoroughly overhauled and refitted, even though this should put him to great expense. Before the ship sailed, however, he succeeded in overcoming these melancholy reflections. He said to himself that she had gone safely through so many voyages and weathered so many storms that it was idle to suppose she would not come safely home from this trip also. He would put his trust in Providence, which could hardly fail to protect all these unhappy families that were leaving their fatherland to seek for better times elsewhere. He would dismiss from his mind all ungenerous suspicions about the honesty of builders and contractors. In such ways he acquired a sincere and comfortable conviction that his vessel was thoroughly safe and seaworthy; he watched her departure with a light heart, and benevolent wishes for the success of the exiles in their strange new home that was to be; and he got his insurance money when she went down in mid-ocean and told no tales.

What shall we say of him? Surely this, that he was verily guilty of the death of those men. It is admitted that he did sincerely believe in the soundness of his ship; but the sincerity of his conviction can in no wise help him, because *he had no right to believe on such evidence as was before him.* He had acquired his belief not by honestly earning it in patient investigation, but by stifling his doubts. And although in the end he may have felt so sure about it that he could not think otherwise, yet inasmuch as he had knowingly and willingly worked himself into that frame of mind, he must be held responsible for it.

Let us alter the case a little, and suppose that the ship was not unsound after all; that she made her voyage safely, and many others after it. Will that diminish the guilt of her owner? Not one jot. When an action is once done, it is right or wrong for ever; no accidental failure of its good or evil fruits can possibly alter that. The man would not have been innocent, he would only have been not found out. The question of right or wrong has to do with the origin of his belief, not the matter of it; not what is was, but how he got it; not whether it turned out to be true of false, but whether he had a right to believe on such evidence as was before him.

There was once an island in which some of the inhabitants professed a religion teaching neither the doctrine of original sin nor that of eternal punishment. A suspicion got abroad that the professors of this religion had made use of unfair means to get their doctrines taught to children. They were accused of wresting the laws of their country in such a way as to remove children from the care of their natural and legal guardians; and even

*From W. K. Clifford, *Lectures and Essays* (New York: Macmillan, 1901), pp. 163–76.

of stealing them away and keeping them concealed from their friends and relations. A certain number of men formed themselves into a society for the purpose of agitating the public about this matter. They published grave accusations against individual citizens of the highest position and character, and did all in their power to injure these citizens in the exercise of their professions. So great was the noise they made that a Commission was appointed to investigate the facts; but after the Commission had carefully inquired into all the evidence that could be got, it appeared that the accused were innocent. Not only had they been accused on insufficient evidence, but the evidence of their innocence was such as the agitators might easily have obtained, if they had attempted a fair inquiry. After these disclosures the inhabitants of that country looked upon the members of the agitating society, not only as persons whose judgement was to be distrusted, but also as no longer to be counted honourable men. For although they had sincerely and conscientiously believed in the charges they had made, *yet they had no right to believe on such evidence as was before them*. Their sincere convictions, instead of being honestly earned by patient inquiring, were stolen by listening to the voice of prejudice and passion.

Let us vary this case also, and suppose, other things remaining as before, that a still more accurate investigation proved the accused to have been really guilty. Would this make any difference in the guilt of the accusers? Clearly not; the question is not whether their belief was true or false, but whether they entertained it on wrong grounds. They would no doubt say, 'Now you see that we were right after all; next time perhaps you will believe us.' And they might be believed, but they would not thereby become honourable men. They would not be innocent, they would only be not found out. Every one of them, if he chose to examine himself *in foro conscientiae*, would know that he had acquired and nourished a belief, when he had no right to believe on such evidence as was before him; and therein he would know that he had done a wrong thing.

It may be said, however, that in both of these supposed cases it is not the belief which is judged to be wrong, but the action following upon it. The shipowner might say, 'I am perfectly certain that my ship is sound, but still I feel it my duty to have her examined, before trusting the lives of so many people to her.' And it might be said to the agitator, 'However convinced you were of the justice of your cause and the truth of your convictions, you ought not to have made a public attack upon any man's character until you had examined the evidence on both sides with the utmost patience and care.'

In the first place, let us admit that, so far as it goes, this view of the case is right and necessary; right, because even when a man's belief is so fixed that he cannot think otherwise, he still has a choice in regard to the action suggested by it, and so cannot escape the duty of investigating on the ground of the strength of his convictions; and necessary, because those who are not yet capable of controlling their feelings and thoughts must have a plain rule dealing with overt acts.

But this being premised as necessary, it becomes clear that it is not sufficient, and that our previous judgment is required to supplement it. For it is not possible so to sever the belief from the action it suggests as to condemn the one without condemning the other. No man holding a strong belief on one side of a question, or even wishing to hold a belief on one side, can investigate it with such fairness and completeness as if he were really in doubt and unbiased; so that the existence of a belief not founded on fair inquiry unfits a man for the performance of this necessary duty.

Nor is that truly a belief at all which has not some influence upon the actions of him who holds it. He who truly believes that which prompts him to an action has looked upon that action to lust after it, he has committed it already in his heart. If a belief is not realized immediately in open deeds, it is stored up for the guidance of the future. It goes to make a part of that aggregate of beliefs which is the link between sensation and action at every moment of all our lives, and which is so organized and compacted together that no part of it can be isolated from the rest, but every new addition modifies the structure of the whole. No real belief, however trifling and fragmentary it may seem, is ever truly insignificant; it prepares us to receive more of its like, confirms those which resembled it before, and weakens others; and so gradually it lays a stealthy train in our inmost thoughts, which may some day explode into overt action, and leave its stamp upon our character for ever.

And no one man's belief is in any case a private matter which concerns himself alone. Our lives are guided by that general conception of the course of things which has been created by society for social purposes. Our words, our phrases, our forms and processes and modes of thought, are common property, fashioned and perfected from age to age; an heirloom which every succeeding generation inherits as a precious deposit and a sacred trust to be handed on to the next one, not unchanged but enlarged and purified, with some clear marks of its proper handiwork. Into this, for good or ill, is woven every belief of every man who has speech of his fellows. An awful privilege, and an awful responsibility, that we should help to create the world in which posterity will live.

In the two supposed cases which have been considered, it has been judged wrong to believe on insufficient evidence, or to nourish belief by suppressing doubts and avoiding investigation. The reason of this judgement is not far to seek: it is that in both these cases the belief held by one man was of great importance to other men. But forasmuch as no belief held by one man, however seemingly trivial the belief, and however obscure the believer, is ever actually insignificant or without its effect on the fate of mankind we have no choice but to extend our judgement to all cases of belief whatever. Belief, that sacred faculty which prompts the decisions of our will, and knits into harmonious working all the compacted energies of our being, is ours not for ourselves, but for humanity. It is rightly used on truths which have been established by long experience and waiting toil, and which have stood in the fierce light of free and fearless questioning. Then it helps to bind men together, and to strengthen and direct their common action. It is desecrated when given to unproved and unquestioned statements, for the solace and private pleasure of the believer; to add a tinsel splendour to the plain straight road of our life and display a bright mirage beyond it; or even to drown the common sorrows of our kind by a self-deception which allows them not only to cast down, but also to degrade us. Whoso would deserve well of his fellows in this matter will guard the purity of his belief with a very fanaticism of jealous care, lest at any time it should rest on an unworthy object, and catch a stain which can never be wiped away.

It is not only the leader of men, statesman, philosopher, or poet, that owes this bounden duty to mankind. Every rustic who delivers in the village alehouse his slow, infrequent sentences, may help to kill or keep alive the fatal superstitions which clog his race. Every hard-worked wife of an artisan may transmit to her children beliefs which shall knit society together, or rend it in pieces. No simplicity of mind, no obscurity of station, can escape the universal duty of questioning all that we believe.

It is true that this duty is a hard one, and the doubt which comes out of it is often a very bitter thing. It leaves us bare and powerless where we thought that we were safe and strong. To know all about anything is to know how to deal with it under all circumstances. We feel much happier and more secure when we think we know precisely what to do, no matter what happens, than when we have lost our way and do not know where to turn. And if we have supposed ourselves to know all about anything, and to be capable

of doing what is fit in regard to it, we naturally do not like to find that we are really ignorant and powerless, that we have to begin again at the beginning, and try to learn what
the thing is and how it is to be dealt with – if indeed anything can be learnt about it. It
is the sense of power attached to a sense of knowledge that makes men desirous of believing, and afraid of doubting.

This sense of power is the highest and best of pleasures when the belief on which it is
founded is a true belief, and has been fairly earned by investigation. For then we may justly
feel that it is common property, and holds good for others as well as for ourselves. Then
we may be glad, not that *I* have learned secrets by which I am safer and stronger, but that
we men have got mastery over more of the world; and we shall be strong, not for ourselves, but in the name of Man and in his strength. But if the belief has been accepted on
insufficient evidence, the pleasure is a stolen one. Not only does it deceive ourselves by
giving us a sense of power which we do not really possess, but it is sinful, because it is
stolen in defiance of our duty to mankind. That duty is to guard ourselves from such beliefs
as from a pestilence, which may shortly master our own body and then spread to the rest
of the town. What would be thought of one who, for the sake of a sweet fruit, should
deliberately run the risk of bringing a plague upon his family and his neighbours?

And, as in other such cases, it is not the risk only which has to be considered; for a
bad action is always bad at the time when it is done, no matter what happens afterwards.
Every time we let ourselves believe for unworthy reasons, we weaken our powers of self-
control, of doubting, of judicially and fairly weighing evidence. We all suffer severely
enough from the maintenance and support of false beliefs and the fatally wrong actions
which they lead to, and the evil born when one such belief is entertained is great and
wide. But a greater and wider evil arises when the credulous character is maintained and
supported, when a habit of believing for unworthy reasons is fostered and made permanent. If I steal money from any person, there may be no harm done by the mere transfer of possession; he may not feel the loss, or it may prevent him from using the money
badly. But I cannot help doing this great wrong towards Man, that I make myself dishonest. What hurts society is not that it should lose its property, but that it should become
a den of thieves; for then it must cease to be society. This is why we ought not to do evil
that good may come; for at any rate this great evil has come, that we have done evil and
are made wicked thereby. In like manner, if I let myself believe anything on insufficient
evidence, there may be no great harm done by the mere belief; it may be true after all,
or I may never have occasion to exhibit it in outward acts. But I cannot help doing this
great wrong towards Man, that I make myself credulous. The danger to society is not
merely that it should believe wrong things, though that is great enough; but that it should
become credulous, and lose the habit of testing things and inquiring into them; for then
it must sink back into savagery.

The harm which is done by credulity in a man is not confined to the fostering of a
credulous character in others, and consequent support of false beliefs. Habitual want of
care about what I believe leads to habitual want of care in others about the truth of what
is told to me. Men speak the truth to one another when each reveres the truth in his own
mind and in the other's mind; but how shall my friend revere that truth in my mind when
I myself am careless about it, when I believe things because I want to believe them, and
because they are comforting and pleasant? Will he not learn to cry, 'Peace,' to me, when
there is no peace? By such a course I shall surround myself with a thick atmosphere of
falsehood and fraud, and in that I must live. It may matter little to me, in my cloud-castle
of sweet illusions and darling lies; but it matters much to Man that I have made my neigh-

bours ready to deceive. The credulous man is father to the liar and the cheat; he lives in the bosom of this his family, and it is no marvel if he should become even as they are. So closely are our duties knit together, that whose shall keep the whole law, and yet offend in one point, he is guilty of all.

To sum up: it is wrong always, everywhere, and for any one, to believe anything upon insufficient evidence.

If a man, holding a belief which he was taught in childhood or persuaded of after-wards, keeps down and pushes away any doubts which arise about it in his mind, pur-posely avoids the reading of books and the company of men that call in question or discuss it, and regards as impious those questions which cannot easily be asked without disturb-ing it – the life of that man is one long sin against mankind.

If this judgement seems harsh when applied to those simple souls who have never known better, who have been brought up from the cradle with a horror of doubt, and taught that their eternal welfare depends on *what* they believe, then it leads to the very serious question, *Who hath made Israel to sin?*

It may be permitted me to fortify this judgement with the sentence of Milton:

A man may be a heretic in the truth; and if he believe things only because his pastor says so, or the assembly so determine, without knowing other reason, though his belief be true, yet the very truth he holds becomes his heresy. (*Areopagitica*)

And with this famous aphorism of Coleridge:

He who begins by loving Christianity better than Truth, will proceed by loving his own sect or Church better than Christianity, and end in loving himself better than all. (*Aids to Reflection*)

Inquiry into the evidence of a doctrine is not to be made once for all, and then taken as finally settled. It is never lawful to stifle a doubt; for either it can be honestly answered by means of the inquiry already made, or else it proves that the inquiry was not complete.

'But,' says one, 'I am a busy man; I have no time for the long course of study which would be necessary to make me in any degree a competent judge of certain question, or even able to understand the nature of the arguments.' Then he should have no time to believe.

---

7 It is Wrong, Everywhere, Always, and for Anyone, to Believe Anything upon Insufficient Evidence*

Peter van Inwagen

My title is a famous sentence from W. K. Clifford's celebrated lecture, "The Ethics of Belief." What I want to do is not so much to challenge (or to vindicate) the principle

* From Jeff Jordan and Daniel Howard-Snyder (eds.), *Faith, Freedom, and Rationality: Philosophy of Religion Today* (Lanham, MD: Rowman & Littlefield, 1996), pp. 137–53. Reprinted with permission.

this sentence expresses as to examine what the consequences of attempting consistently to apply it in our lives would be. Various philosophers have attempted something that might be described in these words, and have argued that a strict adherence to the terms of the principle would lead to a chain of requests for further evidence that would terminate only in such presumably unanswerable questions as "What evidence have you for supposing that your sensory apparatus is reliable?," or "Yes, but what considerations can you adduce in support of the hypothesis that the future *will* resemble the past?"; and they have drawn the conclusion that anyone who accepts such propositions as that one's sensory apparatus is reliable or that the future will resemble the past must do so in defiance of the principle. You will be relieved to learn that an investigation along these lines is not on the program tonight. I am not going to raise the question whether a strict adherence to the principle would land us in the one of those very abstract sorts of epistemological predicaments exemplified by uncertainty about the reliability of sense perception or induction. I shall be looking at consequences of accepting the principle that are much more concrete, much closer to our concerns as epistemically responsible citizens – citizens not only of the body politic but of the community of philosophers.

I shall, as I say, be concerned with Clifford's sentence and the lecture that it epitomizes. But I am going to make my way to this topic by a rather winding path. Please bear with me for a bit.

I begin my indirect approach to Clifford's sentence by stating a fact about philosophy. Philosophers do not agree about anything to speak of. That is, it is not very usual for agreement among philosophers on any important philosophical issue to be describable as being, in a quite unambiguous sense, common. Oh, this philosopher may agree with that philosopher on many philosophical points; for that matter, if this philosopher is a former student of that philosopher, they may even agree on *all* philosophical points. But you don't find universal or near-universal agreement about very many important theses or arguments in philosophy. Indeed, it would be hard to find an important philosophical thesis that, say, 95 percent of, say, American analytical philosophers born between 1930 and 1950 agreed about in, say, 1987.

And why not? How can it be that equally intelligent and well-trained philosophers can disagree about the freedom of the will or nominalism or the covering-law model of scientific explanation when each is aware of all of the arguments and distinctions and other relevant considerations that the others are aware of? How – and now I will drop a broad hint about where I am going – how can we philosophers possibly regard ourselves as justified in believing much of anything of philosophical significance in this embarrassing circumstance? How can *I* believe (as I do) that free will is incompatible with determinism or that unrealized possibilities are not physical objects or that human beings are not four-dimensional things extended in time as well as in space, when David Lewis – a philosopher of truly formidable intelligence and insight and ability – rejects these things I believe and is already aware of and understands perfectly every argument that I could produce in their defense?

Well, I *do* believe these things, and I believe that I am justified in believing them. And I am confident that I am right. But how can I take these positions? I don't know. That is itself a philosophical question, and I have no firm opinion about its correct answer. I suppose my best guess is that I enjoy some sort of philosophical insight (I mean in relation to these three particular theses) that, for all his merits, is somehow denied to Lewis. And this would have to be an insight that is incommunicable – at least *I* don't know how to communicate it – for I have done all I can to communicate it to Lewis, and he has understood perfectly everything I have said, and he has not come to share my conclusions. But maybe my best guess is wrong. I'm confident about only one thing in this area: the question must have some good answer. For not only do my beliefs about these questions seem to me to be undeniably *true*, but (quite independent of any consideration of which theses it is that seem to me to be true), I don't want to be forced into a position in which I can't see my way clear to accepting any philosophical thesis of any consequence. Let us call this unattractive position "philosophical skepticism." (Note that I am not using this phrase in its usual sense of "comprehensive and general skepticism based on philosophical argument." Note also that philosophical skepticism is not a thesis – if it were, it's hard to see how it could be accepted without pragmatic contradiction – but a state: philosophical skeptics are people who can't see their way clear to being nominalists or realists, dualists or monists, ordinary-language philosophers or phenomenologists; people, in short, who are aware of many philosophical options but take none of them, people who have listened to many philosophical debates but have never once declared a winner.) I think that any philosopher who does not wish to be a philosophical skeptic – I know of no philosopher who *is* a philosophical skeptic – must agree with me that this question has some good answer: whatever the reason, it must be possible for one to be justified in accepting a philosophical thesis when there are philosophers who, by *all* objective and external criteria, are at least equally well qualified to pronounce on that thesis and who reject it.

Will someone say that philosophical theses are theses of a very special sort, and that philosophy is therefore a special case? That adequacy of evidential support is much more easily achieved in respect of philosophical propositions than in respect of geological or medical or historical propositions? Perhaps because nothing really hangs on philosophical questions, and a false or unjustified philosophical opinion is therefore harmless? Or because philosophy is in some sense not about matters of empirical fact? As to the first of these two suggestions, I think it is false that nothing hangs on philosophical questions. What people have believed about the philosophical theses advanced by – for example – Plato, Locke, and Marx has had profound effects on history. I don't know what the world would be like if everyone who ever encountered philosophy immediately became, and thereafter remained, a philosophical skeptic, but I'm willing to bet it would be a vastly different world. (In any case, I certainly *hope* this suggestion is false. I'd hate to have to defend my own field of study against a charge of adhering to loose epistemic standards by arguing that it's all right to adopt loose epistemic standards in philosophy because philosophy is detached from life to such a degree that philosophical mistakes can't do any harm.) In a more general, theoretical way, Clifford has argued, and with some plausibility, that it is *in principle* impossible to claim on behalf of any subject-matter whatever – on the ground that mistaken beliefs about the things of which that subject-matter treats are harmless – exemption from the strict epistemic standards to which, say, geological, medical, and historical beliefs are properly held. He argues,

> [That is not] truly a belief at all which has not some influence upon the actions of him who holds it. He who truly believes that which prompts him to an action has looked upon the action to lust after it, he has committed it already in his heart. If a belief is not realized immediately in open deeds, it is stored up for the guidance of the future. It goes to make a part of that aggregate of beliefs which is the link between sensation and action at every moment of all our lives, and which is so organized and compacted together that no part of it can be

isolated from the rest, but every new addition modifies the structure of the whole. No real belief, however trifling and fragmentary it may seem, is ever truly insignificant; it prepares us to receive more of its like, confirms those which resembled it before, and weakens others; and so gradually it lays a stealthy train in our inmost thoughts, which may some day explode into overt action, and leave its stamp upon our character forever. . . . And no one man's belief is in any case a private matter which concerns himself alone . . . no belief held by one man, however seemingly trivial the belief, and however obscure the believer, is actually insignificant or without its effect on the fate of mankind.

Whether or not you find this general, theoretical argument convincing, it does in any case seem quite impossible to maintain, given the actual history of the relation between philosophy and our social life, that it makes no real difference what people believe about philosophical questions.

The second suggestion – that philosophy is "different" (and that philosophers may therefore properly, in their professional work, observe looser epistemic standards than geologists or physicians observe in theirs) because it's not about matters of empirical fact – is trickier. Its premise is not that it doesn't make any difference what people believe about philosophical questions; it's rather that the world would look exactly the same whether any given philosophical thesis were true or false. I think that that's a dubious assertion. If the declarative sentences that philosophers characteristically write and speak in their professional capacity are meaningful at all, then many of them express propositions that are *necessary* truths or *necessary* falsehoods, and it's at least a very doubtful assertion that the world would look the same if some necessary truth were a falsehood or if some necessary falsehood were a truth. (Would anyone argue that mathematicians may properly hold themselves to looser epistemic standards than geologists because the world would look the same whether or not there was a greatest prime?) And even if it were true that philosophy was, in no sense of this versatile word, "about" matters of empirical fact, one might well raise the question why this should lend any support to the suggestion that philosophers were entitled to looser epistemic standards than geologists or physiologists, given that philosophical beliefs actually do have important effects on the behavior of those who hold them. Rather than address the issues that these speculations raise, however, I will simply change the subject.

Let us consider politics.

Almost everyone will admit that it makes a difference what people believe about politics – I am using the word in its broadest possible sense – and it would be absurd to say that propositions like "Capital punishment is an ineffective deterrent" or "Nations that do not maintain a strong military capability actually increase the risk of war" are not about matters of empirical fact. And yet people disagree about these propositions (and scores of others of equal importance), and their disagreements about them bear a disquieting resemblance to the disagreements of philosophers about nominalism and free will and the covering-law model. That is, their disagreements are matters of interminable debate, and impressive authorities can be found on both sides of many of the interminable debates.

It is important to realize that this feature of philosophy and politics is not a universal feature of human discourse. It is clear, for example, that someone who believes in astrology believes in something that is simply indefensible. It would be hard to find a philosopher – I *hope* this is true – who believed that every philosopher who disagreed with his or her position on nominalism held a position that was indefensible in the same way that a belief in astrology was indefensible. It might be easier to find someone who held the corresponding position about disputed and important political questions. I suspect there really are people who think that those who disagree with them about the deterrent effect of capital punishment or the probable consequences of unilateral disarmament are not only mistaken but hold beliefs that are indefensible in the way that a belief in astrology is indefensible. I can only say that I regard this attitude as ludicrous. On each side of many interminably debated political questions – it is not necessary to my argument to say *all* – one can find well-informed (indeed, immensely learned) and highly intelligent men and women who adhere to the very highest intellectual standards. And this is imply not the case with debates about astrology. In fact, it is hardly possible to suppose that there could be a very *interesting* debate about the truth-values of the claims made by astrologers.

Everyone who is intellectually honest will admit this, will admit that there are interminable political debates with highly intelligent and well-informed people on both sides. And yet few will react to this state of affairs by becoming political skeptics, by declining to have any political beliefs that are disputed by highly intelligent and well-informed people. But how can this rejection of political skepticism be defended? How can responsible political thinkers believe that the Syndicalist Party is the last, best hope for Ruritania when they know full well that there are well-informed (even immensely learned) and highly intelligent people who argue vehemently – all the while adhering to the highest intellectual standards – that a Syndicalist government would be the ruin of Ruritania? Do the friends of Syndicalism claim to see gaps in the arguments of their opponents, "facts" that they have cited that are not really facts, real facts that they have chosen not to mention, a hidden agenda behind their opposition to Syndicalism? No doubt they do. Nevertheless, if they are intelligent and intellectually honest, they will be aware that if these claims were made in public debate, the opponents of Syndicalism would probably be able to muster a very respectable rebuttal. The friends of Syndicalism will perhaps be confident that they could effectively meet the points raised in this rebuttal, but, if they are intelligent and intellectually honest, they will be aware . . . and so, for all practical purposes, *ad infinitum*.

I ask again, what could it be that justifies us in rejecting political skepticism? How can *I* believe that my political beliefs are justified when these beliefs are rejected by people whose qualifications for engaging in political discourse are as impressive as David Lewis's qualifications for engaging in philosophical discourse? These people are aware of (at least) all the evidence and all the arguments that I am aware of, and they are (at least) as good at evaluating evidence and arguments as I. How, then, can I maintain that the evidence and arguments I can adduce in support of my beliefs actually justify these beliefs? If this evidence and these arguments are capable of that, then why aren't they capable of convincing these other people that these beliefs are correct? Well, as with philosophy, I am inclined to think that I must enjoy some sort of incommunicable insight that the others, for all their merits, lack. I am inclined to think that "the evidence and arguments I can adduce in support of my beliefs" do not constitute the totality of my justification for these beliefs. But all that I am willing to say for sure is that *something* justifies me in rejecting political skepticism, or at least that it is *possible* that something does: that it is not a necessary truth that one is not justified in holding a political belief that is controverted by intelligent and well-informed political thinkers.

I have now accomplished one of the things I wanted to do in this chapter. I have raised the question how it is possible to avoid philosophical and political skepticism. In the remainder of this chapter, I am going to turn to questions about religious belief. My point in raising the questions I have raised about philosophy and politics was primarily to set the stage for comparing religious beliefs with philosophical and political beliefs. But I think that the questions I have so far raised are interesting in their own right. Even if everything I say in the remainder of the chapter is wrong, even if my comparisons of philosophical and political beliefs with religious beliefs turn out to be entirely wide of the mark, the interest of the questions I have raised so far will remain. How can we philosophers, when we consider the matter carefully, avoid the uncomfortable suspicion that the following words of Clifford might apply to *us*: "Every one of them, if he chose to examine himself *in foro conscientiae*, would know that he had acquired and nourished a belief, when he had no right to believe on such evidence as was before him; and therein he would know that he had done a wrong thing."?

Now as to religion: is religion different from philosophy and politics in the respects we have been discussing? Should religious beliefs perhaps be held to a stricter evidential standard than philosophical and political beliefs? Or, if they are to be held to the same standard, do typical religious beliefs fare worse under this standard than typical philosophical or political beliefs? It is an extremely popular position that religion *is* different. Or, at least, it must be that many antireligious philosophers and other writers hostile to religious belief hold this position, for it seems to be presupposed by almost every aspect of their approach to the subject of religious belief. And yet this position seems never to have been explicitly formulated, much less argued for. Let us call it the Difference Thesis. An explicit formulation of the Difference Thesis is a tricky matter. I tentatively suggest that it be formulated disjunctively: Either religious beliefs should be held to a stricter epistemic standard than beliefs of certain other types – of which philosophical and political beliefs are the paradigms – or, if they are to be held to the same epistemic standard as other beliefs, they typically fare worse under this standard than typical beliefs of most other types, including philosophical and political beliefs. I use this disjunctive formulation because, while I think I see some sort of difference thesis at work in much of the hostile writing on the epistemic status of religious belief, the work of this thesis is generally accomplished at a subliminal level and it is hard to get a clear view of it. I suspect that some of the writers I have alluded to are thinking in terms of one of the disjuncts and some in terms of the other.

A good example of the Difference Thesis at work is provided by Clifford's lecture. One of the most interesting facts about "The Ethics of Belief" is that nowhere in it is religious belief explicitly discussed. There are, to be sure, a few glancing references to religion in the lecture, but the fact that they are references to religion, while it doubtless has its polemical function, is never essential to the point that Clifford professes to be making. Clifford's shipowner, for example, comes to his dishonest belief partly because he puts his trust in Providence, but Clifford could have made the same philosophical point if he had made the shipowner come to his dishonest belief because he had put his trust in his brother-in-law. Clifford's other main illustrative case is built round an actual Victorian scandal (described in coyly abstract terms: "There was once a certain island in which . . .") involving religious persecution. But he could have made the same philosophical point if he had described a case of purely secular persecution, such as those that attended the investigations of Senator McCarthy; his illustration turned simply on the unwillingness of zealous agitators, convinced that the right was on their side, to examine certain matters of public record and to obtain easily available testimony. In both of Clifford's illustrative cases, there is a proposition that is dishonestly accepted, accepted without sufficient attention to the available evidence. In neither case is it a religious or theological proposition. And at no point does Clifford come right out and say that his arguments have any special connection with religious beliefs. It would, however, be disingenuous in the extreme to say that "The Ethics of Belief" is simply about the ethics of belief in general and is no more directed at religious belief than at any other kind of belief. "Everyone knows," as the phrase goes, that Clifford's target is religious belief. (Certainly the editors of anthologies know this. "The Ethics of Belief" appears in just about every anthology devoted to the philosophy of religion. It has never appeared in an anthology devoted to epistemology. I know of only one case in which anyone writing on general epistemological questions has mentioned Clifford's lecture, and that is a very brief footnote in Chisholm's *Perceiving*, in the chapter entitled "The Ethics of Belief." In that note, Chisholm simply says that he holds a weaker thesis about the ethics of belief than Clifford's. Given that he had borrowed Clifford's title for his chapter-title, I suppose that that was the least he could have done.) The real thesis of Clifford's lecture, its subtext as our friends in the literature departments say, is that religious beliefs – belief in God, belief in an afterlife, belief in the central historical claims of Judaism or Christianity or Islam – are always or almost always held in ways that violate the famous ethico-epistemic principle whose quotation-name is my title: It is wrong always, everywhere, and for anyone, to believe anything upon insufficient evidence. If, moreover, he is of the opinion that beliefs in any other general category are always or almost always (or typically or rather often) held in ways that violate his principle, this is certainly not apparent.

This conviction that Clifford's specific target is religious belief is no knee-jerk reaction of overly sensitive religious believers or of antireligious polemicists eager to find yet another stick to beat churchgoers with. If the conviction is not supported by his argument, in the strictest sense of the word, it is well grounded in his rhetoric. For one thing, the lecture abounds in biblical quotations and echoes, which is not a usual feature of Clifford's prose. For another, there are the inessential religious elements in both of his illustrative examples. Much more importantly, however, there are two passing allusions to religious belief, which, although they go by rather quickly, are nevertheless writ in letters that he who runs may read. First, one of the dishonest comforts provided by certain beliefs that are not apportioned to evidence is said to be this: they "add a tinsel splendor to the plain straight road of our life and display a bright mirage beyond it." Secondly, when Clifford raises the question whether it is fair to blame people for holding beliefs that are not supported by evidence if they hold these beliefs as a result of their having been trained from childhood not to raise questions of evidence in certain areas, he refers to these unfortunates as "those simple souls . . . who have been brought up from the cradle with a horror of doubt, and taught that their eternal welfare depends on what they believe."

Let us call Clifford's principle – "It is wrong always, everywhere, and for anyone . . ." – Clifford's Principle, which seems an appropriate enough name for it. I should note that there seems to be another principle that Clifford seems sometimes to be appealing to and which he neither articulates nor distinguishes clearly from Clifford's Principle. Call it Clifford's Other Principle. It is something very much like this: "It is wrong always, everywhere, and for anyone to ignore evidence that is relevant to his beliefs, or to dismiss relevant evidence in a facile way." Clifford's Other Principle is obviously not Clifford's Principle. It is very doubtful whether someone who satisfied the requirements of

Clifford's Principle would necessarily satisfy the requirements of Clifford's Other Principle (it could be argued that it would be possible to have evidence that justified one's accepting a certain proposition even though one had deliberately chosen not to examine certain other evidence that was relevant to the question whether to accept that proposition) and it is pretty certain that someone who satisfied the requirements of Clifford's Other Principle would not necessarily satisfy the requirements of Clifford's Principle. I suspect that Clifford tended to conflate the two principles because of a combination of his antireligious agenda with an underlying assumption that the evidence, such as it is, that people have for their religious beliefs is inadequate because it is incomplete, and incomplete because these believers have declined to examine certain evidence relevant to their beliefs, owing to a subconscious realization that examination of this evidence would deprive even them of the power to continue to hold their cherished beliefs. However this may be, having distinguished Clifford's Other Principle from Clifford's Principle, I am not going to discuss it further, beyond pointing out that there does not seem to be any reason to suppose, whatever Clifford may have thought, that those who hold religious beliefs are any more likely to be in violation of Clifford's Other Principle than those who hold philosophical or political beliefs. We all know that there are a lot of people who have violated Clifford's Other Principle at one point or another in the course of arriving at their political beliefs and a few who have not. As to philosophy, well, I'm sure that violations of Clifford's Other Principle are quite rare among professional philosophers. No doubt there are a few cases, however. One might cite, for example, a recent review of a book by John Searle, in which the author of the review (Dan Dennett) accuses Searle of gross violations of Clifford's Other Principle in his (Searle's) descriptions of current theories in the philosophy of mind. If Dennett's charge is not just, then it is plausible to suppose that *he* is in violation of Clifford's Other Principle. So it can happen, even among us. But let us, as the French say, return to our sheep, prominent among which is Clifford's Principle – Clifford's Principle proper, that is, and not Clifford's Other Principle.

It is interesting to note that Clifford's Principle is almost never mentioned by writers subsequent to Clifford except in hostile examinations of religious belief, and that the antireligious writers who mention it never apply it to anything but religious beliefs. (With the exception of illustrative examples – like Clifford's example of the irresponsible shipowner – that are introduced in the course of explaining its content and arguing for it.) It is this that provides the primary evidence for my contention that many antireligious philosophers and other writers against religion tacitly accept the Difference Thesis: the fact that they apply Clifford's Principle only to religious beliefs is best explained by the assumption that they accept the Difference Thesis. The cases of Marxism and Freudianism are instructive examples of what I am talking about. It is easy to point to philosophers who believe that Marxism and Freudianism are nonsense: absurd parodies of scientific theories that get the real world wildly wrong. Presumably these philosophers do not believe that Marxism and Freudianism were adequately supported by the evidence that was available to Marx and Freud – or that they are adequately supported by the evidence that is available to any of the latterday adherents of Marxism and Freudianism. But never once has any writer charged that Marx or Freud blotted his epistemic escutcheon by failing to apportion belief to evidence. I challenge anyone to find me a passage (other than an illustrative passage of the type I have mentioned) in which any devotee of Clifford's Principle has applied it to anything but religious belief. And yet practically all philosophers – the literature will immediately demonstrate this to the most casual inquirer

– subscribe to theses an obvious logical consequence of which is that the world abounds in gross violations of Clifford's Principle that have nothing to do with religion.

An explanation of the widespread tacit acceptance of the Difference Thesis among those who appeal to Clifford's Principle in their attacks on religious belief is not far to seek. If Clifford's Principle were generally applied in philosophy (or in politics or history or even in many parts of the natural sciences), it would have to be applied practically everywhere. If its use became general, we'd all be constantly shoving it in one another's faces. And there would be no comfortable reply open to most of the recipients of a charge of violating Clifford's Principle. Use every man after his desert, and who shall scape whipping? If, for example, I am an archaeologist who believes that an artifact found in a neolithic tomb was a religious object used in a fertility rite, and if my rival, Professor Graves – a professor, according to the German aphorism, is someone who thinks otherwise – believes that it was used to wind flax, how can I suppose that my belief is supported by the evidence? If my evidence really supports my belief, why doesn't it convert Professor Graves, who is as aware of it as I am, to my position? This example, of course, is made up. But let me mention a real and not entirely dissimilar example that I recently came across in a review (by Malcolm W. Browne) of several books about the Neanderthals in the *New York Times Book Review* (July 4, 1993, p. 1). The review includes the following quotation from the recent book *The Neanderthals* by Erik Trinkhaus and Pat Shipman. The authors are discussing a debate between two people called Stringer and Wolpoff, who are leading experts on the Neanderthals. "What is uncanny – and disheartening – is the way in which each side can muster the fossil record into seemingly convincing and yet utterly different syntheses of the course of human evolution. Reading their review papers side by side gives the reader a distinct feeling of having awakened in a Kafka novel." Assuming that this description of the use Stringer and Wolpoff make of their evidence is accurate, can it really be that their beliefs are adequately supported by this evidence? Will someone say that Stringer and Wolpoff are scientists, and that scientists do not really *believe* the theories they put forward, but rather bear to them some more tentative sort of doxastic relation? "Regard as the best hypothesis currently available," or some such tentative attitude as that? Well, that is certainly not the way the author of the review sees the debate. Stringer, one of the parties in the debate, has written his own book, also discussed in the review, of which the reviewer says, "*In Search of the Neanderthals* is built around Mr Stringer's underlying (and highly controversial) belief that the Neanderthals were an evolutionary dead end, that they simply faded away after a long and unsuccessful competition with their contemporaries, the direct ancestors of modern man." (That the Neanderthals were an evolutionary dead end is, by the way, the proposition that was at issue in the debate between Stringer and Wolpoff that was said to give the reader the feeling of having awakened in a novel by Kafka.) Later in the review, summarizing the book of another expert on human origins, the reviewer says, "In another section of the book, Mr Schwartz defends his belief that modern human beings are more closely related to orangutans than to either chimpanzees or gorillas." It is hard to see how to avoid the conclusion that it is very common for scientists *qua* scientists to have beliefs that are vehemently rejected by other equally intelligent scientists who possess the same scientific qualifications and the same evidence. Even in the more austere and abstract parts of science, even in high-energy physics, the current queen of the sciences, where there is some real plausibility in the thesis that investigators typically hold some more tentative attitude than belief toward the content of the controversial theories they champion, it is possible to find clear examples of this. To find them, one need only direct one's attention away from the *content* of the theories to the judgments that physicists make *about* the theories, their judgments about such matters as the usefulness of the theories, their "physical interest," and their prospects. A former colleague at Syracuse University, an internationally recognized quantum-gravity theorist, has told me, using a simple declarative sentence that contained no hedges whatever, that superstring theory would come to nothing. Many prominent physicists (Sheldon Glashow, for example) agree. They really *believe* this. And many prominent physicists (such as Steven Weinberg and Edward Witten) vehemently disagree. They really *believe* that superstring theory has provided the framework within which the development of fundamental physics will take place for a century.

But let us leave the sciences and return to our central examples, philosophy and politics. If we applied Clifford's Principle generally, we'd all have to become skeptics or agnostics as regards most philosophical and political questions – or we'd have to find some reasonable answer to the challenge, "In what sense can the evidence you have adduced support or justify your belief when there are many authorities as competent as you who regard this evidence as unconvincing?" But no answer to this challenge is evident, and religion seems to be the only area of human life in which very many people are willing to be agnostics about the answers to very many question. (When I say "very many people," I mean very many people like *us*: people who write books. It is, of course, false that a very high proportion of the world population consists of people who are willing to be agnostics about religious questions.)

It might, however, be objected that what I have been representing as obvious considerations are obvious only on a certain conception of the nature of evidence. Perhaps the Difference Thesis is defensible because the evidence that some people have for their philosophical and political (and archaeological and historical . . .) beliefs consists partly of the deliverances of that incommunicable "insight" that I speculated about earlier. This objection would seem to be consistent with everything said in "The Ethics of Belief," for Clifford nowhere tells his readers what evidence is. If "evidence" is evidence in the courtroom or laboratory sense (photographs, transcripts of sworn statements, the pronouncements of expert witnesses, records of meter readings – even arguments, provided that an argument is understood as simply a publicly available piece of text, and that anyone who has read and understood the appropriate piece of text thereby "has" the evidence that the argument is said to constitute), then "the evidence" pretty clearly does not support our philosophical and political beliefs. Let such evidence be eked out with logical inference and private sense experience and the memory of sense experience (my private experience and my memories, as opposed to my testimony about my experience and memories, cannot be entered as evidence in a court of law or published in *Physical Review Letters*, but they can be part of *my* evidence for *my* beliefs – or so the epistemologists tell us) and it still seems to be true that "the evidence" does not support our philosophical and political beliefs. It is not that evidence in this sense is necessarily impotent: it can support – I hope – many life-and-death courtroom judgments and such scientific theses as that the continents are in motion. But it does not seem to be sufficient to justify most of our philosophical and political beliefs, or our philosophical and political beliefs, surely, would be far more uniform than they are. (Socrates told Euthyphro that people do not dispute about matters that can be settled by measurement or calculation. This is certainly false, but there is nevertheless an important grain of truth in it. There is indisputably significantly greater uniformity of opinion about matters that can be settled by measurement and calculation than there is about the nature of justice and the other matters that interested Socrates.) If "evidence" must be of the courtroom-and-laboratory sort, how can the Difference Thesis be defended?

If, however, "evidence" can include "insight" or some other incommunicable element – my private experience and my memories are not necessarily incommunicable – it may be that some of the philosophical and political beliefs of certain people are justified by the evidence available to them. (This, as I have said, is the view I find most attractive, or least unattractive.) But if evidence is understood in this way, how can anyone be confident that some of the religious beliefs of some people are not justified by the evidence available to them? (I say some people; and that is probably all that anyone would be willing to grant in the cases of philosophy and politics. Is there anyone who believes that it makes sense to talk of philosophical beliefs being justified and who also thinks that the philosophical beliefs of both Carnap and Heidegger were justified? Is there anyone who holds the corresponding thesis about the political beliefs of both Henry Kissinger and the late Kim Il-Sung?) If evidence can include incommunicable elements, how can anyone be confident that all religious believers are in violation of Clifford's Principle? If "evidence" can include the incommunicable, how can the Difference Thesis be defended?

What I have said so far amounts to a polemic against what I perceive as a widespread double standard in writings about the relation of religious belief to evidence and argument. This double standard consists in setting religious belief a test it could not possibly pass, and in studiously ignoring the fact that very few of our beliefs on any subject could possibly pass this test.

Let me summarize this polemic by setting out some Socratic questions; a complex, in fact, of alternative lines of Socratic questioning laid out in a sort of flowchart.

Either you accept Clifford's Principle or not. If not, game ends. If so, either you think that religious belief stands convicted of some epistemic impropriety under Clifford's Principle or not. If not, game ends. If so, do you think that other important categories of belief stand convicted of similar epistemic impropriety under Clifford's Principle – preeminently philosophical and political belief? If you do, are you a skeptic as regards these categories of belief, a philosophical and political skeptic (and, in all probability, a skeptic in many other areas)? If not, why not? If you do think that the only important category of belief that stands convicted of epistemic impropriety under Clifford's Principle is religious belief – that is, if you accept the Difference Thesis – how will you defend this position? Do you accept my disjunctive formulation of the Difference Thesis: "Either religious beliefs should be held to a stricter epistemic standard than beliefs of certain other types – of which philosophical and political beliefs are the paradigms – or, if they are to be held to the same epistemic standard as other beliefs, they typically fare worse under this standard than typical beliefs of most other types, including philosophical and political beliefs"? If not, how would *you* formulate the Difference Thesis (and how would you defend the thesis you have formulated)? If you do accept my disjunctive formulation of the Difference Thesis, which of the disjuncts do you accept? And what is your defense of that disjunct? In formulating your defense, be sure to explain how you understand evidence. Does "evidence" consist entirely of objects that can be publicly examined (photographs and pointer readings), or that can, at least for purposes of setting out descriptions of the evidence available for a certain thesis, be adequately described in public language (sensations and memories, perhaps)? Or may what is called "evidence" be, or be somehow contained in or accessible to the subject in the form of, incommunicable states of mind of the kind I have rather vaguely called "insight?" If the former, and if you have chosen to say that a single standard of evidence is appropriate to both religious beliefs (on the one hand) and philosophical and political beliefs (on the other), and if you have decided that religious beliefs fare worse under this one standard than philosophical and political beliefs – well, how can you suppose that philosophical and political beliefs *are* supported by that sort of evidence, public evidence, to any significant degree? If the evidence available to you provides adequate support for, say, your adherence to a certain brand of functionalism, and if it is evidence of this straightforward public sort, then it is no doubt readily available to most philosophers who have paid the same careful attention to questions in the philosophy of mind that you have. But then why aren't most of these philosophers functionalists of your particular stripe? (Why, some respectable philosophers of mind aren't even functionalists at all, shocking as that may seem to some of us.) Wouldn't the possession and careful consideration of adequate, really *adequate*, evidence for a proposition induce belief in that proposition? Or, if evidence that provided adequate support for a philosophical proposition was readily available throughout a sizable population of careful, qualified philosophers, wouldn't this fact at least induce a significant uniformity of opinion as regards that proposition among those philosophers?

If you take the other option as to the nature of evidence, if you grant that evidence may include incommunicable insight, can you be sure, have you any particular reason to suppose, that it is false that there are religious believers who have "insight" that lends the same sort of support to their religious beliefs that the incommunicable insight that justifies *your* disagreement with Kripke or Quine or Davidson or Dummett or Putnam lends to *your* beliefs?

This is the end of my Socratic flowchart. I will close with an attempt to forestall two possible misinterpretations. First, I have not challenged Clifford's Principle, or not unless to point out that most of us would find it awkward to live by a certain principle is to challenge it. Clifford's Principle could be correct as far as anything I have said goes. Secondly, I have not argued that religious beliefs – any religious beliefs of anyone's – *are* justified or enjoy any particular warrant or positive epistemic status or whatever your own favorite jargon is. (For that matter, I have not argued that philosophical and political beliefs – any philosophical or political beliefs of anyone's – are justified or enjoy any particular warrant or positive epistemic status. I have recorded my personal conviction that some philosophical and political beliefs are justified, but I have not *argued* for this conclusion. I do not mind – just for the sake of literary symmetry – recording my personal conviction that some religious beliefs are justified, but that they are is not a part of my thesis.)

There is one important question that bears on the epistemic propriety of religious belief that I have not even touched on: whether some or all religious beliefs may go clean contrary to the available evidence – as many would say the belief in a loving and all-powerful deity goes clean contrary to the plain evidence of everyone's senses. To discuss this question was not my project. My project has been to raise certain points about the relevance of Clifford's Principle to the problem of the epistemic propriety of religious belief. These are different questions: it suffices to point out that the philosopher who argues that some religious belief – or some belief of any sort – should be rejected because it goes contrary to some body of evidence is not appealing to Clifford's Principle. If what I have said is correct, then philosophers who wish to mount some sort of evidential or epistemic attack on religious belief (or, more likely, not on religious belief in general, but on particular religious beliefs) should set Clifford's Principle aside and argue that religious belief (or this or that religious belief) is refuted by the evidence they present.

Epistemology: Suggestions for Further Reading

Laurence BonJour, *The Structure of Empirical Knowledge* (Cambridge, MA: Harvard University Press, 1985).

Keith DeRose and Ted A. Warfield, eds., *Skepticism: A Contemporary Reader* (New York: Oxford University Press, 1999).

Abrol Fairweather and Linda Zagzebski, eds., *Virtue Epistemology: Essays on Epistemic Virtue and Responsibility* (New York: Oxford University Press, 2001).

Sandra Harding, ed., *The Feminist Standpoint Theory Reader: Intellectual and Political Controversies* (New York: Routledge, 2003).

Philip Kitcher, *The Advancement of Science* (New York: Oxford University Press, 1993).

Hilary Kornblith, ed., *Naturalizing Epistemology*, 2nd edn. (Cambridge, MA: MIT Press, 1994).

Paul K. Moser, ed., *The Oxford Handbook of Epistemology* (New York: Oxford University Press, 2002).

Alvin Plantinga, *Warranted Christian Belief* (New York: Oxford University Press, 2000).

John L. Pollock and Joseph Cruz, *Contemporary Theories of Knowledge*, 2nd edn. (Lanham, MD: Rowman & Littlefield, 1999).

Frederick Schmitt, ed., *Socializing Epistemology* (Lanham, MD: Rowman & Littlefield, 1994).

PART TWO

WHAT CAN WE KNOW ABOUT THE NATURE AND EXISTENCE OF GOD?

Introduction

8 From *Proslogium*
   ST. ANSELM

9 In Behalf of the Fool: An Answer to the Argument of Anselm in
   the *Proslogium*
   GAUNILO

10 The Ontological Argument
    WILLIAM L. ROWE

11 The Cosmological Argument
    WILLIAM L. ROWE

12 From *Dialogues Concerning Natural Religion*
    DAVID HUME

13 The Argument from Design
    R. G. SWINBURNE

14 The Wager
    BLAISE PASCAL

15 The Recombinant DNA Debate: A Difficulty for Pascalian-Style
    Wagering
    STEPHEN P. STICH

16 A Central Theistic Argument
    GEORGE SCHLESINGER

17 Evil and Omnipotence
    J. L. MACKIE

18 The Problem of Evil
    ELEONORE STUMP

19 Male-Chauvinist Religion
    DEBORAH MATHIEU
20 Divine Racism: A Philosophical and Theological Analysis
    WILLIAM R. JONES
    Religion: Suggestions for Further Reading

Introduction

Is there a divine being? If so, what attributes does this being possess? Can such a being reasonably be regarded as benevolent? What forces have shaped the conception of God in the major religions?

Throughout history, most cultures have accepted, and in many cases enforced, the belief in the existence of a god. This is still the case, and, when asked, the majority of people throughout the world identify themselves as Christian or Muslim. In addition to the monotheistic religions, there are many adherents of various pantheistic ones such as Hinduism and animism, but relatively few people identify themselves as atheists. As a consequence, much if not most writing on religion begins with a set of theistic assumptions and navigates within a basically religious world-view.

Western thought in particular reflects its predominant monotheism. Religious thinkers have sought to reconcile various doctrines, seemingly in conflict, within their particular religious tradition; they have tried to articulate the nature of religious experience; they have speculated on the nature of sin, an afterlife, and the nature of God's divine moral law. They have offered various theories of what God must, as a divine being, be like. Most religious traditions, Western and non-Western, also offer a *cosmogony*, an account of how the world began. The source of these religious doctrines is often a sacred text, but it can also be traditional religious stories passed from one generation to the next by spoken word. New religious beliefs and practices are still being formed, and many people have adopted doctrines and habits from non-Western religion.

Discursive practices in which the belief in God is taken for granted or on faith are termed "revealed theology." By contrast, "natural" or "rational" theology tries to defend various religious doctrines without relying on fundamentally religious assumptions, and without accepting religious doctrines as a matter of faith. It appeals to earthly or "natural" experience, as opposed to supernatural. Deeply religious philosophers (such as Descartes, featured in the previous section) are interested in the nature and justification of religious belief. A given thinker can, as Descartes did, participate in both rational and revealed religion. Yet both theological approaches reinforce religious doctrine and are fundamentally committed to the reality of the spiritual and the primacy of spiritual goals.[1]

Philosophical reflection on religion is not theological in this sense; it is not fundamentally committed to a spiritual goal, but to understanding the basic structure of reality. This can be consistent with a commitment to spiritual goals, but only in so far as God and religious experience *really are* part of the basic structure of reality. Philosophers do not simply accept traditional religious belief without subjecting it to critical evaluation. Philosophers give and ask for reasons. Even when philosophers argue that religious beliefs require no justification, they feel obligated to give a justification for *that* epistemological view! If a philosopher should, for example, come to accept the existence of miracles (that is, events that happen outside of or contrary to laws of nature as a result of divine intervention), she would do so only after considering and responding to the (considerable) objections to such a belief. The fact that a religious belief is customary is not a philosophical reason to adopt that belief. This puts Western philosophy, to some degree, at odds with theology. While there are many religious philosophers, by no means are all philosophers religious.

In this section we present a selection of writings addressing some of the key issues in the philosophy of religion. We include both classical and contemporary writings in the Western tradition. We focus on the central questions of the nature and existence of God.

Just as monotheism is by no means the only religious doctrine, the existence of a supernatural entity is not the only philosophical debate. Nonetheless, much pro-theistic philosophical argumentation attempts to prove the existence of a single all-powerful, all-knowing, all-benevolent God. Thus we begin with the major attempts to prove that such a unique God exists. First, St. Anselm offers an *ontological* proof that attempts to derive God's existence from the very idea of God. His interlocutor, the Benedictine monk Gaunilo, attempts to refute him. Next, contemporary philosopher William Rowe offers a defense of the *cosmological* argument, in which the existence of God is said to be a pre-requisite for the existence of the universe itself. The *teleological* argument or "argument from design" – a favorite of nineteenth-century natural theologians – is defended by Richard Swinburne as vigorously as it is attacked (and even parodied) by David Hume. We also include Pascal's famous wager, in which he argues not that God exists, but that it is rational to believe that he does – even if it is impossible to have knowledge that he exists. Stephen Stich concisely states one of the most serious objections to Pascal's approach, namely, that it is based on a specious form of "worst-case scenario" proba-bilistic reasoning. George Schlesinger provides a critical but more sympathetic analysis of the wager, arguing that it is more successful (if not completely so) than the other major proofs for the existence of God.

Although there are various approaches to proving that God exists, there is only one major argument that aims to demonstrate the impossibility of God's existence: the problem of evil. Many theologians and philosophers have tried to explain how a perfect God could permit the world to be filled with terrible evil. Some have concluded that it is not possible to reconcile God's existence with the existence of evil. The events of World War II, including the Holocaust, made the problem of evil particularly acute for twenti-eth-century thinkers, and provided a stimulus for existentialist philosophy and literature, much of which is predicated on the belief that God does not exist and thus humans are forced to create their own future. The end of Hume's *Dialogues* contains a famous dis-cussion of this issue, and J. L. Mackie argues that the problem of evil is insurmountable – hence God does not exist, at least as God is traditionally understood. Eleonore Stump offers a specifically Christian response to the problem.

Finally, we address an aspect of the so-called "post-modern" influence in the philoso-phy of religion. Much recent analysis of culture investigates not simply the content of or rationale for particular doctrines, but the genesis of those doctrines and their tendency to reinforce the power of dominant social groups. Of particular interest to us is the issue of racial and gender bias in religion. Those who accept the existence of God seem to have attributed characteristics to God that seem arbitrary (being male, for example) and help to underwrite privilege. Religious thinkers of all sorts have, until recently, regarded reli-gious doctrine in all its detail as fundamentally reflective of the human experience. But to what degree has it actually reflected the interests, views, and values of the privileged group of people who appointed themselves the promulgators and interpreters of religious ideology? Can religious doctrine and practice be reformed sufficiently to defeat the charge of objectionable bias? Some philosophers have recently asked whether religion can be rehabilitated so as to no longer reflect the prejudices of those powerful people who orig-inally promulgated and interpreted it. Deborah Mathieu argues that the major religions are male chauvinist in a fundamental sense. William R. Jones raises the question of the nature of the supreme being in the context of pervasive and deeply harmful racism. The concerns raised by the problem of evil call into question God's presumed benevolence. Would white philosophers of religion be disposed to accept the moral perfection of God if they had experienced slavery and domination akin to that of black Africans and African American slaves? These issues reflect the current philosophical interest in the etiology, rather than simply the logic, of religious belief.

Note

1   For further discussion of this distinction, see Mark Woodhouse, *A Preface to Philosophy*, 6th edn (Belmont, CA: Wadsworth, 2000).

8 From *Proslogium**

St. Anselm

Chapter II

Truly there is a God, although the fool hath said in his heart, There is no God.

And so, Lord, do thou, who dost give understanding to faith, give me, so far as thou knowest it to be profitable, to understand that thou art as we believe; and that thou art that which we believe. And, indeed, we believe that thou art a being than which nothing greater can be conceived. Or is there no such nature, since the fool hath said in his heart, there is not God? (Psalms xiv. I). But, at any rate, this very fool, when he hears of this being of which I speak – a being than which nothing greater can be conceived – understands what he hears, and what he understands is in his understanding; although he does not understand it to exist.

For, it is one thing for an object to be in the understanding, and another to understand that the object exists. When a painter first conceives of what he will afterwards perform, he has it in his understanding, but he does not yet understand it to be, because he has not yet performed it. But after he has made the painting, he both has it in his understanding and he understands that it exists, because he has made it.

Hence, even the fool is convinced that something exists in the understanding, at least, than which nothing greater can be conceived. For, when he hears of this, he understands it. And whatever is understood, exists in the understanding. And assuredly that, than which nothing greater can be conceived, cannot exist in the understanding alone. For, suppose it exists in the understanding alone: then it can be conceived to exist in reality; which is greater.

Therefore, if that, than which nothing greater can be conceived, exists in the understanding alone, the very being, than which nothing greater can be conceived, is one, than which a greater can be conceived. But obviously this is impossible. Hence, there is no doubt that there exists a being, than which nothing greater can be conceived, and it exists both in the understanding and in reality.

Chapter III

God cannot be conceived not to exist. – God is that, than which nothing greater can be conceived. – That which can be conceived not to exist is not God.

And it assuredly exists so truly, that it cannot be conceived not to exist. For, it is possible to conceive of a being which cannot be conceived not to exist; and this is greater than

* St. Anselm, *Proslogium*, chapters II and III, from "Proslogium," in *St. Anselm: Basic Writings*, 2nd edn translated by S. N. Deane (Chicago: Open Court, 1962), pp. 53–5. Reprinted by permission of Open Court Publishing Company, a division of Carus Publishing Company, Peru, IL, © 1962 by Open Court Publishing Company.

one which can be conceived not to exist. Hence, if that, than which nothing greater can be conceived, can be conceived not to exist, it is not that, than which nothing greater can be conceived. But this is an irreconcilable contradiction. There is, then, so truly a being than which nothing greater can be conceived to exist, that it cannot even be conceived not to exist; and this being thou art, O Lord, our God.

So truly, therefore, dost thou exist, O Lord, my God, that thou canst not be conceived not to exist; and rightly. For, if a mind could conceive of a being better than thee, the creature would rise above the Creator; and this is most absurd. And, indeed, whatever else there is, except thee alone, can be conceived not to exist. To thee alone, therefore, it belongs to exist more truly than all other beings, and hence in a higher degree than all others. For, whatever else exists does not exist so truly, and hence in a less degree it belongs to it to exist. Why, then, has the fool said in his heart, there is no God (Psalms xiv. I), since it is so evident, to a rational mind, that thou dost exist in the highest degree of all? Why, except that he is dull and a fool?

9   In Behalf of the Fool: An Answer to the Argument of Anselm in the *Proslogium**

Gaunilo, a monk of Marmoutier

1.   If one doubts or denies the existence of a being of such a nature that nothing greater than it can be conceived, he receives this answer:

The existence of this being is proved, in the first place, by the fact that he himself, in his doubt or denial regarding this being, already has it in his understanding; for in hearing it spoken of he understands what is spoken of. It is proved, therefore, by the fact that what he understands must exist not only in his understanding, but in reality also.

And the proof of this is as follows. – It is a greater thing to exist both in the understanding and in reality than to be in the understanding alone. And if this being is in the understanding alone, whatever has even in the past existed in reality will be greater than this being. And so that which was greater than all beings will be less than some being, and will not be greater than all: which is a manifest contradiction.

And hence, that which is greater than all, already proved to be in the understanding, must exist not only in the understanding, but also in reality: for otherwise it will not be greater than all other beings.

2.   The fool might make this reply:

This being is said to be in my understanding already, only because I understand what is said. Now could it not with equal justice be said that I have in my understanding all

* Gaunilo, "In Behalf of the Fool: An Answer to the Argument of Anselm in the Proslogium," from *St. Anselm: Basic Writings*, 2nd edn, translated by S. N. Deane (Chicago: Open Court, 1962), pp. 303–11. Reprinted by permission of Open Court Publishing Company, a division of Carus Publishing Company, Peru, IL, © 1962 by Open Court Publishing Company.

manner of unreal objects, having absolutely no existence in themselves, because I understand these things if one speaks of them, whatever they may be?

Unless indeed it is shown that this being is of such a character that it cannot be held in concept like all unreal objects, or objects whose existence is uncertain: and hence I am not able to conceive of it when I hear of it, or to hold it in concept; but I must understand it and have it in my understanding; because, it seems, I cannot conceive of it in any other way than by understanding it, that is, by comprehending in my knowledge its existence in reality.

But if this is the case, in the first place there will be no distinction between what has precedence in time – namely, the having of an object in the understanding – and what is subsequent in time – namely, the understanding that an object exists; as in the example of the picture, which exists first in the mind of the painter, and afterwards in his work.

Moreover, the following assertion can hardly be accepted: that this being, when it is spoken of and heard of, cannot be conceived not to exist in the way in which even God can be conceived not to exist. For if this is impossible, what was the object of this argument against one who doubts or denies the existence of such a being?

Finally, that this being so exists that it cannot be perceived by an understanding convinced of its own indubitable existence, unless this being is afterwards conceived of – this should be proved to me by an indisputable argument, but not by that which you have advanced: namely, that what I understand, when I hear it, already is in my understanding. For thus in my understanding, as I still think, could be all sorts of things whose existence is uncertain, or which do not exist at all, if some one whose words I should understand mentioned them. And so much the more if I should be deceived, as often happens, and believe in them: though I do not yet believe in the being whose existence you would prove.

3. Hence, your example of the painter who already has in his understanding what he is to paint cannot agree with this argument. For the picture, before it is made, is contained in the artificer's art itself; and any such thing, existing in the art of an artificer, is nothing but a part of his understanding itself. A joiner, St. Augustine says, when he is about to make a box in fact, first has it in his art. The box which is made in fact is not life; but the box which exists in his art is life. For the artificer's soul lives, in which all these things are, before they are produced. Why, then, are these things life in the living soul of the artificer, unless because they are nothing else than the knowledge or understanding of the soul itself?

With the exception, however, of those facts which are known to pertain to the mental nature, whatever, on being heard and thought out by the understanding, is perceived to be real, undoubtedly that real object is one thing, and the understanding itself, by which the object is grasped, is another. Hence, even if it were true that there is a being than which a greater is inconceivable: yet to this being, when heard of and understood, the not yet created picture in the mind of the painter is not analogous.

4. Let us notice also the point touched on above, with regard to this being which is greater than all which can be conceived, and which, it is said, can be none other than God himself. I, so far as actual knowledge of the object, either from its specific or general character, is concerned, am as little able to conceive of this being when I hear of it, or to have it in my understanding, as I am to conceive of or understand God himself: whom, indeed, for this very reason I can conceive not to exist. For I do not know that reality itself which God is, nor can I form a conjecture of that reality from some other like reality. For you yourself assert that that reality is such that there can be nothing else like it.

For, suppose that I should hear something said of a man absolutely unknown to me, of whose very existence I was unaware. Through that special or general knowledge by which I know what man is, or what men are, I could conceive of him also, according to the reality itself, which man is. And yet it would be possible, if the person who told me of him deceived me, that the man himself, of whom I conceived, did not exist; since that reality according to which I conceived of him, though a no less indisputable fact, was not that man, but any man.

Hence, I am not able, in the way in which I should have this unreal being in concept or in understanding, to have that being of which you speak in concept or in understanding, when I hear the word *God* or the words, *a being greater than all other beings*. For I can conceive of the man according to a fact that is real and familiar to me: but of God, or a being greater than all others, I could not conceive at all, except merely according to the word. And an object can hardly or never be conceived according to the word alone.

For when it is so conceived, it is not so much the word itself (which is, indeed, a real thing – that is, the sound of the letters and syllables) as the signification of the word, when heard, that is conceived. But it is not conceived as by one who knows what is generally signified by the word; by whom, that is, it is conceived according to a reality and in true conception alone. It is conceived as by a man who does not know the object, and conceives of it only in accordance with the movement of his mind produced by hearing the word, the mind attempting to image for itself the signification of the word that is heard. And it would be surprising if in the reality of fact it could ever attain to this.

Thus, it appears, and in no other way, this being is also in my understanding, when I hear and understand a person who says that there is a being greater than all conceivable beings. So much for the assertion that this supreme nature already is in my understanding.

5.   But that this being must exist, not only in the understanding but also in reality, is thus proved to me:

If it did not so exist, whatever exists in reality would be greater than it. And so the being which has been already proved to exist in my understanding, will not be greater than all other beings.

I still answer: if it should be said that a being which cannot be even conceived in terms of any fact, is in the understanding, I do not deny that this being is, accordingly, in my understanding. But since through this fact it can in no wise attain to real existence also, I do not yet concede to it that existence at all, until some certain proof of it shall be given.

For he who says that this being exists, because otherwise the being which is greater than all will not be greater than all, does not attend strictly enough to what he is saying. For I do not yet say, no, I even deny or doubt that this being is greater than any real object. Nor do I concede to it any other existence than this (if it should be called existence) which it has when the mind, according to a word merely heard, tries to form the image of an object absolutely unknown to it.

How, then, is the veritable existence of that being proved to me from the assumption, by hypothesis, that it is greater than all other beings? For I should still deny this, or doubt your demonstration of it, to this extent, that I should not admit that this being is in my understanding and concept even in the way in which many objects whose real existence is uncertain and doubtful, are in my understanding and concept. For it should be proved first that this being itself really exists somewhere; and then, from the fact that it is greater than all, we shall not hesitate to infer that it also subsists in itself.

6. For example: it is said that somewhere in the ocean is an island, which, because of the difficulty, or rather the impossibility, of discovering what does not exist, is called the lost island. And they say that this island has an inestimable wealth of all manner of riches and delicacies in greater abundance than is told of the Islands of the Blest; and that having no owner or inhabitant, it is more excellent than all other countries, which are inhabited by mankind, in the abundance with which it is stored.

Now if some one should tell me that there is such an island, I should easily understand his words, in which there is no difficulty. But suppose that he went on to say, as if by a logical inference: "You can no longer doubt that this island which is more excellent than all lands exists somewhere, since you have no doubt that it is in your understanding. And since it is more excellent not to be in the understanding alone, but to exist both in the understanding and in reality, for this reason it must exist. For if it does not exist, any land which really exists will be more excellent than it; and so the island already understood by you to be more excellent will not be more excellent."

If a man should try to prove to me by such reasoning that this island truly exists, and that its existence should no longer be doubted, either I should believe that he was jesting, or I know not which I ought to regard as the greater fool: myself, supposing that I should allow this proof; or him, if he should suppose that he had established with any certainty the existence of this island. For he ought to show first that the hypothetical excellence of this island exists as a real and indubitable fact, and in no wise as any unreal object, or one whose existence is uncertain, in my understanding.

7. This, in the mean time, is the answer the fool could make to the arguments urged against him. When he is assured in the first place that this being is so great that its non-existence is not even conceivable, and that this in turn is proved on no other ground than the fact that otherwise it will not be greater than all things, the fool may make the same answer, and say:

When did I say that any such being exists in reality, that is, a being greater than all others? – that on this ground it should be proved to me that it also exists in reality to such a degree that it cannot even be conceived not to exist? Whereas in the first place it should be in some way proved that a nature which is higher, that is, greater and better, than all other natures, exists; in order that from this we may then be able to prove all attributes which necessarily the being that is greater and better than all possesses.

Moreover, it is said that the non-existence of this being is inconceivable. It might better be said, perhaps, that its non-existence, or the possibility of its non-existence, is unintelligible. For according to the true meaning of the word, unreal objects are unintelligible. Yet their existence is conceivable in the way in which the fool conceived of the non-existence of God. I am most certainly aware of my own existence; but I know, nevertheless, that my non-existence is possible. As to that supreme being, moreover, which God is, I understand without any doubt both his existence, and the impossibility of his non-existence. Whether, however, so long as I am most positively aware of my existence, I can conceive of my non-existence, I am not sure. But if I can, why can I not conceive of the non-existence of whatever else I know with the same certainty? If, however, I cannot, God will not be the only being of which it can be said, it is impossible to conceive of his non-existence.

8. The other parts of this book are argued with such truth, such brilliancy, such grandeur; and are so replete with usefulness, so fragrant with a certain perfume of devout

and holy feeling, that though there are matters in the beginning which, however rightly sensed, are weakly presented, the rest of the work should not be rejected on this account. The rather ought these earlier matters to be reasoned more cogently, and the whole to be received with great respect and honor.

10   The Ontological Argument*

William L. Rowe

Arguments for the existence of God are commonly divided into a posteriori and a priori arguments. An a posteriori argument depends on a principle or premise that can be known only by means of our experience of the world. An a priori argument, on the other hand, purports to rest on principles which can be known independently of our experience of the world, just by reflecting on and understanding them. Of the three major arguments for the existence of God – the Cosmological, Teleological, and Ontological – only the last is entirely a priori. In the Cosmological argument one starts from some simple fact about the world, such as the fact that it contains things which are caused to exist by other things. In the Teleological argument a somewhat more complicated fact about the world serves as a starting point: the fact that the world exhibits order and design. In the Ontological argument, however, one begins simply with a concept of God.

I

It is perhaps best to think of the Ontological argument as a family of arguments, each member of which begins with a concept of God, and by appealing only to a priori principles, endeavors to establish that God actually exists. Within this family of arguments the most important historically is the argument set forth by Anselm in the second chapter of his *Proslogium* (A Discourse).[1] Indeed, the Ontological argument begins with chapter II of Anselm's *Proslogium*. In an earlier work, *Monologium* (A Soliloquy), Anselm had endeavored to establish the existence and nature of God by weaving together several versions of the Cosmological argument. In the Preface to *Proslogium* Anselm remarks that after the publication of *Monologium* he began to search for a single argument which alone would establish the existence and nature of God. After much strenuous but unsuccessful effort, he reports that he sought to put the project out of his mind in order to turn to more fruitful tasks. The idea, however, continued to haunt him until one day the proof he had so strenuously sought became clear to his mind. Anselm sets forth this proof in the second chapter of *Proslogium*.

* From Joel Feinberg (ed.), *Reason and Responsibility: Readings in Some Basic Problems of Philosophy*, 8th edn (Belmont, CA: Wadsworth, 1993), pp. 8–17. © 1974 by William L. Rowe. Reprinted with permission.

Before discussing Anselm's argument in step-by-step fashion, there are certain concepts that will help us understand some of the central ideas of the argument. Suppose we draw a vertical line in our imagination and agree that on the left side of our line are all the things which exist, while on the right side of the line are all the things which don't exist. We might then begin to make a list of some of the things on both sides of our imaginary line, as follows:

THINGS WHICH EXIST	THINGS WHICH DON'T EXIST
The Empire State Building	The Fountain of Youth
Dogs	Unicorns
The planet Mars	The Abominable Snowman

Now each of the things (or sorts of things) listed thus far has (have) the following feature: it (they) logically might have been on the other side of the line. The Fountain of Youth, for example, is on the right side of the line, but *logically* there is no absurdity in the idea that it might have been on the left side of the line. Similarly, although dogs do exist, we surely can imagine without logical absurdity that they might not have existed, that they might have been on the right side of the line. Let us then record this feature of the things thus far listed by introducing the idea of a *contingent thing* as a thing that logically might have been on the other side of the line from the side it actually is on. The planet Mars and the Abominable Snowman are contingent things, even though the former happens to exist and the latter does not.

Suppose we add to our list the phrase "the object which is completely round and completely square at the same time" on the right side of our line. The round square, however, unlike the other things thus far listed on the right side of our line, is something that *logically could not* have been on the left side of the line. Noting this, let us introduce the idea of an *impossible thing* as a thing that is on the right side of the line and logically could not have been on the left side of the line.

Looking again at our list, we wonder if there is anything on the left side of our imaginary line which, unlike the things thus far listed on the left side, *logically could not* have been on the right side of the line. At this point we don't have to answer this question, but it is useful to have a concept to apply to any such things, should there be any. Accordingly, let us say that a *necessary thing* is a thing on the left side of our imaginary line and logically could not have been on the right side of the line.

Finally, a *possible thing* is any thing that is either on the left side of our imaginary line or logically might have been on the left side of the line. Possible things, then, will be all those things that are not impossible things – that is, all those things that are either contingent or necessary. If there are no necessary things, then all possible things will be contingent and all contingent things will be possible. If there is a necessary thing, however, then there will be a possible thing which is not contingent.

Armed with these concepts, we can clarify certain important distinctions and ideas in Anselm's thought. The first of these is his distinction between *existence in the understanding* and *existence in reality*. Anselm's notion of existence in reality is the same as our notion of existence; that is, being on the left side of our imaginary line. Since the Fountain of Youth is on the right side of the line, it does not exist in reality. The things which exist are, to use Anselm's phrase, the things which exist in reality. Anselm's notion of existence in the understanding, however, is not the same as any idea we normally employ. When we think of a certain thing, say the Fountain of Youth, then that thing, on Anselm's view, exists in the understanding. Also, when we think of an existing thing like the Empire State Building, it, too, exists in the understanding. So some of the things on both sides of our imaginary line exist in the understanding, but only those on the left side of our line exist in reality. Are there any things that don't exist in the understanding? Undoubtedly there are, for there are things, both existing and non-existing, of which we have not really thought. Now suppose I assert that the Fountain of Youth does not exist. Since to meaningfully deny the existence of something I have to have that thing in mind, I have to think of it, it follows on Anselm's view that whenever someone asserts that some thing does not exist, that thing *does* exist in the understanding.[2] So in asserting that the Fountain of Youth does not exist, I imply that the Fountain of Youth does exist in the understanding. And in asserting that it does not exist I have asserted (on Anselm's view) that it does not exist in reality. This means that my simple assertion amounts to the somewhat more complex claim that the Fountain of Youth exists in the understanding but does not exist in reality – in short, that the Fountain of Youth exists *only* in the understanding.

We can now understand why Anselm insists that anyone who hears of God, thinks about God, or even denies the existence of God is, nevertheless, committed to the view that God exists in the understanding. Also, we can understand why Anselm treats what he calls "the fool's claim" that God does not exist as the claim that God exists *only* in the understanding – that is, that God exists in the understanding but does not exist in reality.

In *Monologium* Anselm sought to prove that among those beings which do exist there is one which is the greatest, highest, and the best. But in *Proslogium* he undertakes to prove that among those beings which exist there is one which is not just the greatest among existing beings, but is such that no conceivable being is greater. We need to distinguish these two ideas: (1) a being than which *no existing being* is greater, and (2) a being than which *no conceivable being* is greater. If the only things in existence were a stone, a frog, and a man, the last of these would satisfy our first idea but not our second – for we can conceive of a being (an angel or God) greater than a man. Anselm's idea of God, as he expresses it in *Proslogium* II, is the same as (2) above; it is the idea of "a being than which nothing greater can be conceived." It will facilitate our understanding of Anselm's argument if we make two slight changes in the way he has expressed his idea of God. For his phrase I shall substitute the following: "*the* being than which none greater is possible."[3] This idea says that if a certain being is God then no *possible being* can be greater than it, or conversely, if a certain being is such that it is even *possible* for there to be a being greater than it, then that being is not God. What Anselm proposes to prove, then, is that the being than which none greater is possible exists in reality. If he proves this he will have proved that God, as he conceives of Him, exists in reality.

But what does Anselm mean by "greatness"? Is a building, for example, greater than a man? In *Monologium*, chapter II, Anselm remarks: "But I do not mean physically great, as a material object is great, but that which, the greater it is, is the better or the more worthy – wisdom, for instance." Contrast wisdom with size. Anselm is saying that wisdom is something that contributes to the greatness of a thing. If a thing comes to have more wisdom that it did before then (given that its other characteristics remain the same), that thing has become a greater, better, more worthy thing than it was. Wisdom, Anselm is saying, is a great-making quality. However, the mere fact that something increases in size (physical greatness) does not make that thing a better thing than it was before, so size is not a great-making quality. By "greater than" Anselm means "better than," "superior to," or "more worthy than," and he believes that some characteristics, like wisdom and moral goodness, are great-making characteristics in that anything which has them is a *better thing* than it would be (other characteristics of it remaining the same) were it to lack them.

We come now to what we may call the *key idea* in Anselm's Ontological argument. Anselm believes that *existence in reality is a great-making quality*. Does Anselm mean that anything that exists is a greater thing than anything that doesn't? Although he does not ask or answer the question, it is perhaps reasonable to believe that Anselm did not mean this. When he discusses wisdom as a great-making quality he is careful not to say that any wise thing is better than any unwise thing – for he recognizes that a just but unwise man might be a better being than a wise but unjust man.[4] I suggest that what Anselm means is that anything that doesn't exist but might have existed (is on the right side of our line but might have been on the left) would have been a greater thing if it had existed (if it had been on the left side of our line). He is not comparing two different things (one existing and one not existing) and saying that the first is therefore greater than the second. Rather, he is talking about *one* thing and pointing out that if it does not exist but might have existed, then *it* would have been a greater thing if it had existed. Using Anselm's distinction between existence in the understanding and existence in reality, we may express the key idea in Anselm's reasoning as follows: If something exists only in the understanding but might have existed in reality, then it might have been greater than it is. Since the Fountain of Youth, for example, exists only in the understanding but (unlike the round square) might have existed in reality, it follows by Anselm's principle that the Fountain of Youth might have been a greater thing than it is.

II

We can now consider the step-by-step development of Anselm's Ontological argument. I shall use the term "God" in place of the longer phrase "the being than which none greater is possible" – wherever the term "God" appears we are to think of it as simply an abbreviation of the longer phrase.

    1.   God exists in the understanding.

As we have noted, anyone who hears of the being than which none greater is possible is, on Anselm's view, committed to premise (1).

    2.   God might have existed in reality (God is a possible being).

Anselm, I think, assumes the truth of (2) without making it explicit in his reasoning. By asserting (2) I do not mean to imply that God does not exist in reality, but that, unlike the round square, God is a possible being.

    3.   If something exists only in the understanding and might have existed in reality, then it might have been greater than it is.

As we noted, this is the key idea in Anselm's Ontological argument. It is intended as a general principle, true of anything whatever.

Steps (1)–(3) constitute the basic premises of Anselm's Ontological argument. From these three items, Anselm believes, it follows that God exists in reality. But how does Anselm propose to convince us that if we accept (1)–(3) we are committed by the rules of logic to accept his conclusion that God exists in reality? Anselm's procedure is to offer what is called a *reductio ad absurdum* proof of his conclusion. Instead of showing directly that the existence of God follows from steps (1)–(3), Anselm invites us to *suppose* that God does not exist (i.e., that the conclusion he wants to establish is false) and then shows how this supposition, when conjoined with steps (1)–(3), leads to an absurd result, a result that couldn't possibly be true because it is contradictory. Since the supposition that God does not exist leads to an absurdity, that supposition must be rejected in favor of the conclusion that God does exist.

Does Anselm succeed in reducing the "fool's belief" that God does not exist to an absurdity? The best way to answer this question is to follow the steps of his argument.

4. Suppose God exists only in the understanding.

This supposition, as we saw earlier, is Anselm's way of expressing the belief that God does not exist.

5. God might have been greater than He is. (2, 4, and 3)[5]

Step (5) follows from steps (2), (4), and (3). Since (3), if true, is true of anything whatever, it will be true of God. Therefore, (3) implies that if God exists only in the understanding and might have existed in reality, then God might have been greater than He is. If so, then given (2) and (4), (5) must be true. For what (3) says when applied to God is that given (2) and (4), it follows that (5).

6. God is a being than which a greater is possible. (5)

Surely if God is such that He logically might have been greater, then He is such than which a greater is possible.

We can now appreciate Anselm's *reductio* argument. He has shown that if we accept steps (1)–(4), we must accept step (6). But (6) is unacceptable; it is the absurdity Anselm was after. By replacing "God" in (6) with the longer phrase it abbreviates, we see that (6) amounts to be absurd assertion:

7. The being than which none greater is possible is a being than which a greater is possible.

Now since steps (1)–(4) have led us to an obviously false conclusion, and if we accept Anselm's basic premises (1)–(3) as true, then (4), the supposition that God exists only in the understanding, must be rejected as false. Thus we have shown that:

8. It is false that God exists only in the understanding.

But since premise (1) tells us that God does exist in the understanding and (8) tells us that God does not exist only there, we may infer that

9. God exists in reality as well as in the understanding. (1, 8)

III

Most of the philosophers who have considered this argument have rejected it because of a basic conviction that from the logical analysis of a certain idea or concept we can never determine that there exists in reality anything answering to that idea or concept. We may examine and analyse, for example, the idea of an elephant or the idea of a unicorn, but it is only by our experience of the world that we can determine that there exist things answering to our first idea and not to the second. Anselm, however, believes that the concept of God is utterly unique – from an analysis of this concept he believes that it can be determined that there exists in reality a being which answers to it. Moreover, he presents us with an argument to show that it can be done in the case of the idea of God. We can, of course, simply reject Anselm's argument on the grounds that it violates the basic conviction noted above. Many critics, however, have sought to prove more directly that it is a bad argument and to point out the particular step that is mistaken. Next we shall examine the three major objections that have been advanced by the argument's critics.

The first criticism was advanced by a contemporary of Anselm's, a monk named "Gaunilo," who wrote a response to Anselm entitled, "On Behalf of the Fool."[6] Gaunilo sought to prove that Anselm's reasoning is mistaken by applying it to things other than God, things which we know don't exist. He took as his example the island than which none greater is possible. No such island really exists. But, argues Gaunilo, if Anselm's reasoning were correct we could show that such an island really does exist. For since it is greater to exist than not to exist, if the island than which none greater is possible doesn't exist then it is an island than which a greater is possible. But it is impossible for the island than which none greater is possible to be an island than which a greater is possible. Therefore, the island than which none greater is possible must exist. About this argument Gaunilo remarks:

> If a man should try to prove to me by such reasoning that this island truly exists, and that its existence should no longer be doubted, either I should believe that he was jesting, or I know not which I ought to regard as the greater fool: myself, supposing I should allow this proof; or him, if he should suppose that he had established with any certainty the existence of this island.[7]

Gaunilo's strategy is clear: by using the very same reasoning Anselm employs in his argument, we can prove the existence of things we know don't exist. Therefore, Anselm's reasoning in his proof of the existence of God must be mistaken. In reply to Gaunilo, Anselm insisted that his reasoning applies only to God and cannot be used to establish the existence of things other than God. Unfortunately, Anselm did not explain just why his reasoning cannot be applied to things like Gaunilo's island.

In defense of Anselm against Gaunilo's objection, there are two difficulties in applying Anselm's reasoning to things like Gaunilo's island. The first derives from the fact that Anselm's principle that existence is a great-making quality was taken to mean that if something does not exist then it is not as great *a thing* (being) as it would have been had it existed. Now if we use precisely this principle in Gaunilo's argument, all we will prove is that if Gaunilo's island does not exist then the island than which none greater is possible is an island than which *a greater thing* is possible. But this statement is not an absurdity. For the island than which no greater *island* is possible can be something than which *a greater thing* is possible – an unsurpassable island may be a surpassable thing. (A perfect man might be a greater thing than a perfect island.) Consequently, if we follow Anselm's reasoning exactly, it does not appear that we can derive an absurdity from the supposition that the island than which none greater is possible does not exist.

A second difficulty in applying Anselm's reasoning to Gaunilo's island is that we must accept the premise that Gaunilo's island is a possible thing. But this seems to require us to believe that some finite, limited thing (an island) might have unlimited perfections. It is not at all clear that this is possible. Try to think, for example, of a hockey player than which none greater is possible. How fast would he have to skate? How many goals would he have to score in a game? How fast would he have to shoot the puck? Could he ever fall down, be checked, or receive a penalty? Although the phrase, "the hockey player than which none greater is possible," seems meaningful, as soon as we try to get a clear idea of what such a being would be like we discover that we can't form a coherent idea of it all. For we are being invited to think of some limited, finite thing – a hockey player or an island – and then to think of it as exhibiting unlimited, infinite perfections. Perhaps, then, since Anselm's reasoning applies only to possible things, Anselm can reject its application to Gaunilo's island on the grounds that the island than which none greater is possible is, like the round square, an impossible thing.

By far the most famous objection to the Ontological argument was set forth by Immanuel Kant in the eighteenth century. According to this objection the mistake in the argument is its claim, implicit in premise (3), that existence is a quality or predicate that adds to the greatness of a thing. There are two parts to this claim: (1) existence is a quality or predicate, and (2) existence, like wisdom and unlike physical size, is a great-making quality or predicate. Someone might accept (1) but object to (2); the objection made famous by Kant, however, is directed at (1). According to this objection, existence is not a predicate at all. Therefore, since in its third premise Anselm's argument implies that existence *is* a predicate, the argument must be rejected.

The central point in the philosophical doctrine that existence is not a predicate concerns what we do when we ascribe a certain quality or predicate to something: for example, when we say of a man next door that he is intelligent, six feet tall, or fat. In each case we seem to assert or presuppose that there *exists* a man next door and then go on to ascribe to him a certain predicate – "intelligent," "six feet tall," or "fat." And many proponents of the doctrine that existence is not a predicate claim that this is a *general feature* of predication. They hold that when we ascribe a quality or predicate to anything we assert or presuppose that the thing exists and then ascribe the predicate to it. Now if this is so, then it is clear that existence cannot be a predicate which we may ascribe to or deny of something. For if it were a predicate, then when we assert of some thing (things) that it (they) exists (exist) we would be asserting or presupposing that it (they) exists (exist) and then going on to predicate existence of it (them). For example, if existence were a predicate, then in asserting "tigers exist" we would be asserting or presupposing that tigers exist and then going on to predicate existence of them. Furthermore, in asserting "dragons do not exist" we would be asserting or presupposing, if existence were a predicate, that dragons do exist and then going on to deny that existence attaches to them. In short, if existence were a predicate, the affirmative existential statement "tigers exist" would be a redundancy and the negative existential statement "dragons do not exist" would be contradictory. But clearly "tigers exist" is not a redundancy; and "dragons do not exist" is true and, therefore, not contradictory. What this shows, according to the proponents of Kant's objection, is that existence is not a genuine predicate.

According to the proponents of the above objection, when we assert that tigers exist and that dragons do not we are not saying that certain things (tigers) have and certain other things (dragons) do not have a peculiar predicate, *existence*; rather, we are saying something about the *concept* of a tiger and the *concept* of a dragon. We are saying that the concept of a tiger applies to something in the world and that the concept of a dragon does not apply to anything in the world.

Although this objection to the Ontological argument has been widely accepted, it is doubtful that it provides us with a conclusive refutation of the argument. It may be true that existence is not a predicate, that in asserting the existence of something we are not ascribing a certain predicate or attribute to that thing. But the arguments presented for this view seem to rest on mistaken or incomplete claims about the nature of predication. For example, the argument which we stated earlier rests on the claim that when we ascribe a predicate to anything we assert or presuppose that that thing exists. But this claim appears to be mistaken. In asserting that Dr. Doolittle is an animal lover I seem to be ascribing the predicate "animal lover" to Dr. Doolittle, but in doing so I certainly am not asserting or presupposing that Dr. Doolittle actually exists. Dr. Doolittle doesn't exist, but it is nevertheless true that he is an animal lover. The plain fact is that we can talk about and ascribe predicates to many things which do not exist and never did. Merlin, for example, no less than Houdini, was a magician, although Houdini existed but Merlin did not. If, as these examples suggest, the claim that whenever we ascribe a predicate to something we assert or presuppose that the thing exists is a false claim, then we will need a better argument for the doctrine that existence is not a predicate. There is some question, however, whether anyone has succeeded in giving a really conclusive argument for this doctrine.[8]

A third objection against the Ontological argument calls into question the premise that God might have existed in reality (God is a possible being). As we saw, this premise claims that the being than which none greater is possible is not an impossible object. But is this true? Consider the series of positive integers: 1, 2, 3, 4, etc. We know that any integer in this series, no matter how large, is such that a larger integer than it is possible. Therefore, the positive integer than which none larger is possible is an impossible object. Perhaps this is also true of the being than which none greater is possible. That is, perhaps no matter how great a being may be, it is possible for there to be a being greater than it. If this were so, then, like the integer than which none larger is possible, Anselm's God would not be a possible object. The mere fact that there are degrees of greatness, however, does not entitle us to conclude that Anselm's God is like the integer than which none larger is possible. There are, for example, degrees of size in angles – one angle is larger than another – but it is not true that no matter how large an angle is it is possible for there to be an angle larger than it. It is logically impossible for an angle to exceed four right angles. The notion of an angle, unlike the notion of a positive integer, implies a degree of size beyond which it is impossible to go. Is Anselm's God like a largest integer, and therefore impossible, or like a largest angle, and therefore possible? Some philosophers have argued that Anselm's God is impossible,[9] but the arguments for this conclusion are not very compelling. Perhaps, then, this objection is best construed not as proving that Anselm's God is impossible, but as raising the question whether any of us is in a position to know that the being than which none greater is possible is a possible object. For Anselm's argument cannot be a successful proof of the existence of God unless its premises are not just true but are really *known* to be true. Therefore, if we do not know that Anselm's God is a possible object, then his argument cannot prove the existence of God to us, cannot enable us to know that God exists.

IV

Finally, I want to present a somewhat different critique of Anselm's argument, a critique suggested by the basic conviction noted earlier; namely that from the mere logical analysis of a certain idea or concept we can never determine that there exists in reality anything answering to that idea or concept.

Suppose someone comes to us and says:

> I propose to define the term "God" as *an existing, wholly perfect being*. Now since it can't be true that an existing, wholly perfect being does not exist, it can't be true that God, as I've defined Him, does not exist. Therefore, God must exist.

His argument appears to be a very simple Ontological argument. It begins with a particular idea or concept of God and ends by concluding that God, so conceived, must exist. What can we say in response? We might start by objecting to his definition, claiming: (1) that only predicates can be used to define a term, and (2) that existence is not a predicate. But suppose he is not impressed by this response – either because he thinks that no one has fully explained what a predicate is or proved that existence isn't one, or because he thinks that anyone can define a word in whatever way he pleases. Can we allow him to define the word "God" in any way he pleases and still hope to convince him that it will not follow from that definition that there actually exists something to which his concept of God applies? I think we can. Let us first invite him, however, to consider some concepts other than his peculiar concept of God.

Earlier we noted that the term "magician" may be applied both to Houdini and Merlin, even though the former existed and the latter did not. Noting that our friend has used "existing" as part of his definition of "God," suppose we agree with him that we can define a word in any way we please, and, accordingly, introduce the following definitions:

> A "magican" is defined as *an existing magician*.
> A "magico" is defined as *a non-existing magician*.

Here we have introduced two words and used "existing" or "non-existing" in their definitions. Now something of interest follows from the fact that "existing" is part of our definition of a "magican." For while it is true that Merlin was a *magician*, it is not true that Merlin was a *magican*. And something of interest follows from our including "non-existing" in the definition of a "magico" – it is true that Houdini was a *magician*, but it is not true that Houdini was a *magico*. Houdini was a *magician* and a *magican*, but not a *magico*; Merlin was a *magician* and a *magico*, but not a *magican*.

We have just seen that introducing "existing" or "non-existing" into the definition of a concept has a very important implication. If we introduce "existing" into the definition of a concept, it follows that no non-existing thing can examplify that concept. And if we introduce "non-existing" into the definition of a concept, it follows that no existing thing can exemplify that concept. No non-existing thing can be a *magican*, and no existing thing can be a *magico*.

But must some existing thing exemplify the concept "magican"? No! From the fact that "existing" is included in the definition of "magican" it does not follow that some existing thing is a magican – all that follows is that no non-existing thing is a magican. If there were no magicans in existence there would be nothing to which the term "magican" would apply. This being so, it clearly does not follow merely from our definition of "magican" that some existing thing is a magican. Only if magicians exist will it be true that some existing thing is a magican.

We are now in a position to help our friend see that from the mere fact that "God" is defined as an existing, wholly perfect being it will not follow that some existing being is God. Something of interest does follow from his definition; namely that no non-existing being can be God. But whether some existing thing is God will depend entirely on whether some existing thing is a wholly perfect being. If no wholly perfect being exists there will be nothing to which his concept of God can apply. This being so, it clearly does not follow merely from his definition of "God" that some existing thing is God. Only if a wholly perfect being exists will it be true that God, as he conceives of Him, exists.

The implications of these considerations for Anselm's ingenious argument can now be traced. Anselm conceives of God as a being than which none greater is possible. He then claims that existence is a great-making quality and something that has it is greater than it would have been had it lacked existence. Clearly then, no non-existing thing can exemplify Anselm's concept of God. For if we suppose that some non-existing thing exemplifies Anselm's concept of God and also suppose that that non-existing thing might have existed in reality (is a possible thing) then we are supposing that that non-existing thing (1) might have been a greater thing, and (2) is, nevertheless, a thing than which a greater is not possible. Thus far Anselm's reasoning is, I believe, impeccable. But what follows from it? All that follows from it is that no non-existing thing can be God (as Anselm conceives of God). All that follows is that given Anselm's concept of God, the proposition, "Some non-existing thing is God," cannot be true. But, as we saw earlier, this is also the case with the proposition, "Some non-existing thing is a magican." What remains to be shown is that some existing thing exemplifies Anselm's concept of God. What really does follow from his reasoning is that the only thing that logically could exemplify his concept of God is something which actually exists. And this conclusion is not without interest. But from the mere fact that nothing but an existing thing could exemplify Anselm's concept of God, it does not follow that some existing thing actually does exemplify his concept of God – no more than it follows from the mere fact that no non-existing thing can be a magican that some existing thing is a magican.[10]

There is, however, one major difficulty in this critique of Anselm's argument. This difficulty arises when we take into account Anselm's implicit claim that God is a possible thing. To see just what this difficulty is, let us return to the idea of a possible thing, which is any thing that either is on the left side of our imaginary line or logically might have been on the left side of the line. Possible things, then, will be all those things that, unlike the round square, are not impossible things. Suppose we concede to Anselm that God, as he conceives of Him, is a possible thing. Now, of course, the mere knowledge that something is a possible thing does not enable us to conclude that that thing is an existing thing. Many possible things, like the Fountain of Youth, do not exist. But if something is a possible thing then it is either an existing thing or a non-existing thing. The set of possible things can be exhaustively divided into those possible things which actually exist and those possible things which do not exist. Therefore, if Anselm's God is a possible thing it is either an existing thing or a non-existing thing. We have concluded, however, that no non-existing thing can be Anselm's God; therefore, it seems we must conclude with Anselm that some actually existing thing does exemplify his concept of God.

To see the solution to this major difficulty we need to return to an earlier example. Let us consider again the idea of a "magican," an existing magician. It so happens that some magicians have existed – Houdini, the Great Blackstone, etc. But, of course, it might have been otherwise. Suppose, for the moment that no magicians have ever existed. The concept "magician" would still have application, for it would still be true that Merlin was a magician. But would any possible object be picked out by the concept of a "magican"? No, for no non-existing thing could exemplify the concept "magican." And on the supposition that no magicians ever existed, no existing thing would exemplify the concept "magican."[11] We then would have a coherent concept "magican" which would not be exemplified by any possible object at all. For if all the possible objects which are magicians are non-existing things, none of them would be a magican and, since no possible objects which exist are magicians, none of them would be a magican. Put in this way, our result seems paradoxical. We are inclined to think that only contradictory concepts like "the round square" are not exemplified by any possible things. The truth is, however, that when "existing" is included in or implied by a certain concept, it may be the case that no possible object does in fact exemplify that concept. For no possible object that doesn't exist will exemplify a concept like "magican" in which "existing" is included; and if there are no existing things which exemplify the other features included in the concept – for example, "being a magician" in the case of the concept "magican" – then no possible object that exists will exemplify the concept. Put in its simplest terms, if we ask whether any possible thing is a magican the answer will depend entirely on whether any existing thing is a magician. If no existing things are magicians then no possible things are magicans. Some possible object is a magican just in the case some actually existing thing is a magician.

Applying these considerations to Anselm's argument, we can find the solution to our major difficulty. Given Anselm's concept of God and his principle that existence is a great-making quality, it really does follow that the only thing that logically could exemplify his concept of God is something which actually exists. But, we argued, it doesn't follow from these considerations alone that God actually exists, that some existing thing exemplifies Anselm's concept of God. The difficulty we fell into, however, is that when we add the premise that God is a possible thing, that some possible object exemplifies his concept of God, it really does follow that God actually exists, that some actually existing thing exemplifies Anselm's concept of God. For if some possible object exemplifies his concept of God, that object is either an existing thing or a non-existing thing. But since no non-existing thing could exemplify Anselm's concept of God, it follows that the possible object which exemplifies his concept of God must be a possible object that actually exists. Therefore, given (1) Anselm's concept of God, (2) his principle that existence is a great-making quality, and (3) the premise that God, as conceived by Anselm, is a possible thing, it really does follow that Anselm's God actually exists. But we now can see that in granting Anselm the premise that God is a possible thing we have granted far more than we intended. All we thought we were conceding is that Anselm's concept of God, unlike the concept of a round square, is not contradictory or incoherent. But without realizing it we were in fact granting much more than this, as became apparent when we considered the idea of a magician. There is nothing contradictory in the idea of a magican, an existing magician. But in asserting that a magican is a possible thing we are, as we saw, directly implying that some existing thing is a magician. For if no existing thing is a magician, the concept of a magican will apply to no possible object whatever. The same point holds with respect to Anselm's God. Since Anselm's concept of God logically cannot apply to some non-existing thing, the only possible objects to which it could apply are possible objects which actually exist. Therefore, in granting that Anselm's God is a possible thing we are conceding far more than that his idea of God isn't incoherent or contradictory. Suppose, for example, that every existing being has some defect which it might not have had. Without realizing it we were denying this when we granted that Anselm's God is a possible being. If every existing being has a defect it might not have had, then every existing being might have been greater. But if every existing being might have been greater, then Anselm's concept of God will apply to no possible object whatever. Therefore, if we allow Anselm his concept of God and his principle that existence is a great-making quality, then in granting that God, as Anselm conceives of Him, is a possible being we will be granting much more than that his concept of God is not contradictory. We will be conceding, for example, that some existing thing is as perfect as it can be. The fact is that Anselm's God is a possible thing only if some *existing* thing is as perfect as it can be.

Our final critique of Anselm's argument is simply this. In granting that Anselm's God is a possible thing we are in fact granting that Anselm's God actually exists. But since the purpose of the argument is to prove to us that Anselm's God exists, we cannot be asked to grant as a premise a statement which is virtually equivalent to the conclusion that is to be proved. Anselm's concept of God may be coherent and his principle that existence is a great-making quality may be true. But all that follows from this is that no non-existing thing can be Anselm's God. If we add to all of this the premise that God is a possible thing it will follow that God actually exists. But the additional premise claims more than that Anselm's concept of God isn't incoherent or contradictory. It amounts to the assertion that some existing being is supremely great. And since this is, in part, the point the argument endeavors to prove, the argument begs the question: it assumes the point it is supposed to prove.

If the above critique is correct, Anselm's argument fails as a proof of the existence of God. This is not to say, however, that the argument is not a work of genius. Perhaps no other argument in the history of thought has raised so many basic philosophical questions and stimulated so much hard thought. Even if it fails as a proof of the existence of God, it will remain as one of the high achievements of the human intellect.

Notes

1 Some philosophers believe that Anselm sets forth a different and more cogent argument in chapter III of his *Proslogium*. For this viewpoint see Charles Hartshorne, *Anselm's Discovery* (LaSalle, Ill.: Open Court Publishing Co., 1965); and Norman Malcolm, "Anselm's Ontological Arguments," *The Philosophical Review* 69/1 (Jan. 1960): 41–62. For an illuminating account both of Anselm's intentions in *Proslogium II* and *III* and of recent interpretations of Anselm see Arthur C. McGill's essay "Recent Discussions of Anselm's Argument," in *The Many-faced Argument*, ed. John Hick and Arthur C. McGill (New York: The Macmillan Co., 1967), pp. 33–110.

2   Anselm does allow that someone may assert the sentence "God does not exist" without having in his understanding the object or idea for which the word 'God' stands (see *Proslogium*, chapter IV). But when a person does understand the object for which a word stands, then when he uses that word in a sentence denying the existence of that object he must have that object in his understanding. It is doubtful, however, that Anselm thought that incoherent or contradictory expressions like "the round square" stand for objects which may exist in the understanding.

3   Anselm speaks of "a being" rather than "the being" than which none greater can be conceived. His argument is easier to present if we express his idea of God in terms of "the being." Secondly, to avoid the psychological connotations of "can be conceived" I have substituted "possible."

4   See *Monologium*, chapter XV.

5   The numbers in parentheses refer to the earlier steps in the argument from which the present step is derived.

6   Gaunilo's brief essay, Anselm's reply, and several of Anselm's major works, as translated by S. N. Deane, are collected in *Saint Anselm: Basic Writings* (LaSalle, Ill.: Open Court Publishing Co., 1962).

7   *Saint Anselm: Basic Writings*, p. 151.

8   Perhaps the most sophisticated presentation of the objection that existence is not a predicate is William P. Alston's "The Ontological Argument Revisited," *The Philosophical Review* 69 (1960): 452–74.

9   See, for example, C. D. Broad's discussion of the Ontological Argument in *Religion, Philosophy, and Psychical Research* (New York: Harcourt, Brace & World, 1953).

10   An argument along the lines just presented may be found in J. Shaffer's illuminating essay "Existence, Predication and the Ontological Argument," *Mind* 71 (1962): 307–25.

11   I am indebted to Professor William Wainwright for bringing this point to my attention.

---

11   The Cosmological Argument*

William L. Rowe

Since ancient times thoughtful people have sought to justify their religious beliefs. Perhaps the most basic belief for which justification has been sought is the belief that there is a God. The effort to justify belief in the existence of God has generally started either from facts available to believers and nonbelievers alike or from facts, such as the experience of God, normally available only to believers. [Here] we shall consider some major attempts to justify belief in God by appealing to facts supposedly available to any rational person, whether religious or not. By starting from such facts theologians and philosophers have developed arguments for the existence of God, arguments which, they have claimed, prove beyond reasonable doubt that there is a God.

* From William L. Rowe, *The Philosophy of Religion: An Introduction*, 1st edn (Belmont, CA: Wadsworth, 1978), pp. 16–29. © 1978. Reprinted with permission of Wadsworth, an imprint of the Wadsworth Group, a division of Thomson Learning.

Stating the Argument

Arguments for the existence of God are commonly divided into *a posteriori* arguments and *a priori* arguments. An *a posteriori* argument depends on a principle or premise that can be known only by means of our experience of the world. An *a priori* argument, on the other hand, purports to rest on principles all of which can be known independently of our experience of the world, by just reflecting on and understanding them. Of the three major arguments for the existence of God – the Cosmological, the Teleological, and the Ontological – only the last of these is entirely *a priori*. In the Cosmological Argument one starts from some simple fact about the world, such as that it contains things which are caused to exist by other things. In the Teleological Argument a somewhat more complicated fact about the world serves as a starting point, the fact that the world exhibits order and design. In the Ontological Argument, however, one begins simply with a concept of God. . . .

Before we state the Cosmological Argument itself, we shall consider some rather general points about the argument. Historically, it can be traced to the writings of the Greek philosophers Plato and Aristotle, but the major developments in the argument took place in the thirteenth and in the eighteenth centuries. In the thirteenth century, Aquinas put forth five distinct arguments for the existence of God, and of these, the first three are versions of the Cosmological Argument. In the first of these he started from the fact that there are things in the world undergoing change and reasoned to the conclusion that there must be some ultimate cause of change that is itself unchanging. In the second he started from the fact that there are things in the world that clearly are caused to exist by other things and reasoned to the conclusion that there must be some ultimate cause of existence whose own existence is itself uncaused. And in the third argument he started from the fact that there are things in the world which need not have existed at all, things which do exist but which we can easily imagine might not, and reasoned to the conclusion that there must be some being that had to be, that exists and could not have failed to exist. Now it might be objected that even if Aquinas's arguments do prove beyond doubt the existence of an unchanging changer, an uncaused cause, and a being that could not have failed to exist, the arguments fail to prove the existence of the theistic God. For the theistic God . . . is supremely good, omnipotent, omniscient, and creator of but separate from and independent of the world. How do we know, for example, that the unchanging changer isn't evil or slightly ignorant? The answer to this objection is that the Cosmological Argument has two parts. In the first part the effort is to prove the existence of a special sort of being, for example, a being that could not have failed to exist, or a being that causes change in other things but is itself unchanging. In the second part of the argument the effort is to prove that the special sort of being whose existence has been established in the first part has, and must have the features – perfect goodness, omnipotence, omniscience, and so on – which go together to make up the theistic idea of God. What this means, then, is that Aquinas's three arguments are different versions of only the first part of the Cosmological Argument. Indeed, in later sections of his *Summa Theologica* Aquinas undertakes to show that the unchanging changer, the uncaused cause of existence, and the being which had to exist are one and the same being and that this single being has all of the attributes of the theistic God.

We noted above that a second major development in the Cosmological Argument took place in the eighteenth century, a development reflected in the writings of the German philosopher Gottfried Leibniz (1646–1716), and especially in the writings of the English theologian and philosopher, Samuel Clarke (1675–1729). In 1704 Clarke gave a series of lectures, later published under the title *A Demonstration of the Being and Attributes of God*. These lectures constitute, perhaps, the most complete, forceful, and cogent presentation of the Cosmological Argument we possess. The lectures were read by the major skeptical philosopher of the century, David Hume (1711–1776), and in his brilliant attack on the attempt to justify religion in the court of reason, his *Dialogues Concerning Natural Religion*, Hume advanced several penetrating criticisms of Clarke's arguments, criticisms which have persuaded many philosophers in the modern period to reject the Cosmological Argument. In our study of the argument we shall concentrate our attention largely on its eighteenth-century form and try to assess its strengths and weaknesses in the light of the criticisms which Hume and others have advanced against it.

The first part of the eighteenth-century form of the Cosmological Argument seeks to establish the existence of a self-existent being. The second part of the argument attempts to prove that the self-existent being is the theistic God, that is, has the features which we have noted to be basic elements in the theistic idea of God. We shall consider mainly the first part of the argument, for it is against the first part that philosophers from Hume to Russell have advanced very important objections.

In stating the first part of the Cosmological Argument we shall make use of two important concepts, the concept of a *dependent being* and the concept of a *self-existent being*. By "a dependent being" we mean *a being whose existence is accounted for by the causal activity of other things*. Recalling Anselm's division into the three cases: "explained by another," "explained by nothing," and "explained by itself," it's clear that a dependent being is a being whose existence is explained by another. By "a self-existent being" we mean *a being whose existence is accounted for by its own nature*. This idea . . . is an essential element in the theistic concept of God. Again, in terms of Anselm's three cases, a self-existent being is a being whose existence is explained by itself. Armed with these two concepts, the concept of a dependent being and the concept of a self-existent being, we can now state the first part of the Cosmological Argument.

(1) Every being (that exists or ever did exist) is either a dependent being or a self-existent being.
(2) Not every being can be a dependent being.
(3) Therefore, there exists a self-existent being.

. . . The Cosmological Argument (that is, its first part) is a deductively valid argument. If its premises are or were true its conclusion would have to be true . . . What else is required? Clearly that we know or have rational grounds for believing that the premises are true. If we know that the Cosmological Argument is deductively valid and can establish that its premises are true, we shall thereby have proved that its conclusion is true. Are, then, the premises of the Cosmological Argument true? To this more difficult question we must now turn.

PSR and the first premise

At first glance the first premise might appear to be an obvious or even trivial truth. But it is neither obvious nor trivial. And if it appears to be obvious or trivial, we must be confusing the idea of a self-existent being with the idea of a being that is not a dependent being. Clearly, it is obviously true that any being is either a dependent being (explained by other things) or it is not a dependent being (not explained by other things). But what our premise says is that any being is either a dependent being (explained by other things) or it is a self-existent being (explained by itself). Consider . . . three cases:

(a) explained by another,
(b) explained by nothing,
(c) explained by itself.

What our first premise asserts is that each being that exists (or ever did exist) is either of sort (a) or of sort (c). It denies that any being is of sort (b). And it is this denial that makes the first premise both significant and controversial. The obvious truth we must not confuse it with is the truth that any being is either of sort (a) or not of sort (a). While this is true it is neither very significant nor controversial.

Earlier we saw that Anselm accepted as a basic principle that whatever exists has an explanation of its existence. Since this basic principle denies that any thing of sort (b) exists or ever did exist, it's clear that Anselm would believe the first premise of our Cosmological Argument. The eighteenth-century proponents of the argument also were convinced of the truth of the basic principle we attributed to Anselm. And because they were convinced of its truth, they readily accepted the first premise of the Cosmological Argument. But by the eighteenth century, Anselm's basic principle had been more fully elaborated and had received a name, "the Principle of Sufficient Reason." Since this principle (PSR, as we shall call it) plays such an important role in justifying the premises of the Cosmological Argument, it will help us to consider it for a moment before we continue our enquiry into the truth or falsity of the Cosmological Argument.

The Principle of Sufficient Reason (PSR), as it was expressed by both Leibniz and Samuel Clarke, is a very general principle and is best understood as having two parts. In its first part it is simply a restatement of Anselm's principle that there must be an explanation of the *existence* of any being whatever. Thus if we come upon a man in a room, PSR implies that there must be an explanation of the fact that that particular man exists. A moment's reflection, however, reveals that there are many facts about the man other than the mere fact that he exists. There is the fact that the man in question is in the room he's in, rather than somewhere else, the fact that he is in good health, and the fact that he is at the moment thinking of Paris, rather than, say, London. Now the purpose of the second part of PSR is to require and explanation of these facts as well. We may state PSR, therefore, as the principle that *there must be an explanation (a) of the existence of any being, and (b) of any positive fact whatever*. We are now in a position to study the role this very important principle plays in the Cosmological Argument.

Since the proponent of the Cosmological Argument accepts PSR in both its parts, it is clear that he will appeal to its first part, PSRa, as justification for the first premise of the Cosmological Argument. Of course, we can and should enquire into the deeper question of whether the proponent of the argument is rationally justified in accepting PSR itself. But we shall put this question aside for the moment. What we need to see first is whether he is correct in thinking that *if* PSR is true then both of the premises of the Cosmological Argument are true. And what we have just seen is that if only the first part of PSR, that is, PSRa, is true, the first premise of the Cosmological Argument will be true. But what of the second premise of the Argument? For what reasons does the proponent think that it must be true?

The second premise

According to the second premise, not every being that exists can be a dependent being, that is, can have the explanation of its existence in some other being or beings. Presumably, the proponent of the argument thinks there is something fundamentally wrong with the idea that every being that exists is dependent, that each existing being was caused by some other being which in turn was caused by some other being, and so on. But just what does he think is wrong with it? To help us in understanding his thinking, let's simplify things by supposing that there exists only one thing now, A_1, a living thing perhaps, that was brought into existence by something else A_2, which perished shortly after it brought A_1 into existence. Suppose further that A_2 was brought into existence in similar fashion some time ago by A_3, and A_3 by A_4, and so forth back into the past. Each of these beings is a *dependent* being, it owes its existence to the preceding thing in the series. Now if nothing else ever existed but these beings, then what the second premise says would not be true. For if every being that exists or ever did exist is an A and was produced by a preceding A, then every being that exists or ever did exist would be dependent and, accordingly, premise two of the Cosmological Argument would be false. If the proponent of the Cosmological Argument is correct there must, then, be something wrong with the idea that every being that exists or did exist is an A and that they form a causal series, A_1, caused by A_2, A_2 caused by A_3, A_3 caused by $A_4 \ldots A_n$ caused by A_{n+1}. How does the proponent of the Cosmological Argument propose to show us that there is something wrong with this view?

A popular but mistaken idea of how the proponent tries to show that something is wrong with the view that every being might be dependent is that he uses the following argument to reject it.

(1)   There must be a *first being* to start any causal series.
(2)   If every being were dependent there would be no *first being* to start the causal series.
(3)   Therefore, not every being can be a dependent being.

Although this argument is deductively valid and its second premise is true, its first premise overlooks the distinct possibility that a causal series might be *infinite*, with no first member at all. Thus if we go back to our series of A beings, where each A is dependent, having been produced by the preceding A in the causal series, it's clear that if the series existed it would have no first member, for every A in the series there would be a preceding A which produced it, *ad infinitum*. The first premise of the argument just given assumes that a causal series must stop with a first member somewhere in the distant past. But there seems to be no good reason for making that assumption.

The eighteenth-century proponents of the Cosmological Argument recognized that the causal series of dependent beings could be infinite, without a first member to start the series. They rejected the idea that every being that is or ever was is dependent not because there would then be no first member to the series of dependent beings, but because there would then be no explanation for the fact that there are and have always been dependent beings. To see their reasoning let's return to our simplification of the supposition that the only things that exist or ever did exist are dependent beings. In our simplification of that supposition only one of the dependent beings exists at a time, each one perishing as it produces the next in the series. Perhaps the first thing to note about this supposition is that there is no individual A in the causal series of dependent beings whose existence is unexplained – A_1 is explained by A_2, A_2 by A_3, and A_n by A_{n+1}. So the first part of PSR, PSRa, appears to be satisfied. There is no particular being whose existence lacks an explanation. What, then, is it that lacks an explanation, if every particular A in the causal series of dependent beings has an explanation? It is the *series itself* that lacks an explanation. Or, as I've chosen to express it, *the fact that there are and have always been dependent beings*. For suppose we ask why it is that there are and have always been A_s in existence. It won't do to say that A_s have always been producing other A_s – we can't explain why there have always been A_s by saying there always have always been A_s. Nor, on the supposition that only A_s have ever existed, can we explain the fact that there have always been A_s by appealing to something other than an A – for no such thing would have existed. Thus the supposition that the only things that exist or ever existed are dependent things leaves us with a fact for which there can be no explanation; namely, the fact that there are and have always been dependent beings.

Questioning the justification of the second premise

Critics of the Cosmological Argument have raised several important objections against the claim that if every being is dependent the series or collection of those beings would have no explanation. Our understanding of the Cosmological Argument, as well as of its strengths and weaknesses, will be deepened by a careful consideration of these criticisms.

The first criticism is that the proponent of the Cosmological Argument makes the mistake of treating the collection or series of dependent beings as though it were itself a dependent being, and, therefore, requires an explanation of its existence. But, so the objection goes, the collection of dependent beings in not itself a dependent being any more than a collection of stamps is itself a stamp.

A second criticism is that the proponent makes the mistake of inferring that because each member of the collection of dependent beings has a cause the collection itself must have a cause. But, as Bertrand Russell noted, such reasoning is as fallacious as to infer that the human race (that is, the collection of human beings) must have a mother because each member of the collection (each human being) has a mother.

A third criticism is that the proponent of the argument fails to realize that for there to be an explanation of a collection of things is nothing more than for there to be an explanation of each of the things making up the collection. Since in the infinite collection (or series) of dependent beings, each being in the collection does have an explanation – by virtue of having been caused by some preceding member of the collection – the explanation of the collection, so the criticism goes, has already been given. As David Hume remarked, "Did I show you the particular causes of each individual in a collection of twenty particles of matter, I should think it very unreasonable, should you afterwards ask me, what was the cause of the whole twenty. This is sufficiently explained in explaining the cause of the parts."

Finally, even if the proponent of the Cosmological Argument can satisfactorily answer these objection, he must face one last objection to his ingenious attempt to justify premise two of the Cosmological Argument. For someone may agree that if nothing exists but an infinite collection of dependent beings, the infinite collection will have no explanation of its existence, and still refuse to conclude from this that there is something wrong with the idea that every being is a dependent being. Why, he might ask, should we think that everything has to have an explanation? What's wrong with admitting that the fact that there are and have always been dependent beings is a *brute fact*, a fact having no explanation whatever? Why does everything have to have an explanation anyway? We must now see what can be said in response to these several objections.

Responses to criticism

It is certainly a mistake to think that a collection of stamps is itself a stamp, and very likely a mistake to think that the collection of dependent beings is itself a dependent being. But the mere fact that the proponent of the argument thinks that there must be an explanation not only for each member of the collection of dependent beings but for the collection itself is not sufficient grounds for concluding that he must view the collection as itself a dependent being. The collection of human beings, for example, is certainly not itself a human being. Admitting this, however, we might still seek an explanation of why there is a collection of human beings, of why there are such things as human beings at all. So the mere fact that an explanation is demanded for the collection of dependent beings is no proof that the person who demands the explanation must be supposing that the collection itself is just another dependent being.

The second criticism attributes to the proponent of the Cosmological Argument the following bit of reasoning:

(1) Every member of the collection of dependent beings has a cause or explanation.
(2) Therefore, the collection of dependent beings has a cause or explanation.

As we noted in setting forth this criticism, arguments of this sort are often unreliable. It would be a mistake to conclude that a collection of objects is light in weight simply because each object in the collection is light in weight, for if there were many objects in the collection it might be quite heavy. On the other hand, if we know that each marble weighs more than one ounce we could infer validly that the collection of marbles weighs more than an ounce. Fortunately, however, we don't need to decide whether the inference from (1) to (2) is valid or invalid. We need not decide this question because the proponent of the Cosmological Argument need not use this inference to establish that there must be an explanation of the collection of dependent beings. He need not use this inference because he has in PSR a principle from which it follows immediately that the collection of dependent beings has a cause or explanation. For according to PSR every positive fact must have an explanation. If it is a fact that there exists a collection of dependent beings then, according to PSR, that fact too must have an explanation. So it is PSR that the proponent of the Cosmological Argument appeals to in concluding that there must be an explanation of the collection of dependent beings, and not some dubious inference from the premise that each member of the collection has an explanation. It seems, then, that neither of the first two criticisms is strong enough to do any serious damage to the reasoning used to support the second premise of Cosmological Argument.

The third objection contends that to explain the existence of a collection of things is the same thing as to explain the existence of each of its members. If we consider a collection of dependent beings where each being in the collection is explained by the preceding member which caused it, it's clear that no member of the collection will lack an explanation of its existence. But, so the criticism goes, if we've explained the existence of every member of a collection we've explained the existence of the collection – there's nothing left over to be explained. This forceful criticism, originally advanced by David Hume, has gained considerable support in the modern period. But the criticism rests on

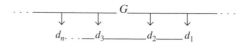

Figure 1

an assumption that the proponent of the Cosmological Argument would not accept. The assumption is that to explain the existence of a collection of things it is *sufficient* to explain the existence of every member in the collection. To see what is wrong with this assumption is to understand the basic issue in the reasoning by which the proponent of the Cosmological Argument seeks to establish that not every being can be a dependent being.

In order for there to be an explanation of the existence of the collection of dependent beings, it's clear that the eighteenth-century proponents would require that the following two conditions be satisfied:

(C1)   There is an explanation of the existence of each of the members of the collection of dependent beings.

(C2)   There is an explanation of why there are *any* dependent beings.

According to the proponents of the Cosmological Argument, if every being that exists or ever did exist is a dependent being – that is, if the whole of reality consists of nothing more than a collection of dependent beings – (C1) will be satisfied, but (C2) will not be satisfied. And since (C2) won't be satisfied there will be no explanation of the collection of dependent beings. The third criticism, therefore, says in effect that if (C1) is satisfied (C2) will be satisfied, and, since in a collection of dependent beings each member will have an explanation in whatever it was that produced it, (C1) will be satisfied. So, therefore, (C2) will be satisfied and the collection of dependent beings will have an explanation.

Although the issue is a complicated one, I think it is possible to see that the third criticism rests on a mistake: the mistake of thinking that if (C1) is satisfied (C2) must also be satisfied. The mistake is a natural one to make for it is easy to imagine circumstances in which if (C1) is satisfied (C2) also will be satisfied. Suppose, for example, that the whole of reality includes not just a collection of dependent beings but also a self-existent being. Suppose further that instead of each dependent being having been produced by some other dependent being every dependent being was produced by the self-existent being. Finally, let us consider both the possibility that the collection of dependent beings is finite in time and has a first member and the possibility that the collection of dependent beings is infinite in past time, having no first member. Using "*G*" for the self-existent being, the first possibility may be diagramed as [in figure 1]: *G*, we shall say, has always existed and always will. We can think of d_1 as some presently existing dependent being, d_2, d_3, and so forth as dependent beings that existed at some time in the past, and d_n as the first dependent being to exist. The second possibility may be portrayed as [in figure 2]. On this diagram there is no first member of the collection of dependent beings. Each member of the infinite collection, however, is explained by reference to the self-existent being *G* which produced it. Now the interesting point about both these cases is that the explanation that has been provided for the members of the collection of dependent beings carries with it, at least in part, an answer to the question of why there are any dependent beings at all. In both cases we may explain why there are dependent beings

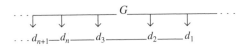

Figure 2

by pointing out that there exists a self-existent being that has been engaged in producing them. So once we have learned that the existence of each member of the collection of dependent beings has its existence explained by the fact that G produced it, we have already learned why there are dependent beings.

Someone might object that we haven't really learned why there are dependent beings until we also learn *why* G has been producing them. But, of course, we could also say that we haven't really explained the existence of a particular dependent being, say d_3, until we also learn not just that G produced it but *why* G produced it. The point we need to grasp, however, is that once we admit that every dependent being's existence is explained by G, we must admit that the fact that there are dependent beings has also been explained. So it is not unnatural that someone should think that to explain the existence of the collection of dependent beings is nothing more than to explain the existence of its members. For, as we've seen, to explain the collection's existence is to explain each member's existence and to explain why there are any dependent beings at all. And in the examples we've considered, in doing the one (explaining why each dependent being exists) we've already done the other (explained why there are any dependent beings at all). We must now see, however, that on the supposition that the whole of reality consists *only* of a collection of dependent beings, to give an explanation of each member's existence is not to provide an explanation of why there are dependent beings.

In the examples we've considered we have gone *outside* of the collection of dependent beings in order to explain the member's existence. But if the only beings that exist or ever existed are dependent beings then each dependent being will be explained by some other dependent being, *ad infinitum*. This does not mean that there will be some particular dependent being whose existence is unaccounted for. Each dependent being has an explanation of its existence; namely, in the dependent being which preceded it and produced it. So (C1) is satisfied: there is an explanation of the existence of each member of the collection of dependent beings. Turning to (C2), however, we can see that it will not be satisfied. We cannot explain why there are (or have ever been) dependent beings by appealing to all the members of the infinite collection of dependent beings. For if the question to be answered is why there are (or have ever been) any dependent beings at all, we cannot answer that question by noting that there always have been dependent beings, each one accounting for the existence of some other dependent being. Thus on the supposition that every being is dependent it seems there will be no explanation of why there are dependent beings. (C2) will not be satisfied. Therefore, on the supposition that every being is dependent there will be no explanation of the existence of the collection of dependent beings.

The truth of PSR

We come now to the final criticism of the reasoning supporting the second premise of the Cosmological Argument. According to this criticism, it is admitted that the supposition that every being is dependent implies that there will be a *brute fact* in the universe, a fact, that is, for which there can be no explanation whatever. For there will be no explanation of the fact that dependent beings exist and have always been in existence. It is this brute fact that the proponents of the argument were describing when they pointed out that if every being is dependent the series or collection of dependent beings would lack and explanation of *its* existence. The final criticism asks what is wrong with admitting that the universe contains such a brute, unintelligible fact. In asking this question the critic challenges the fundamental principle, PSR, on which the Cosmological Argument rests. For, as we've seen, the first premise of the argument denies that there exists a being whose existence has no explanation. In support of this premise the proponent appeals to the first part of PSR. The second premise of the argument claims that not every being can be dependent. In support of this premise the proponent appeals to the second part of PSR, the part which states that there must be an explanation of any positive fact whatever.

The proponent reasons that if every being were a dependent being then although the first part of PSR would be satisfied – every being would have an explanation – the second part would be violated, there would be no explanation for the positive fact that there are and have always been dependent beings. For first, since every being is supposed to be dependent, there would be nothing outside of the collection of dependent beings to explain the collection's existence. Second, the fact that each member of the collection has an explanation in some other dependent being is insufficient to explain why there are and have always been dependent beings. And, finally, there is nothing about the collection of dependent beings that would suggest that it is a self-existent collection. Consequently, if every being were dependent, the fact that there are and have always been dependent beings would have no explanation. But this violates the second part of PSR. So the second premise of the Cosmological Argument must be true, not every being can be a dependent being. This conclusion, however, is no better than the principle, PSR, on which it rests. And it is the point of the final criticism to question the truth of PSR. Why, after all, should we accept the idea that every being and every positive fact must have an explanation? Why, in short, should we believe PSR? These are important questions, and any final judgment of the Cosmological Argument depends on how they are answered.

Most of the theologians and philosophers who accept PSR have tried to defend it in either of two ways. Some have held that PSR is (or can be) known *intuitively* to be true. By this they mean that if we fully understand and reflect on what is said by PSR we can see that it must be true. Now, undoubtedly, there are statements which are known intuitively to be true. "Every triangle has exactly three angles" or "No physical object can be in two different places in space at one and the same time" are examples of statements whose truth we can apprehend just by understanding and reflecting on them. The difficulty with the claim that PSR is intuitively true, however, is that a number of very able philosophers fail to apprehend its truth, and some even claim that the principle is false. It is doubtful, therefore, that many of us, if any, know intuitively that PSR is true.

The second way philosophers and theologians who accept PSR have sought to defend it is by claiming that although it is not known to be true, it is, nevertheless, a presupposition of reason, a basic assumption that rational people make, whether or not they reflect sufficiently to become aware of the assumption. It's probably true that there are some assumptions we all make about our world, assumptions which are so basic that most of us are unaware of them. And, I suppose, it might be true that PSR is such an assumption. What bearing would this view of PSR have on the Cosmological Argument? Perhaps the main point to note is that even if PSR is a presupposition we all share, the premises of the Cosmological Argument could still be false. For PSR itself could still be false. The fact, if it is a fact, that all of us *presuppose* that every existing being and every positive fact has an explanation does not imply that no being exists, and no positive fact obtains, without an explanation. Nature is not bound to satisfy our presuppositions. As the American philosopher William James once remarked in another connection, "In the great boarding house of nature, the cakes and the butter and the syrup seldom come out so even and leave the plates so clear."

Our study of the first part of the Cosmological Argument has led us to the fundamental principle on which its premises rest, the Principle of Sufficient Reason. Since we do not seem to know the PSR is true we cannot reasonably claim to know that the premises of the Cosmological Argument are true. They might be true. But unless we do know them to be true they cannot *establish* for us the conclusion that there exists a being that has the explanation of its existence within its own nature. If it were shown, however, that even though we do not *know* that PSR is true we all, nevertheless, *presuppose* PSR to be true, then, whether PSR is true or not, to be consistent we should accept the Cosmological Argument. For, as we've seen, its premises imply its conclusion and its premises do seem to follow from PSR. But no one has succeeded in *showing* that PSR is an assumption that most or all of us share. So our final conclusion must be that although the Cosmological Argument might be a *sound* argument (valid with true premises), it does not provide us with good rational grounds for believing that among those beings that exist there is one whose existence is accounted for by its own nature. Having come to this conclusion we may safely put aside the second part of the argument. For even if it succeeded in showing that a self-existent being would have the other attributes of the theistic God, the Cosmological Argument would still not provide us with good rational grounds for belief in God, having failed in its first part to provide us with good rational grounds for believing that there is a self-existent being.

12 From *Dialogues Concerning Natural Religion*[*]

David Hume

Part II

I must own, Cleanthes, said Demea, that nothing can more surprise me, than the light, in which you have, all along, put this argument. By the whole tenor of your discourse, one would imagine that you were maintaining the being of a God, against the cavils of atheists and infidels; and were necessitated to become a champion for that fundamental principle of all religion. But this, I hope, is not by any means a question among us. No man; no man, at least, of common sense, I am persuaded, ever entertained a serious

* From David Hume, *Dialogues Concerning Natural Religion*, Parts II and V. Public domain. First published in 1779.

doubt with regard to a truth, so certain and self-evident. The question is not concerning the *being*, but the *nature* of God. This, I affirm, from the infirmities of human understanding, to be altogether incomprehensible and unknown to us. The essence of that supreme mind, his attributes, the manner of his existence, the very nature of his duration; these and every particular, which regards so divine a being, are mysterious to men. Finite, weak, and blind creatures, we ought to humble ourselves in his august presence, and, conscious of our frailties, adore in silence his infinite perfections, which eye hath not seen, ear hath not heard, neither hath it entered into the heart of man to conceive them. They are covered in a deep cloud from human curiosity: it is profaneness to attempt penetrating through these sacred obscurities: and next to the impiety of denying his existence, is the temerity of prying into his nature and essence, decrees and attributes.

But lest you should think, that my *piety* has here got the better of my *philosophy*, I shall support my opinion, if it needs any support, by a very great authority. I might cite all the divines almost, from the foundation of Christianity, who have ever treated of this or any other theological subject: but I shall confine myself, at present, to one equally celebrated for piety and philosophy. It is Father Malebranche, who, I remember, thus expresses himself.[1] 'One ought not so much (says he) to call God a spirit, in order to express positively what he is, as in order to signify that he is not matter. He is a Being infinitely perfect: of this we cannot doubt. But in the same manner as we ought not to imagine, even supposing him corporeal, that he is clothed with a human body, as the Anthropomorphites asserted, under color that that figure was the most perfect of any; so neither ought we to imagine, that the spirit of God has human ideas, or bears *any* resemblance to our spirit; under color that we know nothing more perfect than a human mind. We ought rather to believe, that as he comprehends the perfections of matter without being material. . . . he comprehends also the perfections of created spirits, without being spirit, in the manner we conceive spirit: that his true name is, He *that is*, or, in other words, Being without restriction, All Being, the Being infinite and universal.'

After so great an authority, Demea, replied Philo, as that which you have produced, and a thousand more, which you might produce, it would appear ridiculous in me to add my sentiment, or express my approbation of your doctrine. But surely, where reasonable men treat these subjects, the question can never be concerning the being, but only the nature of the Deity. The former truth, as you well observe, is unquestionable and self-evident. Nothing exists without a cause; and the original cause of this universe (whatever it be) we call God; and piously ascribe to him every species of perfection. Whoever scruples this fundamental truth, deserves every punishment, which can be inflicted among philosophers, to wit, the greatest ridicule, contempt and disapprobation. But as all perfection is entirely relative, we ought never to imagine, that we comprehend the attributes of this divine Being, or to suppose, that his perfections have any analogy or likeness to the perfections of a human creature. Wisdom, thought, design, knowledge; these we justly ascribe to him; because these words are honorable among men, and we have no other language or other conceptions, by which we can express our adoration of him. But let us beware, lest we think, that our ideas any wise correspond to his perfections, or that his attributes have any resemblance to these qualities among men. He is infinitely superior to our limited view and comprehension; and is more the object of worship in the temple, than of disputation in the schools.

In reality, Cleanthes, continued he, there is no need of having recourse to that affected scepticism, so displeasing to you, in order to come at this determination. Our ideas reach no farther than our experience: we have no experience of divine attributes and operations:

I need not conclude my syllogism: you can draw the inference yourself. And it is a pleasure to me (and I hope to you too) that just reasoning and sound piety here concur in the same conclusion, and both of them establish the adorably mysterious and incomprehensible nature of the Supreme Being.

Not to lose any time in circumlocutions, said Cleanthes, addressing himself to Demea, much less in replying to the pious declamations of Philo; I shall briefly explain how I conceive this matter. Look round the world: contemplate the whole and every part of it: you will find it to be nothing but one great machine, subdivided into an infinite number of lesser machines, which again admit of subdivisions, to a degree beyond what human senses and faculties can trace and explain. All these various machines, and even their most minute parts, are adjusted to each other with an accuracy, which ravishes into admiration all men, who have ever contemplated them. The curious adapting of means to ends, throughout all nature, resembles exactly, though it much exceeds, the productions of human contrivance; of human design, thought, wisdom, and intelligence. Since therefore the effects resemble each other, we are led to infer, by all the rules of analogy, that the causes also resemble; and that the Author of Nature is somewhat similar to the mind of men; though possessed of much larger faculties, proportioned to the grandeur of the work, which he has executed. By this argument *a posteriori*, and by this argument alone, do we prove at once the existence of a Deity, and his similarity to human mind and intelligence.

I shall be so free, Cleanthes, said Demea, as to tell you, that from the beginning, I could not approve of your conclusion concerning the similarity of the Deity to men; still less can I approve of the mediums, by which you endeavor to establish it. What! No demonstration of the being of a God! No abstract arguments! No proofs *a priori*! Are these, which have hitherto been so much insisted on by philosophers, all fallacy, all sophism? Can we reach no farther in this subject than experience and probability? I will not say, that this is betraying the cause of a deity: but surely, by this affected candor, you give advantage to atheists, which they never could obtain, by the mere dint of argument and reasoning.

What I chiefly scruple in this subject, said Philo, is not so much, that all religious arguments are by Cleanthes reduced to experience, as that they appear not to be even the most certain and irrefragable of that inferior kind. That a stone will fall, that fire will burn, that the earth has solidity, we have observed thousand and a thousand times; and when any new instance of this nature is presented, we draw without hesitation the accustomed inference. The exact similarity of the cases gives us a perfect assurance of a similar event; and a stronger evidence is never desired nor sought after. But wherever you depart, in the least, from the similarity of the cases, you diminish proportionably the evidence; and may at last bring it to a very weak *analogy*, which is confessedly liable to error and uncertainty. After having experienced the circulation of the blood in human creatures, we make no doubt that it takes place in Titius and Maevius: but from its circulation in frogs and fishes, it is only a presumption, though a strong one, from analogy, that it takes place in men and other animals. The analogical reasoning is much weaker, when we infer the circulation of the sap in vegetables from our experience, that the blood circulates in animals; and those, who hastily followed that imperfect analogy, are found, by more accurate experiments, to have been mistaken.

If we see a house, Cleanthes, we conclude, with the greatest certainty, that it had an architect or builder; because this is precisely that species of effect, which we have experienced to proceed from that species of cause. But surely you will not affirm, that the universe bears such a resemblance to a house, that we can with the same certainty infer a similar cause, or that the analogy is here entire and perfect. The dissimilitude is so striking, that the utmost you can here pretend to is a guess, a conjecture, a presumption concerning a similar cause; and how that pretension will be received in the world, I leave you to consider.

It would surely be very ill received, replied Cleanthes; and I should be deservedly blamed and detested, did I allow, that the proofs of a Deity amounted to no more than a guess or conjecture. But is the whole adjustment of means to ends in a house and in the universe so slight a resemblance? The economy of final causes? The order, proportion, and arrangement of every part? Steps of a stair are plainly contrived, that human legs may use them in mounting; and this inference is certain and infallible. Human legs are also contrived for walking and mounting; and this inference, I allow, is not altogether so certain, because of the dissimilarity which you remark; but does it, therefore, deserve the name only of presumption or conjecture?

Good God! cried Demea, interrupting him, where are we? Zealous defenders of religion allow, that the proofs of a Deity fall short of perfect evidence! And you, Philo, on whose assistance I depended, in proving the adorable mysteriousness of the Divine Nature, do you assent to all these extravagant opinions of Cleanthes? For what other name can I give them? Or why spare my censure, when such principles are advanced, supported by such an authority, before so young a man as Pamphilus?

You seem not to apprehend, replied Philo, that I argue with Cleanthes in his own way; and by showing him the dangerous consequences of his tenets, hope at last to reduce him to our opinion. But what sticks most with you, I observe, is the representation which Cleanthes has made of the argument *a posteriori*; and finding, that that argument is likely to escape your hold and vanish into air, you think it so disguised, that you can scarcely believe it to be set in its true light. Now, however much I may dissent, in other respects, from the dangerous principles of Cleanthes, I must allow, that he has fairly represented that argument; and I shall endeavor so to state the matter to you, that you will entertain no farther scruples with regard to it.

Were a man to abstract from everything which he knows or has seen, he would be altogether incapable, merely from his own ideas, to determine what kind of scene the universe must be, or to give the preference to one state or situation of things above another. For as nothing which he clearly conceives, could be esteemed impossible or implying a contradiction, every chimera of his fancy would be upon an equal footing; nor could he assign any just reason, why he adheres to one idea or system, and rejects the others, which are equally possible.

Again; after he opens his eyes, and contemplates the world, as it really is, it would be impossible for him, at first, to assign the cause of any one event; much less, of the whole of things or of the universe. He might set his fancy a rambling; and she might bring him in an infinite variety of reports and representations. These would all be possible; but being all equally possible, he would never, of himself, give a satisfactory account for his preferring one of them to the rest. Experience alone can point out to him the true cause of any phenomenon.

Now, according to this method of reasoning, Demea, it follows (and is, indeed, tacitly allowed by Cleanthes himself) that order, arrangement, or the adjustment of final causes is not, of itself, any proof of design; but only so far as it has been experienced to proceed from that principle. For aught we can know *a priori*, matter may contain the source or spring of order originally, within itself, as well as mind does; and there is no more difficulty in conceiving, that the several elements, from an internal unknown cause, may fall into the most exquisite arrangement, than to conceive that their ideas, in the great, universal mind, from a like internal, unknown cause, fall into that arrangement. The equal possibility of both these suppositions is allowed. But by experience we find (according to Cleanthes), that there is a difference between them. Throw several pieces of steel together, without shape or form; they will never arrange themselves so as to compose a watch: stone, and mortar, and wood, without an architect, never erect a house. But the ideas in a human mind, we see, by an unknown, inexplicable economy, arrange themselves so as to form the plan of a watch or house. Experience, therefore, proves, that there is an original principle of order in mind, not in matter. From similar effects we infer similar causes. The adjustment of means to ends is alike in the universe, as in a machine of human contrivance. The causes, therefore, must be resembling.

I was from the beginning scandalized, I must own, with this resemblance, which is asserted, between the Deity and human creatures; and must conceive it to imply such a degradation of the Supreme Being as no sound theist could endure. With your assistance, therefore, Demea, I shall endeavor to defend what you justly called the adorable mysteriousness of the Divine Nature, and shall refute this reasoning of Cleanthes, provided he allows, that I have made a fair representation of it.

When Cleanthes had assented, Philo, after a short pause, proceeded in the following manner.

That all inferences, Cleanthes, concerning fact, are founded on experience, and that all experimental reasonings are founded on the supposition, that similar causes prove similar effects, and similar effects similar causes; I shall not, at present, much dispute with you. But observe, I entreat you, with what extreme caution all just reasoners proceed in the transferring of experiments to similar cases. Unless the cases be exactly similar, they repose no perfect confidence in applying their past observation to any particular phenomenon. Every alteration of circumstances occasions a doubt concerning the event; and it requires new experiments to prove certainly, that the new circumstances are of no moment or importance. A change in bulk, situation, arrangement, age, disposition of the air, or surrounding bodies; any of these particulars may be attended with the most unexpected consequences: and unless the objects be quite familiar to us, it is the highest temerity to expect with assurance, after any of these changes, an event similar to that which before fell under our observation. The slow and deliberate steps of philosophers, here, if anywhere, are distinguished from the precipitate march of the vulgar, who, hurried on by the smallest similitudes, are incapable of all discernment or consideration.

But can you think, Cleanthes, that your usual phlegm and philosophy have been preserved in so wide a step as you have taken, when you compared to the universe, houses, ships, furniture, machines; and from their similarity in some circumstances inferred a similarity in their causes? Thought, design, intelligence, such as we discover in men and other animals, is no more than one of the springs and principles of the universe, as well as heat or cold, attraction or repulsion, and a hundred others, which fall under daily observation. It is an active cause, by which some particular parts of nature, we find, produce alterations on other parts. But can a conclusion, with any propriety, be transferred from parts to the whole? Does not the great disproportion bar all comparison and inference? From observing the growth of a hair, can we learn anything concerning the generation of a man? Would the manner of a leaf's blowing, even though perfectly known, afford us any instruction concerning the vegetation of a tree?

But allowing that we were to take the *operations* of one part of nature upon another for the foundation of our judgment concerning the *origin* of the whole (which never can be admitted), yet why select so minute, so weak, so bounded a principle as the reason and design of animals is found to be upon this planet? What peculiar privilege has this little agitation of the brain which we call *thought*, that we must thus make it the model of the whole universe? Our partiality in our own favor does indeed present it on all occasions; but sound philosophy ought carefully to guard against so natural an illusion.

So far from admitting, continued Philo, that the operations of a part can afford us any just conclusion concerning the origin of the whole, I will not allow any one part to form a rule for another part, if the latter be very remote from the former. Is there any reasonable ground to conclude, that the inhabitants of other planets possess thought, intelligence, reason, or anything similar to these faculties in men? When Nature has so extremely diversified her manner of operation in this small globe; can we imagine, that she incessantly copies herself throughout so immense a universe? And if thought, as we may well suppose, be confined merely to his narrow corner, and has even there so limited a sphere of action; with what propriety can we assign it for the original cause of all things? The narrow views of a peasant, who makes his domestic economy the rule for the government of kingdoms, is in comparison a pardonable sophism.

But were we ever so much assured, that a thought and reason, resembling the human, were to be found throughout the whole universe, and were its activity elsewhere vastly greater and more commanding than it appears in this globe; yet I cannot see, why the operations of a world, constituted, arranged, adjusted, can with any propriety be extended to a world, which is in its embryo state, and is advancing towards that constitution and arrangement. By observation, we know somewhat of the economy, action, and nourishment of a finished animal; but we must transfer with great caution that observation to the growth of a fetus in the womb, and still more, to the formation of an animalcule in the loins of its male parent. Nature, we find, even from our limited experience, possesses an infinite number of springs and principles, which incessantly discover themselves on every change of her position and situation. And what new and unknown principles would actuate her in so new and unknown a situation as that of the formation of a universe, we cannot, without the utmost temerity, pretend to determine.

A very small part of this great system, during a very short time, is very imperfectly discovered to us: and do we thence pronounce decisively concerning the origin of the whole?

Admirable conclusion! Stone, wood, brick, iron, brass, have not, at this time, in this minute globe of earth, an order or arrangement without human art and contrivance: therefore the universe could not originally attain its order and arrangement, without something similar to human art. But is a part of nature a rule for another part very wide of the former? Is it a rule for the whole? Is a very small part a rule for the universe? Is nature in one situation, a certain rule for nature in another situation, vastly different from the former? . . .

Part V

But to show you still more inconveniences, continued Philo, in your anthropomorphism; please to take a new survey of your principles. *Like effects prove like causes.* This is the experimental argument; and this, you say too, is the sole theological argument. Now it is certain, that the liker the effects are, which are seen, and the liker the causes, which are inferred, the stronger is the argument. Every departure on either side diminishes the probability, and renders the experiment less conclusive. You cannot doubt of the principle: neither ought you to reject its consequences.

All the new discoveries in astronomy, which prove the immense grandeur and magnificence of the works of nature, are so many additional arguments for a Deity, according to the true system of theism: but according to your hypothesis of experimental theism, they become so many objections, by removing the effect still farther from all resemblance to the effects of human art and contrivance. . . .

The discoveries by microscopes, as they open a new universe in miniature, are still objections, according to you; arguments, according to me. The farther we push our researches of this kind, we are still led to infer the universal causes of all to be vastly different from mankind, or from any object of human experience and observation.

And what say you to the discoveries in anatomy, chemistry, botany?. . . . These surely are no objections, replied Cleanthes: they only discover new instances of art and contrivance. It is still the image of mind reflected on us from innumerable objects. Add, a mind *like the human*, said Philo. I know of no other, replied Cleanthes. And the liker the better, insisted Philo. To be sure, said Cleanthes.

Now, Cleanthes, said Philo, with an air of alacrity and triumph, mark the consequences. *First*, By this method of reasoning, you renounce all claim to infinity in any of the attributes of the Deity. For as the cause ought only to be proportioned to the effect, and the effect, so far as it falls under our cognizance, is not infinite; what pretensions have we, upon your suppositions, to ascribe that attribute to the Divine Being? You will still insist, that, by removing him so much from all similarity to human creatures, we give in to the most arbitrary hypothesis, and at the same time weaken all proofs of his existence.

Secondly, You have no reason, on your theory, for ascribing perfection to the Deity, even in his finite capacity; or for supposing him free from every error, mistake, or incoherence in his undertakings. There are many inexplicable difficulties in the works of nature, which, if we allow a perfect author to be proved *a priori*, are easily solved, and become only seeming difficulties, from the narrow capacity of man, who cannot trace infinite relations. But according to your method of reasoning, these difficulties become all real; and perhaps will be insisted on, as new instances of likeness to human art and contrivance. At least, you must acknowledge, that it is impossible for us to tell, from our limited views, whether this system contains any great faults, or deserves any considerable praise, if compared to other possible, and even real systems. Could a peasant, if the *Aeneid* were read to him, pronounce that poem to be absolutely faultless, or even assign to it its proper rank among the productions of human wit; he, who had never seen any other production?

But were this world ever so perfect a production, it must still remain uncertain, whether all the excellences of the work can justly be ascribed to the workman. If we survey a ship, what an exalted idea must we form of the ingenuity of the carpenter, who framed so complicated, useful, and beautiful a machine? And what surprise must we feel, when we find him a stupid mechanic, who imitated others, and copied an art, which, through a long succession of ages, after multiplied trials, mistakes, corrections, deliberations, and controversies, had been gradually improving? Many worlds might have been botched and bungled, throughout an eternity, ere this system was struck out: much labor lost: many fruitless trials made: and a slow, but continued improvement carried on during infinite ages in the art of world-making. In such subjects, who can determine, where the truth; nay, who can conjecture where the probability lies; amidst a great number of hypotheses which may be proposed, and a still greater number which may be imagined?

And what shadow of an argument, continued Philo, can you produce, from your hypothesis, to prove the unity of the Deity? A great number of men join in building a house or ship, in rearing a city, in framing a commonwealth: why may not several deities combine in contriving and framing a world? This is only so much greater similarity to human affairs? By sharing the work among several, we may so much further limit the attributes of each, and get rid of that extensive power and knowledge, which must be supposed in one deity, and which, according to you, can only serve to weaken the proof of his existence. And if such foolish, such vicious creatures as man can yet often unite in framing and executing one plan; how much more those deities or demons, whom we may suppose several degrees more perfect?

To multiply causes, without necessity, is indeed contrary to true philosophy: but this principle applies not to the present case. Were one deity antecedently proved by your theory, who were possessed of every attribute, requisite to the production of the universe; it would be needless, I own (though not absurd) to suppose any other deity existent. But while it is still a question, whether all these attributes are united in one subject, or dispersed among several independent beings: by what phenomena in nature can we pretend to decide the controversy? Where we see a body raised in a scale, we are sure that there is in the opposite scale, however concealed from sight, some counterpoising weight equal to it: but it is still allowed to doubt, whether that weight be an aggregate of several distinct bodies, or one uniform united mass. And if the weight requisite very much exceeds anything which we have ever seen conjoined in any single body, the former supposition becomes still more probable and natural. An intelligent being of such vast power and capacity, as is necessary to produce the universe, or, to speak in the language of ancient philosophy, so prodigious an animal, exceeds all analogy, and even comprehension.

But farther, Cleanthes; men are mortal, and renew their species by generation; and this is common to all living creatures. The two great sexes of male and female, says Milton, animate the world. Why must this circumstance, so universal, so essential, be excluded from those numerous and limited deities? Behold then the theogony of ancient times brought back upon us.

And why not become a perfect anthropomorphite? Why not assert the deity or deities to be corporeal, and to have eyes, a nose, mouth, ears, etc? Epicurus maintained, that no man had ever seen reason but in a human figure; therefore the gods must have a human figure. And this argument, which is deservedly so much ridiculed by Cicero, becomes, according to you, solid and philosophical.

In a word, Cleanthes, a man, who follows your hypothesis, is able, perhaps, to assert, or conjecture, that the universe, sometime, arose from something like design: but beyond that position he cannot ascertain one single circumstance, and is left afterwards to fix every point of his theology, by the utmost license of fancy and hypothesis. This world, for aught he knows, is very faulty and imperfect compared to a superior standard; and was only the first rude essay of some infant deity, who afterwards abandoned it, ashamed of his lame performance; it is the work only of some dependent, inferior deity; and is the object of derision to his superiors: it is the production of old age and dotage in some superannuated deity; and ever since his death, has run on at adventures, from the first impulse and active force, which it received from him. You justly give signs of horror, Demea, at these strange suppositions: but these, and a thousand more of the same kind, are Cleanthes's suppositions, not mine. From the moment the attributes of the Deity are supposed finite, all these have place. And I cannot, for my part, think, that so wild and unsettled a system of theology is, in any respect, preferable to none at all.

These suppositions I absolutely disown, cried Cleanthes: they strike me, however, with no horror; especially, when proposed in that rambling way in which they drop from you. On the contrary, they give me pleasure, why I see, that, by the utmost indulgence of your imagination, you never get rid of the hypothesis of design in the universe; but are obliged, at every turn, to have recourse to it. To this concession I adhere steadily; and this I regard as a sufficient foundation for religion.

Note

1 *Recherche de la Vérité*, liv. 3, chap. 9.

13   The Argument from Design*

R. G. Swinburne

The object of this paper is to show that there are no valid formal objections to the argument from design, so long as the argument is articulated with sufficient care. In particular I wish to analyse Hume's attack on the argument in *Dialogues Concerning Natural Religion* and to show that none of the formal objections made therein by Philo have any validity against a carefully articulated version of the argument.

The argument from design is an argument from the order or regularity of things in the world to a god or, more precisely, a very powerful free non-embodied rational agent, who is responsible for that order. By a body I understand a part of the material Universe subject, at any rate partially, to an agent's direct control, to be contrasted with other parts not thus subject. An agent's body marks the limits to what he can directly control; he can only control other parts of the Universe by moving his body. An agent who could directly control any part of the Universe would not be embodied. Thus ghosts, if they existed, would be non-embodied agents, because there are no particular pieces of matter subject to their direct control, but any piece of matter may be so subject. I use the word 'design' in such a way that it is not analytic that if anything evinces design, an agent designed it, and so it becomes a synthetic question whether the design of the world shows the activity of a designer.

The argument, taken by itself, as was admitted in the *Dialogues* by Cleanthes the proponent of the argument, does not show that the designer of the world is omnipotent, omniscient, totally good, etc. Nor does it show that he is the God of Abraham, Isaac, and Jacob. To make these points further arguments would be needed. The isolation of the argument from design from the web of Christian apologetic is perhaps a somewhat unnatural step, but necessary in order to analyse its structure. My claim is that the argument does not commit any formal fallacy, and by this I mean that it keeps to the canons

* From *Philosophy*, 43 (July 1968), pp. 199–212. © 1968 by Royal Institute of Philosophy. Reprinted with the permission of Cambridge University Press.

of argument about matters of fact and does not violate any of them. It is, however, an argument by analogy. It argues from an analogy between the order of the world and the products of human art to a god responsible for the former, in some ways similar to man who is responsible for the latter. And even if there are no formal fallacies in the argument, one unwilling to admit the conclusion might still claim that the analogy was too weak and remote for him to have to admit it, that the argument gave only negligible support to the conclusion which remained improbable. In defending the argument I will leave to the objector this way of escape from its conclusion.

I will begin by setting forward the argument from design in a more careful and precise way than Cleanthes did.

There are in the world two kinds of regularity or order, and all empirical instances of order are such because they evince one or other or both kinds of order. These are the regularities of copresence or spatial order, and regularities of succession, or temporal order. Regularities of copresence are patterns of spatial order at some one instant of time. An example of a regularity of copresence would be a town with all its roads at right angles to each other, or a section of books in a library arranged in alphabetical order of authors. Regularities of succession are simple patterns of behaviour of objects, such as their behaviour in accordance with the laws of nature – for example, Newton's law of gravitation, which holds universally to a very high degree of approximation, that all bodies attract each other with forces proportional to the product of their masses and inversely proportional to the square of their distance apart.

Many of the striking examples of order in the world evince an order which is due both to a regularity of copresence and to a regularity of succession. A working car consists of many parts so adjusted to each other that it follows the instructions of the driver delivered by his pulling and pushing a few levers and buttons and turning a wheel to take passengers whither he wishes. Its order arises because its parts are so arranged at some instant (regularity of copresence) that, the laws of nature being as they are (regularity of succession), it brings about the result neatly and efficiently. The order of living animals and plants likewise results from regularities of both types.

Men who marvel at the order of the world may marvel at either or both of the regularities of copresence and of succession. The men of the eighteenth century, that great century of 'reasonable religion', were struck almost exclusively by the regularities of copresence. They marvelled at the design and orderly operations of animals and plants; but since they largely took for granted the regularities of succession, what struck them about the animals and plants, as to a lesser extent about machines made by men, was the subtle and coherent arrangement of their millions of parts. Paley's *Natural Theology* dwells mainly on details of comparative anatomy, on eyes and ears and muscles and bones arranged with minute precision so as to operate with high efficiency, and Hume's Cleanthes produces the same kind of examples: 'Consider, anatomise the eye, survey its structure and contrivance, and tell me from your own feeling, if the idea of a contriver does not immediately flow in upon you with a force like that of sensation'.[1]

Those who argue from the existence of regularities of copresence other than those produced by men, to the existence of a god who produced them are however in many respects on slippery ground when compared with those who rely for their premises on regularities of succession. We shall see several of these weaknesses later in considering Hume's objections to the argument, but it is worth while noting two of them at the outset. First, although the world contains many striking regularities of copresence (some few of which are due to human agency), it also contains many examples of spatial disorder. The uniform distribution of the galactic clusters is a marvellous example of spatial order, but the arrangement of trees in an African jungle is a marvellous example of spatial disorder. Although the proponent of the argument may then proceed to argue that in an important sense or from some point of view (e.g. utility to man) the order vastly exceeds the disorder, he has to argue for this in no way obvious proposition.

Secondly the proponent of the argument runs the risk that the regularities of copresence may be explained in terms of something else by a normal scientific explanation[2] in a way that the regularities of succession could not possibly be. A scientist could show that a regularity of copresence R arose from an apparently disordered state D by means of the normal operation of the laws of nature. This would not entirely 'explain away' the regularity of copresence, because the proponent of this argument from design might then argue that the apparently disordered state D really had a latent order, being the kind of state which, when the laws of nature operate, turns into a manifestly ordered one. So long as only few of the physically possible states of apparent disorder were states of latent order, the existence of many states of latent order would be an important contingent fact which could form a premiss for an argument from design. But there is always the risk that scientists might show that most states of apparent disorder were states of latent order, that is, that if the world lasted long enough considerable order must emerge from whichever of many initial states it began. If a scientist showed that, he would have explained by normal scientific explanation the existence of regularities of copresence in terms of something completely different. The eighteenth-century proponents of the argument from design did not suspect this danger and hence the devasting effect of Darwin's Theory of Evolution by Natural Selection on those who accepted their argument. For Darwin showed that the regularities of copresence of the animal and plant kingdoms had evolved by natural processes from an apparently disordered state and would have evolved equally from many other apparently disordered states. Whether all regularities of copresence can be fully explained in this kind of way no one yet knows, but the danger remains for the proponent of an argument from design of this kind that they can be.

However, those who argue from the operation of regularities of succession other than those produced by men to the existence of a god who produces them do not run into either of these difficulties. Regularities of succession (other than those produced by men) unlike regularities of copresence, are all-pervasive. Simple natural laws rule almost all successions of events. Nor can regularities of succession be given a normal scientific explanation in terms of something else. For the normal scientific explanation of the operation of a regularity of succession is in terms of the operation of a yet more general regularity of succession. Note too that a normal scientific explanation of the existence of regularities of copresence in terms of something different, if it can be provided, is explanation in terms of regularities of succession.

For these reasons the proponent of the argument from design does much better to rely for his premiss more on regularities of succession. St Thomas Aquinas, wiser than the men of the eighteenth century, did just this. He puts forward an argument from design as his fifth and last way to prove the existence of God, and gives his premiss as follows:

'The fifth way is based on the guidedness of nature. An orderedness of actions to an end is observed in all bodies obeying natural laws, even when they lack awareness. For their behaviour hardly ever varies, and will practically always turn out well; which shows that they truly tend to a goal, and do not merely hit it by accident.'[3] If we ignore any value judgment in 'practically always turn out well', St Thomas' argument is an argument from regularities of succession.

The most satisfactory premiss for the argument from design is then the operation of regularities of succession other than those produced by men, that is, the operation of natural laws. Almost all things almost always obey simple natural laws and so behave in a strikingly regular way. Given the premiss, what is our justification for proceeding to the conclusion, that a very powerful free non-embodied rational agent is responsible for their behaving in that way? The justification which Aquinas gives is that 'Nothing . . . that lacks awareness tends to a goal, except under the direction of someone with awareness and with understanding; the arrow, for example requires an archer. Everything in nature, therefore is directed to its goal by someone with understanding and this we call "God".'[4] A similar argument has been given by many religious apologists since Aquinas, but clearly as it stands it is guilty of the grossest *petitio principii*. Certainly *some* things which tend to a goal, tend to a goal because of a direction imposed upon them by someone 'with awareness and with understanding'. Did not the archer place the arrow and pull the string in a certain way the arrow would not tend to its goal. But whether *all* things which tend to a goal tend to a goal for this reason is the very question at issue and that they do cannot be used as a premiss to prove the conclusion. We must therefore reconstruct the argument in a more satisfactory way.

The structure of any plausible argument from design can only be that the existence of a god responsible for the order in the world is a hypothesis well confirmed on the basis of the evidence, viz. that contained in the premiss which we have now stated, and better confirmed than any other hypothesis. I shall begin by showing that there can be no other possible explanation for the operation of natural laws than the activity of a god and then see to what extent the hypothesis is well confirmed on the basis of the evidence.

Almost all phenomena can, as we have seen, be explained by a normal scientific explanation in terms of the operation of natural laws on preceding states. There is however one other way of explaining natural phenomena, and that is explaining in terms of the rational choice of a free agent. When a man marries Jane rather than Anne, becomes a solicitor rather than a barrister, kills rather than shows mercy after considering arguments in favour of each course, he brings about a state of the world by his free and rational choice. To all appearances this is an entirely different way whereby states of the world may come about than through the operation of laws of nature on preceding states. Someone may object that it is necessary that physiological or other scientific laws operate in order for the agent to bring about effects. My answer is that certainly it is necessary that such laws operate in order for effects brought about directly by the agent to have ulterior consequences. But unless there are some effects which the agent brings about directly without the operation of scientific laws acting on preceding physical states bringing them about, then these laws and states could fully explain the effects and there would be no need to refer in explaining them to the rational choice of an agent. True, the apparent freedom and rationality of the human will *may* prove an illusion. Man may have no more option what to do than a machine and be guided by an argument no more than is a piece of iron. But this has never yet been shown and, in the absence of good philosophical and scientific argument to show it, I assume, what is apparent, that when a man acts by free and rational choice, his agency is the operation of a different kind of causality from that of scientific laws. The free choice of a rational agent is the only way of accounting for natural phenomena other than the way of normal scientific explanation, which is recognised as such by all men and has not been reduced to normal scientific explanation.

Almost all regularities of succession are due to the normal operation of scientific laws. But to say this is simply to say that these regularities are instances of more general regularities. The operation of the most fundamental regularities clearly cannot be given a normal scientific explanation. If their operation is to receive an explanation and not merely to be left as a brute fact, that explanation must therefore be in terms of the rational choice of a free agent. What then are grounds for adopting this hypothesis, given that it is the only possible one?

The grounds are that we can explain some few regularities of succession as produced by rational agents and that the other regularities cannot be explained except in this way. Among the typical products of a rational agent acting freely are regularities both of co-presence and of succession. The alphabetical order of books on a library shelf is due to the activity of the librarian who chose to arrange them thus. The order of the cards of a pack by suits and seniority in each suit is due to the activity of the card player who arranged them thus. Among examples of regularities of succession produced by men are the notes of a song sung by a singer or the movements of a dancer's body when he performs a dance in time with the accompanying instrument. Hence knowing that some regularities of succession have such a cause, we postulate that they all have. An agent produces the celestial harmony like a man who sings a song. But at this point an obvious difficulty arises. The regularities of succession, such as songs which are produced by men, are pro-duced by agents of comparatively small power, whose bodies we can locate. If an agent is responsible for the operation of the laws of nature, he must act directly on the whole Universe, as we act directly on our bodies. Also he must be of immense power and intel-ligence compared with men. Hence he can only be somewhat similar to men having, like them, intelligence and freedom of choice, yet unlike them in the degree of these and in not possessing a body. For a body, as I have distinguished it earlier, is a part of the Uni-verse subject to an agent's direct control, to be contrasted with other parts not thus subject. The fact that we are obliged to postulate on the basis of differences in the effects differences in the causes, men and the god, weakens the argument. How much it weakens it depends on how great these differences are.

Our argument thus proves to be an argument by analogy and to exemplify a pattern common in scientific inference. As are caused by Bs. A*s are similar to As. Therefore – given that there is no more satisfactory explanation of the existence of A*s – they are pro-duced by B*s similar to Bs. B*s are postulated to be similar in all respects to Bs except in so far as shown otherwise, viz. except in so far as the dissimilarities between As and A*s force us to postulate a difference. A well-known scientific example of this type of inference is as follows. Certain pressures (As) on the walls of containers are produced by billiard balls (Bs) with certain motions. Similar pressures (A*s) are produced on the walls of containers which contain not billiard balls but gases. Therefore, since we have no better explanation of the existence of the pressures, gases consist of particles (B*s) similar to bil-liard balls except in certain respects – e.g. size. By similar arguments scientists have argued for the existence of many unobservables. Such an argument becomes weaker in so far as the properties which we are forced to attribute to the B*s because of the differences between the As and the A*s become different from those of the Bs. Nineteenth-century physicists postulated the existence of an elastic solid, the aether, to account for the prop-agation of light. But the way in which light was propagated turned out to have such dif-ferences (despite the similarities) from the way in which waves in solids are normally propagated that the physicists had to say that if there was an aether it had very many peculiar properties not possessed by normal liquids or solids. Hence they concluded that the argument for its existence was very weak. The proponent of the argument from design stresses the similarities between the regularities of succession produced by man and those which are laws of nature and so between men and the agent which he postulates as responsible for the laws of nature. The opponent of the argument stresses the dissimilarities. The degree of support which the conclusion obtains from the evidence depends on how great the similarities are.

The degree of support for the conclusion of an argument from analogy does not however depend merely on the similarities between the types of evidence but on the degree to which the resulting theory makes explanation of empirical matters more simple and coherent. In the case of the argument from design the conclusion has an enormous simplifying effect on explanations of empirical matters. For if the conclusion is true, if a very powerful non-embodied rational agent is responsible for the operation of the laws of nature, then normal scientific explanation would prove to be personal explanation. That is, explanation of some phenomenon in terms of the operation of a natural law would ultimately be an explanation in terms of the operation of an agent. Hence (given an initial arrangement of matter) the principles of explanation of phenomena would have been reduced from two to one. It is a basic principle of explanation that we should postulate as few as possible kinds of explanation. To take a more mundane example – if we have as possible alternatives to explain physical phenomena by the operation of two kinds of force, the electromagnetic and the gravitational, and to explain physical phenomena in terms of the operation of only one kind of force, the gravitational, we ought always – *ceteris paribus* – to prefer the latter alternative. Since as we have seen, we are obliged, at any rate at present, to use explanation in terms of the free choice of a rational agent in explaining many empirical phenomena, then if the amount of similarity between the order in the Universe not produced by human agents and that produced by human agents makes it at all plausible to do so, we ought to postulate that an agent is responsible for the former as well as for the latter. So then in so far as regularities of succession produced by the operation of natural laws are similar to those produced by human agents, to postulate that a rational agent is responsible for them would indeed provide a simple unifying and coherent explanation of natural phenomena. What is there against taking this step? Simply that celebrated principle of explanation – *entia non sunt multiplicanda praeter necessitatem* – do not add a god to your ontology unless you have to. The issue turns on whether the evidence constitutes enough of a *necessitas* to compel us to multiply entities. Whether it does depends on how strong is the analogy between the regularities of succession produced by human agents and those produced by the operation of natural laws. I do not propose to assess the strength of the analogy but only to claim that everything turns on it. I claim that the inference from natural laws to a god responsible for them is of a perfectly proper type for inference about matters of fact, and that the only issue is whether the evidence is strong enough to allow us to affirm that it is probable that the conclusion is true.

Now that I have reconstructed the argument from design in what is, I hope, a logically impeccable form, I turn to consider Hume's criticisms of it, and I shall argue that all his criticisms alleging formal fallacies in the argument do not apply to it in the form in which I have stated it. This, we shall see, is largely because the criticisms are bad criticisms of the argument in any form but also in small part because Hume directed his fire against that form of the argument which used as its premiss the existence of regularities of copresence other than those produced by men, and did not appeal to the operation of regularities of succession. I shall begin by considering one general point which he makes only in the *Enquiry* and then consider in turn all the objections which appear on the pages of the *Dialogues*.

1.   The point which appears at the beginning of Hume's discussion of the argument in section XI of the *Enquiry* is a point which reveals the fundamental weakness of Hume's sceptical position. In discussing the argument, Hume puts forward as a general principle that 'when we infer any particular cause from an effect, we must proportion the one to the other, and can never be allowed to ascribe to the cause any qualities but what are exactly sufficient to produce the effect.'[5] Now it is true that Hume uses this principle mainly to show that we are not justified in inferring that the god responsible for the design of the Universe is totally good, omnipotent, and omniscient. I accept, as Cleanthes did, that the argument does not by itself lead to that conclusion. But Hume's use of the principle tends to cast doubt on the validity of the argument in the weaker form in which I am discussing it, for it seems to suggest that although we may conclude that whatever produced the regularity of the world was a regularity-producing object, we cannot go further and conclude that it is an agent who acts by choice, etc., for this would be to suppose more than we need in order to account for the effect. It is, therefore, important to realise that the principle is clearly false on our normal understanding of what are the criteria of inference about empirical matters. For the universal adoption of this celebrated principle would lead to the abandonment of science. Any scientist who told us only that the cause of E had E-producing characteristics would not add an iota to our knowledge. Explanation of matters of fact consists in postulating on reasonable grounds that the cause of an effect has certain characteristics other than those sufficient to produce the effect.

2.   Two objections seem to be telescoped in the following passage of the *Dialogues*. 'When two *species* of objects have always been observed to be conjoined together, I can *infer* by custom the existence of one wherever I *see* the existence of the other; and this I call an argument from experience. But how this argument can have place where the objects, as in the present case, are single, individual, without parallel or specific resemblance, may be difficult to explain.'[6] One argument here seems to be that we can only infer from an observed A to an unobserved B when we have frequently observed As and Bs together, and that we cannot infer to a B unless we have actually observed other Bs. Hence we cannot infer from regularities of succession to an unobserved god on the analogy of the connection between observed regularities and human agents, unless we have observed at other times other gods. This argument, like the first, reveals Hume's inadequate appreciation of scientific method. As we saw in the scientific examples which I cited, a more developed science than Hume knew has taught us that when observed As have a relation R to observed Bs, it is often perfectly reasonable to postulate that observed A*s, similar to As, have the same relation to unobserved and unobservable B*s similar to Bs.

3.   The other objection which seems to be involved in the above passage is that we cannot reach conclusions about an object which is the only one of its kind, and, as the Universe is such an object, we cannot reach conclusions about the regularities characteristic of it as a whole.[7] But cosmologists are reaching very well-tested scientific conclusions about the Universe as a whole, as are physical anthropologists about the origins of our human race, even though it is the only human race of which we have knowledge and perhaps the only human race there is. The principle quoted in the objections is obviously wrong. There is no space here to analyse its errors in detail but suffice it to point out that it becomes hopelessly confused by ignoring the fact that uniqueness is relative to description. Nothing describable is unique under all descriptions (the Universe is, like the solar system, a number of material bodies distributed in empty space) and everything describable is unique under some description.

4. The next argument which we meet in the *Dialogues* is that the postulated existence of a rational agent who produces the order of the world would itself need explaining. Picturing such an agent as a mind, and a mind as an arrangement of ideas, Hume phrases the objection as follows: 'a mental world or Universe of ideas requires a cause as much as does a material world or Universe of objects.'[8] Hume himself provides the obvious answer to this – that it is no objection to explaining X by Y that we cannot explain Y. But then he suggests that the Y in this case, the mind, is just as mysterious as the ordered Universe. Men never 'thought it satisfactory to explain a particular effect by a particular cause which was no more to be accounted for than the effect itself.'[9] On the contrary, scientists have always thought it reasonable to postulate entities merely to explain effects, so long as the postulated entities accounted simply and coherently for the characteristics of the effects. The existence of molecules with their characteristic behaviour was 'no more to be accounted for' than observable phenomena, but the postulation of their existence gave a neat and simple explanation of a whole host of chemical and physical phenomena, and that was the justification for postulating their existence.

5. Next, Hume argues that if we are going to use the analogy of a human agent we ought to go the whole way and postulate that the god who gives order to the Universe is like men in many other respects. 'Why not become a perfect anthropomorphite? Why not assert the deity or deities to be corporeal, and, to have eyes, a nose, mouths, ears, etc.'[10] The argument from design is, as we have seen, an argument by analogy. All analogies break down somewhere; otherwise they would not be analogies. In saying that the relation of A to B is analogous to a relation of A* to a postulated B*, we do not claim that B* is in all respects like B, but only in such respects as to account for the existence of the relation and also in other respects except in so far as we have contrary evidence. For the activity of a god to account for the regularities, he must be free, rational, and very powerful. But it is not necessary that he, like men, should only be able to act on a limited part of the Universe, a body, and by acting on that control the rest of the Universe. And there is good reason to suppose that the god does not operate in this way. For, if his direct control was confined to a part of the Universe, scientific laws outside his control must operate to ensure that his actions have effects in the rest of the Universe. Hence the postulation of the existence of the god would not explain the operations of those laws: yet to explain the operation of all scientific laws was the point of postulating the existence of the god. The hypothesis that the god is not embodied thus explains more and explains more coherently than the hypothesis that he is embodied. Hume's objection would however have weight against an argument from regularities of copresence which did not appeal to the operation of regularities of succession. For one could suppose an embodied god just as well as a disembodied god to have made the animal kingdom and then left it alone, as a man makes a machine, or, like a landscape gardener, to have laid out the galactic cluster. The explanatory force of such an hypothesis is as great as that of the hypothesis that a disembodied god did these things, and argument from analogy would suggest the hypothesis of an embodied god to be more probable. Incidentally, a god whose prior existence was shown by the existence of regularities of copresence might now be dead, but a god whose existence was shown by the present operation of regularities of succession could not be, since the existence of an agent is contemporaneous with the temporal regularities which he produces.

6. Hume urges – why should we not postulate many gods to give order to the Universe, not merely one? 'A great number of men join in building a house or a ship, in rearing a city, in framing a commonwealth, why may not several deities combine in

framing a world?'[11] Hume again is aware of the obvious counter-objection to his suggestion – 'To multiply causes without necessity is . . . contrary to true philosophy'.[12] He claims however that the counter-objection does not apply here, because it is an open question whether there is a god with sufficient power to put the whole Universe in order. The principle, however, still applies whether or not we have prior information that a being of sufficient power exists. When postulating entities, postulate as few as possible. Always suppose only one murderer, unless the evidence forces you to suppose a second. If there were more than one deity responsible for the order of the Universe, we should expect to see characteristic marks of the handiwork of different deities in different parts of the Universe, just as we see different kinds of workmanship in the different houses of a city. We should expect to find an inverse square law of gravitation obeyed in one part of the universe, and in another part a law which was just short of being an inverse square law – without the difference being explicable in terms of a more general law. But it is enough to draw this absurd conclusion to see how ridiculous the Humean objection is.

7.   Hume argues that there are in the Universe other things than rational agents which bestow order. 'A tree bestows order and organisation on that tree which springs from it, without knowing the order; an animal in the same manner on its offspring.'[13] It would therefore, Hume argues, be equally reasonable if we are arguing from analogy, to suppose the cause of the regularities in the world 'to be something similar or analogous to generation or vegetation.'[14] This suggestion makes perfectly good sense if it is the regularities of copresence which we are attempting to explain. But as analogous processes to explain regularities of succession, generation or vegetation will not do, because they only produce regularities of copresence – and those through the operation of regularities of succession outside their control. The seed only produces the plant because of the continued operation of the laws of biochemistry.

8.   The last distinct objection which I can discover in the *Dialogues* is the following. Why should we not suppose, Hume urges, that this ordered Universe is a mere accident among the chance arrangements of eternal matter? In the course of eternity matter arranges itself in all kinds of way. We just happen to live in a period when it is characterised by order, and mistakenly conclude that matter is always ordered. Now, as Hume phrases this objection, it is directed against an argument from design which uses as its premiss the existence of the regularities of copresence. 'The continual motion of matter . . . in less than infinite transpositions must produce this economy or order, and by its very nature, that order, when once established supports itself for many ages if not to eternity'.[15] Hume thus relies here partly on chance and partly on the operation of regularities of succession (the preservation of order) to account for the existence of regularities of copresence. In so far as it relies on regularities of succession to explain regularities of copresence, such an argument has, as we saw earlier, some plausibility. But in so far as it relies on chance, it does not, if the amount of order to be accounted for is very striking. An attempt to attribute the operation of regularities of succession to chance would not thus be very plausible. The claim would be that there are no laws of nature which always apply to matter; matter evinces in the course of eternity all kinds of patterns of behaviour, it is just chance that at the moment the states of the Universe are succeeding each other in a regular way. But if we say that it is chance that in 1960 matter is behaving in a regular way, our claim becomes less and less plausible as we find that in 1961 and 1962 and so on it continues to behave in a regular way. An appeal to chance to account for order becomes less and less plausible, the greater the order. We would be justified attributing a typewritten version of collected works of

Shakespeare to the activity of monkeys typing eternally on eternal typewriters if we had some evidence of the existence of an infinite quantity of paper randomly covered with type, as well as the collected works. In the absence of any evidence that matter behaved irregularly at other temporal periods, we are not justified in attributing its present regular behaviour to chance.

In addition to the objections which I have stated, the *Dialogues* contain a lengthy presentation of the argument that the existence of evil in the world shows that the god who made it and gave it order is not both totally good and omnipotent. But this does not affect the argument from design which, as Cleanthes admits, does not purport to show that the designer of the Universe does have these characteristics. The eight objections which I have stated are all the distinct objections to the argument from design which I can find in the *Enquiry* and in the *Dialogues*, which claim that in some formal respect the argument does not work. As well as claiming that the argument from design is deficient in some formal respect, Hume makes the point that the analogy of the order produced by men to the other order of the Universe is too remote for us to postulate similar causes.[16] I have argued earlier that if there is a weakness in the argument it is here that it is to be found. The only way to deal with this point would be to start drawing the parallels or stressing the dissimilarities, and these are perhaps tasks more appropriate for the preacher and the poet than for the philosopher. The philosopher will be content to have shown that though perhaps weak, the argument has some force. How much force depends on the strength of the analogy.

Notes

1   David Hume, *Dialogues Concerning Natural Religion*, ed. H. D. Aiken (New York, 1948), p. 28.
2   I understand by a 'normal scientific explanation' one conforming to the pattern of deductive or statistical explanation utilised in paradigm empirical sciences such as physics and chemistry, elucidated in recent years by Hempel, Braithwaite, Popper and others. Although there are many uncertain points about scientific explanation, those to which I appeal in the text are accepted by all philosophers of science.
3   St Thomas Aquinas, *Summa Theologiae*, Ia, 2, 3. Translated by Timothy McDermott, O. P. (London, 1964).
4   Ibid., *loc. cit.*
5   David Hume, *An Enquiry Concerning Human Understanding*, ed L. A. Selby Bigge, 2nd edn (1902), p. 136.
6   Hume, *Dialogues Concerning Natural Religion*, ed. Aiken, p. 23.
7   For this argument see also *The Enquiry*, pp. 147f.
8   *Dialogues*, p. 33.
9   Ibid., p. 36.
10   Ibid., p. 40.
11   Ibid., p. 39.
12   Ibid., p. 40.
13   Ibid., p. 50.
14   Ibid., p. 47.
15   Ibid., p. 53.
16   See, for example, *Dialogues*, p. 18 and p. 37.

14   The Wager*

Blaise Pascal

Infinity nothingness. Our soul is thrust into the body, where it finds number, time, dimension. It ponders them and calls them nature, necessity, and can believe nothing else.

A unit added to infinity does not increase it at all, any more than a foot added to an infinite length. The finite dissolves in the presence of the infinite and becomes pure nothingness. So it is with our mind before God, with our justice before divine justice. There is not so great a disproportion between our justice and God's justice as there is between unity and infinity.

God's justice must be as vast as his mercy. But justice towards the damned is not so vast, and ought to shock less than mercy towards the elect.

We know that there is an infinite, but we do not know its nature, as we know that it is false that numbers are finite, so therefore it is true that there is an infinite number, but we do not know what it is: it is false that it is even and false that it is odd, for by adding a unit it does not change its nature; however it is a number, and all numbers are even or odd (it is true that this applies to all finite numbers).

So we can clearly understand that there is a God without knowing what he is.

Is there no substantial truth, seeing that there are so many true things which are not truth itself?

We therefore know the existence and nature of the finite, because we too are finite and have no extension.

We know the existence of the infinite, and do not know its nature, because it has extent like us, but not the same limits as us.

But we know neither the existence nor the nature of God, because he has neither extent nor limits.

But we know of his existence through faith. In glory we will know his nature.

Now I have already shown that we can certainly know the existence of something without knowing its nature.

Let us now speak according to natural lights.

If there is a God, he is infinitely beyond our comprehension, since, having neither parts nor limits, he bears no relation to ourselves. We are therefore incapable of knowing either what he is, or if he is. That being so, who will dare to undertake a resolution of this question? It cannot be us, who bear no relationship to him.

* From Blaise Pascal, *Pensées and Other Writings*, translated by Honor Levi, with an introduction and notes by Anthony Levi, World's Classics (Oxford: Oxford University Press, 1995), pp. 153–6. Translation ©1995 by Honor Levi. Reprinted by permission of Oxford University Press.

Who will then blame the Christians for being unable to provide a rational basis for their belief, they who profess a religion for which they cannot provide a rational basis? They declare that it is a folly, *stultitiam* (1 Cor. 1: 18) in laying it before the world: and then you complain that they do not prove it! If they did prove it, they would not be keeping their word. It is by the lack of proof that they do not lack sense. 'Yes, but although that excuses those who offer their religion as it is, and that takes away the blame from them of producing it without a rational basis, it does not excuse those who accept it.'

Let us therefore examine this point, and say: God is, or is not. But towards which side will we lean? Reason cannot decide anything. There is an infinite chaos separating us. At the far end of this infinite distance a game is being played and the coin will come down heads or tails. How will you wager? Reason cannot make you choose one way or the other, reason cannot make you defend either of the two choices.

So do not accuse those who have made a choice of being wrong, for you know nothing about it! 'No, but I will blame them not for having made this choice, but for having made any choice. For, though the one who chooses heads and the other one are equally wrong, they are both wrong. The right thing is not to wager at all.'

Yes, but you have to wager. It is not up to you, you are already committed. Which then will you choose? Let us see. Since you have to choose, let us see which interests you the least. You have two things to lose: the truth and the good, and two things to stake: your reason and will, your knowledge and beatitude; and your nature has two things to avoid: error and wretchedness. Your reason is not hurt more by choosing one rather than the other, since you do have to make the choice. That is one point disposed of. But your beatitude? Let us weigh up the gain and the loss by calling heads that God exists. Let us assess the two cases: if you win, you win everything; if you lose, you lose nothing. Wager that he exists then, without hesitating! 'This is wonderful. Yes, I must wager. But perhaps I am betting too much.' Let us see. Since there is an equal chance of gain and loss, if you won only two lives instead of one, you could still put on a bet. But if there were three lives to win, you would have to play (since you must necessarily play), and you would be unwise, once forced to play, not to chance your life to win three in a game where there is an equal chance of losing and winning. But there is an eternity of life and happiness. And that being so, even though there were an infinite number of chances of which only one were in your favour, you would still be right to wager one in order to win two, and you would be acting wrongly, since you are obliged to play, by refusing to stake one life against three in a game where out of an infinite number of chances there is one in your favour, if there were an infinitely happy infinity of life to be won. But here there is an infinitely happy infinity of life to be won, one chance of winning against a finite number of chances of losing, and what you are staking is finite. That removes all choice: wherever there is infinity and where there is no infinity of chances of losing againt one of winning, there is no scope for wavering, you have to chance everything. And thus, as you are forced to gamble, you have to have discarded reason if you cling on to your life, rather than risk it for the infinite prize which is just as likely to happen as the loss of nothingness.

For it is no good saying that it is uncertain if you will win, that it is certain you are taking a risk, and that the infinite distance between the CERTAINTY of what you are risking and the UNCERTAINTY of whether you win makes the finite good of what you are certainly risking equal to the uncertainty of the infinite. It does not work like that. Every gambler takes a certain risk for an uncertain gain; nevertheless he certainly risks the finite uncertainty in order to win a finite gain, without sinning against reason. There is no infinite distance between this certainty of what is being risked and the uncertainty of what might be gained: that is untrue. There is, indeed, an infinite distance between the certainty of winning and the certainty of losing. But the uncertainty of winning is proportional to the certainty of the risk, according to the chances of winning or losing. And hence, if there are as many chances on one side as on the other, the odds are even, and then the certainty of what you risk is equal to the uncertainty of winning. It is very far from being infinitely distant from it. So our argument is infinitely strong, when the finite is at stake in a game where there are equal chances of winning and losing, and the infinite is to be won.

That is conclusive, and, if human beings are capable of understanding any truth at all, this is the one.

'I confess it, I admit it, but even so . . . Is there no way of seeing underneath the cards?' 'Yes, Scripture and the rest, etc.' 'Yes, but my hands are tied and I cannot speak a word. I am being forced to wager and I am not free, they will not let me go. And I am made in such a way that I cannot believe. So what do you want me to do?' 'That is true. But at least realize that your inability to believe, since reason urges you to do so and yet you cannot, arises from your passions. So concentrate not on convincing yourself by increasing the number of proofs of God but on diminishing your passions. You want to find faith and you do not know the way? You want to cure yourself of unbelief and you ask for the remedies? Learn from those who have been bound like you, and who now wager all they have. They are people who know the road you want to follow and have been cured of the affliction of which you want to be cured. Follow the way by which they began: by behaving just as if they believed, taking holy water, having masses said, etc. That will make you believe quite naturally, and according to your animal reactions.' 'But that is what I am afraid of.' 'Why? What do you have to lose? In order to show you that this is where it leads, it is because it diminishes the passions, which are your great stumbling-blocks, etc.'

'How these words carry me away, send me into raptures,' etc. If these words please you and seem worthwhile, you should know that they are spoken by a man who knelt both before and afterwards to beg this infinite and indivisible Being, to whom he submits the whole of himself, that you should also submit yourself, for your own good and for his glory, and that strength might thereby be reconciled with this lowliness.

End of this discourse.

But what harm will come to you from taking this course? You will be faithful, honest, humble, grateful, doing good, a sincere and true friend. It is, of course, true; you will not take part in corrupt pleasure, in glory, in the pleasures of high living. But will you not have others?

I tell you that you will win thereby in this life, and that at every step you take along this path, you will see so much certainty of winning and so negligible a risk, that you will realize in the end that you have wagered on something certain and infinite, for which you have paid nothing.

―――――

15 The Recombinant DNA Debate: A Difficulty for Pascalian-Style Wagering*

Stephen P. Stich

In the argument I want to examine the particular moral judgment being defended is that there should be a total ban on recombinant DNA research. The argument begins with the observation that even in so-called low-risk recombinant DNA experiments there is at least a possibility of catastrophic consequences. We are, after all, dealing with a relatively new and unexplored technology. Thus it is at least possible that a bacterial culture whose genetic makeup has been altered in the course of a recombinant DNA experiment may exhibit completely unexpected pathogenic characteristics. Indeed, it is not impossible that we could find ourselves confronted with a killer strain of, say, *E. coli* and, worse, a strain against which humans can marshal no natural defense. Now if this is possible – if we cannot say with assurance that the probability of it happening is zero – then, the argument continues, all recombinant DNA research should be halted. For the negative utility of the imagined catastrophe is so enormous, resulting as it would in the destruction of our society and perhaps even of our species, that no work which could possibly lead to this result would be worth the risk.

The argument just sketched, which might be called the "doomsday scenario" argument, begins with a premise which no informed person would be inclined to deny. It is indeed *possible* that even a low-risk recombinant DNA experiment might lead to totally catastrophic results. No ironclad guarantee can be offered that this will not happen. And while the probability of such an unanticipated catastrophe is surely not large, there is no serious argument that the probability is zero. Still, I think the argument is a sophistry. To go from the undeniable premise that recombinant DNA research might possibly result in unthinkable catastrophe to the conclusion that such research should be banned requires a moral principle stating that *all* endeavors that might possibly result in such a catastrophe should be prohibited. Once the principle has been stated, it is hard to believe that anyone would take it at all seriously. For the principle entails that, along with recombinant DNA research, almost all scientific research and many other commonplace activities having little to do with science should be prohibited. It is, after all, at least logically possible that the next new compound synthesized in an ongoing chemical research program will turn out to be an uncontainable carcinogen many orders of magnitude more dangerous than aerosol plutonium. And, to vary the example, there is a non-zero probability that experiments in artificial pollination will produce a weed that will, a decade from now, ruin the world's food grain harvest.[1]

I cannot resist noting that the principle invoked in the doomsday scenario argument is not new. Pascal used an entirely parallel argument to show that it is in our own best interests to believe in God. For though the probability of God's existence may be very

* From *Philosophy and Public Affairs*, 7/3 (1978), pp. 189–91. © 1978 by Princeton University Press. Reprinted by permission.

low, if He none the less should happen to exist, the disutility that would accrue to the disbeliever would be catastrophic – an eternity in hell. But, as introductory philosophy students should all know, Pascal's argument only looks persuasive if we take our options to be just two: Christianity or atheism. A third possibility is belief in a jealous non-Christian God who will see to our damnation if and only if we *are* Christians. The probability of such a deity existing is again very small, but non-zero. So Pascal's argument is of no help in deciding whether or not to accept Christianity. For we may be damned if we do and damned if we don't.

I mention Pascal's difficulty because there is a direct parallel in the doomsday scenario argument against recombinant DNA research. Just as there is a non-zero probability that unforeseen consequences of recombinant DNA research will lead to disaster, so there is a non-zero probability that unforeseen consequences of *failing* to pursue the research will lead to disaster. There may, for example, come a time when, because of natural or man-induced climatic change, the capacity to alter quickly the genetic constitution of agricultural plants will be necessary to forestall catastrophic famine. And if we fail to pursue recombinant DNA research now, our lack of knowledge in the future may have consequences as dire as any foreseen in the doomsday scenario argument . . .

Note

1   Unfortunately, the doomsday scenario argument is *not* a straw man conjured only by those who would refute it. Consider, for example, the remarks of Anthony Mazzocchi, spokesman for the Oil, Chemical and Atomic Workers International Union, reported in *Science News*, March 19, 1977, p. 181: "When scientists argue over safe or unsafe, we ought to be very prudent. . . . If critics are correct and the Andromeda scenario has *even the smallest possibility* of occurring, we must assume it will occur on the basis of our experience" (emphasis added).

---

16   A Central Theistic Argument*

George Schlesinger

Introduction

Pascal's wager is as a rule more easily appreciated than any other argument in support of religious belief. After all, the locution (which represents the essential structure of the wager), "I have nothing to lose and everything to gain by doing such and such," is a common one and readily understood by everybody.

At the same time the wager has been the target of a number of objections. I propose here to deal with three of these; two are widely known, whereas the third is of very recent origin. Finally, I also point out that the gravest objection to the wager requires a reply

* From Jeff Jordan (ed.), *Gambling on God: Essays on Pascal's Wager* (Lanham, MD: Rowman & Littlefield, 1994), pp. 83–99. Reprinted with permission.

that is based on an argument indispensable in the context of nearly all other theistic proofs. Hence, that argument (of which three different versions are considered in Sections 6 and 7) may well be regarded as the most central theistic argument.

The first objection has no great logical force but carries considerable psychological weight. It is unique insofar that it contends not so much that the wager violates the rules of sound thinking and is therefore invalid but rather that it is repugnant, and in a religious context, it is especially unseemly. The second objection contends that even if the argument were logically impeccable it would lead nowhere. The last one, surprisingly enough, claims that it is overly effective, so much so that it should not at all matter what an individual does or fails to do, because he or she is by virtue of the wager in a maximally advantageous position anyway with regard to eternal salvation.

The Wager and Greed

It is common knowledge that many well-intentioned individuals reject the wager for reasons that do not require much philosophical sophistication. They find it mercenary. They believe it appeals to the scheming, calculating self and are thus repelled by it. Without delving deep into theological issues, it has seemed to many that applying betting rules, relevant to moneymaking ventures, to a supposedly infinitely more exalted subject to lure skeptics by appealing to their grasping instincts offends religious proprieties.

People have found absurd the very notion that there may be any comparison between the seeker of a transcendent goal in life and a patron of a gambling house. We need not assume that greed as such is held generally in our highly acquisitive society in intense contempt. In the present context, however, it appears to offend the very spirit of what one is supposed to pursue. The essence of religion is generally perceived as the conviction that all profane, self-seeking ambitions are incompatible with the quest for piety. The religious seeker is not one to be mired in self indulgent pursuits but passionately devotes oneself to much nobler and more ultimate concerns.

Now of course Pascal was quite explicit in saying that the skeptic's wagering on God is no more than a first step, and those who take no further steps will have achieved nothing. However, his advice to the wagerer is to start behaving as one would if one actually believed, because Pascal believed that such conduct is likely to lead to a truly dedicated life in the service of God. By starting to observe the rituals of religion, associating with pious persons, and studying the sacred literature, individuals are likely to transform their sentiments and feelings and eventually acquire genuine belief.

Yet Pascal's reply has failed to satisfy many of his critics. If grasping is incompatible with the spirit of religion, then it is not to be used as a vehicle with which to reach any destination. Noble ends are debased when pursued by ignoble means.

Pascal's supporters at this stage are usually inclined to offer distinctions between means that do not and means that do justify their end. I believe a more important point should be made: we are free to assume that no objective is ever hallowed enough that it should be impermissible to reach it by anything but impeccable means.

First, a relatively simple point about the offensiveness of greed. Suppose there is a person of an extraordinarily high income who gives away almost all his money to charity, retaining only what is necessary for bare existence. Furthermore, this individual does not seek the gratitude of the beneficiaries of these donations nor the admiration of the community. In fact, this person always makes every possible effort to ensure that no one should be aware of these humanitarian activities. Despite all this, it is conceivable that he could be charged with selfishness and greed: he is surely aware of his almost unparalleled, heroic, moral accomplishments. Evidently therefore he is a highly greedy individual; what he apparently craves is not material possessions nor the prestige accorded for outstanding philanthropy but the ability to relish the knowledge that he has outdone practically everyone in his contempt for stinginess, in his indifference for fame and praise, and the ability to enjoy the deep satisfaction of having been able to reach the pinnacle of otherdirectedness and the heights of noble magnanimity free of the slightest taint of petty self-regard.

Clearly, if we were to take this line, then we would be forced to conclude that every act which fulfills some wish is greedy and selfish and no freely willed act would ever be free of sin. Thus, the sensible thing to say is that the pursuit of a quest is deplorable when it brings harm either to others or to oneself in the sense that it debases the questing individual (which Pascal calls "poisonous pleasures") who could instead strive for more refined, higher order, life-enhancing pleasures.

Now the pleasure that Pascal holds up before his "calculating clients" is of the most exalted kind, one that is simply inaccessible to an individual who has not spent life passionately serving the Master of the Universe and thereby developing and perfecting one's soul, without which one lacks the capacity to partake in the transmundane bliss available to the select few. Only the suitably groomed soul, when released from its earthly fetters, will bask in the radiance of the Divine presence and delight in the adoring communion with a loving God. If craving for such an end is a manifestation of greed, then it is the manifestation of a noble greed that is to be acclaimed. Therefore, only if one were to assume that the ultimate reward of the righteous is the satisfaction of some cruder yearnings could one charge a follower of Pascal with trying to enkindle our unseemly mercenary motives.

Practice and Belief

However, a more important point needs to be made as well. The essence of true religion is not the intellectual assent to a set of propositions nor is it the verbal profession of certain beliefs. It is a full commitment and devotion, having one's heart and soul virtually consumed by a deep reverence and love of God. Maimonides wrote:

> What is the proper love of God? It is the love of the Lord with a great and very strong love so that one's soul shall be tied to the love of the Lord, and one should be continually enraptured by it, like a lovesick individual. . . .[1]

The immediate question one is bound to ask is, how does one achieve such a state of mind? Belief might be obtained through compelling arguments, or credible evidence, but surely exaltation or love is not an epistemic universal and cannot be planted into one's heart by the methodological rules of knowledge acquisition.

A very brief answer has been hinted at by the sagacious Hillel, who, as the famous story goes, was approached by someone demanding to be taught the whole Law while standing on one foot. Hillel agreed and informed the man that the single sentence, "Whatever is hateful to you do not do it to your fellow-human," contains the essence of all there is to be learned.[2] Hillel's fascinating precis of the Law raises many problems. One of them is in Leviticus 19:18: it says, "You all love your fellow-human as yourself."

Why did he believe it necessary to change the wording of the Scriptures? This particular question may have a simple answer, namely, Hillel realized that one cannot be commanded to have certain sentiments; I could be ordered to act or to refrain from acting in a certain way but not to love someone I happen to dislike. Thus, to reach the stage that the Scripture prescribes where one actually loves other human beings, we have to begin with the kind of behavior that is always associated with such a sentiment, that is, our practical conduct toward our fellow humans should be like that toward our own self: never actually do anything injurious to their interests. Desirable behavior is assumed to generate eventually desirable feelings.

Hillel's insight should be applied in the context of one's relation to God as well. The twelfth-century poet-philosopher Judah Halevi was quite explicit on this point, "Man can reach God only by doing His commands" (*Cuzari*, 2.46). Good thoughts, on their own, are too fleeting and insubstantial, and physical acts are concrete; when one has trained oneself to act in accordance with the dictates of religion and actual behavior closely resembles the behavior of those who possess truly deep religious sentiments, then one has provided oneself with the proper grounds on which fervent love for the Divine may grow. The theory behind this view may be compared with what today is called " behavior modification." This kind of therapy is based on the belief that it is possible to induce feelings of aversion to what is harmful and a natural desire for what is beneficial through adopting certain patterns of behavior. On the more extreme version of this view (as held by Halevy), it is not merely possible but essential to begin one's journey toward authentic theism by looking on the practices mandated by religion as the proper first step toward genuine piety. On this view, the wagerer who starts out satisfying the demands of faith before having acquired actual belief is not merely doing what is calculating and mercenary nor even that which is merely commendable but is engaged in what is absolutely indispensable for reaching the noble objective that is sought.

Are There Infinitely Many Equally Viable Hypotheses?

The second, oft-repeated objection is a relatively powerful, clearly articulated objection, known as the "many-gods objection." Pascal has been charged with making the unwarranted assumption that the problem facing the agnostic is confined to the question of which of two options to choose. In reality, however, in addition to the God of the theist, there are any number of other possible ones as well. How is the wagerer to assess the relative benefits associated with betting on Osiris, Baal, Dagon, Zeus, or Blodenwedd? Pascal provides no argument to guide us to the right deity, worshiping whom one is most likely to secure oneself eternal salvation.

Before attempting to advance any reply, I should point out that though the objection is, as already mentioned, a serious one, we find in the literature several versions, depicting a far more threatening portrayal of the difficulty than it is in reality. Richard Gale, for example, sees the following devastating consequences of the many-gods objection:

> . . . from the fact that it is logically possible that God exists it does not follow that the product of the probability of his existence and an infinite number is infinite. In a fair lottery with a denumerable infinity of tickets, for each ticket it is true that it is logically possible that it will win, but the probability of its doing so is infinitesimal and the product of an infinitesimal and an infinite number is itself infinitesimal. Thus the expected gain of buying a ticket

is not infinite but infinitesimal. There is at least a denumerable infinity of logically possible deities . . . and thus betting on any one of them the expected gain is zero according to this argument.[3]

The opponents of the wager have had the tendency to magnify the gravity of the problem by overcalculating the number of alternatives available for the religious seeker and hence depicting Pascal's counsel as quite hopelessly arbitrary. For example, J. L. Mackie, who lists a number of possible deities that seem to have escaped Pascal's notice, also mentions,

> . . . that there might be a god who looked with more favor on honest doubters or atheists who, in Hume's words, proportioned their belief to the evidence, than on mercenary manipulators of their own understanding. Indeed, this would follow from the ascription to God of moral goodness in any sense we can understand.[4]

Also fairly often heard is the argument that among the infinitely many possible deities, we must not overlook one who grants eternal reward to those who firmly deny the existence of a theistic God and punishes all those who believe in him.

Richard Gale goes even further, suggesting that

> there is the logically possible deity who rewards with infinite felicity all and only those who believe in him and step on only one sidewalk crack in the course of their life, as well as the two-crack deity, the three-crack deity, and so on ad infinitum.[5]

There are several lines one may adopt to meet this kind of objection. One may be based on the realization that Pascal is addressing individuals who, though they may be hardened in their disbelief, do have a notion of what genuine religion is about. In other words, though they deny its truth, they acknowledge its meaningfulness and understand that it is based on a highly optimistic view of human potential and of the sublime possible level of existence it postulates. It is a necessary presupposition of the wager that one understands that the notion of "genuine religion" is conceptually associated with a number of other exalted notions, and those people whom Pascal addresses are to be assumed to have a basic grasp of the sublime concerns of its devout practitioners. Divine worship in an authentic sense (as distinct from a pagan sense, where one is trying to propitiate the supernatural powers on whose whims one's fate depends) is in no way to be likened to a commercial transaction. Whatever the probability of the existence of an afterlife worth seeking with all one's might is, it is certainly not to be viewed as a place to which one may be admitted after one has paid the amount demanded by its Divine Proprietor. "The service of God is not intended for God's perfection; it is intended for our own perfection," says Maimonides. On this view, an individual who has devoted his or her life to Divine service has nurtured and refined his or her soul, rendering it capable of receiving and finding felicity in the celestial radiance available for those prepared to absorb it. In brief, the wagerer is supposed to appreciate that in the context of theism, highly involved systems of theologies have been developed over the centuries, theologies that have an internal coherence and consist of many propositions with an appeal to the intellect as well as to the nobler, human sentiments.

Nothing of this sort exists in the context of, say, the sidewalk deity. It is difficult to conceive a reason why one should come to love such a being or why one should desire to be in its proximity. Of course, one might claim that without any rhyme or reason it capriciously rewards those who obey its arbitrary demands. Still, a Pascalian would insist that because a good portion of theistic belief is in harmony with natural, noble aspirations and is embedded in highly developed theology, it has to be ascribed a considerably higher probability than those with little appeal to the human mind and heart.

Thus, we are permitted to assert the following: if we were to agree that different deities have different probabilities, then even if there are infinitely many candidates for the office of the Master of the Universe, it does not follow that each has zero probability. One may, if one wants to, ascribe a finite value to the probability of the existence of each one of them and yet obtain a sum total of all these (which is the value of the probability of the infinite disjunction of "Zeus exists OR Baal exists OR etc."), an amount that does not exceed one. This should be the case if the various finite probabilities are members of a convergent series, for instance, the sum of the series $\frac{1}{2} + \frac{1}{4} + \frac{1}{8} + \ldots$ never actually reaches one. This should be sufficient to lay to rest Gale's fear that if "there is at least a denumerable infinity of logically possible deities . . . [then] betting on any one of them the expected gain is zero."

The Criterion for Betting When the Expected Utilities are Infinite

I submit a crucial point, one that is contrary to what numerous philosophers hold, namely, that when each possible outcome carries an infinite expected value, it is rational to bet on the outcome most probable to occur. Are there solid grounds for my hypothesis? Let me first point out that grounds are provided for this view by common sense (which in itself would not be sufficient to establish my point). Anyone wishing to verify this experimentally may consider the following two cases, A and B:

> A = Of the billions of people alive at the present moment, one and only one is going to enjoy eternal salvation, whereas the rest vanish into nothingness after completing their lives upon this earth. A truly randomizing device is going to determine the identity of the single lucky individual.

> B = Of the billions of people alive at the present moment, one and only one is going to vanish into nothingness after completing one's existence upon this planet; the rest are going to enjoy eternal salvation. A truly randomizing device is going to determine the identity of the one unlucky individual.

Now, without offering preliminary explanations, ask any number of individuals (and you may include among them some mathematicians) which case they would prefer to obtain? If my experience is reliable to any degree, rarely if ever does anybody argue: although if B is true then I am a billion times more likely to be among the blessed, this is quite irrelevant; the expected utilities are equal and therefore it makes no difference which is true.

Now let us look at a truly compelling argument. In cases where the mathematical expectations are infinite, the criterion for choosing the outcome to bet on is its probability. In all betting situations the sum I am charged to participate I am charged with certainty, whereas the prize I may receive is uncertain. Fairness demands that I be compensated through being charged less than the value of the prize and proportionately so, that is, the lower the probability of winning, the less I should be charged. Thus, it is obvious that the same set of rules cannot apply in case the prize is infinite, as in other cases. Justice cannot demand that the cost for being permitted to bet should equal the expected utilities, because then the fair cost should be infinite. But that is absurd: why should I definitely pay an infinite amount for a less than certain chance of winning back the same amount? It is evident therefore that the situation demands that a different principle must be guiding a wagerer faced with the problem of which of the various outcomes – each associated with infinite utilities – to choose. Because neither expected utilities nor the magnitude of the prize can serve as one's criterion, by elimination it should be reasonable to be guided by the value of the probability: wager on the outcome that is most likely to materialize.

Deities with Different Degrees of Plausibility

Let us consider a number of possible solutions to the many-gods problem. First, it is reasonable that a scrupulously just deity who ensures that each person's celestial reward is in direct proportion to the amount of energy and time invested throughout one's earthly life to the refinement of one's soul so as to increase its susceptibility to that reward, is considerably more probable than a fancy-bred capricious power whose awards are not in any obvious way related to earning, meriting, or the enhanced quality of the receptivity or atonement of the worshipper. Thus, we regard it at least fairly plausible that a deity may exist who does not hand out compensation or reimbursement for the trouble his adherents have gone through in serving him but who is so exalted that it seems reasonable to assume that the highest form of felicity is to center one's life around him. The most important task is to do everything in one's power to adjust and attune one's soul so that it has the capacity of fully resonating with the celestial radiance in which it will be submerged. A mere century or two ago theists did not recoil from using such locutions and were unembarrassed by what today may strike some as inflated grandiloquence. Thus we find the eighteenth-century poet and theologian M. H. Luzatto making (in his widely studied *Mesilat Yesharim*) the brief statement, because he regarded the matter too obvious to require elaboration, "Man came into the world only to achieve nearness to God." Surely such a view is bound to permeate every act and every thought of its adherent; it is part of an inclusive outlook on life and belongs to an extensive system of interconnected propositions.

Furthermore, in the context of the sublime god of the theist, many found it not unreasonable to view life's many trials and tribulations as instruments of soul-making or in any case as means to an end that may surpass our understanding. On the other hand, when referring to deities devoid of the various glorious Divine attributes, it seems more natural to speak like Gloucester: "As flies to wanton boys, are we to the gods/ They kill us for their sport."

Thus, the hypothesis is that "a God of faithfulness and without iniquity [one who is] just and right . . ." (Deuteronomy 31:4), who therefore can be a source of emulation and inspiration and whose attributes altogether resonate with our nobler sentiments, makes a great deal of sense and it is therefore reasonable to ascribe a higher probability to his existence than to an unprincipled, arbitrarily acting, wanton god. And if this is conceded, then it should also seem sensible to hold that the greater those sublime properties, the greater the likelihood the one exemplifying them exists. Hence, the being greater than which is inconceivable, who possesses them to a maximum degree, is to be regarded more probable than any other deity.

Simplicity

The Cambridge statistician H. Jeffreys has shown in the 1920s that whenever we have a finite set of experimental results there are indefinitely many hypotheses that satisfy each result. The only way to select the hypothesis to be adopted is by following the principle of simplicity: of all the equally well-confirmed hypotheses, select the one that is simpler than all the others. It is crucial to realize that Jeffreys does not refer to the simplicity of structure of the systems involved or the simplicity of use and so on; he refers solely to descriptive simplicity and says that among the various expressions that represent the law, we are to adopt the one consisting of the minimal number of terms. It is also worth noting that Jeffreys' is not a prescriptive but a descriptive principle: scientists have followed it for hundreds of years without explicitly being aware of it, simply because it has never been articulated before that of the indefinitely many alternative hypotheses present in all cases.

Many people willingly concede that the rules of rational reasoning are invariant with subject matter. Consequently, after Pascal has convinced us that we should wager on some supernatural power, we are confronted with the problem of which of the many possible such powers to adopt. In the absence of any facts to assist us, it stands to reason that we should have to use Jeffreys' principle. It is fairly easy to see that the theistic hypothesis is the simplest in the sense specified by Jeffreys.

It is the simplest because it is the only hypothesis that may be expressed with the use of a single predicate: to describe the God of the theist all that is needed is that he is an absolutely perfect being. By contrast, a statement positing the existence of any deity less than absolutely perfect will be relatively complex. For example, though there is a large body of ancient Greek literature concerning Zeus, there are still many aspects of Zeus's character that remain unknown to us. We know for instance that he was sometimes asleep, but we have no idea how many hours of sleep he needed and what effect sleeplessness had on him. We also know that he ate and drank, but not how much or whether he occasionally overgorged himself or how long he could go without any food at all, and so on.

The Principle of Sufficient Reason

Finally, I should advance an argument based on the principle of sufficient reason why the wagerer should go for the being greater than which is not conceivable. Before doing so, I believe it is necessary to defend the principle because many contemporary philosophers deny its validity. J. L. Mackie was speaking for a large number of adherents of empiricism when he said, "There is no sufficient reason to regard the principle of sufficient reason to be valid."[6] Levelheaded empiricists are not supposed to subscribe to *a priori* principles. For this reason, the majority of contemporary writers strongly object to ascribing equal probabilities on the basis of the principle of indifference, which is no more than a variation on the principle of sufficient reason (PSR).

It seems to me that these objections are based on a serious misconception. They are mostly based on the refusal to acknowledge that "experience is mute" and that it is necessary to assume some unconfirmed principles before we are able to surmise what it tells us. As a matter of fact, no empirically confirmed statement can be found anywhere that did not rely on the PSR. The following illustrate the wide range of its application.

1.   It is universally held that there is, for instance, overwhelming inductive evidence that the melting point of gold is 1,064 degrees Celsius. It is common knowledge, however, that it is illegitimate to argue inductively from biased sample classes. Thus, the question arises why do physicists feel entitled to maintain that 1,064 degrees Celsius is likely to remain the melting point of gold when all their evidence is based on a biased sample class: all the samples of gold hitherto melted occurred in a universe in which the density of matter (which keeps decreasing) was higher, the scaling factor (which is constantly increasing) was lower, and the velocity of the universe's expansion (which according to some cosmologists keeps decreasing all the time) was higher than at this crucial moment.

The answer is not that we have no grounds on which to assume that these changes are relevant to the melting point of any metal. In the past, serious biases turned out to be factors we never suspected before of having relevance: all swans were thought to be white, and the fact that the sample class on which this conclusion was based included only non-Australian swans had not occurred to anyone to be of concern. The presumed law that matter cannot be destroyed was based on the failure of every conceivable attempt to do so; you may break, grind, melt, boil and evaporate, or burn to ashes any lump of matter without succeeding to alter the amount in which it continues to exist. The fact that no relevant observations have been made under exceedingly large pressures and temperatures, the kind of which prevail at the center of the sun where matter does diminish through part of it transforming into energy, did not seem to constitute a source of worry. Indeed, at the pre-twentieth century knowledge of what processes take place on the sub-atomic level, there was no reason why one should suspect that pressure and temperature had relevance to the issue of the conservation of matter. Similarly, our knowledge of physics may be still too deficient for us to be able to see why the scaling factor of the universe should influence the melting point of anything.

The correct answer has to be that we are aware of the possibility of having arrived at our conclusion through the use of a biased sample class, and consequently there are two lines of action available to us. One is to make no predictions at all. This, of course, would imply the complete paralysis of the scientific enterprise, which we should want to resist if at all possible. The alternative is to make use of the principle of sufficient reason. In the particular context of the melting point of gold, we then proceed in the following manner: in the past the melting point of gold has always been observed to be 1,064 degrees Celsius. In the future it may be different. However, there is no good reason to believe that the melting point will be higher than it will be lower or vice versa. Thus, as long as not proven otherwise, we make the unique prediction that it will be neither higher nor lower but will continue to remain the same as in the past.

2.   It was mentioned before that whenever we have a finite set of experimental results there are indefinitely many hypotheses that satisfy each result and that the accepted practice is to select the hypothesis to be adopted by following the principle of simplicity: of all the equally well-confirmed hypotheses, select the one that is simpler than all the others. What justification is there for this rule? One is the PSR. Should we suggest that some alternative hypothesis be adopted it will immediately be asked: what reason is there to make this particular choice? Why not select a simpler or a more complicated hypothesis? However, the simplest hypothesis has an edge over all others. It is unique. It is the only one in connection with which it is not possible to ask why not choose a simpler hypoth-

esis. We thus justify our selection on the basis of the chosen hypothesis having a significant feature no other hypothesis has. The most complex hypothesis would also have such
a feature except that it does not exist (just as the largest integer does not exist).

3. A strong illustration of how compelling the PSR is is the fact that even mathematicians have found it useful as a principle of plausible reasoning. L. C. Larson in his
highly influential book poses the problem: of all the rectangles which can be inscribed in
a given circle, which has greatest area? Larson suggests,

> The principle of insufficient reason leads us to suspect that the rectangle of maximum area
> that can be inscribed in a circle is a square.

He then goes on to give a rigorous proof of his conjecture without regarding it as
necessary to elaborate how precisely the principle led him to it. It is reasonable to assume
that what Larson had in mind was that if it were suggested that the sought-after rectangle was one with length x and width $x + n$ then of course the rectangle with length
$x + n$ and width x must also have the maximum area. And if there are indeed two rectangles with maximum area, then, of course, there are infinitely many couples that might
possibly be the ones we are after. There is, however, one rectangle that is unique in the
sense that it has no counterpart: the rectangle with equal length and width. It "stands to
reason" that this is the privileged figure we are after.

4. Some 2,400 years ago Democritus argued,

> that there are infinite worlds, hypothesizing that the void is infinite; for why would this part
> of the void be filled by a world, but that part not? So, if there is a world in one part of the
> void, then also in all the void. So, since the void is infinite, the worlds will be infinite too.

Democritus's hypothesis would warrant detailed study; here I can point out only first of
all that his "worlds," unlike what we mean when referring to various possible worlds, are
not necessarily causally separated from one another and also that he thought of the actual
world as having tiny size as compared with what we believe it to be. Yet his hypothesis
may be said to have survived to this very day in the form of the far-reaching cosmological principle. It asserts that the universe is the same (i.e., the distribution of galaxies,
stars, and planets) everywhere in space (apart from irregularities of a local nature), or that
the universe is homogeneous.

The reasoning behind Democritus's hypothesis is once more based on the PSR.
Suppose it were suggested that there exist some finite number n worlds. We would be at
loss to offer a reason why it was not a number less or greater than n. However, if n is
infinite then a unique reason can be given why it is not larger than n.

This last example is of special significance as it shows that the PSR, which is customarily
associated with the name of Leibniz, who indeed applied it to numerous issues, was
known and made use of two thousand years before him. It provides therefore further
evidence of the universal appeal of the PSR and its central role in all our conceptual
schemes.

Suppose someone subscribed to a religion that was based on the belief that the deity
governing the universe was very benevolent but not absolutely so, possessing merely 95
percent of full benevolence. (It is not important for our purposes to describe how we
compute the numerical degree of benevolence.) We might then ask an adherent of this

religion: why not ascribe to your deity 96 percent or 94 percent benevolence? No reasonable answer seems available. On the other hand, the theist, when faced with a similar inquiry, might appeal to the PSR. If one settles for any number, like 95 percent, no sufficient reason seems to be available: why not have more or why not have less. However, a reason may be offered for 100 percent benevolence: it is of a unique magnitude, as it is impossible to have more. Suppose someone were to ask: but by the same principle you might as well ascribe 0 percent benevolence and explain your doing so by saying that having less than it is impossible? To this, as mentioned before, the theist reply would be that such a being is not a fit deity to worship, and thus one is to ascribe considerably lower probability to its existence.

Why Wager At All?

We are now in the position to reply to an ingenious objection raised by Antony Duff. Duff points out that the wager works regardless how small the probability, as long as its value is not zero, and that one is going to be the recipient of infinite salvation. If so, he argues, it is quite superfluous that I should follow Pascal's advice and begin acting religiously and make every effort to acquire faith, because,

> . . . suppose I take no steps to make it more likely that I will come to believe in God. There must be some probability, however small, that I will nonetheless come to believe in Him . . . and that probability is enough to generate an infinite expected value for my actions.[7]

Now we have at least two answers to Duff's objection. The briefer answer is to recall the idea advanced previously that it is untenable to maintain that because of the infinitude of the reward it makes no difference how probable is its acquisition. We are instead to assume that it is important to try and increase the probability of obtaining the prospective prize.

The second answer would be based on the principle that a rational wagerer will always want to bet on the outcome associated with the highest expected utilities. But is it possible to gain anything more than infinite salvation? The answer is, in an appropriate sense, yes! An infinitely long string, for example, may be increased in width, or in mass per unit length, and so on. Similarly, eternal life, which of course is infinitely long and cannot be increased in length, may vary in the degree of its depth, intensity, exquisiteness, and so on, during every moment for the eternal duration of that felicitous state. Once we are prepared to entertain the possibility of an afterlife, we are likely to find it reasonable to go along with the traditional view that the magnificence of posthumous reward varies directly with the quality and the portion of the time at one's disposal as well as the magnitude of the exertion invested in acts of piety.

It should also be recalled that as soon as an individual embarks on the road that offers the best chance to lead to the acquisition of genuine religious faith, one is already set on the path of the righteous and is already engaged in the service of God. Clearly, therefore, one who acts upon Pascal's call at once, rather than waiting for the not entirely improbable inspiration to light unassisted upon him at some later time, places oneself in a far more favorable position with respect to the amount of time spent on the purification of one's soul. Thus, even if we conceded that in the context of eternal salvation the value or probability plays no role, the individual following Duff's advice would engage in a conduct associated with a prize of lower quality and thus with lower expected utilities.

A Common Feature to Almost All Theistic Argument

One of the most commonly cited theistic proofs is the Argument from Design. It is based on the wonders of nature we see around us that are unlikely to be, or perhaps unthinkable that they should be, the results of blind forces. Now even if we regard the argument absolutely compelling, it establishes at most – as was pointed out by Hume – that there exists a creator who is many hundreds times more powerful and intelligent than ourselves. But such a creator's power and intelligence may still fall infinitely short of Omnipotence and Omniscience. About benevolence the argument says even less, and the same goes for Omnipresence or Immutability.

Another famous argument is the Cosmological Argument. It shares all the weaknesses just mentioned in connection with the Argument from Design. Indeed, it should be obvious that all other arguments in support of theism (with the exception of the Ontological Argument, of which only a few would claim to have achieved full clarity) face the many gods objection.

Thus, an individual making use of any of numerous known arguments for the existence of God can get no further than to conclude that there exists some supernatural power and intelligence behind the material universe. That individual is thus facing the need to choose among the various candidates who may fulfill this function.

It seems reasonable to conjecture that whatever is deemed the best justification for the theist's choice in one context is also likely to be so in other contexts as well. Therefore, the most acceptable reply to the many-gods objection may well be regarded as an argument of wide application and thus of central importance in the context of theistic arguments in general.

One of the striking features of Pascal's wager is surely the fact that the most often cited stumbling block it runs into has been the many-gods objection, whereas in the context of theistic arguments, I venture to suggest that this may be read as an indication of the unique strength of the wager. The reason why the many-gods objection has been raised less frequently in the context of the wager was because skeptics felt able to clip the wings of a putative argument at the very initial stages, before it could get off the ground and thus prevent even the conclusion that some supernatural being is to be assumed.

Thus, the Argument from Design is nipped in the bud by insisting that the universe does not exhibit any signs of design; the Cosmological Argument has been cut short because of its alleged, unwarranted, basic assumption that there can be no uncaused contingent particulars. On the other hand, it seems that no serious defect could be discovered in Pascal's wager before it reached the relatively advanced stage of establishing the reasonableness of assuming the existence of some transmundane force.

Notes

1 *Mishneh Torah*, Hilkhot Teshuvah, x.
2 *Shabbat*, 31b.
3 *On the Nature and Existence of God* (Cambridge, 1991), p. 350.
4 *The Miracle of Theism* (Oxford, 1982), p. 203.
5 Gale, op. cit., p. 350.
6 "Three Steps Toward Absolutism," *Space, Time and Causality*, ed. R. Swinburne (Dordrecht, 1981), p. 6.
7 "Pascal's Wager and Infinite Utilities," *Analysis* 46 (1986): 107.

17   Evil and Omnipotence*

J. L. Mackie

The traditional arguments for the existence of God have been fairly thoroughly criticised by philosophers. But the theologian can, if he wishes, accept this criticism. He can admit that no rational proof of God's existence is possible. And he can still retain all that is essential to his position, by holding that God's existence is known in some other, non-rational way. I think, however, that a more telling criticism can be made by way of the traditional problem of evil. Here it can be shown, not that religious beliefs lack rational support, but that they are positively irrational, that the several parts of the essential theological doctrine are inconsistent with one another, so that the theologian can maintain his position as a whole only by a much more extreme rejection of reason than in the former case. He must now be prepared to believe, not merely what cannot be proved, but what can be *disproved* from other beliefs that he also holds.

The problem of evil, in the sense in which I shall be using the phrase, is a problem only for someone who believes that there is a God who is both omnipotent and wholly good. And it is a logical problem, the problem of clarifying and reconciling a number of beliefs: it is not a scientific problem that might be solved by further observations, or a practical problem that might be solved by a decision or an action. These points are obvious; I mention them only because they are sometimes ignored by theologians, who sometimes parry a statement of the problem with such remarks as "Well, can you solve the problem yourself?" or "This is a mystery which may be revealed to us later" or "Evil is something to be faced and overcome, not to be merely discussed".

In its simplest form the problem is this: God is omnipotent; God is wholly good; and yet evil exists. These seems to be some contradiction between these three propositions, so that if any two of them were true the third would be false. But at the same time all three are essential parts of most theological positions: the theologian, it seems, at once *must* adhere and *cannot consistently* adhere to all three. (The problem does not arise only for theists, but I shall discuss it in the form in which it presents itself for ordinary theism.)

However, the contradiction does not arise immediately; to show it we need some additional premises, or perhaps some quasi-logical rules connecting the terms 'good', 'evil', and 'omnipotent'. These additional principles are that good is opposed to evil, in such a way that a good thing always eliminates evil as far as it can, and that there are no limits to what an omnipotent thing can do. From these it follows that a good omnipotent thing eliminates evil completely, and then the propositions that a good omnipotent thing exists, and that evil exists, are incompatible.

A. Adequate Solutions

Now once the problem is fully stated it is clear that it can be solved, in the sense that the problem will not arise if one gives up at least one of the propositions that constitute it.

* From *Mind*, NS 64 (April 1955), pp. 200–12. Reprinted by permission of Oxford University Press.

If you are prepared to say that God is not wholly good, or not quite omnipotent, or that evil does not exist, or that good is not opposed to the kind of evil that exists, or that there are limits to what an omnipotent thing can do, then the problem of evil will not arise for you.

There are, then, quite a number of adequate solutions of the problem of evil, and some of these have been adopted, or almost adopted, by various thinkers. For example, a few have been prepared to deny God's omnipotence, and rather more have been prepared to keep the term 'omnipotence' but severely to restrict its meaning, recording quite a number of things that an omnipotent being cannot do. Some have said that evil is an illusion, perhaps because they held that the whole world of temporal, changing things is an illusion, and that what we call evil belongs only to this world, or perhaps because they held that although temporal things *are* much as we see them, those that we call evil are not really evil. Some have said that what we call evil is merely the privation of good, that evil in a positive sense, evil that would really be opposed to good, does not exist. Many have agreed with Pope that disorder is harmony not understood, and that partial evil is universal good. Whether any of these views is *true* is, of course, another question. But each of them gives an adequate solution of the problem of evil in the sense that if you accept it this problem does not arise for you, though you may, of course, have *other* problems to face.

But often enough these adequate solutions are only *almost* adopted. The thinkers who restrict God's power, but keep the term 'omnipotence', may reasonably be suspected of thinking, in other contexts, that his power is really unlimited. Those who say that evil is an illusion may also be thinking, inconsistently, that this illusion is itself an evil. Those who say that "evil" is merely privation of good may also be thinking, inconsistently, that privation of good is an evil. (The fallacy here is akin to some forms of the "naturalistic fallacy" in ethics, where some think, for example, that "good" is just what contributes to evolutionary progress, and that evolutionary progress is itself good.) If Pope meant what he said in the first line of his couplet, that "disorder" is only harmony not understood, the "partial evil" of the second line must, for consistency, mean "that which, taken in isolation, falsely appears to be evil", but it would more naturally mean "that which, in isolation, really is evil". The second line, in fact, hesitates between two views, that "partial evil" isn't really evil, since only the universal quality is real, and that "partial evil" is really an evil, but only a little one.

In addition, therefore, to adequate solutions, we must recognise unsatisfactory inconsistent solutions, in which there is only a half-hearted or temporary rejection of one of the propositions which together constitute the problem. In these, one of the constituent propositions is explicitly rejected, but it is covertly re-asserted or assumed elsewhere in the system.

B. Fallacious Solutions

Besides these half-hearted solutions, which explicitly reject but implicitly assert one of the constituent propositions, there are definitely fallacious solutions which explicitly maintain all the constituent propositions, but implicitly reject at least one of them in the course of the argument that explains away the problem of evil.

There are, in fact, many so-called solutions which purport to remove the contradiction without abandoning any of its constituent propositions. These must be fallacious, as we can see from the very statement of the problem, but it is not so easy to see in each case precisely where the fallacy lies. I suggest that in all cases the fallacy has the general form suggested above: in order to solve the problem one (or perhaps more) of its constituent propositions is given up, but in such a way that it appears to have been retained, and can therefore be asserted without qualification in other contexts. Sometimes there is a further complication: the supposed solution moves to and fro between, say, two of the constituent propositions, at one point asserting the first of these but covertly abandoning the second, at another point asserting the second but covertly abandoning the first. These fallacious solutions often turn upon some equivocation with the words 'good' and 'evil', or upon some vagueness about the way in which good and evil are opposed to one another, or about how much is meant by 'omnipotence'. I propose to examine some of these so-called solutions, and to exhibit their fallacies in detail. Incidentally, I shall also be considering whether an adequate solution could be reached by a minor modification of one or more of the constituent propositions, which would, however, still satisfy all the essential requirements of ordinary theism.

1. *"Good cannot exist without evil" or "Evil is necessary as a counterpart to good."*

It is sometimes suggested that evil is necessary as a counterpart to good, that if there were no evil there could be no good either, and that this solves the problem of evil. It is true that it points to an answer to the question "Why should there be evil?" But it does so only by qualifying some of the propositions that constitute the problem.

First, it sets a limit to what God can do, saying that God *cannot* create good without simultaneously creating evil, and this means either that God is not omnipotent or that there are *some* limits to what an omnipotent thing can do. It may be replied that these limits are always presupposed, that omnipotence has never meant the power to do what is logically impossible, and on the present view the existence of good without evil would be a logical impossibility. This interpretation of omnipotence may, indeed, be accepted as a modification of our original account which does not reject anything that is essential to theism, and I shall in general assume it in the subsequent discussion. It is, perhaps, the most common theistic view, but I think that some theists at least have maintained that God can do what is logically impossible. Many theists, at any rate, have held that logic itself is created or laid down by God, that logic is the way in which God arbitrarily chooses to think. (This is, of course, parallel to the ethical view that morally right actions are those which God arbitrarily chooses to command, and the two views encounter similar difficulties.) And *this* account of logic is clearly inconsistent with the view that God is bound by logical necessities – unless it is possible for an omnipotent being to bind himself, an issue which we shall consider later, when we come to the Paradox of Omnipotence. This solution of the problem of evil cannot, therefore, be consistently adopted along with the view that logic is itself created by God.

But, secondly, this solution denies that evil is opposed to good in our original sense. If good and evil are counterparts, a good thing will not "eliminate evil as far as it can". Indeed, this view suggests that good and evil are not strictly qualities of things at all. Perhaps the suggestion is that good and evil are related in much the same way as great and small. Certainly, when the term 'great' is used relatively as a condensation of 'greater than so-and-so', and 'small' is used correspondingly, greatness and smallness are counterparts and cannot exist without each other. But in this sense greatness is not a quality, not an intrinsic feature of anything; and it would be absurd to think of a movement in favour of greatness and against smallness in this sense. Such a movement would be self-defeating, since relative greatness can be promoted only by a simultaneous promotion of relative smallness. I feel sure that no theists would be content to regard God's goodness as analogous to this – as if what he supports were not the *good* but the *better*, and as if he had the paradoxical aim that all things should be better than other things.

This point is obscured by the fact that 'great' and 'small' seem to have an absolute as well as a relative sense. I cannot discuss here whether there is absolute magnitude or not, but if there is, there could be an absolute sense for 'great', it could mean of at least a certain size, and it would make sense to speak of all things getting bigger, of a universe that was expanding all over, and therefore it would make sense to speak of promoting greatness. But in *this* sense great and small are not logically necessary counterparts: either quality could exist without the other. There would be no logical impossibility in everything's being small or in everything's being great.

Neither in the absolute nor in the relative sense, then, of 'great' and 'small' do these terms provide an analogy of the sort that would be needed to support this solution of the problem of evil. In neither case are greatness and smallness *both* necessary counterparts *and* mutually opposed forces or possible objects for support and attack.

It may be replied that good and evil are necessary counterparts in the same way as any quality and its logical opposite: redness can occur, it is suggested, only if non-redness also occurs. But unless evil is merely the privation of good, they are not logical opposites, and some further argument would be needed to show that they are counterparts in the same way as genuine logical opposites. Let us assume that this could be given. There is still doubt of the correctness of the metaphysical principle that a quality must have a real opposite: I suggest that it is not really impossible that everything should be, say, red, that the truth is merely that if everything were red we should not notice redness, and so we should have no word 'red'; we observe and give names to qualities only if they have real opposites. If so, the principle that a term must have an opposite would belong only to our language or to our thought, and would not be an ontological principle, and, correspondingly, the rule that good cannot exist without evil would not state a logical necessity of a sort that God would just have to put up with. God might have made everything good, though *we* should not have noticed it if he had.

But, finally, even if we concede that this *is* an ontological principle, it will provide a solution for the problem of evil only if one is prepared to say, "Evil exists, but only just enough evil to serve as the counterpart of good". I doubt whether any theist will accept this. After all, the *ontological* requirement that non-redness should occur would be satisfied even if all the universe, except for a minute speck, were red, and, if there were a corresponding requirement for evil as a counterpart to good, a minute dose of evil would presumably do. But theists are not usually willing to say, in all contexts, that all the evil that occurs is a minute and necessary dose.

2. "*Evil is necessary as a means to good.*"

It is sometimes suggested that evil is necessary for good not as a counterpart but as a means. In its simple form this has little plausibility as a solution of the problem of evil, since it obviously implies a severe restriction of God's power. It would be a *causal* law that you cannot have a certain end without a certain means, so that if God has to introduce evil as a means to good, he must be subject to at least some causal laws. This certainly conflicts with what a theist normally means by omnipotence. This view of God as limited by causal laws also conflicts with the view that causal laws are themselves made by God, which is more widely held than the corresponding view about the laws of logic. This conflict would, indeed, be resolved if it were possible for an omnipotent being to bind himself, and this possibility has still to be considered. Unless a favourable answer can be given to this question, the suggestion that evil is necessary as a means to good solves the problem of evil only by denying one of its constituent propositions, either that God is omnipotent or that 'omnipotent' means what it says.

3. *"The universe is better with some evil in it than it could be
if there were no evil."*

Much more important is a solution which at first seems to be a mere variant of the previous one, that evil may contribute to the goodness of a whole in which it is found, so that the universe as a whole is better as it is, with some evil in it, than it would be if there were no evil. This solution may be developed in either of two ways. It may be supported by an aesthetic analogy, by the fact that contrasts heighten beauty, that in a musical work, for example, there may occur discords which somehow add to the beauty of the work as a whole. Alternatively, it may be worked out in connexion with the notion of progress, that the best possible organisation of the universe will not be static, but progressive, that the gradual overcoming of evil by good is really a finer thing than would be the eternal unchallenged supremacy of good.

In either case, this solution usually starts from the assumption that the evil whose existence gives rise to the problem of evil is primarily what is called physical evil, that is to say, pain. In Hume's rather half-hearted presentation of the problem of evil, the evils that he stresses are pain and disease, and those who reply to him argue that the existence of pain and disease makes possible the existence of sympathy, benevolence, heroism, and the gradually successful struggle of doctors and reformers to overcome these evils. In fact, theists often seize the opportunity to accuse those who stress the problem of evil of taking a low, materialistic view of good and evil, equating these with pleasure and pain, and of ignoring the more spiritual goods which can arise in the struggle against evils.

But let us see exactly what is being done here. Let us call pain and misery 'first order evil' or 'evil (1)'. What contrasts with this, namely, pleasure and happiness, will be called 'first order good' or 'good (1)'. Distinct from this is 'second order good' or 'good (2)' which somehow emerges in a complex situation in which evil (1) is a necessary component – logically, not merely causally, necessary. (Exactly *how* it emerges does not matter: in the crudest version of this solution good (2) is simply the heightening of happiness by the contrast with misery, in other versions it includes sympathy with suffering, heroism in facing danger, and the gradual decrease of first order evil and increase of first order good.) It is also being assumed that second order good is more important than first order good or evil, in particular that it more than outweighs the first order evil it involves.

Now this is a particularly subtle attempt to solve the problem of evil. It defends God's goodness and omnipotence on the ground that (on a sufficiently long view) this is the best of all logically possible worlds, because it includes the important second order goods, and yet it admits that real evils, namely first order evils, exist. But does it still hold that good and evil are opposed? Not, clearly, in the sense that we set out originally: good does not tend to eliminate evil in general. Instead, we have a modified, a more complex pattern. First order good (e.g. happiness) *contrasts with* first order evil (e.g. misery): these two are opposed in a fairly mechanical way; some second order goods (e.g. benevolence) try to maximise first order good and minimise first order evil; but God's goodness is not this, it is rather the will to maximise *second* order good. We might, therefore, call God's goodness an example of a third order goodness, or good (3). While this account is different from our original one, it might well be held to be an improvement on it, to give a more accurate description of the way in which good is opposed to evil, and to be consistent with the essential theist position.

There might, however, be several objections to this solution.

First, some might argue that such qualities as benevolence – and *a fortiori* the third order goodness which promotes benevolence – have a merely derivative value, that they are not higher sorts of good, but merely means to good (1), that is, to happiness, so that it would be absurd for God to keep misery in existence in order to make possible the virtues of benevolence, heroism, etc. The theist who adopts the present solution must, of course, deny this, but he can do so with some plausibility, so I should not press this objection.

Secondly, it follows from this solution that God is not in our sense benevolent or sympathetic: he is not concerned to minimise evil (1), but only to promote good (2); and this might be a disturbing conclusion for some theists.

But, thirdly, the fatal objection is this. Our analysis shows clearly the possibility of the existence of a *second* order evil, an evil (2) contrasting with good (2) as evil (1) contrasts with good (1). This would include malevolence, cruelty, callousness, cowardice, and states in which good (1) is decreasing and evil (1) increasing. And just as good (2) is held to be the important kind of good, the kind that God is concerned to promote, so evil (2) will, by analogy, be the important kind of evil, the kind which God, if he were wholly good and omnipotent, would eliminate. And yet evil (2) plainly exists, and indeed most theists (in other contexts) stress its existence more than that of evil (1). We should, therefore, state the problem of evil in terms of second order evil, and against this form of the problem the present solution is useless.

An attempt might be made to use this solution again, at a higher level, to explain the occurrence of evil (2): indeed the next main solution that we shall examine does just this, with the help of some new notions. Without any fresh notions, such a solution would have little plausibility: for example, we could hardly say that the really important good was a good (3), such as the increase of benevolence in proportion to cruelty, which logically required for its occurrence the occurrence of some second order evil. But even if evil (2) could be explained in this way, it is fairly clear that there would be third order evils contrasting with this third order good: and we should be well on the way to an infinite regress, where the solution of a problem of evil, stated in terms of evil (n), indicated the existence of an evil ($n + 1$), and a further problem to be solved.

4. *"Evil is due to human freewill."*

Perhaps the most important proposed solution of the problem of evil is that evil is not to be ascribed to God at all, but to the independent actions of human beings, supposed to have been endowed by God with freedom of the will. This solution may be combined with the preceding one: first order evil (e.g. pain) may be justified as a logically necessary component in second order good (e.g. sympathy) while second order evil (e.g. cruelty) is not *justified*, but is so ascribed to human beings that God cannot be held responsible for it. This combination evades my third criticism of the preceding solution.

The freewill solution also involves the preceding solution at a higher level. To explain why a wholly good God gave men freewill although it would lead to some important evils, it must be argued that it is better on the whole that men should act freely, and sometimes err, than that they should be innocent automata, acting rightly in a wholly determined way. Freedom, that is to say, is now treated as a third order good, and as being more valuable than second order goods (such as sympathy and heroism) would be if they were deterministically produced, and it is being assumed that second order evils, such as cruelty, are logically necessary accompaniments of freedom, just as pain is a logically necessary pre-condition of sympathy.

I think that this solution is unsatisfactory primarily because of the incoherence of the notion of freedom of the will: but I cannot discuss this topic adequately here, although some of my criticisms will touch upon it.

First I should query the assumption that second order evils are logically necessary accompaniments of freedom. I should ask this: if God has made men such that in their free choices they sometimes prefer what is good and sometimes what is evil, why could he not have made men such that they always freely choose the good? If there is no logical impossibility in a man's freely choosing the good on one, or on several, occasions, there cannot be a logical impossibility in his freely choosing the good on every occasion. God was not, then, faced with a choice between making innocent automata and making beings who, in acting freely, would sometimes go wrong: there was open to him the obviously better possibility of making beings who would act freely but always go right. Clearly, his failure to avail himself of this possibility is inconsistent with his being both omnipotent and wholly good.

If it is replied that this objection is absurd, that the making of some wrong choices is logically necessary for freedom, it would seem that 'freedom' must here mean complete randomness or indeterminacy, including randomness with regard to the alternatives good and evil, in other words that men's choices and consequent actions can be "free" only if they are not determined by their characters. Only on this assumption can God escape the responsibility for men's actions; for if he made them as they are, but did not determine their wrong choices, this can only be because the wrong choices are not determined by men as they are. But then if freedom is randomness, how can it be a characteristic of *will*? And, still more, how can it be the most important good? What value or merit would there be in free choices if these were random actions which were not determined by the nature of the agent?

I conclude that to make this solution plausible two different senses of 'freedom' must be confused, one sense which will justify the view that freedom is a third order good, more valuable than other goods would be without it, and another sense, sheer randomness, to prevent us from ascribing to God a decision to make men such that they sometimes go wrong when he might have made them such that they would always freely go right.

This criticism is sufficient to dispose of this solution. But besides this there is a fundamental difficulty in the notion of an omnipotent God creating men with free will, for if men's wills are really free this must mean that even God cannot control them, that is, that God is no longer omnipotent. It may be objected that God's gift of freedom to men does not mean that he *cannot* control their wills, but that he always *refrains* from controlling their wills. But why, we may ask, should God refrain from controlling evil wills? Why should he not leave men free to will rightly, but intervene when he sees them beginning to will wrongly? If God could do this, but does not, and if he is wholly good, the only explanation could be that even a wrong free act of will is not really evil, that its freedom is a value which outweighs its wrongness, so that there would be a loss of value if God took away the wrongness and the freedom together. But this is utterly opposed to what theists say about sin in other contexts. The present solution of the problem of evil, then, can be maintained only in the form that God has made men so free that he *cannot* control their wills.

This leads us to what I call the Paradox of Omnipotence: can an omnipotent being make things which he cannot subsequently control? Or, what is practically equivalent to this, can an omnipotent being make rules which then bind himself? (These are practically equivalent because any such rules could be regarded as setting certain things beyond his control, and *vice versa*.) The second of these formulations is relevant to the suggestions that we have already met, that an omnipotent God creates the rules of logic or causal laws, and is then bound by them.

It is clear that this is a paradox: the questions cannot be answered satisfactorily either in the affirmative or in the negative. If we answer "Yes", it follows that if God actually makes things which he cannot control, or makes rules which bind himself, he is not omnipotent once he has made them: there are *then* things which he cannot do. But if we answer "No", we are immediately asserting that there are things which he cannot do, that is to say that he is already not omnipotent.

It cannot be replied that the question which sets this paradox is not a proper question. It would make perfectly good sense to say that a human mechanic has made a machine which he cannot control: if there is any difficulty about the question it lies in the notion of omnipotence itself.

This, incidentally, shows that although we have approached this paradox from the free will theory, it is equally a problem for a theological determinist. No one thinks that machines have free will, yet they may well be beyond the control of their makers. The determinist might reply that anyone who makes anything determines its ways of acting, and so determines its subsequent behaviour: even the human mechanic does this by his *choice* of materials and structure for his machine, though he does not know all about either of these: the mechanic thus determines, though he may not foresee, his machine's actions. And since God is omniscient, and since his creation of things is total, he both determines and foresees the ways in which his creatures will act. We may grant this, but it is beside the point. The question is not whether God *originally* determined the future actions of his creatures, but whether he can *subsequently* control their actions, or whether he was able in his original creation to put things beyond his subsequent control. Even on determinist principles the answers "Yes" and "No" are equally irreconcilable with God's omnipotence.

Before suggesting a solution of this paradox, I would point out that there is a parallel Paradox of Sovereignty. Can a legal sovereign make a law restricting its own future legislative power? For example, could the British parliament make a law forbidding any future parliament to socialise banking, and also forbidding the future repeal of this law itself? Or could the British parliament, which was legally sovereign in Australia in, say, 1899, pass a valid law, or series of laws, which made it no longer sovereign in 1933? Again, neither the affirmative nor the negative answer is really satisfactory. If we were to answer "Yes", we should be admitting the validity of a law which, if it were actually made, would mean that parliament was no longer sovereign. If we were to answer "No", we should be admitting that there is a law, not logically absurd, which parliament cannot validly make, that is, that parliament is not now a legal sovereign. This paradox can be solved in the following way. We should distinguish between first order laws, that is laws governing the actions of individuals and bodies other than the legislature, and second order laws, that is laws about laws, laws governing the actions of the legislature itself. Correspondingly, we should distinguish two orders of sovereignty, first order sovereignty (sovereignty (1)) which is unlimited authority to make first order laws, and second order sovereignty (sovereignty (2)) which is unlimited authority to make second order laws. If we say that parliament is sovereign we might mean that any parliament at any time has sovereignty (1), or we might mean that parliament has both sovereignty (1) and sovereignty (2) at present, but we cannot without contradiction mean both that the present parliament has sovereignty (2) and that every parliament at every time has sovereignty (1), for if the present parliament has sovereignty (2) it may use it to take away the sovereignty (1) of later parliaments. What the paradox shows is that we cannot ascribe to any continuing institution legal sovereignty in an inclusive sense.

The analogy between omnipotence and sovereignty shows that the paradox of omnipotence can be solved in a similar way. We must distinguish between first order omnipotence (omnipotence (1)), that is unlimited power to act, and second order omnipotence (omnipotence (2)), that is unlimited power to determine what powers to act things shall have. Then we could consistently say that God all the time has omnipotence (1), but if so no beings at any time have powers to act independently of God. Or we could say that God at one time had omnipotence (2), and used it to assign independent powers to act to certain things, so that God thereafter did not have omnipotence (1). But what the paradox shows is that we cannot consistently ascribe to any continuing being omnipotence in an inclusive sense.

An alternative solution of this paradox would be simply to deny that God is a continuing being, that any times can be assigned to his actions at all. But on this assumption (which also has difficulties of its own) no meaning can be given to the assertion that God made men with wills so free that he could not control them. The paradox of omnipotence can be avoided by putting God outside time, but the freewill solution of the problem of evil cannot be saved in this way, and equally it remains impossible to hold that an omnipotent God *bind himself* by causal or logical laws.

Conclusion

Of the proposed solutions of the problem of evil which we have examined, none has stood up to criticism. There may be other solutions which require examination, but this study strongly suggests that there is no valid solution of the problem which does not modify at least one of the constituent propositions in a way which would seriously affect the essential core of the theistic position.

Quite apart from the problem of evil, the paradox of omnipotence has shown that God's omnipotence must in any case be restricted in one way or another, that unqualified omnipotence cannot be ascribed to any being that continues through time. And if God and his actions are not in time, can omnipotence, or power of any sort, be meaningfully ascribed to him?

18   The Problem of Evil*

Eleonore Stump

Introduction

The problem of evil traditionally has been understood as an apparent inconsistency in theistic beliefs.[1] Orthodox believers of all three major monotheisms, Judaism, Christianity, and Islam, are committed to the truth of the following claims about God:

(1)   God is omnipotent;
(2)   God is omniscient;
(3)   God is perfectly good.

Reasonable people of all persuasions are also committed to this claim:

(4)   There is evil in the world;

and many theists in particular are bound to maintain the truth of (4) in virtue of their various doctrines of the afterlife or the injunctions of their religion against evil. The view that (1)–(4) are logically incompatible has become associated with Hume in virtue of Philo's position in the *Dialogues Concerning Natural Religion*, though many other philosophers have maintained it,[2] including in recent years J. L. Mackie[3] and H. J. McCloskey.[4] As other philosophers have pointed out, however, Philo's view that there is a logical inconsistency in (1)–(4) alone is mistaken.[5] To show such an inconsistency, one would need at least to demonstrate that this claim must be true:

(5)   There is no morally sufficient reason for God to allow instances of evil.

Since Hume, there have been attempts to solve the problem of evil by attacking or reinterpreting one of the first four assumptions. Mill, for example, suggested a radical weakening of (1) and (2),[6] and according to Mill, Mansel reinterpreted (3) in such a way as almost to make (4) follow from it, by in effect claiming that God's goodness might include attributes which we consider evil by human standards.[7] But for reasons which I think are obvious, theists have generally been unwilling to avail themselves of such solutions; and most attempts at solving the problem, especially recently, have concentrated on strategies for rejecting (5). Some of these attempted rejections of (5) make significant contributions to our understanding of the problem, but none of them, I think, ultimately constitutes a successful solution of the problem. In this paper, I will briefly review what seem to me three of the most promising discussions of the problem of evil and then develop in detail a different solution of my own by presenting and defending a morally sufficient reason for God to allow instances of evil.

* From *Faith and Philosophy*, 2/4 (1985), pp. 392–5, 397–8, 406–15, and 417–18. Reprinted with permission.

I

Plantinga's presentation of the free will defense is a landmark in contemporary discussions of the problem of evil. As Plantinga expounds it,[8] the free will defense rests on these two philosophical claims, which it adds to the theological assumptions (1)–(3):

(6)   Human beings have free will;

and

(7)   Possession of free will and use of it to do more good than evil is a good of such value that it outweighs all the evil in the world.

Plantinga uses these assumptions to argue that a morally sufficient reason for God to permit evil is possible: the value of man's possession and use of free will is a possible reason for God's permitting moral evil, which is evil caused by man. The value of the fallen angel's possession of free will is a possible reason for God's permitting natural evil, evil which is not caused by human free choice but which (Plantinga suggests) could be attributed to the freely chosen actions of fallen angels. As long as it is possible that there be a morally sufficient reason for God to allow evil, regardless of whether or not that possibility is actualized, the existence of evil is not logically incompatible with the existence of a good God.

Plantinga's work has generated considerable discussion, which cannot be effectively summarized here.[9] But for my purposes perhaps the most interesting criticism is the objection that even if we grant Plantinga's free will defense everything it wants and needs, what results does not seem to be even a candidate for a morally sufficient reason justifying God's permitting instances of evil. In "The Irrelevance of the Free Will Defense,"[10] Steven Boer has argued that nothing in the grant of free will to creatures entails that creatures always be able successfully to inflict the harm which they have willed. It is possible that God allow his creatures to be free with respect to their willing and yet prevent by natural or supernatural means the suffering which their evil will and actions aim at. Thus, for example, God could allow Smith to will to murder Jones and to act on that will by hiring killers to shoot Jones, and at the same time God could warn Jones of Smith's intentions in time for Jones to run away and hide until Smith's wrath had subsided. By warning Jones God would prevent the evil of Jones' murder without interfering with Smith's exercise of free will. Many critics of Plantinga's position are bothered by the fact that they cannot seriously entertain the notion that Plantinga's possible sufficient reason for evil might actually obtain. The thought that all natural evil might be caused by fallen angels seems to many a particularly implausible view. This criticism does not especially worry Plantinga, however, because his purpose was to show not what God's reason for allowing evil is but rather just that there could be such a reason; and this is all he needs to show in order to refute those who think that the existence of God is logically incompatible with the existence of evil. Plantinga's strategy is similar in his arguments against those who hold the weaker view that the existence of evil renders it *improbable* that God exist.[11] He does not attempt a justification for God's allowing evil which would diminish the critic's sense of the improbability of God's existence. Rather he argues that the critic has not made his case. Judgments of a claim's probability are relative to a knower's whole set of beliefs. But a theist's set of beliefs includes the belief that God exists, so that atheists' assessments of the probability of God's existence given the existence of evil will not be the same as theists'. Therefore, the atheist critic's argument that God's existence is improbable is not telling against theism.

The problem with Plantinga's general strategy for the defense of theism against arguments from evil is that it leaves the presence of evil in the actual world mysterious. Plantinga's tendency is to show the weaknesses inherent in arguments from evil, not to provide a theodicy, and so it yields no explanation for why we in this world suffer from evil if our world is governed by a good God. No doubt many people, including Plantinga, would not find this result problematic. In fact, in a recent paper Steven Wykstra has argued that given the limitlessness of God's intellect and the finitude of ours, the mysteriousness of evil in our world is just what we might expect;[12] it is reasonable to suppose that we cannot understand why an omniscient and omnipotent entity does what he does. I think that there is some plausibility in Wykstra's thesis; and if all efforts at theodicy fail utterly, no doubt theists will be glad of arguments like Wykstra's and content with strategies like Plantinga's. The problem with such arguments and strategies, to put it crudely, is that they leave people on both sides of the issue unsatisfied. The atheist is inclined to claim, as William Rowe does in a recent paper,[13] that it is apparent there is *no* justifying or overriding good for some evils that occur in the world. To tell such an atheist that he hasn't succeeded in undermining theists' beliefs in the existence of such a good although they don't know what it is, or that his inability to see such a good is just what theists would expect, is likely to strike him as less than a powerful response. As for the theist struggling with the problem of evil, even if he entertains no anxieties about the rationality of his theistic belief in consequence of the existence of evil, he may well still be weakened in his religious belief by the consideration that the deity in whom he is to place his *trust* seems to act in ways which are unintelligible to him at best and apparently evil at worst. So, if it is at all possible to do so, it seems worth trying to construct a more positive explanation for the compatibility of God and evil; and such an explanation is in fact what we find in the work of Swinburne and Hick. . . .

II

. . . The problem of evil is generally presented as some sort of inconsistency in theistic beliefs, and (1)–(4) present the relevant theistic assumptions. And yet *mere* theists are relatively rare in the history of religion. Most people who accept (1)–(4) are Jews or Christians or Muslims. If we are going to claim that *their* beliefs are somehow inconsistent, we need to look at a more complete set of Jewish or Muslim or Christian beliefs concerning God's goodness and evil in the world, not just at that limited subset of such beliefs which are common to all three religions, because what *appears* inconsistent if we take a partial sampling of beliefs may in fact look consistent when set in the context of a more complete set of beliefs. I do not of course mean to suggest that an inconsistent set of propositions could become consistent if we add more propositions to it. My point is simple and commonsensical: that the appearance of inconsistency in a set of beliefs may arise from our interpretation of those beliefs, and our reinterpretation of them in light of a larger system of beliefs to which they belong may dispel the appearance of inconsistency. A more promising foundation for a solution to the problem of evil, then, might be found if we consider a broader range of beliefs concerning the relations of God to evil in the world, which are specific to a particular monotheism.

Furthermore, attempted solutions to the problem of evil based solely on a few theistic assumptions common to the major monotheisms are likely themselves to be incompatible with Jewish or Christian or Islamic beliefs. Swinburne's attempted solution, for example, seems incompatible with traditional Christian beliefs about heaven. On Swinburne's account, we are more like pets than humans unless we have significant exercise of our free will, and natural evil is necessary for such a significant exercise. But there is no natural evil in heaven and so, according to Swinburne's position, no significant exercise of free will either. Hence, on Swinburne's account, persons in heaven are not perfected in virtue of their translation to heaven, as Christian doctrine has traditionally claimed, but rather diminished in status. Thoughtful Christians troubled by the problem of evil, then, are not likely to be reassured by Swinburne's solution.

For these reasons, in what follows I will focus on one particular monotheism, namely, Christianity; I do not know enough about Judaism or Islam to present a discussion of the problem of evil in the context of those religions. In fact, my account will not deal even with all varieties of Christian belief. Because my account will depend on a number of assumptions, such as that man has free will, it will present a solution to the problem of evil applicable only to those versions of Christianity which accept those assumptions. Christians who reject a belief in free will, for example, will also reject my attempt at a solution to the problem of evil.

Besides (1)–(4), there are three Christian beliefs that seem to me especially relevant to the problem of evil. They are these:

(8) Adam fell.
(9) Natural evil entered the world as a result of Adam's fall.
(10) After death, depending on their state at the time of their death, either (a) human beings go to heaven or (b) they go to hell.[14]

III

According to the Christian beliefs summarized as (8), (9), and (10), all human beings since Adam's fall have been defective in their free wills, so that they have a powerful inclination to will what they ought not to will, to will their own power or pleasure in preference to greater goods. It is not possible for human beings in that condition to go to heaven, which consists in union with God; and hell understood in Dantean terms is arguably the best alternative to annihilation. A good God will want to fix such persons, to save them from hell and bring them to heaven; and as the creator of these persons, God surely bears some responsibility for fixing and saving them if he can. How is he to do so?

It seems to me clear that he cannot fix the defect by using his omnipotence to remove it miraculously. The defect is a defect in *free* will, and it consists in a person's generally failing to will what he ought to will. To remove this defect miraculously would be to force a person's free will to be other than it is; it would consist in causing a person to will freely what he ought to will. But it is logically impossible for anyone to make a person freely will something, and therefore even God in his omnipotence cannot directly and miraculously remove the defect in free will, without destroying the very freedom of the will he wants to fix.

Someone might object here that if the defect in the will is inheritable without prejudice to the freedom of the will, then it is also removable without detriment to the freedom of the will; and if it destroys freedom to have God remove the defect, then it also destroys freedom to have the defect inherited. This objection, I think, is based on a mistaken picture of the inheritance of the defect. If the traditional doctrine were that after the time of Adam's fall, human beings whose wills were in a pre-fall state suddenly acquired fallen, defective wills, then this objection would be sound. And perhaps the use of the word "inheritance," with its suggestions of one individual suddenly receiving something from another, invites such a picture. But in fact the doctrine of Adam's fall makes it clear that in the transmission of the defect there is no change of will on the part of post-fallen men. What the doctrine specifies is that individuals conceived and born after Adam's fall have defective wills from the very beginning of their existence. There is no change of will in this process; rather the process consists in the generation of persons whose free wills from birth are strongly inclined to certain sorts of evil actions. If God were to destroy such post-fall persons and generate new ones with non-defective wills (as I have argued he should not), he would not be violating the free wills of the new persons by so creating them any more than he violated Adam's free will when he created Adam in his pre-fall state. But if God intervenes to remove the defect in the wills of post-fall persons, he brings about a *change* in their wills; and this, I think, he cannot do if their wills are to remain free.[15]

If God cannot by his omnipotence directly fix the defect in free will, it seems that human beings must fix it themselves. Self-repair is a common feature of the natural world, but I do not think self-repair is possible for a person with post-fall free will. People, of course, do sometimes reform their lives and change their habits; but one necessary condition for their doing so is that, for whatever purpose or motive, they will something different from what they previously willed. Analogously, to reform the will requires willing something different from what one previously willed; that is, it requires a change of will. But how to change the will is the problem in the first place. If we want to know whether a man himself can fix a defect in his will, whether he himself can somehow remove his tendency to will what he ought not to will, it is no help to be told that of course he can if he just wills to change his will. We know that a man *can* change his will for the better; otherwise his will would not be free. The problem with a defect in the will is not that there is an inability to will what one ought to will because of some external restraint on the will, but that one does not and will not will what one ought to will because the will itself is bent towards evil. Consequently, changing the will is the end for which we are seeking the means; if one were *willing* to change one's will by willing what one ought to will, there would be no problem of a defect in the will.[16] Self-repair, then, is no more a solution to the problem of a defective will than is God's miraculous intervention.[17]

If God cannot and human beings will not fix the defect in their wills, what possible cure is there? Christianity suggests what seems to me the only remaining alternative. Let a person will that God fix his defective will. In that case, God's alteration of the will is something the person has freely chosen, and God can then alter that person's will without destroying its freedom. It is a fact well-attested in religious literature that people who find it next to impossible to will what (they believe) they ought to will may none the less find it in themselves to will that God alter their wills. Perhaps two of the most famous examples are the sonnet of John Donne in which he prays for God to overwhelm him so that he will be chaste[18] and Augustine's prayers that God give him continence.[19] The traditional formulation of the crucial necessary condition for a person's being a Christian (variously interpreted by Protestants and Catholics) is that he wills God to save him from his sin; and this condition is, I think, logically (and perhaps also psychologically) equivalent to a person's willing that God fix his will. Willing to have God save one from one's sin is willing to have God bring one to a state in which one is free from sin, and that state depends essentially on a will which wills what it ought to will.

What role God plays in man's coming to will that God fix his will is controversial in the history of Christian thought. Some Protestant theologians have argued that God bears sole responsibility for such willing; Pelagius apparently argued that all the responsibility belongs to man. The first of these positions seems to me to have difficulties roughly analogous to those raised above by the suggestion that God might miraculously fix man's will, and the difficulties in the second are like those in the suggestion that a man himself might fix his own will. Perhaps the correct view here too consists in postulating a cooperative divine and human effort. Perhaps Socrates's way with those he encountered can serve as a model. When Socrates pursued a man with wit and care and passion for the truth, that man sometimes converted to philosophy and became Socrates's disciple. Such a man converted freely, so that it is false to say Socrates *caused* his conversion; and yet, on the other hand, it would be ridiculous to say in consequence that the man bears sole responsibility for his conversion. The responsibility and the credit for the conversion belong to Socrates, whose effort and ingenuity were necessary conditions of the conversion. That they were not sufficient conditions, however, and that the man none the less freely willed his conversion is clear from the cases of men such as Alcibiades, whom Socrates sought but did not succeed in converting. Without rashly trying to adjudicate in a paragraph an old and complicated controversy, I think that something along those lines can also be said of the process by which a man comes to will God's help. God's effort on behalf of Augustine are the necessary condition of Augustine's conversion, and the credit for his conversion belongs to God; but God's efforts are not a sufficient condition, and so Augustine's free will is not impugned. Or, as Anselm says with regard to the fall of the angels, "although the good angel received perseverance [in willing what he ought to will] because God gave it, it is not the case that the evil angel did not receive it because God did not give it. But rather, God did not give it because Satan did not receive it, and he did not receive it because he was unwilling to receive it."[20]

At any rate, if a man does will that God fix his will or save him from his sins, then I think that God can do so without detriment to free will, provided that he does so only to the extent to which the man freely wills that God do so. There is in principle no reason why a person could not will at once that God fix the whole defect of his will; but in general, perhaps because of the extent of the defect in the will, people seem to turn from their own evil in a series of small-scale reforms. In book VIII, chapter VII, of the *Confessions*, Augustine describes himself as praying that God give him chastity and making the private reservation "but not yet." If God were immediately to give Augustine chastity in such a case, he would in fact be doing so against Augustine's will. And so, in general, God's fixing the will seems to be a lengthy process, in which a little willing produces a little fixing, which in turn promotes more willing of more fixing. On Christian doctrine, this is the process of sanctification, which is not finally completed until after death when it culminates "in the twinkling of an eye" in the last changes which unite the sanctified person with God.[21]

The fixing of a defective free will by a person's freely willing that God fix his will is, I think, the foundation of a Christian solution to the problem of evil. What sort of world is most conducive to bringing about both the initial human willing of help and also the subsequent process of sanctification? To answer that question, we need to consider the psychological state of a person who wills God's help. Apart from the obvious theological beliefs, such a person must also hold that he tends to do what he ought not to do and does so because he himself wills what he ought not to will, and he must want not to be in such a condition. He must, in other words, have both a humbling recognition of himself as evil and a desire for a better state. So things that contribute to a person's humbling, to his awareness of his own evil, and to his unhappiness with his present state contribute to his willing God's help.

I think that both moral and natural evil make such a contribution. The unprevented gross moral evils in the course of human history show us something about the nature of man, and our own successful carrying out of our no doubt smaller-scaled evil wills shows us that we are undeniably members of the species. Natural evil – the pain of disease, the intermittent and unpredictable destruction of natural disasters, the decay of old age, the imminence of death – takes away a person's satisfaction with himself. It tends to humble him, show him his frailty, make him reflect on the transience of temporal goods and turn his affections towards other-worldly things, away from the things of this world. No amount of moral or natural evil, of course, can *guarantee* that a man will seek God's help. If it could, the willing it produced would not be free. But evil of this sort is the best hope, I think, and maybe the only effective means, for bringing men to such a state.

That natural evil and moral evil, the successful carrying out of evil human wills, serve to make men recognize their own evils, become dissatisfied with things of this world, and turn to God is a controversial claim; and it is clear that a compelling argument for or against it would be very difficult to construct. To produce such an argument we would need a representative sample, whatever that might be, of natural and moral evil. Then we would need to examine that sample case by case to determine the effect of the evil in each case on the human beings who suffered or perpetrated it. To determine the effect we would have to know the psychological and moral state of these people both before and after the evil at issue (since the effect would consist in some alteration of a previous state); and we would have to chart their state for the rest of their lives after that evil because, like the effect of carcinogens, the effect of the experience of evil may take many years to manifest itself. Even with the help of a team of psychologists and sociologists, then, it would be hard to collect the data necessary to make a good argument for or against this claim. Hence, I am unable to present a cogent argument for one of the main claims of this paper, not because of the improbability of the claim but because of the nature of the data an argument for the claim requires; and perhaps it should just be categorized as one more Christian belief and added as (11) to the list of (8), (9), and (10) as a traditionally held, not demonstrably false Christian belief.[22] Still, there is *some* historical evidence for it in the fact that Christianity has tended to flourish among the oppressed and decline among the comfortable, and perhaps the best evidence comes from the raising of children. The phrase "spoiling a child" is ambiguous in current parlance between "turning a child into a unpleasant person" and "giving a child everything he wants," and the ambiguity reflects a truth about human nature. The pains, the hardships, the struggles which children encounter tend to make them better people. Of course, such experiences do not invariably make children better; children, like adults, are also sometimes made worse by their troubles. But that fact would be a counter-example to the general claim about the function of evil in the world only in case it maintained that evil was *guaranteed* to make people better; and that is something this claim could not include and still be compatible with Christianity as long as Christianity is committed to the view that human beings have free will.

Someone may object here that the suffering of children is just what this attempted solution to the problem of evil cannot explain. In *The Brothers Karamazov*, Dostoevsky provides the most eloquent presentation this objection is likely ever to get, concluding with Ivan's passionate insistence (implicit in a question addressed to Alyosha) that even if the whole world could be saved for eternal bliss by the torture of one innocent child, allowing the torture of that child for that purpose would be horribly wrong. I am in sympathy with the attitude Dostoevsky has Ivan express and in agreement with Ivan's conclusion. The suffering of children is in my view unquestionably the instance of evil most difficult for the problem of evil, and there is something almost indecent about any move resembling an attempt to explain it away. The suffering of children is a terrible thing, and to try to see it otherwise is to betray one's humanity. Any attempt to solve the problem of evil must try to provide some understanding of the suffering of children, but it must not lessen our pain over that suffering if it is not to become something monstrous and inhumane.

With considerable diffidence, then, I want to suggest that Christian doctrine is committed to the claim that a child's suffering is out-weighed by the good for the child which can result from that suffering. This is a brave (or foolhardy) thing to say, and the risk inherent in it is only sharpened when one applies it to cases in which infants suffer, for example, or in which children die in their suffering. Perhaps the decent thing to do here is simply to sketch some considerations which may shed light on these hard cases. To begin with, it is important to remember that on Christian doctrine death is not the ultimate evil or even the ultimate end, but rather a transition between one form of life and another. From a Christian point of view, the thing to be avoided at all costs is not dying, but dying badly; what concerns the Christian about death is not that it occurs but that the timing and mode of death be such as to constitute the best means of ensuring that state of soul which will bring a person to eternal union with God. If children who die in their suffering thereby move from the precarious and frequently painful existence of this world to a permanently blissful existence in the other world and if their suffering was among part of the necessary means to effect that change, their suffering is justified. I am not trying to say here that the suffering which a child or any other person experiences is the only way in which that person could be brought to God. Rather, I am trying to avoid constructing the sort of explanation for evil which requires telling the sufferer that God lets him suffer just for the sake of some abstract general good for mankind. Perhaps it is true that such a general good – the significant freedom of created persons, for example – is the ultimate end for the sake of which God permits evil. It seems to me none the less that a perfectly good entity who was also omniscient and omnipotent must govern the evil resulting from the misuse of that significant freedom in such a way that the sufferings of any particular person are out-weighed by the good which the suffering produces *for that person*; otherwise, we might justifiably expect a good God somehow to prevent that *particular suffering*, either by intervening (in one way or another) to protect the victim, while still allowing the perpetrator his freedom, or by curtailing freedom in some select cases.[23] And since on Christian doctrine the ultimate good for persons is union with God, the suffering of any person will be justified if it brings that person nearer to the ultimate good in a way he could not have been without the suffering. I think that Christianity must take some such approach to the suffering or death of children; and perhaps something analogous can be said in connection with the hardest case of all, the suffering of infants. Psychologists tell us that the first year of a child's life is tremendously important in molding the personality and character. For some persons the molding of the personality produced by suffering in infancy may be the best means of insuring a character capable of coming to God.[24]

In all these hard cases, the difficulty of formulating a Christian position which does not appear either implausible or inhuman will be diminished if we have clearly in mind the view of man Christianity starts with. On Christian doctrine, all human beings are suffering from the spiritual equivalent of a terminal disease; they have a defect in the will which if not corrected will cost them life in heaven and consign them to a living death in hell. Now suppose that we are the parents of a child with a terminal brain disease, which includes among its symptoms the child's rejecting the notion that he is sick and refusing to cooperate in any treatments. The doctors tell us that there are treatments which may well cure the child completely, but they hurt and their success is not guaranteed. Would we not choose to subject the child to the treatments, even if they were very painful? The child's suffering would be a terrible thing; we would and we should be grieved at it. But we would none the less be glad of the treatments and hope of a cure. And yet this example is only a pale reflection of what Christianity claims to be the case for all human beings, where the loss inflicted by the disease and the benefits of its cure are infinitely greater. If moral and natural evil contain an essential ingredient of a possible cure, surely the cure is worth the suffering such evil entails.

It might seem to some people that if this is God's plan, it is a tragic failure because the amount of evil in the world produces so few cures. The vast majority of people in the world are not Christians or theists of any kind; and even among those who are Christian many die in serious unrepented evil. But this complaint rests on an assumption for which we have no evidence, namely, that the majority of people end in hell. That even an evildoer who dies a sudden, unexpected death may not die impenitent is shown vividly by Dante:

> I am Buonconte . . . wounded in the throat, flying on foot and bloodying the plain [I came]. There I lost my sight and speech. I ended on the name of Mary, and there I fell, and my flesh remained alone . . . The Angel of God took me, and he from Hell cried, "O you from Heaven, why do you rob me? You carry off with you the eternal part of him for one little tear which takes him from me."[25]

As for those who live and die without the religious knowledge necessary for redemption from evil, it is not incompatible with Christian doctrine to speculate that in the process of their dying God acquaints them with what they need to know and offers them a last chance to choose.[26] Such a speculation might seem to vitiate the justification for evil which I have been developing in this paper, because if the whole process of redemption can be begun and completed in a person's dying hour, why do we need evil in the world? But this is a mistaken objection, because surely in any sort of deathbed repentance the sufferings of the dying person will have had a significant effect on that person's character and consequently on the choices he makes on his deathbed. So as long as some such speculation is not incompatible with Christian doctrine, it is not at all clear that the majority of people end in hell. And without that assumption the complaint that God's plan for the use of evil is a failure is altogether unwarranted.

Someone might also object here that this solution to the problem of evil prohibits us from any attempt to relieve human suffering and in fact suggests that we ought to promote it, as the means of man's salvation. Such an objection is mistaken, I think, and rests on an invalid inference. Because God can use suffering to cure an evil will, it does not follow that we can do so also. God can see into the minds and hearts of human beings and determine what sort and amount of suffering is likely to produce the best results; we cannot. (Our inability to do so is in fact one of the things which make it so difficult to discuss cases of infant suffering, for example.) Furthermore, God as parent creator has a right to, and a responsibility for, painful correction of his creatures, which we as sibling creatures do not have. Therefore, since all human suffering is prima facie evil, and since we do not know with any high degree of probability how much (if any) of it is likely to result in good to any particular sufferer on any particular occasion, it is reasonable for us to eliminate the suffering as much as we can. At any rate, the attempt to eliminate suffering is likely to be beneficial to our characters, and passivity in the face of others' suffering will have no such good effects.[27]

IV

The solution to the problem of evil I have been developing will be clarified further by being applied to an individual instance of evil. The instance I want to consider is the Old Testament story of Cain and Abel. For my purposes here, this biblical story of an instance of evil has several advantages over a description of an instance of evil drawn from such sources as the newspapers. The biblical story contains a description of God's intervention or lack of intervention in human history, and it includes an account of the inner thoughts and motivations of the principal characters. To the extent to which Christians are committed to accepting the Bible as the revealed word of God, to that extent they are committed to accepting this story as veridical also; and that fact obviously contributes to the use I want to make of the story. Finally, although the story of Cain and Abel is regularly taken by Christians as a paradigmatically moral and religious story, suitable for the edification of children, the incidents related in the story are such that a twentieth-century atheistic philosopher might have invented them as a showcase for the problem of evil.

Cain and Abel are two brothers who bring offerings to God. Abel's offering is accepted, but Cain's is not – why, the story does not say. In consequence, Cain is very angry at Abel. The story suggests that acceptance or rejection of the offerings is an (at least temporary) acceptance or rejection of the offerer; and Cain's anger at Abel apparently stems from jealousy over God's favoring Abel rather than Cain. Now there is something double-minded in Cain's anger and jealousy. Either God is right to reject Cain's offering – because there was something about it or about the person who brought it which made it objectively unacceptable – and in that case there are no grounds for anger; or God is wrong to reject Cain's offering – because it was a perfectly good offering brought in an altogether appropriate spirit – and in that case *God* is not good. And although one might then still be afraid of the consequences of incurring God's displeasure or resent those more favored by God, a single-minded belief that God's standards for accepting offerings are bad precludes jealousy towards those who are accepted. That Cain is angry and jealous indicates that he is double-minded about whether God is right to reject his offering.

Although he does reject Cain's offering, God does not leave Cain to himself in his double-minded anger. He comes to him and talks to him, asking Cain Socratic questions designed to get him to recognize and resolve his double-mindedness: "Why are you angry?;" "If you do well, will you not be accepted?" And God goes on to give Cain a warning, that he is in danger of sin. So God apparently anticipates Cain's attack on his brother, and he intervenes to warn Cain.

But Cain attacks and kills his brother. Abel, who has just been accepted by God and is evidently righteous, suffers violent and untimely death. When the killing is over, God speaks to Cain again, asking him more careful questions designed to lead him to confess his deed: first, "Where is Abel?," and then after the evasive response to that question, the stronger question "What have you done?" When Cain is obstinate in his evil, God punishes him by miraculously intervening in nature: the ground will be barren when Cain tills it, and apparently only when Cain tills it. Finally, we have the last piece of God's care for Cain in this story: Cain says his punishment is more than he can bear, and God comforts him by protecting him against being killed by other men, a danger Cain had understood to be part of his punishment.

Now consider God's actions in this story. In the first place, he punishes Cain for the murder of Abel, showing thereby that he regards the murder of Abel as bad and worthy of punishment. And yet he himself allowed the murder to take place, although obviously he could have prevented it. Any decent person who was present when Cain attacked his brother would have made some effort to rescue Abel; but God, who is always present everywhere and who even seems to anticipate Cain's attack, does nothing for Abel. On the other hand, consider what God does to or for Cain. He comes to him and warns him of the coming temptation. After the murder he returns to talk to Cain again, in a way designed to make Cain acknowledge his true state. When he imposes punishment, he does it in a way that seems to require a miracle. He banishes Cain from his land. And when Cain complains that his punishment is too much, God is merciful to him and guards him from being killed by other men. In short, God interferes in Cain's affairs to warn him; he talks to him earnestly to get him to see his true situation; he performs a miracle on his behalf; he sends him away from his own place; and he protects him from being murdered. Clearly, any *one* of these things done on Abel's behalf would have been enough to save him. But God does none of these things for *Abel*, the innocent, the accepted of God; he does them instead for *Cain*, a man whose offering was rejected and who is murderously angry at his brother. When it comes to righteous Abel, God simply stands by and watches him be killed. Why has such a story been allowed to stand as part of the canonical Scriptures?

On the solution to the problem of evil which I have been developing in this paper, if God is good and has a care for his creatures, his over-riding concern must be to insure not that they live as long as possible or that they suffer as little pain as possible in this life but rather that they live in such a way as ultimately to bring them to union with God.

Abel presents God with no problems in this respect. He is apparently righteous at the time of his offering; and hence that is a safe, even a propitious, time for him to die, to make the transition from this life to the next. Given that he will die sometime, Abel's death at this time is if anything in Abel's interest; he dies at a time when he is accepted by God, and he enters into union with God. It is true that Abel dies prematurely and so is deprived of years of life. But on Christian doctrine, what he loses is years of a painful and spiritually perilous pilgrimage through this life, and what he gains is eternal bliss.

Cain, on the other hand, is in trouble as regards both his current moral state and his prospects for the next life. If God were to rescue Abel by striking Cain with heart failure at the outset of Cain's attack on Abel, for example, Cain would die in mortal sin and so would go to hell, while righteous Abel would continue the morally dangerous journey of this life only to die later, perhaps in some less virtuous state. There are, of course, many other ways in which God could have stopped Cain and rescued Abel without going so far as killing Cain. But perhaps stopping Cain even in those other ways would not have been good for Cain. Because God does not step in between Cain's willing and the successful realization of that willing, Cain is brought as forcefully as possible to a recognition of the depth of the evil he willed. And that forceful recognition is, I think, the most powerful means of bringing Cain to an acknowledgment of his own evil and a desire for help, which is a necessary condition for his salvation.

On the solution to the problem of evil which I have been developing here, then, God does not rescue Abel because contrary to appearances Abel is not in danger; and God's failure to rescue Abel, as well as all the other care for Cain recorded in the story, constitutes the best hope of a rescue for Cain, who is in danger, and not just of death but of a perpetual living death.

V

I think, then, that it is possible to produce a defensible solution to the problem of evil by relying both on the traditional theological and philosophical assumptions in (1)–(4) and (6), and on the specifically Christian doctrines in (8)–(10). Like other recent attempted solutions, this one also rests fundamentally on a revised version of (7), namely, this:

> (7‴) Because it is a necessary condition for union with God, the significant exercise of free will employed by human beings in the process which is essential for their being saved from their own evil is of such great value that it outweighs all the evil of the world.

(7‴) constitutes a morally sufficient reason for evil and so is a counter-example to (5), the claim that there is no morally sufficient reason for God to permit instances of evil.

In the brief exposition of this solution in this paper, I cannot hope to have given anything but a sketch and a preliminary defense of it; to do it justice and to consider carefully all the questions and objections it raises would require book-length treatment. For all its complexity, the story of Cain and Abel is the story of a simple instance of evil, which is easily dwarfed by any account of evil culled at random from today's newspapers; and I am under no illusions that by providing an explanation for the simple evil in the story of Cain and Abel, I have given a sufficient and satisfying explanation of even the commonplace evils of ghetto violence, much less the almost unthinkable evils of Belsen or Hiroshima. What I would like to believe I have done is to have shown that with good will and careful attention to the details of the doctrines specific to a particular monotheism there is hope of a successful solution to the problem of evil along the lines developed here.

Notes

1 For a review of recent literature on the problem of evil, see Michael Peterson, "Recent Work on the Problem of Evil," *American Philosophical Quarterly*, 20 (1983), pp. 321–40.

2 Cf. Nelson Pike, "Hume on Evil," *The Philosophical Review*, 72 (1963), pp. 180–1.

3 See "Evil and Omnipotence," *Mind*, 64 (1955), pp. 200–12.

4 "God and Evil," *The Philosophical Quarterly*, 10 (1960), pp. 97–114.

5 Cf., e.g., Nelson Pike, "Hume on Evil."

6 Cf. John Stuart Mill, *Three Essays on Religion* (London: Longmans, Green and Co., 1875), pp. 176–90, 194.

7 John Stuart Mill, *An Examination of Sir William Hamilton's Philosophy* (London: Longman's Green and Co., 1865), ch. 7.

8 Cf. Alvin Plantinga, "The Free Will Defense," in *Philosophy in America*, ed. Max Black (London: Allen and Unwin, 1965), pp. 204–20. A revised version of this paper is included in *God and Other Minds* (Ithaca, N.Y.: Cornell University Press, 1967) pp. 131–55. Cf. also "Which Worlds Could God Have Created?" *Journal of Philosophy*, 70 (1973), pp. 539–52.

9 Among the most interesting criticisms of Plantinga are the following: Robert M. Adams, "Middle Knowledge and the Problem of Evil," *American Philosophical Quarterly*, 14 (1977), pp. 109–17; George Botterill, "Falsification and the Existence of God: A Discussion of Plantinga's Free Will Defense," *Philosophical Quarterly*, 27 (1977), pp. 114–34; Robert Burch, "Plantinga and Leibniz's Lapse," *Analysis*, 39 (1979), pp. 24–9; Nelson Pike, "Plantinga on Free Will and Evil," *Religious Studies*, 15 (1979), pp. 449–73; William Rowe, "God and Other Minds," *Nous*, 3 (1969), pp. 271–7; William Wainwright, "Christian Theism and the Free Will Defense: A Problem," *International Journal for the Philosophy of Religion*, 6 (1975), pp. 243–50; William Wainwright, "Freedom and Omnipotence," *Nous*, 2 (1968), pp. 293–301; and Peter Windt, "Plantinga's Unfortunate God," *Philosophical Studies*, 24 (1973), pp. 335–42.

10 *Analysis* (1975), pp. 110–12.

11 See "The Probabilistic Argument from Evil," *Philosophical Studies*, 35 (1979), pp. 1–53.

12 Steven Wykstra, "The Humean Obstacle to Evidential Arguments from Suffering: On Avoiding the Evils of Appearance," forthcoming in *International Journal for the Philosophy of Religion*.

13 William Rowe, "The Empirical Argument from Evil," in *Rationality, Religious Belief, and Moral Commitment: New Essays in the Philosophy of Religion*, ed. R. Audi and W. Wainwright (Cornell University Press, forthcoming).

14 For an example of this view in prominent Catholic and Protestant theologians, see, e.g., Thomas Aquinas, *Summa theologiae*, Ia–IIae, q. 87, q. 3, and John Calvin, *Institutes of the Christian Religion*, bk. III, ch. xxiv, esp. section 6.

15 Someone might also object that if post-fall persons inherit a disordered will, they are not responsible for the evil they do and so should not be punished for it. But this objection misunderstands the nature of the defect post-fall persons inherit. It is not an external constraint on the will; it is a tendency within the will to will evil. A person with post-fall will *can* will only right actions, but tends not to *want* to do so. Such a person, who can will the right action in certain circumstances but who does not do so because he does not want to, is generally held to be responsible for what he does.

16 I do not mean to suggest that changing one's character is accomplished by a single act of will of any sort, only that a particular sort of act of will is a prerequisite for a change of character.

17 This very sketchy discussion suggests a solution to the sort of quarrel engaged in by Luther and Erasmus. Even the defective will is free, in the sense that it *can* will the good; and to this extent it seems to me that Erasmus was right. But if this ability is not exercised because, in virtue of a defect in the will, the will *does not* will the good, then for practical as distinct from theological purposes Luther was right. Of himself, man will not do what is right; to do so he

must have external help. See Martin Luther, *The Bondage of the Will*, tr. J. I. Packer and A. R. Johnston (London: James Clarke, 1957); and Erasmus, *De Libero Arbitrio, Discourse on the Freedom of the Will*, ed. and tr. Ernest F. Winter (New York, 1967).

18   "Batter my heart, three-personed God; for You

As yet but knock, breathe, shine, and seek to mend;

That I may rise and stand, o'erthrow me, and bend

Your force to break, blow, burn, and make me new.

I, like an usurped town, to another due,

Labor to admit You, but O, to no end;

Reason, Your viceroy in me, me should defend,

But is captived, and proves weak or untrue.

Yet dearly I love You, and would be loved fain,

But am betrothed unto Your enemy.

Divorce me, untie, or break that knot again;

Take me to You, imprison me, for I,

Except You enthrall me, never shall be free,

Nor ever chaste, except you ravish me."

19   Augustine, *Confessions*, tr. Edward Pusey (New York: Macmillan, 1961), bk. viii, pp. 125, 130: "But I wretched, most wretched, in the very commencement of my early youth, had begged chastity of Thee, and said, 'Give me chastity and continence, only not yet.' For I feared lest Thou shouldest hear me soon, and soon cure me of the disease of concupiscence, which I wished to have satisfied, rather than extinguished . . . [Now, however] I cast myself down I know not how, under a certain fig tree, giving full vent to my tears; and the floods of mine eyes gushed out an acceptable sacrifice to Thee . . . I sent up these sorrowful words: how long, how long, 'tomorrow, and tomorrow?' Why not now? Why not is there this hour an end to my uncleanness?"

20   Anselm, *The Fall of Satan*, tr. Iasper Hopkins and Herbert Richardson (New York: Harper and Row, 1967), p. 157.

21   See, for example, the articles on sanctification in *The Encyclopedia of Religion and Ethics*, ed. James Hastings (New York: Charles Scribner's Sons, 1962) and in *A Theological Word Book of the Bible*, ed. Alan Richardson (New York: Macmillan, 1950), and the article on grace in *The Catholic Encyclopedia*, ed. Charles Herbermann et al. (New York: Robert Appleton Co., 1909).

22   That this is a claim Christians are committed to is clear from even a brief perusal of the Old Testament. The Old Testament prophetic books abound with statements such as these: "In vain have I smitten your children; they received no correction" (Jeremiah 2: 30); "Oh Lord, . . . thou has stricken them, but they have not grieved; thou has consumed them, but they have refused to receive correction" (Jeremiah 5: 3); "The people turneth not unto him that smiteth them, neither do they seek the Lord of hosts" (Isaiah 9: 13). Amos 4: 6–11 is a particularly clear statement of this claim. The story of the blind man in John 9: 1–38, which culminates in the blind man's expression of faith and worship, is an example of a New Testament story illustrating this claim.

23   For a Biblical story showing God protecting the victim while allowing the perpetrator the freedom to act on his evil will, cf., e.g., Daniel 3: 8–25; a clear-cut story showing God preventing suffering by curtailing the freedom of a human agent to act on his will is harder to find, but cf., e.g., Genesis 19: 1–11, Genesis 22: 11–12, and such stories of relief from oppression as Judges 6: 11 ff.

24   The death of infants has been variously handled in the history of Christian thought. It seems to me not so much a hard case as a borderline one. Like the suffering of animals, the death of infants is hard to account for in large part because we have an inadequate understanding of the nature of infants and animals. Do infants have free will? Do some of the more intelligent

species of animals other than man have free will? If they do, maybe some version of the solution I am developing here applies to them also. As for creatures to whom no one would want to attribute free will, such as worms and snails, what sort of suffering do they undergo? Until we have a clearer account of the nature of infants and animals, it will not be clear what to say about the death of infants or the suffering of animals in connection with the problem of evil. For that reason, I leave both out of account here.

25 Dante, *Purgatorio*, V. 98–107, tr. Charles Singleton (Princeton, N.J.: Princeton University Press, 1973), p. 51.

26 For an interesting variation on such a speculation, see C. S. Lewis, *The Great Divorce* (New York: Macmillan, 1946).

27 I have made no attempt in this section to discuss the connection, crucial for Christianity, between salvation from one's sins and the Incarnation and Resurrection of Christ. I intend to examine that connection in a forthcoming paper on the Atonement.

19 Male-Chauvinist Religion*

Deborah Mathieu

> *Man for the field and woman for the hearth*
> *Man for the sword and for the needle she*
> *Man with the head and woman with the heart*
> *Man to command and woman to obey*
> *All else confusion.*
>
> ALFRED, LORD TENNYSON[1]

All functioning societies rely on a division of labor: some individuals raise children, some produce food, some construct roads, some adjudicate disputes, and so on. Occasionally these tasks overlap, but often they do not. How do societies decide who does what? How, in other words, are rights and responsibilities allocated?

There is no one universally accepted method of determining which people will perform which roles, and often a given society will employ several methods. One common distributive standard is age: no one over a certain age or under a certain age may perform certain functions. Another distributive standard is ability: an intelligent person with a sense of fairness may adjudicate disputes, for instance, while a brawny person willing to work hard may construct roads. Yet another common standard is gender: males perform one set of tasks while females perform another. There are other allocative standards as well: race, religion, family, class, education, and so on.

The United States has employed all of these (and more) to determine who does what. Most of the criteria are unfair most of the time: your family name, for instance, should be irrelevant to your career (unless you work in the family business), as should your theology (unless you work as a religious official). But I am not concerned with all unfair

* From Joel Feinberg and Russ Shafer-Landau (eds), *Reason and Responsibility*, 11th edn (Belmont, CA: Wadsworth, 2002), pp. 80–9. Reprinted with permission.

standards, just with one: gender. If positions are allocated according to gender, then no female – regardless of her talents, her education, her aspirations – may perform those tasks assigned to males.

During the many decades in which the United States used gender as a principal method of distribution, a woman could wash clothes but she could not shine shoes, she could be a barmaid but not a bartender, she could raise children but could not hold public office. Women could not be lawyers, serve on juries, operate elevators, or mine coal. Indeed, it was once illegal in this country for women to perform *most* jobs outside the home.[2] This type of occupational gender segregation, of course, is very common around the world. One result is that work traditionally performed by women – rearing children, cleaning house, teaching grammar school – though necessary and often arduous, is usually under-valued and underpaid.[3]

The separation of tasks according to gender typically means that males act in the public sphere of politics and paid work while females stay in the private sphere of the home. But why would an intelligent woman with a robust sense of fairness concede that she should spend her time cleaning house instead of refereeing disputes? Why would any woman acquiesce to any sort of gender stereotyping, especially when the results are harmful to her?

The answer is simple and somewhat frightening: she believes that only certain narrowly defined roles are appropriate for her. Why would she believe that? Because every facet of her society – the media, her schools, her books, her friends, her parents, even her toys – have conspired to convince her that it is so.

One of the most powerful tools in this respect is religion, for it tells people not only what is proper and good, but what is holy and unholy, natural and unnatural. Having certain activities branded by a sacred text as unholy or unnatural when performed by females certainly helps ensure that females will avoid those activities. Equally inhibiting are declarations from religious leaders. Public declarations by a few Islamic *ulama* that women may not drive automobiles, for instance, surely have more clout than the private remonstrations of a multitude of husbands. In short, when important distinctions are made along gender lines, religious doctrines and practices are valuable instruments of indoctrination.

Of the many male-chauvinist religions, three have been especially successful in rele-gating females to inferior positions: Christianity, Islam, and Judaism. In addition to the institutionalization of patriarchal, even misogynistic, mores and practices, these familiar religions have much in common: belief in one and only one supreme being, identifica-tion of one book as a record of its god's words and deeds, characterization of its god as male, emphasis on compassion, and status as a major world religion. The relationship among these factors is fascinating, especially the roles they have played in the subjuga-tion of females.

Misogyny On High

The practices of Christianity, Islam, and Judaism originated when males and females were assigned different social roles in life: males in the public sphere, females in the private.[4] Because the males' role included designing the rules, they designed the rules to favor themselves. One of the most important rules, of course, was that only males could craft the rules.

This separation of roles extended to religion, so the males designed the rules there as well: they formulated the beliefs and practices, they created the institutions, they controlled the rituals. It should be no surprise, then, that the resulting religions explicitly reinforced the belief that males are superior to females and endorsed a set of social relations in which males controlled females.[5]

Religious practices demonstrated this message constantly. Females could not be religious leaders, and they could be religious participants only from a distance. They were not permitted near the holy sanctuaries, allowed to speak (or sing) in the church/mosque/synagogue, or even allowed to read the holy books. Of course the religious teachings were often harshly judgmental of females. A leader of the early Christian church, for instance, went so far as to blame human sin and suffering on females:

> The sentence of God on this sex of yours lives in this age: the guilt must of necessity live too. You are the Devil's gateway; you are the first deserter of the divine law; you are she who persuaded him whom the devil was not valiant enough to attack. You so carelessly destroyed man, God's image. On account of your desert, even the Son of God had to die.[6]

Indeed, all facets of the religions could be used to dishonor females, even prayer. Every morning, for instance, the Jewish man was expected to thank God: "Blessed art thou, O Lord our God, King of the Universe, who has not made me a woman."

And yet, despite their malice toward the female sex, these three religions flourished. How could this be? How could a theology that demeaned females become a significant religion throughout the world? How could something so blatantly one-sided and unfair gain such legitimacy? It is easy to imagine the existence of a few all-male cults built around the idea (and it is just an idea) of male superiority. But why would millions of sensible women support three worldwide religions based on that idea? How could reasonable women believe in these gods?

Co-opting Females

The first part of the explanation relates to the high value all three religions place on compassion and equality. All virtuous people are equal in the sight of God, the holy books proclaim. To honor each other is to honor God, the books declare, so be kind to each other, show concern for the vulnerable, help those less fortunate, be fair in all your dealings. No doubt females heard these words and believed them, despite the mountains of evidence to the contrary.

The second, and less comforting, reason females accepted these religions is related to the need of those who wield power to justify that status quo to themselves and to others. Men claiming such inordinate power needed to mollify any misgivings the advantaged might have and to gain the acquiescence of the disadvantaged. The benefits of this to those who make and enforce the rules are obvious: if people believe that the status quo is the best system, they will not fight against it, and the privileged can maintain their position (relatively) peacefully.

Therefore males used their religion to brainwash females into accepting the theory of male superiority as fact. The technique has been effective because of its multi-faceted approach: it appeals to the female's intellect as well as her emotions.

The crux of the male's argument for supremacy over females is inherent in all three religions: the contention that the one and only true god is male. Thus the very cores of all three theologies were deployed to subjugate females. The results were devastatingly successful, as well as successfully devastating.

The basic deductive argument is built around two simple syllogisms of the following classic form:

If P, Then Q.

P

Therefore Q.

The first part of the argument goes like this:

If god is male, then human males are more like god than human females are.

God is male.

Therefore human males are more like god than human females are.

The second part of the argument is:

If human males are more like god than human females are, then human males are superior to human females.

Human males are more like god than human females are.

Therefore human males are superior to human females.

The argument is not a sound one. But it still has power, for if you accept the premises, then the conclusions follow inevitably and indisputably.

Those conclusions have led to the disenfranchisement of females, especially within the religions themselves. Why couldn't Christian women be priests? Because a priest impersonates (the male) Christ during Eucharist. Why must Jewish women sit behind a screen in the synagogue, away from the sanctuary? Because they are too flawed to be near the holy objects. Why must Islamic women cover their entire bodies even though Allah commanded only that they dress modestly? Because the (male) *ulama* interpret Allah otherwise, and they know better. Why were women prevented from conducting the religious ceremonies, setting the rules, designing the practices? Because of their inherent inferiority to the men who do. And why is a woman's labor rewarded less than a man's? Need we ask?

It is curious that the deductive arguments noted above could ever be persuasive, for under scrutiny they collapse. Both syllogisms suffer from the same flaw: they rely on premises that are open to dispute. The first shaky premise is the assertion that god is male. It need not be so. Indeed, there are other, equally plausible alternatives: god may be female, or neither male nor female, or both male and female. In short, one may believe in the existence of god and yet deny that god is male.[7] This seems a sound approach for religious females to take, especially as it is to their advantage to do so.

Feminist theologians have staunchly advocated this approach. But this is a very recent development; for thousands of years women agreed that god was male, and many women still do. Why? Because that contention enjoys powerful support: the holy books of the three religions. According to the Jewish *Tenakh*, the Christian *Bible*, and the Islamic *Qur'an*, god is male. Yahweh, Christ, and Allah all have male attributes and male sobriquets: Lord of Hosts, God the Father, God the Son, King of the Universe, He who gives life and death, He who exalts. If you accept any of these books as literally true, then you are likely to view your god as male.

But if females believe that their god is male, and therefore refuse to challenge that part of the argument, they still may challenge another, equally shaky premise: the contention that, if human males are more like god than human females are, then human males are superior to human females. Other plausible options are available here, too. If the god is an inferior one, for instance, then being similar to him may not be an asset; perhaps being similar to god in some way makes one, not better than another, but more vulnerable. Perhaps being different (i.e., female) makes someone more, not less, fit to rule.

Of course the holy books can be used to rebut this challenge as well. God is magnificent, omnipotent, omniscient, wonderful in every way, the three books declare. To be like him, then, is to have positive attributes. And to be unlike him is to have negative attributes. It follows that because males are like god and females are not, males must be superior to females. And surely superior beings should rule inferior ones.

This argument could be broken down into a set of syllogisms, each of which would have at least one shaky premise. But the response would be the same as above: an appeal could be made to any of the three holy books to attest to the inevitability, the undeniability, the universality of female subordinacy. In short, if god is male, then females are in trouble. It is that simple.

This brings us to the second component of religious brainwashing: the appeal to emotions. The religious ceremonies and teachings were designed to make females feel both accepted (if they conform to certain standards) and unacceptable (because of their inherent unworthiness). They were designed, as well, to make the females doubt themselves.

Imagine how a woman might feel as she listened to St. Paul's Letter to the Ephesians read as part of the day's religious ceremony:

> Wives, submit yourselves unto your own husbands, as unto the Lord. For the husband is the head of the wife, even as Christ is the head of the church, and he is the savior of the body. Therefore, as the church is subject unto Christ, so let the wives be to their own husbands in every thing. (Eph 5:22–24)[8]

How would a female feel, seated in the back of the synagogue behind a screen during every religious service of her life? How would she feel when her presence in the synagogue is not even counted toward the quorum needed for a service? How would she feel, covered in black from head to foot in the blazing sun of a desert summer? Would she be angry? Would she be offended? Or might she instead feel inferior, inadequate?

And how might she feel when she realizes that all meaningful choices in life are denied to her? How might she feel when she is told – in school, at home, and in her place of worship – that males are superior to females? Might she come to believe that her want of options, as well as her lack of power, was natural? On what basis might she think otherwise?

And if she believes that everyone else accepts the proposition that she is second-rate, simply because she is female, is she likely to rebel? Is she even likely to question the system? Or is she more apt to question her own feelings, to distrust her ability to understand? If no one else believes that she is intelligent, or even rational, is she likely to presume it? If no one else believes she is capable of performing anything other than the most routine, mundane tasks, will she? Probably not.

So what is the result? Is she likely to be brimming with confidence and self-respect, eager to strike out on her own to make her way in the world? Is she likely to question the foundations of the dominant religion, to argue forcefully against the unfairness of the system? Or is she more likely to be someone who is fearful and insecure, someone who is subservient to others?

The answer is obvious: she behaves as you would expect someone who has been marginalized all her life would behave. She does what she is told, she acquiesces to the system, she accepts her fate. Perhaps she suffers from low self-esteem, perhaps she is passive and dependent and anxious. She behaves, in other words, like an unempowered female. After all, the whole system is designed to make her this way.

In short, males have heavy-handedly used these three religions to advance their own interests and to justify their having the upper hand. It can even be argued that the basic features of the religions – belief in one and only one supreme being, identification of one book as a record of the god's words and deeds, and characterization of its god as male – were designed to augment male domination over female members of his species. Perhaps even the purported emphasis on compassion and equality was merely a smokescreen hiding the truth, a cruel hoax played on females to entice them to acquiesce in their own destruction.

Misogyny and Monotheism

The question is, then, how important is male chauvinism to these religions? Is the misogyny, in other words, as integral a part as the monotheism?

Four responses to this question merit discussion:

1. "anatomy is destiny"[9]
2. god is a male chauvinist
3. the religious images should be taken symbolically
4. sexism has always been superfluous to these religions.

I will explain each in turn and also offer a rebuttal to each.

1.   Anatomy is destiny

The contention here is that the three religions accurately reflect the fact that males and females are different types of beings. Males are rational while females are emotional; males are rule-oriented while females are relationship-oriented; males are domineering while females are submissive; males are properly heads of households while females are their helpmeets; males belong in the public sphere while females belong in the private sphere. It has been this way since time immemorial. It has been this way, not because males have unfairly dominated females, but because it is the natural course of life. This is the way the world was designed, it is the way the world works, and all reasonable people recognize it. To fight this natural order is to invite disaster.

We have heard declarations like these for centuries; but all of them are wrong, terribly, tragically wrong. A female is not by nature someone who stays home to raise children, wash clothes, and bake bread. Nor is she by nature subservient to males. She becomes that type of person by adopting a certain gender role, a view of what is acceptable for her to do/say/think as a female. Gender roles are social constructions that begin at birth, not biological determinates beginning at conception.

There is one question everyone asks when told of a birth: Is it a boy or a girl? We ask because it makes a difference to us; we need to know how to treat this new being. We dress a male differently from a female; we address a male differently from a female; we expect different behaviors from a male than from a female. The children, of course, internalize these differences, and behave accordingly. They tend to repeat behaviors we have rewarded and reinforced, just as they tend to avoid behaviors we have punished and discouraged. They learn gender differences in other ways as well: from observation, for instance, and by generalizing from one type of experience to another.

These patterns continue throughout their lives, as males and females adapt to the dissimilar social expectations and mores imposed on them. The interplay of their behaviors with variations in treatment by others creates different life experiences. And these different life experiences form different sorts of people – people with the characteristics of distinct genders – with different feelings, beliefs, and skills. This, then, is how gender is constructed. And because gender roles are social constructs, they vary from culture to culture, and may even vary within a culture over time.

This is not to say that there are no biological differences between male and female humans; of course there are. The contrasts are sometimes obvious (such as their dramatically dissimilar reproductive organs), sometimes less noticeable (the two X chromosomes of a typical female, versus the one X chromosome and one Y of a typical male). The point is, rather, that these biological differences are less significant than the cultural ones in determining the ways males and females operate in the world. In other words, in the nature/nurture debate, I am arguing that the evidence indicates that more weight should be given to nurture than nature when it comes to gender differences.[10]

It is difficult, though, to convince skeptics of the validity of an ambiguous stance like this: it is true that there are innate differences between males and females *and* that gender is a largely social construct. In contrast, positions on the outside boundaries of the debate offer the comfort of firm absolutes. At one end are the postmodernists, who reject grand explanatory theories in general and theories of innate human traits in particular; all of our options and preferences, they argue, are the result of cultural influences. And at the other end are their archenemies, the sociobiologists, who argue that myriad human traits are genetically based. I am suggesting, instead, that the truth lies somewhere between the two; that, while genes exert a probabilistic influence on human behavior, their influence is muted dramatically by the environment.

This is not the place, however, to engage at length in the contentious nature/nurture debate that has raged across disciplines for years (and which shows no signs of abating). Suffice it to say that it seems clear to me that anatomy is not destiny (at least with regard to most gender differences), that females are not inherently inferior to males, and that cultural conditioning shapes most gender roles.

2. God is a male chauvinist

Nothing about the nature of god follows from my criticisms of these three religions. And I offer no propositions about the true nature of god, or even about the existence of god. Instead, let us assume for the sake of argument that these three religions are correct: god exists and he is a male chauvinist. In this case, it does not matter whether males and females are inherently different because god has designated separate social roles for them.

And if we wish to obey god's will, then we will treat males and females as different. If one result is that the members of one gender wield most of the power, then so be it.

This position raises a fundamental question about the response of females to god. Would a male chauvinist god be likely to inspire love in females? Would a biased, unfair god inspire awe? Or devotion? Or would such a being inspire some other reaction in females: something closer to wrath, perhaps, or resentment?

When confronted with a god who consigns you to a drab, dull existence, wouldn't you be angry? When told during religious services that you are base and inferior, simply because of the design of your genitalia, wouldn't you be indignant? Or perhaps Nelle Morton illustrates the proper tone for a females to adopt:

> No one is wise enough to know why God made female reproductive organs compact and internal so that woman is physically free to move about unencumbered and take her natural place of leadership in the world of womankind. Or why God made a male's organs external and exposed, so that he would demand sheltering and protection from the outside in order that he may be kept for reproducing the race.[11]

Surely Morton is correct that the situation calls for at least a little irony. Maybe even a good dose of sarcasm. But not love, certainly not love. Fear might be appropriate perhaps, given the unsavory outcomes for females, but not love. And not awe. After all, there is nothing splendid about a sexist god. And should we even consider such a limited being to be a god?

But females did not spurn the gods of these three religions, at least not generally. Nor were anger, indignation, and irony the typical responses of females to these gods or their religions. Instead, Christianity, Islam, and Judaism became powerful in part because of their female adherents.

That is because attitudes such as irony and indignation are possible only if you are able to step back from the god, to view the religion clearly. Females were prevented from doing precisely that. One successful method was to deny them access to education (so they could not read the holy books themselves) as well as access to any decision-making processes. Another, equally effective method was to prey on their emotions, to make them believe they were somehow inadequate, even irrational.

But today these techniques are not nearly so widespread nor so effective. And misogyny is no longer so much in vogue. Eventually, as sexist social systems disappear, so will sexist religions. And as our mores change, so must our gods.

3. The religious images should be taken symbolically, not literally

One way to save these three religions from the charge of unfair sexism is to deny that the holy books are literally true. The religious images, it is argued, should be understood as metaphors, as devices for expounding profound truths too difficult for the average person to describe (or understand) in the abstract. And abstractions are too impersonal and cold to instill the deeply emotional responses that religious faith requires. It seems more natural, for instance, to love and honor the particularized image of Jesus – a god who became a man in order to die for all human sin – than an abstruse concept of forgiveness.

So religious stories use familiar objects to create images we can grasp and to which we are likely to react with reverence and awe. These images are so powerful that we often forget that they are mere symbols. But that is our failing, not the fault of the holy books. We need to remind ourselves that religious discourse was meant to be taken figuratively, that, for instance, Yahweh's promise in Genesis to deliver his chosen people into a "land flowing with milk and honey" is not a contract at all, and certainly not one guaranteeing a future awash in sweetened dairy products; it is, instead, a reassurance of a brighter future, an exhortation to be hopeful.

It should not be surprising, the argument continues, that some of these images are couched in misogynistic language, given the low status of women at the time the religious works were compiled. But this sexism is only a contingent feature of the religions; the religious tenets can be expressed in nonsexist, even nongendered, language. Thus God need not be seen as a male, but understood instead as a perfect nongendered being, "the being than whom a more perfect being cannot be conceived." In short, we should be able to see beyond these time-bound images to appreciate the deeper truths they contain; we should be able to proceed beyond the sexist language of these ancient works to understand the universalist metaphors they express.

As compelling as this argument appears, it is persuasive only if one is willing to deny reality. Among its many weaknesses, three are worth noting here. The first problem is that even the sophisticated have difficulty being abstract. Can you really imagine what it means to be "the being than whom a more perfect being cannot be conceived" or "a ground of all contingency"? Most people cannot. And that is why religious literature continues to maintain a gendered image of god. Even those who seek to expunge sexism from religious practices find it impossible to erase gender altogether. Take, for instance, the Society for the Promotion of Christian Knowledge, Britain's oldest publisher of religious books, which touts its new, nonsexist prayer book. In it, Christianity's most often recited prayer, the Lord's Prayer, has been cleansed of its male chauvinist overtones. Retitled the "Prayer of Jesus," it now appeals not to a male god or an ungendered god but to an androgynous god. Thus where the prayer once began, "Our father, who art in heaven, hallowed be thy name," it now begins: "Beloved, our father and mother, in whom is heaven, hallowed be your name."[12] The new prayer book has met, of course, with considerable resistance. "I think it's heretical," the Archdeacon of York recently said. "I would walk out of a service if that was read."[13] This attitude is reflected in many places, including the Catholic Mass, which still features the centuries-old Nicene Creed:

> We believe in one God, the Father, Almighty, maker of heaven and earth, of all that is seen and unseen. We believe in one Lord, Jesus Christ, the only Son of God, eternally begotten of the Father. . . .

It seems clear that, while change is coming, it is slow and halting, and leaves untouched millions of lives.

A second and related problem is that one may adopt the theoretical principle that religious images are to be taken symbolically yet fail to accept that precept on an emotional level. It often is the case that "images function powerfully long after they have been repudiated intellectually."[14] Thus we find ourselves making declarations on an intellectual level that we simply do not accept on an emotional level. With religious images tending to honor males and dishonor females, we may find ourselves unconsciously doing the same.

Finally, there is the woeful fact that for thousands of years these images were used to subjugate women. Suggesting that the interpretations may have been mistaken, or that we should understand them figuratively, is insufficient; the sexist language is there, and it has caused terrible harm by marginalizing generations of females. And it continues to do so.

4. Male chauvinism is and always has been superfluous to Christianity, Islam, and Judaism

The holy books of all three religions acknowledge the profound value of females: the account of creation in the *Qur'an* describes the common origin of men and women, as does one of the versions of creation in the *Tenakh*, while the Gospels of the *New Testament* indicate that Christ treated females with respect and compassion. Indeed, all of the holy books give the impression that, in ultimate spiritual terms, males and females are equal.[15] Thus the fact that these religions may have been used by males to subjugate females shows only that males will manipulate anything and everything in order to maintain power; it does not show that these religions are necessarily sexist.

This is both the strongest and the weakest of the countervailing considerations. It is the strongest because it is accurate: I have shown only that male chauvinism is a major part of these three religions, I have not demonstrated that it is an essential part. Nor could I. A few Christian sects (such as Christian Scientists and Quakers) have always treated females as the equals of males; the largest Islamic group, Sunni Muslims, believe that females are as competent as males to perform some religious rites; and there have been Jewish female (reform) rabbis since 1972. Surely these are powerful counterexamples to my arguments.

Yes and no. Yes, they demonstrate that these three religions can exist intact minus a certain degree of misogyny. But no, they are not powerful enough to do the job; the examples are too few, and are overwhelmed by the countless instances of raw sexism. Indeed, many religious sects remain robustly male chauvinist, continuing to justify their stance by reference to their sacred texts and customs. The Catholic Church, for instance, declared as recently as 1995 that women may not be priests, not now, not ever.[16] This is to be expected; in the traditional forms of these religions, men continue to keep most of the interesting and influential roles for themselves.

The contention that the male chauvinism of these religions is only contingently a part of them – that they could exist intact without it – is a serious indictment against those who are unwilling to relinquish it. To hold tight to tradition is to embrace patriarchy. And that is not a pretty picture: it conserves an unfair and damaging conception of what it means to be female; it supports a one-sided power grab, allowing males to monopolize key roles; and it may even, as Mary Daly charges, sustain a hoax, "a front for men's plans and a cover for inadequacy, ignorance, and evil."[17]

The traditional forms of these religions are opting, in short, to cast doubt on the nature and value of religion itself. They are opting, as well, to cast doubt on the existence of an infinitely powerful yet benevolent god, for their disgraceful treatment of females raises the same demanding question posed by all great evils: what kind of god would allow this to happen?

Notes

1 Alfred Lord Tennyson, *The Princess: A Medley.* William J. Rolfe, ed. (Cambridge, MA: Riverside Press 1884), lines 437–41.

2   See D. M. Stetson, *Women's Rights in the U.S.A.* (Belmont, CA: Wadsworth, 1991); Carol Hymowitz and Michaele Weissman, *A History of Women in America* (N.Y.: Bantam Books, 1978).

3   See Pamela K. Brubaker, *Women Don't Count* (Atlanta: Scholars Press, 1994); *The State of the World's Women, 1985* (Oxford: New International Publications, 1985).

4   For a thoughtful history of the evolution of these three religious, see Karen Armstrong, *A History of God* (N.Y.: Ballantine Books, 1993).

5   Rachel Biale, *Women and Jewish Law* (N.Y.: Schocken, 1986); Mary Daly, *Beyond God the Father* (Boston: Beacon Press, 1973); Alice L. Hageman, ed., *Sexist Religion and Women in the Church* (N.Y.: Association Press, 1974); John S. Hawley, *Fundamentalism and Gender* (N.Y.: Oxford University Press, 1994); Jean Holm, ed., *Women in Religion* (N.Y.: Pinter, 1994); Rosemary R. Ruether, ed., *Images of Women in the Jewish and Christian Traditions* (N.Y.: Simon and Schuster, 1973).

6   Tertullian, *On Female Dress*, I, i. Tertullian, a North African theologian, lived about a hundred years after the death of Christ.
    Note as well the male chauvinist writings of other well-known Christian writers: Augustine, Cyprian, Jerome, Aquinas, Karl Barth, Dietrich Bonhoeffer, and Reinhold Niebuhr.

7   You may also dispute the premise by claiming that there is no god, or at least not one that matters much. Two directions are then possible: you can reject all religious belief, or you can choose a system of spiritual thought with no central god. You may discover, though, that the second alternative contains its own set of sexist elements. Consider, for instance, Buddhism, a non-theistic religion which emphasizes the human roots of suffering. Although the details of Buddhism change with every culture into which it is introduced, a core set of "Noble Truths" is embraced by nearly all Buddhists: suffering is universal, suffering is a result of desire, to eliminate suffering you must eliminate desire, a path can be followed to achieve freedom from desire and suffering. These tenets are gender-neutral and apply to all, without exception. Yet Buddhism is still tainted by misogyny. According to Buddha himself, for instance, the most senior nun must defer to the most junior monk. And in the system of reincarnation, rebirth as a female is generally considered unfortunate compared to rebirth as a male.

8   See also the words ascribed to Paul in I Tim. 2: 12: "But I suffer not a woman to teach, nor to usurp authority over the man, but to be in silence." Interestingly, many contemporary scholars agree that Paul never made any of these sexist remarks, that they were appended later to his letters. See, e.g., Robin Scroggs, "Paul and the Eschatological Woman," *Journal of the American Academy of Religion*, 40: 283–303, 1972.

9   Freud said this, earning the enmity of feminists. Sigmund Freud, *On Sexuality: Three Essays on the Theory of Sexuality and Other Works*, James Strachey, cn. (London Penguin, 1991).

10 For more on gender socialization see: Pierre Bourdieu, *The Logic of Practice* (Stanford, CA: Stanford University Press, 1990); R. W. Connell, *Gender and Power* (Stanford, CA: Stanford University Press, 1987); Michelle H. Garskof, ed., *Roles Women Play* (Belmont, CA: Belmont/Cole, 1971); Eleanor E. Maccoby, ed., *The Development of Sex Differences* (Stanford, CA: Stanford University Press, 1966); Dorothy E. Smith, *The Everyday World as Problematic* (Toronto: University of Toronto Press, 1987).

11 Nelle Morton, "Preaching the Word," in Alice L. Hageman, ed., *Sexist Religion and Women in the Church* (N.Y.: Association Press, 1974), pp. 30–1.

12 *Including Women: A Non-Sexist Prayer Book* is published by the Society for the Promotion of Christian Knowledge, and has been adopted by some Church of England congregations since 1991.

13 "Equal-opportunity Prayers," *Maclean's* August 5, 1991.

14 Morton, *op. cit.,* p. 32.

15 The *Qur'an* even gave women legal rights of inheritance and divorce, rights most Western women would not gain for over a thousand years.

16 Pope John Paul II issued an apostolic letter in 1994 declaring that the Catholic Church may not ordain women; in 1995 the Vatican's Congregation for the Doctrine of the Faith confirmed that this conclusion was infallible and irrevocable.

17 Mary Daly, *op cit.*, p. 30.

20 Divine Racism: A Philosophical and Theological Analysis*

William R. Jones

Toward a Definition of Divine Racism

Because of the novelty of the concept of divine racism, it is beneficial to describe its essential features by examining some concrete examples in which the concept is highly visible. Thomas Gossett's interpretation of sections of the *Rig Veda*, the Hindu scriptures of ancient India, and I. A. Newby's analysis of "religious racism" provide the desired specimens.

In Gossett's interpretation, Indra, the God of the Aryans, is described as "blowing away with supernatural might from earth and from the heavens the black skin which Indra hates." The account further reports how Indra "slew the flat-nosed barbarians," the dark people called Anasahs. Finally, after Indra conquers the land of the Anasahs for His worshipers, He commands that the Anasahs are to be "flayed of [their] black skin."

Proposition one. The first distinctive trait of divine racism to be noted is its appeal to a "two-category system"; it presupposes a basic division of mankind into an "in" group and an "out" group. In addition, this fundamental division is supported, initiated, or sanctioned by God Himself. God has special concern for the "in" group, and it receives His sustaining aid and grace. By contrast He is indifferent or hostile to the "out" group. In sum, God does not value all men equally; consequently He treats them differently. And this difference is not accidental but central to His will and purpose.

Proposition two. In the context of divine racism, the two-category system is correlated with an imbalance of suffering; the "out" group suffers more than the rest of the population. In the account from the *Rig Veda* we know that God has less affection for the Anasahs, because they suffer far more than the Aryans. The Anasahs are the vanquished, not the victor.

Proposition three. Implicit in the concept of divine racism is a third principle: God is responsible for imbalance of suffering that differentiates the "in" and the "out" groups. Indra is the major warrior on the field of battle bringing about the Anasahs' defeat. Thus honor, praise, and thanksgiving are addressed to Him for His mighty acts

---

* From William R. Jones, *Is God a White Racist? A Preamble to Black Theology* (Garden City, NY: Anchor Press/Doubleday, 1973), pp. 3–22 and 77–8.

in slaying "the flat-nosed barbarians." Perhaps, however, the concept of divine racism is defined too narrowly if it must be God's own hand that flays the ethnic outcasts. For my purpose I would emphasize only that the imbalance of suffering must express God's will or purpose, thus allowing that men or angels, for instance, could be the actual instrument and executioners of the divine plan.

Proposition four. God's favor or disfavor is correlated with the racial or ethnic identity of the group in question. God's wrath and hostility are directed toward the very features that characterize a particular racial or ethnic community. As the account from the *Rig Veda* concludes, Indra hated their blackness.

Proposition five. Newby's analysis of religious racism – "the idea that racial inequality is the work and will of God" – describes another essential feature of divine racism: God must be a member of the "in" group. In the context of this study, God must be white. The argument of an American divine, the Reverend Buchner Payne, is a classic statement of this claim:

> Now as Adam was white, Abraham white and our Savior white, did he enter heaven when he arose from the dead as a white man or as a negro? If as a white man, then the negro is left out; if as a negro then the white man is left out. As Adam was the Son of God and as God is light (white) and in Him is no darkness (black) at all, how could God then be the father of the negro, as like begets like? And if God could not be the father of the blacks because He was white, how could our Savior, "being the express image of God's person," as asserted by St. Paul, carry such a damned color into heaven, where all are white, much less to the throne?

Clearly Payne's analysis presupposes the two-category system, here the saved and the unsaved. This difference is correlated with contrasting racial populations, black and white. Salvation, the highest expression of God's favor, occurs only when the savior and the elect belong to the same ethnic group.

It is necessary at this juncture, for the sake of accuracy, to make certain qualifications. It must be understood that I am not arguing that every concept of divine election or divine preference is divine racism. We must allow that God may select a special group or individual to accomplish the salvation of others. But this type of election is more a specification of function, and need not entail in any way that God's love is less than universal.

Nor should one conclude that God's direct or indirect flaying or even the slaughter of a particular group is sufficient evidence for divine racism. The possibility that flaying is a justified response to prior sin must be granted. It is illegitimate to allow the concept of divine punishment to collapse into a form of divine racism.

Having identified and qualified some of the prominent features of divine racism, it is now necessary to scrutinize each. We must determine if every one of the several traits is essential and what special problems arise when we try to ascertain if divine racism is in fact present. Consider, for instance, that the fourth and fifth propositions introduce unique problems. The fourth requires ultimately that we psychoanalyze God, that we read His mind and fathom His motive and intent, His value system and plan for mankind. The fifth necessitates that the very being of God must be visible to the human observer. The third proposition involves a similar difficulty: We must either identify where God's own hand is at work in human history or at least specify the human acts that are claimed to be the locus of His activity. Merely to state the problem is to illuminate the difficulty.

Some question from another perspective must also be raised regarding the fourth proposition. Is blackness really the object of white hatred and racism? I think not. The racist is not actually affirming that white skin color is superior to black skin color. His emphasis lies elsewhere. The alleged inferiority and undesirability of blacks, which lie at the core of racism, do not inhere in color; it is of a different order, e.g. intelligence. Blackness is simply the most visible indicator of the absence or presence of the latter.

If we doubt the possibility of psychoanalyzing God to determine the presence of divine racism, if the divine side of the coin is obscure, then attention must be directed to the human side. This dictates that we plumb the situation of man, especially the factor of suffering and its uneven distribution. Thus my approach to the issue of divine racism reduces primarily to an analysis of the second proposition, to which we now turn.

The Multievidentiality of Suffering

To speak of divine racism is to raise questions about God's equal love and concern for all men. It is to suggest that He is for some but not for others, or at least not for all equally. It asks whether there is a demonic streak in the divine nature. The charge of divine racism, in the final analysis, is a frontal challenge to the claim of God's benevolence for all.

No doubt the phrase "divine racism" falls on the ear with contradictory import; it is akin to speaking of a married bachelor or a square circle. This is so, precisely because the concept of God's benevolence is being attacked. The case is the same with any God talk that hints at a demonic God. Only by picturing God as a supernatural Dr. Jekyll and Mr. Hyde can space be found for a malevolent deity. Clearly, in the context of Western monotheism, benevolence is as essential to the definition of God as is His existence. Hence there is an instinctive tendency to make God and goodness interchangeable terms and an inclination to make either man or some other creature, e.g. the devil, the ultimate cause of evil. One point is unmistakable in the framework of the Judaeo-Christian tradition: we can establish the legitimacy and irreducibility of the category of divine racism only by a frontal attack on the concept of God's *intrinsic* goodness.

The quickest and most effective way to execute this attack is to show that events are multievidential; specifically, the materials and events that have traditionally been interpreted as evidence of divine benevolence can just as easily support the opposite conclusion, of divine malevolence. Albert Camus makes this point persuasively in his inverted interpretation of Jesus' crucifixion, when he argues that the Cross is not necessarily a sign of God's activity for man's salvation.

Golgotha, a symbol of Jesus' suffering, traditionally represents God's crowning act of self-sacrificing love and vicarious suffering for man's salvation. And if we emphasize Anders Nygren's view, Calvary expresses the very essence of agapaic love, with no hint of divine self-interest.

Camus's interpretation of the inner meaning of Golgotha, however, has a strong flavor of misanthropy and divine self-interest:

> For as long as the Western world has been Christian, the Gospels have been the interpreter between heaven and earth. Each time a solitary cry of rebellion against human suffering was uttered, the answer came in the form of an even more terrible suffering. In that Christ had suffered and had suffered voluntarily, suffering was no longer unjust. . . . From this point of view the New Testament can be considered as an attempt to answer, in advance, every [rebel]

by painting the figure of God in softer colors and by creating an intercessor between God and man. Christ came to solve two major problems, evil and death. . . . His solution consisted first in experiencing them. The man-god suffers, too – with patience. Evil and death can no longer be entirely imputed to Him, since He, too, suffers and dies.

The effect of Camus's interpretation is to deny that Calvary is linked to man's salvation. In this new setting it becomes a public relations gimmick concocted by God to improve His image by reducing His accountability for human suffering. By arguing that human suffering should be endured and accepted because God Himself has suffered even more, the strategy is laid to keep man, particularly the oppressed, docile and reconciled to his suffering. Accordingly, human suffering does not become a springboard to rebellion. The one act that will initiate man's ultimate deliverance and humanization, the one act that will dignify man is nipped in the bud – precluded, as it were, by God's supreme act of love! God's act in Christ, then, becomes not an act for man's highest good, but against it. And the principle that we should love God because He first loved us collapses.

The essential focus of Camus's argument is to call attention to the ambiguity or multievidentiality of events. This means that the same event points with equal validity toward opposing interpretations. Multievidentiality is especially prominent when we are dealing with an individual's motive. Whether we conclude that God is a liberator or a misanthrope on the grounds of Calvary rests finally upon our reading of His motive. The multievidentiality of phenomena is also pronounced when we consider a general situation rather than a single event. It is interesting to compare how different observers describe the black situation in America. The black theologians, particularly James Cone, Joseph Washington, and J. Deotis Roberts, discover the liberating hand of God at work in the present black condition. Samuel Yette, however, sees a different pattern: "a plan to 'destroy' an obsolete people." Liberation or genocide? Take your pick.

The crucial conclusion, therefore, to be drawn from Camus's analysis is this: a demonic deity is a possible deduction – I do not say the only one – from every event asserting God's benevolence. And the step is indeed a short one from a demonic deity to a divine racist.

The divine suffering at Golgotha yields a possible interpretation of divine hostility. A similar conclusion can be drawn from any instance of human suffering; it, too, is multievidential. Any given occurrence of human suffering harmonizes equally well with antithetical positions, divine favor or disfavor, God's grace or God's curse. Consequently, in the face of human suffering, whatever its character, we must entertain the possibility that it is an expression of divine hostility. Moreover, if it is allowed that the general category of human suffering raises the possibility of a demonic deity, then the particular category of black suffering – and this is the crucial point for the argument – at least suggests the possibility of divine racism, a particular form of hostility.

A critical question arises once we acknowledge that suffering is multievidential: can we determine which of the antithetical interpretations is correct by inspecting the suffering itself? As a general principle, I would answer "No." Though black suffering may raise the question of divine racism or malevolence, the answer cannot be determined by an examination of that suffering alone. Camus's analysis of Golgotha illustrates the point. His interpretation of a demonic deity is not based on any peculiarities of suffering; no special aspects of Calvary demand an interpretation of divine hostility. Rather, Camus brings a different theological perspective to his analysis of the materials. The decisive factor appears to be his refusal to presuppose the intrinsic goodness of God because he adopts a different interpretive principle: God is the sum of his acts.

God as the Sum of His Acts

The concept of divine racism becomes clearer when we connect the previous discussion, of the multievidentiality of suffering and a demonic deity, to the principle: man is the sum of his acts. This principle is central to Sartre's doctrine of man, but I will argue subsequently that it is also central to the biblical understanding of God.

When we unpack the essentials of the principle that man is the sum of his acts, we find the following to be crucial for the discussion. First, a man's *character* is the sum of his acts. To speak of a man as loving or honest is always to refer to a complex of loving *acts*, of honest acts. The principle thus places what amounts to exclusive weight on the individual's activity, and this involves a corresponding devaluation of the category of motives. Indeed, in the context of this principle, a motive is an inference from the real acts of the individual. To assign a motive commits one to a particular method of confirmation. A motive must be substantiated – and this is the crucial point for the analysis – by reference to the actual practice of the individual. That is to say, we verify motives, as it were, retrospectively. We look at the individual's actual behavior and then argue backward to a prior motive. Thus the consequence of this principle is clear; we cannot appeal to an alleged self or character that is independent of or in disharmony with the veritable acts of the person.

The principle that man is the sum of his acts also places a premium upon the present and past acts of an individual. The character or motive we assign must be substantiated by reference to one's actual actions, i.e. past and/or present. Appeal cannot be made to one's anticipated or future acts as determinative for an appraisal of one's present character.

This point takes on additional clarity when we consider a third consequence of the principle. To speak of man as the sum of his acts is to advance a specific theory about man's nature, namely that man is freedom. Freedom, in this context, is the essence of man, and it alone is intrinsic. Accordingly we must differentiate between the *given* essence of man and his *achieved* essence. The former designates man's freedom; the latter, the character he weaves through the exercise of his given essence, i.e. freedom. More specifically, love, honesty, etc. must be classified as aspects of one's achieved essence and therefore are never intrinsic. Love, like the other aspects of one's achieved essence, refers, then, to one's actual performance, the sum of one's acts.

Applying the principle that man is the sum of his acts to God, we arrive at some illuminating conclusions, particularly for theological method and treatments of suffering that appeal to a future, or eschatological, resolution. First, it requires that whatever motive or character is assigned to God must be based on His past or present acts or both. Further, one is not permitted to speak of a divine motive of character that is different from His actual performance relative to man.

This principle obviously presents apparently insurmountable difficulties for the black theologian, for it forces him to identify the actual events in which he sees the benevolent and liberating hand of God at work not for man in general, but for blacks. This is not easily accomplished in light of the long history of oppression that is presupposed by each black theologian.

Treatments of suffering that appeal to eschatological, i.e. future, data are also seriously threatened if not effectively demolished by the principle that God is the sum of His acts. The reasons for this conclusion are simple. Every eschatological theory presupposes that man's situation in the future will differ from his past or present condition. According to this theory the shape and character of human existence will be radically modified; the Christian hope is that the undesirable elements of the past and the present will be judiciously eliminated or transformed. Many biblical images come to mind to confirm this observation. "The wolf shall dwell with the lamb." "The blind receive their sight, the lame walk, . . . the dead are raised up." The eschatological approach looks toward a corrective development in the course of human history. Whether the future is interpreted to involve a more complete realization of something already in germ or whether the future is said to involve a radical and qualitative break with present conditions, the corrective element is still clearly visible. And it is the corrective factor that is significant for the subsequent argument.

That many black theologians quickly accept an eschatological approach to black suffering is surprising in light of the troublesome consequences that attend its adoption. Does this acceptance suggest a certain desperation of method or argument? We can get at one weighty problem by asking the question, Why has the anticipated amelioration of black suffering not yet occurred; why is there still a double portion of black suffering? Surely the delay of the new age of black freedom yields at least these two interpretations: (1) being able but not wanting to; (2) wanting to but being unable. And these alternatives correspond roughly to the respective theories of a malevolent and a benevolent deity.

A further point is worthy of consideration: Consider that the anticipated correction can be read as either a gratuitous hope or a question-begging device – if it is not substantiated in a precise way. On what grounds can the black theologian affirm that God's activity will be different in the future – i.e., effecting the liberation of blacks – when the present and past history of blacks is oppression? Must not the evil and suffering that are presupposed in the very hope for future improvement be regarded as possible counterevidence against two claims: that the future will be different and that God will act differently in the future, i.e. in a liberating fashion? And as possible contrary evidence, must it not be considered and refuted by those who adopt the opposite interpretation?

Black religionists appear to beg the question in their appeal to the future. Believing that the past and present oppression of blacks is unjust and that God is just, they can only look toward the future for the actualization of black liberation and thereby the manifestation of God's justice and might. But does not black suffering call into question the very presupposition that undergirds the hope for future improvement, namely the justice of God? Consider as well that the suffering of blacks is deserved; where then is the ground and hope for improvement in the black situation?

Let us make the point more explicitly. The employment of eschatological data as a guide to the future condition of blacks requires a specific method if one's position is not to collapse into an improbable and presumptuous hope. The anticipated jubilee cannot be a mere substitute for the absence or paucity of events in the past and present in which the hand of God is at work for black liberation. Otherwise one is endorsing a blatant "pie in the sky" eschatology, and this view is explicitly denounced by each black theologian.

The logical and theological validation of an eschatological approach must proceed as follows: One must move from (a) the actual acts of God in the past or the present or both to (b) conclusions about His character, motives, and mode of activity. Given the principle that God is the sum of His acts, (b) is equivalent to (a), and (a) is thus the primary basis for speaking of (c) God's future activity. In the final analysis, (a) is determinative for (c). What is ruled out is to make (c) determinative for either (a) or (b). This conclusion seems inevitable unless one argues for a radical conversion on the part of God Himself.

I have suggested that the principle that God is the sum of His acts is Sartrean. A strong case, however, can be made for its essential biblical rootage. This is neither the place nor the time to give a lengthy defense of this claim, and the argument does not require it. The reader can confirm it for himself. What I have in mind is suggested by Bernhard Anderson, who concludes, ". . . for Israel to write history was to narrate the mighty acts of the Lord. . . . The Old Testament is the narration of God's action: what He has done, is doing and will do." I contend that the biblical writers establish Who God is by reference to what He has done or is now doing. Their conviction about the nature of God's future acts is grounded in the character of His past and present acts. . . .

. . . It is easy now to see how the principle of man as the sum of his acts enlarges the contours of the concept of divine racism. When one makes conclusions about *Who God is* on the basis of *what He has done* for black people, when one accents what is central to the black past – oppression and slavery – as the primary materials for reaching conclusions about the divine attributes, if we do not come to our analysis of the divine nature with the presupposition of His intrinsic goodness for all of mankind but let this conclusion emerge, if at all, on the basis of His actual benevolent acts in behalf of all, it is not difficult to see the category of divine racism surfacing. And when we are forced to make conclusions about God's nature and motives in the light of our subsequent discussion of black suffering as a variety of ethnic suffering, the question Is God a white racist? becomes an even more promising point of departure for black theology.

Toward a Biblical View of Suffering

An examination of the biblical treatment of suffering is necessary at this juncture for several reasons. An understanding of the biblical perspective helps to clarify the relation between suffering and divine racism, particularly the multievidential quality of suffering. It also prepares part of the necessary background for the next section: an analysis of ethnic suffering.

An examination of the biblical understanding of suffering confirms the crucial premise of the multievidentiality of suffering. One can find biblical statements to support each of the logical possibilities – suffering as an expression of (a) divine disfavor or deserved punishment, (b) divine favor, and (c) neither favor nor disfavor. Accordingly, suffering in the biblical view is inherently ambiguous.

No doubt the earliest theory advanced to explain human suffering was that it was invariably punishment for man's sin. Adam and Eve's banishment from Eden, the flood that destroyed all but the house of Noah, the razing of Sodom, etc. illustrate the familiar sequence: human sin, divine punishment, human suffering. Suffering, in this context, is evidence that corrective measures are necessary; suffering demands repentance.

One could easily cite a multitude of other biblical references that express this common response to suffering, but such is not my concern. My purpose is simply to call attention to the variety of interpretations, not to demonstrate that any single explanation is the biblical position. In this way, additional support is marshaled for the theory of the multievidential quality of suffering.

The opposite interpretation, human suffering as evidence of God's favor, also finds expression in the biblical record. ". . . the Lord reproves him whom He loves." One finds similar claims as well in the extracanonical literature, that those who are most pleasing to God have to be tried through suffering. Perhaps the suffering-servant theme, however, is the best and most familiar example of the relation of divine favor and suffering. In contrast to the Deuteronomic theory, in which suffering automatically convicts the sufferer of rebellion and disobedience, the suffering of the servant symbolizes perfect conformity to God's will. Accordingly, corrective measures are not necessary; suffering does not demand repentance. The future holds not judgment but reward and exaltation. In sum, suffering is evidence of more than simply divine favor; it manifests God's highest favor.

Numerous New Testament passages could be cited granting that suffering is not only positive, but a glorious and essential aspect of man's salvation. Peter's first letter is a case in point:

> Beloved, think it not strange concerning the fiery trial which is to try you, as though some strange thing happened unto you: But rejoice, inasmuch as ye are partakers of Christ's sufferings; that, when his glory shall be revealed, ye may be glad also with exceeding joy.

Peter affirms here that suffering is inherent in the life of the Christian, just as it was central to Jesus' own life. Further, that to endure suffering will lead to glory and reward, as it did for Jesus. Elsewhere in the same letter, Peter reminds his readers again: "Forasmuch then as Christ hath suffered for us in the flesh, arm yourselves likewise with the same mind."

Surely it is redundant to labor over those familiar parts of the New Testament record which affirm, at least implicitly, the value of Jesus' suffering and death for man's salvation, or those references to His death and suffering as the highest expression of self-sacrificing love.

The conclusion to be drawn from the foregoing is this: not every instance of suffering is negative in quality and thereby to be attacked or circumvented. Some are not only valuable but necessary for one's salvation.

Other interpretations of suffering cannot be neatly classified as evidence of God's favor or disfavor. Some explanations appear to have a foothold in both camps. Consider those treatments which define suffering as a form of divine warning. Here suffering has a dual role. To suffer indicates on the one hand that the wrong path has been taken. However, suffering can also be regarded as a guide to the proper path in so far as it illuminates the actions to be avoided if man is to obtain his highest good. Moreover, since it is a spur to repentance, it it essential to one's salvation. Thus, suffering as a form of divine warning is easily interpreted as a revelation of divine favor.

The duality of this example reinforces the fundamental point: suffering, in the biblical picture, is ambiguous, and this ambiguity is not dissolved by examining the conspicuous characteristics of suffering.

Other interpretations of suffering express a relation of neither favor nor disfavor. It is possible to affirm that suffering is simply an inherent feature of the human condition; to be human is to suffer, regardless of one's status relative to the divine. Certain sufferings express the elementary truth that man is a creature and not Creator, that he is not all-powerful, in sum, that he is man and not God.

Suffering as God's special method of testing man would also appear to fall into this class. Whether suffering is weal or woe, here depends ultimately upon whether one passes or fails the test. The suffering itself is transparently neutral.

The foregoing analysis underscores the claim that suffering is multievidential; it can embody God's grace, God's curse, or neither. We are thus forced to consider the crucial and difficult question, How do we determine in which class a given instance of suffering belongs; how do we differentiate between the suffering that evinces God's marvelous grace and that which signifies his terrible judgment; how do we determine if the sufferer is an agent of God's salvation or a sinner receiving his rightful punishment? The answer is inescapable: a standard or criteriology for separating negative from positive suffering must be formulated.

This issue is by no means an academic matter, but a core issue, as we shall see, for every theology of liberation. To reiterate an earlier conclusion: if we define an instance of suffering as positive or necessary for salvation, we are persuaded to endure it. On the other hand, to define suffering as negative is to prepare the ground for its annihilation. It is on the basis of this observation that we affirm the crucial conclusion: a theology of liberation must provide a basis for defining as negative the suffering that is implicit in oppression.

What do the biblical writers propose as the formula for distinguishing between positive and negative suffering? The criterion, I must confess, is not clear-cut. It is easy, for instance, to detect a developing consensus that not all suffering is divine punishment. The consequence of this development, however, is to increase, not reduce, the ambiguity of suffering.

Nonetheless, there is one clear line of thought that enables us to say at least that a given case of suffering is not divine punishment. Obviously, the fact of suffering itself is not sufficient to decide the case. Suffering is present when the sufferer is the recipient of merited punishment, but suffering can also be present when the sufferer is the object of God's favor. Nor does it appear that the special character of suffering, e.g. its severity, requires or permits the removal of one alternative in favor of the other. The differentiating factor must be something other than the suffering itself, even its peculiar characteristics. An analysis of the suffering-servant theme, in my view, supplies the differentiating factor.

The distinguishing element to be noted is a radical shift in the status of the sufferer. This shift, which I will designate as the *exaltation event*, comprises something akin to the principle "from last to first." In the context of oppression, the exaltation event would be labeled the *liberation* event, e.g. the Exodus. An analysis of the servant passages in Isaiah forces the conclusion that two conditions are required to index an individual or group in the class of suffering servant, which is to say, the object of God's favor. There is (1) the fact of suffering and (2) the exaltation-liberation event. If we call (1) the situation of humiliation, then (2) would designate the exaltation or reward. The two events are antithetical. The exaltation event constitutes the elimination of the suffering and its replacement by the opposite state of affairs.

The references "I will divide his portion with the great" and "he shall divide the spoils with the strong" supply the general sense of what is intended in the exaltation event. Even if the exaltation event is postponed to some future time, that is, interpreted eschatologically, it is on the basis of the anticipated event that the present suffering is claimed to be vindicated. . . .

. . . The eschatological option, in my view, is a theological dead end, for it leaves the issue unresolved until the distant future. Prior to the exaltation event and given the multievidentiality of suffering, God's favor and disfavor remain equally probable. Only the exaltation event appears to weight the scale for the interpretation of God's favor. Further, one is inclined toward the explanation of divine disfavor or deserved punishment to the degree that the exaltation event tarries.

If the foregoing analysis is correct, to refute the charge of divine racism, according to the biblical model, requires the occurrence of the exaltation-liberation event. And it should be clear that this event of emancipation terminates the suffering implicit in oppression. It is also clear that the identification of this event for *blacks* is no small theological task, particularly if we adhere strictly to the text of Isaiah. The liberation event, according to Isaiah, is not restricted to the eyes of the faithful alone but is visible and acknowledged by the oppressor as well.

In sum, it must be asked if the black theologian can legitimately adopt the suffering-servant model to explain black suffering if he (a) does not isolate in a concrete way the crucial exaltation-liberation event(s) or (b) regards this occurrence as a future event.

Ethnic Suffering and Divine Racism

I have attempted thus far to show that the multievidentiality of suffering, in part, forces consideration of the question, Is God a white racist? At this juncture it is necessary to enlarge the complex of categories that generates the issue of divine racism. The concept of ethnic suffering, the correlate of divine racism, will be our immediate focus.

Four essential features constitute ethnic suffering: (a) maldistribution, (b) negative quality, (c) enormity, and (d) non-catastrophic character. By accenting the ethnic factor I wish to call attention to that suffering which is maldistributed; it is not spread, as it were, more or less randomly and impartially over the total human race. Rather, it is concentrated in a particular ethnic group. My concern in utilizing the concept of ethnic suffering is to accentuate the fact that black suffering is balanced by white non-suffering instead of white suffering. Consequently, black suffering in particular and ethnic suffering in general raise the issue of the scandal of particularity.

John Bowker makes the cogent observation that the problem of the maldistribution of suffering is central in the Old Testament. "The problem in Scripture," he contends, "is not why suffering exists, but why it afflicts some people and not others. The problem is not the *fact* of suffering, but its *distribution*." Ethnic suffering underlines and gives emphasis to the same notion.

If we differentiate between positive and negative suffering, ethnic suffering in my stipulative definition would be a subclass of negative suffering. It describes a suffering without essential value for man's salvation or well-being. It leads away from, rather than toward, one's highest good. In contrast, certain advocates of types of asceticism, for instance, would regard suffering positively, as something to be actively pursued.

A third feature of ethnic suffering is its enormity, and here the reference is to several things: There is the factor of numbers, but numbers in relation to the total class, i.e., the number of suffering Jews or blacks in comparison with the total number of Jews or blacks. The factor of numbers raises the issue of divine racism at the point where the level of suffering and death makes the interpretation of genocide feasible.

Enormity also designates suffering unto death. Ethnic suffering reduces the life expectancy or anticipates the immediate death of the individual. The importance of this feature is that it nullifies various explanations of suffering and thereby narrows the spectrum of possible theodicies. Suffering unto death, for instance, negates any interpretation of pedagogical suffering; i.e., we learn from a burn to avoid fire. This makes little sense if the learning method destroys the learner. Suffering as a form of testing is also contradicted if the amount and severity of the suffering are incommensurate with the alleged purpose. It is for this reason that Rabbi Richard Rubenstein, for instance, denies that the horror of the suffering of Jews at Auschwitz could ever be likened to the testing of Job.

The final feature to be discussed is the non-catastrophic aspect. Ethnic suffering does not strike quickly and then leave after a short and terrible siege. Instead, it extends over long historical eras. It strikes not only the father but the son, the grandson, and the great-grandson. In short, non-catastrophic suffering is transgenerational.

When these aspects of ethnic suffering are connected, one is not tempted to account for their presence on the grounds of the operation of indifferent and impersonal laws of nature. Rather, one is more inclined to explain its causal nexus in terms of purpose and consequently person. This, too, is but a short step to seeing God as perhaps that person.

It is my contention that the peculiarities of black suffering make the *question* of divine racism imperative; it is not my position that the special character of black suffering *answers* the question. What I do affirm is that black theology, precisely because of the prominence of ethnic suffering in the black experience, cannot operate as if the goodness of God for all mankind were a theological axiom. . . .

. . . On the basis of the foregoing analysis – and here we arrive at the crucial point for the argument – the black theologian is committed to a total examination of the theological tradition. Once it is concluded that Christianity is infected with "Whitianity," once it is granted that a racist doctrine of the tradition has been perpetuated, the tradition must be scrutinized in the most radical and comprehensive manner. Like the rotten apples in the barrel of good apples, nothing prior to the examination can be regarded as sacrosanct for black theology – be it God, Jesus, or the Bible. Each and every category must be painstakingly inspected, and if it is found to be infected with the virus of racism or oppression, it must be cast aside.

The same point can be made from another perspective: Once the black theologian is convinced that a racist variety of Christian faith has continued, he must proceed, as it were, *de novo*, placing the entire tradition under a rigid theological ban. And this ban can be lifted only when each part proves its orthodoxy by showing its racist quotient to be minimal.

I question whether the black theologians have recognized the sweeping consequences of their presuppositions here. I also take the position that their appraisal has not been sufficiently comprehensive and radical. From my vantage point I see a fatal residue of the oppressor's world view in some of their theistic premises, in particular the intrinsic goodness of God. One of the compelling reasons for raising the issue of divine racism is to force a discussion of traditional concepts of God as possible props for oppression.

The major point can now be made: From a *de novo* perspective, the rival claims, God is a white racist and God is a soul brother, stand on equal footing. Accordingly, the black theologian cannot avoid the issue of divine racism. In fact it can be argued that he contradicts himself methodologically if he emphasizes black suffering and calls for a comprehensive scrutiny of the tradition but fails to raise the question of divine racism.

The presuppositions of the black theologians, in summary, force the conclusion that the foundation for their systems must be a theodicy that effectively rebuts the charge that God is a white racist.

Religion: Suggestions for Further Reading

R. M. Adams, *The Virtue of Faith* (Oxford: Oxford University Press, 1987).

R. M. Adams and M. M. Adams, *The Problem of Evil* (Oxford: Clarendon Press, 1991).

Martin Buber, *I and Thou*, trans. Walter Kaufmann (New York: Charles Scribner, 1970).

John D. Caputo, ed., *The Religious* (Oxford: Blackwell, 2002).

Jeff Jordan, ed., *Gambling on God: Essays on Pascal's Wager* (Lanham, MD: Rowman & Littlefield, 1994).

Jeff Jordan and Daniel Howard-Snyder, eds., *Faith, Freedom and Rationality: Philosophy of Religion Today* (Lanham, MD: Rowman & Littlefield, 1996).

Michael Peterson, William Hasker, David Basinger, and Bruce R. Reichenbach, *Philosophy of Religion: Selected Reading*, 2nd edn. (Oxford: Oxford University Press, 2001).

Michael Peterson, William Hasker, David Basinger, and Bruce R. Reichenbach, *Reason and Religious Belief: An Introduction to the Philosophy of Religion*, 3rd edn. (Oxford: Oxford University Press, 2002).

Alvin Plantinga, *God, Freedom, and Evil* (New York: Harper & Row, 1974).

Alvin Plantinga, *God and Other Minds: A Study of the Rational Justification of the Belief in God* (Cornell, NY: Cornell University Press, 1990).

William Rowe, *Philosophy of Religion: An Introduction* (Belmont, CA: Wadsworth, 1978).

Richard Swinburne, *The Evolution of the Soul* (Oxford: Oxford University Press, 1988).

Cornel West, *Prophesy Deliverance! An Afro-American Revolutionary Christianity* (Louisville, KY: Westminster John Knox Press, 2002).

PART THREE

ARE WE EVER FREE?

Introduction

21 From *The System of Nature*
PAUL HOLBACH

22 Freedom and Necessity
A. J. AYER

23 Human Freedom and the Self
RODERICK M. CHISHOLM

24 Alternate Possibilities and Moral Responsibility
HARRY G. FRANKFURT

25 How to Complete the Compatibilist Account of Free Action
JAMES P. STERBA AND JANET A. KOURANY

26 Living without Free Will: The Case for Hard Incompatibilism
DERK PEREBOOM

27 Metaethics, Metaphilosophy, and Free Will Subjectivism
RICHARD DOUBLE
Freedom and Determinism: Suggestions for Further Reading

Introduction

We like to think that we often choose and act freely. Of course, there will be times when we are forced to do things by other people, or are constrained by circumstances, so that we have no choice about what we do. But such occasions, we assume, are exceptions. Throughout our lives, we are continually faced with options and alternatives, some momentous (should I get married?) and some trivial (should I have a pizza or a hamburger?), and we assume that we can choose freely among them.

But suppose this subjective feeling of freedom is always illusory. Suppose that our decisions and resulting actions have all already been predetermined, so that someone in the know at the time of our birth (an omniscient observer) could map the track that we would follow for the rest of our life? Philosophers have been wrestling with this issue for over two thousand years, and, some would say, are no nearer to a solution today than they were two millennia ago. Part of what makes it such a difficult problem to resolve is that the seemingly simple concepts involved (for example, what it means to say we *could* have done otherwise) turn out, on closer examination, to be filled with deep complexities. Moreover, it is a problem that has major implications for other areas of our lives, for example whether it makes sense to hold people morally responsible for their actions, and whether our lives can really be meaningful. In this section, we start with some classic readings representing the main positions that have historically been taken on this issue, and then end with two more recent essays that, in certain respects, try to transcend the terms of the traditional debate.

Why might freedom be illusory? The issue arises in the first place because of the possible implications of the thesis of determinism: the view that, at least above the sub-atomic level, all events are completely caused. (The strange behavior of sub-atomic particles means that it is uncertain whether straightforward causal relations of the kind we are used to hold at that level.) We would have no difficulty in accepting this thesis as true for the inanimate world – chemical reactions, physical processes – or the animate world (on this planet) outside of ourselves – bacteria, plants, non-human animals. (Intelligent aliens would be another story.) After all, the natural sciences, like chemistry, physics, and biology, are based on precisely this premise. But when it comes to human animals, and intelligent aliens (if they exist), some people have hesitated to affirm the truth of determinism, at least for actions upon which we have deliberated, as against reflexive actions or things we do in a routine and unthinking way. For if all our actions, and the choices upon which they are based, are completely caused, then how could any of them be free? Wouldn't determinism imply that, given the cause, or set of causes, at work, the person *had* to do what she did?

The main positions on the issue can be summarized very simply by focusing on the following three central claims. Let D be the thesis that all events are caused, I be the thesis that causation is incompatible with freedom, and F be the thesis that human freedom exists. (Note that this need not imply that *all* actions are free, just that at least some are.) Affirming and denying these three claims in different combinations results in three main positions: *hard* or *incompatibilist determinism*; *soft* or *compatibilist determinism*; and *libertarian indeterminism*.

Incompatibilist determinism affirms the truth of both D and I, thereby ruling out human freedom. All events are caused, and causation is incompatible with freedom; therefore, F is false. This position is represented here by the selection from Paul Holbach. The idea is that if we really consider, without evasion, the implications of the human race's being part of nature, subject to the same causal laws as the rest of nature, then we have to face the fact that we are no more free than non-human animals. We have the illusion of freedom, but not the reality. When we think we are deciding something, or choosing between alternatives, a pre-existing causal chain is already in place that determines the outcome. And this causal chain stretches backward in time, each link having preceding links, so that Z is caused by Y, which is caused by X, which is caused by W . . . etc. Knowing our heredity (from the Human Genome Project, say), the environment in which we were raised, the resulting character we have, and the particular set of circumstances with which we are now faced, the appropriately informed observer would always be able to tell what we are going to do and so we are not free.

But not all philosophers have accepted this analysis. Compatibilist determinists affirm determinism just as completely as do incompatibilist determinists ("soft" does not imply that they are any the *less* deterministic), but deny that it rules out human freedom. So they accept D, while rejecting I, and endorsing F. All events are indeed caused, but since, they claim, determinism is compatible with freedom, the hard determinist conclusion is false. The classic argument, developed here by A. J. Ayer, is that, if we analyze how we use the term "freedom," we will realize that it is opposed not to *causality* as such, but to *constraint*, in other words, to a particular *kind* of causality. The crucial issue is whether the causal chain at work involves our own wishes and desires or not. If it does, then apart from some weird non-typical cases (hypnosis, obsessive-compulsive motivation, being programmed with electrodes in the brain, etc.), we are acting in a way that is *both* caused and free.

However this "solution" is seen as bogus by philosophers in the third category: libertarian indeterminists. (Note that "libertarianism" here is being used in the metaphysical rather than political sense.) Libertarians, also sometimes known as theorists of "agent" causation, argue that the compatibilist subdividing of causality into constraining and non-constraining kinds of causes is irrelevant, since even if our actions are caused by our desires, the fact that the desires themselves are caused by a pre-existing chain of events means that we could not have *chosen* or *willed* otherwise. So such "freedom" would be illusory. Libertarians agree with hard determinists that incompatibilism, I, is true, but since they believe F, that human freedom exists, they deny the truth of D, determinism. Thus Roderick Chisholm (who uses the term "immanent" causation) claims that, for at least some of our actions, we cause them *ourselves* independently of the determining effects of a previous causal chain. So the contention is not that some of our actions are free because they are *uncaused* (simple indeterminism), since the lack of connection with our selves in such a scenario would rule out their being free in any meaningful sense. Rather, they are *self*-caused. Even given a particular set of preceding causes, metaphysical libertarians believe, the self can still choose to will in different ways, which is why D is not true.

Compatibilists have a comeback to this libertarian critique, though. James Sterba and Janet Kourany argue against Chisholm's analysis (in a related article) of what it means to say we could have acted otherwise. Chisholm and other incompatibilists claim that determinism renders empty or mysteriously unanalyzable the assertion "X could have willed otherwise." But Sterba and Kourany deny that this is so. They contend that this statement can be simply explained with reference to X's alternative "willing," on the basis of his values and reasons to act, in the given choice situation. So compatibilism does not, impossibly, require that the agent in the situation have different knowledge or ability than he actually does. It just requires that if he had, say, made more effort, or paid more attention, he could have willed and acted otherwise. Thus he is legitimately subject to moral evaluation for his actions.

Another perspective on the interconnection between moral responsibility and freedom and determinism is provided by Harry Frankfurt. It might seem obviously, even trivially, true that an agent is morally responsible for her actions only if she could have done otherwise. But in what is now seen as a classic article in the recent literature, Harry Frankfurt argues against this claim, which he calls the principle of alternate possibilities. It is true that coercion (doing something because you're forced to do it) is incompatible with moral responsibility, but Frankfurt denies that this thesis about coercion is just a special case of the more general principle of alternate possibilities. So even if it is true, it does not follow that the principle is true. The crucial requirement for blamelessness is whether or not the agent performed the action *only because* she could not have done otherwise. But it is possible both that she could not have done otherwise, and that she did it because she wanted to, in which case she might indeed be morally responsible. So the principle of alternate possibilities, in Frankfurt's view, is false.

Finally, the two essays by Derk Pereboom and Richard Double represent recent work that develops views at variance with what have become the established positions on the issue. Pereboom argues for what he calls "hard incompatibilism," denying that we have free will as commonly understood but not committing himself to determinism. He explores the implications of his view for such areas as moral responsibility, the meaningfulness of life, and personal relationships, arguing that, despite its depressing initial appearance, his position could actually have "substantial benefits for human life." Double suggests that the main underlying motivation of the free will debate has been to establish what the possibilities are for moral responsibility. If we think of the free will issue, accordingly, as primarily a moral problem, we can draw on the debates in ethical theory over the subjectivity or objectivity of moral claims, and apply these categories to claims about free will. He endorses what he calls "free will subjectivism," which rejects (analogously to subjectivism in ethics with respect to right and wrong) the assumption that there is an objectively correct view of whether the will is free or not. Freedom becomes a matter of how the individual in question subjectively feels about things. Double then shows how, if his analysis were accepted, the traditional compatibilist/incompatibilist mapping of positions would have to be redrawn.

21   From *The System of Nature**

Paul Holbach

Chapter XI
Of the System of Man's Free Agency

Those who have pretended that the *soul* is distinguished from the body, is immaterial, draws its ideas from its own peculiar source, acts by its own energies, without the aid of any exterior object, have, by a consequence of their own system, enfranchised it from those physical laws according to which all beings of which we have a knowledge are obliged to act. They have believed that the soul is mistress of its own conduct, is able to regulate its own peculiar operations, has the faculty to determine its will by its own natural energy; in a word, they have pretended that man is a *free agent*.

It has been already sufficiently proved that the soul is nothing more than the body considered relatively to some of its functions more concealed than others: it has been shown that this soul, even when it shall be supposed immaterial, is continually modified conjointly with the body, is submitted to all its motion, and that without this it would remain inert and dead: that, consequently, it is subjected to the influence of those material and physical causes which give impulse to the body; of which the mode of existence, whether habitual or transitory, depends upon the material elements by which it is surrounded, that form its texture, constitute its temperament, enter into it by means of the aliments, and penetrate it by their subtility. The faculties which are called *intellectual*, and those qualities which are styled *moral*, have been explained in a manner purely physical and natural. In the last place it has been demonstrated that all the ideas, all the systems, all the affections, all the opinions, whether true or false, which man forms to himself, are to be attributed to his physical and material senses. Thus man is a being purely physical; in whatever manner he is considered, he is connected to universal nature, and submitted to the necessary and immutable laws that she imposes on all the beings she contains, according to their peculiar essences or to the respective properties with which, without consulting them, she endows each particular species. Man's life is a line that nature commands him to describe upon the surface of the earth, without his ever being able to swerve from it, even for an instant. He is born without his own consent; his organization does in nowise depend upon himself; his ideas come to him involuntarily; his habits are in the power of those who cause him to contract them; he is unceasingly modified by causes, whether visible or concealed, over which he has no control, which necessarily regulate his mode of existence, give the hue to his way of thinking, and determine his manner of acting. He is good or bad, happy or miserable, wise or foolish, reasonable or irrational, without his will being for any thing in these various states. Nevertheless, in despite of the shackles by which he is bound, it is pretended he is a free agent, or that independent of the causes by which he is moved, he determines his own will, and regulates his own condition. . . .

* From Baron D'Holbach, *The System of Nature: Laws of the Moral and Physical World*, translated by H. D. Robinson (Boston, MA: J. P. Mendum), chapter XI.

... The will, as we have elsewhere said, is a modification of the brain, by which it is disposed to action, or prepared to give play to the organs. This will is necessarily determined by the qualities, good or bad, agreeable or painful, of the object or the motive that acts upon his senses, or of which the idea remains with him, and is resuscitated by his memory. In consequence, he acts necessarily, his action is the result of the impulse he receives either from the motive, from the object, or from the idea which has modified his brain, or disposed his will. When he does not act according to this impulse, it is because there comes some new cause, some new motive, some new idea, which modifies his brain in a different manner, gives him a new impulse, determines his will in another way, by which the action of the former impulse is suspended: thus, the sight of an agreeable object, or its idea, determines his will to set him in action to procure it; but if a new object or a new idea more powerfully attracts him, it gives a new direction to his will, annihilates the effect of the former, and prevents the action by which it was to be procured. This is the mode in which reflection, experience, reason, necessarily arrests or suspends the action of man's will: without this he would of necessity have followed the anterior impulse which carried him towards a then desirable object. In all this he always acts according to necessary laws, from which he has no means of emancipating himself.

If when tormented with violent thirst, he figures to himself in idea, or really perceives a fountain, whose limpid streams might cool his feverish want, is he sufficient master of himself to desire or not to desire the object competent to satisfy so lively a want? It will no doubt be conceded, that it is impossible he should not be desirous to satisfy it; but it will be said – if at this moment it is announced to him that the water he so ardently desires is poisoned, he will, notwithstanding his vehement thirst, abstain from drinking it: and it has, therefore, been falsely concluded that he is a free agent. The fact, however, is, that the motive in either case is exactly the same: his own conservation. The same necessity that determined him to drink before he knew the water was deleterious, upon this new discovery equally determines him not to drink; the desire of conserving himself either annihilates or suspends the former impulse; the second motive becomes stronger than the preceding, that is, the fear of death, or the desire of preserving himself, necessarily prevails over the painful sensation caused by his eagerness to drink: but, it will be said, if the thirst is very parching, an inconsiderate man without regarding the danger will risk swallowing the water. Nothing is gained by this remark: in this case, the anterior impulse only regains the ascendency; he is persuaded that life may possibly be longer preserved, or that he shall derive a greater good by drinking the poisoned water than by enduring the torment, which, to his mind, threatens instant dissolution: thus the first becomes the strongest and necessarily urges him on to action. Nevertheless, in either case, whether he partakes of the water, or whether he does not, the two actions will be equally necessary; they will be the effect of that motive which finds itself most puissant; which consequently acts in the most coercive manner upon his will.

This example will serve to explain the whole phenomena of the human will. This will, or rather the brain, finds itself in the same situation as a bowl, which, although it has received an impulse that drives it forward in a straight line, is deranged in its course whenever a force superior to the first obliges it to change its direction. The man who drinks the poisoned water appears a madman; but the actions of fools are as necessary as those of the most prudent individuals. The motives that determine the voluptuary and the debauchee to risk their health, are as powerful, and their actions are as necessary, as those which decide the wise man to manage his. But, it will be insisted, the debauchee may be prevailed on to change his conduct: this does not imply that he is a free agent; but that motives may be found sufficiently powerful to annihilate the effect of those that previously acted upon him; then these new motives determine his will to the new mode of conduct he may adopt as necessarily as the former did to the old mode. . . .

. . . The errors of philosophers on the free agency of man, have arisen from their regarding his will as the *primum mobile*, the original motive of his actions; for want of recurring back, they have not perceived the multiplied, the complicated causes which, independently of him, give motion to the will itself; or which dispose and modify his brain, whilst he himself is purely passive in the motion he receives. Is he the master of desiring or not desiring an object that appears desirable to him? Without doubt it will be answered, no: but he is the master of resisting his desire, if he reflects on the consequences. But, I ask, is he capable of reflecting on these consequences, when his soul is hurried along by a very lively passion, which entirely depends upon his natural organization, and the causes by which he is modified? Is it in his power to add to these consequences all the weight necessary to counterbalance his desire? Is he the master of preventing the qualities which render an object desirable from residing in it? I shall be told: he ought to have learned to resist his passions; to contract a habit of putting a curb on his desires. I agree to it without any difficulty. But in reply, I again ask, is his nature susceptible of this modification? Does his boiling blood, his unruly imagination, the igneous fluid that circulates in his veins, permit him to make, enable him to apply true experience in the moment when it is wanted? And even when his temperament has capacitated him, has his education, the examples set before him, the ideas with which he has been inspired in early life, been suitable to make him contract this habit of repressing his desires? Have not all these things rather contributed to induce him to seek with avidity, to make him actually desire those objects which you say he ought to resist.

The *ambitious man* cries out: you will have me resist my passion; but have they not unceasingly repeated to me that rank, honours, power, are the most desirable advantages in life? Have I not seen my fellow citizens envy them, the nobles of my country sacrifice every thing to obtain them? In the society in which I live, am I not obliged to feel, that if I am deprived of these advantages, I must expect to languish in contempt; to cringe under the rod of oppression?

The *miser* says: you forbid me to love money, to seek after the means of acquiring it: alas! does not every thing tell me that, in this world, money is the greatest blessing; that it is amply sufficient to render me happy? In the country I inhabit, do I not see all my fellow citizens covetous of riches? but do I not also witness that they are little scrupulous in the means of obtaining wealth? As soon as they are enriched by the means which you censure, are they not cherished, considered and respected? By what authority, then, do you defend me from amassing treasure? what right have you to prevent my using means, which, although you call them sordid and criminal, I see approved by the sovereign? Will you have me renounce my happiness?

The *voluptuary* argues: you pretend that I should resist my desires; but was I the maker of my own temperament, which unceasingly invites me to pleasure? You call my pleasures disgraceful; but in the country in which I live, do I not witness the most dissipated men enjoying the most distinguished rank? Do I not behold that no one is ashamed of adultery but the husband it has outraged? do not I see men making trophies of their debaucheries, boasting of their libertinism, rewarded with applause?

The *choleric man* vociferates: you advise me to put a curb on my passions, and to resist the desire of avenging myself: but can I conquer my nature? Can I alter the received opinions of the world? Shall I not be for ever disgraced, infallibly dishonoured in society, if I do not wash out in the blood of my fellow creature the injuries I have received?

The *zealous enthusiast* exclaims: you recommend me mildness; you advise me to be tolerant; to be indulgent to the opinions of my fellow men; but is not my temperament violent? Do I not ardently love my God? Do they not assure me, that zeal is pleasing to him; that sanguinary inhuman persecutors have been his friends? As I wish to render myself acceptable in his sight, I therefore adopt the same means.

In short, the actions of man are never free; they are always the necessary consequence of his temperament, of the received ideas, and of the notions, either true or false, which he has formed to himself of happiness; of his opinions, strengthened by example, by education, and by daily experience. So many crimes are witnessed on the earth only because every thing conspires to render man vicious and criminal; the religion he has adopted, his government, his education, the examples set before him, irresistibly drive him on to evil: under these circumstances, morality preaches virtue to him in vain. In those societies where vice is esteemed, where crime is crowned, where venality is constantly recompensed, where the most dreadful disorders are punished only in those who are too weak to enjoy the privilege of committing them with impunity, the practice of virtue is considered nothing more than a painful sacrifice of happiness. Such societies chastise, in the lower orders, those excesses which they respect in the higher ranks; and frequently have the injustice to condemn those in the penalty of death, whom public prejudices, maintained by constant example, have rendered criminal.

Man, then, is not a free agent in any one instant of his life; he is necessarily guided in each step by those advantages, whether real or fictitious, that he attaches to the objects by which his passions are roused: these passions themselves are necessary in a being who unceasingly tends towards his own happiness; their energy is necessary, since that depends on his temperament; his temperament is necessary, because it depends on the physical elements which enter into his composition; the modification of this temperament is necessary, as it is the infallible and inevitable consequence of the impulse he receives from the incessant action of moral and physical beings.

In despite of these proofs of the want of free agency in man, so clear to unprejudiced minds, it will, perhaps, be insisted upon with no small feeling of triumph, that if it be proposed to any one, to move or not to move his hand, an action in the number of those called *indifferent*, he evidently appears to be the master of choosing; from which it is concluded that evidence has been offered of his free agency. The reply is, this example is perfectly simple; man in performing some action which he is resolved on doing, does not by any means prove his free agency: the very desire of displaying this quality, excited by the dispute, becomes a necessary motive, which decides his will either for the one or the other of these actions: what deludes him in this instance, or that which persuades him he is a free agent at this moment, is, that he does not discern the true motive which sets him in action, namely, the desire of convincing his opponent: if in the heat of the dispute he insists and asks, "Am I not the master of throwing myself out of the window?" I shall answer him, no; that whilst he preserves his reason there is no probability that the desire of proving his free agency, will become a motive sufficiently powerful to make him sacrifice his life to the attempt: if, notwithstanding this, to prove he is a free agent, he should actually precipitate himself from the window, it would not be a sufficient warranty to conclude he acted freely, but rather that it was the violence of his temperament which spurred him on to this folly. Madness is a state, that depends upon the heat of the blood, not upon the will. A fanatic or a hero, braves death as necessarily as a more phlegmatic man or a coward flies from it.[1]

It is said that free agency is the absence of those obstacles competent to oppose themselves to the actions of man, or to the exercise of his faculties: it is pretended that he is a free agent whenever, making use of these faculties, he produces the effect he has proposed to himself. In reply to this reasoning, it is sufficient to consider that it in nowise depends upon himself to place or remove the obstacles that either determine or resist him; the motive that causes his action is no more in his own power than the obstacle that impedes him, whether this obstacle or motive be within his own machine or exterior of his person: he is not master of the thought presented to his mind, which determines his will; this thought is excited by some cause independent of himself.

To be undeceived on the system of his free agency, man has simply to recur to the motive by which his will is determined; he will always find this motive is out of his own controul. It is said: that in consequence of an idea to which the mind gives birth, man acts freely if he encounters no obstacle. But the question is, what gives birth to this idea in his brain? was he the master either to prevent it from presenting itself, or from renewing itself in his brain? Does not this idea depend either upon objects that strike him exteriorly and in despite of himself, or upon causes, that without his knowledge, act within himself and modify his brain? Can he prevent his eyes, cast without design upon any object whatever, from giving him an idea of this object, and from moving his brain? He is not more master of the obstacles; they are the necessary effects of either interior or exterior causes, which always act according to their given properties. A man insults a coward, this necessarily irritates him against his insulter, but his will cannot vanquish the obstacle that cowardice places to the object of his desire, because his natural conformation, which does not depend upon himself, prevents his having courage. In this case, the coward is insulted in despite of himself; and against his will is obliged patiently to brook the insult he has received.

The partisans of the system of free agency appear ever to have confounded constraint with necessity. Man believes he acts as a free agent, every time he does not see any thing that places obstacles to his actions; he does not perceive that the motive which causes him to will, is always necessary and independent of himself. A prisoner loaded with chains is compelled to remain in prison; but he is not a free agent in the desire to emancipate himself; his chains prevent him from acting, but they do not prevent him from willing; he would save himself if they would loose his fetters; but he would not save himself as a free agent; fear or the idea of punishment would be sufficient motives for his action.

Man may, therefore, cease to be restrained, without, for that reason, becoming a free agent: in whatever manner he acts, he will act necessarily, according to motives by which he shall be determined. He may be compared to a heavy body that finds itself arrested in its descent by any obstacle whatever: take away this obstacle, it will gravitate or continue to fall; but who shall say this dense body is free to fall or not? Is not its descent the necessary effect of its own specific gravity? The virtuous Socrates submitted to the laws of his country, although they were unjust; and though the doors of his jail were left open to him, he would not save himself; but in this he did not act as a free agent: the invisible chains of opinion, the secret love of decorum, the inward respect for the laws, even when they were iniquitous, the fear of tarnishing his glory, kept him in his prison; they were motives sufficiently powerful with this enthusiast for virtue, to induce him to wait death with tranquillity; it was not in his power to save himself, because he could find no potential motive to bring him to depart, even for an instant, from those principles to which his mind was accustomed.

Man, it is said, frequently acts against his inclination, from whence it is falsely concluded he is a free agent; but when he appears to act contrary to his inclination, he is always determined to it by some motive sufficiently efficacious to vanquish this inclination. A sick man, with a view to his cure, arrives at conquering his repugnance to the most disgusting remedies: the fear of pain, or the dread of death, then become necessary motives; consequently this sick man cannot be said to act freely.

When it is said, that man is not a free agent, it is not pretended to compare him to a body moved by a simple impulsive cause: he contains within himself causes inherent to his existence; he is moved by an interior organ, which has its own peculiar laws, and is itself necessarily determined in consequence of ideas formed from perceptions resulting from sensations which it receives from exterior objects. As the mechanism of these sensations, of these perceptions, and the manner they engrave ideas on the brain of man, are not known to him; because he is unable to unravel all these motions; because he cannot perceive the chain of operations in his soul, or the motive principle that acts within him, he supposes himself a free agent; which, literally translated, signifies, that he moves himself by himself; that he determines himself without cause: when he rather ought to say, that he is ignorant how or for why he acts in the manner he does. It is true the soul enjoys an activity peculiar to itself: but it is equally certain that this activity would never be displayed, if some motive or some cause did not put it in a condition to exercise itself: at least it will not be pretended that the soul is able either to love or to hate without being moved, without knowing the objects, without having some idea of their qualities. Gunpowder has unquestionably a particular activity, but this activity will never display itself, unless fire be applied to it; this, however, immediately sets it in motion.

It is the great complication of motion in man, it is the variety of his action, it is the multiplicity of causes that move him, whether simultaneously or in continual succession, that persuades him he is a free agent: if all his motions were simple, if the causes that move him did not confound themselves with each other, if they were distinct, if his machine were less complicated, he would perceive that all his actions were necessary, because he would be enabled to recur instantly to the cause that made him act. A man who should be always obliged to go towards the west, would always go on that side; but he would feel that, in so going, he was not a free agent: if he had another sense, as his actions or his motion, augmented by a sixth, would be still more varied and much more complicated, he would believe himself still more a free agent than he does with his five senses.

It is, then, for want of recurring to the causes that move him; for want of being able to analyze, from not being competent to decompose the complicated motion of his machine, that man believes himself a free agent: it is only upon his own ignorance that he founds the profound yet deceitful notion he has of his free agency; that he builds those opinions which he brings forward as a striking proof of his pretended freedom of action. If, for a short time, each man was willing to examine his own peculiar actions, search out their true motives to discover their concatenation, he would remain convinced that the sentiment he has of his natural free agency, is a chimera that must speedily be destroyed by experience.

Nevertheless it must be acknowledged that the multiplicity and diversity of the causes which continually act upon man, frequently without even his knowledge, render it impossible, or at least extremely difficult for him to recur to the true principles of his own peculiar actions, much less the actions of others: they frequently depend upon causes so fugitive, so remote from their effects, and which, superficially examined, appear to have so little analogy, so slender a relation with them, that it requires singular sagacity to bring them into light. This is what renders the study of the moral man a task of such difficulty; this is the reason why his heart is an abyss, of which it is frequently impossible for him to fathom the depth. . . .

. . . If he understood the play of his organs, if he was able to recall to himself all the impulsions they have received, all the modifications they have undergone, all the effects they have produced, he would perceive that all his actions are submitted to that *fatality*, which regulates his own particular system, as it does the entire system of the universe: no one effect in him, any more than in nature, produces itself by *chance*; this, as has been before proved, is a word void of sense. All that passes in him; all that is done by him; as well as all that happens in nature, or that is attributed to her, is derived from necessary causes, which act according to necessary laws, and which produce necessary effects from whence necessarily flow others.

Fatality, is the eternal, the immutable, the necessary order, established in nature; or the indispensable connexion of causes that act, with the effects they operate. Conforming to this order, heavy bodies fall; light bodies rise; that which is analogous in matter reciprocally attracts; that which is heterogeneous mutually repels; man congregates himself in society, modifies each his fellow; becomes either virtuous or wicked; either contributes to his mutual happiness, or reciprocates his misery; either loves his neighbour, or hates his companion necessarily, according to the manner in which the one acts upon the other. From whence it may be seen, that the same necessity which regulates the physical, also regulates the moral world, in which every thing is in consequence submitted to fatality. Man, in running over, frequently without his own knowledge, often in despite of himself, the route which nature has marked out for him, resembles a swimmer who is obliged to follow the current that carries him along: he believes himself a free agent, because he sometimes consents, sometimes does not consent, to glide with the stream, which notwithstanding, always hurries him forward; he believes himself the master of his condition, because he is obliged to use his arms under the fear of sinking.

Note

1   There is, in point of fact, no difference between the man that is cast out of the window by another, and the man who throws himself out of it, except that the impulse in the first instance comes immediately from without, whilst that which determines the fall in the second case, springs from within his own peculiar machine, having its more remote cause also exterior. When Mutius Scævola held his hand in the fire, he was as much acting under the influence of necessity (caused by interior motives) that urged him to this strange action, as if his arm had been held by strong men: pride, despair, the desire of braving his enemy, a wish to astonish him, an anxiety to intimidate him, &c., were the invisible chains that held his hand bound to the fire. The love of glory, enthusiasm for their country, in like manner caused Codrus and Decius to devote themselves for their fellow-citizens. The Indian Colanus and the philosopher Peregrinus were equally obliged to burn themselves, by desire of exciting the astonishment of the Grecian assembly.

22   Freedom and Necessity*

A. J. Ayer

12.   Freedom and Necessity

When I am said to have done something of my own free will it is implied that I could have acted otherwise; and it is only when it is believed that I could have acted otherwise that I am held to be morally responsible for what I have done. For a man is not thought to be morally responsible for an action that it was not in his power to avoid. But if human behaviour is entirely governed by causal laws, it is not clear how any action that is done could ever have been avoided. It may be said of the agent that he would have acted otherwise if the causes of his action had been different, but they being what they were, it seems to follow that he was bound to act as he did. Now it is commonly assumed both that men are capable of acting freely, in the sense that is required to make them morally responsible, and that human behaviour is entirely governed by causal law: and it is the apparent conflict between these two assumptions that gives rise to the philosophical problem of the freedom of the will.

Confronted with this problem, many people will be inclined to agree with Dr. Johnson: 'Sir, we *know* our will is free, and *there's* an end on't'. But, while this does very well for those who accept Dr. Johnson's premiss, it would hardly convince anyone who denied the freedom of the will. Certainly, if we do know that our wills are free, it follows that they are so. But the logical reply to this might be that since our wills are not free, it follows that no one can know that they are: so that if anyone claims, like Dr. Johnson, to know that they are, he must be mistaken. What is evident, indeed, is that people often believe themselves to be acting freely; and it is to this 'feeling' of freedom that some philosophers appeal when they wish, in the supposed interests of morality, to prove that not all human action is causally determined. But if these philosophers are right in their assumption that a man cannot be acting freely if his action causally determined, then the fact that someone feels free to do, or not to do, a certain action does not prove that he really is so. It may prove that the agent does not himself know what it is that makes him act in one way rather than another: but from the fact that a man is unaware of the causes of his action, it does not follow that no such causes exist.

So much may be allowed to the determinist; but his belief that all human actions are subservient to causal laws still remains to be justified. If, indeed, it is necessary that every event should have a cause, then the rule must apply to human behaviour as much as to anything else. But why should it be supposed that every event must have a cause? The contrary is not unthinkable. Nor is the law of universal causation a necessary pre-supposition of scientific thought. The scientist may try to discover causal laws, and in many cases he succeeds; but sometimes he has to be content with statistical laws, and sometimes he comes upon events which, in the present state of his knowledge, he is

* From A. J. Ayer, *Philosophical Essays* (London: Macmillan and New York: St. Martin's Press, 1954), pp. 271–84. Reprinted with permission of Bedford/St. Martin's.

not able to subsume under any law at all. In the case of these events he assumes that if he knew more he would be able to discover some law, whether causal or statistical, which would enable him to account for them. And this assumption cannot be disproved. For however far he may have carried his investigation, it is always open to him to carry it further; and it is always conceivable that if he carried it further he would discover the connection which had hitherto escaped him. Nevertheless, it is also conceivable that the events with which he is concerned are not systematically connected with any others: so that the reason why he does not discover the sort of laws that he requires is simply that they do not obtain.

Now in the case of human conduct the search for explanations has not in fact been altogether fruitless. Certain scientific laws have been established; and with the help of these laws we do make a number of successful predictions about the ways in which different people will behave. But these predictions do not always cover every detail. We may be able to predict that in certain circumstances a particular man will be angry, without being able to prescribe the precise form that the expression of his anger will take. We may be reasonably sure that he will shout, but not sure how loud his shout will be, or exactly what words he will use. And it is only a small proportion of human actions that we are able to forecast even so precisely as this. But that, it may be said, is because we have not carried our investigations very far. The science of psychology is still in its infancy and, as it is developed, not only will more human actions be explained, but the explanations will go into greater detail. The ideal of complete explanation may never in fact be attained: but it is theoretically attainable. Well, this may be so: and certainly it is impossible to show *a priori* that it is not so: but equally it cannot be shown that it is. This will not, however, discourage the scientist who, in the field of human behaviour, as elsewhere, will continue to formulate theories and test them by the facts. And in this he is justified. For since he has no reason *a priori* to admit that there is a limit to what he can discover, the fact that he also cannot be sure that there is no limit does not make it unreasonable for him to devise theories, nor, having devised them, to try constantly to improve them.

But now suppose it to be claimed that, so far as men's actions are concerned, there is a limit: and that this limit is set by the fact of human freedom. An obvious objection is that in many cases in which a person feels himself to be free to do, or not to do, a certain action, we are even now able to explain, in causal terms, why it is that he acts as he does. But it might be argued that even if men are sometimes mistaken in believing that they act freely, it does not follow that they are always so mistaken. For it is not always the case that when a man believes that he has acted freely we are in fact able to account for his action in causal terms. A determinist would say that we should be able to account for it if we had more knowledge of the circumstances, and had been able to discover the appro-priate natural laws. But until those discoveries have been made, this remains only a pious hope. And may it not be true that, in some cases at least, the reason why we can give no causal explanation is that no causal explanation is available; and that this is because the agent's choice was literally free, as he himself felt it to be?

The answer is that this may indeed be true, inasmuch as it is open to anyone to hold that no explanation is possible until some explanation is actually found. But even so it does not give the moralist what he wants. For he is anxious to show that men are capable of acting freely in order to infer that they can be morally responsible for what they do. But if it is a matter of pure chance that a man should act in one way rather than another, he may be free but he can hardly be responsible. And indeed when a men's actions seem to us quite unpredictable, when, as we say, there is no knowing what he will do, we do not look upon him as a moral agent. We look upon him rather as a lunatic.

To this it may be objected that we are not dealing fairly with the moralist. For when he makes it a condition of my being morally responsible that I should act freely, he does not wish to imply that it is purely a matter of chance that I act as I do. What he wishes to imply is that my actions are the result of my own free choice: and it is because they are the result of my own free choice that I am held to be morally responsible for them.

But now we must ask how it is that I come to make my choice. Either it is an accident that I choose to act as I do or it is not. If it is an accident, then it is merely a matter of chance that I did not choose otherwise; and if it is merely a matter of chance that I did not choose otherwise, it is surely irrational to hold me morally responsible for choosing as I did. But if it is not an accident that I choose to do one thing rather than another, then presumably there is some causal explanation of my choice: and in that case we are led back to determinism.

Again, the objection may be raised that we are not doing justice to the moralist's case. His view is not that it is a matter of chance that I choose to act as I do, but rather that my choice depends upon my character. Nevertheless he holds that I can still be free in the sense that he requires; for it is I who am responsible for my character. But in what way am I responsible for my character? Only, surely, in the sense that there is a causal connection between what I do now and what I have done in the past. It is only this that justifies the statement that I have made myself what I am: and even so this is an over-simplification, since it takes no account of the external influences to which I have been subjected. But, ignoring the external influences, let us assume that it is in fact the case that I have made myself what I am. Then it is still legitimate to ask how it is that I have come to make myself one sort of person rather than another. And if it be answered that it is a matter of my strength of will, we can put the same question in another form by asking how it is that my will has the strength that it has and not some other degree of strength. Once more, either it is an accident or it is not. If it is an accident, then by the same argument as before, I am not morally responsible, and if it is not an accident we are led back to determinism.

Furthermore, to say that my actions proceed from my character or, more colloquially, that I act in character, is to say that my behaviour is consistent and to that extent pre-dictable: and since it is, above all, for the actions that I perform in character that I am held to be morally responsible, it looks as if the admission of moral responsibility, so far from being incompatible with determinism, tends rather to presuppose it. But how can this be so if it is a necessary condition of moral responsibility that the person who is held responsible should have acted freely? It seems that if we are to retain this idea of moral responsibility, we must either show that men can be held responsible for actions which they do not do freely, or else find some way of reconciling determinism with the freedom of the will.

It is no doubt with the object of effecting this reconciliation that some philosophers have defined freedom as the consciousness of necessity. And by so doing they are able to say not only that a man can be acting freely when his action is causally determined, but even that his action must be causally determined for it to be possible for him to be acting freely. Nevertheless this definition has the serious disadvantage that it gives to the word 'freedom' a meaning quite different from any that it ordinarily bears. It is indeed obvious that if we are allowed to give the word 'freedom' any meaning that we please, we can find a meaning that will reconcile it with determinism: but this is no more a solution of our present problem than the fact that the word 'horse' could be arbitrarily used to mean what is ordinarily meant by 'sparrow' is a proof that horses have wings. For suppose that I am compelled by another person to do something 'against my will'. In that case, as the word 'freedom' is ordinarily used, I should not be said to be acting freely: and the fact that I am fully aware of the constraint to which I am subjected makes no difference to the matter. I do not become free by becoming conscious that I am not. It may, indeed, be possible to show that my being aware that my action is causally determined is not incompatible with my acting freely: but it by no means follows that it is in this that my freedom consists. Moreover, I suspect that one of the reasons why people are inclined to define freedom as the consciousness of necessity is that they think that if one is conscious of necessity one may somehow be able to master it. But this is a fallacy. It is like someone's saying that he wishes he could see into the future, because if he did he would know what calamities lay in wait for him and so would be able to avoid them. But if he avoids the calamities then they don't lie in the future and it is not true that he foresees them. And similarly if I am able to master necessity, in the sense of escaping the operation of a necessary law, then the law in question is not necessary. And if the law is not necessary, then neither my freedom nor anything else can consist in my knowing that it is.

Let it be granted, then, that when we speak of reconciling freedom with determinism we are using the word 'freedom' in an ordinary sense. It still remains for us to make this usage clear: and perhaps the best way to make it clear is to show what it is that freedom, in this sense, is contrasted with. Now we began with the assumption that freedom is contrasted with causality: so that a man cannot be said to be acting freely if his action is causally determined. But this assumption has led us into difficulties and I now wish to suggest that it is mistaken. For it is not, I think, causality that freedom is to be contrasted with, but constraint. And while it is true that being constrained to do an action entails being caused to do it, I shall try to show that the converse does not hold. I shall try to show that from the fact that my action is causally determined it does not necessarily follow that I am constrained to do it: and this is equivalent to saying that it does not necessarily follow that I am not free.

If I am constrained, I do not act freely. But in what circumstances can I legitimately be said to be constrained? An obvious instance is the case in which I am compelled by another person to do what he wants. In a case of this sort the compulsion need not be such as to deprive one of the power of choice. It is not required that the other person should have hypnotized me, or that he should make it physically impossible for me to go against his will. It is enough that he should induce me to do what he wants by making it clear to me that, if I do not, he will bring about some situation that I regard as even more undesirable than the consequences of the action that he wishes me to do. Thus, if the man points a pistol at my head I may still choose to disobey him: but this does not prevent its being true that if I do fall in with his wishes he can legitimately be said to have compelled me. And if the circumstances are such that no reasonable person would be expected to choose the other alternative, then the action that I am made to do is not one for which I am held to be morally responsible.

A similar, but still somewhat different, case is that in which another person has obtained an habitual ascendancy over me. Where this is so, there may be no question of my being induced to act as the other person wishes by being confronted with a still more disagreeable alternative: for if I am sufficiently under his influence this special stimulus will not be necessary. Nevertheless I do not act freely, for the reason that I have been deprived of the power of choice. And this means that I have acquired so strong a habit of obedience that I no longer go through any process of deciding whether or not to do what the other person wants. About other matters I may still deliberate; but as regards the fulfilment of this other person's wishes, my own deliberations have ceased to be a causal factor in my behaviour. And it is in this sense that I may be said to be constrained. It is not, however, necessary that such constraint should take the form of subservience to another person. A kleptomaniac is not a free agent, in respect of his stealing, because he does not go through any process of deciding whether or not to steal. Or rather, if he does go through such a process, it is irrelevant to his behaviour. Whatever he resolved to do, he would steal all the same. And it is this that distinguishes him from the ordinary thief.

But now it may be asked whether there is any essential difference between these cases and those in which the agent is commonly thought to be free. No doubt the ordinary thief does go through a process of deciding whether or not to steal, and no doubt it does affect his behaviour. If he resolved to refrain from stealing, he could carry his resolution out. But if it be allowed that his making or not making this resolution is causally determined, then how can he be any more free than the kleptomaniac? It may be true that unlike the kleptomaniac he could refrain from stealing if he chose: but if there is a cause, or set of causes, which necessitate his choosing as he does, how can he be said to have the power of choice? Again, it may be true that no one now compels me to get up and walk across the room: but if my doing so can be causally explained in terms of my history or my environment, or whatever it may be, then how am I any more free than if some other person had compelled me? I do not have the feeling of constraint that I have when a pistol is manifestly pointed at my head; but the chains of causation by which I am bound are no less effective for being invisible.

The answer to this is that the cases I have mentioned as examples of constraint do differ from the others: and they differ just in the ways that I have tried to bring out. If I suffered from a compulsion neurosis, so that I got up and walked across the room, whether I wanted to or not, or if I did so because somebody else compelled me, then I should not be acting freely. But if I do it now, I shall be acting freely, just because these conditions do not obtain; and the fact that my action may nevertheless have a cause is, from this point of view, irrelevant. For it is not when my action has any cause at all, but only when it has a special sort of cause, that it is reckoned not to be free.

But here it may be objected that, even if this distinction corresponds to ordinary usage, it is still very irrational. For why should we distinguish, with regard to a person's freedom, between the operations of one sort of cause and those of another? Do not all causes equally necessitate? And is it not therefore arbitrary to say that a person is free when he is necessitated in one fashion but not when he is necessitated in another?

That all causes equally necessitate is indeed a tautology, if the word 'necessitate' is taken merely as equivalent to 'cause': but if, as the objection requires, it is taken as equivalent to 'constrain' or 'compel', then I do not think that this proposition is true. For all that is needed for one event to be the cause of another is that, in the given circumstances, the event which is said to be the effect would not have occurred if it had not been for the occurrence of the event which is said to be the cause, or *vice versa*, according as causes are interpreted as necessary, or sufficient, conditions: and this fact is usually deducible from some causal law which states that whenever an event of the one kind occurs then, given suitable conditions, an event of the other kind will occur in a certain temporal or spatio-temporal relationship to it. In short, there is an invariable concomitance between the two classes of events; but there is no compulsion, in any but a metaphorical sense. Suppose, for example, that a psycho-analyst is able to account for some aspect of my behaviour by referring it to some lesion that I suffered in my childhood. In that case, it may be said that my childhood experience, together with certain other events, necessitates my behaving as I do. But all that this involves is that it is found to be true in general that when people have had certain experiences as children, they subsequently behave in certain specifiable ways; and my case is just another instance of this general law. It is in this way indeed that my behaviour is explained. But from the fact that my behaviour is capable of being explained, in the sense that it can be subsumed under some natural law, it does not follow that I am acting under constraint.

If this is correct, to say that I could have acted otherwise is to say, first, that I should have acted otherwise if I had so chosen; secondly, that my action was voluntary in the sense in which the actions, say, of the kleptomaniac are not; and thirdly, that nobody compelled me to choose as I did: and these three conditions may very well be fulfilled. When they are fulfilled, I may be said to have acted freely. But this is not to say that it was a matter of chance that I acted as I did, or, in other words, that my action could not be explained. And that my actions should be capable of being explained is all that is required by the postulate of determinism.

If more than this seems to be required it is, I think, because the use of the very word 'determinism' is in some degree misleading. For it tends to suggest that one event is somehow in the power of another, whereas the truth is merely that they are factually correlated. And the same applies to the use, in this context, of the word 'necessity' and even of the word 'cause' itself. Moreover, there are various reasons for this. One is the tendency to confuse causal with logical necessitation, and so to infer mistakenly that the effect is contained in the cause. Another is the uncritical use of a concept of force which is derived from primitive experiences of pushing and striking. A third is the survival of an animistic conception of causality, in which all causal relationships are modelled on the example of one person's exercising authority over another. As a result we tend to form an imaginative picture of an unhappy effect trying vainly to escape from the clutches of an overmastering cause. But, I repeat, the fact is simply that when an event of one type occurs, an event of another type occurs also, in a certain temporal or spatio-temporal relation to the first. The rest is only metaphor. And it is because of the metaphor, and not because of the fact, that we come to think that there is an antithesis between causality and freedom.

Nevertheless, it may be said, if the postulate of determinism is valid, then the future can be explained in terms of the past: and this means that if one knew enough about the past one would be able to predict the future. But in that case what will happen in the future is already decided. And how then can I be said to be free? What is going to happen is going to happen and nothing that I do can prevent it. If the determinist is right, I am the helpless prisoner of fate.

But what is meant by saying that the future course of events is already decided? If the implication is that some person has arranged it, then the proposition is false. But if all that is meant is that it is possible, in principle, to deduce it from a set of particular facts about the past, together with the appropriate general laws, then, even if this is true, it does not in the least entail that I am the helpless prisoner of fate. It does not even entail that my actions make no difference to the future: for they are causes as well as effects; so that if they were different their consequences would be different also. What it does entail is that my behaviour can be predicted: but to say that my behaviour can be predicted is not to say that I am acting under constraint. It is indeed true that I cannot escape my destiny if this is taken to mean no more than that I shall do what I shall do. But this is a tautology, just as it is a tautology that what is going to happen is going to happen. And such tautologies as these prove nothing whatsoever about the freedom of the will.

23   Human Freedom and the Self*

Roderick M. Chisholm

A staff moves a stone, and is moved by a hand, which is moved by a man.

Aristotle, *Physics*, 256a.

1.   The metaphysical problem of human freedom might be summarized in the following way: Human beings are responsible agents; but this fact appears to conflict with a deterministic view of human action (the view that every event that is involved in an act is caused by some other event); and it *also* appears to conflict with an indeterministic view of human action (the view that the act, or some event that is essential to the act, is not caused at all). To solve the problem, I believe, we must make somewhat far-reaching assumptions about the self or the agent – about the man who performs the act.

Perhaps it is needless to remark that, in all likelihood, it is impossible to say anything significant about this ancient problem that has not been said before.[1]

2.   Let us consider some deed, or misdeed, that may be attributed to a responsible agent: one man, say, shot another. If the man *was* responsible for what he did, then, I would urge, what was to happen at the time of the shooting was something that was entirely up to the man himself. There was a moment at which it was true, both that he could have fired the shot and also that he could have refrained from firing it. And if this is so, then, even though he did fire it, he could have done something else instead. (He didn't find himself firing the shot "against his will," as we say.) I think we can say, more generally, then, that if a man is responsible for a certain event or a certain state of affairs (in our example, the shooting of another man), then that event or state of affairs was brought about by some act of his, and the act was something that was in his power either to perform or not to perform.

But now if the act which he *did* perform was an act that was also in his power *not* to perform, then it could not have been caused or determined by any event that was not itself within his power either to bring about or not to bring about. For example, if what we say he did was really something that was brought about by a second man, one who forced his hand upon the trigger, say, or who, by means of hypnosis, compelled him to perform the act, then since the act was caused by the *second* man it was nothing that was within the power of the *first* man to prevent. And precisely the same thing is true, I think, if instead of referring to a second man who compelled the first one, we speak instead of

* From John Bricke (ed.), *Freedom and Morality: The Lindley Lectures* (Lawrence: University of Kansas, 1976), pp. 23–35. Reprinted with permission. This essay was originally delivered as an E. H. Lindley Lecture at the University of Kansas in 1964.

the *desires* and *beliefs* which the first man happens to have had. For if what we say he did was really something that was brought about by his own beliefs and desires, if these beliefs and desires in the particular situation in which he happened to have found himself caused him to do just what it was that we say he did do, then, since *they* caused it, *he* was unable to do anything other than just what it was that he did do. It makes no difference whether the cause of the deed was internal or external; if the cause was some state or event for which the man himself was not responsible, then he was not responsible for what we have been mistakenly calling his act. If a flood caused the poorly constructed dam to break, then, given the flood and the constitution of the dam, the break, we may say, *had* to occur and nothing could have happened in its place. And if the flood of desire caused the weak-willed man to give in, then he, too, had to do just what it was that he did do and he was no more responsible than was the dam for the results that followed. (It is true, of course, that if the man is responsible for the beliefs and desires that he happens to have, then he may also be responsible for the things they lead him to do. But the question now becomes: *is* he responsible for the beliefs and desires he happens to have? If he is, then there was a time when they were within his power either to acquire or not to acquire, and we are left, therefore, with our general point.)

One may object: But surely if there were such a thing as a man who is really *good*, then he would be responsible for things that he would do; yet, he would be unable to do anything other than just what it is that he does do, since, being good, he will always choose to do what is best. The answer, I think, is suggested by a comment that Thomas Reid makes upon an ancient author. The author had said of Cato, "He was good because he could not be otherwise," and Reid observes: "This saying, if understood literally and strictly, is not the praise of Cato, but of his constitution, which was no more the work of Cato than his existence."[2] If Cato was himself responsible for the good things that he did, then Cato, as Reid suggests, was such that, although he had the power to do what was not good, he exercised his power only for that which was good.

All of this, if it is true, may give a certain amount of comfort to those who are tender-minded. But we should remind them that it also conflicts with a familiar view about the nature of God – with the view that St. Thomas Aquinas expresses by saying that "every movement both of the will and of nature proceeds from God as the Prime Mover."[3] If the act of the sinner *did* proceed from God as the Prime Mover, then God was in the position of the second agent we just discussed – the man who forced the trigger finger, or the hypnotist – and the sinner, so-called, was *not* responsible for what he did. (This may be a bold assertion, in view of the history of western theology, but I must say that I have never encountered a single good reason for denying it.)

There is one standard objection to all of this and we should consider it briefly.

3. The objection takes the form of a stratagem – one designed to show that determinism (and divine providence) is consistent with human responsibility. The stratagem is one that was used by Jonathan Edwards and by many philosophers in the present century, most notably, G. E. Moore.[4]

One proceeds as follows: The expression

(a)   He could have done otherwise,

it is argued, means no more nor less than

(b)   If he had chosen to do otherwise, then he would have done otherwise.

(In place of "chosen," one might say "tried," "set out," "decided," "undertaken," or "willed.") The truth of statement (b), it is then pointed out, is consistent with determinism (and with divine providence); for even if all of the man's actions were causally determined, the man could still be such that, *if* he had chosen otherwise, then he would have done otherwise. What the murderer saw, let us suppose, along with his beliefs and desires, *caused* him to fire the shot; yet he was such that *if,* just then, he had chosen or decided *not* to fire the shot, then he would not have fired it. All of this is certainly possible. Similarly, we could say, of the dam, that the flood caused it to break and also that the dam was such that, *if* there had been no flood or any similar pressure, then the dam would have remained intact. And therefore, the argument proceeds, if (b) is consistent with determinism, and if (a) and (b) say the same thing, then (a) is also consistent with determinism; hence we can say that the agent *could* have done otherwise even though he was caused to do what he did do; and therefore determinism and moral responsibility are compatible.

Is the argument sound? The conclusion follows from the premises, but the catch, I think, lies in the first premise – the one saying that statement (a) tells us no more nor less than what statement (b) tells us. For (b), it would seem, could be true while (a) is false. That is to say, our man might be such that, if he had chosen to do otherwise, then he would have done otherwise, and yet *also* such that he could not have done otherwise. Suppose, after all, that our murderer could not have *chosen,* or could not have *decided,* to do otherwise. Then the fact that he happens also to be a man such that, if he had chosen not to shoot he would not have shot, would make no difference. For if he could *not* have chosen *not* to shoot, then he could not have done anything other than just what it was that he did do. In a word: from our statement (b) above ("If he had chosen to do otherwise, then he would have done otherwise"), we cannot make an inference to (a) above ("He could have done otherwise") unless we can *also* assert:

(c)   He could have chosen to do otherwise.

And therefore, if we must reject this third statement (c), then, even though we may be justified in asserting (b), we are not justified in asserting (a). If the man could not have chosen to do otherwise, then he would not have done otherwise – *even if* he was such that, if he *had* chosen to do otherwise, then he would have done otherwise.

The stratagem in question, then, seems to me not to work, and I would say, therefore, that the ascription of responsibility conflicts with a deterministic view of action.

4.   Perhaps there is less need to argue that the ascription of responsibility also conflicts with an indeterministic view of action – with the view that the act, or some event that is essential to the act, is not caused at all. If the act – the firing of the shot – was not caused at all, if it was fortuitous or capricious, happening so to speak out of the blue, then, presumably, no one – and nothing – was responsible for the act. Our conception of action, therefore, should be neither deterministic nor indeterministic. Is there any other possibility?

5.   We must not say that every event involved in the act is caused by some other event; and we must not say that the act is something that is not caused at all. The possibility that remains, therefore, is this: We should say that at least one of the events that are involved in the act is caused, not by any other events, but by something else instead. And this something else can only be the agent – the man. If there is an event that is caused, not by other events, but by the man, then there are some events involved in the act that are not caused by other events. But if the event in question is caused by the man then it *is* caused and we are not committed to saying that there is something involved in the act that is not caused at all.

But this, of course, is a large consequence, implying something of considerable importance about the nature of the agent or the man.

6. If we consider only inanimate natural objects, we may say that causation, if it occurs, is a relation between *events* or *states of affairs*. The dam's breaking was an event that was caused by a set of other events – the dam being weak, the flood being strong, and so on. But if a man is responsible for a particular deed, then, if what I have said is true, there is some event, or set of events, that is caused, *not* by other events or states of affairs, but by the agent, whatever he may be.

I shall borrow a pair of medieval terms, using them, perhaps, in a way that is slightly different from that for which they were originally intended. I shall say that when one event or state of affairs (or set of events or states of affairs) causes some other event or state of affairs, then we have an instance of *transeunt* causation. And I shall say that when an *agent*, as distinguished from an event, causes an event or state of affairs, then we have an instance of *immanent* causation.

The nature of what is intended by the expression "immanent causation" may be illustrated by this sentence from Aristotle's *Physics*: "Thus, a staff moves a stone, and is moved by a hand, which is moved by a man." (VII, 5, 256a, 6–8) If the man was responsible, then we have in this illustration a number of instances of causation – most of them transeunt but at least one of them immanent. What the staff did to the stone was an instance of transeunt causation, and thus we may describe it as a relation between events: "the motion of the staff caused the motion of the stone." And similarly for what the hand did to the staff: "the motion of the hand caused the motion of the staff." And, as we know from physiology, there are still other events which caused the motion of the hand. Hence we need not introduce the agent at this particular point, as Aristotle does – we *need* not, though we *may*. We *may* say that the hand was moved by the man, but we may *also* say that the motion of the hand was caused by the motion of certain muscles; and we may say that the motion of the muscles was caused by certain events that took place within the brain. But some event, and presumably one of those that took place within the brain, was caused by the agent and not by any other events.

There are, of course, objections to this way of putting the matter; I shall consider the two that seem to me to be most important.

7. One may object, firstly: "If the *man* does anything, then, as Aristotle's remark suggests, what he does is to move the *hand*. But he certainly does not *do* anything to his brain – he may not even know that he *has* a brain. And if he doesn't do anything to the brain, and if the motion of the hand was caused by something that happened within the brain, then there is no point in appealing to 'immanent causation' as being something incompatible with 'transeunt causation' – for the whole thing, after all, is a matter of causal relations among events or states of affairs."

The answer to this objection, I think, is this: It is true that the agent does not *do* anything with his brain, or to his brain, in the sense in which he *does* something with his hand and does something to the staff. But from this it does not follow that the agent was not the immanent cause of something that happened within his brain.

We should note a useful distinction that has been proposed by Professor A. I. Melden – namely, the distinction between "making something A happen" and "doing A."[5] If I reach for the staff and pick it up, then one of the things that I *do* is just that – reach for the staff and pick it up. And if it is something that I do, then there is a very clear sense in which it may be said to be something that I know that I do. If you ask me, "Are you doing something, or trying to do something, with the staff?", I will have no difficulty in finding an answer. But in doing something with the staff, I also make various things happen which are not in this same sense things that I do: I will make various air-particles move; I will free a number of blades of grass from the pressure that had been upon them; and I may cause a shadow to move from one place to another. If these are merely things that I make happen, as distinguished from things that I do, then I may know nothing whatever about them; I may not have the slightest idea that, in moving the staff, I am bringing about any such thing as the motion of air-particles, shadows, and blades of grass.

We may say, in answer to the first objection, therefore, that it is true that our agent does nothing to his brain or with his brain; but from this it does not follow that the agent is not the immanent cause of some event within his brain; for the brain event may be something which, like the motion of the air-particles, he made happen in picking up the staff. The only difference between the two cases is this: in each case, he made something happen when he picked up the staff; but in the one case – the motion of the air-particles or of the shadows – it was the motion of the staff that caused the event to happen; and in the other case – the event that took place in the brain – it was this event that caused the motion of the staff.

The point is, in a word, that whenever a man does something A, then (by "immanent causation") he makes a certain cerebral event happen, and this cerebral event (by "transeunt causation") makes A happen.

8.   The second objection is more difficult and concerns the very concept of "immanent causation," or causation by an agent, as this concept is to be interpreted here. The concept is subject to a difficulty which has long been associated with that of the prime mover unmoved. We have said that there must be some event A, presumably some cerebral event, which is caused not by any other event, but by the agent. Since A was not caused by any other event, then the agent himself cannot be said to have undergone any change or produced any other event (such as "an act of will" or the like) which brought A about. But if, when the agent made A happen, there was no event involved other than A itself, no event which could be described as *making* A happen, what did the agent's causation consist of? What, for example, is the difference between A's just happening, and the agent's *causing* A to happen? We cannot attribute the difference to any event that took place within the agent. And so far as the event A itself is concerned, there would seem to be no discernible difference. Thus Aristotle said that the activity of the prime mover is nothing in addition to the motion that it produces, and Suarez said that "the action is in reality nothing but the effect as it flows from the agent."[6] Must we conclude, then, that there is no more to the man's action in causing event A than there is to the event A's happening by itself? Here we would seem to have a distinction without a difference – in which case we have failed to find a *via media* between a deterministic and an indeterministic view of action.

The only answer, I think, can be this: that the difference between the man's causing A, on the one hand, and the event A just happening, on the other, lies in the fact that, in the first case but not the second, the event A *was* caused and was caused by the man. There was a brain event A; the agent did, in fact, cause the brain event; but there was nothing that he did to cause it.

This answer may not entirely satisfy and it will be likely to provoke the following question: "But what are you really *adding* to the assertion that A happened when you utter the words 'The agent *caused* A to happen'?" As soon as we have put the question this way, we see, I think, that whatever difficulty we may have encountered is one that may be traced to the concept of causation generally – whether "immanent" or "transeunt." The problem, in other words, is not a problem that is peculiar to our conception of human action. It is a problem that must be faced by anyone who makes use of the concept of causation at all; and therefore, I would say, it is a problem for everyone but the complete indeterminist.

For the problem, as we put it, referring just to "immanent causation," or causation by an agent, was this: "What is the difference between saying, of an event A, that A just happened and saying that someone caused A to happen?" The analogous problem, which holds for "transeunt causation," or causation by an event, is this: "What is the difference between saying, of two events A and B, that B happened and then A happened, and saying that B's happening was the *cause* of A's happening?" And the only answer that one can give is this – that in the one case the agent was the cause of A's happening and in the other case event B was the cause of A's happening. The nature of transeunt causation is no more clear than is that of immanent causation.

9.   But we may plausibly say – and there is a respectable philosophical tradition to which we may appeal – that the notion of immanent causation, or causation by an agent, is in fact more clear than that of transeunt causation, or causation by an event, and that it is only by understanding our own causal efficacy, as agents, that we can grasp the concept of *cause* at all. Hume may be said to have shown that we do not derive the concept of *cause* from what we perceive of external things. How, then, do we derive it? The most plausible suggestion, it seems to me, is that of Reid, once again: namely that "the conception of an efficient cause may very probably be derived from the experience we have had . . . of our own power to produce certain effects."[7] If we did not understand the concept of immanent causation, we would not understand that of transeunt causation.

10.   It may have been noted that I have avoided the term "free will" in all of this. For even if there is such a faculty as "the will," which somehow sets our acts agoing, the question of freedom, as John Locke said, is not the question "*whether the will be free*"; it is the question "*whether a man be free*."[8] For if there is a "will," as a moving faculty, the question is whether the man is free to will to do those things that he does will to do – and also whether he is free *not* to will any of those things that he does will to do, and, again, whether he is free to will any of those things that he does not will to do. Jonathan Edwards tried to restrict himself to the question – "Is the man free to do what it is that he wills?" – but the answer to this question will not tell us whether the man is responsible for what it is that he *does* will to do. Using still another pair of medieval terms, we may say that the metaphysical problem of freedom does not concern the *actus imperatus*; it does not concern the question whether we are free to accomplish whatever it is that we will or set out to do; it concerns the *actus elicitus*, the question whether we are free to will or to set out to do those things that we do will or set out to do.

11.   If we are responsible, and if what I have been trying to say is true, then we have a prerogative which some would attribute only to God: each of us, when we act, is a prime mover unmoved. In doing what we do, we cause certain events to happen, and nothing – or no one – causes us to cause those events to happen.

12.   If we are thus prime movers unmoved and if our actions, or those for which we are responsible, are not causally determined, then they are not causally determined by our *desires*. And this means that the relation between what we want or what we desire, on the one hand, and what it is that we do, on the other, is not as simple as most philosophers would have it.

We may distinguish between what we might call the "Hobbist approach" and what we might call the "Kantian approach" to this question. The Hobbist approach is the one that is generally accepted at the present time, but the Kantian approach, I believe, is the one that is true. According to Hobbism, if we *know*, of some man, what his beliefs and desires happen to be and how strong they are, if we know what he feels certain of, what he desires more than anything else, and if we know the state of his body and what stimuli he is being subjected to, then we may *deduce*, logically, just what it is that he will do – or, more accurately, just what it is that he will try, set out, or undertake to do. Thus Professor Melden has said that "the connection between wanting and doing is logical."⁹ But according to the Kantian approach to our problem, and this is the one that I would take, there is no such logical connection between wanting and doing, nor need there even be a causal connection. No set of statements about a man's desires, beliefs, and stimulus situation at any time implies any statement telling us what the man will try, set out, or undertake to do at that time. As Reid put it, though we may "reason from men's motives to their actions and, in many cases, with great probability," we can never do so "with absolute certainty."¹⁰

This means that, in one very strict sense of the terms, there can be no science of man. If we think of science as a matter of finding out what laws happen to hold, and if the statement of a law tells us what kinds of events are caused by what other kinds of events, then there will be human actions which we cannot explain by subsuming them under any laws. We cannot say, "It is causally necessary that, given such and such desires and beliefs, and being subject to such and such stimuli, the agent will do so and so." For at times the agent, if he chooses, may rise above his desires and do something else instead.

But all of this is consistent with saying that, perhaps more often than not, our desires do exist under conditions such that those conditions necessitate us to act. And we may also say, with Leibniz, that at other times our desires may "incline without necessitating."

13. Leibniz's phrase presents us with our final philosophical problem. What does it mean to say that a desire, or a motive, might "incline without necessitating"? There is a temptation, certainly, to say that "to incline" means to cause and that "not to necessitate" means not to cause, but obviously we cannot have it both ways.

Nor will Leibniz's own solution do. In his letter to Coste, he puts the problem as follows: "When a choice is proposed, for example to go out or not to go out, it is a question whether, with all the circumstances, internal and external, motives, perceptions, dispositions, impressions, passions, inclinations taken together, I am still in a contingent state, or whether I am necessitated to make the choice, for example, to go out; that is to say, whether this proposition true and determined in fact, *In all these circumstances taken together I shall choose to go out*, is contingent or necessary."¹¹ Leibniz's answer might be put as follows: in one sense of the terms "necessary" and "contingent," the proposition "In all these circumstances taken together I shall choose to go out," may be said to be contingent and not necessary, and in another sense of these terms, it may be said to be necessary and not contingent. But the sense in which the proposition may be said to be contingent, according to Leibniz, is only this: there is no logical contradiction involved in denying the proposition. And the sense in which it may be said to be necessary is this: since "nothing ever occurs without cause or determining reason," the proposition is causally necessary. "Whenever all the circumstances taken together are such that the balance of deliberation is heavier on one side than on the other, it is certain and infallible that that is the side that is going to win out." But if what we have been saying is true, the proposition "In all these circumstances taken together I shall choose to go out," may be causally as well as logically contingent. Hence we must find another interpretation for Leibniz's statement that our motives and desires may incline us, or influence us, to choose without thereby necessitating us to choose.

Let us consider a public official who has some moral scruples but who also, as one says, could be had. Because of the scruples that he does have, he would never take any positive steps to receive a bribe – he would not actively solicit one. But his morality has its limits and he is also such that, if we were to confront him with a *fait accompli* or to let him see what is about to happen ($10,000 in cash is being deposited behind the garage), then he would succumb and be unable to resist. The general situation is a familiar one and this is one reason that people pray to be delivered from temptation. (It also justifies Kant's remark: "And how many there are who may have led a long blameless life, who are only *fortunate* in having escaped so many temptations."[12]) Our relation to the misdeed that we contemplate may not be a matter simply of being able to bring it about or not to bring it about. As St. Anselm noted, there are at least four possibilities. We may illustrate them by reference to our public official and the event which is his receiving the bribe, in the following way: (i) he may be able to bring the event about himself (*facere esse*), in which case he would actively cause himself to receive the bribe; (ii) he may be able to refrain from bringing it about himself (*non facere esse*), in which case he would not himself do anything to insure that he receive the bribe; (iii) he may be able to do something to prevent the event from occurring (*facere non esse*), in which case he would make sure that the $10,000 was *not* left behind the garage; or (iv) he may be unable to do anything to prevent the event from occurring (*non facere non esse*), in which case, though he may not solicit the bribe, he would allow himself to keep it.[13] We have envisaged our official as a man who can resist the temptation to (i) but cannot resist the temptation to (iv): he can refrain from bringing the event about himself, but he cannot bring himself to do anything to prevent it.

Let us think of "inclination without necessitation," then, in such terms as these. First we may contrast the two propositions:

(1)   He can resist the temptation to do something in order to make A happen;
(2)   He can resist the temptation to allow A to happen (i.e., to do nothing to prevent A from happening).

We may suppose that the man has some desire to have A happen and thus has a motive for making A happen. His motive for making A happen, I suggest, is one that *necessitates* provided that, because of the motive, (1) is false; he cannot resist the temptation to do something in order to make A happen. His motive for making A happen is one that *inclines* provided that, because of the motive, (2) is false; like our public official, he cannot bring himself to do anything to prevent A from happening. And therefore we can say that his motive for making A happen is one that *inclines but does not necessitate* provided that, because of the motive, (1) is true and (2) is false; he can resist the temptation to make it happen but he cannot resist the temptation to allow it to happen.

Notes

1   The general position to be presented here is suggested in the following writings, among others: Aristotle, *Eudemian Ethics*, Book II, Ch. 6; *Nicomachean Ethics*, Book III, Chs. 1–5; Thomas

Reid, *Essays on the Active Powers of Man*; C. A. Campbell, "Is 'Free Will' a Pseudo-Problem?" *Mind*, NS vol. LX (1951), pp. 441–65; Roderick M. Chisholm, "Responsibility and Avoidability," and Richard Taylor, "Determination and the Theory of Agency," in Sidney Hook, ed., *Determinism and Freedom in the Age of Modern Science* (New York 1958).

2 Thomas Reid, *Essays on the Active Powers of Man*, Essay IV, Chapter 4 (*Works*, p. 600).

3 *Summa Theologica*, First Part of the Second Part, Question VI ("On the Voluntary and Involuntary").

4 Jonathan Edwards, *Freedom of the Will* (New Haven 1957); G. E. Moore, *Ethics* (Home University Library 1912), Chapter Six.

5 A. I. Melden, *Free Action* (London 1961), especially Chapter Three. Mr. Melden's own views, however, are quite the contrary of those that are proposed here.

6 Aristotle, *Physics*, Book III, Chapter 3; Suarez, *Disputationes Metaphysicae*, Disputation 18, Section 10.

7 Reid, *Works*, p. 524.

8 *Essay concerning Human Understanding*, Book II, Chapter XXI.

9 *Op. cit.*, p. 166.

10 Reid, *Works*, pp. 608, 612.

11 "Lettre a Mr. Coste de la Nécessité et de la Contingence" (1707) in *Opera Philosophica*, ed. Erdmann, pp. 447–9.

12 In the Preface to the *Metaphysical Elements of Ethics*, in T. K. Abbott, ed., *Kant's Critique of Practical Reason and Other Works on the Theory of Ethics* (London 1959), p. 303.

13 Cf. D. P. Henry, "Saint Anselm's *De 'Grammatico'*," *Philosophical Quarterly*, vol. X (1960), pp. 115–26. St. Anselm noted that (i) and (iii), respectively, may be thought of as forming the upper left and the upper right corners of a square of opposition, and (ii) and (iv) the lower left and the lower right.

---

24 Alternate Possibilities and Moral Responsibility*

Harry G. Frankfurt

A dominant role in nearly all recent inquiries into the free-will problem has been played by a principle which I shall call "the principle of alternate possibilities." This principle states that a person is morally responsible for what he has done only if he could have done otherwise. Its exact meaning is a subject of controversy, particularly concerning whether someone who accepts it is thereby committed to believing that moral responsibility and determinism are incompatible. Practically no one, however, seems inclined to deny or even to question that the principle of alternate possibilities (construed in some way or other) is true. It has generally seemed so overwhelmingly plausible that some philosophers have even characterized it as an *a priori* truth. People whose accounts of free will or of moral responsibility are radically at odds evidently find in it a firm and convenient common ground upon which they can profitably take their opposing stands.

* From *The Journal of Philosophy*, 66/23 (December 4, 1969), pp. 829–39. Reprinted with permission of *The Journal of Philosophy* and Harry Frankfurt.

But the principle of alternate possibilities is false. A person may well be morally responsible for what he has done even though he could not have done otherwise. The principle's plausibility is an illusion, which can be made to vanish by bringing the relevant moral phenomena into sharper focus.

I

In seeking illustrations of the principle of alternate possibilities, it is most natural to think of situations in which the same circumstances both bring it about that a person does something and make it impossible for him to avoid doing it. These include, for example, situations in which a person is coerced into doing something, or in which he is impelled to act by a hypnotic suggestion, or in which some inner compulsion drives him to do what he does. In situations of these kinds there are circumstances that make it impossible for the person to do otherwise, and these very circumstances also serve to bring it about that he does whatever it is that he does.

However, there may be circumstances that constitute sufficient conditions for a certain action to be performed by someone and that therefore make it impossible for the person to do otherwise, but that do not actually impel the person to act or in any way produce his action. A person may do something in circumstances that leave him no alternative to doing it, without these circumstances actually moving him or leading him to do it – without them playing any role, indeed, in bringing it about that he does what he does.

An examination of situations characterized by circumstances of this sort casts doubt, I believe, on the relevance to questions of moral responsibility of the fact that a person who has done something could not have done otherwise. I propose to develop some examples of this kind in the context of a discussion of coercion and to suggest that our moral intuitions concerning these examples tend to disconfirm the principle of alternate possibilities. Then I will discuss the principle in more general terms, explain what I think is wrong with it, and describe briefly and without argument how it might appropriately be revised.

II

It is generally agreed that a person who has been coerced to do something did not do it freely and is not morally responsible for having done it. Now the doctrine that coercion and moral responsibility are mutually exclusive may appear to be no more than a somewhat particularized version of the principle of alternate possibilities. It is natural enough to say of a person who has been coerced to do something that he could not have done otherwise. And it may easily seem that being coerced deprives a person of freedom and of moral responsibility simply because it is a special case of being unable to do otherwise. The principle of alternate possibilities may in this way derive some credibility from its association with the very plausible proposition that moral responsibility is excluded by coercion.

It is not right, however, that it should do so. The fact that a person was coerced to act as he did may entail both that he could not have done otherwise and that he bears no moral responsibility for his action. But his lack of moral responsibility is not entailed by his having been unable to do otherwise. The doctrine that coercion excludes moral responsibility is not correctly understood, in other words, as a particularized version of the principle of alternate possibilities.

Let us suppose that someone is threatened convincingly with a penalty he finds unacceptable and that he then does what is required of him by the issuer of the threat. We can imagine details that would make it reasonable for us to think that the person was coerced to perform the action in question, that he could not have done otherwise, and that he bears no moral responsibility for having done what he did. But just what is it about situations of this kind that warrants the judgment that the threatened person is not morally responsible for his act?

This question may be approached by considering situations of the following kind. Jones decides for reasons of his own to do something, then someone threatens him with a very harsh penalty (so harsh that any reasonable person would submit to the threat) unless he does precisely that, and Jones does it. Will we hold Jones morally responsible for what he has done? I think this will depend on the roles we think were played, in leading him to act, by his original decision and by the threat.

One possibility is that $Jones_1$ is not a reasonable man: he is, rather, a man who does what he has once decided to do no matter what happens next and no matter what the cost. In that case, the threat actually exerted no effective force upon him. He acted without any regard to it, very much as if he were not aware that it had been made. If this is indeed the way it was, the situation did not involve coercion at all. The threat did not lead $Jones_1$ to do what he did. Nor was it in fact sufficient to have prevented him from doing otherwise: if his earlier decision had been to do something else, the threat would not have deterred him in the slightest. It seems evident that in these circumstances the fact that $Jones_1$ was threatened in no way reduces the moral responsibility he would otherwise bear for his act. This example, however, is not a counterexample either to the doctrine that coercion excuses or to the principle of alternate possibilities. For we have supposed that $Jones_1$ is a man upon whom the threat had no coercive effect and, hence, that it did not actually deprive him of alternatives to doing what he did.

Another possibility is that $Jones_2$ was stampeded by the threat. Given that threat, he would have performed that action regardless of what decision he had already made. The threat upset him so profoundly, moreover, that he completely forgot his own earlier decision and did what was demanded of him entirely because he was terrified of the penalty with which he was threatened. In this case, it is not relevant to his having performed the action that he had already decided on his own to perform it. When the chips were down he thought of nothing but the threat, and fear alone led him to act. The fact that at an earlier time $Jones_2$ had decided for his own reasons to act in just that way may be relevant to an evaluation of his character; he may bear full moral responsibility for having made *that* decision. But he can hardly be said to be morally responsible for his action. For he performed the action simply as a result of the coercion to which he was subjected. His earlier decision played no role in bringing it about that he did what he did, and it would therefore be gratuitous to assign it a role in the moral evaluation of his action.

Now consider a third possibility. $Jones_3$ was neither stampeded by the threat nor indifferent to it. The threat impressed him, as it would impress any reasonable man, and he would have submitted to it wholeheartedly if he had not already made a decision that coincided with the one demanded of him. In fact, however, he performed the action in question on the basis of the decision he had made before the threat was issued. When he acted, he was not actually motivated by the threat but solely by the considerations that had originally commended the action to him. It was not the threat that led him to act, though it would have done so if he had not already provided himself with a sufficient motive for performing the action in question.

No doubt it will be very difficult for anyone to know, in a case like this one, exactly what happened. Did Jones$_3$ perform the action because of the threat, or were his reasons for acting simply those which had already persuaded him to do so? Or did he act on the basis of two motives, each of which was sufficient for his action? It is not impossible, however, that the situation should be clearer than situations of this kind usually are. And suppose it is apparent to us that Jones$_3$ acted on the basis of his own decision and not because of the threat. Then I think we would be justified in regarding his moral responsibility for what he did as unaffected by the threat even though, since he would in any case have submitted to the threat, he could not have avoided doing what he did. It would be entirely reasonable for us to make the same judgment concerning his moral responsibility that we would have made if we had not known of the threat. For the threat did not in fact influence his performance of the action. He did what he did just as if the threat had not been made at all.

III

The case of Jones$_3$ may appear at first glance to combine coercion and moral responsibility, and thus to provide a counterexample to the doctrine that coercion excuses. It is not really so certain that it does so, however, because it is unclear whether the example constitutes a genuine instance of coercion. Can we say of Jones$_3$ that he was coerced to do something, when he had already decided on his own to do it and when he did it entirely on the basis of that decision? Or would it be more correct to say that Jones$_3$ was not coerced to do what he did, even though he himself recognized that there was an irresistible force at work in virtue of which he had to do it? My own linguistic intuitions lead me toward the second alternative, but they are somewhat equivocal. Perhaps we can say either of these things, or perhaps we must add a qualifying explanation to whichever of them we say.

This murkiness, however, does not interfere with our drawing an important moral from an examination of the example. Suppose we decide to say that Jones$_3$ was *not* coerced. Our basis for saying this will clearly be that it is incorrect to regard a man as being coerced to do something unless he does it *because of* the coercive force exerted against him. The fact that an irresistible threat is made will not, then, entail that the person who receives it is coerced to do what he does. It will also be necessary that the threat is what actually accounts for his doing it. On the other hand, suppose we decide to say that Jones$_3$ *was* coerced. Then we will be bound to admit that being coerced does not exclude being morally responsible. And we will also surely be led to the view that coercion affects the judgment of a person's moral responsibility only when the person acts as he does because he is coerced to do so – i.e., when the fact that he is coerced is what accounts for his action.

Whichever we decide to say, then, we will recognize that the doctrine that coercion excludes moral responsibility is not a particularized version of the principle of alternate possibilities. Situations in which a person who does something cannot do otherwise because he is subject to coercive power are either not instances of coercion at all, or they are situations in which the person may still be morally responsible for what he does if it is not because of the coercion that he does it. When we excuse a person who has been coerced, we do not excuse him because he was unable to do otherwise. Even though a person is subject to a coercive force that precludes his performing any action but one, he may nonetheless bear full moral responsibility for performing that action.

IV

To the extent that the principle of alternate possibilities derives its plausibility from association with the doctrine that coercion excludes moral responsibility, a clear understanding of the latter diminishes the appeal of the former. Indeed the case of $Jones_3$ may appear to do more than illuminate the relationship between the two doctrines. It may well seem to provide a decisive counterexample to the principle of alternate possibilities and thus to show that this principle is false. For the irresistibility of the threat to which $Jones_3$ is subjected might well be taken to mean that he cannot but perform the action he performs. And yet the threat, since $Jones_3$ performs the action without regard to it, does not reduce his moral responsibility for what he does.

This following objection will doubtless be raised against the suggestion that the case of $Jones_3$ is a counterexample to the principle of alternate possibilities. There is perhaps a sense in which $Jones_3$ cannot do otherwise than perform the action he performs, since he is a reasonable man and the threat he encounters is sufficient to move any reasonable man. But it is not this sense that is germane to the principle of alternate possibilities. His knowledge that he stands to suffer an intolerably harsh penalty does not mean that $Jones_3$, strictly speaking, *cannot* perform any action but the one he does perform. After all it is still open to him, and this is crucial, to defy the threat if he wishes to do so and to accept the penalty his action would bring down upon him. In the sense in which the principle of alternate possibilities employs the concept of "could have done otherwise," $Jones_3$'s inability to resist the threat does not mean that he cannot do otherwise than perform the action he performs. Hence the case of $Jones_3$ does not constitute an instance contrary to the principle.

I do not propose to consider in what sense the concept of "could have done otherwise" figures in the principle of alternate possibilities, nor will I attempt to measure the force of the objection I have just described.[1] For I believe that whatever force this objection may be thought to have can be deflected by altering the example in the following way.[2] Suppose someone – Black, let us say – wants $Jones_4$ to perform a certain action. Black is prepared to go to considerable lengths to get his way, but he prefers to avoid showing his hand unnecessarily. So he waits until $Jones_4$ is about to make up his mind what to do, and he does nothing unless it is clear to him (Black is an excellent judge of such things) that $Jones_4$ is going to decide to do something *other* than what he wants him to do. If it does become clear that $Jones_4$ is going to decide to do something else, Black takes effective steps to ensure that $Jones_4$ decides to do, and that he does do, what he wants him to do.[3] Whatever $Jones_4$'s initial preferences and inclinations, then, Black will have his way.

What steps will Black take, if he believes he must take steps, in order to ensure that $Jones_4$ decides and acts as he wishes? Anyone with a theory concerning what "could have done otherwise" means may answer this question for himself by describing whatever measures he would regard as sufficient to guarantee that, in the relevant sense, $Jones_4$ cannot do otherwise. Let Black pronounce a terrible threat, and in this way both force $Jones_4$ to perform the desired action and prevent him from performing a forbidden one. Let Black give $Jones_4$ a potion, or put him under hypnosis, and in some such way as these generate in $Jones_4$ an irresistible inner compulsion to perform the act Black wants performed and to avoid others. Or let Black manipulate the minute processes of $Jones_4$'s brain and nervous system in some more direct way, so that causal forces running in and out of his synapses and along the poor man's nerves determine that he chooses to act and that he does act in the one way and not in any other. Given any conditions under which it will be maintained that Jones$_4$ cannot do otherwise, in other words, let Black bring it about that those conditions prevail. The structure of the example is flexible enough, I think, to find a way around any charge of irrelevance by accommodating the doctrine on which the charge is based.[4]

Now suppose that Black never has to show his hand because Jones$_4$, for reasons of his own, decides to perform and does perform the very action Black wants him to perform. In that case, it seems clear, Jones$_4$ will bear precisely the same moral responsibility for what he does as he would have borne if Black had not been ready to take steps to ensure that he do it. It would be quite unreasonable to excuse Jones$_4$ for his action, or to with- hold the praise to which it would normally entitle him, on the basis of the fact that he could not have done otherwise. This fact played no role at all in leading him to act as he did. He would have acted the same even if it had not been a fact. Indeed, everything happened just as it would have happened without Black's presence in the situation and without his readiness to intrude into it.

In this example there are sufficient conditions for Jones$_4$'s performing the action in question. What action he performs is not up to him. Of course it is in a way up to him whether he acts on his own or as a result of Black's intervention. That depends upon what action he himself is inclined to perform. But whether he finally acts on his own or as a result of Black's intervention, he performs the same action. He has no alternative but to do what Black wants him to do. If he does it on his own, however, his moral respon- sibility for doing it is not affected by the fact that Black was lurking in the background with sinister intent, since this intent never comes into play.

V

The fact that a person could not have avoided doing something is a sufficient condition of his having done it. But, as some of my examples show, this fact may play no role what- ever in the explanation of why he did it. It may not figure at all among the circumstances that actually brought it about that he did what he did, so that his action is to be accounted for on another basis entirely. Even though the person was unable to do otherwise, that is to say, it may not be the case that he acted as he did *because* he could not have done otherwise. Now if someone had no alternative to performing a certain action but did not perform it because he was unable to do otherwise, then he would have performed exactly the same action even if he *could* have done otherwise. The circumstances that made it impossible for him to do otherwise could have been subtracted from the situation without affecting what happened or why it happened in any way. Whatever it was that actually led the person to do what he did, or that made him do it, would have led him to do it or made him do it even if it had been possible for him to do something else instead.

Thus it would have made no difference, so far as concerns his action or how he came to perform it, if the circumstances that made it impossible for him to avoid performing it had not prevailed. The fact that he could not have done otherwise clearly provides no basis for supposing that he *might* have done otherwise if he had been able to do so. When a fact is in this way irrelevant to the problem of accounting for a person's action it seems quite gratuitous to assign it any weight in the assessment of his moral responsibility. Why should the fact be considered in reaching a moral judgment concerning the person when it does not help in any way to understand either what made him act as he did or what, in other circumstances, he might have done?

This, then, is why the principle of alternate possibilities is mistaken. It asserts that a person bears no moral responsibility – that is, he is to be excused – for having performed an action if there were circumstances that made it impossible for him to avoid performing it. But there may be circumstances that make it impossible for a person to avoid performing some action without those circumstances in any way bringing it about that he performs that action. It would surely be no good for the person to refer to circumstances of this sort in an effort to absolve himself of moral responsibility for performing the action in question. For those circumstances, by hypothesis, actually had nothing to do with his having done what he did. He would have done precisely the same thing, and he would have been led or made in precisely the same way to do it, even if they had not prevailed.

We often do, to be sure, excuse people for what they have done when they tell us (and we believe them) that they could not have done otherwise. But this is because we assume that what they tell us serves to explain why they did what they did. We take it for granted that they are not being disingenuous, as a person would be who cited as an excuse the fact that he could not have avoided doing what he did but who knew full well that it was not at all because of this that he did it.

What I have said may suggest that the principle of alternate possibilities should be revised so as to assert that a person is not morally responsible for what he has done if he did it because he could not have done otherwise. It may be noted that this revision of the principle does not seriously affect the arguments of those who have relied on the original principle in their efforts to maintain that moral responsibility and determinism are incompatible. For if it was causally determined that a person perform a certain action, then it will be true that the person performed it because of those causal determinants. And if the fact that it was causally determined that a person perform a certain action means that the person could not have done otherwise, as philosophers who argue for the incompatibility thesis characteristically suppose, then the fact that it was causally determined that a person perform a certain action will mean that the person performed it because he could not have done otherwise. The revised principle of alternate possibilities will entail, on this assumption concerning the meaning of 'could have done otherwise', that a person is not morally responsible for what he has done if it was causally determined that he do it. I do not believe, however, that this revision of the principle is acceptable.

Suppose a person tells us that he did what he did because he was unable to do otherwise; or suppose he makes the similar statement that he did what he did because he had to do it. We do often accept statements like these (if we believe them) as valid excuses, and such statements may well seem at first glance to invoke the revised principle of alternate possibilities. But I think that when we accept such statements as valid excuses it is because we assume that we are being told more than the statements strictly and literally convey. We understand the person who offers the excuse to mean that he did what he did *only because* he was unable to do otherwise, or *only because* he had to do it. And we understand him to mean, more particularly, that when he did what he did it was not because that was what he really wanted to do. The principle of alternate possibilities should thus be replaced, in my opinion, by the following principle: a person is not morally responsible for what he has done if he did it only because he could not have done otherwise. This principle does not appear to conflict with the view that moral responsibility is compatible with determinism.

The following may all be true: there were circumstances that made it impossible for a person to avoid doing something; these circumstances actually played a role in bringing it about that he did it, so that it is correct to say that he did it because he could not have done otherwise; the person really wanted to do what he did; he did it because it was what he really wanted to do, so that it is not correct to say that he did what he did only because he could not have done otherwise. Under these conditions, the person may well be morally responsible for what he has done. On the other hand, he will not be morally responsible for what he has done if he did it only because he could not have done otherwise, even if what he did was something he really wanted to do.

Notes

1   The two main concepts employed in the principle of alternate possibilities are "morally responsible" and "could have done otherwise." To discuss the principle without analyzing either of these concepts may well seem like an attempt at piracy. The reader should take notice that my Jolly Roger is now unfurled.

2   After thinking up the example that I am about to develop I learned that Robert Nozick, in lectures given several years ago, had formulated an example of the same general type and had proposed it as a counterexample to the principle of alternate possibilities.

3   The assumption that Black can predict what $Jones_4$ will decide to do does not beg the question of determinism. We can imagine that $Jones_4$ has often confronted the alternative – A and B – that he now confronts, and that his face has invariably twitched when he was about to decide to do A and never when he was about to decide to do B. Knowing this, and observing the twitch, Black would have a basis for prediction. This does, to be sure, suppose that there is some sort of causal relation between $Jones_4$'s state at the time of the twitch and his subsequent states. But any plausible view of decision or of action will allow that reaching a decision and performing an action both involve earlier and later phases, with causal relations between them, and such that the earlier phases are not themselves part of the decision or of the action. The example does not require that these earlier phases be deterministically related to still earlier events.

4   The example is also flexible enough to allow for the elimination of Black altogether. Anyone who thinks that the effectiveness of the example is undermined by its reliance on a human manipulator, who imposes his will on $Jones_4$, can substitute for Black a machine programmed to do what Black does. If this is still not good enough, forget both Black and the machine and suppose that their role is played by natural forces involving no will or design at all.

25   How to Complete the Compatibilist Account of Free Action*

James P. Sterba and Janet A. Kourany

In its long and venerable career as a subject of philosophical debate, determinism has appeared in many forms: sometimes as a very general factual truth about the world,

*From *Philosophy and Phenomenological Research*, 41/4 (1981), pp. 508–23. Reprinted with permission.

variously explicated and illustrated, a truth sometimes known a priori, sometimes known inductively, sometimes simply assumed as a presupposition of scientific enquiry, sometimes simply believed as an article of scientific faith, as an expression of the scientist's confidence in the possibility of solving his problems; sometimes appearing, again, as a methodological principle of scientific enquiry rather than a truth about the world, expressing by its directives the goals of science rather than the facts of nature; sometimes, again, appearing in other forms as well. And in one or another of these forms, determinism has managed to tempt, if not actually seduce, nearly all philosophers at some stage or another of their philosophical careers. Indeed, in one form or another, determinism has symbolized to these philosophers and others nothing less than the world's intelligibility.

But if determinism in one form or another has always seemed enticing, it has always seemed threatening as well. For it has always seemed that a universe described in terms of determinism (now construed as a factual truth about the world), or described in terms that at least approximate here and there to determinism (now construed as a descriptive and explanatory scientific ideal), is a universe that rules out, in whole or in part, those valuable human commodities of freedom and responsibility. And this, despite all the effort and ingenuity that have been expended at least since the time of Hume toward showing that freedom and determinism are fully compatible.

This is not to say, of course, that determinism has not appeared *less* threatening as a result of all this effort and ingenuity. Hume, Mill, Schlick, and their followers have argued persuasively, after all, that a deterministic universe is not a universe in which all things, including human beings, are necessitated or compelled to do what they do, in which all things, that is, *must* do what they do, *cannot but* do what they do, and hence, cannot do *other* than what they do. It is *not*, therefore, a universe in which human beings, in particular, never "could have acted otherwise than they did" – the hallmark of freedom for most writers on the subject. A deterministic universe, they tell us, is simply a predictable universe, is simply a universe whose complete set of laws of nature, together with relevant statements of fact, allow the deduction of statements describing everything that will in fact occur, including everything that human beings will in fact do (irrespective of what they could do, or could have done), just as an indeterministic universe is one whose complete set of laws of nature, together with relevant statements of fact, allow the deduction of statements describing only some things that will occur and only some things that human beings will do, the rest being a matter of absolute, inexorable, inexplicable chance. Hume, Mill, Schlick, and their followers have told us all that, and, needless to say, it is all very comforting, especially after the chilling accounts of determinism that antedated Hume. But still, it has been widely felt, the threat posed by determinism to our freedom is there, and will remain so long as a detailed and fully acceptable analysis of freedom, showing its compatibility with determinism, is not produced. And, at least some have claimed, the prospects for such an eventuation have been significantly diminished by a problem in the compatibilist program pointed out by Chisholm.

This problem of Chisholm's applies to a broad range of suggested compatibilist analyses of freedom, in fact, according to Chisholm, "applies . . . in all probability, to any attempt to define 'can' in terms of 'will if,' " though he actually applies it only to an analysis of "can" that he himself suggests.[1] According to this analysis, broadly construed, to say that a person X could have acted otherwise than he did is to say that there was in the choice situation some physically possible action a such that, had X willed (or chosen or tried or tried hard, etc.) to perform a, he would have acted otherwise than he did. Thus, for example, to say that Harry, hard-core smoker that he is, could have stopped smoking when his friend Freda did is to say that there was some specific action (or series of actions), e.g., buying and using a set of graduated cigarette filters, or joining Smokers Anonymous, or showing up for hypnosis, or the like, such that, had Harry willed to perform that action (or series of actions), then he *would* have stopped smoking when his friend Freda did. Notice that, according to this analysis, Harry might actually have *tried* to stop smoking when his friend Freda did, might have failed to do so, and nonetheless might actually have *had* the ability, then and there, to do so – a point to Chisholm's credit, as many ex-smokers will doubtless attest. Indeed, it was the possibility of just this kind of case – of having an ability to do something and yet trying and failing to do it – that led Chisholm to formulate the analysis he did, in replacement of an earlier analysis proposed by Moore and criticized by Austin.[2] For according to Moore's analysis, to say that a person X could have acted otherwise than he did is to say that X *would* have acted otherwise if he had but tried (or chosen or willed, etc.) – from which it does follow, embarrassingly enough, as Austin pointed out, that X could not have tried and failed and yet been able to act otherwise nonetheless.

If Chisholm's analysis of "X could have acted otherwise" does not fall prey to the major (as well as other) criticisms Austin leveled at Moore's analysis, however, it yet falls prey to another criticism at least equally devastating – at least according to Chisholm; and that is, that its analysans, but not its analysandum, will be satisfied by situations in which X could not have willed to perform *a*. Thus, returning to hard-core Harry, there might have been some one particular action, such as buying and using a set of graduated cigarette filters, such that, had Harry willed to perform that action, then he would have stopped smoking when his friend Freda did. But it might *also* have been the case that Harry could not have willed to buy and use such a set of graduated cigarette filters, that, hard-core smoker that he is, he could not have brought himself to will (or try or choose) to do it. And if that *were* also the case, then we would want to say that Harry really *could not* have stopped smoking when his friend Freda did – that the analysandum of our example is false – even though the proposed analysans is true. And this is, of course, to say that the analysis of "X could have acted otherwise" proposed by Chisholm is, as it stands, inadequate. But so will be any other analysis, any other "attempt to define 'can' in terms of 'will if.'" For any such attempt will presumably introduce a verb of which 'he' may be made the subject; it will then be grammatically permissible to insert 'cannot' between the subject 'he' and the verb, and then it will be possible to describe a situation in which the *analysans* is true and 'He can' is false . . . "All of which confirms," so Chisholm concludes, "Austin's profound remark: 'In philosophy it is *can* in particular that we seem so often to uncover, just when we had thought some problem settled, grinning residually up at us like the frog at the bottom of the beer mug.'"[3]

Small wonder that we all too frequently find an "absolute," "unanalyzable" "X could have willed otherwise" grinning residually up at us at the end of an analysis of "X could have acted otherwise" in the contemporary compatibilist literature, an "X could have willed otherwise" which is then casually declared to be fully compatible with determinism, which is then casually declared to be "prima facie neutral" or "nondeterminist" (as in the case of Lawrence H. Davis[4]), or similar to the kinds of descriptions of abilities we apply to automobiles and other such objects (as in the case of Wilfrid Sellars[5]), or the like. And small wonder that the so-called threat to our freedom posed by determinism is still so widely felt. But the situation *need* not be this way. Indeed, all that follows from the problem posed by Chisholm is that any adequate analysis of "can" in terms of "will if" must include another "can." It does *not* follow that any such analysis must include an unanalyzable, an "absolute," "can." And although philosophers have tended, whenever they have actually *tried* to formulate a suitable analysis of, for example, "*X* could have willed otherwise," to gravitate toward something like "*X* would have willed otherwise if he had willed to will otherwise," have thereupon declared *that* to be nonsense, and have concluded, as a result, that "*X* could have willed otherwise" is unanalyzable, the possibility of intelligent and intelligible analysis is certainly there. Thus, returning to the analysis of "*X* could have acted otherwise than he did at time *t*" suggested by Chisholm, we can *agree* that the analysans should include something like:

a.   There was in the choice situation some physically possible action *a* such that, had *X* willed to perform *a* at time *t'* (*t'* $\lessgtr$ *t*), he would have acted otherwise than he did at *t*;

and we can *agree*, as was suggested by the discussion of Chisholm's problem, that the analysans must *also* include something like:

b.   *X* could have willed to perform *a* at *t'*.

But we *cannot agree that the latter is unanalyzable. Indeed, we suggest that the latter amounts to something like*:

X would have willed to perform *a* at *t'* if
i.   The facts of the choice situation that were reasons motivating *X* to act had been relevantly different from what they were at *t'*; and/or
ii.   *X*'s values had been relevantly different from what they were at *t'*

where "the facts of the choice situation that were reasons motivating *X* to act" means those facts of *X*'s environment that were both reasons for acting and were taken by *X* to be reasons for acting; and where "relevantly different facts" means physically possible facts that would provide sufficient reasons to motivate *X* to prefer to do *a* without altering the basic opportunities that *X* justifiably believes obtain in the choice situation, and "relevantly different values" means physically possible values that likewise would have been sufficient to motivate *X* to prefer to do *a* without altering the basic opportunities that *X* justifiably believes obtain in the choice situation. Again, we can agree that the problem pointed out by Chisholm forces us to further include in the analysis:

c.   The facts of the choice situation that were reasons motivating *X* to act could have been relevantly different from what they were at *t'*; and/or
d.   *X*'s values could have been relevantly different from what they were at *t'*.

But, again, we cannot agree that the latter are unanalyzable. Indeed, we suggest that the latter amount to something like:

c.   The facts of the choice situation that were reasons motivating *X* to act could have been relevantly different from what they were at *t'*; that is to say, they would have been relevantly different if still earlier facts had been relevantly different; and these earlier facts could have been relevantly different, that is to say . . . ; and/or

d. X's values could have been relevantly different from what they were at t'; that is to say, X's values would have been relevantly different from what they were at t' if

    i. the facts of the choice situation that were reasons motivating X to have the values that he did at t' had been relevantly different from what they were at t', so as to motivate X to prefer relevantly different values; and these facts of the choice situation could have been relevantly different from what they were at t', that is to say, they would have been relevantly different if still earlier facts had been relevantly different; and these earlier facts could have been relevantly different, that is to say . . . ; and/or

    ii. the facts of previous choice situations that were reasons motivating X to acquire the values that he had at t' had been relevantly different from what they were, so that X would have acquired relevantly different values by t'; and these facts of previous choice situations could have been relevantly different from what they were, that is to say, they would have been relevantly different; and these still earlier facts could have been relevantly different, that is to say . . .

At no time, therefore, must we settle for an "absolute," unanalyzable "can" "grinning residually up at us like the frog at the bottom of the beer mug"; and therefore, at no time must we settle for something less than a detailed demonstration of the compatibility of freedom and determinism.

What's more, the foregoing analysis of freedom would seem to accommodate at least the most important ways in which we ordinarily envision persons could have acted otherwise. Consider, for example, the question of effort and attention. On many occasions we want to say of someone that he could have acted otherwise in the sense that he could have exerted more (or less) effort or paid more (or less) attention to what he was doing. Thus, we say of the safecracker who took too long opening a bank's vault and was caught in the act that she could have attended more carefully to the movements of the vault's tumblers, and thereby escaped undetected. Or the jeweler who succeeded in adjusting the extremely delicate mainspring of an old watch, we say, could have applied but normal effort and broken it. Or the child who exerted too much effort on his arithmetic assignment and had no time left for his spelling, we say, could have exerted less effort and gotten everything done. Or the motorist who ran a red light, colliding with an oncoming automobile, we say, could have attended more carefully to his driving and avoided the accident. Even the husband who failed to lighten the mood of his grumpy wife, we are sure, could have put more effort into preparing her favorite dinner and thereby succeeded.

Such actions as these that could have been performed with more or less effort or attention, it should be clear, are subject to the entire spectrum of moral evaluation. Thus, such actions can be blameworthy (as in the safecracker example), excusable (as in the jeweler example), morally neutral (as in the child example), morally required and possibly praiseworthy (as in the motorist example), or praiseworthy but not morally required (as in the husband example). Even so, our attention is normally focused on alternative actions that are morally required, since failure to perform such actions either causes harm or risks doing so, and is accordingly subject (and justifiably so) to moral sanctions (e.g., blaming a host for failing to attend to the needs of his guests) or to both moral and coercive sanctions (e.g., suspending a person's license for reckless driving).

Perhaps the most significant feature of this freedom to act with a different degree of effort or attention, however, is the feature that principally serves to distinguish it from a second variety of freedom, the freedom to act with different knowledge or ability. For while the freedom to act with a different degree of effort or attention normally defines an option open to an agent at the time he performs his action, the freedom to act with different knowledge or ability normally does not. That is to say, acting with more or less effort or attention is usually open to an agent at the time he performs whatever action he does perform, and this, because such more or less effortful or attentive actions are so similar to the action the agent does perform – similar with respect to the abilities and reasons for acting they involve. But, acting with different knowledge or ability is usually *not* open to an agent at the time he performs whatever action he does perform – unless, of course, he can acquire the relevant knowledge or ability on the spot (which sometimes may be possible). Thus, for example, to say of a student, who failed his history exam on Monday morning due to his ignorance of the details of the Treaty of Versailles that he could have passed the exam – could have known more about the treaty of Versailles – does not normally imply that the student had the option of passing the exam on Monday morning. What it implies is that at some time earlier than Monday morning the student could have acquired the knowledge necessary to pass the exam, that at that earlier time the option of acquiring the relevant knowledge was indeed open to the student when he in fact chose to do something else (e.g., stay out late on a date). To say, in short, that an agent could have acted, on some particular occasion, with a different degree of effort or attention normally implies that he had the option *on that occasion* of applying the different degree of effort or attention and thereby acting differently. To say, on the other hand, that an agent could have acted, on some particular occasion, with different knowledge or ability normally implies that he could have acquired the relevant knowledge or ability at some *previous* time, and thereby acted otherwise on that occasion.[6]

Of course, in order for an agent to be able to act with different knowledge or ability, it does not suffice that he was simply physically able at some earlier time to acquire the relevant knowledge or ability. For clearly we are all physically able to acquire all kinds of knowledge and abilities which would then effectively motivate us to perform many actions that are quite different from those we do perform. And we should not infer from this that we can perform, or could have performed, all of these different actions. Indeed, in determining whether a person could have acted otherwise than he did on some particular occasion, we must go beyond what is simply physically possible and carefully attend to the agent's own personal history; in particular, we must determine what basic opportunities that history provided for acquiring knowledge and ability that the agent does not in fact possess. Thus, in order to determine whether a person could have acted otherwise when he broke a law of which he was ignorant, we must examine his personal history to determine whether that history provided the basic opportunities for acquiring the knowledge of the law. Needless to say, in determining whether an agent could have acted with a different degree of effort or attention, we must also take as given the agent's basic opportunities. But for that kind of freedom, the relevant opportunities are normally the basic opportunities of the agent at the time of his action, and not, as in the case of the freedom to act with different knowledge or ability, the basic opportunities of the agent at a time before his action.

Finally, as in the case of the freedom to act with a different degree of effort or attention, so too in the case of the freedom to act with different knowledge or ability, there is the possibility of the entire spectrum of moral evaluation. To grant that an agent could have acted otherwise on some particular occasion, since he could have taken advantage of certain basic opportunities in his past, does not, that is, imply any particular moral evaluation of either the action he does perform or the action he could have performed. Of course, if the agent's action is to be blameworthy, he must not only have caused or risked causing harm, he must also have had a reasonably good opportunity to acquire the knowledge or ability necessary for alternative action. And a similar requirement holds where morally required actions are concerned, but obviously not where excusable, morally neutral, or praiseworthy but not morally required actions are concerned.

So, too, a third variety of freedom, the freedom to act with different reasons or values, also covers the entire spectrum of moral evaluation. But here, different relations with our two previous varieties of freedom are possible. Thus, acting with a different degree of effort or attention obviously requires somewhat different reasons for acting or values from those which motivated the action that was performed. Hence, every case of our first variety of freedom will be an instance of our third. Similarly, acting with different knowledge or ability obviously requires different reasons for acting or values to motivate the acquisition of the different knowledge or ability. And hence, every case of our second variety of freedom will be an instance of our third. But just as obviously, acting with different reasons for acting or values does *not* require a different degree of effort or attention or different knowledge or ability – so long, that is, as knowledge is not equated with virtue, or ability with achievement. Hence, not every case of our third variety of freedom will be an instance of our first or second. Thus, we might say of a young woman who has chosen to pursue the less demanding of two contemplated careers that she could have chosen the more demanding career. And we might mean thereby that the explanation of the woman's choice is motivational in nature – which is to say that it lies not in any lack of knowledge or ability or effort or attention on her part, but solely in her reasons for acting or values. Under such circumstances the woman's husband might have attempted to change his wife's mind by reasoning with her. But in so doing he would not have been trying to provide her with new knowledge or ability that would lead her to a different choice. Rather, he would only have been trying to change her reasons for acting or values, having assumed that she already had sufficient knowledge and ability to make a different choice, but was simply not motivated to do so.

The exercise of the varieties of freedom we have been discussing, it should be noted, is not restricted to the performance of uncoerced or noncompulsive actions. For example, it may well be that a traveler coerced at the point of a gun to hand over his valuables could have acted with more effort – e.g., could have handed over his valuables more quickly – or could have acted with more knowledge – e.g., could have refrained from pleading with the robber to spare his life, knowing as a consequence that he would be treated less roughly. Similarly, it may well be that a person under a compulsion to change his clothes seven times a day could have paid more attention to his task on some particular occasion, or could have taken advantage of several opportunities he had to get psychiatric help, and thereby rid himself of his compulsion. Indeed, what normally contrasts with acting under coercion or acting from compulsion is not the exercise of the three varieties of freedom we have been considering, but rather the exercise of freedom of the will.

What the exercise of freedom of the will by an agent entails is that the agent acts in accordance with what he believes after considerable reflection is one of his "higher order life plans." That is to say, we can envision an agent as having a range of "life plans" that specify his preferences under various possible circumstances, and are ordered so as to correspond to the degree to which they assume the cooperation or noninterference of others with respect to the agent's preferences. Thus, Jones's life plan will specify Jones's preferences assuming the full cooperation of her husband, family, friends, and others with respect to her preferences. And Jones's husband's life plan will specify his preferences assuming the full cooperation of his wife, family, friends, and others with respect to his preference. And similarly for other agents. Life plans of a somewhat lower order will assume that other agents at least do not interfere with what pertains to the preferences of the agent concerned, and life plans of a still lower order will assume varying degrees of interference by other agents. Given that people's preferences can and do conflict, most people will not be able to realize their highest order life plan. Nevertheless, the exercise of freedom of the will does presuppose that they act in accordance with what they believe after considerable reflection is one of their higher order life plans.

By contrast, acting under coercion entails that an agent is prevented by others from doing something he could otherwise do – prevented by the use of considerable force or by the threat of some highly undesirable consequence. Accordingly, coercion usually impedes the exercise of an agent's freedom of the will because the performance of the coerced action normally conflicts with the agent's higher order life plans. Occasionally, however, an action that an agent is coerced into performing does turn out to be in accord with the agent's higher order life plans – as, for example, when the application of coercive sanctions helps an agent overcome some particularly unruly desire or impulse. On such occasions, therefore, acting under coercion does not impede the exercise of the agent's freedom of the will. Likewise, acting under compulsion usually impedes the exercise of an agent's freedom of the will. For to act under compulsion is to act from desires that a person is normally incapable of resisting, or at least resisting to any significant degree, even if he believes he has conclusive reasons for doing so. For example, acting under a compulsion not to touch anyone normally interferes with an agent's acting in accordance with his higher order life plans, and hence, normally interferes with the exercise of his freedom of the will. Still, it is possible – as, for example, with some cases of drug addiction – for compulsive actions to play essential roles in an agent's higher order life plans. This does not mean, however, that an agent would be fully rational in such cases. For in order to be fully rational, an agent in exercising his freedom of the will would have to (1) give sufficient consideration to life plans based upon preferences that differ from those he in fact accepts, and (2) have the ability to make changes in his preferences and his life plans whenever he discovered conclusive reasons for doing so. And while an agent acting under a compulsion might be able to satisfy condition (1), he would not be able to satisfy condition (2).

We have now, in effect, distinguished three basic varieties of freedom – the freedom to act with a different degree of effort or attention, the freedom to act with different knowledge or ability, and the freedom to act with different reasons or values – along with three subsidiary varieties of freedom – the freedom from coercion, the freedom from compulsion, and the freedom of the will. These varieties of freedom would seem to capture at least the more important ways in which we ordinarily envision persons could have acted otherwise. And these varieties of freedom would seem to be accommodated by the analysis of freedom with which we began – the one, you will recall, that allows a detailed demonstration of the compatibility of freedom and determinism. But if all this is so, then the foregoing comes close to a complete justification of compatibilism. Nonetheless, some objections might still be raised. Thus, it might be said, people not infrequently claim to know, sometimes on very plausible grounds, that they or others "could have acted otherwise than they did." But according to the analysis of freedom on which our justification of compatibilism is based, a potentially infinite number of general conditions have to be satisfied before any statement of the form "X could have acted otherwise than he did" is true. And that being the case, how could anyone ever *know* that such a statement is true? But is there really any problem here? To say that a potentially infinite number of general conditions have to be satisfied before any statement of the form "X could have acted otherwise than he did" is true is not to say that one must *know* that an infinite number of conditions have been satisfied before one can plausibly be said to *know* that the statement is true.[7] Nor is it to say that any one of these conditions, or the evidence relevant to determining whether or not it has been satisfied, is just as significant as any other for deciding whether or not it has been satisfied, is just as significant as any other for deciding whether the statement of the form "X could have acted otherwise than he did" is true. In short, it does not follow from our analysis of freedom that any particular kind or amount of evidence is needed to warrant a claim of the form "X could have acted otherwise than he did." And this seems to be as it should be. For the question of the kind and amount of evidence that is needed to warrant a claim of the form "X could have acted otherwise than he did" seems to be just the kind of question whose answer will very properly vary from context to context, and cannot, therefore, be decided in the abstract, in conjunction with a general analysis of "X could have acted otherwise than he did." At any rate, our analysis cannot be faulted for not providing such an answer.

Is, then, any problem provided for our justification of compatibilism by recent criticisms of compatibilism?[8] According to these criticisms, to say that some agent X could have acted otherwise than he did at time t is at least to say that X could have prevented his action at t. And, so the argument goes, this is the only insight into the concept of freedom that is needed to demonstrate the incompatibility of freedom and determinism. For, imagine that agent X performed action a at time t. Then, if determinism is true, there is some state of the universe, call it s, that occurred at time t' before X was even born, whose description, together with the laws of nature, entails that X performed a at t. But if, in addition to the truth of determinism, it is also true that X could have acted otherwise than he did at t, then it is also true that X could have prevented his action a at t. And if it is also true that X could have prevented his action a at t, then it is also true that X could have prevented s at t' as well (since, it is claimed, preventing action a at t entails preventing s at t'). But X obviously could *not* have prevented s at t', a state of the universe that occurred before X was even born. And hence, if determinism is true, it cannot also be true that X could have acted otherwise than he did at t.

Does the above argument render doubtworthy our justification of compatibilism? Hardly. For from the argument's three suppositions – (1) X did a at t; (2) determinism is true, from which it follows that there is some state s of the universe that occurred at t' before X was born, whose description, together with the laws of nature, entails that X did a at t; and (3) X could have acted otherwise than he did at t, that is, X could have prevented his action a at t – from these three suppositions it simply does not follow that X could have prevented s at t'. Indeed, it seems perfectly consistent to say that X did a at t; the description of s at t', together with the laws of nature, entails that X did a at t; X could have prevented his action a at t; and X could *not* have prevented s at t'. But if the claim that X could have prevented s at t' does not follow from the argument's three suppositions, then the falsity of this claim does not demonstrate the falsity of at least one of those three suppositions – or more particularly, the falsity of "X could have acted otherwise than he did at t," given the truth of determinism. In short, the line of argument presented above and recently taken by some philosophers does not provide any problem for our justification of compatibilism.

But is our justification of compatibilism finally all that important? To say that a person "could have acted otherwise than he did" is not, after all, to imply that his liberty was unrestricted.[9] Indeed, as we have before observed, it is possible that a person was *coerced* to do what he did and *also* "could have acted otherwise" – both handed over his money to a robber at the point of a gun, for example, *and* could have resisted and been shot, or could have tried to trick the robber, or bargain with him, etc. To say that a person "could have acted otherwise than he did" is not, then, to provide a *sufficient* condition for moral responsibility. Nor is it, according to Harry Frankfurt, at least, even to provide a *necessary* condition.[10] For, as Frankfurt sees it, a person may well be morally responsible for some action he performed even though he could not have acted otherwise – on the grounds that he performed the action because he wanted to rather than because he could not have done otherwise. And if Frankfurt's view is correct, then the question of the compatibility of freedom and determinism, together with our proposed answer to that question, is at least somewhat irrelevant to its supposed source of importance, moral responsibility.

But *is* Frankfurt's view correct? Frankfurt attempts to justify it by appealing to the following case: – Suppose that Black wants Jones to perform some particular action, and is prepared to go to considerable lengths to get his way. "What steps will Black take . . . to ensure that Jones decides and acts as he wishes? Anyone with a theory concerning what 'could have done otherwise' means may answer this question for himself by describing whatever measures he would regard as sufficient to guarantee that, in the relevant sense, Jones cannot do otherwise." Thus, Black might "pronounce a terrible threat," or "give Jones a potion, or put him under hypnosis," or "manipulate the minute processes of Jones's brain and nervous system." Suppose, however, that Black will do none of these things "unless it [becomes] clear to him (Black is an excellent judge of such things) that Jones is going to decide to do something *other* than what he wants him to do." Finally, "suppose that Black never has to show his hand because Jones, for reasons of his own, decides to perform and does perform the very action Black wants him to perform."[11] In that case, Frankfurt concludes, Jones will bear moral responsibility for his action even though he could not have acted otherwise – which is to say that it is *not* a necessary condition of an agent's moral responsibility that he "could have acted otherwise than he did."

Is this conclusion justified? That is, has it really been shown that, under the supposed circumstances, Jones would be *both* morally responsible for his action *and* unable to act otherwise? Or more specifically – since it seems clear that Jones *would be* morally responsible for his action – has it really been shown that Jones would be unable to act otherwise? According to our analysis of "could have acted otherwise," which we have been invited to consider, it is the case that Jones could have acted otherwise only if the following condition obtains:

If the facts of the choice situation that were reasons motivating Jones to act, and/or if Jones's values, had been relevantly different from what they were just before Jones acted, that is, if they had been different in such a way as to provide sufficient reasons to motivate Jones to prefer to act otherwise without altering the basic opportunities of the choice situation, then Jones would have willed to act otherwise, and thence, would have acted otherwise.

And apparently this condition (as well as the other conditions necessary for Jones's ability to act otherwise) *would* have obtained had Black not been on the scene ready to intrude. But with Black on the scene, if the factors motivating Jones had been relevently different, Black would have altered Jones – would have drugged him, or hypnotized him, or temporarily or permanently altered his brain, or the like – in such a way that, then, Jones would *not* have willed to act otherwise, and thence, would *not* have acted otherwise, and, in all probability, *could* not (strictly speaking) have willed or acted at all. But does this show that, with Black on the scene, the above condition for "Jones could have acted otherwise" does *not* obtain? Not at all. For in deciding whether the above condition obtains, it is not permissible to consider just any hypothetical difference in Jones's choice situation or just any hypothetical difference in Jones's nature. On the contrary, any hypothetical difference in Jones's choice situation that is permissible must leave the basic opportunities of his choice situation unaltered; otherwise we would not be deciding whether Jones could have acted otherwise *in that choice situation*. Similarly, any hypothetical difference in Jones that is permissible must leave Jones's nature basically unaltered; otherwise we would not be deciding whether *Jones* could have acted otherwise in that choice situation. And it is precisely this second requirement that is violated by Frankfurt's example. A drugged or hypnotized or neurologically altered Jones is, after all, a Jones whose nature has, at least temporarily, been basically altered. Any consideration of the actions that would or would not result after such an alteration would obscure rather than illuminate Jones's capacities. Thus, we could no more infer that "Jones could not have acted otherwise" from the fact that a basically altered Jones, under relevantly different conditions, would not have acted otherwise than we could infer that "A Chevy Scooter could not have gotten 26 miles to the gallon" from the fact that a basically altered Chevy Scooter, under relevantly different (greatly improved) driving conditions, would not have gotten 26 miles to the gallon (e.g., imagine that the Chevy Scooter's 4 cylinder engine were replace with a gas guzzling 8 cylinder engine).

Frankfurt has, then, failed to justify his skepticism regarding the traditionally-conceived relation between freedom and moral responsibility, and in consequence, has failed to justify his (at least latent) skepticism regarding the importance of the freedom-determinism debate. And that being the case, the contribution to that debate contained in the foregoing is at least to some extent vouched for. What still needs to be done, of course, is to show that the compatibilist analysis of freedom we have offered is superior to any analysis of freedom available to the incompatibilist. But that is a task for another occasion.

Notes

1 See Roderick Chisholm. "J. L. Austin's Philosophical Papers," *Mind* (1964), pp. 20–5.
2 See G. E. Moore, *Ethics* (1913), chapter VI, and J. L. Austin, "Ifs and Cans," reprinted in Myles Brand, *The Nature of Human Action* (Glenview, 1970), pp. 161–78.
3 Chisholm. p. 25.
4 Cf. Lawrence H. Davis, *Theory of Action* (Englewood Cliffs, 1979), chapters 5 and 6.
5 Cf. Wilfrid Sellars, "Reply to Donagan," *Philosophical Studies* (1975), pp. 154, 175, and "Fatalism and Determinism" in *Freedom and Determinism*, edited by Keith Lehrer (New York, 1966), p. 173.
6 For a different account, see Alvin I. Goldman. *A Theory of Human Action* (1970), pp. 207–15.
7 For example, one can know that a scientific theory is true without knowing that all the empirical implications of that theory are true.

8   Cf. Carl Ginet, "Might We Have No Choice?" in Lehrer, pp. 87–104; Peter van Inwagen, "The Incompatibility of Free Will and Determinism," *Philosophical Studies* (1975), pp. 185–99; James W. Lamb, "On a Proof of Incompatibilism," *Philosophical Review* (1977), pp. 20–35.

9   For the relevant account of what constitutes restricting a person's liberty, see James P. Sterba, "Neo-Libertarianism," *American Philosophical Quarterly* (1978), pp. 115–21.

10 Harry Frankfurt, "Alternate Possiblities and Moral Responsibility." *The Journal of Philosophy* (1969), pp. 829–39.

11 Ibid., pp. 835–6.

26   Living without Free Will: The Case for Hard Incompatibilism*

Derk Pereboom

The central thesis of the position I defend is that we do not have the sort of free will required for moral responsibility.[1] My argument for this claim has the following structure: An agent's moral responsibility for an action depends primarily on its actual causal history, and not on the existence of alternative possibilities. Absent agent causation, indeterministic causal histories pose no less of a threat to moral responsibility than do deterministic histories, and a generalization argument from manipulation cases shows that deterministic histories indeed undermine moral responsibility. Agent causation is a coherent possibility, but it is not credible given our best physical theories. Consequently, no position that affirms the sort of free will required for moral responsibility is left standing. I also contend that a conception of life without this sort of free will would not be devastating to our sense of meaning and purpose, and in certain respects it may even be beneficial. Although this position is clearly similar to hard determinism, it does not endorse determinism itself, and thus I call it *hard incompatibilism*.

1.   Outline of the Argument

I reject an alternative-possibilities type of incompatibilism and accept instead a type of incompatibilism that ascribes the more significant role to an action's causal history. My view is that an agent's responsibility for an action is explained not by the existence of alternative possibilities available to her, but rather by the action's having a causal history of a sort that allows the agent to be the source of her action in a specific way. Following Ted Honderich and Robert Kane, the crucial condition emphasizes that an agent must be the origin of her action in a particular way.[2] According to my version of this condition, if an agent is morally responsible for her decision to perform an action, then the production of this decision must be something over which the agent has control, and an

* From Robert Kane (ed.), *Oxford Handbook of Free Will* (Oxford: Oxford University Press, 2002), pp. 477–88. © 2001 by Robert Kane. Used by permission of Oxford University Press Inc.

agent is not morally responsible for the decision if it is ultimately produced by a source over which she has no control.

The grounding for this kind of incompatibilism includes the argument that certain Frankfurt-style cases rule out the notion that having alternative possibilities explains an agent's responsibility for action and the argument that a deterministic causal history would make it impossible for the agent to be the source of her action in the way required.[3] The best strategy for establishing the latter claim involves devising manipulation cases in which the agent is covertly induced to perform an action by some external cause and for that reason is not responsible for her action, and then generalizing to nonresponsibility in more ordinary deterministic cases. I contend that no relevant and principled difference can distinguish an action that results from responsibility-undermining manipulation from an action that has a more ordinary deterministic causal history.[4] Moreover, exclusively event-causal indeterministic histories are no less threatening to moral responsibility than deterministic histories, and since deterministic causal histories undermine moral responsibility, so do such event-causal indeterministic histories.[5] If the crucial indeterministic events were appropriately produced by a randomizing manipulator, then one would have the intuition that the agent is not morally responsible.[6] But there is no relevant and principled difference between the manipulated action and one that is indeterministic in a more ordinary way. Among available models for agency, to my mind only agent causation allows for moral responsibility, but simply because it builds into the agent, as a primitive power, the capacity to be a source of action that is required for moral responsibility. The agent-causation model is coherent as far as we can tell, but given evidence from our best scientific theories, it is not credible that we are in fact agent-causes. We are therefore left with the view that we do not have free will of the kind required for moral responsibility.

2. Wrongdoing

Accepting hard incompatibilism demands giving up our ordinary view of ourselves as blameworthy for immoral actions and praiseworthy for those that are morally exemplary. One might argue that giving up our belief in moral responsibility would have very harmful consequences, or even that they would be so damaging that thinking and acting as if hard incompatibilism is true is not a practical possibility for us. Thus even if the claim that we are morally responsible turns out to be false, there may yet be a practical argument for continuing to treat ourselves and others as if we were. One might find this proposal attractive because acting as if people are at times blameworthy is typically required for moral reform and education. If we began to act as if people were not morally responsible, then one might fear that we would be left with insufficient leverage to change immoral ways of behaving.

It is nevertheless important to understand that this option would have the hard incompatibilist treating people as blameworthy – by, for example, expressing indignation toward them – when they do not deserve it, which would seem morally wrong. As Bruce Waller argues, if people are not responsible for immoral behavior, treating them as if they were would be unfair.[7] However, it is possible to achieve moral reform and education by methods that would not suffer from this sort of unfairness, and in ordinary situations such practices could arguably be as successful as those that presuppose moral responsibility. Instead of treating people as if they were deserving of blame, the hard incompatibilist can draw upon moral admonishment and encouragement, which presuppose only that the offender has done wrong. These methods can effectively communicate a sense of what is right and result in beneficial reform. Similarly, rather than treating oneself as blameworthy, one could admonish oneself for one's wrongdoing and resolve to avoid similar behavior in the future.

But what resources does hard incompatibilism have for dealing with criminal behavior? Here hard incompatibilism would appear to be at a disadvantage, and if so, practical considerations might force us nevertheless to treat criminals as if they were morally responsible. Indeed, if hard incompatibilism is true, a retributivist justification for criminal punishment is ruled out, for it assumes that we deserve blame or pain or deprivation just for performing an immoral action, while hard incompatibilism denies this claim. Hard incompatibilism must therefore forswear retributivism – one of the most naturally compelling ways for justifying criminal punishment.

By contrast, the moral education theory of punishment is not challenged by hard incompatibilism specifically. Still, without strong empirical evidence that punishment of criminals would bring about moral education, it would be wrong to punish them for the sake of achieving this goal. In general, it is morally wrong to harm someone in order to realize some good if there is insufficient evidence that the harm can produce the good. Moreover, even if we knew that punishment could be effective in moral education, we should prefer nonpunitive methods for producing this result – whether or not we are morally responsible.

Although the two most prominent deterrence theories are not challenged by hard incompatibilism in particular, they are questionable on other grounds. The utilitarian version is dubious for well-known reasons – it would at times demand punishing the innocent, in some circumstances it would prescribe punishment that is unduly severe, and it would authorize using people merely as means. I contend that the type of deterrence theory that justifies punishment on the basis of the right to harm in self-defense is also objectionable.[8] For at the time when a criminal is sentenced, he is typically not an immediate threat to anyone, and this fact about his circumstances distinguishes him from those who may legitimately be harmed on the basis of the right of self-defense.

A theory of crime prevention whose legitimacy is independent of hard incompatibilism draws an analogy between treatment of criminals and policy toward carriers of dangerous diseases. Ferdinand Schoeman argues that if we have the right to quarantine people who are carriers of severe communicable diseases to protect society, then we also have the right to isolate the criminally dangerous to protect society.[9] Schoeman's claim is true independently of any legitimate attribution of moral responsibility. If a child is infected with the Ebola virus because it has been passed on to her at birth by her parent, quarantine may nevertheless be justified. By analogy, suppose that someone poses a known danger to society by having demonstrated a sufficiently strong tendency to commit murder. Even if he is not in general a morally responsible agent, society would nevertheless seem to have as much right to detain him as it does to quarantine a carrier of a deadly communicable disease who is not responsible for being a carrier.

One must note, however, that it would be morally wrong to treat carriers of a disease more severely than is required to defuse the threat to society. Similarly, given the quarantine model, it would be wrong to treat those with violent criminal tendencies more harshly than is needed to remove the danger to society. In addition, just as moderately dangerous diseases may only license measures less intrusive than quarantine, so tendencies to moderately serious crimes may only justify responses less intrusive than detention. Shoplifting, for example, may warrant merely some degree of monitoring. Furthermore, I suspect that a theory modeled on quarantine would never justify criminal punishment of the sort whose legitimacy is most in doubt, such as the death penalty or confinement in the worst prisons in our society. Moreover, it would require a degree of concern for the rehabilitation and well being of the criminal that would decisively alter current policy. Just as society has a duty to try to cure the diseased it quarantines, so it would have a duty to attempt to rehabilitate the criminals it detains. And when rehabilitation is impossible, and if the protection of society were to demand indefinite confinement, there would be no justification for taking measures that aim only to make the criminal's life miserable.

3. Meaning in Life

Would it be practically impossible for us to live without a conception of ourselves as praiseworthy for achieving what makes our lives fulfilled, happy, satisfactory, or worthwhile – for realizing what Honderich has called our *life-hopes*?[10] Honderich argues that there is an aspect of these life-hopes that is undermined by determinism, but that nevertheless determinism leaves them largely intact. I agree with this type of position, and develop it in the following way. It is not unreasonable to object that life-hopes involve an aspiration for praiseworthiness, which hard incompatibilism would undercut. For life-hopes are aspirations for achievement, and because it cannot be that one has an achievement for which one is not also praiseworthy, giving up praiseworthiness would deprive us of life-hopes altogether. However, achievement and life-hopes are not obviously connected to praiseworthiness in the way this objection supposes. If an agent hopes for success in some endeavor, and if she accomplishes what she hoped for, intuitively this outcome can be her achievement even if she is not praiseworthy for it – although the sense in which it is her achievement may be diminished. If an agent hopes that her efforts as a teacher will result in well-educated children, and they do, it seems clear that she achieved what she hoped for, even if, according to the truth of hard incompatibilism, she is not praiseworthy for her efforts.

Furthermore, one might think that acceptance of hard incompatibilism would instill an attitude of resignation to whatever one's behavioral dispositions together with environmental conditions hold in store. But this is not clearly true. In the hard incompatibilist view, given that we lack knowledge of how our futures will turn out, we can still reasonably hope for success in achieving what we want most even if we turn out to be creatures of our environments and our dispositions. It may sometimes be crucial that we lack complete knowledge of our environments and dispositions. Suppose that there is some disposition that an agent reasonably believes might be an obstacle to realizing a life-hope. However, because he does not know whether this disposition will in fact function this way, it remains epistemically possible for him to have a further disposition that will allow him to transcend the potential obstacle. For example, suppose that someone aspires to become a successful clinical psychologist but is concerned that his irritability will stand in the way. He does not know whether his irritability will in fact frustrate his life-hope, since it is epistemically possible for him that he will overcome this problem, perhaps due to a disposition for resolute self-discipline. As a result, he might reasonably hope that he will overcome his irritability and succeed in his aspiration. In the hard incompatibilist view, if he in fact does overcome his problem and becomes a successful clinical psychologist, his achievement will not be as robust as one might naturally have believed, but it will be his achievement in a substantial sense nevertheless.

But how significant is the aspect of our life-hopes that we must forgo if hard determinism or hard incompatibilism is true? Saul Smilansky argues that although determinism leaves room for a limited foundation for the sense of self-worth that derives from achievement or virtue, the hard determinist's (and also, by extension, the hard incompatibilist's) perspective can nevertheless be "extremely damaging to our view of ourselves, to our sense of achievement, worth, and self-respect," and in response we should foster the illusion that we have free will.[11] I agree with Smilansky that there is a type of self-respect that presupposes an incompatibilist foundation, and that it would be undermined if hard determinism (or hard incompatibilism) were true. I do question, however, whether he is right about how damaging it would be for us to find that we must give up this sort of self-respect, and thus whether his move to illusion would be justified.

One should note that our sense of self-worth, our sense that we are valuable and that are lives are worth living, is to a significant extent due to factors that are not produced by our volitions at all, let alone by free will. People place great value, both in others and in themselves, on beauty, intelligence, and native athletic ability, none of which are produced voluntarily. However, we also value voluntary efforts, hard work and generous actions, for example, and their results. But how much does it matter to us that the voluntary efforts are also freely willed? In my view, Smilansky overestimates how much we care.

Consider the formation of moral character. It is not implausible that good moral character is to a large extent the function of upbringing, and furthermore, the belief that this is so is common in our society. Parents typically regard themselves as failures if their children turn out to be immoral, and many take great care to raise their children to prevent this result. Accordingly, people often come to believe that they have a good moral character largely because they were brought up with parental love and skill. But I suspect that hardly anyone who comes to this realization experiences dismay because of it. We tend not at all to be dispirited upon coming to understand that our moral character is not our own doing, and that we deserve at best diminished respect for having this character. Rather, we feel fortunate and thankful for the upbringing we have enjoyed, and not that something significant has been lost.

Moreover, people typically do not become dispirited when they come to believe that success in a career depends very much on one's upbringing, opportunities in one's society, the assistance of colleagues, and good fortune. Realizations of this sort frequently give rise to a sense of thankfulness, and almost never, if at all, to dismay. Why then should we suppose that we would generally become dispirited were we to adopt a hard incompatibilist stance? We would then relinquish the view that character and accomplishments are due to free will and that we for this reason deserve respect, but given our response to the more commonplace beliefs in external determination, we have little reason to think that we would be overcome with dismay. But suppose that there are people who would become disheartened even upon coming to believe that moral character is largely due to upbringing. Then would it be justified or even desirable for them to sustain the illusion that they nevertheless deserve respect for producing their moral character? Most people are capable of facing the truth without incurring much loss, and those for whom it would be painful will typically have the psychological resources to cope with the new understanding. I suspect that the same would be true for those who come to accept hard incompatibilism.

4. Personal Relationships

P. F. Strawson contends that the justification for claims of blameworthiness and praiseworthiness terminates in the system of human reactive attitudes, and because moral responsibility has this kind of foundation, the truth or falsity of universal determinism is irrelevant to whether we are justified in holding agents morally responsible.[12] These reactive attitudes, such as indignation, gratitude, forgiveness, and love are required for the kinds of relationships that make our lives meaningful, and so even if we could give up the attitudes – and Strawson believes that this is impossible – we would never have practical reason to do so. Accordingly, we would never have practical reason to give up on moral responsibility. On the other hand, if universal determinism did threaten the reactive attitudes, we would face the prospect of the "objective attitude," a cold and calculating stance toward others that would undermine the possibility of meaningful personal relationships.

Strawson is clearly right to believe that an objective attitude would destroy relationships, but I deny that we would adopt this stance or that it would be appropriate if we came to believe universal determinism (or hard incompatibilism) and it did pose a threat to the reactive attitudes. In my conception, some of the reactive attitudes would in fact be undermined by hard determinism, or more broadly by hard incompatibilism. For some of them, such as indignation, presuppose that the person who is the object of the attitude is morally responsible. I claim, however, that the reactive attitudes that we would want to retain either are not threatened by hard incompatibilism in this way or else have analogues or aspects that would not have false presuppositions. The complex of attitudes that would survive by no means amount to Strawson's objectivity, and they would be sufficient to sustain good relationships.

To a certain degree indignation is likely to be beyond our power to affect, and thus even supposing that a hard incompatibilist is thoroughly committed to morality and rationality, and that she is admirably in control of her emotional life, she might nevertheless be unable to eradicate this attitude. Thus, as hard incompatibilists, we might expect that people will become indignant under certain circumstances, and we would regard it as inevitable and exempt from blame when they do. However, we also have the ability to prevent, temper, and sometimes to dispel indignation, and given a belief in hard incompatibilism, we might attempt these measures for the sake of morality and rationality. Modifications of this sort, aided by a hard incompatibilist conviction, could well be good for relationships.

In response, one might contend that indignation is crucial to communication of wrongdoing in relationships, and if we were to diminish or eliminate this attitude, relationships would suffer as a result. But when one is wronged in a relationship, one typically experiences additional attitudes that are not threatened by hard incompatibilism, whose expression can play the communicative role at issue. These attitudes include feeling hurt, alarmed, or distressed about what the other has done, and moral sadness or concern for the other. Indignation, then, is not clearly required for communication in personal relationships.

Forgiveness might appear to presuppose that the person being forgiven is blameworthy, and if this is so, it would indeed be threatened by hard incompatibilism. But this attitude has central features that are unaffected by hard incompatibilism, and they are sufficient to sustain the typical role of forgiveness as a whole in good relationships. Suppose a friend repeatedly mistreats you, and because of this you have resolved to end your relationship with him. However, he then apologizes to you, in such a way that (in harmony with hard incompatibilism) he thereby signifies his recognition of the wrongness of his actions, his wish that he had not mistreated you, and his sincere commitment to refraining from the offensive behavior. Because of this you decide not to terminate the friendship. The feature of forgiveness that is consistent with hard incompatibilism in this case is the willingness to cease to regard past immoral behavior as a reason to dissolve or weaken a relationship. In another type of case, independently of the other's repentance, you might simply dismiss the wrong as a reason to end or change the character of your relationship. This feature of forgiveness is also not jeopardized by a hard incompatibilist conviction. The only aspect of forgiveness that is undercut by hard incompatibilism is the willingness to disregard deserved blame or punishment. Having relinquished the belief in moral responsibility, however, the hard incompatibilist no longer needs the willingness to overlook deserved blame and punishment to have good relationships.

One might contend that hard incompatibilism also threatens the self-directed attitudes of guilt and repentance. There is much at stake here, one could argue, since these attitudes are not only necessary for maintaining good relationships for agents prone to wrongdoing, but are also required for sustaining their moral integrity. Without guilt and repentance, such an agent would not only be incapable of restoring relationships damaged because he has done wrong, but he would also be kept from restoring his moral integrity. For other than the attitudes of guilt and repentance we have no psychological mechanisms that can play these roles. But hard incompatibilism would seem to jeopardize guilt because it essentially involves a belief that one is blameworthy for something one has done. And if guilt is undermined by hard incompatibilism, the attitude of repentance might also be threatened, for it could well be that feeling guilty is required for motivating repentance. But suppose that you perpetrate some wrongdoing, but because you endorse hard incompatibilism, you deny that you are blameworthy. Instead, you agree that you have done wrong, you feel sad that you were the agent of wrongdoing, you deeply regret what you have done.[13] Also, because you are committed to doing what is right and to moral advancement, you resolve to forbear from wrongdoing of this kind in the future, and you seek the help of others in sustaining your resolve. None of this is threatened by hard incompatibilism.

Gratitude might well presuppose that the person to whom one is grateful is morally responsible for a beneficial act, and for this reason hard incompatibilism would imperil gratitude. Still, certain aspects of this attitude would be unaffected, and these aspects can play the role gratitude as a whole has in good relationships. Gratitude involves, first of all, thankfulness toward someone who has acted beneficially. True, being thankful toward someone often involves the belief that she is praiseworthy for an action. But at the same time one can also be thankful to a pet or a small child for some kindness, even though in these cases one does not believe that the agent is morally responsible. Given hard incompatibilism, the aspect of thankfulness could be retained even if the presupposition of praiseworthiness is relinquished. Gratitude also typically involves joy occasioned by the beneficent act of another. But hard incompatibilism fully harmonizes with being joyful and expressing joy when others are considerate or generous on one's behalf. Such expression of joy can bring about the sense of harmony and goodwill often occasioned by gratitude, and so in this respect hard incompatibilism is not at a disadvantage.

Is mature love endangered by hard incompatibilism? Consider first whether loving someone requires that she be free in the sense required for moral responsibility. Parents love their children rarely, if ever, because they possess this sort of free will, or because they choose to do what is right by free will, or because they deserve to be loved because of their freely willed choices. Moreover, when adults love each other, it is also seldom, if at all, for such reasons. Undoubtedly the kinds of reasons we have for loving someone are complex. Besides moral character and behavior, considerations such as intelligence, appearance, style, and resemblance to others in one's personal history all might have a part. But let us suppose that moral character and action are especially important in occasioning, enriching, and sustaining love. Even if there is a significant feature of love that is a deserved response to moral character and action, it is unlikely that love would be undermined if one came to believe that these moral qualities did not come about through freely willed decision. Moral character and action are loveable whether or not they merit praise. Love of another involves, fundamentally, wishing for the other's good, taking on her aims and desires, and a desire to be together with her. Hard incompatibilism threatens none of this.

One might argue that we very much want to be loved by others as a result of their free will – we want freely willed love. Against this, the love parents have for their children is typically engendered independently of the parents' will, and we do not find this love deficient. Kane agrees with this claim about parental love, and with a similar view about romantic love, but he nevertheless contends that there is a kind of love we want of which we would feel deprived if we knew that factors beyond the other's control determined it.[14] The plausibility of this view might be enhanced by reflecting on how you would feel if you found out that someone you love was causally determined to love you by a benevolent manipulator.

Setting aside *free* will for now, when does the will play a role in producing love for another at all? When an intimate relationship is deteriorating, people sometimes make a decision to try to restore the love they once felt for each other. When a student finds herself at odds with a roommate from the outset, she may decide to attempt nevertheless to form an emotional bond. Or when one's marriage is arranged, one may choose to do whatever one can to love one's spouse. But first of all, in such situations we might want the other person to make a decision to love, but it is not clear that we would have reason to want the decision to be freely willed in the sense required for moral responsibility. A decision to love on the part of another might greatly enhance one's personal life, but it is not clear what value the decision's being free and therefore praiseworthy would supply in addition. Second, although under these kinds of circumstances we might desire that the other make a decision to love, we would typically prefer love that was not mediated by a decision. This is true not only when romantic love is at issue – when it is manifestly obvious – but also for friendships and for love between parents and children.

Suppose Kane's view could be defended, and we do want love that is freely willed in the sense required for moral responsibility. If we indeed desire love of this kind, then we desire a kind of love that is impossible if hard incompatibilism is true. Still, the kinds of love that are invulnerable to hard incompatibilism are surely sufficient for good relationships. If we can aspire to the sort of love parents typically have toward children, or the kind romantic lovers ideally have toward one another, or the type shared by friends who are immediately attracted to one another, and whose relationship is deepened by their interactions, then the possibility of fulfillment in personal relationships is far from undermined.

Hard incompatibilism, therefore, endangers neither relationships with others nor personal integrity. It might well jeopardize certain attitudes that typically have a role in these domains. Indignation and guilt would likely be theoretically irrational for a hard incompatibilist. But such attitudes are either not essential to good relationships, or they have analogues that could play the same role they typically have. Moreover, love – the reactive attitude most essential to good personal relationships – is not clearly threatened by hard incompatibilism at all.

5. The Benefits of Hard Incompatibilism

Furthermore, hard incompatibilism holds out the promise of substantial benefits for human life. Of all the attitudes associated with moral responsibility, anger seems most closely connected with it. It is significant that discussions about moral responsibility typically focus not on how we should regard morally exemplary agents, but rather on how we should consider those that are morally offensive. The kinds of cases most often employed in producing a strong conviction of moral responsibility feature especially malevolent actions, and the sense of moral responsibility evoked typically involves sympathetic anger. It may be, then, that our attachment to moral responsibility derives in part from the role of anger in our emotional lives, and perhaps we feel hard incompatibilism poses a serious threat because it challenges the rationality of anger.

The type of anger at issue is directed toward someone who is believed to have done wrong. Let us call this attitude *moral anger*. Not all anger is moral anger. One type of nonmoral anger is directed at someone because his abilities in some respect are lacking or because he has performed badly under some circumstance. Sometimes we are angry with machines for malfunctioning. On occasion our anger has no object. But still, by far most human anger is moral anger.

Moral anger forms an important part of the moral life as we ordinarily conceive it. Anger motivates us to resist oppression, injustice, and abuse. But at the same time expressions of moral anger frequently have harmful effects, and they fail to contribute to the well being of those against whom they are directed. Often expressions of moral anger are intended to cause physical or emotional pain. As a result, moral anger tends to damage or destroy relationships. In extreme cases, it can motivate people to torture and kill.

The sense that expressions of moral anger can be damaging gives rise to a robust demand that they be morally justified when they occur. The demand to morally justify behavior that is harmful to others is always strong, and expressions of moral anger are typically harmful to others. Moreover, this demand is made more pressing by the fact that we are often attached to moral anger; we often in a sense enjoy displaying it, and this is partly why we want these displays to be morally justifiable. Most commonly we justify expressions of moral anger by arguing that wrongdoers fundamentally deserve to endure them. If hard incompatibilism is true, however, this justifying claim is false. But even if we knew it was false, we might still have a strong interest in retaining the belief in moral responsibility to satisfy our need to justify expressions of moral anger.

Accepting hard incompatibilism is not likely to modify human psychology so that anger is no longer a problem for us. Nevertheless, anger is often nourished by the presupposition that its object is blameworthy for wrongdoing. Destructive anger in relationships is nurtured by the belief that the other deserves blame for immoral behavior. The anger that fuels many ethnic conflicts often derives from the conviction that a group of people deserves blame for some past evil. Hard incompatibilism advocates relinquishing these anger-sustaining beliefs because they are false, and as a result the anger might be weakened, and its expressions curtailed.

Would the benefits that result if anger were reduced in this way outweigh the losses? Moral anger does indeed motivate us to oppose wrongdoing. But even when the assumption that wrongdoers are blameworthy is withdrawn for hard incompatibilist reasons, the conviction that they have in fact done wrong could legitimately survive. Such a moral conviction could still engender a strong resolve to resist oppression, injustice, and abuse. Perhaps, then, the hard incompatibilist could retain the benefits that moral anger can also produce, while diminishing its destructive consequences.

Notes

1 Derk Pereboom, "Determinism Al Dente," *Nous*, 29 (1995), 21–45; Pereboom, *Living without Free Will* (Cambridge: Cambridge University Press, 2001).

2 Ted Honderich, *A Theory of Determinism* (Oxford: Clarendon Press, 1988), vol. 1, 194–206; Robert Kane, *The Significance of Free Will* (Oxford: Oxford University Press, 1996), 35.

3 Harry Frankfurt, "Alternate Possibilities and Moral Responsibility," *Journal of Philosophy*, 66 (1969), 829–39.

4 Richard Taylor, *Metaphysics* (Englewood Cliffs, N.J.: Prentice-Hall, 1974), 43–4; Kane, *Significance of Free Will*, 65–71.

5 Randolph Clarke, "On the Possibility of Rational Free Action," *Philosophical Studies*, 88 (1997), 37–57.

6 Peter van Inwagen, *An Essay on Free Will* (Oxford: Clarendon Press, 1983), 132–4; Alfred Mele, "Ultimate Responsibility and Dumb Luck," *Social Philosophy and Policy*, 16 (1999), 277.

7 Bruce Waller, *Freedom without Responsibility* (Philadelphia: Temple University Press, 1990), 130–5.

8 Daniel Farrell, "The Justification of General Deterrence," *The Philosophical Review*, 104 (1985), 176–210.

9 Ferdinand Schoeman, "On Incapacitating the Dangerous," *American Philosophical Quarterly*, 16 (1979), 56–67.

10 Honderich, *Theory of Determinism*, vol. 2, 382.

11 Saul Smilansky, "Can a Determinist Help Herself?", in C. H. Manekin and M. Kellner, eds., *Freedom and Moral Responsibility: General and Jewish Perspectives* (College Park: University of Maryland Press, 1997), 94; Smilansky, *Free Will and Illusion* (Oxford: Clarendon Press, 2000); Smilansky, "Free Will, Fundamental Dualism, and the Centrality of Illusion," in Robert Kane, ed., *The Oxford Handbook of Free Will* (New York: Oxford University Press, 2002), 489–505.

12 Peter F. Strawson, "Freedom and Resentment," *Proceedings of the British Academy*, 48 (1962), 1–25; repr. in Gary Watson, ed., *Free Will* (Oxford: Oxford University Press, 1982), 59–80.

13 Waller, *Freedom without Responsibility*.

14 Kane, *Significance of Free Will*, 88. Similar claims are made in Galen Strawson, *Freedom and Belief* (Oxford: Oxford University Press, 1986), 309, and W. S. Anglin, *Free Will and the Christian Faith* (Oxford: Oxford University Press, 1990), 20.

27   Metaethics, Metaphilosophy, and Free Will Subjectivism*

Richard Double

1.   Free Will Subjectivism and Metaethical Subjectivism

Anyone who argues for the *actual existence* of moral responsibility must make plausible the existence of a variety of free choice strong enough to underpin moral responsibility. Anyone who claims to vindicate the *possibility* of moral responsibility must show that such a variety of free choice is possible. Although there are other things philosophers care about when discussing free will (dignity, autonomy, genuine creativity, worthiness of love and friendship),[1] "the fundamental motor of the free will debate is the worry about moral responsibility".[2] A handy reminder of the fact that free will is supposed to sanction assignments of moral responsibility is to define "free will" (the "faculty" of making free choices) in terms of "moral responsibility." I define "free choice" as "whatever degree of freedom of choice that, all other factors being equal, is necessary and sufficient for moral responsibility." Other thinkers emphasize the connection between moral responsibility and free will by using the term "moral freedom." A third way to cast the free will problem as a moral problem eliminates the term "free will" altogether: We could pose the problem this way: "Is it morally permissible to hold (determined, undetermined, naturalistic, supernaturalistic) persons morally responsible?"

Holding persons morally responsible encompasses a range of behaviors: expressed positive and negative reactive attitudes, verbal recrimination, praise and blame, retributive punishment, and just-deserts rewards, all the way to torment in hell and bliss in heaven. Philosophers disagree over how much of that range moral responsibility includes. But, because even the mildest of the adverse behaviors harms persons, assigning moral responsibility serves as a justificatory mantra that turns otherwise immoral treatment into just-deserts goods. Because of this justificatory role, I take "moral responsibility" to be a moral concept.

Believing the free will issue is a moral problem carries a little-noted implication. We may submit free will theories to metalevel analysis just as we do to theories in normative ethics. Making objectively true claims about what sort of choices underpin moral responsibility requires metaethical objectivism, just as does making objectively true claims about consequentialism or deontologism. So, if the claims of, for example, the compatibilists and incompatibilists can take objective answers, then there can exist objective (existing beyond subjective attitudes and opinions of individuals or groups) moral facts that reveal what sort of choices are needed to underpin persons' moral responsibility. This *if* there are no objective moral facts, as metaethical subjectivists such as A. J. Ayer and J. L. Mackie

* From Robert Kane (ed.), *Oxford Handbook of Free Will* (Oxford: Oxford University Press, 2002), pp. 507–16 and 525. © 2001 by Robert Kane. Used by permission of Oxford University Press Inc.

aver, then logically there are no such facts regarding moral responsibility. I call this position "free will subjectivism."[3]

Free will subjectivism is like metaethical subjectivism in important ways. Metaethical subjectivism does not claim that "X is wrong" means "I or my society approve of X" (as Ayer observes), but that judgments assigning moral characteristics cannot be objectively true. Similarly, free will subjectivism does not hold that "S is morally responsible" means "I or my society hold S morally responsible," but that judgments assigning moral responsibility cannot be objectively true.[4]

If we accept free will subjectivism, we may elect to be vitally concerned with lower-level accounts of persons' free will and moral responsibility. Subjectivists can take free will theories as explicating our important feelings and attitudes about free will and moral responsibility, just as Hume and J. L. Mackie take seriously their substantive normative theories despite their subjectivist metaethics. Nonetheless, espousing free will subjectivism does not leave everything as is. Concluding that there are no objectively true statements that assign moral responsibility is important to philosophers who are concerned with reaching the most plausible overall worldview. Moreover, for many subjectivists, accepting the theory may modulate the stridency of their free will theorizing.

In addition, uncovering the ambiguity of talk about the *incompatibility* (or compatibility) of moral responsibility and determined or undetermined choices can liberate metaethical subjectivists to engage in free will theorizing. There are at least three relevant kinds of incompatibility: analytic, factual, and moral. Examples of each category follow: *analytic incompatibility*: "S is a bachelor" and "S is married." *Factual incompatibility*: "S is in New York" and "S is in the Pacific time-zone." *Moral incompatibility*: "S is cruel to animals" and "S is morally exemplary." In principle, philosophers who talk about the incompatibility of moral responsibility and determinism (or indeterminism) might mean any of these three.

Compatibilists who think that the free will problem can be settled by linguistic analysis of *can*, *could*, and *free*, represent that first view. Other philosophers apparently believe the compatibility issue is not analytic, but perhaps synthetic a priori. Note that if one sees the incompatibility or compatibility at stake in either of these two ways, one must consider assignments of moral responsibility to be capable of being true. So, if these two groups of thinkers accept my view that assignments of moral responsibility are moral claims, then they are committed to holding that an important class of moral claims is capable of being true, and, ipso facto, accept moral objectivism.

Things are different if one takes the incompatibility at stake as *moral incompatibility*. This would amount to saying, "It is morally wrong to hold determined (undetermined) persons morally responsible." Metaethical objectivists *could* assert this, but so could metaethical subjectivists. For example, the metaethical subjectivist Bruce Waller is a moral incompatibilist who is stridently opposed to holding naturalistic persons morally responsible, whether they are determined or not.[5] His subjectivist metaethics prevents him from saying that "S is a naturalistic being" and "S is morally responsible" have contradictory truth-values, but Waller believes the two judgments are morally incompatible. This means that it is wrong to hold naturalistic persons morally responsible. Waller is passionately opposed to the practice of blame and provides moral reasons for thinking we ought not blame, while admitting his position has no other grounding than the way he (and other like-minded persons) feel. So, interpreting the incompatibility at stake as moral brings metaethical subjectivists into the free will debate.

Metaethical subjectivists can also enter the free will debate through what I call "metaphilosophies." By a "metaphilosophy" I mean a view of what philosophy is and what philosophers should try to accomplish by philosophizing.[6] The metaphilosophy I hold is *Philosophy as Worldview Construction*, specifically, *Philosophy as Continuous with Science*. The former tries to construct a view of reality that is most likely to be accurate given our most reliable sources of epistemic justification. The latter takes science as the best model for philosophical theory construction, using methods of scientific theory construction such as inference to the best explanation and Occam's Razor. Philosophy as Continuous with Science accepts science as a Sellarsian measure "of what is that it is, and of what is not that it is not." Philosophy as Continuous with Science is a posteriori and defeasible. If another method is better able to reach the most accurate worldview, then some other species of Worldview Construction such as *Philosophy as Phenomenology*, or *Philosophy as Mysticism* would be better.

Philosophy as Praxis sees philosophy as an instrument to improve the world, as exemplified in Marx's claim in his eleventh thesis against Feuerbach that *the point* of philosophy is not to *interpret* the world, but to *change* it.[7] There are two ways for Praxis metaphilosophy to influence one's reasoning concerning philosophical problems. First, a Praxis thinker might think that moral urgency justifies giving nonepistemically justifying, Praxis considerations an important role in the picture of the world we construct. Second, a Praxis thinker might bend the objectivist's vocabulary by portraying a subjective theory as an objective one, or "objective enough" to serve the purposes that unobtainable objectivist theories are designed to serve.

Exemplifying the first type of Praxis argument, the metaethical objectivist David Brink argues:

> If . . . rejection of moral realism would undermine the nature of existing practices and beliefs, then the metaphysical queerness of moral realism may seem a small price to pay to preserve these practices and beliefs. I am not claiming that the presumption in favor of moral realism could not be overturned on a posteriori metaphysical grounds. I am claiming only that we could not determine the appropriate reaction to the success of this (Mackie's, R. D.) metaphysical argument until we determined, among other things, the strength of the presumption in favor of moral realism.[8]

Here Brink pits the Praxis desirability of believing in metaethical objectivism against the argument against objectivism from ontological simplicity provided by Mackie and concludes that our overall ontological picture should contain objective moral truths. This reasoning is similar to the sort William James allowed regarding the existence of God and libertarian free will. I reject this kind of Praxis argument because it assigns weight in ontological theory construction to a factor that even its proponents admit does not increase the probability that the hoped-for entities exist. I do not support this appeal to wishful thinking in constructing a worldview, although I admit that in dire enough cases it is forgivable or, arguably, even morally obligatory.[9]

Exemplifying the second kind of Praxis argument are philosophers whom Stephen Darwall calls "constructivists" and "practical-reasoning theorists," who believe they can underpin morality without including objective moral truths within our theoretical worldview.[10] Hobbes, Kurt Baier, and David Gauthier all claim that although moral truth is not waiting to be found, we can build contractual systems of ethics on top of an egoistic foundation that suffices to underpin normative ethics.[11] Kant, John Rawls, and Thomas Nagel all argue that there are purely logical constraints on practical reasoning that make moral claims objectively true.[12] In my view, constructivism and practical-reasoning theories are manifestations of Praxis metaphilosophy. If one sees the point of moral philosophy as providing an appealing theory of normative ethics, then, given the difficulties with *finding* moral truths, it is natural to try to *construct* them.

I regard constructivists and practical-reasoning theorists as metaethical subjectivists, because they portray moral truth as dependent upon features of humans' social arrangements and their psychological states. In this sense, these theories are just as subjective as "projectionist" theories.[13] Constructivism regarding postulated entities in scientific theories has a name" "scientific instrumentalism," which is a variety of subjectivism (nonrealism). If moral truth is created by human conventions or the putative nature of human reason, then logically there is nothing outside of those conventions or our minds to serve as the truth conditions of realistic moral truths. As a Worldview metaphilosopher, I treat *realism* and *true* as univocal for the moral and the nonmoral domains. Worldview Construction demands a correspondence theory of truth for moral judgments, as it does for nonmoral claims. The most coherent moral system – and I deny that any moral system can be *very* coherent anyway – logically cannot be sufficient for objective moral truth. So the second Praxis argument fails also. Neither it nor the first argument can be adapted to provide epistemic justification for free will objectivism.

Nonetheless, Praxis free will theorists are not left out of substantive free will theorizing. When I propound free will subjectivism, I take myself to be doing metaphysics on a scientific model. I do *not* say, "It is useless to construct theories for use in criminal justice and everyday life." My point is theoretical, that the traditional theorists cannot claim to have objective truth on their side, just as utilitarians and Kantians cannot claim metaethical truth on their side if metaethical subjectivism is true. I therefore have no objection to Praxis theorizing in ethics and free will. I merely criticize traditional theorists who purport to provide the real thing, when the real thing turns out to be logically impossible. Let us not confuse the issues of what practices are the most beneficial and what is the most likely to be true worldview. There are other prominent metaphilosophies,[14] but the major ones for the purposes of this chapter are Worldview Construction and Praxis.

2. My View Defended

I endorse top-down and bottom-up strategies to argue for free will subjectivism. The *top-down argument* uses two premises. The first premise is the doctrine of metaethical subjectivism, and the second is the claim that *free will*, defined in terms of moral responsibility, is a moral term. Although I find this a powerful argument with the advantage of revealing the connection between lower level theorizing in normative ethics and free will, the top-down argument is weakened by its controversial first premise. Although I believe the general philosophical case for metaethical subjectivism is strong and have argued for it at length, in this essay I shall not press the top-down argument.[15] The *bottom-up argument* does not rely on metaethical subjectivism but argues that free will subjectivism is the best explanation for our logically conflicting intuitions regarding the claims of compatibilists and incompatibilists.

The bottom-up argument faces a broadly metaphilosophical preliminary objection. Free will objectivists can criticize my appeal to intuitions about moral responsibility, just as some metaethical objectivists look askance at using moral intuitions to criticize normative theories. I emphasize that I do not view our intuitions concerning whether a person would be morally responsible in a certain thought-experiment as infallible or even as having great epistemic weight, but simply as providing thoughtful judgments about responsibility. Just as I do not see how we could evaluate egoism or relativism without appealing to our intuitive judgments of their implications, I do not see how to evaluate theories of moral responsibility without appealing to our intuitions.

Free will subjectivism of the kind I defend in this chapter entails two unfamiliar views regarding the free will problem. The first view is *metacompatibilism*, the doctrine that regarding persons we believe to be determined, logically we may hold them morally responsible *despite* our belief that they are determined (as compatibilists might) *and* we may fully exonerate them *because* we think they are determined (as incompatibilists would).[16] The second view is that because free will subjectivism holds that persons' "being" morally responsible is simply a matter of what attitudes persons hold toward them, subjectivists commit no error when they decide to hold strong views about moral responsibility *despite* their belief in free will subjectivism *or* to hold mild views *because* they believe their views are only subjective. I call these two options "strident subjectivism" and "sheepish subjectivism." Free will subjectivists might be stridently in favor of holding persons responsible (perhaps Peter Strawson is close to this view) or stridently opposed to holding persons responsible, as Waller is.[17] Subjectivists might be sheepish, given their belief that their opinions about the assignment of moral responsibility have no grounding beyond their own feelings. Subjectivists might also vacillate between endorsing responsibility and exonerating all persons of responsibility, as I do myself.

Strident and sheepish subjectivist views in the free will problem are parallel to the two stances metaethical subjectivists might take regarding normative ethics. Strident metaethical subjectivists make judgments in normative ethics with full force despite their metaethical beliefs. J. L. Mackie would be an example. Sheepish metaethical subjectivists would take their metaethical positions as reason to assert normative claims with modulated or even no force.[18] Perhaps some of the twentieth-century logical positivists came close to this position.

To clarify the free will vocabulary I use and to begin the bottom-up argument, I offer a taxonomy of five theories rather than the traditional dichotomy of compatibilism and incompatibilism. I arrive at the first four by distinguishing between the positive and negative answers to two questions: *Can determined choices be free (underpin moral responsibility)?* And *Can undetermined choices be free (underpin moral responsibility)?* I reach free will subjectivism by considering the first four claims from the perspective of metaethical subjectivism.

Here are the idealized positive and negative theses of traditional incompatibilists and compatibilists:

(IN)   *Incompatibilism's Negative Claim*: "Determined choices cannot be free."

(IP)   *Incompatibilism's Positive Claim*: "Indeterminism (suitably located) within our choice-making process can give rise to, or at least be consistent with, free choice."

(CN)   *Compatibilism's Negative Claim*: "Undetermined choices cannot be free."

(CP)   *Compatibilism's Positive Claim*: "Under certain conditions, determined choices can be free."

Here are the logical relations that hold between these four claims on the assumption that "free choice" is a univocal and logically coherent concept. The incompatibilists'

Table 1 Theories regarding free will

	(IN)	(IP)	(CN)	(CP)
Classical incompatibilism	True	True	False	False
Classical compatibilism	False	False	True	True
No-free-will-either-way theory	True	False	True	False
Free-will-either-way theory	False	True	False	True

claims (IN) and (IP) are logically consistent, though not equivalent; the compatibilists' claims (CN) and (CP) are consistent though nonequivalent also. There are two pairs of contradictories, namely, the negative and the positive claims of the respective theorists ([IN] contradicts [CP], and [IP] contradicts [CN]). Because there are four statements, each of which may be viewed as being true or false, there are sixteen mathematically possible results; but given the assumption about the contradictories, we can extract only four different theories (table 1).

Even if we prefer one of the first two theories, we have to admit the conceptual possibility of the latter two. Peter Strawson calls the third theory "moral skepticism" but does not examine it in that article.[19] Waller and Derk Pereboom endorse the third position without using my term for it.[20] The closest to the fourth theory is Alfred Mele's conjecture which he calls "agnostic autonomism."[21]

Now consider what happens if we set aside the assumption that the pair (IN) and (CP) and the pair (IP) and (CN) are contradictories and instead try to evaluate each statement on its own merits.

I often feel inclined to accept (IN) ("Determined choices cannot be free") and (CN) ("Undetermined choices cannot be free"). Incompatibilists seem correct to disparage the freedom of determined choices (which categorically could not have been different than they were), and the compatibilist complaint that locating indeterminacy within our choices would lessen the control over our choices required for moral responsibility seems correct also. Nonetheless, I do not always find that the pessimism generated by (and contributing to) my acceptance of (IN) and (CN) carries over to my evaluation of (IP) ("Indeterminism can give rise to free choices") and (CP) ("Determined choices can be free"). Sometimes I do not hesitate to assent to the positive accounts (IP) and (CP).

By accepting all four statements I seem to have done something logically odd, but have I? The *rejection* of all candidates is not remarkable in philosophical disputes. For instance, many thinkers in normative ethics reject every normative theory that comes along, without concluding that there can be no true normative account. Such ethicists simply see their endeavor as forever trying to approximate a best account. Havoc occurs, though, when theorists *affirm* conflicting theories. Imagine what it would mean to say that Kantian and utilitarian theories are both true, instead of saying that they are both false. If we can show that these *apparently* contradictory theories are "equally true," then we have undone the claim of normative ethics to objective truth. Both theories could be "true" only if moral truth were subjectivized to individuals or groups of individuals, which is to say that the theories are not objectively true at all. By analogy, by accepting all four claims of the incompatibilists and compatibilists, I commit myself to the claim that "free choice" can have no objective reference, that free will and moral responsibility can exist only in the eye of the beholder.

There seem to be just three things to say about my acceptance of (IN), (IP), (CN), and (CP). Either (1) "free choice," in the sense I am using it, is unambiguous and logically coherent, in which case I have contradicted myself; or (2) I mean different things by "free choice" when I consider the four statements, and hence, there is no contradiction, only ambiguity; or (3) I am not guilty of contradicting myself and I have not used "free choice" ambiguously, in which case "free choice," when taken to have objective reference, logically cannot denote. I believe (3) is the most plausible.

Although various philosophers mean different things by "free will," it is easy to eliminate (2). I have defined "free will" (and "free choice") throughout as "whatever degree of freedom of choice that is necessary for moral responsibility." I find it easy to remember that I mean this responsibility-enabling sense of "free choice" when I consider (IN), (IP), (CN), and (CP). I do not claim that individuals always know what meanings they assign to words, but I am confident I know what I mean in this instance.

This leaves (1). I do not countenance the rebuttal that I *must* be contradicting myself because we know that "free choice" is coherent; that would be question-begging. Instead, we should investigate the question on its own merits. Here is my argument.

Our acceptance of (IN), (IP), (CN), and (CP) depends on our judgments concerning the conditions in which our choices can be "good enough" to warrant moral responsibility. As argued earlier, I believe these are moral judgments. So, if we are metaethical subjectivists, we have quick support for the bottom-up argument. But I have claimed that the bottom-up argument is independent of the top-down argument, so I cannnot leave matters there. I believe that even metaethical objectivists can find reasons to accept free will subjectivism, and I propose these now.

To ask whether determined choices can be free frames the issue in a historical context. It prompts us to consider whether a choice can be good enough to count as free if we theoretically can trace its causes back to the laws of nature and events occurring before the chooser was born.[22] When we frame the question with this historical perspective, it is tempting to assign determined choices a negative grade. When we assign this negative grade, we affirm (IN). On the other hand, to ask whether an *undetermined* choice can be free frames matters so that we think about the perils of indeterminism, bringing to mind the specter of choices that are not under the control of the chooser chronicled by Hobart and Ayer.[23] When we are in such a frame of mind, we are likely to be impressed that such cases are destructive to freedom, and we assent to (CN).

Nonetheless, having assented to (IN) and (CN), we have no reason – beyond self-imposed constraints that we might *think* are logical constraints – why we cannot give the high marks to certain choices that are implicit in (CP) and (IP). If we focus on the internal rationality of choices, as Harry Frankfurt does, the fact that they are determined, and, hence, theroretically predictable since before the chooser was even born, seems irrelevant to their freedom. This prompts us to affirm (CP).[24] If we do not demand that free choices be so rigidly connected to what went before, as Robert Kane tries to get us to do, we have little difficulty in giving up the claim that undetermined choices are unfree. This is to accept (IP).[25]

I claim that the freeness of choices is not a characteristic that exists in the choices; all "freeness" amounts to is how we feel about or *grade* choices. The grades we give do not track a characteristic of choices but depend upon our opinions and feelings about the actual characteristics of choices. Such opinions and feelings are moved by a disorganized variety of factors that have little to do with the choices themselves. Instead, they involve such subjective factors as the context in which we consider the free will issue, our personal histories, our temperaments, philosophical schooling, ideologies, and other idiosyncratic elements. Also relevant in our judgments of the goodness of choices are the competing exemplars of freedom that philosophers use throughout the free will debate.[26] Taken together, these considerations (as well as doubtless others that I have failed to list) explain why we *do* affirm (IN), (IP), (CN), and (CP). This explanation creates a positive case for thinking that we are *correct* to do so.

This leaves (3) standing: If we take *free* to denote a characteristic of choices itself, that characteristic is contradictory. A free choice may be determined (CP) and cannot be determined (IN), can be undetermined (IP) and cannot be undetermined (CN). Such a "characteristic" cannot belong to a choice itself. Because the "freeness" of choices themselves is a logically impossible characteristic, it cannot – not only does not – exist. We are thus forced to understand talk about the freeness of choices in a subjectivized way. Speakers may give coherent senses to *free* in their own idiolects, just as we may for any subjective word. But this fact does not count against the claim that the meaning of "free choice" is idiosyncratic, with no possibility of denoting a class of choices that objectively underpin moral responsibility. . . .

4. The Free Will Problem Psychologized

Given my metaphilosophy of Philosophy as Worldview Construction, metaethical subjectivism, and free will subjectivism, I view philosophers' debates over free will as more a psychological topic than do most philosophers. According to my view, the free will debate ceases to be a conceptual puzzle over the correct analysis of "free will" followed by a metaphysical inquiry over whether persons in fact have free will. The debate between the compatibilists and incompatibilists over *the objectively correct view* of free will becomes fruitless. The free will problem becomes psychologized, much as metaethical subjectivism turns the search for moral truth into moral psychology and the phenomenology of moral thinking.

Notes

1 Robert Kane, *The Significance of Free Will* (Oxford: Oxford University Press, 1996), 81–9.
2 Galen Strawson, "Free Will," in Edward Craig, ed., *Routledge Encyclopedia of Philosophy* (New York: Routledge, 1998), vol. 3, 746.
3 A. J. Ayer, *Language, Truth and Logic*, 2nd edn. (New York: Dover, 1952); J. L. Mackie, *Ethics: Inventing Right and Wrong* (New York: Penguin, 1977).
4 Ayer, *Language, Truth and Logic*, 104.
5 Bruce Waller, *Freedom without Responsibility* (Philadelphia: Temple University Press, 1990).
6 Richard Double, *Metaphilosophy and Free Will* (Oxford: Oxford University Press, 1996).
7 Lewis Feuer, ed., *Marx and Engels: Basic Writings* (New York: Doubleday, 1959), 245.
8 David O. Brink, *Moral Realism and the Foundations of Ethics* (Cambridge: Cambridge University Press, 1989), 173–4.
9 Suppose the only options an individual had were (1) adoption of false, self-flattering beliefs (such as thinking one is better liked or more competent than one really is) or poor epistemic strategies (such as never entertaining criticisms of you-the-person as opposed to your behavior) and (2) leading a deeply depressed, suicide-prone life. In this case, I think there is a compelling moral case for adopting (1). See Richard Double, "What's Wrong with Self-Serving Epistemic Strategies?," *Philosophical Psychology*, 2 (1988), 341–8.

10 Stephen Darwall, "Ethical Theory," in Donald M. Borchert, ed., *The Encyclopedia of Philosophy Supplement* (New York: Simon & Schuster/Macmillan, 1996).

11 Kurt Baier, *The Moral Point of View* (Ithaca, N.Y.: Cornell University Press, 1958); David Gauthier, *Morals by Agreement* (Oxford: Clarendon Press, 1986).

12 John Rawls, *A Theory of Justice* (Cambridge, MA: Harvard University Press, 1971). Thomas Nagel, *The Possibility of Altruism* (New York: Oxford University Press, 1970).

13 Mackie, *Ethics*; Simon Blackburn, *Essays in Quasi-Realism* (New York: Oxford University Press, 1993).

14 What I call *Philosophy as Conversation* after Richard Rorty (*Philosophy and the Mirror of Nature* [Princeton, N.J.: Princeton University Press, 1979]; *Contingency, Irony and Solidarity* [Cambridge: Cambridge University Press, 1989]) sees philosophy as a kind of literature that contributes to our intellectual lives without pronouncing on the character of ultimate reality. This contribution may be viewed aesthetically and evaluated as one does literary works, or viewed as a technical genre, full of modal operators and analyses of subjective conditionals, the sort of philosophy Rorty sees promulgated in the elite philosophy graduate schools of our day.

   Philosophy as Underpinnings sees philosophy's role as supporting some other area or areas of intellectual interest. Historically, philosophy has served religion, science, and common sense. Unsympathetically portrayed, the Underpinning metaphilosophy can be characterized as *Philosophy for Defending What I Already Believe* or *Philosophy Supporting Conventional Wisdom*. Other metaphilosophies could be included such as *Philosophy as Flaunting Common Sense*, *Philosophy as Stirring Up Controversy*, *Philosophy as Furthering My Dissertation Advisor's Research Program*, and *Philosophy as Ego Aggrandizement*. Also, there is a blurred line between a metaphilosophy and a favorite strategy one uses in a pinch. For example, we could consider the following as metaphilosophies or argumentative strategies. *Philosophical Snootiness*: Here philosophers give extra points to views simply because philosophers-in-the-right-circles endorse them. *Studied Myopia to Avoid Critical Challenges*: Here philosophers treat minutiae with great precision, while ignoring broader challenges to their technical concerns. Because philosophers have various motivations, they might instance more than one metaphilosophy.

15 Richard Double, *The Non-Reality of Free Will* (Oxford: Oxford University Press, 1991), ch. 7.

16 Ibid., ch. 6.

17 Peter F. Strawson, "Freedom and Resentment," *Proceedings of the British Academy*, 48 (1962), 1–25; repr. in Gary Watson, ed., *Free Will* (Oxford: Oxford University Press, 1982), 59–80. Waller, *Freedom without Responsibility*.

18 Mackie, *Ethics*.

19 Strawson, "Freedom and Resentment."

20 Waller, *Freedom without Responsibility*; Derk Pereboom, "Alternate Possibilities and Causal Histories," *Philosophical Perspectives*, 14 (2000), 119–38.

21 Alfred Mele, *Autonomous Agents: From Self-Control to Autonomy* (New York: Oxford University Press, 1995), 253. See also Derk Pereboom, "Living without Free Will: The Case for Hard Incompatibilism," in this volume, and Alfred R. Mele, "Autonomy, Self-Control, and Weakness of Will," in Robert Kane, ed., *The Oxford Handbook of Free Will* (New York: Oxford University Press, 2002), 529–48.

22 Peter van Inwagen, *An Essay on Free Will* (Oxford: Clarendon Press, 1983), ch. 1.

23 R. E. Hobart, "Free Will as Involving Determinism and Inconceivable without It," *Mind*, 43 (1934), 1–27; repr. in Bernard Berofsky, ed., *Free Will and Determinism* (New York: Harper & Row, 1966), 63–95. A. J. Ayer, "Freedom and Necessity," in Ayer, *Philosophical Essays* (New York: St. Martin's Press, 1954), 3–20.

24 Harry Frankfurt, "Freedom of the Will and the Concept of a Person," *Journal of Philosophy*, 68 (1971), 5–20.

25 Kane, *Significance of Free Will*.

26 Double, *Non-Reality*, ch. 5.

Freedom and Determinism:
Suggestions for Further Reading

Daniel Dennett, *Elbow Room* (Cambridge, MA: MIT Press, 1984).

John Martin Fischer, ed., *God, Freedom and Foreknowledge* (Stanford: Stanford University Press, 1989).

John Martin Fischer and Mark Ravizza, eds., *Responsibility and Control: A Theory of Moral Responsibility* (Cambridge: Cambridge University Press, 1998).

Ted Honderich, *How Free Are You?* (Oxford: Oxford University Press, 1993).

Robert Kane, ed., *The Oxford Handbook of Free Will* (New York: Oxford University Press, 2002).

Benjamin Libet, Anthony Freeman, and Keith Sunderland, eds., *The Volitional Brain: Towards a Neuroscience of Free Will* (Thorverton, UK: Imprint Academic, 1999).

Timothy O'Connor, *Reasons and Causes: The Metaphysics of Free Will* (New York: Oxford University Press, 2000).

Saul Smilansky, *Free Will and Illusion* (Oxford: Clarendon Press, 2000).

Gary Watson, ed., *Free Will* (Oxford: Oxford University Press, 1982).

Susan Wolf, *Freedom within Reason* (Oxford: Oxford University Press, 1990).

PART FOUR

DOES OUR EXISTENCE HAVE A MEANING OR PURPOSE?

Introduction

28 From *My Confession*
LEO TOLSTOY

29 The Absurdity of Life without God
WILLIAM LANE CRAIG

30 On the Vanity of Existence
ARTHUR SCHOPENHAUER

31 An Absurd Reasoning
ALBERT CAMUS

32 Existentialism Is a Humanism
JEAN-PAUL SARTRE

33 The Absurd
THOMAS NAGEL

34 What Makes Life Worth Living?
OWEN FLANAGAN

35 The Meaning of Life
JOHN KEKES

36 Tolstoi and the Meaning of Life
ANTHONY FLEW
The Meaning of Life: Suggestions for Further Reading

Introduction

One of the most interesting philosophical questions concerns whether there is any significance to human existence. Many people have given it serious thought, long before
taking a first course in philosophy. Nonetheless, many introductory courses in philosophy do not address this issue. This, in our judgment, is a mistake. At the risk of seeming
quaint, here we include a series of readings that offer various understandings of the question as well as different answers.

These readings represent the range of responses to the problem of life's meaning: religious and secular, nihilistic and optimistic. Some have regarded the problem as serious
and perhaps insurmountable, and others have viewed it as to some degree illusory and
manageable. All of the readings date back no farther than the nineteenth century. The
reason for this is that the question was really posed most starkly by existentialist writers
of that era. Ancient philosophers such as Aristotle are famous for inquiring into the nature
of the good life and happiness for humans. In a sense, they address the issue of what
makes life worth living. But the issues of the purpose of human existence and its apparent meaninglessness were made explicit and addressed more extensively in the last two
centuries, particularly by existentialist writers.

We begin with Tolstoy's *My Confession*, in which he comes to the conclusion that the
only solution to the apparent meaninglessness of human existence is faith in God. Here
Tolstoy argues for the practical necessity of belief in God. His argument bears a resemblance to that of Pascal (featured in part II, in "The Wager," where Pascal asks, "What
can we know about the nature and existence of God?"). Pascal, who is sometimes regarded
as an existentialist, argued for the practical necessity of believing in God on the basis of
the possibility of infinitely bad and infinitely good outcomes. Those outcomes are eternal
misery (hell) or eternal bliss (heaven). But Pascal takes for granted that our misery or
bliss have overriding significance. Tolstoy is interested in the question of whether *we should
care* about our own life if it should turn out that there is no God. He does not try to
prove that God exists – only that belief in God is in some sense necessary. Similarly,
William Lane Craig defends the view that belief in God is a practical necessity, and that
a biblically based Christian faith can solve the apparent problem of life's meaninglessness.
As with Tolstoy and Pascal, he does not try to argue that God exists. Nor does he try to
argue that Christianity is the only solution to this problem. His claim is that an atheistic
solution is not available.

Of course, one might suspect that there is a secular answer to this question.
Schopenhauer believes that there is, and answers in the negative: human existence is
utterly meaningless, and only brute instinct can explain how human beings are able to
go on in the awareness of this fact. Camus takes this idea further, and puts forth the
radical idea that, in the face of "the absurd," suicide becomes the most important philosophical question – more important than any other. The ridiculousness of human existence is a function of our "transcendence," our ability to stand back from our world,
conceptualize it, and assess its value. Human beings are doomed to this kind of transcendent consciousness; there is no retirement from being human, short of death. Sartre
addresses this issue more optimistically (at least in this instance) in his understanding of

human existence as ongoing self-creation. Human beings, he argues, are those beings whose existence precedes their essence, making us different from any other kind of being. The significance of our existence comes not from an external maker or authority such as God, but from our own free acts. Thus he puts forth "atheistic existentialism" as the answer to the search for meaning, rejecting despair as the logical outcome of this view.

For nearly every philosophical question, philosophers have questioned the question itself. Thomas Nagel asks whether Camus is right, whether life really is absurd, and what this could mean. If life seems pointless because in the end we all die, would it actually have more of a point if we lived for ever? If eternal life would not make life meaningful, then what would? He argues that, although life is not absurd for the reasons that people typically invoke, there is an element of truth to the *sense* of absurdity that many of us feel. Yet, he argues, it is not cause for despair. Owen Flanagan offers an account of what may make our lives worth living for us. His analysis of "naturalistic transcendence" converges with the common thought that our actions need to matter in some more permanent way. John Kekes does not deny that the question is meaningful, but rejects previous religious and moral approaches, claiming that the meaning of life calls for a "pluralistic" answer. Meaningful lives may take a variety of forms, but there is no general answer to the question of what makes life meaningful that applies "equally to all lives." No particular religious world-view, and no particular moral commitment, is necessary for a meaningful life. Finally, Antony Flew provides an interpretation of Tolstoy's *My Confession* and an analysis of where he went right – and wrong. Tolstoy, Flew contends, was right in his suggestion that a meaningful life involves a certain kind of attitude and way of living: "something combining dignity, realism, and peace of mind." Yet he denies what Tolstoy apparently insisted upon: that this meaning could only be found in some "mystic truth."

28   From *My Confession**

Leo Tolstoy

Although I regarded authorship as a waste of time, I continued to write during those fifteen years. I had tasted of the seduction of authorship, of the seduction of enormous monetary remunerations and applauses for my insignificant labour, and so I submitted to it, as being a means for improving my material condition and for stifling in my soul all questions about the meaning of my life and life in general.

In my writings I advocated, what to me was the only truth, that it was necessary to live in such a way as to derive the greatest comfort for oneself and one's family.

Thus I proceeded to live, but five years ago something very strange began to happen with me: I was overcome by minutes at first of perplexity and then of an arrest of life, as though I did not know how to live or what to do, and I lost myself and was dejected. But that passed, and I continued to live as before. Then those minutes of perplexity were repeated oftener and oftener, and always in one and the same form. These arrests of life found their expression in ever the same questions: "Why? Well, and then?"

At first I thought that those were simply aimless, inappropriate questions. It seemed to me that that was all well known and that if I ever wanted to busy myself with their solution, it would not cost me much labour, – that now I had no time to attend to them, but that if I wanted to I should find the proper answers. But the questions began to repeat themselves oftener and oftener, answers were demanded more and more persistently, and, like dots that fall on the same spot, these questions, without any answers, thickened into one black blotch.

There happened what happens with any person who falls ill with a mortal internal disease. At first there appear insignificant symptoms of indisposition, to which the patient pays no attention; then these symptoms are repeated more and more frequently and blend into one temporally indivisible suffering. The suffering keeps growing, and before the patient has had time to look around, he becomes conscious that what he took for an indisposition is the most significant thing in the world to him, – is death.

The same happened with me. I understood that it was not a passing indisposition, but something very important, and that, if the questions were going to repeat themselves, it would be necessary to find an answer for them. And I tried to answer them. The questions seemed to be so foolish, simple, and childish. But the moment I touched them and tried to solve them, I became convinced, in the first place, that they were not childish and foolish, but very important and profound questions in life, and, in the second, that, no matter how much I might try, I should not be able to answer them. Before attending to my Samára estate, to my son's education, or to the writing of a book, I ought to know why I should do that. So long as I did not know why, I could not do anything. I could not live. Amidst my thoughts of farming, which interested my very much during that time, there would suddenly pass through my head a question like this: "All right, you are going to have six thousand desyatínas of land in the Government of Samára, and

* From Leo Tolstoy, *My Confession*, translated by Leo Wierner (London: J. M. Dent, 1905), pp. 11–20.

three hundred horses, – and then?" And I completely lost my senses and did not know what to think farther. Or, when I thought of the education of my children, I said to myself: "Why?" Or, reflecting on the manner in which the masses might obtain their welfare, I suddenly said to myself: "What is that to me?" Or, thinking of the fame which my works would get me, I said to myself: "All right, you will be more famous than Gógol, Púshkin, Shakespeare, Molière, and all the writers in the world, – what of it?" And I was absolutely unable to make any reply. The questions were not waiting, and I had to answer them at once; if I did not answer them, I could not live.

I felt that what I was standing on had given way, that I had no foundation to stand on, that that which I lived by no longer existed, and that I had nothing to live by. . . .

All that happened with me when I was on every side surrounded by what is considered to be complete happiness. I had a good, loving, and beloved wife, good children, and a large estate, which grew and increased without any labour on my part. I was respected by my neighbours and friends, more than ever before, was praised by strangers, and, without any self-deception, could consider my name famous. With all that, I was not deranged or mentally unsound, – on the contrary, I was in full command of my mental and physical powers, such as I had rarely met with in people of my age: physically I could work in a field, mowing, without falling behind a peasant; mentally I could work from eight to ten hours in succession, without experiencing any consequences from the strain. And while in such condition I arrived at the conclusion that I could not live, and, fearing death, I had to use cunning against myself, in order that I might not take my life.

This mental condition expressed itself to me in this form: my life is a stupid, mean trick played on me by somebody. Although I did not recognize that "somebody" as having created me, the form of the conception that some one had played a mean, stupid trick on me by bringing me into the world was the most natural one that presented itself to me.

Involuntarily I imagined that there, somewhere, there was somebody who was now having fun as he looked down upon me and saw me, who had lived for thirty or forty years, learning, developing, growing in body and mind, now that I had become strengthened in mind and had reached that summit of life from which it lay all before me, standing as a complete fool on that summit and seeing clearly that there was nothing in life and never would be. And that was fun to him –

But whether there was or was not that somebody who made fun of me, did not make it easier for me. I could not ascribe any sensible meaning to a single act, or to my whole life. I was only surprised that I had not understood that from the start. All that had long ago been known to everybody. Sooner or later there would come diseases and death (they had come already) to my dear ones and to me, and there would be nothing left but stench and worms. All my affairs, no matter what they might be, would sooner or later be forgotten, and I myself should not exist. So why should I worry about all these things? How could a man fail to see that and live, – that was surprising? A person could live only so long as he was drunk; but the moment he sobered up, he could not help seeing that all that was only a deception, and a stupid deception at that! Really, there was nothing funny and ingenious about it, but only something cruel and stupid.

Long ago has been told the Eastern story about the traveller who in the steppe is overtaken by an infuriated beast. Trying to save himself from the animal, the traveller jumps into a waterless well, but at its bottom he sees a dragon who opens his jaws in order to swallow him. And the unfortunate man does not dare climb out, lest he perish from the infuriated beast, and does not dare jump down to the bottom of the well, lest he be devoured by the dragon, and so clutches the twig of a wild bush growing in a cleft of the well and holds on to it. His hands grow weak and he feels that soon he shall have to surrender to the peril which awaits him at either side; but he still holds on and sees two mice, one white, the other black, in even measure making a circle around the main trunk of the bush to which he is clinging, and nibbling at it on all sides. Now, at any moment, the bush will break and tear off, and he will fall into the dragon's jaws. The traveller sees that and knows that he will inevitably perish; but while he is still clinging, he sees some drops of honey hanging on the leaves of the bush, and so reaches out for them with his tongue and licks that leaves. Just so I hold on to the branch of life, knowing that the dragon of death is waiting inevitably for me, ready to tear me to pieces, and I cannot understand why I have fallen on such suffering. And I try to lick that honey which used to give me pleasure; but now it no longer gives me joy, and the white and the black mouse day and night nibble at the branch to which I am holding on. I clearly see the dragon, and the honey is no longer sweet to me. I see only the inevitable dragon and the mice, and am unable to turn my glance away from them. That is not a fable, but a veritable, indisputable, comprehensible truth.

The former deception of the pleasures of life, which stifled the terror of the dragon, no longer deceives me. No matter how much one should say to me, "You cannot understand the meaning of life, do not think, live!" I am unable to do so, because I have been doing it too long before. Now I cannot help seeing day and night, which run and lead me up to death. I see that alone, because that alone is the truth. Everything else is a lie.

The two drops of honey that have longest turned my eyes away from the cruel truth, the love of family and of authorship, which I have called an art, are no longer sweet to me.

"My family –" I said to myself, "but my family, my wife and children, they are also human beings. They are in precisely the same condition that I am in: they must either live in the lie or see the terrible truth. Why should they live? Why should I love them, why guard, raise, and watch them? Is it for the same despair which is in me, or for dullness of perception? Since I love them, I cannot conceal the truth from them, – every step in cognition leads them up to this truth. And the truth is death."

"Art, poetry?" For a long time, under the influence of the success of human praise, I tried to persuade myself that that was a thing which could be done, even though death should come and destroy everything, my deeds, as well as my memory of them; but soon I came to see that that, too, was a deception. It was clear to me that art was an adornment of life, a decoy of life. But life lost all its attractiveness for me. How, then, could I entrap others? So long as I did not live my own life, and a strange life bore me on its waves; so long as I believed that life had some sense, although I was not able to express it, – the reflections of life of every description in poetry and in the arts afforded me pleasure, and I was delighted to look at life through this little mirror of art; but when I began to look for the meaning of life, when I experienced the necessity of living myself, that little mirror became either useless, superfluous, and ridiculous, or painful to me. I could no longer console myself with what I saw in the mirror, namely, that my situation was stupid and desperate. It was all right for me to rejoice so long as I believed in the depth of my soul that life had some sense. At that time the play of lights – of the comical, the tragical, the touching, the beautiful, the terrible in life – afforded me amusement. But when I knew that life was meaningless and terrible, the play in the little mirror could no longer amuse me. No sweetness of honey could be sweet to me, when I saw the dragon and the mice that were nibbling down my support. . . .

In my search after the question of life I experienced the same feeling which a man who has lost his way in the forest may experience.

He comes to a clearing, climbs a tree, and clearly sees an unlimited space before him; at the same time he sees that there are no houses there, and that there can be none; he goes back to the forest, into the darkness, and he sees darkness, and again there are no houses.

Thus I blundered in this forest of human knowledge, between the clearings of the mathematical and experimental sciences, which disclosed to me clear horizons, but such in the direction of which there could be no house, and between the darkness of the speculative sciences, where I sunk into a deeper darkness, the farther I proceeded, and I convinced myself at last that there was no way out and could not be.

By abandoning myself to the bright side of knowledge I saw that I only turned my eyes away from the question. No mater how enticing and clear the horizons were that were disclosed to me, no matter how enticing it was to bury myself in the infinitude of this knowledge, I comprehended that these sciences were the more clear, the less I needed them, the less they answered my question.

"Well, I know," I said to myself, "all which science wants so persistently to know, but there is no answer to the question about the meaning of my life." But in the speculative sphere I saw that, in spite of the fact that the aim of the knowledge was directed straight to the answer of my question, or because of that fact, there could be no other answer than what I was giving to myself: "What is the meaning of my life?" – "None." Or, "What will come of my life?" – "Nothing." Or, "Why does everything which exists exist, and why do I exist?" – "Because it exists."

Putting the question to the one side of human knowledge, I received an endless quantity of exact answers about what I did not ask: about the chemical composition of the stars, about the movement of the sun toward the constellation of Hercules, about the origin of species and of man, about the forms of infinitely small, imponderable particles of ether; but the answer in this sphere of knowledge to my question what the meaning of my life was, was always: " you are what you call your life; you are a temporal, accidental conglomeration of particles. The interrelation, the change of these particles, produces in you that which you call life. This congeries will last for some time; then the interaction of these particles will cease, and that which you call life and all your questions will come to an end. You are an accidentally cohering globule of something. The globule is fermenting. This fermentation the globule calls its life. The globule falls to pieces, and all fermentation and all questions will come to an end." Thus the clear side of knowledge answers, and it cannot say anything else, if only it strictly follows its principles.

With such an answer it appears that the answer is not a reply to the question. I want to know the meaning of my life, but the fact that it is a particle of the infinite not only gives it no meaning, but even destroys every possible meaning.

Those obscure transactions, which this side of the experimental, exact science has with speculation, when it says that the meaning of life consists in evolution and the cooperation with this evolution, because of their obscurity and inexactness cannot be regarded as answers.

The other side of knowledge, the speculative, so long as it sticks strictly to its fundamental principles in giving a direct answer to the question, everywhere and at all times has answered one and the same: "The world is something infinite and incomprehensible. Human life is an incomprehensible part of this incomprehensible *all. . . .*"

I lived for a long time in this madness, which, not in words, but in deeds, is particularly characteristic of us, the most liberal and learned of men. But, thanks either to my strange, physical love for the real working class, which made me understand it and see that it is not so stupid as we suppose, or to the sincerity of my conviction, which was that I could know nothing and that the best that I could do was to hang myself, – I felt that if I wanted to live and understand the meaning of life, I ought naturally to look for it, not among those who had lost the meaning of life and wanted to kill themselves, but among those billions departed and living men who had been carrying their own lives and ours upon their shoulders. And I looked around at the enormous masses of deceased and living men, – not learned and wealthy, but simple men, – and I saw something quite different. I saw that all these billions of men that lived or had lived, all, with rare exceptions, did not fit into my subdivisions, and that I could not recognize them as not understanding the question, because they themselves put it and answered it with surprising clearness. Nor could I recognize them as Epicureans, because their lives were composed rather of privations and suffering than of enjoyment. Still less could I recognize them as senselessly living out their meaningless lives, because every act of theirs and death itself was explained by them. They regarded it as the greatest evil to kill themselves. It appeared, then, that all humanity was in possession of a knowledge of the meaning of life, which I did not recognize and which I condemned. It turned out that rational knowledge did not give any meaning to life, excluded life, while the meaning which by billions of people, by all humanity, was ascribed to life was based on some despised, false knowledge.

The rational knowledge in the person of the learned and the wise denied the meaning of life, but the enormous masses of men, all humanity, recognized this meaning in an irrational knowledge. This irrational knowledge was faith, the same that I could not help but reject. That was God as one and three, the creation in six days, devils and angels, and all that which I could not accept so long as I had not lost my senses.

My situation was a terrible one. I knew that I should not find anything on the path of rational knowledge but the negation of life, and there, in faith, nothing but the negation of reason, which was still more impossible than the negation of life. From the rational knowledge it followed that life was an evil and men knew it, – it depended on men whether they should cease living, and yet they lived and continued to live, and I myself lived, though I had known long ago that life was meaningless and an evil. From faith it followed that, in order to understand life, I must renounce reason, for which alone a meaning was needed.

There resulted a contradiction, from which there were two ways out: either what I called rational was not so rational as I had thought; or that which to me appeared irrational was not so irrational as I had thought. And I began to verify the train of thoughts of my rational knowledge.

In verifying the train of thoughts of my rational knowledge, I found that it was quite correct. The deduction that life was nothing was inevitable; but I saw a mistake. The mistake was that I had not reasoned in conformity with the question put by me. The question was, "Why should I live?" that is, "What real, indestructible essence will come from my phantasmal, destructible life? What meaning has my finite existence in this infinite world?" And in order to answer this question, I studied life.

The solutions of all possible questions of life apparently could not satisfy me, because my question, no matter how simple it appeared in the beginning, included the necessity of explaining the finite through the infinite, and vice versa.

I asked, "What is the extra-temporal, extra-causal, extra-spatial meaning of life?" But I gave an answer to the question, "What is the temporal, causal, spatial meaning of my life?" The result was that after a long labour of mind I answered, "None."

In my reflections I constantly equated, nor could I do otherwise, the finite with the finite, the infinite with the infinite, and so from that resulted precisely what had to result: force was force, matter was matter, will was will, infinity was infinity, nothing was nothing, – and nothing else could come from it.

There happened something like what at times takes place in mathematics: you think you are solving an equation, when you have only an identity. The reasoning is correct, but you receive as a result the answer: $a = a$, or $x = x$, or $o = o$. The same happened with my reflection in respect to the question about the meaning of my life. The answers given by all science to that question are only identities.

Indeed, the strictly scientific knowledge, that knowledge which, as Descartes did, begins with a full doubt in everything, rejects all knowledge which has been taken on trust, and builds everything anew on the laws of reason and experience, cannot give any other answer to the question of life than what I received, – an indefinite answer. It only seemed to me at first that science gave me a positive answer, – Schopenhauer's answer: "Life has no meaning, it is an evil." But when I analyzed the matter, I saw that the answer was not a positive one, but that it was only my feeling which expressed it as such. The answer, strictly expressed, as it is expressed by the Brahmins, by Solomon, and by Schopenhauer, is only an indefinite answer, or an identity, $o = o$, life is nothing. Thus the philosophical knowledge does not negate anything, but only answers that the question cannot be solved by it, that for philosophy the solution remains insoluble.

When I saw that, I understood that it was not right for me to look for an answer to my question in rational knowledge, and that the answer given by rational knowledge was only an indication that the answer might be got if the question were differently put, but only when into the discussion of the question should be introduced the question of the relation of the finite to the infinite. I also understood that, no matter how irrational and monstrous the answers might be that faith gave, they had this advantage that they intro-duced into each answer the relation of the finite to the infinite, without which there could be no answer.

No matter how I may put the question, "How must I live?" the answer is, "Accord-ing to God's law." "What real result will there be from my life?" – "Eternal torment or eternal bliss." "What is the meaning which is not destroyed by death?" – "The union with infinite God, paradise."

Thus, outside the rational knowledge, which had to me appeared as the only one, I was inevitably led to recognize that all living humanity had a certain other irrational knowledge, faith, which made it possible to live.

All the irrationality of faith remained the same for me, but I could not help recog-nizing that it alone gave to humanity answers to the questions of life, and, in consequence of them, the possibility of living.

The rational knowledge brought me to the recognition that life was meaningless, – my life stopped, and I wanted to destroy myself. When I looked around at people, at all humanity, I saw that people lived and asserted that they knew the meaning of life. I looked back at myself: I lived so long as I knew the meaning of life. As to other people, so even to me, did faith give the meaning of life and the possibility of living.

Looking again at the people of other countries, contemporaries of mine and those passed away, I saw again the same. Where life had been, there faith, ever since humanity had existed, had given the possibility of living, and the chief features of faith were everywhere one and the same.

No matter what answers faith may give, its every answer gives to the finite existence of man the sense of the infinite, – a sense which is not destroyed by suffering, privation, and death. Consequently in faith alone could we find the meaning and possibility of life. What, then, was faith? I understood that faith was not merely an evidence of things not seen, and so forth, not revelation (that is only the description of one of the symptoms of faith), not the relation of man to man (faith has to be defined, and then God, and not first God, and faith through him), not merely and agreement with what a man was told, as faith was generally understood, – that faith was the knowledge of the meaning of human life, in consequence of which man did not destroy himself, but lived. Faith is the power of life. If a man lives he believes in something. If he did not believe that he ought to live for some purpose, he would not live. If he does not see and understand the phantasm of the finite, he believes in that finite; if he understands the phantasm of the finite, he must believe in the infinite. Without faith one cannot live. . . .

In order that all humanity may be able to live, in order that they may continue living, giving a meaning to live, they, those billions, must have another, a real knowledge of faith, for not the fact that I, with Solomon and Schopenhauer, did not kill myself convinced me of the existence of faith, but that these billions had lived and had borne us, me and Solomon, on the waves of life.

Then I began to cultivate the acquaintance of the believers from among the poor, the simple and unlettered folk, of pilgrims, monks, dissenters, peasants. The doctrine of these people from among the masses was also the Christian doctrine that the quasi-believers of our circle professed. With the Christian truths were also mixed in very many superstitions, but there was this difference: the superstitions of our circle were quite unnecessary to them, had no connection with their lives, were only a kind of a Epicurean amusement, while the superstitions of the believers from among the labouring classes were to such an extent blended with their life that it would have been impossible to imagine it without these superstitions, – it was a necessary condition of that life. I began to examine closely the lives and beliefs of these people, and the more I examined them, the more did I become convinced that they had the real faith, that their faith was necessary for them, and that it alone gave them a meaning and possibility of life. In contradistinction to what I saw in our circle, where life without faith was possible, and where hardly one in a thousand professed to be a believer, among them there was hardly one in a thousand who was not a believer. In contradistinction to what I saw in our circle, where all life passed in idleness, amusements, and tedium of life, I saw that the whole life of these people was passed in hard work, and that they were satisfied with life. In contradistinction to the people of our circle, who struggled and murmured against fate because of their privations and their suffering, these people accepted diseases and sorrows without any perplexity or opposition, but with the calm and firm conviction that it was all for good. In contradistinction to the fact that the more intelligent we are, the less do we understand the meaning of life and the more do we see a kind of a bad joke in our suffering and death, these people live, suffer, and approach death, and suffer in peace and more often in joy. In contradistinction to the fact that a calm death, a death without terror or despair, is the greatest exception in our circle, a restless, insubmissive, joyless death is one of the greatest exceptions among the masses. And of such people, who are deprived of everything which for Solomon and for me constitutes the only good of life, and who withal experience the greatest happiness, there is an enormous number. I cast a broader glance about me. I examined the life of past and present vast masses of men, and I saw people who in like manner had understood the meaning of life, who had known how to live and die, not two, not three, not ten, but hundreds, thousands, millions. All of them, infinitely diversified as to habits, intellect, culture, situation, all equally and quite contrary to my ignorance knew the meaning of life and of death, worked calmly, bore privations and suffering, lived and died, seeing in that not vanity, but good.

I began to love those people. The more I penetrated into their life, the life of the men now living, and the life of men departed, of whom I had read and heard, the more did I love them, and the easier it became for me to live. Thus I lived for about two years, and within me took place a transformation, which had long been working within me, and the germ of which had always been in me. What happened with me was that the life of our circle, – of the rich and the learned, – not only disgusted me, but even lost all its meaning. All our acts, reflections, sciences, arts, – all that appeared to me in a new light. I saw that all that was mere pampering of the appetites, and that no meaning could be found in it; but the life of all the working masses, of all humanity, which created life, presented itself to me in its real significance. I saw that that was life itself and that the meaning given to this life was truth, and I accepted it.

---

29 The Absurdity of Life without God*

William Lane Craig

Assessment

The Necessity of God and Immortality

Man, writes Loren Eiseley, is the Cosmic Orphan. He is the only creature in the universe who asks, "Why?" Other animals have instincts to guide them, but man has learned to ask questions.

"Who am I?" man asks. "Why am I here? Where am I going?" Since the Enlightenment, when he threw off the shackles of religion, man has tried to answer these questions without reference to God. But the answers that came back were not exhilarating,

* From William Lane Craig, *Reasonable Faith: Christian Truth and Apologetics* (Wheaton, ILL: Crossway Books), pp. 57–75, © 1984. Used by permission of Good News Publishers/Crossway Books, Wheaton, Illinois 60187, www.crosswaybooks.org.

but dark and terrible. "You are the accidental by-product of nature, a result of matter plus time plus chance. There is no reason for your existence. All you face is death."

Modern man thought that when he had gotten rid of God, he had freed himself from all that repressed and stifled him. Instead, he discovered that in killing God, he had also killed himself.

For if there is no God, then man's life becomes absurd.

If God does not exist, then both man and the universe are inevitably doomed to death. Man, like all biological organisms, must die. With no hope of immortality, man's life leads only to the grave. His life is but a spark in the infinite blackness, a spark that appears, flickers, and dies forever. Compared to the infinite stretch of time, the span of man's life is but an infinitesimal moment; and yet this is all the life he will ever know. Therefore, everyone must come face to face with what theologian Paul Tillich has called "the threat of non-being." For though I know now that I exist, that I am alive, I also know that someday I will no longer exist, that I will no longer be, that I will die. This thought is staggering and threatening: to think that the person I call "myself" will cease to exist, that I will be no more!

I remember vividly the first time my father told me that someday I would die. Somehow as a child the thought had just never occurred to me. When he told me, I was filled with fear and unbearable sadness. And though he tried repeatedly to reassure me that this was a long way off, that did not seem to matter. Whether sooner or later, the undeniable fact was that I would die and be no more, and the thought overwhelmed me. Eventually, like all of us, I grew to simply accept the fact. We all learn to live with the inevitable. But the child's insight remains true. As the French existentialist Jean-Paul Sartre observed, several hours or several years make no difference once you have lost eternity.

Whether it comes sooner or later, the prospect of death and the threat of non-being is a terrible horror. But I met a student once who did not feel this threat. He said he had been raised on the farm and was used to seeing the animals being born and dying. Death was for him simply natural – a part of life, so to speak. I was puzzled by how different our two perspectives on death were and found it difficult to understand why he did not feel the threat of non-being. Years later, I think I found my answer in reading Sartre. Sartre observed that death is not threatening so long as we view it as the death of the other, from a third-person standpoint, so to speak. It is only when we internalize it and look at it from the first-person perspective – "*my* death: *I* am going to die" – that the threat of non-being becomes real. As Sartre points out, many people never assume this first-person perspective in the midst of life; one can even look at one's own death from the third-person standpoint, as if it were the death of another or even of an animal, as did my friend. But the true existential significance of *my death* can only be appreciated from the first-person perspective, as I realize that I am going to die and forever cease to exist. My life is just a momentary transition out of oblivion into oblivion.

And the universe, too, faces death. Scientists tell us that the universe is expanding, and everything in it is growing farther and farther apart. As it does so, it grows colder and colder, and its energy is used up. Eventually all the stars will burn out and all matter will collapse into dead stars and black holes. There will be no light at all; there will be no heat; there will be no life; only the corpses of dead stars and galaxies, ever expanding into the endless darkness and the cold recesses of space – a universe in ruins. The entire universe marches irreversibly toward its grave. So not only is the life of each individual person doomed; the entire human race is doomed. The universe is plunging toward inevitable extinction – death is written throughout its structure. There is no escape. There is no hope.

The Absurdity of Life without God and Immortality

If there is no God, then man and the universe are doomed. Like prisoners condemned to death, we await our unavoidable execution. There is no God, and there is no immortality. And what is the consequence of this? It means that life itself is absurd. It means that the life we have is without ultimate significance, value, or purpose. Let's look at each of these.

No ultimate meaning without immortality and God

If each individual person passes out of existence when he dies, then what ultimate meaning can be given to his life? Does it really matter whether he ever existed at all? It might be said that his life was important because it influenced others or affected the course of history. But this only shows a relative significance to his life, not an ultimate significance. His life may be important relative to certain other events, but what is the ultimate significance of any of those events? If all the events are meaningless, then what can be the ultimate meaning of influencing any of them? Ultimately it makes no difference.

Look at it from another perspective: Scientists say that the universe originated in an explosion called the "Big Bang" about 15 billion years ago. Suppose the Big Bang had never occurred. Suppose the universe had never existed. What ultimate difference would it make? The universe is doomed to die anyway. In the end it makes no difference whether the universe ever existed or not. Therefore, it is without ultimate significance.

The same is true of the human race. Mankind is a doomed race in a dying universe. Because the human race will eventually cease to exist, it makes no ultimate difference whether it ever did exist. Mankind is thus no more significant than a swarm of mosquitos or a barnyard of pigs, for their end is all the same. The same blind cosmic process that coughed them up in the first place will eventually swallow them all again.

And the same is true of each individual person. The contributions of the scientist to the advance of human knowledge, the researches of the doctor to alleviate pain and suffering, the efforts of the diplomat to secure peace in the world, the sacrifices of good men everywhere to better the lot of the human race – all these come to nothing. In the end they don't make one bit of difference, not one bit. Each person's life is therefore without ultimate significance. And because our lives are ultimately meaningless, the activities we fill our lives with are also meaningless. The long hours spent in study at the university, our jobs, our interests, our friendships – all these are, in the final analysis, utterly meaningless. This is the horror of modern man: because he ends in nothing, he is nothing.

But it is important to see that it is not just immortality that man needs if life is to be meaningful. Mere duration of existence does not make that existence meaningful. If man and the universe could exist forever, but if there were no God, their existence would still have no ultimate significance. To illustrate: I once read a science-fiction story in which an astronaut was marooned on a barren chunk of rock lost in outer space. He had with him two vials: one containing poison and the other a potion that would make him live forever. Realizing his predicament, he gulped down the poison. But then to his horror, he discovered he had swallowed the wrong vial – he had drunk the potion for immortality. And that meant that he was cursed to exist forever – a meaningless, unending life. Now if God does not exist, our lives are just like that. They could go on and on and still be utterly without meaning. We could still ask of life, "So what?" So it is not just immortality man needs if life is to be ultimately significant; he needs God and immortality. And if God does not exist, then he has neither.

Twentieth-century man came to understand this. Read *Waiting for Godot* by Samuel Beckett. During this entire play two men carry on trivial conversation while waiting for a third man to arrive, who never does. Our lives are like that, Beckett is saying; we just kill time waiting – for what, we don't know. In a tragic portrayal of man, Beckett wrote another play in which the curtain opens revealing a stage littered with junk. For thirty long seconds, the audience sits and stares in silence at that junk. Then the curtain closes. That's all.

One of the most devastating novels I've ever read was *Steppenwolf*, by Hermann Hesse. At the novel's end, Harry Haller stands looking at himself in a mirror. During the course of his life he had experienced all the world offers. And now he stands looking at himself, and he mutters, "Ah, the bitter taste of life!" He spits at himself in the looking-glass, and then he kicks it to pieces. His life has been futile and meaningless.

French existentialists Jean-Paul Sartre and Albert Camus understood this, too. Sartre portrayed life in his play *No Exit* as hell – the final line of the play are the words of resignation, "Well, let's get on with it." Hence, Sartre writes elsewhere of the "nausea" of existence. Camus, too, saw life as absurd. At the end of his brief novel *The Stranger*, Camus's hero discovers in a flash of insight that the universe has no meaning and there is no God to give it one. The French biochemist Jacques Monod seemed to echo those sentiments when he wrote in his work *Chance and Necessity*, "Man finally knows he is alone in the indifferent immensity of the universe."

Thus, if there is no God, then life itself becomes meaningless. Man and the universe are without ultimate significance.

No ultimate value without immortality and God

If life ends at the grave, then it makes no difference whether one has lived as a Stalin or as a saint. Since one's destiny is ultimately unrelated to one's behavior, you may as well just live as you please. As Dostoyevsky put it: "If there is no immortality then all things are permitted." On this basis, a writer like Ayn Rand is absolutely correct to praise the virtues of selfishness. Live totally for self; no one holds you accountable! Indeed, it would be foolish to do anything else, for life is too short to jeopardize it by acting out of anything but pure self-interest. Sacrifice for another person would be stupid. Kai Nielsen, an atheist philosopher who attempts to defend the viability of ethics without God, in the end admits,

> We have not been able to show that reason requires the moral point of view, or that all really rational persons, unhoodwinked by myth or ideology, need not be individual egoists or classical amoralists. Reason doesn't decide here. The picture I have painted for you is not a pleasant one. Reflection on it depresses me . . . Pure practical reason, even with a good knowledge of the facts, will not take you to morality.[1]

But the problem becomes even worse. For, regardless of immortality, if there is no God, then there can be no objective standards of right and wrong. All we are confronted with is, in Jean-Paul Sartre's words, the bare, valueless fact of existence. Moral values are either just expressions of personal taste or the by-products of socio-biological evolution and conditioning. In the words of one humanist philosopher, "The moral principles that govern our behavior are rooted in habit and custom, feeling and fashion.[2] In a world without God, who is to say which values are right and which are wrong? Who is to judge that the values of Adolf Hitler are inferior to those of a saint? The concept of morality loses all meaning in a universe without God. As one contemporary atheistic ethicist points out, "to say that something is wrong because . . . it is forbidden by God, is . . . perfectly understandable to anyone who believes in a law-giving God. But to say that something is wrong . . . even though no God exists to forbid it, is *not* understandable . . . ." "The concept of moral obligation [is] unintelligible apart from the idea of God. The words remain but their meaning is gone.[3] In a world without God, there can be no objective right and wrong, only our culturally and personally relative, subjective judgments. This means that it is impossible to condemn war, oppression, or crime as evil. Nor can one praise brotherhood, equality, and love as good. For in a universe without God, good and evil do not exist – there is only the bare valueless fact of existence, and there is no one to say you are right and I am wrong.

No ultimate purpose without immortality and God

If death stands with open arms at the end of life's trail, then what is the goal of life? To what end has life been lived? Is it all for nothing? Is there no reason for life? And what of the universe? Is it utterly pointless? If its destiny is a cold grave in the recesses of outer space, the answer must be yes – it is pointless. There is no goal, no purpose, for the universe. The litter of a dead universe will just go on expanding and expanding – forever.

And what of man? Is there no purpose at all for the human race? Or will it simply peter out someday lost in the oblivion of an indifferent universe? The English writer H. G. Wells foresaw such a prospect. In his novel *The Time Machine* Wells's time traveler journeys far into the future to discover the destiny of man. All he finds is a dead earth, save for a few lichens and moss, orbiting a gigantic red sun. The only sounds are the rush of the wind and the gentle ripple of the sea. "Beyond these lifeless sounds," writes Wells, "the world was silent. Silent? It would be hard to convey the stillness of it. All the sounds of man, the bleating of sheep, the cries of birds, the hum of insects, the stir that makes the background of our lives – all that was over."[4] And so Wells's time traveler returned. But to what? – to merely an earlier point on the purposeless rush toward oblivion. When as a non-Christian I first read Wells's book, I thought, "No, no! It can't end that way!" But if there is no God, it will end that way, like it or not. This is reality in a universe without God: there is no hope; there is no purpose. . . .

What is true of mankind as a whole is true of each of us individually: we are here to no purpose. If there is no God, then our life is not qualitatively different from that of a dog. I know that's harsh, but it's true. As the ancient writer of Ecclesiastes put it: "The fate of the sons of men and the fate of beasts is the same. As one dies so dies the other; indeed, they all have the same breath and there is no advantage for man over beast, for all is vanity. All go to the same place. All come from the dust and all return to the dust" (Eccles. 3:19–20). In this book, which reads more like a piece of modern existentialist literature than a book of the Bible, the writer shows the futility of pleasure, wealth, education, political fame, and honor in a life doomed to end in death. His verdict? "Vanity of vanities! All is vanity" (1:2). If life ends at the grave, then we have no ultimate purpose for living.

But more than that: even if it did not end in death, without God life would still be without purpose. For man and the universe would then be simple accidents of chance, thrust into existence for no reason. Without God the universe is the result of a cosmic accident, a chance explosion. There is no reason for which it exists. As for man, he is a freak of nature – a blind product of matter plus time plus chance. Man is just a lump of slime that evolved into rationality. There is no more purpose in life for the human race than for a species of insect; for both are the result of the blind interaction of chance and necessity. As one philosopher has put it: "Human life is mounted upon a subhuman pedestal and must shift for itself alone in the heart of a silent and mindless universe."[5]

What is true of the universe and of the human race is also true of us as individuals. Insofar as we are individual human beings, we are the results of certain combinations of heredity and environment. We are victims of a kind of genetic and environmental roulette. Psychologists following Sigmund Freud tell us our actions are the result of various repressed sexual tendencies. Sociologists following B. F. Skinner argue that all our choices are determined by conditioning, so that freedom is an illusion. Biologists like Francis Crick regard man as an electro-chemical machine that can be controlled by altering its genetic code. If God does not exist, then you are just a miscarriage of nature, thrust into a purposeless universe to live a purposeless life.

So if God does not exist, that means that man and the universe exist to no purpose – since the end of everything is death – and that they came to be for no purpose, since they are only blind products of chance. In short, life is utterly without reason.

Do you understand the gravity of the alternatives before us? For if God exists, then there is hope for man. But if God does not exist, then all we are left with is despair. Do you understand why the question of God's existence is so vital to man? As one writer has aptly put it, "If God is dead, then man is dead, too."

Unfortunately, the mass of mankind do not realize this fact. They continue on as though nothing has changed. I'm reminded of Nietzsche's story of the madman who in the early morning hours burst into the marketplace, lantern in hand, crying, "I seek God! I seek God!" Since many of those standing about did not believe in God, he provoked much laughter. "Did God get lost?" they taunted him. "Or is he hiding? Or maybe he has gone on a voyage or emigrated!" Thus they yelled and laughed. Then, writes Nietzsche, the madman turned in their midst and pierced them with his eyes.

> 'Whither is God?' he cried, 'I shall tell you. *We have killed him* – you and I. All of us are his murderers. But how have we done this? How were we able to drink up the sea? Who gave us the sponge to wipe away the entire horizon? What did we do when we unchained this earth from its sun? Whither is it moving now? Away from all suns? Are we not plunging continually? Backward, sideward, forward, in all directions? Is there any up or down left? Are we not straying as through an infinite nothing? Do we not feel the breath of empty space? Has it not become colder? Is not night and more night coming on all the while? Must not lanterns be lit in the morning? Do we not hear anything yet of the noise of the gravediggers who are burying God? . . . God is dead . . . And we have killed him. How shall we, the murderers of all murderers, comfort ourselves?'[6]

The crowd stared at the madman in silence and astonishment. At last he dashed his lantern to the ground. "I have come too early," he said. "This tremendous event is still on its way – it has not yet reached the ears of man." Men did not yet truly comprehend the consequences of what they had done in killing God. But Nietzsche predicted that someday people would realize the implications of their atheism; and this realization would usher in an age of nihilism – the destruction of all meaning and value in life. The end of Christianity, wrote Nietzsche, means the advent of nihilism. This most gruesome of guests is standing already at the door. "Our whole European culture is moving for some time now," wrote Nietzsche, "with a tortured tension that is growing from decade to decade, as toward a catastrophe: restlessly, violently, headlong, like a river that wants to reach the end, that no longer reflects, that is afraid to reflect."[7]

Most people still do not reflect on the consequences of atheism and so, like the crowd in the marketplace, go unknowingly on their way. But when we realize, as did Nietzsche, what atheism implies, then his question presses hard upon us: how *shall* we, the murderers of all murderers, comfort ourselves?

The Practical Impossibility of Atheism

About the only solution the atheist can offer is that we face the absurdity of life and live bravely. Bertrand Russell, for example, wrote that we must build our lives upon "the firm foundation of unyielding despair."[8] Only by recognizing that the world really is a terrible place can we successfully come to terms with life. Camus said that we should honestly recognize life's absurdity and then live in love for one another.

The fundamental problem with this solution, however, is that it is impossible to live consistently and happily within such a world view. If one lives consistently, he will not be happy; if one lives happily, it is only because he is not consistent. Francis Schaeffer has explained this point well. Modern man, says Schaeffer, resides in a two-story universe. In the lower story is the finite world without God; here life is absurd, as we have seen. In the upper story are meaning, value, and purpose. Now modern man lives in the lower story because he believes there is no God. But he cannot live happily in such an absurd world; therefore, he continually makes leaps of faith into the upper story to affirm meaning, value, and purpose, even though he has no right to, since he does not believe in God. Modern man is totally inconsistent when he makes this leap, because these values cannot exist without God, and man in his lower story does not have God.

Let's look again, then, at each of the three areas in which we saw life was absurd without God, to show how man cannot live consistently and happily with his atheism.

Meaning of life

First, the area of meaning. We saw that without God, life has no meaning. Yet philosophers continue to live as though life does have meaning. For example, Sartre argued that one may create meaning for his life by freely choosing to follow a certain course of action. Sartre himself chose Marxism.

Now this is utterly inconsistent. It is inconsistent to say life is objectively absurd and then to say one may create meaning for his life. If life is really absurd, then man is trapped in the lower story. To try to create meaning in life represents a leap to the upper story. But Sartre has no basis for this leap. Without God, there can be no objective meaning in life. Sartre's program is actually an exercise in self-delusion. For the universe does not really acquire meaning just because *I* give it one. This is easy to see: for suppose I give the universe one meaning, and you give it another. Who is right? The answer, of course, is neither one. For the universe without God remains objectively meaningless, no matter how *we* regard it. Sartre is really saying, "Let's *pretend* the universe has meaning." And this is just fooling ourselves.

The point is this: if God does not exist, then life is objectively meaningless; but man cannot live consistently and happily knowing that life is meaningless; so in order to be happy he pretends life has meaning. But this is, of course, entirely inconsistent – for without God, man and the universe are without any real significance.

Value of life

Turn now to the problem of value. Here is where the most blatant inconsistencies occur. First of all, atheistic humanists are totally inconsistent in affirming the traditional values of love and brotherhood. Camus has been rightly criticized for inconsistently holding both to the absurdity of life and the ethics of human love and brotherhood. The two are logically incompatible. Bertrand Russell, too, was inconsistent. For though he was an atheist, he was an outspoken social critic, denouncing war and restrictions on sexual freedom. Russell admitted that he could not live as though ethical values were simply a matter of personal taste, and that he therefore found his own views "incredible." I do not know the solution," he confessed.[9] The point is that if there is no God, then objective right and wrong cannot exist. As Dostoyevsky said, "All things are permitted."

But Dostoyevsky also showed that man cannot live this way. He cannot live as though it is perfectly all right for soldiers to slaughter innocent children. He cannot live as though it is all right for dictatorial regimes to follow a systematic program of physical torture of political prisoners. He cannot live as though it is all right for dictators like Pol Pot to exterminate millions of their own countrymen. Everything in him cries out to say these acts are wrong – really wrong. But if there is no God, he cannot. So he makes a leap of faith and affirms values anyway. And when he does so, he reveals the inadequacy of a world without God.

The horror of a world devoid of value was brought home to me with new intensity a few years ago as I viewed a BBC television documentary called "The Gathering." It concerned the reunion of survivors of the Holocaust in Jerusalem, where they redis-covered lost friendships and shared their experiences. Now, I had heard stories of the Holocaust before and had even visited Dachau and Buchenwald, and I thought I was beyond shocking by further tales of horror. But I found that I was not. Perhaps I had been made more sensitive by the recent birth of our beautiful baby girl, so that I applied the situations to her as they were related on the television. In any case, one woman pris-oner, a nurse, told of how she was made the gynecologist at Auschwitz. She observed that pregnant women were grouped together by the soldiers under the direction of Dr. Mengele and housed in the same barracks. Some time passed, and she noted that she no longer saw any of these women. She made inquiries. "Where are the pregnant women who were housed in that barracks?" "Haven't you heard?" came the reply. "*Dr. Mengele used them for vivisection.*"

Another woman told of how Mengele had bound up her breasts so that she could not suckle her infant. The doctor wanted to learn how long an infant could survive without nourishment. Desperately this poor woman tried to keep her baby alive by giving it pieces of bread soaked in coffee, but to no avail. Each day the baby lost weight, a fact that was eagerly monitored by Dr. Mengele. A nurse then came secretly to this woman and told her, "I have arranged a way for you to get out of here, but you cannot take your baby with you. I have brought a morphine injection that you can give to your child to end its life." When the woman protested, the nurse was insistent: "Look, your baby is going to die anyway. At least save yourself." And so *this mother took the life of her own baby.* Dr. Mengele was furious when he learned of it because he had lost his experimental specimen, and he searched among the dead to find the baby's discarded corpse so that he could have one last weighing.

My heart was torn by these stories. One rabbi who survived the camp summed it up well when he said that at Auschwitz it was as though there existed a world in which all the Ten Commandments were reversed. Mankind had never seen such a hell.

And yet, if God does not exist, then in a sense, our world *is* Auschwitz: there is no absolute right and wrong; *all things* are permitted. But no atheist, no agnostic, can live consistently with such a view. Nietzsche himself, who proclaimed the necessity of living "beyond good and evil," broke with his mentor Richard Wagner precisely over the issue of the composer's anti-Semitism and strident German nationalism. Similarly Sartre, writing in the aftermath of the Second World War, condemned anti-Semitism, declaring that a doctrine that leads to extermination is not merely an opinion or matter of personal taste, of equal value with its opposite.[10] In his important essay "Existentialism Is a Humanism," Sartre struggles vainly to elude the contradiction between his denial of divinely pre-established values and his urgent desire to affirm the value of human persons. Like Russell, he could not live with the implications of his own denial of ethical absolutes.

A second problem is that if God does not exist and there is no immortality, then all the evil acts of men go unpunished and all the sacrifices of good men go unrewarded. But who can live with such a view? Richard Wurmbrand, who has been tortured for his faith in communist prisons, says,

> The cruelty of atheism is hard to believe when man has no faith in the reward of good or the punishment of evil. There is no reason to be human. There is no restraint from the depths of evil which is in man. The communist torturers often said, 'There is no God, no Hereafter, no punishment for evil. We can do what we wish.' I have heard one torturer even say, 'I thank God, in whom I don't believe, that I have lived to this hour when I can express all the evil in my heart.' He expressed it in unbelievable brutality and torture inflicted on prisoners.[11]

The English theologian Cardinal Newman once said that if he believed that all evils and injustices of life throughout history were not to be made right by God in the afterlife, "Why I think I should go mad." Rightly so.

And the same applies to acts of self-sacrifice. A number of years ago, a terrible midwinter air disaster occurred in which a plane leaving the Washington, D.C. airport smashed into a bridge spanning the Potomac River, plunging its passengers into the icy waters. As the rescue helicopters came, attention was focused on one man who again and again pushed the dangling rope ladder to other passengers rather than be pulled to safety himself. Six times he passed the ladder by. When they came again, he was gone. He had freely given his life that others might live. The whole nation turned its eyes to this man in respect and admiration for the selfless and good act he had performed. And yet, if the atheist is right, that man was not noble – he did the stupidest thing possible. He should have gone for the ladder first, pushed others away if necessary in order to survive. But to die for others he did not even know, to give up all the brief existence he would ever have

– what for? For the atheist there can be no reason. And yet the atheist, like the rest of us, instinctively reacts with praise for this man's selfless action. Indeed, one will probably never find an atheist who lives consistently with his system. For a universe without moral accountability and devoid of value is unimaginably terrible.

Purpose of life

Finally, let's look at the problem of purpose in life. The only way most people who deny purpose in life live happily is either by making up some purpose, which amounts to self-delusion as we saw with Sartre, or by not carrying their view to its logical conclusions. Take the problem of death, for example. According to Ernst Bloch, the only way modern man lives in the face of death is by subconsciously borrowing the belief in immortality that his forefathers held to, even though he himself has no basis for this belief, since he does not believe in God. Bloch states that the belief that life ends in nothing is hardly, in his words, "sufficient to keep the head high and to work as if there were no end." By borrowing the remnants of a belief in immortality, writes Bloch, "modern man does not feel the chasm that unceasingly surrounds him and that will certainly engulf him at last. Through these remnants, he saves his sense of self-identity. Through them the impression arises that man is not perishing, but only that one day the world has the whim no longer to appear to him." Bloch concludes, "This quite shallow courage feasts on a borrowed credit card. It lives from earlier hopes and the support that they once had provided."[12] Modern man no longer has any right to that support, since he rejects God. But in order to live purposefully, he makes a leap of faith to affirm a reason for living.

We often find the same inconsistency among those who say that man and the universe came to exist for no reason or purpose, but just by chance. Unable to live in an impersonal universe in which everything is the product of blind chance, these persons begin to ascribe personality and motives to the physical processes themselves. It is a bizarre way of speaking and represents a leap from the lower to the upper story. For example, the brilliant Russian physicists Zeldovich and Novikov, in contemplating the properties of the universe, ask, Why did "Nature" choose to create this sort of universe instead of another? "Nature" has obviously become a sort of God-substitute, filling the role and function of God. Francis Crick halfway through his book *The Origin of the Genetic Code* begins to spell nature with a capital "N" and elsewhere speaks of natural selection as being "clever" and as "thinking" of what it will do. Fred Hoyle, the English astronomer, attributes to the universe itself the qualities of God. For Carl Sagan the "Cosmos," which he always spells with a capital letter, obviously fills the role of a God-substitute. Though all these men profess not to believe in God, they smuggle in a God-substitute through the back door because they cannot bear to live in a universe in which everything is the chance result of impersonal forces.

And it's interesting to see many thinkers betray their views when they're pushed to their logical conclusions. For example, certain feminists have raised a storm of protest over Freudian sexual psychology because it is chauvinistic and degrading to women. And some psychologists have knuckled under and revised their theories. Now this is totally inconsistent. If Freudian psychology is really true, then it doesn't matter if it's degrading to women. You can't change the truth because you don't like what it leads to. But people cannot live consistently and happily in a world where other persons are devalued. Yet if God does not exist, then nobody has any value. Only if God exists can a person consistently support women's rights. For if God does not exist, then natural selection dictates that the male of the species is the dominant and aggressive one. Women would no more have rights than a female goat or chicken have rights. In nature whatever is, is right. But who can live with such a view? Apparently not even Freudian psychologists, who betray their theories when pushed to their logical conclusions.

Or take the sociological behaviorism of a man like B. F. Skinner. This view leads to the sort of society envisioned in George Orwell's *1984*, where the government controls and programs the thoughts of everybody. If Pavlov's dog can be made to salivate when a bell rings, so can a human being. If Skinner's theories are right, then there can be no objection to treating people like the rats in Skinner's rat-box as they run through their mazes, coaxed on by food and electric shocks. According to Skinner, all our actions are determined anyway. And if God does not exist, then no moral objection can be raised against this kind of programming, for man is not qualitatively different from a rat, since both are just matter plus time plus chance. But again, who can live with such a dehumanizing view?

Or finally, take the biological determinism of a man like Francis Crick. The logical conclusion is that man is like any other laboratory specimen. The world was horrified when it learned that at camps like Dachau the Nazis had used prisoners for medical experiments on living humans. But why not? If God does not exist, there can be no objection to using people as human guinea pigs. A memorial at Dachau says *Nie Wieder* – "Never Again" – but this sort of thing is still going on. It was revealed a few years ago that in the United States several people had been injected, unknown to them, with a sterilization drug by medical researchers. Must we not protest that this is wrong – that man is more than an electro-chemical machine? The end of this view is population control in which the weak and unwanted are killed off to make room for the strong. But the only way we can consistently protest this view is if God exists. Only if God exists can there be purpose in life.

The dilemma of modern man is thus truly terrible. And insofar as he denies the existence of God and the objectivity of value and purpose, this dilemma remains unrelieved for "post-modern" man as well. Indeed, it is precisely the awareness that modernism issues inevitably in absurdity and despair that constitutes the anguish of post-modernism. In some respects, post-modernism just *is* the awareness of the bankruptcy of modernity. The atheistic world view is insufficient to maintain a happy and consistent life. Man cannot live consistently and happily as though life were ultimately without meaning, value, or purpose. If we try to live consistently within the atheistic world view, we shall find ourselves profoundly unhappy. If instead we manage to live happily, it is only by giving the lie to our world view.

Confronted with this dilemma, man flounders pathetically for some means of escape. In a remarkable address to the American Academy for the Advancement of Science in 1991, Dr. L. D. Rue, confronted with the predicament of modern man, boldly advocated that we deceive ourselves by means of some "Noble Lie" into thinking that we and the universe still have value.[13] Claiming that "The lesson of the past two centuries is that intellectual and moral relativism is profoundly the case," Dr. Rue muses that the consequence of such a realization is that one's quest for personal wholeness (or self-fulfillment) and the quest for social coherence become independent from one another. This is because on the view of relativism the search for self-fulfillment becomes radically privatized: each person chooses his own set of values and meaning. "There is no final, objective reading on the world or the self. There is no universal vocabulary for integrating cosmology and morality." If we are to avoid "the madhouse option," where self-fulfillment is pursued regardless of social coherence, and "the totalitarian option," where social coherence is imposed at the expense of personal wholeness, then we have no choice but to embrace some Noble Lie that will inspire us to live beyond selfish interests and so achieve social coherence. A Noble Lie "is one that deceives us, tricks us, compels us beyond self-interest, beyond ego, beyond family, nation, [and] race." It is a lie, because it tells us that the universe is infused with value (which is a great fiction), because it makes a claim to universal truth (when there is none), and because it tells me not to live for self-interest (which is evidently false). "But without such lies, we cannot live."

This is the dreadful verdict pronounced over modern man. In order to survive, he must live in self-deception. But even the Noble Lie option is in the end unworkable. For if what I have said thus far is correct, belief in a Noble Lie would not only be necessary to achieve social coherence and personal wholeness for the masses, but it would also be necessary to achieve one's *own* personal wholeness. For one cannot live happily and consistently on an atheistic world view. In order to be happy, one must believe in objective meaning, value, and purpose. But how can one believe in those Noble Lies while at the same time believing in atheism and relativism? The more convinced you are of the necessity of a Noble Lie, the less you are able to believe in it. Like a placebo, a Noble Lie works only on those who believe it is the truth. Once we have seen through the fiction, then the Lie has lost its power over us. Thus, ironically, the Noble Lie cannot solve the human predicament for anyone who has come to see that predicament.

The Noble Lie option therefore leads at best to a society in which an elitist group of *illuminati* deceive the masses for their own good by perpetuating the Noble Lie. But then why should those of us who are enlightened follow the masses in their deception? Why should we sacrifice self-interest for a fiction? If the great lesson of the past two centuries is moral and intellectual relativism, then why (if we could) pretend that we do not know this truth and live a lie instead? If one answers, "for the sake of social coherence," one may legitimately ask why I should sacrifice my self-interest for the sake of social coherence? The only answer the relativist can give is that social coherence is in my self-interest – but the problem with this answer is that self-interest and the interest of the herd do not always coincide. Besides, if (out of self-interest) I do care about social coherence, the totalitarian option is always open to me: forget the Noble Lie and maintain social coherence (as well as my self-fulfillment) at the expense of the personal wholeness of the masses. Generations of Soviet leaders who extolled proletarian virtues while they rode in limousines and dined on caviar in their country *dachas* found this alternative quite workable. Rue would undoubtedly regard such an option as repugnant. But therein lies the rub. Rue's dilemma is that he obviously values deeply both social coherence and personal wholeness for their own sakes; in other words, they are objective values, which according to his philosophy do not exist. He has already leapt to the upper story. The Noble Lie option thus affirms what it denies and so refutes itself.

The Success of Biblical Christianity

But if atheism fails in this regard, what about biblical Christianity? According to the Christian world view, God does exist, and man's life does not end at the grave. In the resurrection body man may enjoy eternal life and fellowship with God. Biblical Christianity therefore provides the two conditions necessary for a meaningful, valuable, and purposeful life for man: God and immortality. Because of this, we can live consistently and happily. Thus, biblical Christianity succeeds precisely where atheism breaks down.

Conclusion

Now I want to make it clear that I have not yet shown biblical Christianity to be true. But what I have done is clearly spell out the alternatives. If God does not exist, then life is futile. If the God of the Bible does exist, then life is meaningful. Only the second of these two alternatives enables us to live happily and consistently. Therefore, it seems to me that even if the evidence for these two options were absolutely equal, a rational person ought to choose biblical Christianity. It seems to me positively irrational to prefer death, futility, and destruction to life, meaningfulness, and happiness. As Pascal said, we have nothing to lose and infinity to gain.

Practical Application

The foregoing discussion makes clear the role I conceive cultural apologetics to play: it is not one's whole apologetic but rather an introduction to positive argumentation. It serves to lay out in a dramatic way the alternatives facing the unbeliever in order to create a felt need in him. When he realizes the predicament he is in, he will see why the gospel is so important to him; and many a non-Christian will be impelled by these considerations alone to give his life to Christ.

In sharing this material with an unbeliever, we need to push him to the logical conclusions of his position. If I am right, no atheist or agnostic really lives consistently with his world view. In some way he affirms meaning, value, or purpose without an adequate basis. It is our job to discover those areas and lovingly show him where those beliefs are groundless. We need not attack his values themselves – for they are probably largely correct – but we may agree with him concerning them, and then point out only that he lacks any foundation for those values, whereas the Christian has such a foundation. Thus, we need not make him defensive by a frontal attack on his personal values; rather we offer him a foundation for the values he already possesses.

I have found the material on the absence of objective moral value in an atheistic world view to be an especially powerful apologetic to university students. Although students may give lip-service to relativism, my experience is that 95% can be very quickly convinced that objective moral values do exist after all. All you have to do is produce a few illustrations and let them decide for themselves. Ask what they think of the Hindu practice of *suttee* (burning widows alive on the funeral pyres of their husbands) or the ancient Chinese custom of crippling women for life by tightly binding their feet from childhood to resemble lotus-blossoms. Point out that without God to provide a trans-cultural basis for moral values, we're left with sociocultural relativism, so that such practices are morally unobjectionable – which scarcely anyone can sincerely accept.

Of course, sometimes you find some hard-liners, but usually their position is seen to be so extreme that others are repulsed by it. For example, at a recent meeting of the Society of Biblical Literature, I attended a panel discussion on "Biblical Authority and

Homosexuality," in which all the panelists endorsed the legitimacy of homosexual activity. One panelist dismissed scriptural prohibitions against such activity on the grounds that they reflect the cultural milieu in which they were written. Since this is the case for all of Scripture's commands (it wasn't written in a vacuum), he concluded that "there are no timeless, normative, moral truths in Scripture." In discussion from the floor, I pointed out that such a view leads to sociocultural relativism, which makes it impossible to criticize *any* society's moral values, including those of a society which persecutes homosexuals. He responded with a fog of theological double-talk and claimed that there's no place outside Scripture where we can find timeless moral values either. "But that just *is* what we mean by moral relativism," I said. "In fact, on your view there's no content to the notion of the goodness of God. He might as well be dead. And Nietzsche recognized that the death of God leads to nihilism." At this point another panelist came in with that knock-down refutation: "Well, if you're going to get pejorative, we might as well not discuss it."

I sat down, but the point wasn't lost on the audience. The next man who stood up said, "Wait a minute. I'm rather confused. I'm a pastor and people are always coming to me, asking if something they have done is wrong and if they need forgiveness. For example, isn't it always wrong to abuse a child?" I couldn't believe the panelist's response. She replied: "What counts as abuse differs from society to society, so we can't really use the word 'abuse' without tying it to a historical context." "Call it whatever you like," the pastor insisted, "but child abuse is damaging to children. Isn't it wrong to damage children?" And still she wouldn't admit it! This sort of hardness of heart ultimately backfires on the moral relativist and exposes in the minds of most people the bankruptcy of such a world view.

In sharing this material with unbelievers, it's important also to ask ourselves exactly what part of our case his objections are meant to refute. Thus, if he says that values are merely social conventions pragmatically adopted to ensure mutual survival, what does this purport to refute? Not that life without God really is without value, for this the objection admits. Therefore, it would be a mistake to react by arguing that values are not social conventions but are grounded in God. Rather the objection is really aimed at the claim that one cannot live as though values do not exist; it holds that one may live by social conventions alone.

Seen in this light, however, the objection is entirely implausible, for we have argued precisely that man cannot live as though morality were merely a matter of social convention. We believe certain acts to be genuinely wrong or right. Therefore, one ought to respond to the unbeliever on this score by saying, "You're exactly right: if God does not exist, then values are merely social conventions. But the point I'm trying to make is that it is impossible to live consistently and happily with such a world view." Push him on the Holocaust or some issue of popular concern like ethnic cleansing, apartheid, or child abuse. Bring it home to him personally and if he's honest and you are not threatening, I think he will admit that he does hold to some absolutes. Thus, it's very important to analyze exactly what the unbeliever's objection actually attacks before we answer.

I believe that this mode of apologetics can be very effective in helping to bring people to Christ because it does not concern neutral matters but cuts to the heart of the unbeliever's own existential situation. I remember that once, when I was delivering a series of talks at the University of Birmingham in England, the audience the first night was very hostile and aggressive. The second night I spoke on the absurdity of life without God. This time the largely same audience was utterly subdued: the lions had turned to lambs, and now their questions were no longer attacking but sincere and searching. The remarkable transformation was due to the fact that the message had penetrated their intellectual facade and struck at the core of their existence. I would encourage you to employ this material in evangelistic dorm meetings and fraternity/sorority meetings, where you can compel people to really *think* about the desperate human predicament in which we all find ourselves.

Notes

1 Kai Nielsen, "Why Should I Be Moral?" *American Philosophical Quarterly*, 21 (1984), 90.
2 Paul Kurtz, *Forbidden Fruit* (Buffalo, NY: Prometheus, 1988), p. 73.
3 Richard Taylor, *Ethics, Faith, and Reason* (Englewood Cliffs, NJ: Prentice Hall, 1985), pp. 90, 84.
4 H. G. Wells, *The Time Machine* (New York: Berkeley, 1957), ch. 11.
5 W. E. Hocking, *Types of Philosophy* (New York: Scribner's, 1959), p. 27.
6 Friedrich Nietzsche, "The Gay Science," in *The Portable Nietzsche*, ed. and trans. W. Kaufmann (New York: Viking, 1954), p. 95.
7 Friedrich Nietzsche, "The Will to Power," trans. W. Kaufmann, in *Existentialism from Dostoyevsky to Sartre*, 2nd edn., ed. with an introduction by W. Kaufmann (New York: New American Library, Meridian, 1975), pp. 130–1.
8 Bertrand Russell, "A Free Man's Worship," In *Why I Am Not a Christian*, ed. P. Edwards (New York: Simon & Schuster, 1957), p. 107.
9 Bertrand Russell, Letter to the *Observer*, 6 October 1957.
10 Jean-Paul Sartre, "Portrait of the Antisemite," trans. M. Guggenheim, in *Existentialism*, p. 30.
11 Richard Wurmbrand, *Tortured for Christ* (London: Hodder & Stoughton, 1967), p. 34.
12 Ernst Bloch, *Das Prinzip Hoffnung*, 2nd edn., 2 vols. (Frankfurt am Main: Suhrkamp Verlag, 1959), 2: 360–1.
13 Loyal D. Rue, "The Saving Grace of Noble Lies," address to the American Academy for the Advancement of Science, February 1991.

---

30 On the Vanity of Existence*

Arthur Schopenhauer

1

The vanity of existence is revealed in the whole form existence assumes: in the infiniteness of time and space contrasted with the finiteness of the individual in both; in the fleeting present as the sole form in which actuality exists; in the contingency and relativity of all things; in continual becoming without being; in continual desire without satisfaction; in the continual frustration of striving of which life consists. *Time* and that *perishability*

* From Schopenhauer, *Essays and Aphorisms*, translated by R. J. Hollingdale (Harmondsworth: Penguin, 1970). Translation © 1970 by R. J. Hollingdale. Reproduced by permission of Penguin Books Ltd.

of all things existing in time that time itself brings about is simply the form under which the will to live, which as thing in itself is imperishable, reveals to itself the vanity of its striving. Time is that by virtue of which everything becomes nothingness in our hands and loses all real value.

2

That which *has been* no longer *is*, it as little exists as does that which has *never* been. But everything that *is* in the next moment *has been*. Thus the most insignificant present has over the most significant past the advantage of *actuality*, which means that the former bears to the latter the relation of something to nothing.

To our amazement we suddenly exist, after having for countless millennia not existed; in a short while we will again not exist, also for countless millennia. That cannot be right, says the heart: and even upon the crudest intelligence there must, when it considers such an idea, dawn a presentiment of the ideality of time. This however, together with that of space, is the key to all true metaphysics, because it makes room for a quite different order of things than that of nature. That is why Kant is so great.

Every moment of our life belongs to the present only for a moment; then it belongs forever to the past. Every evening we are poorer by a day. We would perhaps grow frantic at the sight of this ebbing away of our short span of time were we not secretly conscious in the profoundest depths of our being that we share in the inexhaustible well of eternity, out of which we can for ever draw new life and renewed time.

You could, to be sure, base on considerations of this kind a theory that the greatest *wisdom* consists in enjoying the present and making this enjoyment the goal of life, because the present is all that is real and everything else merely imaginary. But you could just as well call this mode of life the greatest *folly*: for that which in a moment ceases to exist, which vanishes as completely as a dream, cannot be worth any serious effort.

3

Our existence has no foundation on which to rest except the transient present. Thus its form is essentially unceasing *motion*, without any possibility of that repose which we continually strive after. It resembles the course of a man running down a mountain who would fall over if he tried to stop and can stay on his feet only by running on; or a pole balanced on the tip of the finger; or a planet which would fall into its sun if it ever ceased to plunge irresistibly forward. Thus existence is typified by unrest.

In such a world, where no stability of any kind, no enduring state is possible, where everything is involved in restless change and confusion and keeps itself on its tightrope only by continually striding forward – in such a world, happiness is not so much as to be thought of. It cannot dwell where nothing occurs but Plato's "continual becoming and never being." In the first place, no man is happy but strives his whole life long after a supposed happiness which he seldom attains, and even if he does it is only to be disappointed with it; as a rule, however, he finally enters harbour ship-wrecked and dismasted. In the second place, however, it is all one whether he has been happy or not in a life which has consisted merely of a succession of transient present moments and is now at an end.

4

The scenes of our life resemble pictures in rough mosaic; they are ineffective from close up, and have to be viewed from a distance if they are to seem beautiful. That is why to attain something desired is to discover how vain it is; and why, though we live all our lives in expectation of better things, we often at the same time long regretfully for what is past. The present, on the other hand, is regarded as something quite temporary and serving only as the road to our goal. That is why most men discover when they look back on their life that they have the whole time been living *ad interim*, and are surprised to see that which they let go by so unregarded and unenjoyed was precisely their life, was precisely that in expectation of which they lived.

5

Life presents itself first and foremost as a task: the task of maintaining itself, *de gagner sa vie*. If this task is accomplished, what has been gained is a burden, and there then appears a second task: that of doing something with it so as to ward off boredom, which hovers over every secure life like a bird of prey. Thus the first task is to gain something and the second to become unconscious of what has been gained, which is otherwise a burden.

That human life must be some kind of mistake is sufficiently proved by the simple observation that man is a compound of needs which are hard to satisfy; that their satisfaction achieves nothing but a painless condition in which he is only given over to boredom; and that boredom is a direct proof that existence is in itself valueless, for boredom is nothing other than the sensation of the emptiness of existence. For if life, in the desire for which our essence and existence consists, possessed in itself a positive value and real content, there would be no such thing as boredom: mere existence would fulfil and satisfy us. As things are, we take no pleasure in existence except when we are striving after something – in which case distance and difficulties make our goal look as if it would satisfy us (an illusion which fades when we reach it) – or when engaged in purely intellectual activity, in which case we are really stepping out of life so as to regard it from outside, like spectators at a play. Even sensual pleasure itself consists in a continual striving and ceases as soon as its goal is reached. Whenever we are not involved in one or other of these things but directed back to existence itself we are overtaken by its worthlessness and vanity and this is the sensation called boredom.

6

That the most perfect manifestation of the will to live represented by the human organism, with its incomparably ingenious and complicated machinery, must crumble to dust and its whole essence and all its striving be palpably given over at last to annihilation – this is nature's unambiguous declaration that all the striving of this will is essentially vain. If it were something possessing value in itself, something which ought unconditionally to exist, it would not have non-being as its goal.

Yet what a difference there is between our beginning and our end! We begin in the madness of carnal desire and the transport of voluptuousness, we end in the dissolution of all our parts and the musty stench of corpses. And the road from the one to the other too goes, in regard to our well-being and enjoyment of life, steadily downhill: happily dreaming childhood, exultant youth, toil-filled years of manhood, infirm and often wretched old age, the torment of the last illness and finally the throes of death – does it not look as if existence were an error the consequences of which gradually grow more and more manifest?

We shall do best to think of life as a *desengaño*, as a process of disillusionment: since this is, clearly enough, what everything that happens to us is calculated to produce.

31   An Absurd Reasoning*

Albert Camus

Absurdity and Suicide

There is but one truly serious philosophical problem, and that is suicide. Judging whether life is or is not worth living amounts to answering the fundamental question of philosophy. All the rest – whether or not the world has three dimensions, whether the mind has nine or twelve categories – comes afterwards. These are games; one must first answer. And if it is true, as Nietzsche claims, that a philosopher, to deserve our respect, must preach by example, you can appreciate the importance of that reply, for it will precede the definitive act. These are facts the heart can feel; yet they call for careful study before they become clear to the intellect.

If I ask myself how to judge that this question is more urgent than that, I reply that one judges by the actions it entails. I have never seen anyone die for the ontological argument. Galileo, who held a scientific truth of great importance, abjured it with the greatest ease as soon as it endangered his life. In a certain sense, he did right.[1] That truth was not worth the stake. Whether the earth or the sun revolves around the other is a matter of profound indifference. To tell the truth, it is a futile question. On the other hand, I see many people die because they judge that life is not worth living. I see others paradoxically getting killed for the ideas or illusions that give them a reason for living (what is called a reason for living is also an excellent reason for dying). I therefore conclude that the meaning of life is the most urgent of questions. How to answer it? On all essential problems (I mean thereby those that run the risk of leading to death or those that intensify the passion of living) there are probably but two methods of thought: the method of La Palisse and the method of Don Quixote. Solely the balance between evidence and lyricism can allow us to achieve simultaneously emotion and lucidity. In a subject at once so humble and so heavy with emotion, the learned and classical dialectic must yield, one

* From Albert Camus, *The Myth of Sisyphus and Other Essays*, translated by Justin O'Brien (New York: Alfred A. Knopf, 1955), pp. 3–9, 12–16, 21, 28–30, and 51–5. © 1955 by Alfred A. Knopf, a division of Random House Inc. Used by permission.

can see, to a more modest attitude of mind deriving at one and the same time from common sense and understanding.

Suicide has never been dealt with except as a social phenomenon. On the contrary, we are concerned here, at the outset, with the relationship between individual thought and suicide. An act like this is prepared within the silence of the heart, as is a great work of art. The man himself is ignorant of it. One evening he pulls the trigger or jumps. Of an apartment-building manager who had killed himself I was told that he had lost his daughter five years before, that he had changed greatly since, and that that experience had "undermined" him. A more exact word cannot be imagined. Beginning to think is beginning to be undermined. Society has but little connection with such beginnings. The worm is in man's heart. That is where it must be sought. One must follow and understand this fatal game that leads from lucidity in the face of existence to flight from light.

There are many causes for a suicide, and generally the most obvious ones were not the most powerful. Rarely is suicide committed (yet the hypothesis is not excluded) through reflection. What sets off the crisis is almost always unverifiable. Newspapers often speak of "personal sorrows" or of "incurable illness." These explanations are plausible. But one would have to know whether a friend of the desperate man had not that very day addressed him indifferently. He is the guilty one. For that is enough to precipitate all the rancors and all the boredom still in suspension.[2]

But if it is hard to fix the precise instant, the subtle step when the mind opted for death, it is easier to deduce from the act itself the consequences it implies. In a sense, and as in melodrama, killing yourself amounts to confessing. It is confessing that life is too much for you or that you do not understand it. Let's not go too far in such analogies, however, but rather return to everyday words. It is merely confessing that that "is not worth the trouble." Living, naturally, is never easy. You continue making the gestures commanded by existence for many reasons, the first of which is habit. Dying voluntarily implies that you have recognized, even instinctively, the ridiculous character of that habit, the absence of any profound reason for living, the insane character of that daily agitation, and the uselessness of suffering.

What, then, is that incalculable feeling that deprives the mind of the sleep necessary to life? A world that can be explained even with bad reasons is a familiar world. But, on the other hand, in a universe suddenly divested of illusions and lights, man feels an alien, a stranger. His exile is without remedy since he is deprived of the memory of a lost home or the hope of a promised land. This divorce between man and his life, the actor and his setting, is properly the feeling of absurdity. All healthy men having thought of their own suicide, it can be seen, without further explanation, that there is a direct connection between this feeling and the longing for death.

The subject of this essay is precisely this relationship between the absurd and suicide, the exact degree to which suicide is a solution to the absurd. The principle can be established that for a man who does not cheat, what he believes to be true must determine his action. Belief in the absurdity of existence must then dictate his conduct. It is legitimate to wonder, clearly and without false pathos, whether a conclusion of this importance requires forsaking as rapidly as possible an incomprehensible condition. I am speaking, of course, of men inclined to be in harmony with themselves.

Stated clearly, this problem may seem both simple and insoluble. But it is wrongly assumed that simple questions involve answers that are no less simple and that evidence implies evidence. *A priori* and reversing the terms of the problem, just as one does or does not kill oneself, it seems that there are but two philosophical solutions, either yes or no. This would be too easy. But allowance must be made for those who, without concluding, continue questioning. Here I am only slightly indulging in irony: this is the majority. I notice also that those who answer "no" act as if they thought "yes." As a matter of fact, if I accept the Nietzschean criterion, they think "yes" in one way or another. On the other hand, it often happens that those who commit suicide were assured of the meaning of life. These contradictions are constant. It may even be said that they have never been so keen as on this point where, on the contrary, logic seems so desirable. It is a commonplace to compare philosophical theories and the behavior of those who profess them. But it must be said that of the thinkers who refused a meaning to life none except Kirilov who belongs to literature, Peregrinos who is born of legend,[3] and Jules Lequier who belongs to hypothesis, admitted his logic to the point of refusing that life. Schopenhauer is often cited, as a fit subject for laughter, because he praised suicide while seated at a well-set table. This is no subject for joking. That way of not taking the tragic seriously is not so grievous, but it helps to judge a man.

In the face of such contradictions and obscurities must we conclude that there is no relationship between the opinion one has about life and the act one commits to leave it? Let us not exaggerate in this direction. In a man's attachment to life there is something stronger than all the ills in the world. The body's judgment is as good as the mind's, and the body shrinks from annihilation. We get into the habit of living before acquiring the habit of thinking. In that race which daily hastens us toward death, the body maintains its irreparable lead. In short, the essence of that contradiction lies in what I shall call the act of eluding because it is both less and more than diversion in the Pascalian sense. Eluding is the invariable game. The typical act of eluding, the fatal evasion that constitutes the third theme of this essay, is hope. Hope of another life one must "deserve" or trickery of those who live not for life itself but for some great idea that will transcend it, refine it, give it a meaning, and betray it.

Thus everything contributes to spreading confusion. Hitherto, and it has not been wasted effort, people have played on words and pretended to believe that refusing to grant a meaning to life necessarily leads to declaring that it is not worth living. In truth, there is no necessary common measure between these two judgments. One merely has to refuse to be misled by the confusions, divorces, and inconsistencies previously pointed out. One must brush everything aside and go straight to the real problem. One kills oneself because life is not worth living, that is certainly a truth – yet an unfruitful one because it is a truism. But does that insult to existence, that flat denial in which it is plunged come from the fact that it has no meaning? Does its absurdity require one to escape it through hope or suicide – this is what must be clarified, hunted down, and elucidated while brushing aside all the rest. Does the Absurd dictate death? This problem must be given priority over others, outside all methods of thought and all exercises of the disinterested mind. Shades of meaning, contradictions, the psychology that an "objective" mind can always introduce into all problems have no place in this pursuit and this passion. It calls simply for an unjust – in other words, logical – thought. That is not easy. It is always easy to be logical. It is almost impossible to be logical to the bitter end. Men who die by their own hand consequently follow to its conclusion their emotional inclination. Reflection on suicide gives me an opportunity to raise the only problem to interest me: is there a logic to the point of death? I cannot know unless I pursue, without reckless passions in the sole light of evidence, the reasoning of which I am here suggesting the source. This is what I call an absurd reasoning. Many have begun it. I do not yet know whether or not they kept to it . . .

*   *   *

All great deeds and all great thoughts have a ridiculous beginning. Great works are often born on a street-corner or in a restaurant's revolving door. So it is with absurdity. The absurd world more than others derives its nobility from that abject birth. In certain situations, replying "nothing" when asked what one is thinking about may be pretense in a man. Those who are loved are well aware of this. But if that reply is sincere, if it symbolizes that odd state of soul in which the void becomes eloquent, in which the chain of daily gestures is broken, in which the heart vainly seeks the link that will connect it again, then it is as it were the first sign of absurdity.

It happens that the stage sets collapse. Rising, street-car, four hours in the office or the factory, meal, street-car, four hours of work, meal, sleep, and Monday Tuesday Wednesday Thursday Friday and Saturday according to the same rhythm – this path is easily followed most of the time. But one day the "why" arises and everything begins in that weariness tinged with amazement. "Begins" – this is important. Weariness comes at the end of the acts of a mechanical life, but at the same time it inaugurates the impulse of consciousness. It awakens consciousness and provokes what follows. What follows is the gradual return into the chain or it is the definitive awakening. At the end of the awakening comes, in time, the consequence: suicide or recovery. In itself weariness has something sickening about it. Here, I must conclude that it is good. For everything begins with consciousness and nothing is worth anything except through it. There is nothing original about these remarks. But they are obvious; that is enough for a while, during a sketchy reconnaissance in the origins of the absurd. Mere "anxiety," as Heidegger says, is at the source of everything.

Likewise and during every day of an unillustrious life, time carries us. But a moment always comes when we have to carry it. We live on the future: "tomorrow," "later on," "when you have made your way," "you will understand when you are old enough." Such irrelevancies are wonderful, for, after all, it's a matter of dying. Yet a day comes when a man notices or says that he is thirty. Thus he asserts his youth. But simultaneously he situates himself in relation to time. He takes his place in it. He admits that he stands at a certain point on a curve that he acknowledges having to travel to its end. He belongs to time, and by the horror that seizes him, he recognizes his worst enemy. Tomorrow, he was longing for tomorrow, whereas everything in him ought to reject it. That revolt of the flesh is the absurd.[4]

A step lower and strangeness creeps in: perceiving that the world is "dense," sensing to what a degree a stone is foreign and irreducible to us, with what intensity nature or a landscape can negate us. At the heart of all beauty lies something inhuman, and these hills, the softness of the sky, the outline of these trees at this very minute lose the illusory meaning with which we had clothed them, henceforth more remote than a lost paradise. The primitive hostility of the world rises up to face us across millennia. For a second we cease to understand it because for centuries we have understood in it solely the images and designs that we had attributed to it beforehand, because henceforth we lack the power to make use of that artifice. The world evades us because it becomes itself again. That stage scenery masked by habit becomes again what it is. It withdraws at a distance from us. Just as there are days when under the familiar face of a woman, we see as a stranger her we had loved months or years ago, perhaps we shall come even to desire what suddenly leaves us so alone. But the time has not yet come. Just one thing: that denseness and that strangeness of the world is the absurd.

Men, too, secrete the inhuman. At certain moments of lucidity, the mechanical aspect of their gestures, their meaningless pantomime makes silly everything that surrounds them. A man is talking on the telephone behind a glass partition; you cannot hear him, but you see his incomprehensible dumb show: you wonder why he is alive. This discomfort in the face of man's own inhumanity, this incalculable tumble before the image of what we are, this "nausea," as a writer of today calls it, is also the absurd. Likewise the stranger who at certain seconds comes to meet us in a mirror, the familiar and yet alarming brother we encounter in our own photographs is also the absurd.

I come at last to death and to the attitude we have toward it. On this point everything has been said and it is only proper to avoid pathos. Yet one will never be sufficiently surprised that everyone lives as if no one "knew." This is because in reality there is no experience of death. Properly speaking, nothing has been experienced but what has been lived and made conscious. Here, it is barely possible to speak of the experience of others' deaths. It is a substitute, an illusion, and it never quite convinces us. That melancholy convention cannot be persuasive. The horror comes in reality from the mathematical aspect of the event. If time frightens us, this is because it works out the problem and the solution comes afterward. All the pretty speeches about the soul will have their contrary convincingly proved, at least for a time. From this inert body on which a slap makes no mark the soul has disappeared. This elementary and definitive aspect of the adventure constitutes the absurd feeling. Under the fatal lighting of that destiny, its uselessness becomes evident. No code of ethics and no effort are justifiable *a priori* in the face of the cruel mathematics that command our condition.

Let me repeat: all this has been said over and over. I am limiting myself here to making a rapid classification and to pointing out these obvious themes. They run through all literatures and all philosophies. Everyday conversation feeds on them. There is no question of reinventing them. But it is essential to be sure of these facts in order to be able to question oneself subsequently on the primordial question. I am interested – let me repeat again – not so much in absurd discoveries as in their consequences. If one is assured of these facts, what is one to conclude, how far is one to go to elude nothing? Is one to die voluntarily or to hope in spite of everything? Beforehand, it is necessary to take the same rapid inventory on the plane of the intelligence. . .

. . . I said that the world is absurd, but I was too hasty. This world in itself is not reasonable, that is all that can be said. But what is absurd is the confrontation of this irrational and the wild longing for clarity whose call echoes in the human heart. The absurd depends as much on man as on the world. For the moment it is all that links them together. It binds them one to the other as only hatred can weld two creatures together. This is all I can discern clearly in this measureless universe where my adventure takes place. . . .

Philosophical Suicide

The feeling of the absurd is not, for all that, the notion of the absurd. It lays the foundations for it, and that is all. It is not limited to that notion, except in the brief moment when it passes judgment on the universe. Subsequently it has a chance of going further. It is alive; in other words, it must die or else reverberate. So it is with the themes we have gathered together. But there again what interests me is not works or minds, criticism of which would call for another from and another place, but the discovery of what their conclusions have in common. Never, perhaps, have minds been so different. And yet we recognize as identical the spiritual landscapes in which they get under way. Likewise, despite such dissimilar zones of knowledge, the cry that terminates their itinerary rings out in the same way. It is evident that the thinkers we have just recalled have a common climate. To say that that climate is deadly scarcely amounts to playing on words. Living under that stifling sky forces one to get away or to stay. The important thing is to find out how people get away in the first case and why people stay in the second case. This is how I define the problem of suicide and the possible interest in the conclusions of existential philosophy.

But first I want to detour from the direct path. Up to now we have managed to circumscribe the absurd from the outside. One can, however, wonder how much is clear in that notion and by direct analysis try to discover its meaning on the one hand and, on the other, the consequences it involves.

If I accuse an innocent man of a monstrous crime, if I tell a virtuous man that he has coveted his own sister, he will reply that this is absurd. His indignation has its comical aspect. But it also has its fundamental reason. The virtuous man illustrates by that reply the definitive antinomy existing between the deed I am attributing to him and his life-long principles. "It's absurd" means "It's impossible" but also "It's contradictory." If I see a man armed only with a sword attack a group of machine guns, I shall consider his act to be absurd. But it is so solely by virtue of the disproportion between his intention and the reality he will encounter, of the contradiction I notice between his true strength and the aim he has in view. Likewise we shall deem a verdict absurd when we contrast it with the verdict the facts apparently dictated. And, similarly, a demonstration by the absurd is achieved by comparing the consequences of such a reasoning with the logical reality one wants to set up. In all these cases, from the simplest to the most complex, the magnitude of the absurdity will be in direct ratio to the distance between the two terms of my comparison. There are absurd marriages, challenges, rancors, silences, wars, and even peace treaties. For each of them the absurdity springs from a comparison. I am thus justified in saying that the feeling of absurdity does not spring from the mere scrutiny of a fact or an impression, but that it bursts from the comparison between a bare fact and a certain reality, between an action and the world that transcends it. The absurd is essentially a divorce. It lies in neither of the elements compared; it is born of their confrontation. . . .

Absurd Freedom

Now the main thing is done, I hold certain facts from which I cannot separate. What I know, what is certain, what I cannot deny, what I cannot reject – this is what counts. I can negate everything of that part of me that lives on vague nostalgias, except this desire for unity, this longing to solve, this need for clarity and cohesion. I can refute everything in this world surrounding me that offends or enraptures me, except this chaos, this sovereign chance and this divine equivalence which springs from anarchy. I don't know whether this world has a meaning that transcends it. But I know that I do not know that meaning and that it is impossible for me just now to know it. What can a meaning outside my condition mean to me? I can understand only in human terms. What I touch, what resists me – that is what I understand. And these two certainties – my appetite for the absolute and for unity and the impossibility of reducing this world to rational and reasonable principle – I also know that I cannot reconcile them. What other truth can I admit without lying, without bringing in a hope I lack and which means nothing within the limits of my condition?

If I were a tree among trees, a cat among animals, this life would have a meaning, or rather this problem would not arise, for I should belong to this world. I should *be* this world to which I am now opposed by my whole consciousness and my whole insistence upon familiarity. This ridiculous reason is what sets me in opposition to all creation. I cannot cross it out with a stroke of the pen. What I believe to be true I must therefore preserve. What seems to me so obvious, even against me, I must support. And what constitutes the basis of that conflict, of that break between the world and my mind, but the awareness of it? If therefore I want to preserve it, I can through a constant awareness, ever revived, ever alert. This is what, for the moment, I must remember. At this moment the absurd, so obvious and yet so hard to win, returns to a man's life and finds its home there. At this moment, too, the mind can leave the arid, dried-up path of lucid effort. That path now emerges in daily life. It encounters the world of the anonymous impersonal pronoun "one," but henceforth man enters in with his revolt and his lucidity. He has forgotten how to hope. This hell of the present is his Kingdom at last. All problems recover their sharp edge. Abstract evidence retreats before the poetry of forms and colors. Spiritual conflicts become embodied and return to the abject and magnificent shelter of man's heart. None of them is settled. But all are transfigured. Is one going to die, escape by the leap, rebuild a mansion of ideas and forms to one's own scale? Is one, on the contrary, going to take up the heart-rending and marvelous wager of the absurd? Let's make a final effort in this regard and draw all our conclusions. The body, affection, creation, action, human nobility will then resume their places in this mad world. At last man will again find there the wine of the absurd and the bread of indifference on which he feeds his greatness.

Let us insist again on the method: it is a matter of persisting. At a certain point on his path the absurd man is tempted. History is not lacking in either religions or prophets, even without gods. He is asked to leap. All he can reply is that he doesn't fully understand, that it is not obvious. Indeed, he does not want to do anything but what he fully understands. He is assured that this is the sin of pride, but he does not understand the notion of sin; that perhaps hell is in store, but he has not enough imagination to visualize that strange future; that he is losing immortal life, but that seems to him an idle consideration. An attempt is made to get him to admit his guilt. He feels innocent. To tell the truth, that is all he feels – his irreparable innocence. This is what allows him everything. Hence, what he demands of himself is to live *solely* with what he knows, to accommodate himself to what is, and to bring in nothing that is not certain. He is told that nothing is. But this at least is a certainty. And it is with this that he is concerned: he wants to find out if it is possible to live *without appeal*.

* * *

Now I can broach the notion of suicide. It has already been felt what solution might be given. At this point the problem is reversed. It was previously a question of finding out whether or not life had to have a meaning to be lived. It now becomes clear, on the contrary, that it will be lived all the better if it has no meaning. Living an experience, a particular fate, is accepting it fully. Now, no one will live this fate, knowing it to be absurd, unless he does everything to keep before him that absurd brought to light by consciousness. Negating one of the terms of the opposition on which he lives amounts to escaping it. To abolish conscious revolt is to elude the problem. The theme of permanent revolution is thus carried into individual experience. Living is keeping the absurd alive. Keeping it alive is, above all, contemplating it. Unlike Eurydice, the absurd dies only when we turn away from it. One of the only coherent philosophical positions is thus revolt. It is a constant confrontation between man and his own obscurity. It is an insistence upon an impossible transparency. It challenges the world anew every second. Just as danger provided man the unique opportunity of seizing awareness, so metaphysical revolt extends awareness to the whole of experience. It is that constant presence of man in his own eyes. It is not aspiration, for it is devoid of hope. That revolt is the certainty of a crushing fate, without the resignation that ought to accompany it.

This is where it is seen to what a degree absurd experience is remote from suicide. It may be thought that suicide follows revolt – but wrongly. For it does not represent the logical outcome of revolt. It is just the contrary by the consent it presupposes. Suicide, like the leap, is acceptance at its extreme. Everything is over and man returns to his essential history. His future, his unique and dreadful future – he sees and rushes toward it. In its way, suicide settles the absurd. It engulfs the absurd in the same death. But I know that in order to keep alive, the absurd cannot be settled. It escapes suicide to the extent that it is simultaneously awareness and rejection of death. It is, at the extreme limit of the condemned man's last thought, that shoelace that despite everything he sees a few yards away, on the very brink of his dizzying fall. The contrary of suicide, in fact, is the man condemned to death.

That revolt gives life its value. Spread out over the whole length of a life, it restores its majesty to that life. To a man devoid of blinders, there is no finer sight than that of the intelligence at grips with a reality that transcends it. The sight of human pride is unequaled. No disparagement is of any use. That discipline that the mind imposes on itself, that will conjured up out of nothing, that face-to-face struggle have something exceptional about them. To impoverish that reality whose inhumanity constitutes man's majesty is tantamount to impoverishing him himself. I understand then why the doctrines that explain everything to me also debilitate me at the same time. They relieve me of the weight of my own life, and yet I must carry it alone. At this juncture, I cannot conceive that a skeptical metaphysics can be joined to an ethics of renunciation.

Consciousness and revolt, these rejections are the contrary of renunciation. Everything that is indomitable and passionate in a human heart quickens them, on the contrary, with its own life. It is essential to die unreconciled and not of one's own free will. Suicide is a repudiation. The absurd man can only drain everything to the bitter end, and deplete himself. The absurd is his extreme tension, which he maintains constantly by solitary effort, for he knows that in that consciousness and in that day-to-day revolt he gives proof of his only truth, which is defiance. This is a first consequence.

Notes

1 From the point of view of the relative value of truth. On the other hand, from the point of view of virile behavior, this scholar's fragility may well make us smile.

2 Let us not miss this opportunity to point out the relative character of this essay. Suicide may indeed be related to much more honorable considerations – for example, the political suicides of protest, as they were called, during the Chinese revolution.

3 I have heard of an emulator of Peregrinos, a post-war writer who, after having finished his first book, committed suicide to attract attention to his work. Attention was in fact attracted, but the book was judged no good.

4 But not in the proper sense. This is not a definition, but rather an *enumeration* of the feelings that may admit of the absurd. Still, the enumeration finished, the absurd has nevertheless not been exhausted.

---

32 Existentialism Is a Humanism*

Jean-Paul Sartre

I should like on this occasion to defend existentialism against some charges which have been brought against it.

First, it has been charged with inviting people to remain in a kind of desperate quietism because, since no solutions are possible, we should have to consider action in this world as quite impossible. We should then end up in a philosophy of contemplation; and since contemplation is a luxury, we come in the end to a bourgeois philosophy. The Communists in particular have made these charges.

On the other hand, we have been charged with dwelling on human degradation, with pointing up everywhere the sordid, shady, and slimy, and neglecting the gracious and beautiful, the bright side of human nature; for example, according to Mlle. Mercier, a Catholic critic, with forgetting the smile of the child. Both sides charge us with having ignored human solidarity, with considering man as an isolated being. The Communists say that the main reason for this is that we take pure subjectivity, the Cartesian *I think*, as our starting point; in other words, the moment in which man becomes fully aware of what it means to him to be an isolated being; as a result, we are unable to return to a state of solidarity with the men who are not ourselves, a state which we can never reach in the *cogito*.

From the Christian standpoint, we are charged with denying the reality and seriousness of human undertakings, since, if we reject God's commandments and the eternal verities, there no longer remains anything but pure caprice, with everyone permitted to do as he pleases and incapable, from his own point of view, of condemning the points of view and acts of others.

I shall try today to answer these different charges. Many people are going to be surprised at what is said here about humanism. We shall try to see in what sense it is to be understood. In any case, what can be said from the very beginning is that by Existentialism we mean a doctrine which makes human life possible and, in addition, declares that every truth and every action implies a human setting and a human subjectivity.

* From Jean-Paul Sartre, *Existentialism*, trans. Bernard Frechtman (New York: Philosophical Library, 1947), pp. 11–38 and 59–61. © 1947 by The Philosophical Library Inc.

As is generally known, the basic charge against us is that we put the emphasis on the dark side of human life. Someone recently told me of a lady who, when she let slip a vulgar word in a moment of irritation, excused herself by saying, "I guess I'm becoming an Existentialist." Consequently, Existentialism is regarded as something ugly; that is why we are said to be naturalists; and if we are, it is rather surprising that in this day and age we cause so much more alarm and scandal than does naturalism, properly so called. The kind of person who can take in his stride such a novel as Zola's *The Earth* is disgusted as soon as he starts reading an Existentialist novel; the kind of person who is resigned to the wisdom of the ages – which is pretty sad – finds us even sadder. Yet, what can be more disillusioning than saying "true charity begins at home" or "a scoundrel will always return evil for good"?

We know the commonplace remarks made when this subject comes up, remarks which always add up to the same thing: we shouldn't struggle against the powers that be; we shouldn't resist authority; we shouldn't try to rise above our station; any station which doesn't conform to authority is romantic; any effort not based on past experience is doomed to failure; experience shows that man's bent is always toward trouble, that there must be a strong hand to hold him in check, if not, there will be anarchy. There are still people who go on mumbling these melancholy old saws, the people who say, "It's only human!" whenever a more or less repugnant act is pointed out to them, the people who glut themselves on *chansons réalistes* [satirical songs about contemporary persons or events]; these are the people who accuse Existentialism of being too gloomy, and to such an extent that I wonder whether they are complaining about it, not for its pessimism, but much rather its optimism. Can it be that what really scares them in the doctrine I shall try to present here is that it leaves to man a possibility of choice? To answer this question, we must reexamine it on a strictly philosophical plane. What is meant by the term *Existentialism*?

Most people who use the word would be rather embarrassed if they had to explain it, since, now that the word is all the rage, even the work of a musician or painter is being called "existentialist." A gossip columnist in *Clartés* signs himself *The Existentialist*, so that by this time the word has been so stretched and has taken on so broad a meaning, that it no longer means anything at all. It seems that for want of an advance-guard doctrine analogous to surrealism, the kind of people who are eager for scandal and flurry turn to this philosophy, which in other respects does not at all serve their purposes in this sphere.

Actually, it is the least scandalous, the most austere of doctrines. It is intended strictly for specialists and philosophers. Yet it can be defined easily. What complicates matters is that there are two kinds of Existentialist; first, those who are Christian, among whom I would include Jaspers and Gabriel Marcel, both Catholic; and on the other hand the atheistic Existentialists, among whom I class Heidegger, and then the French Existentialists and myself. What they have in common is that they think that existence precedes essence, or, if you prefer, that subjectivity must be the starting point.

Just what does that mean? Let us consider some object that is manufactured, for example, a book or a paper cutter; here is an object which has been made by an artisan whose inspiration came from a concept. He referred to the concept of what a paper cutter is and likewise to a known method of production, which is part of the concept, something which is, by and large, a routine. Thus, the paper cutter is at once an object produced in a certain way and, on the other hand, one having a specific use; and one cannot postulate a man who produces a paper cutter but does not know what it is used for. Therefore, let us say that, for the paper cutter, essence – that is, the ensemble of both the production routines and the properties which enable it to be both produced and defined – precedes existence. Thus, the presence of the paper cutter or book in front of me is determined. Therefore, we have here a technical view of the world whereby it can be said that production precedes existence.

When we conceive God as the Creator, he is generally thought of as a superior sort of artisan. Whatever doctrine we may be considering, whether one like that of Descartes or that of Leibnitz, we always grant that will more or less follows understanding or, at the very least, accompanies it, and that when God creates He knows exactly what He is creating. Thus, the concept of man in the mind of God is comparable to the concept of paper cutter in the mind of the manufacturer, and, following certain techniques and a conception, God produces man, just as the artisan, following a definition and a technique, makes a paper cutter. Thus, the individual man is the realization of a certain concept in the divine intelligence.

In the eighteenth century, the atheism of the *philosophes* discarded the idea of God, but not so much for the notion that essence precedes existence. To a certain extent, this idea is found everywhere; we find it in Diderot, in Voltaire, and even in Kant. Man has a human nature; this human nature, which is the concept of the human, is founded in all men, which means that each man is a particular example of a universal concept, man. In Kant, the result of this universality is that the wild man, the natural man, as well as the bourgeois, are circumscribed by the same definition and have the same basic qualities. Thus, here too the essence of man precedes the historical existence that we find in nature.

Atheistic Existentialism, which I represent, is more coherent. It states that if God does not exist, there is at least one being in whom existence precedes essence, a being who exists before he can be defined by any concept, and that this being is man, or, as Heidegger says, human reality. What is meant here by saying that existence precedes essence? It means that, first of all, man exists, turns up, appears on the scene, and only afterwards, defines himself. If man, as the Existentialist conceives him, is indefinable, it is because at first he is nothing. Only afterward will he be something, and he himself will have made what he will be. Thus, there is no human nature, since there is no God to conceive it. Not only is man what he conceives himself to be, but he is also only what he wills himself to be after this thrust toward existence.

Man is nothing else but what he makes of himself. Such is the first principle of Existentialism. It is also what is called "subjectivity," the name we are labeled with when charges are brought against us. But what do we mean by this, if not that man has a greater dignity than a stone or table? For we mean that man first exists, that is, that man first of all is the being who hurls himself toward a future and who is conscious of imagining himself as being in the future. Man is at the start a plan which is aware of itself, rather than a patch of moss, a piece of garbage, or a cauliflower; nothing exists prior to this plan; there is nothing in heaven; man will be what he will have planned to be. Not what he will want to be. Because by the word "will" we generally mean a conscious decision, which is subsequent to what we have already made of ourselves. I may want to belong to a political party, write a book, get married; but all this is only a manifestation of an earlier, more spontaneous choice that is called "will." But if existence really does precede essence, man is responsible for what he is. Thus, Existentialism's first move is to make every man aware of what he is and to make the full responsibility of his existence rest on him. And when we say that a man is responsible for himself, we do not only mean that he is responsible for his own individuality, but that he is responsible for all men.

The word "subjectivism" has two meanings, and our opponents play on the two. Subjectivism means, on the one hand, that an individual chooses and makes himself; and, on the other, that it is impossible for man to transcend human subjectivity. The second of these is the essential meaning of Existentialism. When we say that man chooses his own self, we mean that every one of us does likewise; but we also mean by that that in making this choice he also chooses all men. In fact, in creating the man that we want to be, there is not a single one of our acts which does not at the same time create an image of man as we think he ought to be. To choose to be this or that is to affirm at the same time the value of what we choose, because we can never choose evil. We always choose the good, and nothing can be good for us without being good for all.

If, on the other hand, existence precedes essence, and if we grant that we exist and fashion our image at one and the same time, the image is valid for everybody and for our whole age. Thus, our responsibility is much greater than we might have supposed, because it involves all mankind. If I am a working man and choose to join a Christian trade union rather than be a Communist, and if by being a member I want to show that the best thing for man is resignation, that the kingdom of man is not of this world, I am not only involving my own case – I want to be resigned for everyone. As a result, my action has involved all humanity. To take a more individual matter, if I want to marry, to have children, even if this marriage depends solely on my own circumstances or passion or wish, I am involving all humanity in monogamy and not merely myself. Therefore, I am responsible for myself and for everyone else. I am creating a certain image of man of my own choosing. In choosing myself, I choose man.

This helps us understand what the actual content is of such rather grandiloquent words as anguish, forlornness, despair. As you will see, it's all quite simple.

First, what is meant by "anguish"? The Existentialists say at once that man is anguish. What that means is this: the man who involves himself and who realizes that he is not only the person he chooses to be, but also a lawmaker who is, at the same time, choosing all mankind as well as himself, cannot escape the feeling of his total and deep responsibility. Of course, there are many people who are not anxious; but we claim that they are hiding their anxiety, that they are fleeing from it. Certainly, many people believe that when they do something, they themselves are the only ones involved, and when someone says to them, "What if everyone acted that way?" they shrug their shoulders and answer, "Everyone doesn't act that way." But really, one should always ask himself, "What would happen if everybody looked at things that way?" There is no escaping this disturbing thought except by a kind of double-dealing. A man who lies and makes excuses for himself by saying "not everybody does that," is someone with an uneasy conscience, because the act of lying implies that a universal value is conferred upon the lie.

Anguish is evident even when it conceals itself. This is the anguish that Kierkegaard called the "anguish of Abraham." You know the story: an angel has ordered Abraham to sacrifice his son; if it really were an angel who has come and said, "You are Abraham, you shall sacrifice your son," everything would be all right. But everyone might first wonder, "Is it really an angel, and am I really Abraham? What proof do I have?"

There was a madwoman who had hallucinations; someone used to speak to her on the telephone and give her orders. Her doctor asked her, "Who is it who talks to you?" She answered, "He says it's God." What proof did she really have that it was God? If an angel comes to me, what proof is there that it's an angel; and if I hear voices, what proof is there that they come from heaven and not from hell, or from the subconscious, or a pathological condition? What proves that they are addressed to me? What proof is there that I have been appointed to impose my choice and my conception of man on humanity? I'll never find any proof or sign to convince me of that. If a voice addresses me, it is always for me to decide that this is the angel's voice; if I consider that such an act is a good one, it is I who will choose to say that it is good rather than bad.

Now, I'm not being singled out as an Abraham, and yet at every moment I'm obliged to perform exemplary acts. For every man, everything happens as if all mankind had its eyes fixed on him and were guiding itself by what he does. And every man ought to say to himself, "Am I really the kind of man who has the right to act in such a way that humanity might guide itself by my actions?" And if he does not say that to himself, he is masking his anguish.

There is no question here of the kind of anguish which would lead to quietism, to inaction. It is a matter of a simple sort of anguish that anybody who has had responsibilities is familiar with. For example, when a military officer takes the responsibility for an attack and sends a certain number of men to death, he chooses to do so, and in the main he alone makes the choice. Doubtless, orders come from above, but they are too broad; he interprets them, and on this interpretation depend the lives of ten or fourteen or twenty men. In making a decision he cannot help having a certain anguish. All leaders know this anguish. That doesn't keep them from acting; on the contrary, it is the very condition of their action. For it implies that they envisage a number of possibilities, and when they choose one, they realize that it has value only because it is chosen. We shall see that this kind of anguish, which is the kind that Existentialism describes, is explained, in addition, by a direct responsibility to the other men whom it involves. It is not a curtain separating us from action, but is part of the action itself.

When we speak of "forlornness," a term Heidegger was fond of, we mean only that God does not exist and that we have to face all the consequences of this. The Existentialist is strongly opposed to a certain kind of secular ethics which would like to abolish God with the least possible expense. About 1880, some French teachers tried to set up a secular ethics which went something like this: God is a useless and costly hypothesis; we are discarding it; but, meanwhile, in order for there to be an ethics, a society, a civilization, it is essential that certain values be taken seriously and that they be considered as having an *a priori* existence. It must be obligatory, *a priori*, to be honest, not to lie, not to beat your wife, to have children, etc., etc. So we're going to try a little device which will make it possible to show that values exist all the time, inscribed in a heaven of ideas, though otherwise God does not exist. In other words – and this, I believe, is the tendency of everything called "reformism" in France – nothing will be changed if God does not exist. We shall find ourselves with the same norms of honesty, progress, and humanism, and we shall have made of God an outdated hypothesis which will peacefully die off by itself.

The Existentialist, on the contrary, thinks it very distressing that God does not exist, because all possibility of finding values in a heaven of ideas disappears along with Him; there can no longer be an *a priori* Good, since there is no infinite and perfect consciousness to think it. Nowhere is it written that the Good exists, that we must be honest, that we must not lie; because the fact is we are on a plane where there are only men. Dostoyevsky said, "If God didn't exist, everything would be possible." That is the very starting point of Existentialism. Indeed, everything is permissible if God does not exist, and as a result man is forlorn, because neither within him nor without does he find anything to cling to. He can't start making excuses for himself.

If existence really does precede essence, there is no explaining things away by reference to a fixed and given human nature. In other words, there is no determinism, man is free, man is freedom. On the other hand, if God does not exist, we find no values or commands to turn to which legitimize our conduct. So, in the bright realm of values, we have no excuse behind us, nor justification before us. We are alone, with no excuses.

That is the idea I shall try to convey when I say that man is condemned to be free. Condemned, because he did not create himself, yet, in other respects is free; because, once thrown into the world, he is responsible for everything he does. The Existentialist does not believe in the power of passion. He will never agree that a sweeping passion is a ravaging torrent which fatally leads a man to certain acts and is therefore an excuse. He thinks that man is responsible for his passion.

The Existentialist does not think that man is going to help himself by finding in the world some omen by which to orient himself. Because he thinks that man will interpret the omen to suit himself. Therefore, he thinks that man, with no support and no aid, is condemned every moment to invent man. Ponge, in a very fine article, has said, "Man is the future of man." That's exactly it. But if it is taken to mean that this future is recorded in heaven, that God sees it, then it is false, because it would really no longer be a future to be forged, a virgin future before him, then this remark is sound. But then we are forlorn.

To give you an example which will enable you to understand forlornness better, I shall cite the case of one of my students who came to see me under the following circumstances: his father was on bad terms with his mother, and, moreover, was inclined to be a collaborationist; his older brother had been killed in the German offensive of 1940, and the young man, with somewhat immature but generous feelings, wanted to avenge him. His mother lived alone with him, very much upset by the half-treason of her husband and the death of her older son; the boy was her only consolation.

The boy was faced with the choice of leaving for England and joining the Free French Forces – that is, leaving his mother behind – or remaining with his mother and helping her to carry on. He was fully aware that the woman lived only for him and that his going off – and perhaps his death – would plunge her into despair. He was also aware that every act that he did for his mother's sake was a sure thing, in the sense that it was helping her to carry on, whereas every effort he made toward going off and fighting was an uncertain move which might run aground and prove completely useless; for example, on his way to England he might, while passing through Spain, be detained indefinitely in a Spanish camp; he might reach England or Algiers and be stuck in an office at a desk job. As a result, he was faced with two very different kinds of action: one, concrete, immediate, but concerning only one individual; the other concerned an incomparably vaster group, a national collectivity, but for that very reason was dubious, and might be interrupted en route. And, at the same time, he was wavering between two kinds of ethics. On the one hand, an ethics of sympathy, of personal devotion; on the other, a broader ethics, but one whose efficacy was more dubious. He had to choose between the two.

Who could help him choose? Christian doctrine? No. Christian doctrine says, "Be charitable, love your neighbor, take the more rugged path, etc., etc." But which is the more rugged path? Whom should he love as a brother? The fighting man or his mother? Which does the greater good, the vague act of fighting in a group, or the concrete one of helping a particular human being to go on living? Who can decide *a priori*? Nobody. No book of ethics can tell him. The Kantian ethics says, "Never treat any person as a means, but as an end." Very well, if I stay with my mother, I'll treat her as an end and not as a means; but by virtue of this very fact, I'm running the risk of treating the people around me who are fighting, as means; and, conversely, if I go to join those who are fighting, I'll be treating them as an end, and, by doing that, I run the risk of treating my mother as a means.

If values are vague, and if they are always too broad for the concrete and specific case that we are considering, the only thing left for us is to trust our instincts. That's what this young man tried to do; and when I saw him, he said, "In the end, feeling is what counts. I ought to choose whichever pushes me in one direction. If I feel that I love my mother enough to sacrifice everything else for her – my desire for vengeance, for action, for adventure – then I'll stay with her. If, on the contrary, I feel that my love for my mother isn't enough, I'll leave."

But how is the value of a feeling determined? What gives his feeling for his mother value? Precisely the fact that he remained with her. I may say that I like so-and-so well enough to sacrifice a certain amount of money for him, but I may say so only if I've done it. I may say, "I love my mother well enough to remain with her" if I have remained with her. The only way to determine the value of this affection is, precisely, to perform an act which confirms and defines it. But, since I require this affection to justify my act, I find myself caught in a vicious circle.

On the other hand, Gide has well said that a mock feeling and a true feeling are almost indistinguishable; to decide that I love my mother and will remain with her, or to remain with her by putting on an act, amount somewhat to the same thing. In other words, the feeling is formed by the acts one performs; so, I cannot refer to it in order to act upon it. Which means that I can neither seek within myself the true condition which will impel me to act, nor apply to a system of ethics for concepts which will permit me to act. You will say, "At least, he did go to a teacher for advice." But if you seek advice from a priest, for example, you have chosen this priest; you already knew, more or less, just about what advice he was going to give you. In other words, choosing your adviser is involving yourself. The proof of this is that if you are a Christian, you will say, "Consult a priest." But some priests are collaborating, some are just marking time, some are resisting. Which to choose? If the young man chooses a priest who is resisting or collaborating, he has already decided on the kind of advice he's going to get. Therefore, in coming to see me he knew the answer I was going to give him, and I had only one answer to give: "You're free, choose, that is, invent." No general ethics can show you what is to be done; there are no omens in the world. The Catholics will reply, "But there are." Granted – but, in any case, I myself choose the meaning they have.

When I was a prisoner, I knew a rather remarkable young man who was a Jesuit. He had entered the Jesuit order in the following way: he had had a number of very bad breaks; in childhood, his father died, leaving him in poverty, and he was a scholarship student at a religious institution where he was constantly made to feel that he was being kept out of charity; then, he failed to get any of the honors and distinctions that children like; later on, at about eighteen, he bungled a love affair; finally, at twenty-two, he failed in military training, a childish enough matter, but it was the last straw.

This young fellow might well have felt that he had botched everything. It was a sign of something, but of what? He might have taken refuge in bitterness or despair. But he very wisely looked upon all this as a sign that he was not made for secular triumphs, and that only the triumphs of religion, holiness, and faith were open to him. He saw the hand of God in all this, and so he entered the order. Who can help seeing that he alone decided what the sign meant?

Some other interpretation might have been drawn from this series of setbacks; for example, that he might have done better to turn carpenter or revolutionist. Therefore, he is fully responsible for the interpretation. Forlornness implies that we ourselves choose our being. Forlornness and anguish go together.

As for "despair," the term has a very simple meaning. It means that we shall confine ourselves to reckoning only with what depends upon our will, or on the ensemble of probabilities which make our action possible. When we want something, we always have to reckon with probabilities. I may be counting on the arrival of a friend. The friend is coming by rail or streetcar; this supposes that the train will arrive on schedule, or that the streetcar will not jump the track. I am left in the realm of possibility; but possibilities are to be reckoned with only to the point where my action comports with the ensemble of these possibilities, and no further. The moment the possibilities I am considering are not rigorously involved by my action, I ought to disengage myself from them, because no God, no scheme, can adapt the world and its possibilities to my will. When Descartes said, "Conquer yourself rather than the world," he meant essentially the same thing.

The Marxists to whom I have spoken reply, "You can rely on the support of others in your action, which obviously has certain limits, because you're not going to live forever. That means: rely on both what others are doing elsewhere to help you, in China, in Russia, and what they will do later on, after your death, to carry on the action and lead it to its fulfillment, which will be the revolution. You even *have* to rely upon that, otherwise you're immoral." I reply at once that I will always rely on fellow fighters insofar as these comrades are involved with me in a common struggle, in the unity of a party or a group in which I can more or less make my weight felt; that is, one whose ranks I am in as a fighter and whose movements I am aware of at every moment. In such a situation, relying on the unity and will of the party is exactly like counting on the fact that the train will arrive on time or that the car won't jump the track. But, given that man is free and that there is no human nature for me to depend on, I cannot count on men whom I do not know by relying on human goodness or man's concern for the good of society. I don't know what will become of the Russian revolution; I may make an example of it to the extent that at the present time it is apparent that the proletariat plays a part in Russia that it plays in no other nation. But I can't swear that this will inevitably lead to a triumph of the proletariat. I've got to limit myself to what I see.

Given that men are free and that tomorrow they will freely decide what man will be, I cannot be sure that, after my death, fellow fighters will carry on my work to bring it to its maximum perfection. Tomorrow, after my death, some men may decide to set up fascism, and the others may be cowardly and muddled enough to let them do it. Fascism will then be the human reality, so much the worse for us.

Actually, things will be as man will have decided they are to be. Does that mean that I should abandon myself to quietism? No. First, I should involve myself; then, act on the old saw, "Nothing ventured, nothing gained." Nor does it mean that I shouldn't belong to a party, but rather that I shall have no illusions and shall do what I can. For example, suppose I ask myself, "Will socialism, as such, ever come about?" I know nothing about it. All I know is that I'm going to do everything in my power to bring it about. Beyond that, I can't count on anything. Quietism is the attitude of people who say, "Let others do what I can't do." The doctrine I am presenting is the very opposite of quietism, since it declares, "There is no reality except in action." Moreover, it goes further, since it adds, "Man is nothing else than his plan; he exists only to the extent that he fulfills himself; he is therefore nothing else than the ensemble of his acts, nothing else than his life." . . .

I've been reproached for asking whether Existentialism is humanistic. It's been said, "But you said in *Nausea* that the humanists were all wrong. You made fun of a certain kind of humanist. Why come back to it now?" Actually, the word "humanism" has two very different meanings. By "humanism" one can mean a theory which takes man as an end and as a higher value. Humanism in this sense can be found in Cocteau's tale *Around the World in Eighty Hours*, when a character, because he is flying over some mountains in an airplane, declares, "Man is simply amazing." That means that I, who did not build the airplanes, shall personally benefit from these particular inventions, and that I, as man, shall personally consider myself responsible for, and honored by, acts of a few particular men. This would imply that we ascribe a value to man on the basis of the highest deeds of certain men. This humanism is absurd, because only the dog or the horse would be able to make such an overall judgment about man, which they are careful not to do, at least to my knowledge.

But it cannot be granted that a man may make a judgment about man. Existentialism spares him from any such judgment. The Existentialist will never consider man as an end because he is always in the making. Nor should we believe that there is a mankind to which we might set up a cult in the manner of Auguste Comte. The cult of mankind ends in the self-enclosed humanism of Comte, and let it be said, of fascism. This kind of humanism we can do without.

But there is another meaning of humanism. Fundamentally it is this: man is constantly outside of himself; in projecting himself, in losing himself outside of himself, he makes for man's existing; and, on the other hand, it is by pursuing transcendent goals that he is able to exist; man, being this state of passing beyond, and seizing upon things only as they bear upon this passing beyond, is at the heart, at the center of this passing beyond. There is no universe other than a human universe, the universe of human subjectivity. This connection between transcendency, as a constituent element of man – not in the sense that God is transcendent, but in the sense of passing beyond – and subjectivity, in the sense that man is not closed in on himself but is always present in a human universe, is what we call "Existentialist humanism." Humanism, because we remind man that there is no lawmaker other than himself, and that in his forlornness he will decide by himself; because we point out that man will fulfill himself as man, not in turning toward himself, but in seeking outside of himself a goal which is just this liberation, just this particular fulfillment.

From these few reflections it is evident that nothing is more unjust than the objections that have been raised against us. Existentialism is nothing else than an attempt to draw all the consequences of a coherent atheistic position. It isn't trying to plunge man into despair at all. But if one calls every attitude of unbelief despair, like the Christians, then the word is not being used in its original sense. Existentialism isn't so atheistic that it wears itself out showing that God doesn't exist. Rather, it declares that even if God did exist, that would change nothing. There you've got our point of view. Not that we believe that God exists, but we think that the problem of His existence is not the issue. In this sense Existentialism is optimistic, a doctrine of action, and it is plain dishonesty for Christians to make no distinction between their own despair and ours and then to call us despairing.

33   The Absurd*

Thomas Nagel

Most people feel on occasion that life is absurd, and some feel it vividly and continually. Yet the reasons usually offered in defense of this conviction are patently inadequate: they *could* not really explain why life is absurd. Why then do they provide a natural expression for the sense that it is?

I

Consider some examples. It is often remarked that nothing we do now will matter in a million years. But if that is true, then by the same token, nothing that will be the case in a million years matters now. In particular, it does not matter now that in a million years nothing we do now will matter. Moreover, even if what we did now *were* going to matter in a million years, how could that keep our present concerns from being absurd? If their mattering now is not enough to accomplish that, how would it help if they mattered a million years from now?

Whether what we do now will matter in a million years could make the crucial difference only if its mattering in a million years depended on its mattering, period. But then to deny that whatever happens now will matter in a million years is to beg the question against its mattering, period; for in that sense one cannot know that it will not matter in a million years whether (for example) someone now is happy or miserable, without knowing that it does not matter, period.

What we say to convey the absurdity of our lives often has to do with space or time: we are tiny specks in the infinite vastness of the universe; our lives are mere instants even on a geological time scale, let alone a cosmic one; we will all be dead any minute. But of course none of these evident facts can be what *makes* life absurd, if it is absurd. For suppose we lived forever; would not a life that is absurd if it lasts seventy years be infinitely absurd if it lasted through eternity? And if our lives are absurd given our present size, why would they be any less absurd if we filled the universe (either because we were larger or because the universe was smaller)? Reflection on our minuteness and brevity appears to be intimately connected with the sense that life is meaningless; but it is not clear what the connection is.

Another inadequate argument is that because we are going to die, all chains of justification must leave off in mid-air: one studies and works to earn money to pay for clothing, housing, entertainment, food, to sustain oneself from year to year, perhaps to support a family and pursue a career – but to what final end? All of it is an elaborate journey leading nowhere. (One will also have some effect on other people's lives, but that simply reproduces the problem, for they will die too.)

* From *The Journal of Philosophy*, 68 (1971), pp. 716–27. Reprinted with permission of The Journal of Philosophy and Thomas Nagel.

There are several replies to this argument. First, life does not consist of a sequence of activities each of which has as its purpose some later member of the sequence. Chains of justification come repeatedly to an end within life, and whether the process as a whole can be justified has no bearing on the finality of these end-points. No further justification is needed to make it reasonable to take aspirin for a headache, attend an exhibit of the work of a painter one admires, or stop a child from putting his hand on a hot stove. No larger context or further purpose is needed to prevent these acts from being pointless.

Even if someone wished to supply a further justification for pursuing all the things in life that are commonly regarded as self-justifying, that justification would have to end somewhere too. If *nothing* can justify unless it is justified in terms of something outside itself, which is also justified, then an infinite regress results, and no chain of justification can be complete. Moreover if a finite chain of reasons cannot justify anything, what could be accomplished by an infinite chain, each link of which must be justified by something outside itself?

Since justifications must come to an end somewhere, nothing is gained by denying that they end where they appear to, within life – or by trying to subsume the multiple, often trivial ordinary justifications of action under a single, controlling life scheme. We can be satisfied more easily than that. In fact, through its misrepresentation of the process of justification, the argument makes a vacuous demand. It insists that the reasons available within life are incomplete, but suggests thereby that all reasons that come to an end are incomplete. This makes it impossible to supply any reasons at all.

The standard arguments for absurdity appear therefore to fail as arguments. Yet I believe they attempt to express something that is difficult to state but fundamentally correct.

II

In ordinary life a situation is absurd when it includes a conspicuous discrepancy between pretension or aspiration and reality: someone gives a complicated speech in support of a motion that has already been passed; a notorious criminal is made president of a major philanthropic foundation; you declare your love over the telephone to a recorded announcement; as you are being knighted, your pants fall down.

When a person finds himself in an absurd situation, he will usually attempt to change it, by modifying his aspirations, or by trying to bring reality into better accord with them, or by removing himself from the situation entirely. We are not always willing or able to extricate ourselves from a position whose absurdity has become clear to us. Nevertheless, it is usually possible to imagine some change that would remove the absurdity – whether or not we can or will implement it. The sense that life as a whole is absurd arises when we perceive, perhaps dimly, an inflated pretension or aspiration which is inseparable from the continuation of human life and which makes its absurdity inescapable, short of escape from life itself.

Many people's lives are absurd, temporarily or permanently, for conventional reasons having to do with their particular ambitions, circumstances, and personal relations. If there is a philosophical sense of absurdity, however, it must arise from the perception of something universal – some respect in which pretension and reality inevitably clash for us all. This condition is supplied, I shall argue, by the collision between the seriousness with which we take our lives and the perpetual possibility of regarding everything about which we are serious as arbitrary, or open to doubt.

We cannot live human lives without energy and attention, nor without making choices which show that we take some things more seriously than others. Yet we have always available a point of view outside the particular form of our lives, from which the seriousness appears gratuitous. These two inescapable viewpoints collide in us, and that is what makes life absurd. It is absurd because we ignore the doubts that we know cannot be settled, continuing to live with nearly undiminished seriousness in spite of them.

This analysis requires defense in two respects: first as regards the unavoidability of seriousness; second as regards the inescapability of doubt.

We take ourselves seriously whether we lead serious lives or not and whether we are concerned primarily with fame, pleasure, virtue, luxury, triumph, beauty, justice, knowledge, salvation, or mere survival. If we take other people seriously and devote ourselves to them, that only multiplies the problem. Human life is full of effort, plans, calculation, success and failure: we *pursue* our lives, with varying degrees of sloth and energy.

It would be different if we could not step back and reflect on the process, but were merely led from impulse to impulse without self-consciousness. But human beings do not act solely on impulse. They are prudent, they reflect, they weigh consequences, they ask whether what they are doing is worth while. Not only are their lives full of particular choices that hang together in larger activities with temporal structure: they also decide in the broadest terms what to pursue and what to avoid, what the priorities among their various aims should be, and what kind of people they want to be or become. Some men are faced with such choices by the large decisions they make from time to time; some merely by reflection on the course their lives are taking as the product of countless small decisions. They decide whom to marry, what profession to follow, whether to join the Country Club, or the Resistance; or they may just wonder why they go on being salesmen or academics or taxi drivers, and then stop thinking about it after a certain period of inconclusive reflection.

Although they may be motivated from act to act by those immediate needs with which life presents them, they allow the process to continue by adhering to the general system of habits and the form of life in which such motives have their place – or perhaps only by clinging to life itself. They spend enormous quantities of energy, risk, and calculation on the details. Think of how an ordinary individual sweats over his appearance, his health, his sex life, his emotional honesty, his social utility, his self-knowledge, the quality of his ties with family, colleagues, and friends, how well he does his job, whether he understands the world and what is going on in it. Leading a human life is a full-time occupation, to which everyone devotes decades of intense concern.

This fact is so obvious that it is hard to find it extraordinary and important. Each of us lives his own life – lives with himself twenty-four hours a day. What else is he supposed to do – live someone else's life? Yet humans have the special capacity to step back and survey themselves, and the lives to which they are committed, with that detached amazement which comes from watching an ant struggle up a heap of sand. Without developing the illusion that they are able to escape from their highly specific and idiosyncratic position, they can view it *sub specie aeternitatis* – and the view is at once sobering and comical.

The crucial backward step is not taken by asking for still another justification in the chain, and failing to get it. The objections to that line of attack have already been stated; justifications come to an end. But this is precisely what provides universal doubt with its object. We step back to find that the whole system of justification and criticism, which controls our choices and supports our claims to rationality, rests on responses and habits that we never question, that we should not know how to defend without circularity, and to which we shall continue to adhere even after they are called into question.

The things we do or want without reasons, and without requiring reasons – the things that define what is a reason for us and what is not – are the starting points of our skepticism. We see ourselves from outside, and all the contingency and specificity of our aims and pursuits become clear. Yet when we take this view and recognize what we do as arbitrary, it does not disengage us from life, and there lies our absurdity: not in the fact that such an external view can be taken of us, but in the fact that we ourselves can take it, without ceasing to be the persons whose ultimate concerns are so coolly regarded.

III

One may try to escape the position by seeking broader ultimate concerns, from which it is impossible to step back – the idea being that absurdity results because what we take seriously is something small and insignificant and individual. Those seeking to supply their lives with meaning usually envision a role or function in something larger than themselves. They therefore seek fulfillment in service to society, the state, the revolution, the progress of history, the advance of science, or religion and the glory of God.

But a role in some larger enterprise cannot confer significance unless that enterprise is itself significant. And its significance must come back to what we can understand, or it will not even appear to give us what we are seeking. If we learned that we were being raised to provide food for other creatures fond of human flesh, who planned to turn us into cutlets before we got too stringy – even if we learned that the human race had been developed by animal breeders precisely for this purpose – that would still not give our lives meaning, for two reasons. First, we would still be in the dark as to the significance of the lives of those other beings; second, although we might acknowledge that this culinary role would make our lives meaningful to them, it is not clear how it would make them meaningful to us.

Admittedly, the usual form of service to a higher being is different from this. One is supposed to behold and partake of the glory of God, for example, in a way in which chickens do not share in the glory of coq au vin. The same is true of service to a state, a movement, or a revolution. People can come to feel, when they are part of something bigger, that it is part of them too. They worry less about what is peculiar to themselves, but identify enough with the larger enterprise to find their role in it fulfilling.

However, any such larger purpose can be put in doubt in the same way that the aims of an individual life can be, and for the same reasons. It is as legitimate to find ultimate justification there as to find it earlier, among the details of individual life. But this does not alter the fact that justifications come to an end when we are content to have them end – when we do not find it necessary to look any further. If we can step back from the purposes of individual life and doubt their point, we can step back also from the progress of human history, or of science, or the success of a society, or the kingdom, power, and glory of God,[1] and put all these things into question in the same way. What seems to us to confer meaning, justification, significance, does so in virtue of the fact that we need no more reasons after a certain point.

What makes doubt inescapable with regard to the limited aims of individual life also makes it inescapable with regard to any larger purpose that encourages the sense that life is meaningful. Once the fundamental doubt has begun, it cannot be laid to rest.

Camus maintains in *The Myth of Sisyphus* that the absurd arises because the world fails to meet our demands for meaning. This suggests that the world might satisfy those demands if it were different. But now we can see that this is not the case. There does not appear to be any conceivable world (containing us) about which unsettlable doubts could not arise. Consequently the absurdity of our situation derives not from a collision between our expectations and the world, but from a collision within ourselves.

IV

It may be objected that the standpoint from which these doubts are supposed to be felt does not exist – that if we take the recommended backward step we will land on thin air, without any basis for judgment about the natural responses we are supposed to be surveying. If we retain our usual standards of what is important, then questions about the significance of what we are doing with our lives will be answerable in the usual way. But if we do not, then those questions can mean nothing to us, since there is no longer any content to the idea of what matters, and hence no content to the idea that nothing does.

But this objection misconceives the nature of the backward step. It is not supposed to give us an understanding of what is *really* important, so that we see by contrast that our lives are insignificant. We never, in the course of these reflections, abandon the ordinary standards that guide our lives. We merely observe them in operation, and recognize that if they are called into question we can justify them only by reference to themselves, uselessly. We adhere to them because of the way we are put together; what seems to us important or serious or valuable would not seem so if we were differently constituted.

In ordinary life, to be sure, we do not judge a situation absurd unless we have in mind some standards of seriousness, significance, or harmony with which the absurd can be contrasted. This contrast is not implied by the philosophical judgment of absurdity, and that might be thought to make the concept unsuitable for the expression of such judgments. This is not so, however, for the philosophical judgment depends on another contrast which makes it a natural extension from more ordinary cases. It departs from them only in contrasting the pretensions of life with a larger context in which *no* standards can be discovered, rather than with a context from which alternative, overriding standards may be applied.

V

In this respect, as in others, philosophical perception of the absurd resembles epistemological skepticism. In both cases the final, philosophical doubt is not contrasted with any unchallenged certainties, though it is arrived at by extrapolation from examples of doubt within the system of evidence or justification, where a contrast with other certainties *is* implied. In both cases our limitedness joins with a capacity to transcend those limitations in thought (thus seeing them as limitations, and as inescapable).

Skepticism begins when we include ourselves in the world about which we claim knowledge. We notice that certain types of evidence convince us, that we are content to allow justifications of belief to come to an end at certain points, that we feel we know many things even without knowing or having grounds for believing the denial of others which, if true, would make what we claim to know false.

For example, I know that I am looking at a piece of paper, although I have no adequate grounds to claim I know that I am not dreaming; and if I am dreaming then I am not looking at a piece of paper. Here an ordinary conception of how appearance may diverge from reality is employed to show that we take our world largely for granted; the certainty that we are not dreaming cannot be justified except circularly, in terms of those very appearances which are being put in doubt. It is somewhat farfetched to suggest I may be dreaming; but the possibility is only illustrative. It reveals that our claims to knowledge depend on our not feeling it necessary to exclude certain incompatible alternatives, and the dreaming possibility or the total-hallucination possibility are just representatives for limitless possibilities most of which we cannot even conceive.[2]

Once we have taken the backward step to an abstract view of our whole system of beliefs, evidence, and justification, and seen that it works only, despite its pretensions, by taking the world largely for granted, we are *not* in a position to contrast all these appearances with an alternative reality. We cannot shed our ordinary responses, and if we could it would leave us with no means of conceiving a reality of any kind.

It is the same in the practical domain. We do not step outside our lives to a new vantage point from which we see what is really, objectively significant. We continue to take life largely for granted while seeing that all our decisions and certainties are possible only because there is a great deal we do not bother to rule out.

Both epistemological skepticism and a sense of the absurd can be reached via initial doubts posed within systems of evidence and justification that we accept, and can be stated without violence to our ordinary concepts. We can ask not only why we should believe there is a floor under us, but also why we should believe the evidence of our senses at all – and at some point the framable questions will have outlasted the answers. Similarly, we can ask not only why we should take aspirin, but why we should take trouble over our own comfort at all. The fact that we shall take the aspirin without waiting for an answer to this last question does not show that it is an unreal question. We shall also continue to believe there is a floor under us without waiting for an answer to the other question. In both cases it is this unsupported natural confidence that generates skeptical doubts; so it cannot be used to settle them.

Philosophical skepticism does not cause us to abandon our ordinary beliefs, but it lends them a peculiar flavor. After acknowledging that their truth is incompatible with possibilities that we have no grounds for believing do not obtain – apart from grounds in those very beliefs which we have called into question – we return to our familiar convictions with a certain irony and resignation. Unable to abandon the natural responses on which they depend, we take them back, like a spouse who has run off with someone else and then decided to return; but we regard them differently (not that the new attitude is necessarily inferior to the old, in either case).

The same situation obtains after we have put in question the seriousness with which we take our lives and human life in general and have looked at ourselves without presuppositions, we then return to our lives, as we must, but our seriousness is laced with irony. Not that irony enables us to escape the absurd. It is useless to mutter: "Life is meaningless; life is meaningless . . ." as an accompaniment to everything we do. In continuing to live and work and strive, we take ourselves seriously in action no matter what we say.

What sustains us, in belief as in action, is not reason or justification, but something more basic than these – for we go on in the same way even after we are convinced that the reasons have given out.[3] If we tried to rely entirely on reason, and pressed it hard, our lives and beliefs would collapse – a form of madness that may actually occur if the inertial force of taking the world and life for granted is somehow lost. If we lose our grip on that, reason will not give it back to us.

VI

In viewing ourselves from a perspective broader than we can occupy in the flesh, we become spectators of our own lives. We cannot do very much as pure spectators of our own lives, so we continue to lead them, and devote ourselves to what we are able at the same time to view as no more than a curiosity, like the ritual of an alien religion.

This explains why the sense of absurdity finds its natural expression in those bad arguments with which the discussion began. Reference to our small size and short lifespan and to the fact that all of mankind will eventually vanish without a trace are metaphors for the backward step which permits us to regard ourselves from without and to find the particular form of our lives curious and slightly surprising. By feigning a nebula's-eye view, we illustrate the capacity to see ourselves without presuppositions, as arbitrary, idiosyncratic, highly specific occupants of the world, one of countless possible forms of life.

Before turning to the question whether the absurdity of our lives is something to be regretted and if possible escaped, let me consider what would have to be given up in order to avoid it.

Why is the life of a mouse not absurd? The orbit of the moon is not absurd either, but that involves no strivings or aims at all. A mouse, however, has to work to stay alive. Yet he is not absurd, because he lacks the capacities for self-consciousness and self-transcendence that would enable him to see that he is only a mouse. If that *did* happen, his life would become absurd, since self-awareness would not make him cease to be a mouse and would not enable him to rise above his mousely strivings. Bringing his new-found self-consciousness with him, he would have to return to his meagre yet frantic life, full of doubts that he was unable to answer, but also full of purposes that he was unable to abandon.

Given that the transcendental step is natural to us humans, can we avoid absurdity by refusing to take that step and remaining entirely within our sublunar lives? Well, we cannot refuse consciously, for to do that we would have to be aware of the viewpoint we were refusing to adopt. The only way to avoid the relevant self-consciousness would be either never to attain it or to forget it – neither of which can be achieved by the will.

On the other hand, it is possible to expend effort on an attempt to destroy the other component of the absurd – abandoning one's earthly, individual, human life in order to identify as completely as possible with that universal viewpoint from which human life seems arbitrary and trivial. (This appears to be the ideal of certain Oriental religions.) If one succeeds, then one will not have to drag the superior awareness through a strenuous mundane life, and absurdity will be diminished.

However, insofar as this self-etiolation is the result of effort, will-power, asceticism, and so forth, it requires that one take oneself seriously as an individual – that one be willing to take considerable trouble to avoid being creaturely and absurd. Thus one may undermine the aim of unworldliness by pursuing it too vigorously. Still, if someone simply allowed his individual, animal nature to drift and respond to impulse, without making the pursuit of its needs a central conscious aim, then he might, at considerable dissociative cost, achieve a life that was less absurd than most. It would not be a meaningful life either, of course; but it would not involve the engagement of a transcendent awareness in the assiduous pursuit of mundane goals. And that is the main condition of absurdity – the dragooning of an unconvinced transcendent consciousness into the service of an immanent, limited enterprise like a human life.

VII

The final escape is suicide; but before adopting any hasty solutions, it would be wise to consider carefully whether the absurdity of our existence truly presents us with a *problem*, to which some solution must be found – a way of dealing with prima facie disaster. That is certainly the attitude with which Camus approaches the issue, and it gains support from the fact that we are all eager to escape from absurd situations on a smaller scale.

Camus – not on uniformly good grounds – rejects suicide and the other solutions he regards as escapist. What he recommends is defiance or scorn. We can salvage our dignity, he appears to believe, by shaking a fist at the world which is deaf to our pleas, and continuing to live in spite of it. This will not make our lives un-absurd, but it will lend them a certain nobility.[4]

This seems to me romantic and slightly self-pitying. Our absurdity warrants neither that much distress nor that much defiance. At the risk of falling into romanticism by a different route, I would argue that absurdity is one of the most human things about us: a manifestation of our most advanced and interesting characteristics. Like skepticism in epistemology, it is possible only because we possess a certain kind of insight – the capacity to transcend ourselves in thought.

If a sense of the absurd is a way of perceiving our true situation (even though the situation is not absurd until the perception arises), then what reason can we have to resent or escape it? Like the capacity for epistemological skepticism, it results from the ability to understand our human limitations. It need not be a matter for agony unless we make it so. Nor need it evoke a defiant contempt of fate that allows us to feel brave or proud. Such dramatics, even if carried on in private, betray a failure to appreciate the cosmic unimportance of the situation. If *sub specie aeternitatis* there is no reason to believe that anything matters, then that doesn't matter either, and we can approach our absurd lives with irony instead of heroism or despair.

Notes

1 Cf. Robert Nozick, "Teleology," *Mosaic*, XII, 1 (Spring 1971), 27/8.
2 I am aware that skepticism about the external world is widely thought to have been refuted, but I have remained convinced of its irrefutability since being exposed at Berkeley to Thompson Clarke's largely unpublished ideas on the subject.
3 As Hume says in a famous passage of the *Treatise*: "Most fortunately it happens, that since reason is incapable of dispelling these clouds, nature herself suffices to that purpose, and cures me of this philosophical melancholy and delirium, either by relaxing this bent of mind, or by some avocation, and lively impression of my senses, which obliterate all these chimeras. I dine, I play a game of backgammon, I converse, and am merry with my friends; and when after three or

four hours' amusement, I would return to these speculations, they appear so cold, and strain'd, and ridiculous, that I cannot find in my heart to enter into them any farther" (Book 1 Part 4, Section 7; Selby-Bigge, p. 269).

4 "Sisyphus, proletarian of the gods, powerless and rebellious, knows the whole extent of his wretched condition: it is what he thinks of during his descent. The lucidity that was to constitute his torture at the same time crowns his victory. There is no fate that cannot be surmounted by scorn" (*The Myth of Sisyphus*, Vintage edition, p. 90).

34   What Makes Life Worth Living?*

Owen Flanagan

Identity and Self-Expression

The question "What makes life worth living?" assumes that life is or can be worth living. Perhaps this is an unwarranted assumption. The question "Is life worth living?" comes first. The question is not "Is life lived?" or even "Do people seek to live out their lives?" Nor is it "Do people care about going on – possibly for as long as possible – sometimes even longer than is sensible?" These are easy questions.

We live our lives in the sense that we spend time *not* dead. And by and large people try to go on, to survive. But this proves nothing about worth. Mosquitoes spend time not dead, and they too will do what it takes to live as long as they can. Is it worth anything to live out a mosquito's life? Objectively, the answer is probably yes. It contributes ecologically to the planet that mosquitoes live lives. Does it matter to the individual mosquito? Does it matter subjectively? This is not a question that should worry us since mosquitoes don't worry about it. They can't. But we have minds, and we can ask the question "Is life worth living?" and if it is, "What, or what sorts of things make it so?" And the answers matter to us.

For us, the objective fact that we live out our lives – and even the fact that we have passion to do so (perhaps the result of biological imperatives) – proves nothing. One can do worthless things. I do them all the time. One can even have passion for worthless things. Perhaps a life is one extended worthless thing.

Why entertain this depressing thought? The answer is that it forces reflection on the question "Is life worth living, and if it is, what makes it so?" Why is reflection on this question worthwhile? I'm not sure how to answer. It may well be that a life can be worth living even for an unreflective agent, unreflective generally, or unreflective enough to be befuddled by this two-part question. Asking the question may even move a life that is worth living to fear and trembling, to sickness unto death, to the edge of despair; and not because the life is not worth living. It may be that the person to whom the question

* From *Self Expressions: Mind, Morals, and the Meaning of Life* (Oxford: Oxford University Press, 1996), pp. 3–11. © 1996 by Oxford University Press Inc. Used by permission of Oxford University Press Inc.

is addressed can't see her way to the answer that her life in fact reveals. She cannot articulate value or worth and wrongly thinks value and worth are not there.

On the other side, the question may move us to consider what matters, how it matters, and why it matters. Mattering might, if we are lucky, add up to value, to worth.

The question "Is life worth living and if it is, what makes it so?" is hard enough. It is connected to a more basic and equally bewildering question. "What does it mean to *live* a life?" Again, there is a trivial sense in which we know the answer: To live a life is to spend time *not* dead. Some people choose death quite deliberately while they are alive. Their suicide is partly constitutive of their life. Perhaps the question, intended as it is existentially, can be put this way: Do we *live* our lives? Do we in any sense make ourselves and control our characters and destinies, or are we just puppets, live puppets – whose lives are lived, but not lived or directed by us – the organisms who live these very lives by being, as it were, alive? The question is about living in some stronger sense than simply being alive, and it involves issues of self and agency.

Some philosophers distinguish between things that have some property – for example, value – intrinsically and things that have the property derivatively. Money is worthless until we make it worth something. Happiness is said to have worth in and of itself. Suppose this is true. Would it follow that a life with many happy times in it was worth living? Not necessarily. Properties of parts do not confer the property on the whole. My parts are small, I am large. Happy times, even many of them, might not constitute a worthwhile life. But I am skeptical in any case that a life's meaning could be intrinsic – could come from just being alive or from something that has value, no matter what. Life's meaning must derive from things other than just being alive. Happiness is probably one of the things that confers worth, but it is not enough. After all, one might perversely find happiness in evil things. Perhaps happiness is not necessary even. One might live a life largely devoid of happiness but still live a good and worthwhile life – even as seen from the subjective point of view.

Suppose, however, that happiness is normally a desired component of a life worth living, what else is needed? Having an identity and expressing it. This is the answer that strikes me as most promising: self and self-expression. The idea is romantic, Western, Nietzschean even. But it is also non-romantic, non-Western, Buddhist even. To make myself a "not-self," to work at creating in myself a mode to transcend caring about mundane things is a form of self-expression, as is suicide. But normally in the West and in the East, having a self and expressing it is not a matter of doing things alone, or doing them only your way, or of being Zarathustra-like. Many, probably most, worthwhile forms of self-expression, require others in crucial ways. Even the decision of the cloistered Christian monk or nun or the ascetic Buddhist *arahant* to remove himself or herself from certain dependencies on other people requires that there be social practices in place – certain economies of desire, for example – that are thought to be worth transcending. Sometimes stopping caring about money, fame, and sex are thought to be worthwhile because these things take time and energy away from more worthwhile human things: love, friendship, peace of mind, for example. Other times, the attempt to shift one's orientation from mundane desire is not motivated by the desire to connect with other, more worthwhile, human goods, but with the transcendental – God, or something of that sort.

Wherever one looks, or so I claim, humans seek, and sometimes find worth in possessing an identity and expressing it. This is why I think having a self and expressing it reign when it comes to answering the question of what makes life worth living. Of course, self and self-expression are not sufficient for living well, but they are necessary. If something – if anything, that is – is necessary for a life worth living, it is this: that I develop an identity and that I express it. The idea awaits refinement since, of course, not any identity or form of expressing it will do. But you get the drift.

It is important that I not be understood as promoting a particular conception of self or identity, especially not some controversial individualistic one. Philosophers from Aristotle to the present, as well as anthropologists, have taught us that in every culture, becoming a self capable of expressing anything of worth requires a community, as does self-expression. Furthermore, what an individual is like and what he or she seeks to express may be things of largely communal *or* largely personal value. This will be a matter of great contingency, as will the degree to which a particular individual develops powers of self-authorship and occupies a world in which she can use these powers in creative ways (luck matters – indeed, it matters far too much). What will *not* be contingent, I am claiming, is that there will be individual selves and that if they find meaning and worth, it will be through self-expression. This, I claim, is true of Nietzscheans, Libertarians, Buddhists, and Benedictines. It is as true of Mother Teresa as it is of Madonna.[1]

The Death of the Subject

I'll be alone when I die. Or better: Dying is something I will do alone. Or better: My passing from being alive to being dead is something that will happen to me alone. This is true even if loved ones are there for the event. When I die, I'll be nothing. But for the time being, I am something rather than nothing.[2]

One thing that would undermine the idea that *this* subject of experience will die, as well as the ideas about the importance of self and self-expression would be if there were no subjects, no agents. If there were no subjects there would be no selves, and if my self was nothing it could hardly die, and self-expression would be illusory. The very thought I just had, "that for the time being I am something rather than nothing," might be considered to be some sort of mistake. Indeed, there is talk in the air of the "death of the subject." Why think there are no subjects? There are three standard sorts of argument that one sees in the postmodern literature.

First, there is a metaphysical argument that promotes the idea that I am merely a location at which and through which, like all other locations, certain things happen. The universe just is a complex causal network and what is "me" is just a location, one among an uncountable number of other locations – locations that *sub specie aeternitatis* just nudge each other from place to place.

Second, there is a sociological argument according to which I am just a bunch of roles melded together in the here and now, as differentiated and complex and situation-specific as the various social niches that I occupy require me to be. *Homo sapiens* learns how to be a "self," but a self is no more than a name like "the university," which names nothing in particular, but only a disparate collection that seems to possess, but invariably lacks, any more than nominal unity.

Third, there are developmental, life span sorts of arguments according to which "I" am a series of self-stages. There is no I, no ego, no self, that is me over time. "I" – now in raised-eyebrow quotes to indicate that grammar is causing trouble – have a name. It stays the same. But my body changes, my beliefs, my desires, my projects, and commitments, my interpersonal relations change radically over the course of life. Owen Flanagan is the name, but changing is my game. The illusion of identity or sameness is just that: an illusion. Its cause is that all these changes happen incrementally. But just as it does not follow from the fact that 2 is not far from 1, nor 23 from 22, nor 6,000,000 from 5,900,000, that 6,000,000 is not far from 1, so too it does not follow that Owen Flanagan at 45 is remotely close to Owen Flanagan at 1 or even at 20.

Strategically, and ever so briefly, here is how I recommend dealing with all three arguments. First, concede the last argument. There are subjects, they change, some more than others, across a variety of dimensions over the course of a life. The argument proves nothing about the death of the subject, only that subjects are not identical over time. But those philosophers are right who have taught us that self-sameness is not what matters. Continuity and connectedness matter, not strict identity. Second, there is something to the social-role argument. Before and after we gain powers of self-authorship we express ourselves in ways particular situations call upon us to be. But even supposing that I am nothing more than some package of socially responsible roles, I am still something rather than nothing. So the argument hardly establishes the death of the subject; it simply makes the subject a social construction all the way down. But houses are completely constructed, and they exist. Being constructed hardly makes something into nothing. Usually it is the other way round.

Third, regarding the metaphysical argument: It is based upon two tricks at once: one, it evokes the specter of determinism to undermine the idea that there are metaphysically free subjects; two, it paints a picture in which "I" am caused by things, but never cause anything. Even if there are no metaphysically autonomous agents, there still might be agents. A finch may not be metaphysically free, but it expresses its needs and satisfies them when it finds and eats from my bird feeder. Furthermore, even under the deterministic picture, each thing that is an effect is in turn a cause, a something-that-makes-other-things-happen. So the existence of agents, in the sense of systems with beliefs and desires and complex motivational economies, who do things is hardly undermined by the argument. Furthermore, even if nothing matters *sub specie aeternitatis*, the fact remains that evolution has resulted in the existence of organisms that have temporally extended lives and are self-organizing and self-moving in certain well-understood ways.

Death-of-subject arguments, even if interpreted generously, do not show that there are no subjects of experience nor that there are no agents. Depending on the type of argument, they deflate our conception(s) of subjects and agents, but they hardly destroy these conceptions – indeed they presuppose invariably that subjects and agents exist.

The arguments just rehearsed are heard among poststructuralists and postmodernists who are enchanted with human contingency and disenchanted with the idea that a person might be essentially constituted by an immutable soul or transcendental ego. I share the enchantment and disenchantment, respectively, but resist the conclusion. There is another quarter from which worries about self and meaning and worth continue to be heard – the ferment here is caused by the attempt to mix the scientific image of the cosmos and of biological evolution with more traditional pictures of persons. I'll explain a bit.

Why Me?

Why is there something rather than nothing? Why is there anything at all? And why in particular am *I* among the things that there are? Here are two answers:

1. An omniscient, omnipotent, all-good, and all-loving God decided in his infinite wisdom that the universe and its creatures should exist. He created humans in his own image. He endows us with immortal souls, souls that will join him and all the other saved persons if we use our free will to follow the right path, to worship him, and follow his moral commandments.

2. It is an inexplicable and irrational feature of things that there is something rather than nothing, that there is anything at all, and that there are particular individuals. But once there was something purely natural up and running, the aftermath of the Big Bang perhaps, then we can give some sketchy accounts of how life emerged on earth, and how natural selection worked to produce *Homo sapiens*, a new kind of animal.

One feature the stories have in common is that they both start by positing an originary force that seems to answer, but does not answer the original question. They both say that there just always was something rather than nothing. To which the original question can then be posed: Why anything at all? And why this, a God who always was, in the first instance, or some set of physical facts, a "singularity" from which the Big Bang emerged, in the second? Both stories stop further questioning and are found satisfying by different groups of people. But this cannot be due to their satisfactoriness as answers. Their appeal must lie elsewhere.

Transcendent Meaning

One reasonable suspect for where the appeal of the first story lies is in the fact that it provides the possibility that life has transcendent meaning – an omniscient God shows the way, I follow, and I achieve personal immortality. His plan must be the right one; it must make sense and ground a good and meaningful life. He is God, after all.

The second story generates a host of worries. If there is no God, if I am just an animal subject to the same finite fate – becoming nothing when I die as I was before my birth – then of what significance am I? And what basis could there be for thinking that one way of living is better than another? And if my time is limited, why should anything else matter than that I get pleasure, as much and as quickly as I can get it? And why, as I push the thought of my utter contingency to the limit, why think that I am in fact anything at all, rather than some sort of chimera or ephemera, at most a location from which self-expressive and self-generative forces seemingly emerge, but which in fact is simply, like all else, a place where certain things come together in a manner that creates the illusion that I am an agent, a self.

The second image, the scientific image, is thought by many to be deflationary and nihilistic, destroying at once the very idea that *I* am an agent as I conceive of myself, that my life matters, and that being ethical matters in this scheme where nothing matters. There is Dostoevsky's worry that if there is no God then everything is permitted. How could anything be better than anything else if there is no transcendent ground for meaning? But then there is Nietzsche's question: Why should the fact that a certain plan is God's plan assure its meaningfulness? Even if it does assure that the plan is meaningful for God, what makes it meaningful for me? And what assures that the plan is good, or that it grounds meaning, just because it is God's plan. If God always was and always shall be, isn't it the case that he just came with this plan. How could something (two things: God and his plan) so inexplicable, reassure me that the meaning of my life is secure, that it is in good hands, that it is not simply a derivative surd – an offshoot of the originary surd, a God who always was and just had this plan. How is this different from the second picture according to which I am nature's surd?

If it seems like the originary force of all things including this life lies in something personal and spiritual rather than material, then the next philosophical move is to motivate skepticism that God's creation, and God himself are good. I am to be reassured because I was made in *his* image. Why?

William James quotes this poem by James Thomson in his essay "Is Life Worth Living?" The poem makes the worry vivid:[3]

> Who is most wretched in this dolorous place?
> I think myself; yet I would rather be
> My miserable self than He, than He
> Who formed such creatures to his own disgrace.
>
> The vilest thing must be less vile than Thou
> From whom it had its being, God and Lord!
> Creator of all woe and sin! abhorred,
> Malignant and implacable! I vow
>
> That not for all Thy power furled and unfurled,
> For all the temples to Thy glory built,
> Would I assume the ignominious guilt
> Of having made such men in such a world.

My Way

It is hard to see why or how either story, the theological one or the naturalistic one, could ground meaning and worth in something instrinsic, timeless, and itself comprehensible. The scientific image seems no worse off at any rate than the theological one.

Perhaps looking for the ground of meaning and worth in origins is the wrong place to be looking. Still, the theological story contains an interesting suggestion. It claims that God needs us as much as we need him for the plan to work. This leads Robert Nozick to ask, "[I]f it were possible for man and God to shore up each other's meaningfulness in this fashion, why could not two people do this for each other as well?"[4]

Or, to put the point more generally: If meaning and worth come with relations of certain sorts, perhaps in the first instance to other selves, but possibly also to nature, to work, to oneself, then perhaps we are wisest to look for grounds of meaning and worth in this life – in relations we can have during this life. Does science say that this life doesn't exist, or that it doesn't matter? I don't see how, any more than I see that "death-of-the subject" arguments in the humanities succeed.

The claim is that it matters a lot that I do what *I* want to do. And it matters at least as much that what I do is something worth doing, something of value. These things of value need not be momentously important – ordinary things matter, eating a tasty meal, throwing a stick for the dog to fetch, shooting a basketball. These are things worth doing. If life was comprised only of such ordinary short-term goods, we might feel that something was missing. Why? Because we think that a person ought to have some long-term projects and plans and these ought to be about things that matter, things that are worth caring about, worth a bit more than the things just mentioned. Love and friend-ship and work, creative work, are among these things.

What I do and think reflect on me, on who I am. What I think and do also help con-stitute who I am. Expressing myself, making and modifying myself, and respecting myself all matter, and they are interconnected. Questions of meaning only arise because I am a thinking thing and, in particular, because I am a conscious thinking thing. My conscious thinking abilities stretch to knowing such things as that I will someday be dead. Being dead means once again being nothing at all. For creatures who thrive on self-expression, no longer being able first-personally to express anything thwarts a basic desire. Here is where leaving parts of ourselves in the world, by having changed that world in directions that matter, that are positive, lessens the threat of my demise. This is a kind of naturalistic transcendence, a way each of us, if we are lucky, can leave good-making traces beyond the time between our birth and death. To believe this sort of tran-scendence is possible is, I guess, to have a kind of religion. It involves believing that there are selves, that we can in self-expression make a difference, and if we use our truth detec-tors and good detectors well, that difference might be positive, a contribution to the cosmos.

Notes

1   In this passage, Richard Rorty expresses the sort of picture I want to endorse: "[E]very human life is the working out of a sophisticated idiosyncratic fantasy, and a reminder that no such working out gets completed before death interrupts. It cannot get completed because there is nothing to complete, there is only a web of relations to be rewoven, a web which time length-ens every day.

"But if we avoid Nietzsche's inverted Platonism – his suggestion that a life of self-creation can be as complete and as autonomous as Plato thought a life of contemplation might be – then we shall be content to think of any human life as the always incomplete, yet sometimes heroic, reweaving of such a web. We shall see the conscious need of the strong poet to *demonstrate* that he is not a copy or replica as merely a special form of an unconscious need everyone has: the need to come to terms with the blind impress which chance has given him, to make a self for himself by redescribing that impress in terms which are, if only marginally, his own" (Richard Rorty, *Contingency, Irony, and Solidarity* [Cambridge: Cambridge University Press, 1989], 42–3).

2   Robert Nozick, like me, has a relational rather than intrinsic view of how life's meaning must accrue, and he captures nicely the deep psychological urge to avoid becoming totally nothing. "Death wipes you out. Dead, you are no longer around – around *here* at any rate – and if there is nowhere else where you'll be (heaven, hell, with the white light) then all that will be left of you is your effects, leavings, traces. People do seem to think it important to continue to be around somehow. The root notion seems to be this one: it shouldn't *ever* be as if you had never existed at all. A significant life leaves its mark on the world. A significant life is, in some sense, permanent; it makes a permanent difference to the world – it leaves traces" (*Philosophical Expla-nations* [Cambridge: Harvard University Press, 1979], 582).

3   William James, "Is Life Worth Living?" In *The Will to Believe and Other Essays in Popular Philosophy* (1897; reprint, New York: Dover, 1956).

4   Nozick, *Philosophical Explanations*, 589.

35   The Meaning of Life*

John Kekes

I

Most of our lives are spent in routine activities. We sleep, wash, dress, eat; go to work, work, shop, relax; balance the checkbook, clean house, do the laundry, have the car serviced; chat, pay bills, worry about this or that, take small pleasure in small things. We do all this in the intervals between familiar milestones: we are born, mature, age, and die; we have children and lose our parents; we graduate, find a job, get married, divorce, fall in and out of love, set up house; succeed at some things, fail at others; make friends and have fights; move house, change jobs, get fired or promoted, fall ill and recover, save for retirement and retire. So life goes for me, you, and just about everyone, allowing for small individual and cultural variations that affect the form but not the fact of routine. These activities constitute everyday life. Everyday life is what life mostly is. Keeping it going, however, involves constant struggle. From a birth we did not choose to a death we rarely desire, we have to cope with endless problems. If we fail, we suffer. And what do we gain from success? No more than some pleasure, a brief sense of triumph, perhaps a little peace of mind. But these are only interludes of well-being, because our difficulties do not cease. It is natural to ask then why we should continue on this treadmill. After all, we could stop.

The tough-minded answer is that the question falsely suggests that we need reasons for continuing to live. The truth is that our nature impels us to carry on. We have wants and the capacity to satisfy them, and instinct and training dictate that we do so. We live as long as we can, as well as we can, and we do so because we are the kind of organisms we are. It is our nature to struggle. To look for reasons beyond this is to misuse the respite we occasionally enjoy from the difficult business of living.

This bleak view correctly depicts the past and present condition of the majority of humanity. People struggle because they are hungry, cold, and threatened, and they want comfort. One should have compassion for the multitudes living in this way. The fact is, however, that many of us, living in civilized societies, no longer face such unrelenting adversity. For us, fortunate ones, the primitive struggle is over. We enjoy the comforts for which the less favored billions yearn. The point of the struggle in primitive conditions is to overcome obstacles to living. But what should we live for once the obstacles are overcome? What should we do with our comfortable lives? Having a comfortable life does not mean that the struggle is over, only that it takes less deadly forms. The threat is to income, prestige, status, self-esteem; the dangers are social and psychological. Nonetheless, these we also want to avoid. Why should we not say then that in primitive conditions our aim is to attain comfort, whereas in civilized conditions it is to protect and enhance the comfort we already have? We struggle to win such prizes as our society affords and to avoid being adversely judged by the prevailing standards.

* From *Midwest Studies in Philosophy*, 24 (2000), pp. 17–34. Reprinted with permission.

This is a superficial view. No doubt, in civilized societies many are motivated in this way, but we also have some freedom and opportunity to stand back and reflect. Much of this reflection needs to be concentrated on the strategy and tactics of the daily struggle. Yet we often have some time and energy left to ponder life and our own lives, to ask why we should live in whatever happen to be the socially accredited ways. We know the standards by which success is judged and the rewards and costs of failure. If we are honest, we admit that we care about success and want to avoid failure, at least in the projects that matter to us. Reflection, however, may prompt us to ask whether they should matter. It may seem to us that the whole business we are caught up in is bogus. We see that children are indoctrinated, adolescents are goaded and guided, and adults are rewarded by the vast, impersonal, ubiquitous molds into which civilized societies press their members. And we may ask why we should put up with it. Why should we care about the emblems of success and the stigma of failure? What does it really matter to us in the dark hours of a sleepless night what our neighbors, acquaintances, or colleagues think about us? They employ standards and judge according to them, but we have come to question the standards. Life will seem hollow if we reflect in this way and we shall rightly ask what meaning it has.

Maybe it has none. Maybe evolution has brought it about that we have a capacity to ask questions about our condition, and in civilized societies some even have the opportunity to employ their capacity. But it is folly to suppose that just because we can ask a question there is going to be an answer to it that we like. There are plenty of useless things in nature, and perhaps this capacity is one of them. Maybe life just is, as black holes, electrons, and hurricanes are. Each has an explanation in terms of the laws of nature and antecedent conditions, but there is no meaning beyond that.

One may meet this answer with despair or cynicism. Both are injurious. They poison the enjoyment there is in life by corrupting the innocent connection between a want and its satisfaction. There intrudes the gnawing question about the point of it all. Despair and cynicism cleave us into a natural self and a preying, harping, jeering, or self-pitying reflective self. We are thus turned against ourselves. Reflection sabotages our own projects. If this is the truth, then the human prospect is dim. Maybe a capacity has evolved in us, and it will undo us.

It is not surprising, therefore, that many people of sturdy common sense simply ignore the question. They go on with the business of living, do as well as they can, enjoy the comforts they may, and prudently keep out of deep waters. This evasion, however, is likely to be possible only for those who are succeeding in navigating life's treacherous waters. The young who are about to start tend to ask why they should follow their elders' mode of life. The old who look back may wonder about whether it was worth it. And the sick, poor, unlucky, and untalented may well ask, with various degrees of resentment, about the point of the enterprise in which they have not done well. It is not possible to ignore the question because it is persistently asked.

Nor is it reasonable to avoid putting the question to ourselves, quite independently of external challenges. It is demeaning to participate in all manner of activities, expending great effort, giving and getting hard knocks, obeying rules we have not made, chasing goals said by others to be rewarding, without asking why we should do all this. Is it not the very opposite of prudence and common sense to invest our lives in projects whose value we have not ascertained? Furthermore, there are exceptionally few lives uninterrupted by serious crises. Grief, ill health, social cataclysms, injustice, setbacks, lack of merited appreciation, being in the power of those who abuse it, and many similar adversities are likely to interfere with even the most prudently lived lives. The questions such adversities raise in us can be answered, if at all, only by reminding ourselves of the point of facing them. Doing that, however, requires having thought about the meaning of our lives.

II

In chapter 5 of his *Autobiography*,[1] John Stuart Mill makes wonderfully concrete what it is like for one's life to have meaning and then to lack it. He writes:

> I had what might truly be called an object in life: to be a reformer of the world. My conception of my own happiness was entirely identified with this object. The personal sympathies I wished for were those of my fellow labourers in this enterprise. . . . [A]s a serious and permanent personal satisfaction . . . my whole reliance was placed on this; and I was accustomed to felicitate myself on the certainty of a happy life which I enjoyed, through placing my happiness in something durable and distant, in which some progress might always be making, while it could never be exhausted by complete attainment. This did very well for several years, during which the general improvement going on in the world and the idea of myself as engaged with others in struggling to promote it, seemed enough to fill up an interesting and animated existence.

Mill lived in this manner until "the time came when I was awakened from this as from a dream. . . . [I]t occurred to me to put the question directly to myself: 'Suppose that all your objects in life were realized; that all the changes in institutions and opinions which you are looking forward to, could be completely effected at this very instant: would this be a great joy and happiness to you?' And an irrepressible self-consciousness answered: 'No!' At this my heart sank within me: the whole foundation on which my life was constructed fell down. . . . The end has ceased to charm, and how could there ever again be any interest in the means? I seemed to have nothing left to live for."

Reflecting on what has gone wrong, Mill offers the following diagnosis:

> All those to whom I looked up, were of the opinion that the pleasure of sympathy with human beings, and the feelings which made the good of others . . . the objects of existence, were the greatest and surest sources of happiness. Of the truth of this I was convinced, but to know that a feeling would make me happy if I had it, did not give me the feeling. My education, I thought, had failed to create these feelings in sufficient strength to resist the dissolving influence of analysis, while the whole course of my intellectual cultivation had made . . . analysis the inveterate habit of my mind. I was thus left stranded . . . without any desire for the ends which I had been so carefully fitted out to work for: no delight in virtue, or the general good, but also as little in anything else.

Mill's explanation of what has deprived his life of meaning is convincing, but we can go beyond it. He became indifferent to his projects and ceased to care about the goals he used to pursue because he became disengaged from them. The circumstances of his disengagement and the nature of his projects are peculiar to Mill, and so is the extraordinary education that was partly responsible for both his achievements and his life's lost meaning. But we can abstract from these peculiarities and recognize Mill's case as typical of many lives whose meaning has been lost. The precipitating experience is that we awaken, as if from a dream, and realize that what mattered before no longer does. Loss of religious faith, the death of a deeply loved person, the recognition that our decisive choices were based on self-deception, the realization that we have devoted our lives to pursuing a hollow goal, the discovery that our passionate commitment is to an irremediably tainted cause are such experiences. The result is disillusion, and life becomes a tedious burden.

These experiences may bring us to regard our activities as worthless. We see ourselves as engaged in the endless drudgery of some soul-destroying job. We do what we do, not to attain some positive good, but to avoid poverty or starvation. Yet some intrinsically worthless activities may have a point if they lead to goals we value. If, however, chores lacking in either intrinsic or instrumental value dominate in our lives, such as tightening screws day in, day out, as in Chaplin's *Modern Times*, then we can rightly judge them meaningless because they are pointless. In other cases, the activities that dominate our lives may have a point, and yet our lives may still be meaningless, because our goals are destructive, like having enough drugs to support an addiction. Lives of this sort are misdirected. Other lives are meaningless because their goals are trivial, like keeping our childhood toys in working order. There are also lives directed at goals impossible even of approximation, like communicating with the dead. These lives are futile.

It will deepen our understanding of what it would be like for our lives to have meaning if we see that it is not enough to avoid these defects. Mill reasonably judged his life meaningless, yet it had worth, for it was dedicated to a good cause; it aimed at the important goal of bettering the condition of humanity, thus it was not pointless, misdirected, destructive, or trivial; and it was not futile either, for the amelioration of misery and the increase of general happiness are feasible goals. Mill recognized that his project in life had these meaning-conferring attributes, yet they were insufficient to give it meaning.

One element that Mill's life lacked was his wanting to continue to be engaged in his project. Before his crisis, he identified himself with it, he actively wanted to pursue it; after it, he did not. There appeared a break between Mill and the worthwhile, purposeful, well-directed, important, and possible project of improving the condition of humanity. The connecting link is Mill's identification with his project, and that is what has come to an end. Mill's case shows that it is a mistake to suppose that there are some types of lives in which meaning is inherent, so that if we live them, we cannot fail to find them meaningful. Meaningful lives must have the features just described, but we must also identify with them, we must want to engage in them. Our motivation is as essential as the intrinsic features of the lives.

The fact is, however, that the combination of the intrinsic features and our motivation is still not sufficient for meaning. We may come to think that reflection excludes the possibility of meaning because it brings home to us the absurdity of even the most reasonable projects. Thomas Nagel gives an account of the philosophical sense of absurdity that "must arise from the perception of something universal – some respect in which pretension and reality inevitably clash for all of us."[2] What is this clash? "Two inevitable standpoints collide in us, and that is what makes life absurd." One is that we "cannot live lives without energy and attention, nor without making choices which show that we take some things more seriously than others. . . . Think of how an ordinary individual sweats over his appearance, his health, his sex life, his emotional honesty, his social utility, his self-knowledge, the quality of his ties with family, colleagues, and friends, how well he does his job, whether he understands the world and what is going on in it." The other viewpoint is that "humans have the capacity to stand back and survey themselves, and the lives to which they are committed, with that detached amazement which comes from watching an ant struggle up a heap of sand. Without developing the illusion that they are able to escape from their specific and idiosyncratic position, they can view it *sub specie aeternitatis*. . . . Yet when we take this view . . . it does not disengage us from life, and there lies our absurdity: not in the fact that such an external view can be taken of us, but in the fact that we ourselves take it, without ceasing to be the persons whose ultimate concerns are so coolly regarded."[3]

This is a perceptive analysis of the philosophical sense of absurdity, but it does not help to understand the kind of meaninglessness that overtook Mill. It is true that we have a capacity to view ourselves from an impersonal cosmic perspective, but the fact is that few of us do so and those who do are by no means uniformly assailed by a sense of meaninglessness. Plato, Spinoza, and Kant among philosophers, Sophocles and Wordsworth among poets, Einstein among scientists come to mind as combining a cosmic view with an intense concern with human welfare. The truths that in the long run we shall all be dead and that from Alpha Centauri we seem like ants lead many reflective people to a heightened appreciation of the importance of human concerns. Nor do people find their lives meaningless, as Mill did, because of a philosophical sense of absurdity. Mill's trouble was not that from a cosmic perspective it appeared absurd to care about his project. What bothered him was that he lost the capacity to "sweat over his appearance, his health, his sex life . . . whether he understands the world and what is going on in it." His life became desultory because he stopped caring, not because his caring appeared to be absurd from a nonhuman point of view.

The experience we need to understand is the break that sometimes occurs in everyday life between us and our projects. The projects used to matter, but they no longer do. This may happen because our projects are worthless, pointless, misdirected, trivial, destructive, or futile. Or it may happen because although our projects have none of these defects, they may still lack meaning because of our attitude toward them. Our attitudes may sometimes be sapped by a sense of absurdity, but they are more often sapped by a disengagement of our will and emotions that has nothing to do with absurdity. It must also be allowed that people may find their lives meaningless because they are meaningless. But not all lives are. The question is: what is it that engages our will and emotions, gives meaning to our lives, given that our projects are not defective and we do not suffer from a sense of absurdity? There are two types of answers: the religious and the moral, and we shall examine them in turn.

III

The religious approach to the question is pithily expressed by Wittgenstein: "The sense of the world must lie outside the world. In the world everything is as it is, and everything happens as it does happen: *in* it no value exists. . . . If there is any value . . . it must lie outside the whole sphere of what happens and is the case."[4] The world is the natural world, and it is a world of facts, not of values. If anything in the natural world has meaning or value, it must come from the outside of it. And it is on the outside that the religious answer concentrates. As Wittgenstein puts it, "Ethics is transcendental,"[5] and he means that "Ethics is the enquiry into what is valuable, or, into what is really important, or . . . into the meaning of life, or into what makes life worth living, or into the right way of living."[6]

We know then the direction in which to look for the religious answer, but before we can look an obstacle needs to be overcome. Religious answers vary greatly in scope, ranging from the very general to the quite specific. Specific religious answers are given by Christianity, Buddhism, Islam, and so forth. The general religious answer is based on the belief that there is a cosmic order that is the ultimate source of meaning. Specific religious answers, then, are interpretations of this supposed cosmic order in terms of revelation, religious experience, miracles, sacred books, the deliverances of prophets, sages, mystics, and various gnostics. In trying to understand the religious answer, it is best to begin with the general one, leaving aside the respective merits of different specific interpretations of it.

Part of the general answer is then that there is a cosmic order in reality. The natural world in which we live is a part of reality and it reflects that order. Through science we may discover some aspects of this order, but there are large and deep questions to which there can be no scientific answers. Why is there a natural world? How did it come into being? Why does it have the order it has? Why is it that of the countless alternative possibilities in the natural world it is self-conscious human beings that have been realized? What is the human significance of the cosmic order? Scientific theories about the big bang and evolution do not even begin to answer these questions because the questions can easily accommodate the scientific answers and go beyond them. What was there before the big bang? Why was there one? Why were there natural entities that could evolve? Why were the conditions that shaped the direction of evolution as they were? Science asks and answers questions internal to the natural world. Religion, if it is reasonable, accepts these answers, asks questions external to the natural world, and endeavors to answer them. That some specific religious answers are myths tells no more against the general religious answer than alchemy, astrology, and phrenology tell against science.

Let us suppose for a moment that there is a cosmic order and that the natural world that science aims to understand is but a part of it. Why, if that were so, would it have anything to do with the meaning of life? A Stoic parable will help here. Take a dog tied to a cart drawn by a horse. The dog's position is unenviable, but it can still be made better or worse depending on what the dog does. It can understand its position and act accordingly: move when the cart moves, rest when the cart does. Or, it can try to resist, in which case it will be dragged, and the going will be much rougher than it needs to be. And so it is for us. We can try to understand and live according to the cosmic order, or we can ignorantly or unreasonably pit ourselves against it. The meaning of human lives is given by our place in the cosmic order, and our lives will go well or badly, depending on how well we understand and conform to it.

The Stoics did not think that human beings have a special place in the cosmic order, or that if we live reasonably, then we shall somehow free ourselves from the necessity it imposes on us. They thought that the only freedom we can have is to understand the necessity to which we are subject. Platonists, Jews, Christians, and a host of philosophers and theologians go beyond this and take the more optimistic view that the cosmic order is not just necessary, but also good. If our lives are governed by understanding it, then we shall not only avoid unnecessary suffering, but enjoy positive benefits. This is called salvation, and the hope that its possibility creates is the dominant tradition in religious thought. Ethics is transcendental because whatever has meaning in the natural world has it as a result of being in harmony with the good cosmic order. Meaning is not made, but found, and it is found outside of the natural world. The key to meaningful lives thus is to cultivate our understanding of the necessary and good cosmic order and to bring our projects in harmony with what we have thus understood.

One problem with the religious answer becomes apparent if we reflect on the mythical fate of Sisyphus, as Albert Camus did in *The Myth of Sisyphus*.[7] Sisyphus revealed divine secrets to humanity, and for this he was condemned by the gods to roll a heavy rock uphill to the crest of a mountain until it rolls down, then to roll it up again and again after it rolls down, and to do this for all eternity. Sisyphus's life is the epitome of meaninglessness. Camus's suggestion is that our time-bound lives are like Sisyphus's, albeit on a less heroic scale. The religious answer needs to show that this is not true.

Richard Taylor offers an interesting suggestion that bears on this.[8] He says:

Let us suppose that the gods, while condemning Sisyphus . . . at the same time, as an afterthought, waxed perversely merciful by implanting in him . . . a compulsive impulse to roll stones. . . . I call this perverse, because from our point of view there is clearly no reason why anyone should have a persistent and insatiable desire to do something as pointless as that. Nevertheless, suppose that is Sisyphus' condition. He has but one obsession, which is to roll stones. . . . Now it can be seen why this little afterthought of the gods . . . was . . . merciful. For they have by this device managed to give Sisyphus precisely what he wants – by making him want precisely what they inflict on him. . . . Sisyphus' . . . life is now filled with mission and meaning, and he seems to himself to have been given an entry to heaven.[9]

Taylor's suggestion provokes a doubt. Sisyphus's belief that his life has meaning is false. He believes that his meaningless life has meaning only because the gods have manipulated him. We may wonder, however, whether meaning can be based on false beliefs. But let us set this doubt aside for the moment and observe that, whatever we may think of Taylor's suggestion, it is not the religious one. Taylor suggests that the meaning of life comes from living the way we want to live, whereas the religious answer is that meaning comes from living according to the cosmic order. A further twist to the myth of Sisyphus, however, will show how it might give rise to the religious answer.

Suppose that Sisyphus's fate remains as before, but when he reaches the crest, the rocks are incorporated into a gigantic monument glorifying the gods. Sisyphus's life then is no longer pointless or futile. He is part of a larger scheme, and his activities, difficult as they are, have a purpose. It may be further supposed that Sisyphus understands this purpose because the gods have explained it to him. This, of course, is the religious answer to the question about the meaning of our own lives as we face the endless struggles our various projects involve. The cosmic order is God's self-designed monument, and the ultimate purpose of all reasonable projects is to enact the small role assigned to us in this monumental scheme. We know that there is such a scheme, and we know that it is good, even if its details remain obscure to our limited intellects, because it has been revealed to us by a sacred book, by prophets, or by our own interpretations of our experiences.

IV

The religious answer is unpersuasive. In the first place, it is impossible to adduce any evidence in its favor because all evidence available to human beings comes from the natural world. There can thus be no evidence of what may be the case beyond the reach of evidence. Sacred texts and prophets, of course, make various claims about what there is beyond the natural world, but there can be no reason to believe their claims because the authors of the texts and the prophets are human beings who, like us, have access only to the natural world. There undoubtedly are events and experiences that have, at least at present, no natural explanation. But to call the events miracles or the experiences religious is once again to go beyond what the evidence permits. To acknowledge that there are events and experiences in the natural world that we cannot explain lends no support whatsoever for explaining them in terms of a cosmic order. If there is a cosmic order, we cannot know anything about it: not *that* it exists, and even less *what* form it takes. The questions that religion asks about what there is external to the natural world have no rationally defensible answers. This does not make the questions uninteresting or illegitimate, but it does make all answers to them arbitrary. Arbitrary answers can be accepted on faith, but that does not make them less arbitrary. If the meaning of life depends on understanding and being motivated to live according to a cosmic order, then life has no meaning because we cannot understand the cosmic order and consequently cannot be motivated by it.

Assume, however, that these doubts about the religious answer are misplaced. Assume that the natural world points toward a cosmic order. That would still be insufficient to give life meaning. To know that there is a cosmic order is not to know what it is. But assume further that we can extrapolate from features of the natural world and form some views about what the cosmic order is because the natural world reflects the cosmic order. Knowing some things about the cosmic order, however, is still not enough for meaning, as the last twist to the myth of Sisyphus makes it obvious. Why would it make Sisyphus's life meaningful if he knew that the rocks he is rolling help to construct a monument for the glory of the gods? He knows that he is part of a plan, that his endless drudgery has a purpose, but neither the plan nor the purpose is his own. He is, in effect, enslaved by the gods. Having a part in monument building gives no more meaning to Sisyphus's life than having had a part in pyramid building gave to the slaves of the Egyptians. Of course, neither Sisyphus nor the real slaves had a choice in the matter; they both had to do what they had to do – just like the dog tied to the cart. They may resign themselves to it; they may accept the inevitable; but why would that make their lives meaningful? Meaningful lives require more than understanding the uselessness of opposing the immense force that coerces us to do its bidding.

What would have to be added to the cosmic order to make our lives meaningful is that it is not merely necessary, but also good. If we understood this about it, it would motivate us to live according to it. We would then see its necessity as the key to living a good life, and this, of course, is just what the dominant tradition in Western religious thought claims. But is this a reasonable claim? Why should we think that the cosmic order is good? Perhaps it is indifferent; perhaps it is not good, but bad; or perhaps it is a mixture of good, bad, and indifferent. What reason is there for accepting one of these possibilities, rather than the others?

In trying to answer this question, we need to remember the assumption we have accepted for the sake of argument: that it is reasonable to derive inferences from the natural world about the cosmic order. What features of the natural world, then, imply that the cosmic order is good? These features, it might be said, are that the natural world sustains life and the human form of life; that many human beings live happy and beneficial lives; that there are many acts of honor, decency, and self-sacrifice; and that people often strive to be kind and just. In general, we can read back our moral successes into the cosmic order.

This approach, however, is fundamentally flawed. For any form of life that the natural world sustains, there are numerous others that have perished in the struggle for survival. Alongside happy and beneficial human lives there are at least as many that are unhappy and destructive, and, probably more than either, lives that sometimes go one way and sometimes the other. Selfishness, cruelty, greed, aggression, envy, and malice also motivate people and often lead them to cause serious unjustified harm to others. If we extrapolate from how things are in the natural world to what the cosmic order must be like, then we cannot just concentrate on the good and ignore what is bad and indifferent. If the natural world reflects a cosmic order, then there is much that is bad and indifferent in the cosmic order, in addition to what may be good.

If the cosmic order has to be good in order to endow our lives with meaning, then we have no reason to believe that our lives have meaning. For understanding the cosmic order will not then motivate us to try to live according to it, but to try to avoid its malignity or indifference. If Sisyphus had remained reasonable in the midst of what the gods forced him to endure, he would not have concluded that the monument the gods were building to glorify themselves was good or that his enforced contribution to it gave meaning to his drudgery.

There is then no reason to accept the religious answer to the question of whether our lives have meaning, because we have no reason to believe that there is a cosmic order; because if there is one, we have no reason to believe anything about what it is; and because if we hold beliefs about what it is on the basis of what the natural world implies, then reason prompts the belief that the cosmic order is a mixture of good, bad, and indifferent elements.

V

Let us, then, turn from the religious to the moral approach to the meaning of life. The distinction between the two approaches has been broached by Plato in *Euthyphro*.[10] The subject there is piety or holiness, but it has become customary to pose the question Socrates puts to Euthyphro in more general terms to be about the source of the good. Assuming that there is a God, what is the relation between God and the good? Does God make the good good or does God's will reflect the good that exists independently of it? The religious answer is the first, the moral answer is the second. Because morality is about the good, regardless of whether there is a God whose will could or would reflect the good, the concern of morality is not with God, but with what God's will might reflect.

According to the moral approach, Wittgenstein was wrong to think that "[e]thics is transcendental."[11] It is revealing, however, to bear in mind Wittgenstein's reason for thinking as he did. Commenting on Schlick's view about "two conceptions of the essence of the Good," Wittgenstein says that "according to the superficial interpretation, the Good is good because God wills it; according to the deeper interpretation, God wills the Good because it is good." Wittgenstein, then, goes on: "I think that the first conception is the deeper one: Good is what God orders. For this cuts off the path to any and every explanation of 'why' it is good, while the second conception is precisely the superficial, the rationalistic one, which proceeds as if what is good could still be given some foundation."[12] The moral approach to the meaning of life assumes, for reasons given in the preceding section, the failure of what Wittgenstein thinks of as the deeper conception. Wittgenstein is wrong to regard the moral approach as "the superficial, the rationalistic one," precisely because it recognizes the obligation that Wittgenstein spurns of giving reasons for claims about what the good is, if its pursuit is to endow life with meaning. It is a further feature of the moral approach that it looks for these reasons within the natural world, rather than outside of it.

Before we can address the question of where in the natural world these reasons could be found, clarity requires distinguishing between a wide and a narrow sense of morality. In the narrow sense, the concern of morality is with what is right. In this sense, morality is about the formulation of impersonal, impartial, disinterested rules that ought to govern human interactions. In the wide sense, the concern of morality is not merely with what is right, but also with what is good. In this sense, morality is not only about rules, actions, and obligations, but also about ideals, virtues, conceptions of a good life, personal aspirations, intimate relationships, private projects, supererogation, and so forth. The moral approach to the meaning of life is moral in the wide sense: what gives meaning to life is the pursuit of good projects. Doing what is right is an important part of that, but it is only a part. Right actions are impersonal conditions of a moral life, whereas the meaningfulness of moral lives derives from the personal sphere in which there are great individual variations. (A technical expression of this point is that the meaning of life is to be found in the aretaic/eudaimonist, rather than in the deontological, aspect of morality.)

We can once again begin by returning to the earlier suggestion of Richard Taylor about where in the wide sense of morality (or in the aretaic/eudaimonist aspect of it) the source of meaning may be found. Taylor thought that Sisyphus's life would have meaning if he wanted to pursue the project to which the gods have doomed him. According to Taylor, the crux is the wanting, not the nature of the projects or how we came to have them. Meaning thus comes from us, not from our projects. We confer meaning on them. On this view, meaning is subjective.

The distinction between "subjective" and "objective" can be drawn in a number of different ways, and there is much confusion about the whole question. It is important, therefore, to make it clear that what is meant by the meaning of life being subjective is that its meaning depends wholly on how the agents regard their lives. According to this view, a life has meaning if the agent sincerely thinks so, and it lacks meaning if the agent sincerely denies it. The subjective view, then, is that the agents' thinking that their lives have meaning is the necessary and sufficient condition for their lives having meaning. The objective view, by contrast, grants that the agents' attribution of meaning to their lives is necessary for their lives' having meaning, but it denies that it is sufficient. According to the objective view, lives may lack meaning even if their agents think otherwise, for they may be mistaken.

There are three reasons for rejecting the subjective view and accepting the objective one. The first emerges if we recall the doubt we ignored earlier. We may want to pursue a project only because we have been manipulated, just as Sisyphus was by the gods in the last twist to the myth. It seems clear, however, that there is a difference between wanting to pursue a project because of indoctrination or artificial stimulation of the cortex and wanting to pursue it as a result of having reflected and discovered that it makes out lives meaningful. If meaning were subjective, if it were created merely by our wants and beliefs, it would make no difference to meaning whether our wanting to pursue a project is genuine or manipulated. And it would be inexplicable how the discovery of manipulation could lead us to regard as meaningless a project that we regarded as mean-ingful before the discovery. Wanting to pursue a project is certainly connected with the meaning of life, but there is more to meaningful lives than that we want to pursue some project.

The second reason grows out of the first. Suppose that we genuinely want to pursue a project, so that we have not been manipulated. Suppose that Sisyphus just found himself wanting to roll rocks. That this is not sufficient for meaning is shown by the fact that the bare having of a want is not enough to move us to try satisfy it. The satisfaction of a want has to matter to us. And its mattering depends on its fitting into the overall causal nexus that connects that want to our other wants, and to our hopes, plans, goals, ambitions, and memories. If we all of a sudden discovered in ourselves an urge to roll rocks, we would not automatically act on it. We would ask ourselves why we want to do that and how it would affect our lives and projects if we did it. There is an explanation that we would want to give ourselves, especially since the want in question is assumed not to be trivial, like scratching one's nose, but a meaning-conferring one, like deciding to make rock rolling one's project in life.

It might be thought, however, that excluding manipulation and having an explanation of why the satisfaction of a want is important to us are requirements that the subjective view can meet. But this is not so. To ascertain whether we have been manipulated, or to explain why something is important to us, inevitably involves reference to objective considerations that exist independently of what we think. Manipulation is interference from the outside by people, the media, the gods, or whatever. To exclude it requires having reasons to believe that we have not been unduly influenced in these ways. And the explanation of why something matters to us must have to do with the influence on us of our upbringing, education, family, society, and so forth. The nature and strength of these influences are independent of what we think about them.

The third reason against the subjective view emerges from the recognition that we want to pursue a project because we believe that it would make our lives better than other available alternatives. But whether this is true depends on whether its pursuit would actually make our lives better. After all, we may pursue a project because we mistakenly believe that it would make our lives better, we may discover that we are mistaken, and we may change our minds about the meaningfulness of the project. If the mere belief that a project is better than the alternatives were sufficient to make the project meaningful, this change of mind could not occur.

It may be said in defense of the subjective view – that the sincere belief that our lives have meaning is necessary and sufficient for our lives' having meaning – that what these three objections show is that the truth of our beliefs may affect how good our projects are, but it will not affect our sense that our lives are meaningful, if we believe them to be so. This is partly right and partly wrong. It is right that we may find our projects meaningful even if, unbeknownst to us, our wants are manipulated and our beliefs in the importance and goodness of our projects are false. But it is wrong to conclude from this that the subjective view that meaning depends merely on our beliefs is correct. The very recognition that meaning requires both that we should fail to know that our wants are being manipulated and that we should fail to realize that our beliefs are false implies the relevance of objective considerations. For the knowledge that our wants are manipulated and beliefs false would destroy our belief in the meaningfulness of our projects. That we may be ignorant of the objective conditions of our projects' having meaning does not show that those conditions are irrelevant to their meaning. It shows that we may be mistaken in believing that our projects have meaning. If we realize that we are mistaken, that our wants are manipulated, or that our beliefs in the importance or goodness of our projects are false, then we would be the first to think that the projects we regarded as meaning-ful were in fact meaningless. This is just what would happen to Sisyphus if he knew the facts.

We are justified in concluding, therefore, that, in addition to the relevant wants and beliefs, there are objective conditions that must be met by meaningful lives. One of these conditions is that the wants must be genuine; and the other is that the beliefs must be true. Consequently, meaning depends on both subjective and objective conditions. To think otherwise, as Taylor does, is not to suppose that meaning depends on what God wills, as the religious approach claims, but that it depends on what the agent wills. As the religious approach relativizes meaning to God's will, so the subjective moral approach rel-ativizes it to the agent's will. Both leave it unexplained how the subjective state of willing, whether it be God's or human agents', could be sufficient to establish what it is that makes lives meaningful.

The strongest case for the moral approach to the meaning of life will therefore rec-ognize that meaning depends on both the subjective and the objective conditions. The subjective condition requires us to be in the appropriate psychological states of wanting and believing. The objective condition requires that our projects actually make our lives better. Meaning then depends on the coincidence of these two conditions: on our psy-chological states' being successfully directed toward the appropriate objects. As David Wiggins puts it: "psychological states and their objects [are] equal and reciprocal part-ners. . . . It can be true both that we desire x because we think x good, and that x is good because we desire x. . . . The quality by which the thing qualifies as good and the desire *for* the thing are equals and 'made for one another.'"[13]

It need not be supposed that this presupposes commitment to a cosmic order. It is not surprising that in the course of evolution there has emerged something like a correlation between what we want and what is good for us. We would be extinct if it were otherwise. Yet the correlation is less than perfect. Objective conditions both shape and constrain our wants, but within the limits they impose on our projects, there is much scope for experiments in living. Evolutionary success has not freed us from neces-sity, but it has opened numerous possibilities that we may pursue within the limits of necessity.

We may conclude, then, that according to the moral approach our lives have meaning if the following conditions are met: first, they are not worthless, pointless, misdirected, trivial, or futile; second, we have not succumbed to the view that all human projects are absurd; third, we have identified with projects that we genuinely want to pursue; and fourth, our belief that successful engagement in our projects will make our lives good or better is true.

VI

The problems of the moral answer begin to emerge if we recognize that the fourth con-dition of meaningful lives is ambiguous. It may mean that successful engagement in our projects will make our lives *morally* better or that it will make them better in *nonmoral* ways. This ambiguity derives from the ambiguity of the "good" in good lives. Our lives may be good because they conform to the requirements of morality, or they may be good because we find them satisfying. Satisfaction in this context should not be identified either with pleasure or with the feeling that results from having met one's own physiological or psychological needs. To be sure, meeting them is an example of satisfaction, but satisfaction may also be derived from doing our duty at considerable cost to ourselves, imposing hard discipline on ourselves, beholding the success of others that does not reflect on us at all, or seeing that justice is done even though we do not benefit from it. These two constituents of good lives may coincide, or they may not. Morally good lives may not be satisfying, and satisfying lives may not be morally good. It is a moral ideal dating back at least to Socrates that our satisfactions should derive from living in conformity to the requirements of morality. If the ideal holds, the ambiguity of the "good" will disappear. The projects we pursue then will be morally good, and our lives will be at once good and meaningful because we will find our engagement in our morally good projects satisfying. This is the ideal that motivates the moral answer to the meaning of life. The ideal, however, is flawed, and the moral answer fails.

There are two different lines of argument that lead to this conclusion. The first is that morally good projects need not be satisfying. What happened to Mill makes this point obvious. Morally good projects may be tedious or painful; they may involve doing our duty at the cost of self-sacrifice, self-denial, the frustration of our desires, and going against our strong feelings. The modicum of satisfaction we may take in doing what we feel we ought to do is often greatly outweighed by the dissatisfactions that are the by-products of having to act contrary to our nonmoral projects.

The second line of argument that leads to the failure of the moral answer is that even if it were true that morally good projects are satisfying, it would not follow that *only* morally good projects are satisfying. There may be satisfying immoral and nonmoral projects, and successful engagement in them may give meaning to our lives. That immoral lives may be meaningful is shown by the countless dedicated Nazi and Communist mass murderers, by those many sincerely committed terrorists who aim to destabilize one society or another through committing outrageous crimes against innocent civilians, and by people whose rage, resentment, greed, ambition, selfishness, sense of superiority or inferiority give purpose to their lives and lead them to inflict grievous unjustified harm on others. Such people may be successfully engaged in their projects, derive great satisfaction from them, and find their lives as scourges of their literal or metaphorical gods very meaningful.

The moral answer, however, is vitiated not only by moral monsters, but also by lives dedicated to the pursuit of nonmoral projects, which may be athletic, aesthetic, horticultural, erotic, or scholarly, or may involve collecting, learning languages, travel, connoisseurship, the invention of ingenious gadgets, and so forth. The lives of many people are given meaning by projects that are neither morally good nor immoral, but morally indifferent. People engaged in them may by and large conform to morality. The meaning of their lives, however, derives from their engagement in nonmoral projects and not from living in conformity with the requirements of morality. It follows from the possibility that immoral and nonmoral projects may give meaning to lives that the moral answer is mistaken in regarding successful engagement in morally good projects as a necessary condition of meaningful lives.

In sum, the moral answer that meaning derives from living good lives founders because of the ambiguity of the "good." If the "good" is taken to be "morally good," then the claim is false because morally good lives may not be meaningful and meaningful lives may not be morally good. If, on the other hand, the "good" is interpreted as "nonmoral good," then the answer ceases to be moral, since it allows that meaningful lives may be immoral or nonmoral. The moral answer, therefore, turns out to be either false or not moral. Its defenders, of course, normally intend it to be interpreted in the moral sense, so the likely charge they have to contend with is that their answer is false.

VII

There are, then, strong and independent reasons that show that neither religion nor morality provides a satisfactory approach to the meaning of life. But there is yet another and deeper reason why they both fail: they seek a general answer. Their basic assumption is that finding meaning depends on finding something that applies equally to all lives. The religious approach looks for that something to a cosmic order; the moral approach seeks it in morality. They recognize individual differences, but they treat them as mere variations on the same basic theme. Individual differences matter to them only because they compel us to do different things to conform to the same general meaning-conferring requirement. Given our characters and circumstances, we may have to serve the will of God in different ways, you as an artist, I as a soldier, or we may have to apply the categorical imperative in different situations or pursue the common good by means of different actions. But they both assume that, for all of us, meaning is derived from the same source, be it the will of God or some moral principle. It is this assumption that makes it impossible for both approaches to recognize the possibility that different individuals may derive meaning for their lives from radically different sources. This is the assumption that prevents them from acknowledging that individual differences have a fundamental influence not only on what we must do to pursue a meaning-conferring project, but also on which of many meaning-conferring projects we should aim to pursue. It is the assumption that all meaning-conferring projects must ultimately be variations of some one or few patterns that is responsible for the mistaken view that the phrase "the meaning of life is . . ." can be completed by some general formula that will make the resulting sentence hold true of all lives.

The problem is that if we give up the assumption that there is a general answer to the question of what gives meaning to life, then we seem to be led back to the subjective view that we had three good reasons to reject earlier. But these reasons continue to hold even if no general answer provides the additional necessary and sufficient condition that must be added to the subjective condition. The wants whose satisfaction we seek may be manipulated, self-destructive, trivial, inconsistent, or otherwise detrimental and thus fail to make our lives meaningful. And the beliefs we hold about the kind of life that would be meaningful may be false. Conformity to the subjective condition is necessary, but insufficient, for meaningful lives, and conformity to the objective by searching for a general answer exacts the unacceptable cost of denying that different lives may be made meaningful by conformity to different meaning-conferring requirements.

It is in this way that answering the question: Does life have a meaning? has become a perennial philosophical problem. The problem originates in a disruption of everyday life. Because we are unsuccessful, bored, poor, tired, unlucky, sick, grief-stricken, victims of injustice, or readers of subversive books, we start reflecting on the point of the routine activities we endlessly perform. Once we embark on this reflection, it is hard to stop. Reflection puts an end to the unreflective innocence with which we have unquestioningly lived in accordance to the prevailing conventions. As we question, so we feel the need for answers, and we turn to religion or morality. But the religious answer fails because no reason can be given for thinking that there is a cosmic order that would confer meaning on lives lived in conformity to it. And the moral answer fails because meaningful lives may be immoral or nonmoral and moral lives may not be meaningful. Defenders of the religious answer insist that the problems of morality can be met only by appealing to a cosmic order that would guarantee the identity of good and meaningful lives. Defenders of the moral answer insist that there must be moral reasons for regarding the cosmic order as good and that these reasons are either unavailable, or, if available, cannot themselves be transcendental. The religious and moral answers to this perennial problem agree in seeking a general answer, but they disagree whether it is to be found in the transcendental or in the natural world.

VIII

The way out of this impasse is to give up the search for a general answer. That brings us to an approach to the meaning of life that is free of the defects of the religious and moral answers. Let us call this approach "pluralistic." Its description is now a simple matter, because it involves no more than assembling the conclusions that have been reached by the preceding arguments. These conclusions may be formulated as conditions of meaningful lives. According to the pluralistic approach, then, lives have meaning if they meet the following conditions:

1. They are not dominated by worthless, pointless, misdirected, trivial, or futile activities.
2. They are not vitiated by the belief that all human projects are absurd.
3. They involve the pursuit of projects with which the agents have genuinely identified; they thus exclude all forms of manipulation.
4. Their agents' genuine identification with their projects is based on their true belief that successful engagement in them will make their lives better by providing the satisfactions they seek; they thus exclude all projects in which the agents' subjective identification is not correlated with objective conditions.
5. Their objective conditions are located in the natural world, not outside of it; they thus exclude the religious answer.
6. Their agents' subjective identifications are based on the pursuit of projects that yield either morally good, or immoral, or nonmoral satisfactions; they thus exclude the moral answer.
7. Their agents' subjective identifications with their projects reflect individual differences; they thus exclude all general answers.

These conditions are individually necessary and jointly sufficient to make lives meaningful. The main purpose of all the preceding arguments has been to attempt to explain and justify them.

The argument has been meant also to make it evident that the proposed approach is pluralistic, not in the trivial sense that there are many conditions that meaningful lives must meet, but in the important sense that meaningful lives may take a wide plurality of forms. The plurality of meaningful lives reflects, in addition to individual differences in our characters and circumstances, also individual differences in the type of projects that we pursue. These projects may be religious or moral, but they may also be scientific, aesthetic, athletic, scholarly, horticultural, military, commercial, political, poetic, and so on. The pluralistic approach recognizes that any project may contribute to making a life meaningful, provided it meets the conditions listed above. Meeting these conditions excludes many possibilities, but for present purposes, the most important among them is the possibility of a general answer to the question of what project or what type of project would make all lives meaningful. The basic difference between the pluralistic approach, on the one hand, and the religious and moral modes of reflection, on the other, is that the first denies and the second assert that there is a general answer.

It remains to point out that this difference constitutes a radical break between the pluralistic approach and traditional philosophical and religious thinking about the meaning of life. For one central claim of the pluralistic approach is that individuals must make their lives meaningful by genuinely identifying themselves with their projects and that doing so must reflect the differences of their capacities, interests, and preferences. It is because of these differences that there can be no acceptable general answers to questions about the meaning of life. A general answer must apply to all human lives, but if meaningful lives must reflect individual differences, then general answers, by their very nature, are doomed.

Part of the reason why the pluralistic approach constitutes a radical break with traditional philosophical and religious ways of thinking about the meaning of life is that all these ways aim to provide a general answer. This is what all the major religions, metaphysical systems, and moral theories aim to do. For Jews, it is the Covenant; for Christians, it is the life of Christ; for Buddhists, it is the Karma; for Moslems, it is the law as laid down in the Koran; for Platonists, it is the Form of the Good; for Stoics, it is natural necessity; for Hegelians, it is the dialectic; for utilitarians, it is the maximization of general happiness; and so on. If the pluralistic approach is right, then all these, and other, general answers are fundamentally misguided because they are essentially committed to denying individual differences in what lives can be meaningful. The pluralistic approach is an attempt to proceed in a different way.

Another central claim of the pluralistic approach is that meaningful lives may not be morally good and morally good lives may not be meaningful. The fundamental reason for this is that meaningful lives often depend on engagement in nonmoral projects. Such projects may be crucial to making lives meaningful, but engagement in them may violate or be indifferent to the requirements of morality. This claim is also contrary to the traditional ways of thinking about meaningful lives because the traditional assumption is that only morally good projects could make lives meaningful.

The assumption that underlies this tradition is that the scheme of things is such that ultimately only morally good lives will be satisfying and immoral or nonmoral lives cannot be. The pluralistic approach rejects this assumption as groundless. Immoral or nonmoral lives could have sufficient satisfactions to make them meaningful. This is hard to accept because it outrages our moral sensibility, which is deeply influenced by this tradition. Accepting it, however, has the virtue of doing justice to the plain fact that many evil and morally unconcerned people live meaningful lives. It also explains what this tradition has great difficulty with explaining, namely, why so many people live lives in which immoral and nonmoral satisfactions dominate moral ones. The explanation is that such satisfactions may make their lives meaningful. It is thus a consequence of the pluralistic approach that the questions of what makes lives meaningful and what makes them morally good are distinct and should not be conflated as it is traditionally done.

Notes

1 John Stuart Mill, *Autobiography* (New York: Columbia University Press, 1924).
2 Thomas Nagel, "The Absurd," in his *Mortal Questions* (Cambridge: Cambridge University Press, 1979), pp. 11–23; quoted passage on p. 13.
3 Nagel, "The Absurd," pp. 14–15.
4 Ludwig Wittgenstein, *Tractatus Logico-Philosophicus*, trans. D. F. Pears and B. F. McGuinness (London: Routledge, 1961), 6.41.
5 Wittgenstein, *Tractatus*, 6.421.
6 Ludwig Wittgenstein, "A Lecture on Ethics," *Philosophical Review*, 74 (1965), pp. 3–12; quoted passage on p. 5.
7 Albert Camus, *The Myth of Sisyphus*, trans. Justin O'Brien (London: Hamish Hamilton, 1955).
8 Richard Taylor, *Good and Evil* (New York: Macmillan, 1970).
9 Taylor, *Good and Evil*, p. 259.
10 Plato, *Euthyphro*, trans. Lane Cooper, in *Plato: The Collected Dialogues*, ed. Edith Hamilton and Huntington Cairns (Princeton: Princeton University Press, 1961).
11 Wittgenstein, *Tractatus*, 6.421.
12 Friedrich Waismann, "Notes on Talks with Wittgenstein," *Philosophical Review*, 74 (1965), pp. 15–16; quoted passage on p. 15.
13 David Wiggins, "Truth, Invention, and the Meaning of Life," *Proceedings of the British Academy*, 62 (1976), pp. 331–378; quoted passage on pp. 348–9.

36 Tolstoi and the Meaning of Life*

Anthony Flew

I

Tolstoi's autobiographical fragment, *A Confession*, marks one of the turning points in his development.[1] It was the first work of the period of his intensive study of the Gospels: the period which begins after the completion of *War and Peace* and *Anna Karenina*, and which continues until the return to fiction in *The Death of Ivan Ilych* and *The Power of Darkness*. In this work Tolstoi recounts his personal search for the meaning of life. It is a powerful revealing document, remarkable in many ways. But on this occasion we propose to use it as the object of a case study. This case study is intended mainly to throw light upon the meaning of the question: "What is the meaning of life?" Once the close examination of Tolstoi's argument is complete there may be room for one or two more general suggestions.

* From *Ethics*, 73 (1963), pp. 110–18. Reprinted by permission of the University of Chicago Press.

II

A. Tolstoi begins by explaining that he was both baptized and raised in the Orthodox Christian faith. "But when I abandoned the second course at the University at the age of eighteen I no longer believed any of the things I had been taught" (p. 3). Tolstoi's loss of faith came about not as the result of any spiritual struggle but seemed to have been rather a recognition of the fact that he had never really had and lived by any real Christian conviction. In his late teens and for most of his twenties he lived the sort of life that was expected of an aristocrat of his country and period. Then he took up with literature: "faith in the meaning of poetry and in the development of life was a religion, and I was one of its priests" (p. 9). He recognized that his fellow professional writers were a poor lot. Nevertheless: "I naively imagined that I was a poet and artist and could teach everybody without myself knowing what I was teaching" (p. 10). Travel in Europe confirmed him in "the faith of striving after perfection" (p. 12). But in this period he suffered two traumata: he witnessed in Paris an execution by the guillotine; and his brother died young after a long and painful illness "not understanding why he had lived and still less why he had to die" (p. 13). Compare in *Anna Karenina* the impact on Constantine Levin of the death of his brother Nicholas.[2]

Marriage swept all cosmic concerns out of Tolstoi's head, temporarily: "The new conditions of happy family life completely diverted me from all search for the general meaning of life. . . . So another fifteen years passed. . . . But five years ago something very strange began to happen to me. At first I experienced moments of perplexity and arrest of life, as though I did not know what to do or how to live . . . these moments of perplexity began to recur oftener and oftener. . . . They were always expressed by the questions: What is it for? What does it lead to?" (pp. 14–15).

Tolstoi's phrasing is perhaps more apt here than he realized. For interpreted as requests for information the questions he was asking would be rather silly. It is better to construe them as expressions of "arrest of life" formulated in a way which is partly misleading. He explains: "Before occupying myself with my Samara estate, the education of my son, or the writing of a book, I had to know *why* I was doing it?" (p. 16; italics in original). So far of course so good. It is perfectly reasonable to ask why you are doing what you are doing. But Tolstoi in this phase "of perplexity and arrest of life" would not take an answer for an answer. To all the replies which came into his mind he responded again: "What of it? What for?" He asks himself why he is making plans for the education of his son. The obvious reply is that he wants to do his best for the boy. Since this is both what he wants to do and what he ought to do it is hard to see what further or better reason there could be for doing what he is doing. As Hume once said: "It is impossible there can be progress in infinitum, and that one thing can always be a reason why another is desired. Something must be desirable on its own account, and because of its immediate accord or agreement with human sentiment and affection."[3] So to go on, as Tolstoi does, asking "What for?" after you have already seen how your contemplated course of action is rooted in your fundamental sentiments and affections might seem to be just silly, an indication of a failure to appreciate the scope and function of the question "What for?"

But, of course, in Tolstoi there is much more to it than that. The point is that all ordinary desires, affections, and satisfactions have lost their power and appeal: precisely this is that "arrest of life" of which the obsessively reiterated interrogatives are symptomatic. "I could find no reply at all. The questions would not wait, they had to be answered at once, and if I did not answer them it was impossible to live" (p. 17). Compare again *Anna Karenina*, and how "though he was a happy and healthy family man Levin was several times so near to suicide that he hid a cord he had lest he should hang himself, and he feared to carry a gun lest he should shoot himself."[4]

So far it has been suggested only that the interrogative forms here are partly misleading: for it is hard to see what answers, other than those of the kind already rejected, could be given to Tolstoi's symptomatic questioning straightforwardly construed. But they are not wholly misleading: for it is at least quite clearly a genuine question of what would remedy the pervasive disease of which they were expressions, of what would enable him to pick up again after this "arrest of life": "My life came to a standstill" (p. 17).

B.   At the beginning of the following section (Section IV) a fresh idea is introduced. It is that what makes Tolstoi's life meaningless, and what apparently should make all human life equally meaningless, is the (presumed) fact that every individual ends in "suffering and real death – complete annihilation" (p. 18). The passage runs: "My life came to a standstill . . . there were no wishes the fulfilment of which I could consider reasonable. . . . The truth was that life is meaningless. . . . It was impossible to . . . avoid seeing that there was nothing ahead but suffering and real death – complete annihilation" (pp. 17–18). As usual there are passages in the great novels where ideas of much the same sort had been expressed. Thus in *War and Peace* Pierre Bezhukov thinks to himself: "All such 'words of honour' are conventional things with no definite meaning, especially if one considers that tomorrow one may be dead. . . ." But there the author adds: "Pierre often indulged in reflections of this sort, nullifying all his decisions and intentions."[5]

In the document which we are considering Tolstoi is speaking in his own person, and there is no similarly astringent comment. Here and now what began as clinical autobiography is developing pretensions to wider insight into the depths of the supposedly universal human situation. Tolstoi is sliding from the merely autobiographical: "there were no wishes the fulfilment of which I could consider reasonable"; to the ostensibly objective conclusion that suffering and mortality really must withdraw all reasonableness from every attempt to satisfy any ordinary human desire. It is the notion of the meaninglessness of life which appears to provide the crucial middle term: if life is meaningless, then there can be no desires the fulfilment of which would be reasonable; but if there is nothing ahead but "suffering and real death," then life must be meaningless. Yet whatever plausibility this argument may have depends on interpreting this crucial middle term ambiguously: the basic sense for Tolstoi is that in which to say that life is meaningless is to say that there are no human desires the fulfilment of which would be reasonable, but sometimes, as in the present argument, the expression is also so construed as in effect simply to mean that life does end in "suffering and real death."

There is a price to be paid even for an unequivocal interpretation of "the meaninglessness of life" as equivalent to "the fact that all our lives end in suffering and real death." If we give the words this meaning then any attempt to press the question "What is the meaning of life?" must amount to a prejudicial insistence that after all we do not really suffer and die – or, at any rate, not finally. Similarly, to lament the meaninglessness of life will not be to lament something which may or may not be the tragic consequence of our mortality and passibility: it will be to express distress over just those very facts of the human condition. But the result of using the expression "the meaninglessness of life," as Tolstoi does, ambiguously, is to make it seem as if some reason had been given for taking it that the only truly deep and adequate response to the facts so labeled is a final decisive arrest of life by suicide. That is the conclusion of Section IV, although it is developed later in Section VII.

C.   In Section V Tolstoi tells us how he proceeded to look for answers to his questions in the sciences, but unsuccessfully: "I sought in all the sciences, but far from finding what I wanted, became convinced that all who like myself had sought in knowledge for the meaning of life had found nothing" (p. 23). These questions are all, he thinks, fundamentally the same question, differently formulated. One, considered in IIA above, is: "Why should I live, why wish for anything, or do anything?" This, for reasons elucidated in IIB above, is taken to be the same thing as asking: "Is there any meaning in my life that the inevitable death awaiting me does not destroy?" (p. 24). In Section VI, by way of Socrates and Schopenhauer Tolstoi reaches *Ecclesiastes* and the story of the Buddha's discovery of disease, death, and decay. For all this, except the reference to the Buddha, compare again the spiritual struggles of Levin in *Anna Karenina.*[6]

In Section VII Tolstoi lists what he regards as the only four possible reactions to this supposed fact of the meaninglessness of life. The first, ignorance, is only for the naïvely innocent: it consists in "not understanding that life is an evil and an absurdity." This is out: "one cannot cease to know what one does know" (p. 39). The second, called epicureanism, is substantially that of the author of *Ecclesiastes.* Although "That is the way in which the majority of people of our circle make life possible for themselves," such epicureanism can, in Tolstoi's view, result only from shallowness and lack of imagination. This, again, is out: "I could not imitate these people; not having their dullness of imagination I could not artificially produce it in myself" (p. 40). The third option "is that of strength and energy." This consists in suicide. "I saw that this was the worthiest way of escape and I wished to adopt it" (p. 41). "The fourth way is that of weakness. It consists in seeing the truth of the situation and yet clinging to life, knowing that nothing will come of it" (p. 41). This was Tolstoi's own first response, as well as that of Pierre Bezhukov and Constantine Levin.

If these were merely the musings of some character in a novel they might perhaps be allowed to pass. Though even here it is as worthwhile as it is unfashionable to emphasize that if the novel or indeed creative literature generally is to be anything more than a pastime, then men of letters must be prepared for a criticism of content which presses beyond all purely literary and dramatic considerations. Certainly, presented as they are, as in part some contribution to our thinking about the problems of world outlook, Tolstoi's ideas categorically must be challenged. It just will not do at all to offer the facts, or supposed facts, of "suffering and real death" as if they must be, or would have to be, taken as compulsive reasons for deciding "that life is an evil and an absurdity." The fact that all lives contain evils gives no ground sufficient for inferring that all or even any lives are wholly or even predominantly evil. The fact that no life lives forever does not necessarily devalue all the possible activities and achievements of a lifetime.

Apparently Tolstoi was one of those inclined to hold, as if this were a necessary truth, that nothing can matter unless it goes on forever, or at any rate, eventually leads to something else which does. But there really is nothing at all ineluctable, or even especially profound, about this particular value commitment. It is at least no less rational to hold that it is precisely our mortality which makes what we do, or fail to do, so overwhelmingly important. And there is not the slightest warrant for suggesting that this alternative and opposite reaction is possible only for those who are lacking in imagination. Consider the words of another character in another novel: "You don't realize how much more noble it is, how much more tragic and yet exhilarating . . . to have a life ephemeral but infinitely precious, precious *because* it is the only life we have."[7] Or consider the concluding lines of Auden's *Spain*:

> We are left alone with our day, and the time is short, and
> > History to the defeated
> May say Alas but cannot help nor pardon.

D.   "Life is a senseless evil, that is certain, said I to myself" (p. 42). Just when he thinks this unsatisfactory conclusion satisfactorily established Tolstoi is struck by a paradoxical observation: "The reasoning showing the vanity of life is not so difficult, and has long been familiar to the very simplest folk; yet they have lived and still live. How is it that they all live and never think of doubting the reasonableness of life?" (p. 43). It is, apparently, because they know the contrary: "from the most distant times . . . people have lived knowing the argument about the vanity of life, which has shown me its senselessness, and yet they lived attributing some meaning to it" (p. 44).

This is a turning point, both of Tolstoi's personal story and of the development of his argument. It is here that he begins to find what he is prepared to call the meaning of life. To appreciate the logic, or the lack of logic, of what is going on, it is essential to bear clearly in mind the various distinctions already drawn. It is one thing to ask what would in fact relieve Tolstoi's disease, the "arrest of life" considered simply as a paralyzing psychological condition. It is quite another to inquire what sense, if any, has been given in this particular and peculiar context to the interrogative sentences the utterance of which is symptomatic of this distressing psychological condition. Again, we must distinguish between the facts of suffering and universal mortality which sometimes are taken as being, and sometimes as showing, the senselessness of life and these evaluative conclusions – about the unreasonableness and the pointlessness of it all – which are sometimes supposed to follow from, and are sometimes equated with, those supposed facts. Certainly, as a matter of biography, the idea of "suffering and real death" presented itself to Tolstoi as if it must involve a devaluation of all values. But, as we have seen, there is no general necessity about this at all, whether logical or psychological; and there is nothing uniquely deep or dignified about the approved suicidal response to these fundamental facts of the human condition.

What at this point struck Tolstoi so forcibly becomes paradoxical only when you take it, as he apparently does, that these simple people must somehow know something which has completely eluded his inquiry. This assumption can be seen in his saying that "there is a whole humanity that lived and lives as if it understood the meaning of its life, *for without understanding it it could not live*" (p. 43; italics mine). Now, of course, it clearly is true that these people have, in a sense, got something that Tolstoi then had not: for they are clearly not suffering from the condition which he so strikingly dubs "arrest of life." But, as we have seen, this condition is by no means a necessary response to, nor a necessary consequence of, a recognition of certain fundamental facts. He is, therefore, not warranted to assume that the absence of this pathological condition in the simplest folk, combined with the presence of a capacity to appreciate some trite reasonings, provides any sort of indication that they must possess knowledge of life's meaning, in the senses in which he has been employing that expression.

Simply by not suffering from arrests of life, and by being acquainted with such trite arguments, they do not show that they must possess some fount of secret knowledge – philosophical knowledge that and why his earlier reasonings are unsound, or metaphysical knowledge that after all we are not really mortal, or that suffering is somehow not what it seems. Nevertheless Tolstoi was not altogether wrong in thinking that there was something to be learned from the mere existence of such simple folk, unworried by his tormenting sense of cosmic futility. It might, for instance, lead one to suspect that there are flaws in his questions and in his arguments, which there are. It might also suggest that he could learn from these unsophisticated examples at least one way to escape from his psychological condition, as in fact he did. What we surely need here is Ryle's distinction between knowing *how* and knowing *that*; the peasants may indeed know how to live their lives free of all sophisticated psychological disabilities, but this by no means presupposes the possession of any theoretical knowledge not vouch-safed to their unfortunate social superiors.[8]

E. In Section VIII Tolstoi tells how an independent force came to the rescue in his dissatisfactions: "something else was also working which I can only call a consciousness of life." This force dragged Tolstoi's attention away from "that narrow circle of rich, learned, and leisured people to which I belonged" and toward "the whole life of mankind that surrounded me on all sides" (p. 45). But he does not now want merely to break down what he has come to regard as his unhealthy isolation from the life of ordinary people. He begins to develop a mystique of the masses: "Rational knowledge, presented by the learned and wise, denies the meaning of life, but the enormous masses of men, the whole of mankind, receive that meaning in irrational knowledge. And that irrational knowledge is faith" (p. 47). This mystique later betrays him into some memorably unper-suasive utterances: "All that people sincerely believe in must be true; it may be differently expressed but it cannot be a lie, and therefore if it presents itself to me as a lie, that only means I have not understood it" (p. 68). It would surely be hard to find, even in the prophetic writings of D. H. Lawrence, anything more egregiously grotesque.

Yet Tolstoi was no wilful irrationalist. He was tormented by this apparent contradic-tion between the deliverances of reason and of faith: "By faith it appears that in order to understand the meaning of life I must renounce my reason, the very thing for which alone a meaning is required" (p. 47). He begins in Section IX to explore as a possible way to the resolution of his antinomy the idea that "rational knowledge" deals only with the finite, whereas "irrational knowledge" is always concerned with a relation between the finite and the infinite. But, like others who have tried to separate two exclusive spheres of influence, he finds difficulty both in determining appropriate territories and in maintaining the necessary barriers. At the end of Section IX, he writes: "I began to understand that in the replies given by faith is stored up the deepest human wisdom and that I had no right to deny them on the ground of reason, and that those answers are the only ones which reply to life's question" (p. 53). Yet at the beginning of Section X Tolstoi, like everybody else, finds himself confronted with rival faiths and rival interpre-tations; and he in fact resorts to some sort of rational criticism as the only sensible method of attempting to decide between their different claims. It is with an account of the first stages of this process that the rest of *A Confession* is occupied; and in the whole period of his life to which this forms a prologue Tolstoi devoted himself to a strenuous, and radically protestant, study both of the Gospels and of systematical theologies. The upshot was something very far indeed from the uncritical and superstitious faith of a muzhik.

However, we are here concerned with all this only insofar as it bears on his argument about the meaning of life. For present purposes what needs to be underlined once again is that the peasants who seem able to teach Tolstoi a lesson in *how* to live do not thereby and necessarily reveal any knowledge *that* something is the case. There is, therefore, no call, at least on this account, to search for some sphere of the infinite for such "irrational knowledge" to be about. Again, the secret of the peasants is not knowledge *that* the finite and the infinite are thus and thus arranged, but knowledge of *how* to go on living, and to allege that they – along surely with the despised epicureans and others – possess this sort of knowledge is in this case only another way of saying that they all enjoy rude mental health. Even if it were to be established that for some men, or for all men, to hold certain metaphysical beliefs is a condition of full well-being, this suspiciously Jungian fact would still have not the slightest tendency to show that any such therapeutic beliefs are actually true. The antinomy, which was at the end of Section VIII tormenting Tolstoi, thus disappears, not because "rational knowledge" and "irrational knowledge" tell the truth about different spheres, but because no sufficient reason has been provided for believing that the latter tells any truth at all.

III

A.   Tolstoi has told us: "I sought in all the sciences, but far from finding what I wanted, became convinced that all who like myself had sought in knowledge for the meaning of life had found nothing"; and now he confesses: "The solution of all the possible questions of life could evidently not satisfy me" (pp. 23 and 48). Here it is interesting to compare some oracular utterances of a philosopher whom we know to have been deeply influenced by Tolstoi.[9] In the *Tractatus Logico-Philosophicus* Wittgenstein writes:

> We feel that even if all possible scientific questions be answered, the problems of life have still not been touched at all. Of course there is then no question left, and just this is the answer. The solution of the problem of life is seen in the vanishing of this problem. (Is not this the reason why men to whom after long doubting the sense of life became clear, could not then say wherein this sense consisted?)

He then adds, in a vein still more apocalyptic: "There is indeed the inexpressible. This shows itself; it is the mystical."[10]

In her hierophantic exposition of the *Tractatus* Miss Anscombe urges that Wittgenstein cannot be interpreted as saying only the negative thing which he seems to be saying in the first four of the six sentences quoted: quite rightly, for the two following sentences are used to insist that there is after all something to be said, albeit something which unfortunately happens to be unsayable. She goes on to write of Tolstoi, "whose explanations of what he thought he understood are miserable failures; but whose understanding is manifested, and whose preaching comes through, in a story like Hadji Murad."[11] In the light of the whole previous argument it becomes possible to see that and how this is both partly right and partly wrong.

It is right in its suggestion that what Tolstoi was seeking, and preaching, was primarily an attitude to life and a way of life; something combining dignity, realism, and peace of mind. It is wrong in assuming that such a way and such an attitude must be connected necessarily with some mystic truth: no good reason whatsoever has been given for believing that the peace of mind of Platon Karataev, and that eventually achieved by Pierre Bezhukov, by Constantine Levin, or by Hadji Murad either validates or presupposes logically any propositions about some infinite shadow world outside the world.

Indeed what should strike the ideologically minded reader is that although Murad was a Hadji – one, that is, who has made the great pilgrimage to Mecca – his character is not in fact presented as formed by the doctrines of Islam. Again, in *War and Peace*, Pierre Bezhukov's "mental change" is not a conversion to a dogma – not even to an inexpressible dogma – but rather the acquisition of "that tranquillity of mind, that inner harmony, which had so impressed him in the soldiers at the battle of Borodino."[12] His new-found "faith" is a faith wholly devoid of intellectual content; and the "answers" which he now accepts are as empty as the original symptomatic "questions."[13] In *Anna Karenina*, similarly, Constantine Levin is not initiated into any truths necessary to salvation. Yet he too comes to feel that "my whole life, independently of anything that may happen to me, is in every moment no longer meaningless as it was before, but has an unquestionable meaning of goodness with which I have the power to invest it."[14]

The appreciation of this antithesis between the concern about a way of life and the discovery of mystic truth may provide a clue to a constructive understanding of Tolstoi's later religious teaching. We have seen how Tolstoi was "brought to acknowledge that all live humanity has another irrational knowledge – faith which makes it possible to live"; and this, at least in *A Confession*, he mistakes to be a knowledge that something is the case. Thus, though Miss Anscombe dismisses all his attempts to formulate this putative knowledge as "miserable failures", this description scarcely applies to the catechism: "What real result will come of my life? – Eternal torment or eternal bliss. What meaning has life that death does not destroy? – Union with the eternal God: heaven" (p. 50). But later, in such specifically religious works as the studies of the Gospels and *What I Believe*, this traditional doctrine seems to disappear; and the teaching is of a way of life, without benefit of any eschatological threats and promises. Indeed we seem to have there a religion which looks as if it really might be completely analyzable in terms of ethics and psychology only.

In the course of the recent revival of lay interest in the philosophy of religion it has been suggested that traditional Christianity might be analyzed in some such manner. Thus, in the early days, a writer in *Mind* urged: that "God exists" might be interpreted as "some men and women have had, and all may have, experiences called 'meeting God'"; and that "God created the world from nothing" should be construed as "everything which we call 'material' can be used in such a way that it contributes to the well-being of men."[15] More recently the somewhat more sophisticated proposal has been made that a religious assertion is to be taken as "the assertion of an intention to carry out a certain behaviour policy, subsumable under a sufficiently general principle to be a moral one, together with the implicit or explicit statement, but not necessarily the assertion of certain stories."[16] Perhaps the most interesting aspect of this second proposal lies in its emphatic recognition that stories which are not even believed to be literally true may nevertheless have an enormous influence: "Next to the Bible and the Prayer Book the most influential work in English Christian religious life has been a book whose stories are frankly recognized as fictitious – Bunyan's *Pilgrim's Progress*; and some of the most influential works in setting the moral tone of my generation were the novels of Dostoievsky."[17]

Now to proffer anything on these lines as an adequate descriptive analysis of the religion of the Saints and the Fathers would, of course, be quite absurd, not but what it has actually been done. But if we are considering Tolstoi's own rather special interpretation of Christianity, then it is at least not obviously impracticable to attempt an analysis in these terms, or in some variation on or combination of them. And to the extent that this is possible his final goal becomes altogether appropriate to the urge which originally drove him on his religious quest. That quest arose from an intolerable dissatisfaction with his condition. Certainly that "arrest of life" expressed itself in interrogatives. But, as we have seen, these are most charitably to be regarded not as questions requiring an answer but as symptomatic utterances. Similarly in Wittgenstein too we can find suggestions of a religion without reference to any world beyond the world. Thus in the *Notebooks, 1914–1916*, filled while he was working on the *Tractatus*, he writes: "To believe in God means to see that life has a meaning. The world is *given* me, i.e. my will enters into the world completely from the outside as into something that is already there. . . . That is why we have the feeling of being dependent on an alien will. *However this may be*, at any rate we *are* in a certain sense dependent, and what we are dependent on we can call God."[18]

Notes

1 All references given in parentheses in the text are to the "World's Classics" edition (London and New York: Oxford University Press, 1940).
2 Part III, chap. xxxi.
3 *An Inquiry Concerning the Principles of Morals*, Appendix I.
4 Part VIII, chap. ix.
5 Book I, chap. iii.
6 Part VIII, chaps. viii and ix.
7 Pierre-Henri Simon, Les Raisins Verts, p. 97. (My italics.)
8 See G. Ryle, *The Concept of Mind*, chap. ii.
9 See G. H. von Wright's biographical sketch in the *Philosophical Review* (1955), p. 534.
10 6.52, 6.521, and 6.522: I follow, although omitting the italics, the old translation (A.V.) rather than the new (R.V.) because the former seems here to be no less accurate while generally it does more justice to the literary quality of the original.
11 G. E. M. Anscombe, *An Introduction to Wittgenstein's Tractatus*, p. 170.
12 Book XIII, chap. iii.
13 Book XV, chap. v.
14 Part VIII, chap. xix: cf. chaps. x, xi, and xiii.
15 D. Cox, "The Significance of Christianity," *Mind* (1949), p. 216.
16 R. B. Braithwaite, *An Empiricist's View of the Nature of Religious Belief* (Cambridge: Cambridge University Press, 1955), p. 32.
17 Ibid., p. 27.
18 Oxford: Basil Blackwell, 1961, p. 74; italics in original.

The Meaning of Life:
Suggestions for Further Reading

Victor Frankl, *Man's Search for Meaning* (New York: Beacon, 1963).
Sigmund Freud, *Civilization and its Discontents*, trans. James Strachey, ed. Peter Gay (New York: W. W. Norton, 1989).
Charles Guignon, ed., *The Good Life* (Indianapolis: Hackett Publishing, 1999).
Walter Kaufmann, ed., *The Portable Nietzsche* (New York: Viking, 1997).

E. D. Klemke, ed., *The Meaning of Life*, 2nd edn. (Oxford: Oxford University Press, 2000).

Carl Levenson and Jonathan Westphal, eds., *Life and Death* (Indianapolis: Hackett Publishing, 1994).

Kai Nielsen, *Ethics without God*, rev. edn. (Buffalo: Prometheus Books, 1990).

Blaise Pascal, *Pensées and Other Writings*, trans. Honor Levi (Oxford: Oxford University Press, 1999).

Jean-Paul Sartre, *Being and Nothingness*, trans. Hazel Barnes (New York: Washington Square Press, 1992).

Leo Tolstoy, *The Death of Ivan Ilych*, trans. A. Maude (New York: New American Library, 1960).

PART FIVE

HOW SHOULD WE LIVE?

Introduction

37 Morality as Good in Itself
PLATO

38 The Problem of Rationality: Is Morality Rationally Required?
JAMES P. STERBA

39 From *Utilitarianism*
JOHN STUART MILL

40 Fundamental Principles of the Metaphysic of Morals
IMMANUEL KANT

41 From *Two Treatises of Government*
JOHN LOCKE

42 From *A Theory of Justice*
JOHN RAWLS

43 Distributive Justice
ROBERT NOZICK

44 Gender Inequality and Cultural Difference
SUSAN MOLLER OKIN

45 Race/Gender and the Ethics of Difference
JANE FLAX

46 A Response to Jane Flax
SUSAN MOLLER OKIN

47 Equality, Discrimination and Preferential Treatment
BERNARD R. BOXILL

48   All Animals Are Equal . . .
     PETER SINGER
49   The Ethics of Respect for Nature
     PAUL W. TAYLOR
     Ethics: Suggestions for Further Reading

Introduction

Ethics is the philosophical study of morality, and philosophers have returned to a few questions again and again. These questions are: What is the nature of morality? What is its justification? What are its requirements? What important challenges have been raised against it? Here we present a selection of readings, ancient and modern, that address these perennial issues.

We begin with an excerpt from Plato's *Republic*. This excerpt from Book II discusses the question of what reason a person has to comply with moral standards. The central character, Glaucon, challenges Socrates to show that a moral life is better than an immoral life, even when one can engage in immoral acts without being caught. In his reply, Socrates argues that a just or moral life is always worth living, but an immoral one is not. James Sterba, in an excerpt from his book *Three Challenges to Ethics*, elaborates his own response to Glaucon's challenge. Sterba presents an account of how one might begin from a perspective of egoism (i.e., the view that the only reasons that we have for action are those that promote our own selfish interests) and end up seeing morality as rational to accept.

If we agree, despite what Glaucon argues, that some moral standard binds us, how do we know which moral standard or standards are correct? John Stuart Mill proposed one of the simplest and most appealing theories of morality: that acts are right insofar as they tend to promote the general welfare, or happiness, of people. In defending this view, called "utilitarianism," Mill offered an alternative to the most important ethical theory to emerge from the Enlightenment period of the eighteenth century: that of Immanuel Kant. Kant had argued that, when assessing the morality of an action, one had to test the maxim or principle upon which one was acting by measuring it against the Categorical Imperative. Kant's view aimed to defend (without appealing to religious doctrine) a morality in which treating other rational beings – humans – with respect and dignity is paramount. The views of Mill and Kant have formed the foundation of most ethical theory since the time of their writing.

In addition to the question of how we ought to individually regulate our behavior, philosophers have asked the question of how we are to live together, and what the purpose of government should be. The seventeenth-century philosopher John Locke offered an account of government that substantially influenced both the Declaration of Independence and the Constitution of the United States. Locke's view, that government is the servant of the people and constructed for the purpose of their mutual advantage, has served as the model for limited government ever since. He explicitly appealed to the idea that the legitimacy of government depends upon the consent of the governed – an idea that was dangerous and heretical in seventeenth-century England. It also inspired many libertarians such as Robert Nozick, who argue against extensive government taxation on the grounds that it is illegitimately taking property from citizens without their consent. This view contradicts that of John Rawls, who appeals to both Locke and Kant in his defense of a welfare state. Rawls argues that, if citizens were to negotiate under fair circumstances, they would agree to a very substantial redistribution of the current holdings of wealth within their nation. Enforcing such a welfare state is fair because anyone who is committed to a just state would consent to it under ideal conditions of deliberation.

Once again, contemporary critics of ethics and social philosophy (including feminists and multiculturalists) ask how the particular history of philosophical debate has affected the theories that seem plausible to us. In particular, some feminists have argued that social contract theory (such as that of Kant, Locke, Rawls, and Nozick) excludes women, and has been used to legitimize unjust social institutions. But even if social contract theory can accommodate feminism, can feminism accommodate multiculturalism? Susan Okin argues that feminists should not shy away from critiquing oppressive institutions other than our own. Jane Flax responds that Okin's feminism amounts to a new kind of imperialism, imposing the views of a dominant group on a subordinate one. To suggest that white women share a common oppression with women of color only reinforces the view of Western women, who see themselves as "free" but see women in developing nations as determined by circumstances. In her reply to Flax, Okin argues that only by regarding women as sharing a common situation, no matter how different each individual woman's situation is, will we be able to address the sexual injustices that permeate all cultures.

In addition to these writings, we include three pieces addressing timely and applied issues in ethics. Bernard Boxill, writing on the morality of affirmative action, argues that these policies are most successfully defended by 'forward-looking' arguments that appeal to desirable outcomes rather than 'backward-looking' claims appealing solely to the history of prior injustices. When these considerations are taken into account, he contends, affirmative action does not necessarily violate the rights of white men. In an excerpt from his book *Animal Liberation*, utilitarian Peter Singer argues that treating animals as worthy of lesser moral regard than humans is unjustified. Our tendency to assign higher moral status to more intelligent beings is irrational because intelligence is not the source of moral status – the ability to perceive and sense is. Paul Taylor argues for an environmental ethic that goes even further, rejecting the idea that right conduct for humans pertains solely to the sentient animal kingdom. Nature itself is worthy of respect. These applications show how more general considerations of ethics can be extended to specific topics of particular relevance today.

37 Morality as Good in Itself*

Plato

With these words I was thinking that I had made an end of the discussion; but the end, in truth, proved to be only a beginning. For Glaucon, who is always the most pugnacious of men, was dissatisfied at Thrasymachus' retirement; he wanted to have the battle out. So he said to me: Socrates, do you wish really to persuade us, or only to seem to have persuaded us, that to be moral is always better than to be immoral?

I should wish really to persuade you, I replied, if I could.

Then you certainly have not succeeded. Let me ask you now: how would you arrange goods – are there not some which we welcome for their own sakes, and independently of their consequences, as, for example, harmless pleasures and enjoyments, which delight us at the time, although nothing follows from them?

I agree in thinking that there is such a class, I replied.

Is there not also a second class of goods, such as knowledge, sight, health, which are desirable not only in themselves, but also for their results?

Certainly, I said.

And would you not recognize a third class, such as gymnastics, and the care of the sick, and the physician's art; also the various ways of money-making – these do us good but we regard them as disagreeable; and no one would choose them for their own sakes, but only for the sake of some reward or result which flows from them?

There is, I said, this third class also. But why do you ask?

Because I want to know in which of the three classes you would place morality?

In the highest class, I reply – among those goods which he who would be happy desires both for their own sake and for the sake of their results.

Then the many are of another mind; they think that morality is to be reckoned in the troublesome class, among goods which are to be pursued for the sake of rewards and of reputation, but in themselves are disagreeable and rather to be avoided.

I know, I said, that this is their manner of thinking, and that this was the thesis which Trasymachus was maintaining just now, when he censured morality and praised immorality. But I am too stupid to be convinced by him.

I wish, he said, that you would hear me as well as him, and then I shall see whether you and I agree. For Thrasymachus seems to me, like a snake, to have been charmed by your voice sooner than he ought to have been; but to my mind the natures of morality and immorality have not yet been made clear. Setting aside their rewards and results, I want to know what they are in themselves, and how they inwardly work in the soul. If you please, then, I will revive the argument of Thrasymachus. And first I will speak of the nature and origin of morality according to the common view of them. Secondly, I will show that all men who practise morality do so against their will, of necessity, but not as a good. And thirdly, I will argue that there is reason in this view, for the life of the immoral is after all better by far than the life of the moral – if what they say is true,

* From *The Republic*, Book II. Public domain.

Socrates, since I myself am not of their opinion. But still I acknowledge that I am perplexed when I hear the voices of Thrasymachus and myriads of others dinning in my ears; and, on the other hand, I have never yet heard the superiority of morality to injustice maintained by anyone in a satisfactory way. I want to hear morality praised in respect of itself; then I shall be satisfied, and you are the person from whom I think that I am most likely to hear this; and therefore I will praise the immoral life to the utmost of my power, and my manner of speaking will indicate the manner in which I desire to hear you too praising morality and censuring immorality. Will you say whether you approve of my proposal?

Indeed I do; nor can I imagine any theme about which a man of sense would oftener wish to converse.

I am delighted, he replied, to hear you say so, and shall begin by speaking, as I proposed, of the nature and origin of morality.

They say that to do wrong is, by nature, good; to have wrong done to you, evil; but that the evil is greater than the good. And so when men have both done and suffered wrong and have had experience of both, not being able to avoid the one and obtain the other, they think that they had better agree among themselves to have neither; hence there arise laws and mutual covenants; and that which is ordained by law is termed by them lawful and right. This they affirm to be the origin and nature of morality; it is a mean or compromise, between the best of all, which is to do wrong and not be punished, and the worst of all, which is to have wrong done to you without the power of retaliation; and justice, being at a middle point between the two, is tolerated not as a good, but as the lesser evil, and honoured by reason of the inability of men to do wrong. For no man who is worthy to be called a man would ever submit to such an agreement if he were able to resist; he would be mad if he did. Such is the received account, Socrates, of the nature and origin of morality.

Now that those who practise morality do so involuntarily and because they have not the power to do what is wrong will best appear if we imagine something of this kind: having given both to the moral and the immoral power to do what they will, let us watch and see whither desire will lead them; then we shall discover in the very act the moral and the immoral man to be proceeding along the same road, following their interest, which all natures deem to be their food, and are only diverted into the path of morality by the force of law. The liberty which we are supposing may be most completely given to them in the form of such a power as is said to have been possessed by Gyges, the ancestor of Croesus the Lydian. According to the tradition, Gyges was a shepherd in the service of the king of Lydia; there was a great storm, and an earthquake made an opening in the earth at the place where he was feeding his flock. Amazed at the sight, he descended into the opening, where, among other marvels, he beheld a hollow brazen horse, having doors, at which he stooping and looking in saw a dead body of stature, as appeared to him, more than human, and having nothing on but a gold ring; this he took from the finger of the dead and reascended. Now the shepherds met together, according to custom, that they might send their monthly report about the flocks to the king; into their assembly he came having the ring on his finger, and as he was sitting among them he chanced to turn the collet of the ring inside his hand, when instantly he became invisible to the rest of the company and they began to speak of him as if he were no longer present. He was astonished at this, and again touching the ring he turned the collet outwards and reappeared; he made several trials of the ring, and always with the same result – when he turned the collet inwards he became invisible, when outwards he reappeared.

Whereupon he contrived to be chosen one of the messengers who were sent to the court; where as soon as he arrived he seduced the queen, and with her help conspired against the king and slew him, and took the kingdom. Suppose now that there were two such magic rings, and the moral put on one of them and the immoral the other, no man can be imagined to be of such an iron nature that he would stand fast in morality. No man would keep his hands off what was not his own when he could safely take what he liked out of the market, or go into houses and lie with anyone of his pleasure, or kill or release from prison whom he would, and in all respects be like a God among men. Then the actions of the moral would be as the actions of the immoral; they would both come at last to the same point. And this we may truly affirm to be a great proof that a man is moral, not willingly or because he thinks that morality is any good to him individually, but of necessity, for wherever anyone thinks that he can safely be immoral, there he is immoral. For all men believe in their hearts that immorality is far more profitable to the individual than morality, and he who argues as I have been supposing, will say that they are right. If you could imagine anyone obtaining this power of becoming invisible, and never doing any wrong or touching what was another's, he would be thought by the lookers-on to be a most wretched idiot, although they would praise him to one another's faces, and keep up appearances with one another from a fear that they too might be wronged. Enough of this.

Now, if we are to form a real judgment of the life of the moral and the immoral, we must isolate them; there is no other way; and how is the isolation to be effected? I answer: Let the immoral man be entirely immoral, and the moral man entirely moral, nothing is to be taken away from either of them, and both are to be perfectly furnished for the work of the respective lives. First, let the immoral be like other distinguished masters of craft; like the skilful pilot or physician, who knows intuitively his own powers and keeps within their limits, and who, if he fails at any point, is able to recover himself. So let the immoral make his immoral attempts in the right way, and lie hidden if he means to be great in his immorality (he who is found out is nobody): for the highest reach of immorality is, to be deemed moral when you are not. Therefore I say that in the perfectly immoral man we must assume the most perfect immorality; there is to be no deduction, but we must allow him, while doing the most immoral acts, to have acquired the greatest reputation for morality. If he has taken a false step he must be able to recover himself; he must be one who can speak with effect, if any of his deeds come to light, and who can force his way where force is required by his courage and strength, and command of money and friends. And at his side let us place the moral man in his nobleness and simplicity, wishing, as Aeschylus says, to be and not to seem good. There must be no seeming, for if he seem to be moral he will be honoured and rewarded, and then we shall not know whether he is moral for the sake of morality or for the sake of honours and rewards; therefore, let him be clothed in morality only, and have no other covering; and he must be imagined in a state of life the opposite of the former. Let him be the best of men, and let him be thought the worst; then he will have been put to the proof; and we shall see whether he will be affected by the fear of infamy and its consequences. And let him continue thus to the hour of death; being just and seeming to one unjust. When both have reached the uttermost extreme, the one of morality and the other of immorality, let judgment be given which of them is the happier of the two.

Heavens! my dear Glaucon, I said, how energetically you polish them up for the decision, first one and then the other, as if they were two statues.

I do my best, he said. And now that we know what they are like there is no difficulty in tracing out the sort of life which awaits either of them. This I will proceed to describe; but as you may think the description a little too coarse, I ask you to suppose, Socrates, that the words which follow are not mine. Let me put them into the mouths of the eulogists of immorality: they will tell you that the moral man who is thought immoral will be scourged, racked, bound – will have his eyes burnt out; and, at last, after suffering every kind of evil, he will be impaled: Then he will understand that he ought to seem only, and not to be, moral; the words of Aeschylus may be more truly spoken of the immoral than of the moral. For the immoral is pursuing a reality; he does not live with a view to appearances – he wants to be really immoral and not to seem only:

> His mind has a soil deep and fertile,
> Out of which spring his prudent counsels.

In the first place, he is thought moral, and therefore bears rule in the city; he can marry whom he will, and give in marriage to whom he will; also he can trade and deal where he likes, and always to his own advantage, because he has no misgivings about immorality, and at every contest, whether in public or private, he gets the better of his antagonists, and gains at their expense, and is rich, and out of his gains he can benefit his friends, and harm his enemies; moreover, he can offer sacrifices, and dedicate gifts to the gods abundantly and magnificently, and can honour the gods or any man whom he wants to honour in a far better style than the just, and therefore he is likely to be dearer than they are to the gods. And thus, Socrates, gods and men are said to unite in making the life of the immoral better than the life of the moral.

I was going to say something in answer to Glaucon, when Adeimantus, his brother, interposed: Socrates, he said, you do not suppose that there is nothing more to be urged?

Why, what else is there? I answered.

The strongest point of all has not been even mentioned, he replied.

Well, then, according to the proverb, 'Let brother help brother' – if he fails in any part do you assist him; although I must confess that Glaucon has already said quite enough to lay me in the dust, and take from me the power of helping morality.

Nonsense, he replied. But let me add something more: There is another side to Glaucon's argument about the praise and censure of morality and immorality, which is equally required in order to bring out what I believe to be his meaning. Parents and tutors are always telling their sons and their wards that they are to be moral; but why? Not for the sake of morality, but for the sake of character and reputation; in the hope of obtaining for him who is reputed just some of those offices, marriages and the like which Glaucon has enumerated among the advantages accruing to the immoral from the reputation of being moral. More, however, is made of appearances by this class of persons than by the others; for they throw in the good opinion of the gods, and will tell you of a shower of benefits which the heavens, as they say, rain upon the pious; and this accords with the testimony of the noble Hesiod and Homer, the first of whom says that the gods make the oaks of the just:

> To bear acorns at their summit, and bees in the middle;
> And the sheep are bowed down with the weight of their fleeces,

and many other blessings of a like kind are provided for them. And Homer has a very similar strain; for he speaks of one whose fame is

> As the fame of some blameless king who, like a god,
> Maintains justice; to whom the black earth brings forth
> Wheat and barley, whose trees are bowed with fruit,
> And his sheep never fail to bear, and the sea gives him fish.

Still grander are the gifts of heaven which Musaeus and his son vouchsafe to the moral; they take them down into the world below, where they have the saints lying on couches at a feast, everlastingly drunk, crowned with garlands; their idea seems to be that an immortality of drunkenness is the [finest wage] of virtue. Some extend their rewards yet further; the posterity, as they say, of the faithful shall survive to the third and fourth generation. This is the style in which they praise morality. But about the wicked there is another strain; they bury them in a slough in Hades, and make them carry water in a sieve; also while they are yet living they bring them to infamy, and inflict upon them the punishments which Glaucon described as the portion of the moral who are reputed to be immoral; nothing else does their invention supply. Such is their manner of praising the one and censuring the other.

Once more, Socrates, I will ask you to consider another way of speaking about morality and immorality, which is not confined to the poets, but is found in prose writers. The universal voice of mankind is always declaring that morality and virtue are honourable, but grievous and toilsome; and that the pleasures of vice . . . are easy of attainment, and are only censured by law and opinion. They say also that honesty is for the most part less profitable than dishonesty; and they are quite ready to call wicked men happy, and to honour them both in public and private when they are rich or in any other way influential, while they despise and overlook those who may be weak and poor, even though acknowledging them to be better than the others. But most extraordinary of all is their mode of speaking about virtue and the gods: they say that the gods apportion calamity and misery to many good men, and good and happiness to the wicked. And mendicant prophets go to rich men's doors and persuade them that they have a power committed to them by the gods of making an atonement for a man's own or his ancestor's sins by sacrifices or charms, with rejoicings and feasts; and they promise to harm an enemy, whether moral or immoral, at a small cost; with magic arts and incantations binding heaven, as they say, to execute their will. And the poets are the authorities to whom they appeal, now smoothing the path of vice with the words of Hesiod:

> Vice may be had in abundance without trouble; the way is smooth and her dwelling-place is near. But before virtue the gods have set toil,

and a tedious and uphill road: then citing Homer as a witness that the gods may be influenced by men; for he also says:

> The gods, too, may be turned from their purpose; and men pray to them and avert their wrath by sacrifices and soothing entreaties, and by libations and the odour of fat, when they have sinned and transgressed.

And they produce a host of books written by Musaeus and Orpheus, who were children of the Moon and the Muses – that is what they say – according to which they perform their ritual, and persuade not only individuals, but whole cities, that expiations and atonements for sin may be made by sacrifices and amusements which fill a vacant hour, and are equally at the service of the living and the dead; the latter sort they call mysteries, and they redeem us from the pains of hell, but if we neglect them no one knows what awaits us.

He proceeded: And now when the young hear all this said about virtue and vice, and the way in which gods and men regard them, how are their minds likely to be affected, my dear Socrates – those of them, I mean, who are quickwitted and, like bees on the wing, light on every flower, and from all that they hear are prone to draw conclusions as to what manner of persons they should be and in what way they should walk if they would make the best of life? Probably the youth will say to himself in the words of Pindar:

> Can I by honesty or by crooked ways of deceit ascend a loftier tower which may be a fortress to me all my days?

For what men say is that, if I am really moral and am not also thought to be moral, profit there is none, but the pain and loss on the other hand are unmistakable. But if, though immoral, I acquire the reputation of being moral, a heavenly life is promised to me. Since then, as philosophers prove, appearance tyrannizes over truth and is lord of happiness, to appearance I must devote myself. I will describe around me a picture and shadow of virtue to be the vestibule and exterior of my house; behind I will trail the subtle and crafty fox, as Archilochus, greatest of sages, recommends. But I hear someone exclaiming that the concealment of wickedness is often difficult; to which I answer, Nothing great is easy. Nevertheless, the argument indicates this, if we would be happy, to be the path along which we should proceed. With a view to concealment we will establish secret brotherhoods and political clubs. And there are professors of rhetoric who teach the art of persuading courts and assemblies; and so, partly by persuasion and partly by force, I shall make unlawful gains and not be punished. Still I hear a voice saying that the gods cannot be deceived, neither can they be compelled. But what if there are no gods? or, suppose them to have no care of human things – why in either case should we mind about concealment? And even if there are gods, and they do care about us, yet we know of them only from tradition and the genealogies of the poets; and these are the very persons who say that they may be influenced and turned by 'sacrifices and soothing entreaties and by offerings'. Let us be consistent then, and believe both or neither. If the poets speak truly, why then we had better do wrong, and offer of the fruits of our crimes; for if we are moral, although we may escape the vengeance of heaven, we shall lose the gains of doing wrong; but, if we are immoral we shall keep the gains, and by our sinning and praying, and praying and sinning, the gods will be propitiated, and we shall not be punished. 'But there is a world below in which either we or our posterity will suffer for our immoral deeds.' Yes, my friend, will be the [reply], but there are mysteries and atoning deities, and these have great power. That is what mighty cities declare; and the children of the gods, who were their poets and prophets, bear a like testimony. On what principle, then, shall we any longer choose morality rather than the worst immorality? When, if we only unite the latter with a deceitful regard to appearance, we shall fare well to our mind both with gods and men, in life and after death, as the most numerous and the highest authorities tell us. Knowing all this, Socrates, how can a man who has any superiority of mind or person or rank or wealth, be willing to honour morality; or indeed to refrain from laughing when he hears morality praised? And even if there should be someone who is able to disprove the truth of my words, and who is satisfied that morality is best, still he is not angry with the immoral, but is very ready to forgive them, because he also knows that men are not moral of their own free will; unless, peradventure, there be someone whom the divinity within him may have inspired with a hatred of immorality, or who has attained knowledge of the truth – but no other man. He only blames immorality who, owing to cowardice or age or some weakness, has not the power of doing wrong. And this is proved by the fact that when he obtains the power, he immediately does what is immoral as far as he can.

The cause of all this, Socrates, was indicated by us at the beginning of the argument, when my brother and I told you how astonished we were to find that of all the professing panegyrists of morality – beginning with the ancient heroes of whom any memorial has been preserved to us, and ending with the men of our own time – no one has ever blamed immorality or praised morality except with a view to the glories, honours and benefits which flow from them. No one has ever adequately described either in verse or prose the true essential nature of either of them abiding in the soul, and invisible to any human or divine eye; or shown that of all the things of a man's soul which he has within him, morality is the greatest good, and immorality the greatest evil. Had this been the universal strain, had you sought to persuade us of this from our youth upwards, we should not have been on the watch to keep one another from doing wrong, but everyone would have been his own watchman, because afraid, if he did wrong, of harbouring in himself the greatest of evils. I dare say that Thrasymachus and others would seriously hold the language which I have been merely repeating, and words even stronger than these about morality and immorality, grossly, as I conceive, perverting their true nature. But I speak in this vehement manner, as I must frankly confess to you, because I want to hear from you the opposite side; and I would ask you to show not only the superiority which morality has over immorality, but what effect they have on the possessor of them which makes the one to be a good and the other an evil to him. And please, as Glaucon requested of you, to exclude reputations; for unless you take away from each of them his true reputation and add on the false, we shall say that you do not praise morality, but the appearance of it; we shall think that you are only exhorting us to keep immorality dark, and that you really agree with Thrasymachus in thinking that morality is another's good and the interest of the stronger, and that immorality is a man's own profit and interest, though injurious to the weaker. Now as you have admitted that morality is one of that highest class of goods which are desired indeed for their results, but in a far greater degree for their own sakes – like sight or hearing or knowledge or health, or any other real and natural and not merely conventional good – I would ask you in your praise of morality to regard one point only: I mean the essential good and evil which morality and immorality work in the possessors of them. Let others praise morality and censure immorality, magnifying the rewards and honours of the one and abusing the other; that is a manner of arguing which, coming from them, I am ready to tolerate, but from you who have spent your whole life in the consideration of this question, unless I hear the contrary from your own lips, I expect something better. And therefore, I say, not only prove to us that morality is better than immorality, but show what either of them does to the possessor of them, which makes the one to be a good and the other an evil, whether seen or unseen by gods and men.

38 The Problem of Rationality: Is Morality Rationally Required?*

James P. Sterba

The main obstacle to showing that morality is rationally required is ethical egoism, which denies the priority of morality over self-interest. Basically, ethical egoism takes two forms: individual ethical egoism and universal ethical egoism. The basic principle of individual ethical egoism is:

Everyone ought to do what is in the overall self-interest of just one particular individual.

The basic principle of universal ethical egoism is:

Everyone ought to do what is in his or her overall self-interest.

Obviously, the practical requirements of these two forms of egoism would conflict significantly with the practical requirements of morality. How then can we show that the practical requirements of morality are rationally preferable to those of egoism?

Individual Ethical Egoism

In individual ethical egoism, all practical requirements are derived from the overall interests of just one particular individual. Let's call that individual Gladys. Because Gladys's interests constitute the sole basis for determining practical requirements according to individual ethical egoism, there should be no problem of inconsistent requirements, assuming, of course, that Gladys's own particular interests are in harmony. The crucial problem for individual ethical egoism, however, is justifying that only Gladys's interests should count in determining practical requirements. Individual ethical egoism must provide at least some reason for accepting that view. Otherwise, it would be irrational to accept the theory. But what reason or reasons could serve this function? Clearly, it will not do to cite some characteristic Gladys shares with other persons because whatever justification such a characteristic would provide for favoring Gladys's interests, it would also provide for favoring the interests of those other persons. Nor will it do to cite as a reason some unique characteristic of Gladys's, such as knowing all of Shakespeare's writings by heart, because such a characteristic involves a comparative element; consequently, others with similar characteristics, like knowing some or most of Shakespeare by heart, would still have some justification, although a proportionally lesser justification, for having their

* From James P. Sterba, *Three Challenges to Ethics: Environmentalism Feminism, and Multiculturalism* (New York and Oxford: Oxford University Press, 2001), pp. 5–19. © 2001 by Oxford University Press Inc. Used by permission of Oxford University Press Inc.

interests favored. But again the proposed characteristic would not justify favoring only Gladys's interests.

A similar objection could be raised if a unique relational characteristic were proposed as a reason for Gladys's special status – such as that Gladys is Seymour's wife. Because other persons would have similar but not identical relational characteristics, similar but not identical reasons would hold for them. Nor will it do to argue that the reason for Gladys's special status is not the particular unique traits that she possesses, but rather the mere fact that she has unique traits. The same would hold true of everyone else. Every individual has unique traits. If recourse to unique traits is dropped and Gladys claims that she is special simply because she is herself and wants to further her own interests, every other person could claim the same.

For the individual ethical egoist to argue that the same or similar reasons do *not* hold for other people with the same or similar characteristics as those of Gladys, she must explain *why* they do not hold. It must always be possible to understand how a characteristic serves as a reason in one case but not in another. If no explanation can be provided, and in the case of individual ethical egoism none has been forthcoming, the proposed characteristic either serves as a reason in both cases or does not serve as a reason at all.

Universal Ethical Egoism

Unfortunately, these objections to individual ethical egoism do not work against universal ethical egoism because the latter does provide a reason why the egoist should be concerned simply about maximizing his or her own interests. The reason is simply that the egoist is herself and wants to further her own interests. The individual ethical egoist could not recognize such a reason without giving up his view, but the universal ethical egoist is willing and able to universalize her claim and recognize that everyone has a similar justification for adopting universal ethical egoism.

Accordingly, the objections that typically have been raised against universal ethical egoism take a different tack and attempt to show that the view is fundamentally inconsistent. For the purpose of evaluating these objections, let's consider the case of Gary Gyges, an otherwise normal human being who, for reasons of personal gain, has embezzled $1,000,000 while working at People's National Bank, and is in the process of escaping to a South Sea island where he will be able to live a pleasant life protected by the local authorities and untroubled by any qualms of conscience. Suppose that Hedda Hawkeye, a coworker, knows that Gyges has been embezzling money from the bank and is about to escape. Suppose, further, that it is in Hawkeye's overall self-interest to prevent Gyges from escaping with the embezzled money because she will be generously rewarded for doing so by being appointed vice president of the bank. Given that it is in Gyges's overall self-interest to escape with embezzled money, it now appears that we can derive a contradiction from the following:

1. Gyges ought to escape with the embezzled money.
2. Hawkeye ought to prevent Gyges from escaping with the embezzled money.
3. By preventing Gyges from escaping with the embezzled money, Hawkeye is preventing Gyges from doing what he ought to do.
4. One ought never to prevent someone from doing what he or she ought to do.

5.   Therefore, Hawkeye ought not to prevent Gyges from escaping with the embezzled money.

Because premises 2 and 5 are contradictory, universal ethical egoism appears to be inconsistent.

The soundness of this argument depends, however, on premise 4, and defenders of universal ethical egoism believe there are grounds for rejecting this premise. For if "preventing an action" means "rendering the action impossible," it would appear that there *are* cases in which a person is justified in preventing someone else from doing what he or she ought to do. Suppose for example, that Irma and Igor are both actively competing for the same position at a prestigious law firm. If Irma accepts the position, she obviously renders it impossible for Igor to obtain the position. But surely this is *not* what we normally think of as an unacceptable form of prevention. Nor would Hawkeye's prevention of Gyges's escape appear to be unacceptable. Thus, to sustain the argument against universal ethical egoism, one must distinguish between acceptable and unacceptable forms of prevention and then show that the argument succeeds even for forms of prevention that a universal ethical egoist should regard as unacceptable. This requires elucidating the force of "ought" in universal ethical egoism.

To illustrate the sense in which a universal ethical egoist claims that other persons ought to do what is in their overall self-interest, defenders often appeal to an analogy of competitive games. For example, in football a defensive player might think that the opposing team's quarterback ought to pass on third down with five yards to go, while not wanting the quarterback to do so and planning to prevent any such attempt. Or to use Jesse Kalin's example:

> I may see how my chess opponent can put my king in check. This is how he ought to move. But believing that he ought to move his bishop and check my king does not commit me to wanting him to do that, nor to persuading him to do so. What I ought to do is sit there quietly, hoping he does not move as he ought.

The point of these examples is to suggest that a universal ethical egoist may, like a player in a game, judge that others ought to do what is in their overall self-interest while simultaneously attempting to prevent such actions, or at least refraining from encouraging them.

The analogy of competitive games also illustrates the sense in which a universal ethical egoist claims that she herself ought to do what is in her overall self-interest. For just as a player's judgment that she ought to make a particular move is followed, other things being equal, by an attempt to perform the appropriate action, so likewise when a universal ethical egoist judges that she ought to do some particular action, other things being equal, an attempt to perform the appropriate action follows. In general, defenders of universal ethical egoism stress that because we have little difficulty understanding the implications of the use of "ought" in competitive games, we should also have little difficulty understanding the analogous use of "ought" by the universal ethical egoist.

To claim, however, that the "oughts" in competitive games are analogous to the "oughts" of universal ethical egoism does not mean there are no differences between them. Most importantly, competitive games are governed by moral constraints such that when everyone plays the game properly, there are acceptable moral limits as to what one can do. For example, in football one cannot poison the opposing quarterback in order to win the game. By contrast, when everyone holds self-interested reasons to be supreme, the only limit to what one can do is the point beyond which one ceases to benefit. But this important difference between the "oughts" of universal ethical egoism and the "oughts" found in publicly recognized activities like competitive games does not defeat the appropriateness of the analogy. That the "oughts" found in publicly recognized activities are always limited by various moral constraints (What else would get publicly recognized?) does not preclude their being a suggestive model for the unlimited action-guiding character of the "oughts" of universal ethical egoism. What all this shows is that the most promising attempt to show that universal ethical egoism is inconsistent unfortunately fails to do so.

From Rationality to Morality

Yet despite our inability to show that universal ethical egoism is inconsistent, there are still grounds for showing that morality is rationally preferable to universal ethical egoism. This is because it can be shown that the universal ethical egoist, although consistent, acts contrary to reason in rejecting morality.

To see this, let us imagine that each of us is capable of entertaining and acting upon both self-interested and moral reasons and that the question we are seeking to answer is what sort of reasons for action it would be rational for us to accept. This question is not about what sort of reasons we should publicly affirm, since people will sometimes publicly affirm reasons that are quite different from those they are prepared to act upon. Rather it is a question about what reasons it would be rational for us to accept at the deepest level – in our heart of hearts.

Of course, there are people who are incapable of acting upon moral reasons. For such people, there is no question about their being required to act morally or altruistically. Yet the interesting philosophical question is not about such people but about people like ourselves, who are capable of acting morally as well as self-interestedly and are seeking a rational justification for following a particular course of action.

In trying to determine how we should act, let us assume that we would like to be able to construct a *good* argument favoring morality over egoism, and given that good arguments are non-question-begging, we accordingly would like to construct an argument that, as far as possible, does not beg the question. The question at issue here is what reasons each of us should take as supreme, and this question would be begged against egoism if we proposed to answer it simply by assuming from the start that moral reasons are the reasons that each of us should take as supreme. But the question would be begged against morality as well if we proposed to answer the question simply by assuming from the start that self-interested reasons are the reasons that each of us should take as supreme. This means, of course, that we cannot answer the question of what reasons we should take as supreme simply by assuming the general principle of egoism:

Each person ought to do what best serves his or her overall self-interest.

We can no more argue for egoism simply by denying the relevance of moral reasons to rational choice than we can argue for pure altruism simply by denying the relevance of self-interested reasons to rational choice and assuming the following general principle of pure altruism:

Each person ought to do what best serves the overall interest of others.

Consequently, in order not to beg the question, we have no other alternative but to grant the prima facie relevance of both self-interested and moral reasons to rational choice and then try to determine which reasons we would be rationally required to act upon, all things considered. Notice that in order not to beg the question, it is necessary to back off from both the general principle of egoism and the general principle of pure altruism, thus granting the prima facie relevance of both self-interested and moral reasons to rational choice. From this standpoint, it is still an open question whether either egoism or pure altruism will be rationally preferable, all things considered.

In this regard, there are two kinds of cases that must be considered: cases in which there is a conflict between the relevant self-interested and moral reasons, and cases in which there is no such conflict.

It seems obvious that where there is no conflict and both reasons are conclusive reasons of their kind, both reasons should be acted upon. In such contexts, we should do what is favored both by morality and by self-interest.

Consider the following example. Suppose you accepted a job marketing a baby formula in a developing country where the formula was improperly used, leading to increased infant mortality. Imagine that you could just as well have accepted an equally attractive and rewarding job marketing a similar formula in a developed country, where the misuse does not occur, so that a rational weighing of the relevant self-interested reasons alone would not have favored your acceptance of one of these jobs over the other. At the same time, there were obviously moral reasons that condemned your acceptance of the first job – reasons that you presumably are or were able to acquire. Moreover, by assumption in this case, the moral reasons do not clash with the relevant self-interested reasons; they simply made a recommendation where the relevant self-interested reasons were silent. Consequently, a rational weighing of all the relevant reasons in this case could not but favor acting in accord with the relevant moral reasons.

Yet it might be objected that in cases of this sort there would frequently be other reasons significantly opposed to these moral reasons – other reasons that you are or were able to acquire. Such reasons would be either *malevolent*, seeking to bring about the suffering and death of other human beings; *benevolent*, concerned to promote nonhuman welfare even at the expense of human welfare; or *aesthetic*, concerned to produce valuable results irrespective of the effects on human or nonhuman welfare. But assuming that such malevolent reasons are ultimately rooted in some conception of what is good for oneself or others, these reasons would have already been taken into account, and by assumption outweighed by the other relevant reasons in this case. And although neither benevolent reasons (concerned to promote nonhuman welfare) nor aesthetic reasons would have been taken into account, such reasons are not directly relevant to justifying morality over egoism. Consequently, even with the presence of these three kinds of reasons, your acceptance of the first job can still be seen to be contrary to the relevant reasons in this case.

Needless to say, defenders of egoism cannot but be disconcerted with this result since it shows that actions in accord with egoism are contrary to reason at least when there are two equally good ways of pursuing one's self-interest, only one of which does not conflict with the basic requirements of morality. Notice also that in cases where there are two equally good ways of fulfilling the basic requirements of morality, only one of which does not conflict with what is in a person's overall self-interest, it is not at all disconcerting for defenders of morality to admit that we are rationally required to choose the way that does not conflict with what is in our overall self-interest. Nevertheless, exposing this defect in egoism for cases where moral reasons and self-interested reasons do not conflict would be but a small victory for defenders of morality if it were not also possible to show that in cases where such reasons do conflict, moral reasons would have priority over self-interested reasons.

Now when we rationally assess the relevant reasons in conflict cases, it is best to cast the conflict not as a conflict between self-interested reasons and moral reasons but instead as a conflict between self-interested reasons and altruistic reasons. Viewed in this way, three solutions are possible. First, we could say that self-interested reasons always have priority over conflicting altruistic reasons. Second, we could say just the opposite, that altruistic reasons always have priority over conflicting self-interested reasons. Third, we could say that some kind of compromise is rationally required. In this compromise, sometimes self-interested reasons would have priority over altruistic reasons, and sometimes altruistic reasons would have priority over self-interested reasons.

Once the conflict is described in this manner, the third solution can be seen to be the one that is rationally required. This is because the first and second solutions give exclusive priority to one class of relevant reasons over the other, and only a completely question-begging justification can be given for such an exclusive priority. Only by employing the third solution, and sometimes giving priority to self-interested reasons, and sometimes giving priority to altruistic reasons, can we avoid a completely question-begging resolution.

Suppose for example, that you are in the waste disposal business and you have decided to dispose of toxic wastes in a manner that is cost-efficient for you but predictably causes significant harm to future generations. Imagine that there are alternative methods available for disposing of the waste that are only slightly less cost-efficient and will not cause any significant harm to future generations. In this case, you are to weigh your self-interested reasons favoring the most cost-efficient disposal of the toxic wastes against the relevant altruistic reasons favoring the avoidance of significant harm to future generations. If we suppose that the projected loss of benefit to yourself was ever so slight and the projected harm to future generations was ever so great, then a nonarbitrary compromise between the relevant self-interested and altruistic reasons would have to favor the altruistic reasons in this case. Hence, as judged by a non-question-begging standard of rationality, your method of waste disposal was contrary to the relevant reasons.

Notice also that this standard of rationality will not support just any compromise between the relevant self-interested and altruistic reasons. The compromise must be a nonarbitrary one, for otherwise it would beg the question with respect to the opposing egoistic and altruistic perspectives. Such a compromise would have to respect the rankings of self-interested and altruistic reasons imposed by the egoistic and altruistic perspectives, respectively. Since for each individual there is a separate ranking of that individual's relevant self-interested and altruistic reasons (which will vary, of course, depending on the individual's capabilities and circumstances), we can represent these rankings from the most important reasons to the least important reasons as shown in table 1. Accordingly, any nonarbitrary compromise among such reasons in seeking not to beg the question against either egoism or pure altruism will have to give priority to those reasons that rank highest in each category. Failure to give priority to the highest-ranking altruistic or self-interested reasons would, other things being equal, be contrary to reason.

Table 1

Individual A		Individual B	
Self-interested reasons	Altruistic reasons	Self-interested reasons	Altruistic reasons
1	1	1	1
2	2	2	2
3	3	3	3
•	•	•	•
•	•	•	•
•	•	•	•
N	N	N	N

Of course, there will be cases in which the only way to avoid being required to do what is contrary to your highest-ranking reasons is by requiring someone else to do what is contrary to her highest-ranking reasons. Some of these cases will be "lifeboat cases," as, for example, where you and two others are stranded on a lifeboat that has only enough resources for two of you to survive before you will be rescued. But although such cases are surely difficult to resolve (maybe only a chance mechanism, like flipping a coin, can offer a reasonable resolution), they surely do not reflect the typical conflict between the relevant self-interested and altruistic reasons that we are or were able to acquire. Typically, one or the other of the conflicting reasons will rank significantly higher on its respective scale, thus permitting a clear resolution.

Now we can see how morality can be viewed as just such a nonarbitrary compromise between self-interested and altruistic reasons. First, a certain amount of self-regard is morally required or at least morally acceptable. Where this is the case, high-ranking self-interested reasons have priority over low-ranking altruistic reasons. Second, morality obviously places limits on the extent to which people should pursue their own self-interest. Where this is the case, high-ranking altruistic reasons have priority over low-ranking self-interested reasons. In this way, morality can be seen to be a nonarbitrary compromise between self-interested and altruistic reasons, and the "moral reasons" that constitute that compromise can be seen as having an absolute priority over the self-interested or altruistic reasons that conflict with them.

It is also important to see how this compromise view has been supported by a two-step argument that is not question-begging at all. In the first step, our goal was to determine what sort of reasons for action it would be rational for us to accept on the basis of a good argument, and this required a non-question-begging starting point. Noting that both egoism, which favored exclusively self-interested reasons, and pure altruism, which favored exclusively altruistic reasons, offered only question-begging starting points, we took as our non-question-begging starting point the prima facie relevance of both self-interested and altruistic reasons to rational choice. The logical inference here is analogous to the inference of equal probability sanctioned in decision theory when we have no evidence that one alternative is more likely than another. Here we had no non-question-begging justification for excluding either self-interested or altruistic reasons as relevant to rational choice, so we accepted both kinds of reasons as prima facie relevant to rational choice. The conclusion of this first step of the argument for the compromise view does not beg the question against egoism or pure altruism because if defenders of either view had any hope of providing a good and, hence, non-question-begging argument for their view, they too would have to grant this very conclusion as necessary for a non-question-begging defense of either egoism, pure altruism, or the compromise view. In accepting it, therefore, the compromise view does not beg the question against a possible non-question-begging defense of these other two perspectives, and that is all that should concern us.

Now once both self-interested and altruistic reasons are recognized as prima facie relevant to rational choice, the second step of the argument for the compromise view offers a nonarbitrary ordering of those reasons on the basis of rankings of self-interested and altruistic reasons imposed by the egoistic and altruistic perspectives respectively. According to that ordering, high-ranking self-interested reasons have priority over low-ranking altruistic reasons and high-ranking altruistic reasons have priority over low-ranking self-interested reasons. There is no other plausible nonarbitrary ordering of these reasons. Hence, it certainly does not beg the question against either the egoistic or altruistic perspective, once we imagine those perspectives (or their defenders) to be suitably reformed so that they too are committed to a standard of non-question-beggingness. In the end, if one is committed to a standard of non-question-beggingness, one has to be concerned only with how one's claims and arguments stack up against others who are also committed to such a standard. If you yourself are committed to the standard of non-question-beggingness, you don't beg the question by simply coming into conflict with the requirements of other perspectives, unless those other perspectives (or their defenders) are also committed to the same standard of non-question-beggingness. In arguing for one's view, when one comes into conflict with bigots, one does not beg the question against them unless one is a bigot oneself.

Suppose, for example, that we are trying to decide who are the two greatest moral and political philosophers of the twentieth century. Suppose some of us assume from the start that the two must belong to the British-American tradition and proceed to nominate John Rawls and R. M. Hare, while the others assume from the start that the two must belong to the Continental tradition and nominate Jürgen Habermas and Jean-Paul Sartre. By contrast, a compromise view, in order not to beg the question, would start by assuming that the two greatest moral and political philosopher of the twentieth century could belong to either the British-American or the Continental tradition or, for that matter, to any philosophical tradition, and it might well proceed to nominate John Rawls and Jurgen Habermas. This would put the compromise view partly in conflict and partly in agreement with the two other views taken in this discussion, but it would not show that it begged the question against them, because they did not approach the discussion in a non-question-begging manner. Again, being in conflict with bigots does not necessarily make one a bigot; to be a bigot, you yourself must also be arguing from a question-begging standpoint.

Accordingly, it would be a mistake to think that the conflicts that exist between the compromise view and either an unreformed egoistic or an unreformed altruistic perspective is grounds for thinking that the compromise view begs the question against those perspectives. Thus, we can imagine an unreformed altruistic perspective as holding that:

(1) All high-ranking altruistic reasons have priority over conflicting lower-ranking self-interested reasons.
(2) All low-ranking altruistic reasons have priority over conflicting higher-ranking self-interested reasons.

And we can also imagine an unreformed egoistic perspective as holding that:

(1′)   All high-ranking self-interested reasons have priority over conflicting lower-ranking altruistic reasons.
(2′)   All low-ranking self-interested reasons have priority over conflicting higher-ranking altruistic reasons.

By contrast, the compromise view holds (1) and (1′). Now one might think that part of what the compromise view holds about the priority of reasons – i.e., (1) – begs the question against an unreformed egoistic perspective, and another part – i.e., (1′) – begs the question against an unreformed altruistic perspective; hence, to that extent, one might conclude that the compromise view does beg the question against each view. But there is no reason to view the conflicts between the compromise view and an unreformed egoistic perspective or an unreformed altruistic perspective as begging the question against those perspectives. To beg the question, it is not enough that one is in complete or partial conflict with someone else's view; you, or both you and they, must also be proceeding from a question-begging standpoint. And this is clearly not the case with respect to the compromise view.

Now it might be objected that even if morality is required by a standard of non-question-beggingness, that does not provide us with the right kind of reason to be moral. It might be argued that avoiding non-question-beggingness is too formal a reason to be moral and that we need a more substantive reason. Happily, the need for a substantive reason to be moral can be met, because in this case the formal reason to be moral – namely, avoiding non-question-beggingness – itself entails a substantive reason to be moral – namely, to give high-ranking altruistic reasons priority over conflicting lower-ranking self-interested reasons and high-ranking self-interested reasons priority over conflicting lower-ranking altruistic reasons, or, to put the reason more substantively still, to avoid inflicting basic harm for the sake of nonbasic benefit. So, as it turns out, morality as compromise can be shown to provide both formal and substantive reasons to be moral.

Of course, exactly how this compromise is to be worked out is a matter of considerable debate, which brings us to our third problem of traditional ethics – the problem of practical requirements. Yet however this debate over practical requirements is resolved, it is clear that some sort of compromise moral solution is rationally preferable to either egoism or pure altruism when judged from a non-question-begging standpoint.

39   From *Utilitarianism**

John Stuart Mill

Chapter I: General Remarks

There are few circumstances among those which make up the present condition of human knowledge more unlike what might have been expected, or more significant of the backward state in which speculation on the most important subjects still lingers, than the little progress which has been made in the decision of the controversy respecting the criterion of right and wrong. From the dawn of philosophy, the question concerning the *summum bonum*, or, what is the same thing, concerning the foundation of morality, has been accounted the main problem in speculative thought, has occupied the most gifted intellects and divided them into sects and schools carrying on a vigorous warfare against one another. And after more than two thousand years the same discussions continue, philosophers are still ranged under the same contending banners, and neither thinkers nor mankind at large seem nearer to being unanimous on the subject than when the youth Socrates listened to the old Protagoras and asserted (if Plato's dialogue be grounded on a real conversation) the theory of utilitarianism against the popular morality of the so-called sophist.

It is true that similar confusion and uncertainty and, in some cases, similar discordance exist respecting the first principles of all the sciences, not excepting that which is deemed the most certain of them – mathematics, without much impairing, generally indeed without impairing at all, the trustworthiness of the conclusions of those sciences. An apparent anomaly, the explanation of which is that the detailed doctrines of a science are not usually deduced from, nor depend for their evidence upon, what are called its first principles. Were it not so, there would be no science more precarious, or whose conclusions were more insufficiently made out, than algebra, which derives none of its certainty from what are commonly taught to learners as its elements, since these, as laid down by some of its most eminent teachers, are as full of fictions as English law, and of mysteries as theology. The truths which are ultimately accepted as the first principles of a science are really the last results of metaphysical analysis practiced on the elementary notions with which the science is conversant; and their relation to the science is not that of foundations to an edifice, but of roots to a tree, which may perform their office equally well though they be never dug down to and exposed to light. But though in science the particular truths precede the general theory, the contrary might be expected to be the case with a practical art, such as morals or legislation. All action is for the sake of some end, and rules of action, it seems natural to suppose, must take their whole character and color from the end to which they are subservient. When we engage in a pursuit, a clear and precise conception of what we are pursuing would seem to be the first thing we need, instead of the last we are to look forward to. A test of right and wrong must be the means, one would think, of ascertaining what is right or wrong, and not a consequence of having already ascertained it.

---

* From *Utilitarianism*, chapters I, II and IV. First published in 1863. Public domain.

The difficulty is not avoided by having recourse to the popular theory of a natural faculty, a sense of instinct, informing us of right and wrong. For – besides that the existence of such a moral instinct is itself one of the matters in dispute – those believers in it who have any pretensions to philosophy have been obliged to abandon the idea that it discerns what is right or wrong in the particular case in hand, as our other senses discern the sight or sound actually present. Our moral faculty, according to all those of its interpreters who are entitled to the name of thinkers, supplies us only with the general principles of moral judgments; it is a branch of our reason, not of our sensitive faculty, and must be looked to for the abstract doctrines of morality, not for perception of it in the concrete. The intuitive, no less than what may be termed the inductive, school of ethics insists on the necessity of general laws. They both agree that the morality of an individual action is not a question of direct perception, but of the application of a law to an individual case. They recognize also, to a great extent, the same moral laws, but differ as to their evidence and the source from which they derive their authority. According to the one opinion, the principles of morals are evident a priori, requiring nothing to command assent except that the meaning of the terms be understood. According to the other doctrine, right and wrong, as well as truth and falsehood, are questions of observation and experience. But both hold equally that morality must be deduced from principles; and the intuitive school affirm as strongly as the inductive that there is a science of morals. Yet they seldom attempt to make out a list of the a priori principles which are to serve as the premises of the science; still more rarely do they make any effort to reduce those various principles to one first principle or common ground of obligation. They either assume the ordinary precepts of morals as of a priori authority, or they lay down as the common groundwork of those maxims some generality much less obviously authoritative than the maxims themselves, and which has never succeeded in gaining popular acceptance. Yet to support their pretensions there ought either to be some one fundamental principle or law at the root of all morality, or, if there be several, there should be a determinate order of precedence among them; and the one principle, or the rule for deciding between the various principles when they conflict, ought to be self-evident.

To inquire how far the bad effects of this deficiency have been mitigated in practice, or to what extent the moral beliefs of mankind have been vitiated or made uncertain by the absence of any distinct recognition of an ultimate standard, would imply a complete survey and criticism of past and present ethical doctrine. It would, however, be easy to show that whatever steadiness or consistency these moral beliefs have attained has been mainly due to the tacit influence of a standard not recognized. Although the non-existence of an acknowledged first principle has made ethics not so much a guide as a consecration of men's actual sentiments, still, as men's sentiments, both of favor and of aversion, are greatly influenced by what they suppose to be the effects of things upon their happiness, the principle of utility, or, as Bentham latterly called it, the greatest happiness principle, has had a large share in forming the moral doctrines even of those who most scornfully reject its authority. Nor is there any school of thought which refuses to admit that the influence of actions on happiness is a most material and even predominant consideration in many of the details of morals, however unwilling to acknowledge it as the fundamental principle of morality and the source of moral obligation. I might go much further and say that to all those a priori moralists who deem it necessary to argue at all, utilitarian arguments are indispensable. It is not my present purpose to criticize these thinkers; but I cannot help referring, for illustration, to a systematic treatise by one of the most illustrious of them, the *Metaphysics of Ethics* by Kant. This remarkable man, whose system of thought will long remain one of the landmarks in the history of philo-sophical speculation, does, in the treatise in question, lay down a universal first principle as the origin and ground of moral obligation; it is this: "So act that the rule on which thou actest would admit of being adopted as a law by all rational beings." But when he begins to deduce from this precept any of the actual duties of morality, he fails, almost grotesquely, to show that there would be any contradiction, any logical (not to say phys-ical) impossibility, in the adoption by all rational beings of the most outrageously immoral rules of conduct. All he shows is that the *consequences* of their universal adoption would be such as no one would choose to incur.

On the present occasion, I shall, without further discussion of the other theories, attempt to contribute something toward the understanding and appreciation of the "util-itarian" or "happiness" theory, and toward such proof as it is susceptible of. It is evident that this cannot be proof in the ordinary and popular meaning of the term. Questions of ultimate ends are not amenable to direct proof. Whatever can be proved to be good must be so by being shown to be a means to something admitted to be good without proof. The medical art is proved to be good by its conducing to health; but how is it possible to prove that health is good? The art of music is good, for the reason, among others, that it produces pleasure; but what proof is it possible to give that pleasure is good? If, then, it is asserted that there is a comprehensive formula, including all things which are in themselves good, and that whatever else is good is not so as an end but as a means, the formula may be accepted or rejected, but is not a subject of what is commonly under-stood by proof. We are not, however, to infer that its acceptance or rejection must depend on blind impulse or arbitrary choice. There is a large meaning of the word "proof," in which this question is as amenable to it as any other of the disputed questions of philos-ophy. The subject is within the cognizance of the rational faculty; and neither does that faculty deal with it solely in the way of intuition. Considerations may be presented capable of determining the intellect either to give or withhold its assent to the doctrine; and this is equivalent to proof.

We shall examine presently of what nature are these considerations; in what manner they apply to the case, and what rational grounds, therefore, can be given for accepting or rejecting the utilitarian formula. But it is a preliminary condition of rational accept-ance or rejection that the formula should be correctly understood. I believe that the very imperfect notion ordinarily formed of its meaning is the chief obstacle which impedes its reception, and that, could it be cleared even from only the grosser misconceptions, the question would be greatly simplified and a large proportion of its difficulties removed. Before, therefore, I attempt to enter into the philosophical grounds which can be given for assenting to the utilitarian standard, I shall offer some illustrations of the doctrine itself, with the view of showing more clearly what it is, distinguishing it from what it is not, and disposing of such of the practical objections to it as either originate in, or are closely connected with, mistaken interpretations of its meaning. Having thus prepared the ground, I shall afterwards endeavor to throw such light as I can call upon the ques-tion considered as one of philosophical theory.

Chapter II: What Utilitarianism Is

A passing remark is all that needs be given to the ignorant blunder of supposing that those who stand up for utility as the test of right and wrong use the term in that restricted and merely colloquial sense in which utility is opposed to pleasure. An apology is due to the philosophical opponents of utilitarianism for even the momentary appearance of confounding them with anyone capable of so absurd a misconception; which is the more extraordinary, inasmuch as the contrary accusation, of referring everything to pleasure, and that, too, in its grossest form, is another of the common charges against utilitarianism: and, as has been pointedly remarked by an able writer, the same sort of persons, and often the very same persons, denounce the theory "as impracticably dry when the word 'utility' precedes the word 'pleasure,' and as too practically voluptuous when the word 'pleasure' precedes the word 'utility.'" Those who know anything about the matter are aware that every writer, from Epicurus to Bentham, who maintained the theory of utility meant by it, not something to be contradistinguished from pleasure, but pleasure itself, together with exemption from pain; and instead of opposing the useful to the agreeable or the ornamental, have always declared that the useful means these, among other things. Yet the common herd, including the herd of writers, not only in newspapers and periodicals, but in books of weight and pretension, are perpetually falling into this shallow mistake. Having caught up the word "utilitarian," while knowing nothing whatever about it but its sound, they habitually express by it the rejection or the neglect of pleasure in some of its forms: of beauty, of ornament, or of amusement. Nor is the term thus ignorantly misapplied solely in disparagement, but occasionally in compliment, as though it implied superiority to frivolity and the mere pleasures of the moment. And this perverted use is the only one in which the word is popularly known, and the one from which the new generation are acquiring their sole notion of its meaning. Those who introduced the word, but who had for many years discontinued it as a distinctive appellation, may well feel themselves called upon to resume it if by doing so they can hope to contribute anything toward rescuing it from this utter degradation.[1]

The creed which accepts as the foundation of morals "utility" or the "greatest happiness principle" holds that actions are right in proportion as they tend to promote happiness; wrong as they tend to produce the reverse of happiness. By happiness is intended pleasure and the absence of pain; by unhappiness, pain and the privation of pleasure. To give a clear view of the moral standard set up by the theory, much more requires to be said; in particular, what things it includes in the ideas of pain and pleasure, and to what extent this is left an open question. But these supplementary explanations do not affect the theory of life on which this theory of morality is grounded – namely, that pleasure and freedom from pain are the only things desirable as ends; and that all desirable things (which are as numerous in the utilitarian as in any other scheme) are desirable either for pleasure inherent in themselves or as means to the promotion of pleasure and the prevention of pain.

Now such a theory of life excites in many minds, and among them in some of the most estimable in feeling and purpose, inveterate dislike. To suppose that life has (as they express it) no higher end than pleasure – no better and nobler object of desire and pursuit – they designate as utterly mean and groveling, as a doctrine worthy only of swine, to whom the followers of Epicurus were, at a very early period, contemptuously likened; and modern holders of the doctrine are occasionally made the subject of equally polite comparisons by its German, French, and English assailants.

When thus attacked, the Epicureans have always answered that it is not they, but their accusers, who represent human nature in a degrading light, since the accusation supposes human beings to be capable of no pleasures except those of which swine are capable. If this supposition were true, the charge could not be gainsaid, but would then be no longer an imputation; for if the sources of pleasure were precisely the same to human beings and to swine, the rule of life which is good enough for the one would be good enough for the other. The comparison of the Epicurean life to that of beasts is felt as degrading, precisely because a beast's pleasures do not satisfy a human being's conceptions of happiness. Human beings have faculties more elevated than the animal appetites and, when once made conscious of them, do not regard anything as happiness which does not include their gratification. I do not, indeed, consider the Epicureans to have been by any means faultless in drawing out their scheme of consequences from the utilitarian principle. To do this in any sufficient manner, many Stoic, as well as Christian, elements require to be included. But there is no known Epicurean theory of life which does not assign to the pleasures of the intellect, of the feelings and imagination, and of the moral sentiments a much higher value as pleasures than to those of mere sensation. It must be admitted, however, that utilitarian writers in general have placed the superiority of mental over bodily pleasures chiefly in the greater permanency, safety, uncostliness, etc., of the former – that is, in their circumstantial advantages rather than in their intrinsic nature. And on all these points utilitarians have fully proved their case; but they might have taken the other and, as it may be called, higher ground with entire consistency. It is quite compatible with the principle of utility to recognize the fact that some kinds of pleasure are more desirable and more valuable than others. It would be absurd that, while in estimating all other things quality is considered as well as quantity, the estimation of pleasure should be supposed to depend on quantity alone.

If I am asked what I mean by difference of quality in pleasures, or what makes one pleasure more valuable than another, merely as a pleasure, except its being greater in amount, there is but one possible answer. Of two pleasures, if there be one to which all or almost all who have experience of both give a decided preference, irrespective of any feeling of moral obligation to prefer it, that is the more desirable pleasure. If one of the two is, by those who are competently acquainted with both, placed so far above the other that they prefer it, even though knowing it to be attended with a greater amount of discontent, and would not resign it for any quantity of the other pleasure which their nature is capable of, we are justified in ascribing to the preferred enjoyment a superiority in quality so far outweighing quantity as to render it, in comparison, of small account.

Now it is an unquestionable fact that those who are equally acquainted with and equally capable of appreciating and enjoying both do give a most marked preference to the manner of existence which employs their higher faculties. Few human creatures would consent to be changed into any of the lower animals for a promise of the fullest allowance of a beast's pleasures; no intelligent human being would consent to be a fool, no instructed person would be an ignoramus, no person of feeling and conscience would be selfish and base, even though they should be persuaded that the fool, the dunce, or the rascal is better satisfied with his lot than they are with theirs. They would not resign what they possess more than he for the most complete satisfaction of all the desires which they have in common with him. If they ever fancy they would, it is only in cases of unhappiness so extreme that to escape from it they would exchange their lot for almost any other, however undesirable in their own eyes. A being of higher faculties requires more to make him happy, is capable probably of more acute suffering, and certainly accessible to it at more points, than one of an inferior type; but in spite of these liabilities, he can never really wish to sink into what he feels to be a lower grade of existence. We may give what explanation we please of this unwillingness; we may attribute it to pride, a name which is given indiscriminately to some of the most and to some of the least estimable feelings of which mankind are capable; we may refer it to the love of liberty and personal independence, an appeal to which was with the Stoics one of the most effective means for the inculcation of it; to the love of power or to the love of excitement, both of which do really enter into and contribute to it; but its most appropriate appellation is a sense of dignity, which all human beings possess in one form or other, and in some, though by no means in exact, proportion to their higher faculties, and which is so essential a part of the happiness of those in whom it is strong that nothing which conflicts with it could be otherwise than momentarily an object of desire to them. Whoever supposes that this preference takes place at a sacrifice of happiness – that the superior being, in anything like equal circumstances, is not happier than the inferior – confounds the two very different ideas of happiness and content. It is indisputable that the being whose capacities of enjoyment are low has the greatest chance of having them fully satisfied; and a highly endowed being will always feel that any happiness which he can look for, as the world is constituted, is imperfect. But he can learn to bear its imperfections, if they are at all bearable; and they will not make him envy the being who is indeed unconscious of the imperfections, but only because he feels not at all the good which those imperfections qualify. It is better to be a human being dissatisfied than a pig satisfied; better to be Socrates dissatisfied than a fool satisfied. And if the fool, or the pig, are of a different opinion, it is because they only know their own side of the question. The other party to the comparison knows both sides.

It may be objected that many who are capable of the higher pleasures occasionally, under the influence of temptation, postpone them to the lower. But this is quite compatible with a full appreciation of the intrinsic superiority of the higher. Men often, from infirmity of character, make their election for the nearer good, though they know it to be the less valuable; and this no less when the choice is between two bodily pleasures than when it is between bodily and mental. They pursue sensual indulgences to the injury of health, though perfectly aware that health is the greater good. It may be further objected that many who begin with youthful enthusiasm for everything noble, as they advance in years, sink into indolence and selfishness. But I do not believe that those who undergo this very common change voluntarily choose the lower description of pleasures in preference to the higher. I believe that, before they devote themselves exclusively to the one, they have already become incapable of the other. Capacity for the nobler feelings is in most natures a very tender plant, easily killed, not only by hostile influences, but by mere want of sustenance; and in the majority of young persons it speedily dies away if the occupations to which their position in life has devoted them, and the society into which it has thrown them, are not favorable to keeping that higher capacity in exercise. Men lose their high aspirations as they lose their intellectual tastes, because they have not time or opportunity for indulging them; and they addict themselves to inferior pleasures, not because they deliberately prefer them, but because they are either the only ones to which they have access or the only ones which they are any longer capable of enjoying. It may be questioned whether anyone who has remained equally susceptible to both classes of pleasures ever knowingly and calmly preferred the lower, though many, in all ages, have broken down in an ineffectual attempt to combine both.

From this verdict of the only competent judges, I apprehend there can be no appeal. On a question which is the best worth having of two pleasures, or which of two modes of existence is the most grateful to the feelings, apart from its moral attributes and from its consequences, the judgment of those who are qualified by knowledge of both, or, if they differ, that of the majority among them, must be admitted as final. And there needs be the less hesitation to accept this judgment respecting the quality of pleasures, since there is no other tribunal to be referred to even on the question of quantity. What means are there of determining which is the acutest of two pains, or the intensest of two pleasurable sensations, except the general suffrage of those who are familiar with both? Neither pains nor pleasures are homogeneous, and pain is always heterogeneous with pleasure. What is there to decide whether a particular pleasure is worth purchasing at the cost of a particular pain, except the feelings and judgment of the experienced? When, therefore, those feelings and judgment declare the pleasures derived from the higher faculties to be preferable *in kind*, apart from the question of intensity, to those of which the animal nature, disjoined from the higher faculties, is susceptible, they are entitled on this subject to the same regard.

I have dwelt on this point as being a necessary part of a perfectly just conception of utility or happiness considered as the directive rule of human conduct. But it is by no means an indispensable condition to the acceptance of the utilitarian standard; for that standard is not the agent's own greatest happiness, but the greatest amount of happiness altogether; and if it may possibly be doubted whether a noble character is always the happier for its nobleness, there can be no doubt that it makes other people happier, and that the world in general is immensely a gainer by it. Utilitarianism, therefore, could only attain its end by the general cultivation of nobleness of character, even if each individual were only benefited by the nobleness of others, and his own, so far as happiness is concerned, were a sheer deduction from the benefit. But the bare enunciation of such an absurdity as this last renders refutation superfluous.

According to the greatest happiness principle, as above explained, the ultimate end, with reference to and for the sake of which all other things are desirable – whether we are considering our own good or that of other people – is an existence exempt as far as possible from pain, and as rich as possible in enjoyments, both in point of quantity and quality; the test of quality and the rule for measuring it against quantity being the preference felt by those who, in their opportunities of experience, to which must be added their habits of self-consciousness and self-observation, are best furnished with the means of comparison. This, being according to the utilitarian opinion the end of human action, is necessarily also the standard of morality, which may accordingly be defined "the rules and precepts for human conduct," by the observance of which an existence such as has been described might be, to the greatest extent possible, secured to all mankind; and not to them only, but, so far as the nature of things admits, to the whole sentient creation. . . .

Unquestionably it is possible to do without happiness; it is done involuntarily by nineteen-twentieths of mankind, even in those parts of our present world which are least deep in barbarism; and it often has to be done voluntarily by the hero or the martyr, for the sake of something which he prizes more than his individual happiness. But this something, what is it, unless the happiness of others or some of the requisites of happiness? It is noble to be capable of resigning entirely one's own portion of happiness, or chances of it; but, after all, this self-sacrifice must be for some end; it is not its own end; and if we are told that its end is not happiness but virtue, which is better than happiness, I ask, would the sacrifice be made if the hero or martyr did not believe that it would earn for others immunity from similar sacrifices? Would it be made if he thought that his renunciation of happiness for himself would produce no fruit for any of his fellow creatures, but to make their lot like his and place them also in the condition of persons who have renounced happiness? All honor to those who can abnegate for themselves the personal enjoyment of life when by such renunciation they contribute worthily to increase the amount of happiness in the world; but he who does it or professes to do it for any other purpose is no more deserving of admiration than the ascetic mounted on his pillar. He may be an inspiriting proof of what men *can* do, but assuredly not an example of what they *should*.

Though it is only in a very imperfect state of the world's arrangements that anyone can best serve the happiness of others by the absolute sacrifice of his own, yet, so long as the world is in that imperfect state, I fully acknowledge that the readiness to make such a sacrifice is the highest virtue which can be found in man. I will add that in this condition of the world, paradoxical as the assertion may be, the conscious ability to do without happiness gives the best prospect of realizing such happiness as is attainable. For nothing except that consciousness can raise a person above the chances of life by making him feel that, let fate and fortune do their worst, they have not power to subdue him; which, once felt, frees him from excess of anxiety concerning the evils of life and enables him, like many a Stoic in the worst times of the Roman Empire, to cultivate in tranquility the sources of satisfaction accessible to him, without concerning himself about the uncertainty of their duration any more than about their inevitable end.

Meanwhile, let utilitarians never cease to claim the morality of self-devotion as a possession which belongs by as good a right to them as either to the Stoic or to the Transcendentalist. The utilitarian morality does recognize in human beings the power of sacrificing their own greatest good for the good of others. It only refuses to admit that the sacrifice is itself a good. A sacrifice which does not increase or tend to increase the sum total of happiness, it considers as wasted. The only self-renunciation which it applauds is devotion to the happiness, or to some of the means of happiness, of others, either of mankind collectively or of individuals within the limits imposed by the collective interests of mankind.

I must again repeat what the assailants of utilitarianism seldom have the justice to acknowledge, that the happiness which forms the utilitarian standard of what is right in conduct is not the agent's own happiness but that of all concerned. As between his own happiness and that of others, utilitarianism requires him to be as strictly impartial as a disinterested and benevolent spectator. In the golden rule of Jesus of Nazareth, we read the complete spirit of the ethics of utility. "To do as you would be done by," and "to love your neighbor as yourself," constitute the ideal perfection of utilitarian morality. As the means of making the nearest approach to this ideal, utility would enjoin, first, that laws and social arrangements should place the happiness or (as, speaking practically, it may be called) the interest of every individual as nearly as possible in harmony with the interest of the whole; and, secondly, that education and opinion, which have so vast a power over human character, should so use that power as to establish in the mind of every individual an indissoluble association between his own happiness and the good of the whole, especially between his own happiness and the practice of such modes of conduct, negative and positive, as regard for the universal happiness prescribes; so that not only he may be unable to conceive the possibility of happiness to himself, consistently with conduct opposed to the general good, but also that a direct impulse to promote the general good may be in every individual one of the habitual motives of action, and the sentiments connected therewith may fill a large and prominent place in every human being's sentient existence. If the impugners of the utilitarian morality represented it to their own minds in this its true character, I know not what recommendation possessed by any other morality they could possibly affirm to be wanting to it; what more beautiful or more exalted developments of human nature any other ethical system can be supposed to foster, or what springs of action, not accessible to the utilitarian, such systems rely on for giving effect to their mandates.

The objectors to utilitarianism cannot always be charged with representing it in a discreditable light. On the contrary, those among them who entertain anything like a just idea of its disinterested character sometimes find fault with its standard as being too high for humanity. They say it is exacting too much to require that people shall always act from the inducement of promoting the general interests of society. But this is to mistake the very meaning of a standard of morals and confound the rule of action with the motive of it. It is the business of ethics to tell us what are our duties, or by what test we may know them; but no system of ethics requires that the sole motive of all we do shall be a feeling of duty; on the contrary, ninety-nine hundredths of all our actions are done from other motives, and rightly so done if the rule of duty does not condemn them. It is the more unjust to utilitarianism that this particular misapprehension should be made a ground of objection to it, inasmuch as utilitarian moralists have gone beyond almost all others in affirming that the motive has nothing to do with the morality of the action, though much with the worth of the agent. He who saves a fellow creature from drowning does what is morally right, whether his motive be duty or the hope of being paid for his trouble; he who betrays the friend that trusts him is guilty of a crime, even if his object be to serve another friend to whom he is under greater obligations.[2] But to speak only of actions done from the motive of duty, and in direct obedience to principle: it is a misapprehension of the utilitarian mode of thought to conceive it as implying that people should fix their minds upon so wide a generality as the world, or society at large. The great majority of good actions are intended not for the benefit of the world, but for that of individuals, of which the good of the world is made up; and the thoughts of the most virtuous man need not on these occasions travel beyond the particular persons concerned, except so far as is necessary to assure himself that in benefiting them he is not violating the rights, that is, the legitimate and authorized expectations, of anyone else. The multiplication of happiness is, according to the utilitarian ethics, the object of virtue: the occasions on which any person (except one in a thousand) has it in his power to do this on an extended scale – in other words, to be a public benefactor – are but exceptional; and on these occasions alone is he called on to consider public utility; in every other case, private utility, the interest or happiness of some few persons, is all he has to attend to. Those alone the influence of whose actions extends to society in general need concern themselves habitually about so large an object. In the case of abstinences indeed – of things which people forbear to do from moral considerations, though the consequences in the particular case might be beneficial – it would be unworthy of an intelligent agent not to be consciously aware that the action is of a class which, if practiced generally, would be generally injurious, and that this is the ground of the obligation to abstain from it. The amount of regard for the public interest implied in this recognition is no greater than is demanded by every system of morals, for they all enjoin to abstain from whatever is manifestly pernicious to society. . . .

It may not be superfluous to notice a few more of the common misapprehensions of utilitarian ethics, even those which are so obvious and gross that it might appear impossible for any person of candor and intelligence to fall into them; since persons, even of considerable mental endowment, often give themselves so little trouble to understand the bearings of any opinion against which they entertain a prejudice, and men are in general so little conscious of this voluntary ignorance as a defect that the vulgarest misunderstandings of ethical doctrines are continually met with in the deliberate writings of persons of the greatest pretensions both to high principle and to philosophy. We not uncommonly hear the doctrine of utility inveighed against as a *godless* doctrine. If it be necessary to say anything at all against so mere an assumption, we may say that the question depends upon what idea we have formed of the moral character of the Deity. If it be a true belief that God desires, above all things, the happiness of his creatures, and that this was his purpose in their creation, utility is not only not a godless doctrine, but more profoundly religious than any other. If it be meant that utilitarianism does not recognize the revealed will of God as the supreme law of morals, I answer that a utilitarian who believes in the perfect goodness and wisdom of *God* necessarily believes that whatever God has thought fit to reveal on the subject of morals must fulfill the requirements of utility in a supreme degree. But others besides utilitarians have been of opinion that the Christian revelation was intended, and is fitted, to inform the hearts and minds of mankind with a spirit which should enable them to find for themselves what is right, and incline them to do it when found, rather than to tell them, except in a very general way, what it is; and that we need a doctrine of ethics, carefully followed out, to *interpret* to us the will of God. Whether this opinion is correct or not, it is superfluous here to discuss; since whatever aid religion, either natural or revealed, can afford to ethical investigation is as open to the utilitarian moralist as to any other. He can use it as the testimony of God to the usefulness or hurtfulness of any given course of action by as good a right as others can use it for the indication of a transcendental law having no connection with usefulness or with happiness. . . .

Again, defenders of utility often find themselves called upon to reply to such objections as this – that there is not time, previous to action, for calculating and weighing the effects of any line of conduct on the general happiness. This is exactly as if anyone were to say that it is impossible to guide our conduct by Christianity because there is not time, on every occasion on which anything has to be done, to read through the Old and New Testaments. The answer to the objection is that there has been ample time, namely, the whole past duration of the human species. During all that time mankind have been learning by experience the tendencies of actions; on which experience all the prudence as well as all the morality of life are dependent. People talk as if the commencement of this course of experience had hitherto been put off, and as if, at the moment when some man feels tempted to meddle with the property or life of another, he had to begin considering for the first time whether murder and theft are injurious to human happiness. Even then I do not think that he would find the question very puzzling; but, at all events, the matter is now done to his hand. It is truly a whimsical supposition that, if mankind were agreed in considering utility to be the test of morality, they would remain without any agreement as to what *is* useful, and would take no measures for having their notions on the subject taught to the young and enforced by law and opinion. There is no difficulty in proving any ethical standard whatever to work ill if we suppose universal idiocy to be conjoined with it; but on any hypothesis short of that, mankind must by this time have acquired positive beliefs as to the effects of some actions on their happiness; and the beliefs which have thus come down are the rules of morality for the multitude, and for the philosopher until he has succeeded in finding better. That philosophers might easily do this, even now, on many subjects; that the received code of ethics is by no means of divine right; and that mankind have still much to learn as to the effects of actions on the general happiness, I admit or rather earnestly maintain. The corollaries from the principle of utility, like the precepts of every practical art, admit of indefinite improvement, and, in a progressive state of the human mind, their improvement is prepetually going on. But to consider the rules of morality as improvable is one thing; to pass over the intermediate generalization entirely and endeavor to test each individual action directly by the first principle is another. It is a strange notion that the acknowledgment of a first principle is inconsistent with the admission of secondary ones. To inform a traveler respecting the place of his ultimate destination is not to forbid the use of landmarks and direction-posts on the way. The proposition that happiness is the end and aim of morality does not mean that no road ought to be laid down to that goal, or that persons going thither should not be advised to take one direction rather than another. Men really ought to leave off talking a kind of nonsense on this subject, which they would neither talk nor listen to on other matters of practical concernment. Nobody argues that the art of navigation is not founded on astronomy because sailors cannot wait to calculate the Nautical Almanac. Being rational creatures, they go to sea with it ready calculated; and all rational creatures go out upon the sea of life with their minds made up on the common questions of right and wrong, as well as on many of the far more difficult questions of wise and foolish. And this, as long as foresight is a human quality, it is to be presumed they will continue to do. Whatever we adopt as the fundamental principle of morality, we require subordinate principles to apply it by; the impossibility of doing without them, being common to all systems, can afford no argument against any one in particular; but gravely to argue as if no such secondary principles could be had, and as if mankind had remained till now, and always must remain, without drawing any general conclusions from the experience of human life is as high a pitch, I think, as absurdity has ever reached in philosophical controversy.

The remainder of the stock arguments against utilitarianism mostly consist in laying to its charge the common infirmities of human nature, and the general difficulties which embarrass conscientious persons in shaping their course through life. We are told that a utilitarian will be apt to make his own particular case an exception to moral rules, and, when under temptation, will see a utility in the breach of a rule, greater than he will see in its observance. But is utility the only creed which is able to furnish us with excuses for evil-doing and means of cheating our own conscience? They are afforded in abundance by all doctrines which recognize as a fact in morals the existence of conflicting considerations, which all doctrines do that have been believed by sane persons. It is not the fault of any creed, but of the complicated nature of human affairs, that rules of conduct cannot be so framed as to require no exceptions, and that hardly any kind of action can safely be laid down as either always obligatory or always condemnable. There is no ethical creed which does not temper the rigidity of its laws by giving a certain latitude, under the moral responsibility of the agent, for accommodation to peculiarities of circumstances; and under every creed, at the opening thus made, self-deception and dishonest casuistry get in. There exists no moral system under which there do not arise unequivocal cases of conflicting obligation. These are the real difficulties, the knotty points both in the theory of ethics and in the conscientious guidance of personal conduct. They are overcome practically, with greater or with less success, according to the intellect and virtue of the individual; but it can hardly be pretended that anyone will be the less qualified for dealing with them, from possessing an ultimate standard to which conflicting rights and duties can be referred. If utility is the ultimate source of moral obligations, utility may be invoked to decide between them when their demands are incompatible. Though the application of the standard may be difficult, it is better than none at all; while in other systems, the moral laws all claiming independent authority, there is no common umpire entitled to interfere between them; their claims to precedence one over another rest on little better than sophistry, and, unless determined, as they generally are, by the unacknowledged influence of consideration of utility, afford a free scope for the action of personal desires and partialities. We must remember that only in these cases of conflict between secondary principles is it requisite that first principles should be appealed to. There is no case of moral obligation in which some secondary principle is not involved; and if only one, there can seldom be any real doubt which one it is, in the mind of any person by whom the principle itself is recognized. . . .

Chapter IV: Of What Sort of Proof the Principle of Utility Is Susceptible

It has already been remarked that questions of ultimate ends do not admit of proof, in the ordinary acceptation of the term. To be incapable of proof by reasoning is common to all first principles; to the first premises of our knowledge, as well as to those of our conduct. But the former, being matters of fact, may be the subject of a direct appeal to the faculties which judge of fact – namely, our senses and our internal consciousness. Can an appeal be made, to the same faculties on questions of practical ends? Or by what other faculty is cognizance taken of them?

Questions about ends are, in other words, questions about what things are desirable. The utilitarian doctrine is that happiness is desirable, and the only thing desirable, as an end; all other things being only desirable as means to that end. What ought to be required of this doctrine – what conditions is it requisite that the doctrine should fulfill – to make good its claim to be believed?

The only proof capable of being given that an object is visible, is that people actually see it. The only proof that a sound is audible, is that people hear it: and so of the other sources of our experience. In like manner, I apprehend, the sole evidence it is possible to produce that anything is desirable, is that people do actually desire it. If the end which the utilitarian doctrine proposes to itself were not, in theory and in practice, acknowledged to be an end, nothing could ever convince any person that it was so. No reason can be given why the general happiness is desirable, except that each person, so far as he believes it to be attainable, desires his own happiness. This, however, being a fact, we have not only all the proof which the case admits of, but all which it is possible to require, that happiness is a good: that each person's happiness is a good to that person, and the general happiness, therefore, a good to the aggregate of all persons. Happiness has made out its title as *one* of the ends of conduct, and consequently one of the criteria of morality.

But it has not, by this alone, proved itself to be the sole criterion. To do that, it would seem, by the same rule, necessary to show, not only that people desire happiness, but that they never desire anything else. Now it is palpable that they do desire things which, in common language, are decidedly distinguished from happiness. They desire, for example, virtue, and the absence of vice, no less really than pleasure and the absence of pain. The desire of virtue is not as universal; but it is as authentic a fact, as the desire of happiness. And hence the opponents of the utilitarian standard deem that they have a right to infer that there are other ends of human action besides happiness, and that happiness is not the standard of approbation and disapprobation.

But does the utilitarian doctrine deny that people desire virtue, or maintain that virtue is not a thing to be desired? The very reverse. It maintains not only that virtue is to be desired, but that it is to be desired disinterestedly, for itself. Whatever may be the opinion of utilitarian moralists as to the original conditions by which virtue is made virtue; however they may believe (as they do) that actions and dispositions are only virtuous because they promote another end than virtue; yet this being granted, and it having been decided, from considerations of this description, what *is* virtuous, they not only place virtue at the very head of the things which are good as means to the ultimate end, but they also recognize as a psychological fact the possibility of its being, to the individual, a good in itself, without looking to any end beyond it; and hold, that the mind is not in a right state, not in a state conformable to utility, not in the state most conducive to the general happiness, unless it does love virtue in this manner – as a thing desirable in itself, even although, in the individual instance, it should not produce those other desirable consequences which it tends to produce and on account of which it is held to be virtue. This opinion is not, in the smallest degree, a departure from the happiness principle. The ingredients of happiness are very various, and each of them is desirable in itself, and not merely when considered as swelling an aggregate. The principle of utility does not mean that any given pleasure, as music for instance, or any given exemption from pain, as for example health, are to be looked upon as a means to a collective something termed happiness, and to be desired on that account. They are desired and desirable in and for themselves; besides being means, they are part of the end. Virtue, according to the utilitarian doctrine, is not naturally and originally part of the end, but it is capable of becoming so; and in those who love it disinterestedly it has become so, and is desired and cherished, not as a means to happiness, but as a part of their happiness.

To illustrate this farther, we may remember that virtue is not the only thing, originally a means, and which if it were not a means to anything else, would be and remain indifferent, but which by association with what it is a means to, comes to be desired for itself, and that too with the utmost intensity. What, for example, shall we say of the love of money? There is nothing originally more desirable about money than about any heap of glittering pebbles. Its worth is solely that of the things which it will buy; the desires for other things than itself, which it is a means of gratifying. Yet the love of money is not only one of the strongest moving forces of human life, but money is, in many cases, desired in and for itself; the desire to possess it is often stronger than the desire to use it, and goes on increasing when all the desires which point to ends beyond it, to be encompassed by it, are falling off. It may be then said truly, that money is desired not for the sake of an end, but as part of the end. From being a means to happiness, it has come to be itself a principal ingredient of the individual's conception of happiness. The same may be said of the majority of the great objects of human life – power, for example, or fame; except that to each of these there is a certain amount of immediate pleasure annexed, which has at least the semblance of being naturally inherent in them; a thing which cannot be said of money. Still, however, the strongest natural attraction, both of power and of fame, is the immense aid they give to the attainment of our other wishes; and it is the strong association thus generated between them and all our objects of desire, which gives to the direct desire of them the intensity it often assumes, so as in some characters to surpass in strength all other desires. In these cases the means have become a part of the end, and a more important part of it than any of the things which they are means to. What was once desired as an instrument for the attainment of happiness, has come to be desired for its own sake. In being desired for its own sake it is, however, desired as *part* of happiness. The person is made, or thinks he would be made, happy by its mere possession; and is made unhappy by failure to obtain it. The desire of it is not a different thing from the desire of happiness, any more than the love of music or the desire of health. They are included in happiness. They are some of the elements of which the desire of happiness is made up. Happiness is not an abstract idea, but a concrete whole; and these are some of its parts. And the utilitarian standard sanctions and approves there being so. Life would be a poor thing, very ill provided with sources of happiness, if there were not this provision of nature, by which things originally indifferent, but conducive to, or otherwise associated with, the satisfaction of our primitive desires, become in themselves sources of pleasure more valuable than the primitive pleasures, both in permanency, in the space of human existence than they are capable of covering, and even in intensity.

Virtue, according to the utilitarian conception, is a good of this description. There was no original desire of it, or motive to it, save its conduciveness to pleasure, and especially to protection from pain. But through the association thus formed, it may be felt a good in itself, and desired as such with as great intensity as any other good; and with this difference between it and the love of money, of power, or of fame, that all of these may, and often do, render the individual noxious to the other members of the society to which he belongs, whereas there is nothing which makes him so much a blessing to them as the cultivation of the disinterested love of virtue. And consequently, the utilitarian standard, when it tolerates and approves those other acquired desires, up to the point beyond which they would be more injurious to the general happiness than promotive of it, enjoins and requires the cultivation of the love of virtue up to the greatest strength possible, as being above all things important to the general happiness.

It results from the preceding considerations, that there is in reality nothing desired except happiness. Whatever is desired otherwise than as a means to some end beyond itself, and ultimately to happiness, is desired as itself a part of happiness, and is not desired for itself until it has become so. Those who desire virtue for its own sake, desire it either because the consciousness of it is a pleasure, or because the consciousness of being without it is a pain, or for both reasons united; as in truth the pleasure and pain seldom exist separately, but almost always together, the same person feeling pleasure in the degree of virtue attained, and pain in not having attained more. If one of these gave him no pleasure, and the other no pain, he would not love or desire virtue, or would desire it only for the other benefits which it might produce to himself or to persons whom he cared for.

We have now, then, an answer to the question, of what sort of proof the principle of utility is susceptible. If the opinion which I have now stated is psychologically true – if human nature is so constituted as to desire nothing which is not either a part of happiness or a means of happiness, we can have no other proof, and we require no other, that these are the only things desirable. If so, happiness is the sole end of human action, and the promotion of it the test by which to judge of all human conduct; from whence it necessarily follows that it must be the criterion of morality, since a part is included in the whole.

And now to decide whether this is really so; whether mankind do desire nothing for itself but that which is a pleasure to them, or of which the absence is a pain; we have evidently arrived at a question of fact and experience, dependent like all similar questions, upon evidence. It can only be determined by practiced self-consciousness and self-observation, assisted by observation of others. I believe that these sources of evidence, impartially consulted, will declare that desiring a thing and finding it pleasant, aversion to it and thinking of it as painful, are phenomena entirely inseparable, or rather two parts of the same phenomenon; in strictness of language, two different modes of naming the same psychological fact: that to think of an object as desirable (unless for the sake of its consequences), and to think of it as pleasant, are one and the same thing; and that to desire anything, except in proportion as the idea of it is pleasant, is a physical and metaphysical impossibility.

So obvious does this appear to me, that I expect it will hardly be disputed: and the objection made will be, not that desire can possibly be directed to anything ultimately except pleasure and exemption from pain, but that the will is a different thing from desire; that a person of confirmed virtue, or any other person whose purposes are fixed, carries out his purposes without any thought of the pleasure he has in contemplating them, or expects to derive from their fulfillment; and persists in acting on them, even though these pleasures are much diminished, by changes in his character or decay of his passive sensibilities, or are outweighed by the pains which the pursuit of the purposes may bring upon him. All this I fully admit, and have stated it elsewhere, as positively and emphatically as any one. Will, the active phenomenon, is a different thing from desire, the state of passive sensibility, and though originally an offshoot from it, may in time take root and detach itself from the parent stock; so much so that in the case of an habitual purpose, instead of willing the thing because we desire it, we often desire it only because we will it. This, however, is but an instance of that familiar fact, the power of habit, and is nowise confined to the case of virtuous actions. Many indifferent things, which men originally did from a motive of some sort, they continue to do from habit. Sometimes this is done unconsciously, the consciousness coming only after the action: at other times with conscious volition, but volition which has become habitual, and is put into operation by the force of habit, in opposition perhaps to the deliberate preference, as often happens with those who have contracted habits of vicious or hurtful indulgence. Third and last comes the case in which the habitual act of will in the individual instance is not in contradiction to the general intention prevailing at other times, but in fulfillment of it; as in the case of the person of confirmed virtue, and of all who pursue deliberately and consistently any determinate end. The distinction between will and desire thus understood, is an authentic and highly important psychological fact; but the fact consists solely in this – that will, like all other parts of our constitution, is amenable to habit, and that we may will from habit what we no longer desire for itself, or desire only because we will it. It is not the less true that will, in the beginning, is entirely produced by desire; including in that term the repelling influence of pain as well as the attractive one of pleasure. Let us take into consideration, no longer the person who has a firmed will to do right, but him in whom that virtuous will is still feeble, conquerable by temptation, and not to be fully relied on; by what means can it be strengthened? How can the will to be virtuous, where it does not exist in sufficient force, be implanted or awakened? Only by making the person *desire* virtue – by making him think of it in a pleasurable light, or of its absence in a painful one. It is by associating the doing right with pleasure, or the doing wrong with pain, or by eliciting and impressing and bringing home to the person's experience the pleasure naturally involved in the one or the pain in the other, that it is possible to call forth that will to be virtuous, which, when confirmed, acts without any thought of either pleasure or pain. Will is the child of desire, and passes out of habit. That which is the result of habit affords no presumption of being intrinsically good; and there would be no reason for wishing that the purpose of virtue should become independent of pleasure and pain, were it not that the influence of the pleasurable and painful associations which prompt to virtue is not sufficiently to be depended on for unerring constancy of action until it has acquired the support of habit. Both in feeling and in conduct, habit is the only thing which imparts certainty; and it is because of the importance to others of being able to rely absolutely on one's feelings and conduct, and to oneself of being able to rely on one's own, that the will to do right ought to be cultivated into this habitual independence. In other words, this state of the will is a means to good, not intrinsically a good; and does not contradict the doctrine that nothing is a good to human beings but in so far as it is either itself pleasurable, or a means of attaining pleasure or averting pain.

But if this doctrine be true, the principle of utility is proved. Whether it is so or not, must now be left to the consideration of the thoughtful reader.

Notes

1   The author of this essay has reason for believing himself to be the first person who brought the word "utilitarian" into use. He did not invent it, but adopted it from a passing expression in Mr [John] Galt's *Annals of the Parish*. After using it as a designation for several years, he and others abandoned it from a growing dislike to anything resembling a badge or watchword of sectarian distinction. But as a name for one single opinion, – not a set of opinions – to denote the recognition of utility as a standard, not any particular way of applying it – the term supplies a want in the language, and offers, in many cases, a convenient mode of avoiding tiresome circumlocution.

2   An opponent, whose intellectual and moral fairness it is a pleasure to acknowledge (the Revd. J. Llewellyn Davies), has objected to this passage, saying, "Surely the rightness or wrongness of saving a man from drowning does depend very much upon the motive with which it is done. Suppose that a tyrant, when his enemy jumped into the sea to escape from him, saved him from drowning simply in order that he might inflict upon him more exquisite tortures, would it tend to clearness to speak of that rescue as 'a morally right action'? Or suppose again, according to one of the stock illustrations of ethical inquiries, that a man betrayed a trust received from a friend, because the discharge of it would fatally injure that friend himself or someone belonging to him, would utilitarianism compel one to call the betrayal 'a crime' as much as if it had been done from the meanest motive?"

I submit that he who saves another from drowning in order to kill him by torture afterwards does not differ only in motive from him who does the same thing from duty or benevolence; the act itself is different. The rescue of the man is, in the case supposed, only the necessary first step of an act far more atrocious than leaving him to drown would have been. Had Mr Davies said, "The rightness or wrongness of saving a man from drowning does depend very much" – not upon the motive, but – "upon the *intention*," no utilitarian would have differed from him. Mr Davies, by an oversight too common not to be quite venial, has in this case confounded the very different ideas of Motive and Intention. There is no point which utilitarian thinkers (and Bentham pre-eminently) have taken more pains to illustrate than this. The morality of the action depends entirely upon the intention – that is, upon what the agent *wills to do*. But the motive, that is, the feeling which makes him will so to do, if it makes no difference in the act, makes none in the morality: though it makes a great difference in our moral estimation of the agent, especially if it indicates a good or a bad habitual *disposition* – a bent of character from which useful, or from which hurtful actions are likely to arise.

40 Fundamental Principles of the Metaphysic of Morals*

Immanuel Kant

Transition from the Common Rational Knowledge of Morality to the Philosophical

Nothing can possibly be conceived in the world, or even out of it, which can be called good, without qualification, except a Good Will. Intelligence, wit, judgment, and the other *talents* of the mind, however they may be named, or courage, resolution, perseverance, as qualities of temperament, are undoubtedly good and desirable in many respects; but these gifts of nature may also become extremely bad and mischievous if the will which is to make use of them, and which, therefore, constitutes what is called *character*, is not good. It is the same with the *gifts of fortune*. Power, riches, honor, even health, and the general well-being and contentment with one's condition which is called *happiness*, inspire pride, and often presumption, if there is not a good will to correct the influence of these on the mind, and with this also to rectify the whole principle of acting, and adapt it to its end. The sight of a being who is not adorned with a single feature of a pure and good will, enjoying unbroken prosperity, can never give pleasure to an impartial rational spectator. Thus a good will appears to constitute the indispensable condition even of being worthy of happiness.

There are even some qualities which are of service to this good will itself, and may facilitate its action, yet which have no intrinsic unconditional value, but always presuppose a good will, and this qualifies the esteem that we justly have for them, and does not permit us to regard them as absolutely good. Moderation in the affections and passions, self-control, and calm deliberation are not only good in many respects, but even seem to constitute part of the intrinsic worth of the person; but they are far from deserving to be called good without qualification, although they have been so unconditionally praised by the ancients. For without the principles of a good will, they may become extremely bad; and the coolness of a villain not only makes him far more dangerous, but also directly makes him more abominable in our eyes than he would have been without it.

A good will is good not because of what it performs or effects, not by its aptness for the attainment of some proposed end, but simply by virtue of the volition, that is, it is good in itself, and considered by itself is to be esteemed much higher than all that can be brought about by it in favor of any inclination, nay, even of the sum-total of all inclinations. Even if it should happen that, owing to special disfavor of fortune, or the niggardly provision of a stepmotherly nature, this will should wholly lack power to accomplish its purpose, if with its greatest efforts it should yet achieve nothing, and there should remain only the good will (not, to be sure, a mere wish, but the summoning of all means in our power), then, like a jewel, it would still shine by its own light, as a thing which

* From *Kant's Critique of Practical Reason and Other Works on the Theory of Ethics*, 6th edn, trans. Thomas Kingsmill Abbott (London: Longman, 1909), pp. 9–22 and 29–59.

has its whole value in itself. Its usefulness or fruitlessness can neither add to nor take away anything from this value. It would be, as it were, only the setting to enable us to handle it the more conveniently in common commerce, or to attract to it the attention of those who are not yet connoisseurs, but not to recommend it to true connoisseurs, or to determine its value. . . .

We have then to develop the notion of a will which deserves to be highly esteemed for itself, and is good without a view to anything further, a notion which exists already in the sound natural understanding, requiring rather to be cleared up than to be taught, and which in estimating the value of our actions always takes the first place, and constitutes the condition of all the rest. In order to do this, we will take the notion of duty, which includes that of a good will, although implying certain subjective restrictions and hindrances. These, however, far from concealing it, or rendering it unrecognizable, rather bring it out by contrast, and make it shine forth so much the brighter.

I omit here all actions which are already recognized as inconsistent with duty, although they may be useful for this or that purpose, for with these the question whether they are done *from duty* cannot arise at all, since they even conflict with it. I also set aside those actions which really conform to duty, but to which men have *no direct inclination*, performing them because they are impelled thereto by some other inclination. For in this case we can readily distinguish whether the action which agrees with duty is done *from duty*, or from a selfish view. It is much harder to make this distinction when the action accords with duty, and the subject has besides a *direct* inclination to it. For example, it is always a matter of duty that a dealer should not overcharge an inexperienced purchaser; and whenever there is much commerce the prudent tradesman does not overcharge, but keeps a fixed price for everyone, so that a child buys of him as well as any other. Men are thus *honestly* served; but this is not enough to make us believe that the tradesman had so acted from duty and from principles of honesty: his own advantage required it; it is out of the question in this case to suppose that he might besides have a direct inclination in favor of the buyers, so that, as it were, from love he should give no advantage to one over another. Accordingly the action was done neither from duty nor from direct inclination, but merely with a selfish view.

On the other hand, it is a duty to maintain one's life; and, in addition, everyone has also a direct inclination to do so. But on this account the often anxious care which most men take for it has no intrinsic worth, and their maxim has no moral import. They preserve their life *as duty requires* no doubt, but not *because duty requires*. On the other hand, if adversity and hopeless sorrow have completely taken away the relish for life; if the unfortunate one, strong in mind, indignant at his fate rather than desponding or dejected, wishes for death, and yet preserves his life without loving it – not from inclination or fear, but from duty – then his maxim has a moral worth.

To be beneficent when we can is a duty; and besides this, there are many minds so sympathetically constituted that, without any other motive of vanity or self-interest, they find a pleasure in spreading joy around them, and can take delight in the satisfaction of others so far as it is their own work. But I maintain that in such a case an action of this kind, however proper, however amiable it may be, has nevertheless no true moral worth, but is on a level with other inclinations, e.g. the inclination to honor, which, if it is happily directed to that which is in fact of public utility and accordant with duty, and consequently honorable, deserves praise and encouragement, but not esteem. For the maxim lacks the moral import, namely, that such actions be done *from duty*, not from inclination. Put the case that the mind of that philanthropist was clouded by sorrow of his own, extinguishing all sympathy with the lot of others, and that while he still has the power to benefit others in distress, he is not touched by their trouble because he is absorbed with his own; and now suppose that he tears himself out of this dead insensibility, and performs the action without any inclination to it, but simply from duty, then first had his action its genuine moral worth. Further still; if nature has put little sympathy in the heart of this or that man; if he, supposed to be an upright man, is by temperament cold and indifferent to the sufferings of others, perhaps because in respect of his own he is provided with the special gift of patience and fortitude, and supposes, or even requires, that others should have the same – and such a man would certainly not be the meanest product of nature – but if nature had not specially framed him for a philanthropist, would he not still find in himself a source from whence to give himself a far higher worth than that of a good-natured temperament could be? Unquestionably. It is just in this that the moral worth of the character is brought out which is incomparably the highest of all, namely, that he is beneficent, not from inclination, but from duty.

To secure one's own happiness is a duty, at least indirectly; for discontent with one's condition, under a pressure of many anxieties and amidst unsatisfied wants, might easily become a great *temptation to transgression of duty*. But here again, without looking to duty, all men have already the strongest and most intimate inclination to happiness, because it is just in this idea that all inclinations are combined in one total. But the precept of happiness is often of such a sort that it greatly interferes with some inclinations, and yet a man cannot form any definite and certain conception of the sum of satisfaction of all of them which is called happiness. It is not then to be wondered at that a single inclination, definite both as to what it promises and as to the time within which it can be gratified, is often able to overcome such a fluctuating idea, and that a gouty patient, for instance, can choose to enjoy what he likes, and to suffer what he may, since, according to his calculation, on this occasion at least, he has [only] not sacrificed the enjoyment of the present moment to a possible mistaken expectation of a happiness which is supposed to be found in health. But even in this case, if the general desire for happiness did not influence his will, and supposing that in his particular case health was not a necessary element in this calculation, there yet remains in this, as in all other cases, this law, namely, that he would promote his happiness not from inclination but from duty, and by this would his conduct first acquire true moral worth.

It is in this manner, undoubtedly, that we are to understand those passages of Scripture also in which we are commanded to love our neighbor, even our enemy. For love, as an affection, cannot be commanded, but beneficence for duty's sake may; even though we are not impelled to it by any inclination – nay, are even repelled by a natural and unconquerable aversion. This is *practical* love, and not *pathological* – a love which is seated in the will, and not in the propensions of sense – in principles of action and not of tender sympathy; and it is this love alone which can be commanded.

The second[1] proposition is: That an action done from duty derives its moral worth, *not from the purpose* which is to be attained by it, but from the maxim by which it is determined, and therefore does not depend on the realization of the object of the action, but merely on the *principle of volition* by which the action has taken place, without regard to any object of desire. It is clear from what precedes that the purposes which we may have in view in our actions, or their effects regarded as ends and springs of the will, cannot give to actions any unconditional or moral worth. In what, then, can their worth lie, if it is not to consist in the will and in reference to its expected effect? It cannot lie anywhere but in the *principle of the will* without regard to the ends which can be attained by the action. For the will stands between its a priori principle, which is formal, and its a posteriori spring, which is material, as between two roads, and as it must be determined by something, it follows that it must be determined by the formal principle of volition when an action is done from duty, in which case every material principle has been withdrawn from it.

The third proposition, which is a consequence of the two preceding, I would express thus: *Duty is the necessity of acting from respect for the law*. I may have *inclination* for an object as the effect of my proposed action, but I cannot have respect for it, just for this reason, that it is an effect and not an energy of will. Similarly, I cannot have respect for inclination, whether my own or another's; I can at most, if my own, approve it; if another's, sometimes even love it; i.e. look on it as favorable to my own interest. It is only what is connected with my will as a principle, by no means as an effect – what does not subserve my inclination, but overpowers it, or at least in case of choice excludes it from its calculation – in other words, simply the law of itself, which can be an object of respect, and hence a command. Now an action done from duty must wholly exclude the influence of inclination, and with it every object of the will, so that nothing remains which can determine the will except objectively the *law*, and subjectively *pure respect* for this practical law, and consequently the maxim[2] that I should follow this law even to the thwarting of all my inclinations.

Thus the moral worth of an action does not lie in the effect expected from it, nor in any principle of action which requires to borrow its motive from this expected effect. For all these effects – agreeableness of one's condition, and even the promotion of the happiness of others – could have been also brought about by other causes, so that for this there would have been no need of the will of a rational being; whereas it is in this alone that the supreme and unconditional good can be found. The pre-eminent good which we call moral can therefore consist in nothing else than *the conception of law* in itself, *which certainly is only possible in a rational being*, so far as this conception, and not the expected effect, determines the will. This is a good which is already present in the person who acts accordingly, and we have not to wait for it to appear first in the result.[3] . . .

Transition from Popular Moral Philosophy to the Metaphysic of Morals

. . . Everything in nature works according to laws. Rational beings alone have the faculty of acting according *to the conception* of laws, that is according to principles, i.e. have a *will*. Since the deduction of actions from principles requires *reason*, the will is nothing but practical reason. If reason infallibly determines the will, then the actions of such a being which are recognized as objectively necessary are subjectively necessary also, i.e. the will is a faculty to choose *that only* which reason independent of inclination recognizes as practically necessary, i.e. as good. But if reason of itself does not sufficiently determine the will, if the latter is subject also to subjective conditions (particular impulses) which do not always coincide with the objective conditions; in a word, if the will does not *in itself* completely accord with reason (which is actually the case with men), then the actions which objectively are recognized as necessary are subjectively contingent, and the determination of such a will according to objective laws is *obligation*, that is to say, the relation of the objective laws to a will that is not thoroughly good is conceived as the determination of the will of a rational being by principles of reason, but which the will from its nature does not of necessity follow.

The conception of an objective principle, in so far as it is obligatory for a will, is called a command (of reason), and the formula of the command is called an Imperative.

All imperatives are expressed by the word *ought* [or *shall*], and thereby indicate the relation of an objective law of reason to a will, which from its subjective constitution is not necessarily determined by it (an obligation). They say that something would be good to do or to forbear, but they say it to a will which does not always do a thing because it is conceived to be good to do it. That is practically *good*, however, which determines the will by means of the conceptions of reason, and consequently not from subjective causes, but objectively, that is on principles which are valid for every rational being as such. It is distinguished from the *pleasant*, as that which influences the will only by means of sensation from merely subjective causes, valid only for the sense of this or that one, and not as a principle of reason, which holds for every one.[4]

A perfectly good will would therefore be equally subject to objective laws (viz. laws of good), but could not be conceived as *obliged* thereby to act lawfully, because of itself from its subjective constitution it can only be determined by the conception of good. Therefore no imperatives hold for the Divine will, or in general for a *holy* will; *ought* is here out of place, because the volition is already of itself necessarily in unison with the law. Therefore imperatives are only formulae to express the relation of objective laws of all volition to the subjective imperfection of the will of this or that rational being, e.g. the human will.

Now all *imperatives* command either *hypothetically* or *categorically*. The former represent the practical necessity of a possible action as means to something else that is willed (or at least which one might possibly will). The categorical imperative would be that which represented an action as necessary of itself without reference to another end, i.e. as objectively necessary.

Since every practical law represents a possible action as good, and on this account, for a subject who is practically determinable by reason, necessary, all imperatives are formulae determining an action which is necessary according to the principle of a will good in some respects. If now the action is good only as a means *to something else*, then the imperative is *hypothetical*; if it is conceived as good *in itself* and consequently as being necessarily the principle of a will which of itself conforms to reason, then it is *categorical*.

Thus the imperative declares what action possible by me would be good, and presents the practical rule in relation to a will which does not forthwith perform an action simply because it is good, whether because the subject does not always know that it is good, or because, even if it know this, yet its maxims might be opposed to the objective principles of practical reason.

Accordingly the hypothetical imperative only says that the action is good for some purpose, *possible* or *actual*. In the first case it is a Problematical, in the second an Assertorial practical principle. The categorical imperative which declares an action to be objectively necessary in itself without reference to any purpose, i.e. without any other end, is valid as an Apodictic (practical) principle.

Whatever is possible only by the power of some rational being may also be conceived as a possible purpose of some will; and therefore the principles of action as regards the means necessary to attain some possible purpose are in fact infinitely numerous. All sciences have a practical part, consisting of problems expressing that some end is possible for us, and of imperatives directing how it may be attained. These may, therefore, be called in general imperatives of Skill. Here there is no question whether the end is rational and good, but only what one must do in order to attain it. The precepts for the physician to make his patient thoroughly healthy, and for a poisoner to ensure certain death, are of equal value in this respect, that each serves to effect its purpose perfectly. Since in early youth it cannot be known what ends are likely to occur to us in the course of life, parents seek to have their children taught *a great many things*, and provide for their *skill* in the use of means for all sorts of arbitrary ends, of none of which can they determine whether it may not perhaps hereafter be an object to their pupil, but which it is at all events *possible* that he might aim at; and this anxiety is so great that they commonly neglect to form and correct their judgment on the value of the things which may be chosen as ends.

There is *one* end, however, which may be assumed to be actually such to all rational beings (so far as imperatives apply to them, viz. as dependent beings), and, therefore, one purpose which they not merely *may* have, but which we may with certainty assume that they all actually *have* by a natural necessity, and this is *happiness*. The hypothetical imperative which expresses the practical necessity of an action as means to the advancement of happiness is Assertorial. We are not to present it as necessary for an uncertain and merely possible purpose, but for a purpose which we may presuppose with certainty and a priori in every man, because it belongs to his being. Now skill in the choice of means to his own greatest wellbeing may be called *prudence*[5] in the narrowest sense. And thus the imperative which refers to the choice of means to one's own happiness, i.e. the precept of prudence, is still always *hypothetical*; the action is not commanded absolutely, but only as means to another purpose.

Finally, there is an imperative which commands a certain conduct immediately, without having as its condition any other purpose to be attained by it. This imperative is Categorical. It concerns not the matter of the action, or its intended result, but its form and the principle of which it is itself a result; and what is essentially good in it consists in the mental disposition, let the consequence be what it may. This imperative may be called that of Morality.

There is a marked distinction also between the volitions on these three sorts of principles in the *dissimilarity* of the obligation of the will. In order to mark this difference more clearly, I think they would be most suitably named in their order if we said they are either *rules* of skill, or *counsels* of prudence, or *commands* (*laws*) of morality. For it is *law* only that involves the conception of an *unconditional* and objective necessity, which is consequently universally valid; and commands are laws which must be obeyed, that is, must be followed, even in opposition to inclination. *Counsels*, indeed, involve necessity, but one which can only hold under a contingent subjective condition, viz. they depend on whether this or that man reckons this or that as part of his happiness; the categorical imperative, on the contrary is not limited by any condition, and as being absolutely, although practically, necessary, may be quite properly called a command. We might also call the first kind of imperatives *technical* (belonging to art), the second *pragmatic*[6] (to welfare), the third *moral* (belonging to free conduct generally, that is, to morals).

Now arises the question, how are all these imperatives possible? This question does not seek to know how we can conceive the accomplishment of the action which the imperative ordains, but merely how we can conceive the obligation of the will which the imperative expresses. No special explanation is needed to show how an imperative of skill is possible. Whoever wills the end, wills also (so far as reason decides his conduct) the means in his power which are indispensably necessary thereto. This proposition is, as regards the volition, analytical for, in willing an object as my effect, there is already thought the causality of myself as an acting cause, that is to say, the use of the means; and the imperative educes from the conception of volition of an end the conception of actions necessary to this end. Synthetical propositions must no doubt be employed in defining the means to a proposed end; but they do not concern the principle, the act of the will, but the object and its realization. E.g., that in order to bisect a line on an unerring principle I must draw from its extremities two intersecting arcs; this no doubt is taught by mathematics only in synthetical propositions; but if I know that it is only by this process that the intended operation can be performed, then to say that if I fully will the operation, I also will the action required for it, is an analytical proposition; for it is one and the same thing to conceive something as an effect which I can produce in a certain way, and to conceive myself as acting in this way.

If it were only equally easy to give a definite conception of happiness, the imperatives of prudence would correspond exactly with those of skill, and would likewise be analytical. For in this case as in that, it could be said, whoever wills the end, wills also (according to the dictate of reason necessarily) the indispensable means thereto which are in his power. But, unfortunately, the notion of happiness is so indefinite that although every man wishes to attain it, yet he never can say definitely and consistently what it is that he really wishes and wills. The reason of this is that all the elements which belong to the notion of happiness are altogether empirical. i.e. they must be borrowed from experience, and nevertheless the idea of happiness requires an absolute whole, a maximum of welfare in my present and all future circumstances. Now it is impossible that the most clear-sighted and at the same time most powerful being (supposed finite) should frame to himself a definite conception of what he really wills in this. Does he will riches, how much anxiety, envy, and snares might he not thereby draw upon his shoulders? Does he will knowledge and discernment, perhaps it might prove to be only an eye so much the sharper to show him so much the more fearfully the evils that are now concealed from him, and that cannot be avoided, or to impose more wants on his desires, which already give him concern enough. Would he have long life? Who guarantees to him that it would not be a long misery? Would he at least have health? How often has uneasiness of the body restrained from excesses into which perfect health would have allowed one to fall? And so on. In short, he is unable, on any principle, to determine with certainty what would make him truly happy; because to do so he would need to be omniscient. We cannot therefore act on any definite principles to secure happiness, but only on empirical counsels, e.g. of regimen, frugality, courtesy, reserve, etc., which experience teaches do, on the average, most promote well-being. Hence it follows that the imperatives of prudence do not, strictly speaking, command at all, that is, they cannot present actions objectively as practically *necessary*, that they are rather to be regarded as counsels (*consilia*) than precepts (*praecepta*) of reason, that the problem to determine certainly and universally what action would promote the happiness of a rational being is completely insoluble, and consequently no imperative respecting it is possible which should, in the strict sense, command to do what makes happy; because happiness is not an ideal of reason but of imagination, resting solely on empirical grounds, and it is vain to expect that these should define an action by which one could attain the totality of a series of consequences which is really endless. This imperative of prudence would, however, be an analytical proposition if we assume that the means to happiness could be certainly assigned; for it is distinguished from the imperative of skill only by this, that in the latter the end is merely possible, in the former it is given; as, however, both only ordain the means to that which we suppose to be willed as an end, it follows that the imperative which ordains the willing of the means to him who wills the end is in both cases analytical. Thus there is no difficulty in regard to the possibility of an imperative of this kind either.

On the other hand, the question, how the imperative of *morality* is possible, is undoubtedly one, the only one, demanding a solution, as this is not at all hypothetical, and the objective necessity which it presents cannot rest on any hypothesis, as is the case with the hypothetical imperatives. Only here we must never leave out of consideration that we *cannot* make out *by any example*, in other words empirically, whether there is such an imperative at all; but it is rather to be feared that all those which seem to be categorical may yet be at bottom hypothetical. For instance, when the precept is: Thou shalt not promise deceitfully; and it is assumed that the necessity of this is not a mere counsel to avoid some other evil, so that it should mean: Thou shalt not make a lying promise, lest if it become known thou shouldst destroy thy credit, but that an action of this kind must be regarded as evil in itself, so that the imperative of the prohibition is categorical; then we cannot show with certainty in any example that the will was determined merely by the law, without any other spring of action, although it may appear to be so. For it is always possible that fear of disgrace, perhaps also obscure dread of other dangers, may have a secret influence on the will. Who can prove by experience the non-existence of a cause when all that experience tells us is that we do not perceive it? But in such a case the so-called moral imperative, which as such appears to be categorical and unconditional, would in reality be only a pragmatic precept, drawing our attention to our own interests, and merely teaching us to take these into consideration.

We shall therefore have to investigate a priori the possibility of a categorical imperative, as we have not in this case the advantage of its reality being given in experience, so that [the elucidation of] its possibility should be requisite only for its explanation, not for its establishment. In the meantime it may be discerned beforehand that the categorical imperative alone has the purport of a practical law: all the rest may indeed be called *principles* of the will but not laws, since whatever is only necessary for the attainment of some arbitrary purpose may be considered as in itself contingent, and we can at any time be free from the precept if we give up the purpose: on the contrary, the unconditional command leaves the will no liberty to choose the opposite; consequently it alone carries with it that necessity which we require in a law.

Secondly, in the case of this categorical imperative or law of morality, the difficulty (of discerning its possibility) is a very profound one. It is an a priori synthetical practical proposition;[7] and as there is so much difficulty in discerning the possibility of speculative propositions of this kind, it may readily be supposed that the difficulty will be no less with the practical.

In this problem we will first inquire whether the mere conception of a categorical imperative may not perhaps supply us also with the formula of it, containing the proposition which alone can be a categorical imperative; for even if we know the tenor of such an absolute command, yet how it is possible will require further special and laborious study, which we postpone to the last section.

When I conceive a hypothetical imperative, in general I do not know beforehand what it will contain until I am given the condition. But when I conceive a categorical imperative, I know at once what it contains. For as the imperative contains besides the law only the necessity that the maxims[8] shall conform to this law, while the law contains no conditions restricting it, there remains nothing but the general statement that the maxim of the action should conform to a universal law, and it is this conformity alone that the imperative properly represents as necessary.

There is therefore but one categorical imperative, namely, this: *Act only on that maxim whereby thou canst at the same time will that it should become a universal law.*

Now if all imperatives of duty can be deduced from this one imperative as from their principle, then, although it should remain undecided whether what is called duty is not merely a vain notion, yet at least we shall be able to show what we understand by it and what this notion means.

Since the universality of the law according to which effects are produced constitutes what is properly called *nature* in the most general sense (as to form), that is the existence of things so far as it is determined by general laws, the imperative of duty may be expressed thus: *Act as if the maxim of the action were to become by thy will a universal law of nature.*

We will now enumerate a few duties, adopting the usual division of them into duties to ourselves and to others, and into perfect and imperfect duties.[9]

1. A man reduced to despair by a series of misfortunes feels wearied of life, but is still so far in possession of his reason that he can ask himself whether it would not be contrary to his duty to himself to take his own life. Now he inquires whether the maxim of his actions could become a universal law of nature. His maxim is: From self-love I adopt it as a principle to shorten my life when its longer duration is likely to bring more evil than satisfaction. It is asked then simply whether this principle founded on self-love can become a universal law of nature. Now we see at once that a system of nature of which it should be a law to destroy life by means of the very feeling whose special nature it is to impel to the improvement of life would contradict itself, and therefore could not exist as a system of nature; hence that maxim cannot possibly exist as a universal law of nature, and consequently would be wholly inconsistent with the supreme principle of all duty.

2. Another finds himself forced by necessity to borrow money. He knows that he will not be able to repay it, but sees also that nothing will be lent to him, unless he promises stoutly to repay it in a definite time. He desires to make this promise, but he has still so much conscience as to ask himself: Is it not unlawful and inconsistent with duty to get out of a difficulty in this way? Suppose, however, that he resolves to do so, then the maxim of his action would be expressed thus: When I think myself in want of money, I will borrow money and promise to repay it, although I know that I never can do so. Now this principle of self-love or of one's own advantage may perhaps be consistent with my whole future welfare; but the question now is, Is it right? I change then the suggestion of self-love into a universal law, and state the question thus: How would it be if my maxim were a universal law? Then I see at once that it could never hold as a universal law of nature, but would necessarily contradict itself. For supposing it to be a universal law that everyone when he thinks himself in a difficulty should be able to promise whatever he pleases, with the purpose of not keeping his promise, the promise itself would become impossible, as well as the end that one might have in view in it, since no one would consider that anything was promised to him, but would ridicule all such statements as vain pretenses.

3. A third finds in himself a talent which with the help of some culture might make him a useful man in many respects. But he finds himself in comfortable circumstances, and prefers to indulge in pleasure rather than to take pains in enlarging and improving his happy natural capacities. He asks, however, whether his maxim of neglect of

his natural gifts, besides agreeing with his inclination to indulgence, agrees also with what is called duty. He sees then that a system of nature could indeed subsist with such a universal law although men (like the South Sea Islanders) should let their talents rest, and resolve to devote their lives merely to idleness, amusement, and propagation of their species – in a word, to enjoyment; but he cannot possibly *will* that this should be a universal law of nature, or be implanted in us as such by a natural instinct. For, as a rational being, he necessarily wills that his faculties be developed, since they serve him, and have been given him, for all sorts of possible purposes.

4. A fourth, who is in prosperity, while he sees that others have to contend with great wretchedness and that he could help them, thinks: What concern is it of mine? Let everyone be as happy as Heaven pleases, or as he can make himself; I will take nothing from him nor even envy him, only I do not wish to contribute anything to his welfare or to his assistance in distress! Now no doubt if such a mode of thinking were a universal law, the human race might very well subsist, and doubtless even better than in a state in which everyone talks of sympathy and goodwill, or even takes care occasionally to put it into practice, but, on the other side, also cheats when he can, betrays the rights of men, or otherwise violates them. But although it is possible that a universal law of nature might exist in accordance with that maxim, it is impossible to *will* that such a principle should have the universal validity of a law of nature. For a will which resolved this would contradict itself, inasmuch as many cases might occur in which one would have need of the love and sympathy of others, and in which, by such a law of nature, sprung from his own will, he would deprive himself of all hope of the aid he desires.

These are a few of the many actual duties, or at least what we regard as such, which obviously fall into two classes on the one principle that we have laid down. We must be *able to will* that a maxim of our action should be a universal law. This is the canon of the moral appreciation of the action generally. Some actions are of such a character that their maxim cannot without contradiction be even *conceived* as a universal law of nature, far from it being possible that we should *will* that it *should* be so. In others this intrinsic impossibility is not found, but still it is impossible to *will* that their maxim should be raised to the universality of a law of nature, since such a will would contradict itself. It is easily seen that the former violate strict or rigorous (inflexible) duty; the latter only laxer (meritorious) duty. Thus it has been completely shown by these examples how all duties depend as regards the nature of the obligation (not the object of the action) on the same principle.

If now we attend to ourselves on occasion of any transgression of duty, we shall find that we in fact do not will that our maxim should be a universal law, for that is impossible for us; on the contrary, we will that the opposite should remain a universal law, only we assume the liberty of making an *exception* in our own favor or (just for this time only) in favor of our inclination. Consequently if we considered all cases from one and the same point of view, namely, that of reason, we should find a contradiction in our own will, namely, that a certain principle should be objectively necessary as a universal law, and yet subjectively should not be universal, but admit of exceptions. As, however, we at one moment regard our action from the point of view of a will wholly conformed to reason, and then again look at the same action from the point of view of a will affected by inclination, there is not really any contradiction, but an antagonism of inclination to the precept of reason, whereby the universality of the principle is changed into a mere generality, so that the practical principle of reason shall meet the maxim half way. Now, although this cannot be justified in our own impartial judgment, yet it proves that we do really recognize the validity of the categorical imperative and (with all respect for it) only allow ourselves a few exceptions, which we think unimportant and forced from us. . . .

Supposing, however, that there were something *whose existence* has *in itself* an absolute worth, something which, being *an end in itself*, could be a source of definite laws, then in this and this alone would lie the source of a possible categorical imperative, i.e. a practical law.

Now I say: man and generally any rational being *exists* as an end in himself, *not merely as a means* to be arbitrarily used by this or that will, but in all his actions, whether they concern himself or other rational beings, must be always regarded at the same time as an end. All objects of the inclinations have only a conditional worth; for if the inclinations and the wants founded on them did not exist, then their object would be without value. But the inclinations themselves being sources of want are so far from having an absolute worth for which they should be desired, that, on the contrary, it must be the universal wish of every rational being to be wholly free from them. Thus the worth of any object which is *to be acquired* by our action is always conditional. Beings whose existence depends not on our will but on nature's, have nevertheless, if they are rational beings, only a relative value as means, and are therefore called things; rational beings, on the contrary, are called *persons*, because their very nature points them out as ends in themselves, that is as something which must not be used merely as means, and so far therefore restricts freedom of action (and is an object of respect). These, therefore, are not merely subjective ends whose existence has a worth *for us* as an effect of our action, but *objective ends*, that is things whose existence is an end in itself: an end moreover for which no other can be substituted, which they should subserve *merely* as means, for otherwise nothing whatever would possess *absolute worth*; but if all worth were conditioned and therefore contingent, then there would be no supreme practical principle of reason whatever.

If then there is a supreme practical principle or, in respect of the human will, a categorical imperative, it must be one which, being drawn from the conception of that which is necessarily an end for everyone because it is *an end in itself*, constitutes an *objective* principle of will, and can therefore serve as a universal practical law. The foundation of this principle is: *rational nature exists as an end in itself.* Man necessarily conceives his own existence as being so: so far then this is a *subjective* principle of human actions. But every other rational being regards its existence similarly, just on the same rational principle that holds for me: so that it is at the same time an objective principle, from which as a supreme practical law all laws of the will must be capable of being deduced. Accordingly the practical imperative will be as follows: *So act as to treat humanity whether in thine own person or in that of any other, in every case as an end withal, never as means only.* We will now inquire whether this can be practically carried out.

To abide by the previous examples:

Firstly, under the head of necessary duty to oneself: He who contemplates suicide should ask himself whether his action can be consistent with the idea of humanity *as an end in itself.* If he destroys himself in order to escape from painful circumstances, he uses a person merely as *a means* to maintain a tolerable condition up to the end of life. But a man is not a thing, that is to say, something which can be used merely as means, but must in all his actions be always considered as an end in himself. I cannot, therefore, dispose in any way of a man in my own person so as to mutilate, to damage or kill him.

It belongs to ethics proper to define this principle more precisely, so as to avoid all misunderstanding, e.g. as to the amputation of the limbs in order to preserve myself; as to exposing my life to danger with a view to preserve it, etc. (This question is therefore omitted here.)

Secondly, as regards necessary duties, or those of strict obligation, toward others; he who is thinking of making a lying promise to others will see at once that he would be using another man *merely as a means*, without the latter containing at the same time the end in himself. For he whom I propose by such a promise to use for my own purposes cannot possibly assent to my mode of acting toward him, and therefore cannot himself contain the end of this action. This violation of the principle of humanity in other men is more obvious if we take in examples of attacks on the freedom and property of others. For then it is clear that he who transgresses the rights of men intends to use the person of others merely as means, without considering that as rational beings they ought always to be esteemed also as ends, that is, as beings who must be capable of containing in themselves the end of the very same action.

Thirdly, as regards contingent (meritorious) duties to oneself; it is not enough that the action does not violate humanity in our own person as an end in itself, it must also *harmonize with* it. Now there are in humanity capacities of greater perfection which belong to the end that nature has in view in regard to humanity in ourselves as the subject: to neglect these might perhaps be consistent with the *maintenance* of humanity as an end in itself, but not with the *advancement* of this end.

Fourthly, as regards meritorious duties toward others: the natural end which all men have is their own happiness. Now humanity might indeed subsist, although no one should contribute anything to the happiness of others, provided he did not intentionally withdraw anything from it; but after all, this would only harmonize negatively, not positively, with *humanity as an end in itself*, if everyone does not also endeavor, as far as in him lies, to forward the ends of others. For the ends of any subject which is an end in himself, ought as far as possible to be *my* ends also, if that conception is to have its *full* effect with me. . . .

Looking back now on all previous attempts to discover the principle of morality, we need not wonder why they all failed. It was seen that man was bound to laws by duty, but it was not observed that the laws to which he is subject are *only those of his own giving*, though at the same time they are *universal*. And that he is only bound to act in conformity with his own will; a will, however, which is designed by nature to give universal laws. For when one has conceived man only as subject to a law (no matter what), then this law required some interest, either by way of attraction or constraint, since it did not originate as a law from *his own* will, but this will was according to a law obliged by *something else* to act in a certain manner. Now by this necessary consequence all the labor spent in finding a supreme principle of *duty* was irrevocably lost. For men never elicited duty, but only a necessity of acting from a certain interest. Whether this interest was private or otherwise, in any case the imperative must be conditional, and could not by any means be capable of being a moral command. I will therefore call this the principle of *Autonomy* of the will, in contrast with every other which I accordingly reckon as *Heteronomy*.

The conception of every rational being as one which must consider itself as giving in all the maxims of its will universal laws, so as to judge itself and its actions from this point of view – this conception leads to another which depends on it and is very fruitful, namely, that of a *kingdom of ends*.

By a *kingdom* I understand the union of different rational beings in a system by common laws. Now since it is by laws that ends are determined as regards their universal validity, hence, if we abstract from the personal differences of rational beings, and likewise from all the content of their private ends, we shall be able to conceive all ends combined in a systematic whole (including both rational beings as ends in themselves, and also the special ends which each may propose to himself), that is to say, we can conceive a kingdom of ends, which on the preceding principles is possible.

For all rational beings come under the *law* that each of them must treat itself and all others *never merely as means*, but in every case *at the same times as ends in themselves*. Hence results a systematic union of rational beings by common objective laws, i.e. a kingdom which may be called a kingdom of ends, since what these laws have in view is just the relation of these beings to one another as ends and means. It is certainly only an ideal.

A rational being belongs as a *member* to the kingdom of ends when, although giving universal laws in it, he is also himself subject to these laws. He belongs to it *as sovereign* when, while giving laws, he is not subject to the will of any other.

A rational being must always regard himself as giving laws either as member or as sovereign in a kingdom of ends which is rendered possible by the freedom of will. He cannot, however, maintain the latter position merely by the maxims of his will, but only in case he is a completely independent being without wants and with unrestricted power adequate to his will. . . .

We can now end where we started at the beginning, namely, with the conception of a will unconditionally good. *That will* is *absolutely good* which cannot be evil – in other words, whose maxim, if made a universal law, could never contradict itself. This principle, then, is its supreme law: Act always on such a maxim as thou canst at the same time will to be a universal law; this is the sole condition under which a will can never contradict itself; and such an imperative is categorical. Since the validity of the will as a universal law for possible actions is analogous to the universal connection of the existence of things by general laws, which is the formal notion of nature in general, the categorical imperative can also be expressed thus; *Act on maxims which can at the same time have for their object themselves as universal laws of nature.* Such then is the formula of an absolutely good will.

Rational nature is distinguished from the rest of nature by this, that it sets before itself an end. This end would be the matter of every good will. But since in the idea of a will that is absolutely good without being limited by any condition (of attaining this or that end) we must abstract wholly from every end *to be effected* (since this would make every will only relatively good), it follows that in this case the end must be conceived, not as an end to be effected, but as an *independently* existing end. Consequently it is conceived only negatively, i.e. as that which we must never act against, and which, therefore, must never be regarded merely as means, but must in every volition be esteemed as an end likewise. Now this end can be nothing but the subject of all possible ends, since this is also the subject of a possible absolutely good will; for such a will cannot without contradiction be postponed to any other object. This principle: So act in regard to every rational being (thyself and others), that he may always have place in thy maxim as an end in himself, is accordingly essentially identical with this other; Act upon a maxim which, at the same time, involves its own universal validity for every rational being. For that in using means for every end I should limit my maxim by the condition of its holding good as a law for every subject, this comes to the same thing as that the fundamental principle of all maxims of action must be that the subject of all ends, i.e. the rational being himself, be never employed merely as means, but as the supreme condition restricting the use of all means, that is in every case as an end likewise.

It follows incontestably that, to whatever laws any rational being may be subject, he being an end in himself must be able to regard himself as also legislating universally in respect of these same laws, since it is just this fitness of his maxims for universal legislation that distinguishes him as an end in himself; also it follows that this implies his dignity (prerogative) above all mere physical beings, that he must always take his maxims from the point of view which regards himself, and likewise every other rational being, as lawgiving beings (on which account they are called persons). In this way a world of rational beings (*mundus intelligibilis*) is possible as a kingdom of ends, and this by virtue of the legislation proper to all persons as members. Therefore every rational being must so act as if he were by his maxims in every case a legislating member in the universal kingdom of ends. The formal principle of these maxims is: So act as if thy maxim were to serve likewise as the universal law (of all rational beings). A kingdom of ends is thus only possible on the analogy of a kingdom of nature, the former, however, only by maxims, that is selfimposed rules, the latter only by the laws of efficient causes acting under necessitation from without. Nevertheless, although the system of nature is looked upon as a machine, yet so far as it has reference to rational beings as its ends, it is given on this account the name of a kingdom of nature. Now such a kingdom of ends would be actually realized by means of maxims conforming to the canon which the categorical imperative prescribes to all rational beings, *if they were universally followed*. But although a rational being, even if he punctually follows this maxim himself, cannot reckon upon all others being therefore true to the same, nor expect that the kingdom of nature and its orderly arrangements shall be in harmony with him as a fitting member, so as to form a kingdom of ends to which he himself contributes, that is to say, that it shall favor his expectation of happiness, still that law: Act according to the maxims of a member of a merely possible kingdom of ends legislating in it universally, remains in its full force, inasmuch as it commands categorically. And it is just in this that the paradox lies; that the mere dignity of man as a rational creature, without any other end or advantage to be attained thereby, in other words, respect for a mere idea, should yet serve as an inflexible precept of the will, and that it is precisely in this independence of the maxim of all such springs of action that its sublimity consists; and it is this that makes every rational subject worthy to be a legislative member in the kingdom of ends: for otherwise he would have to be conceived only as subject to the physical law of his wants. And although we should suppose the kingdom of nature and the kingdom of ends to be united under one sovereign, so that the latter kingdom thereby ceased to be a mere idea and acquired true reality, then it would no doubt gain the accession of a strong spring, but by no means any increase of its intrinsic worth. For this sole absolute lawgiver must, notwithstanding this, be always conceived as estimating the worth of rational beings only by their disinterested behavior, as prescribed to themselves from that idea [the dignity of man] alone. The essence of things is not altered by their external relations, and that which, abstracting from these, alone constitutes the absolute worth of man, is also that by which he must be judged, whoever the judge may be, and even by the Supreme Being. *Morality*, then, is the relation of actions to the autonomy of the will, that is, to the potential universal legislation by its maxims. An action that is consistent with the autonomy of the will is *permitted*; one that does not agree therewith is *forbidden*. A will whose maxims necessarily coincide with the laws of autonomy is a *holy* will, good absolutely. The dependence of a will not absolutely good on the principle of autonomy (moral necessitation) is obligation. This, then, cannot be applied to holy being. The objective necessity of actions from obligation is called *duty*.

From what has just been said, it is easy to see how it happens that although the conception of duty implies subjection to the law, we yet ascribe a certain *dignity* and sublimity to the person who fulfills all his duties. There is not, indeed, any sublimity in him, so far as he is *subject* to the moral law; but inasmuch as in regard to that very law he is likewise a *legislator*, and on that account alone subject to it, he has sublimity. We have also shown above that neither fear nor inclination, but simply respect for the law, is the spring which can give actions a moral worth. Our own will, so far as we suppose it to act only under the condition that its maxims are potentially universal laws, this ideal will which is possible to us is the proper object of respect; and the dignity of humanity consists just in this capacity of being universally legislative, though with the condition that it is itself subject to this same legislation.

Notes

1 The first proposition was that to have moral worth an action must be done from duty.

2 A *maxim* is the subjective principle of volition. The objective principle (i.e. that which would also serve subjectively as a practical principle to all rational beings if reason had full power over the faculty of desire) is the practical *law*.

3 It might be here objected to me that I take refuge behind the word *respect* in an obscure feeling, instead of giving a distinct solution of the question by a concept of the reason. But although respect is a feeling, it is not a feeling *received* through influence, but is *self-wrought* by a rational concept, and, therefore, is specifically distinct from all feelings of the former kind, which may be referred either to inclination or fear. What I recognize immediately as a law for me, I recognize with respect. This merely signifies the consciousness that my will is *subordinate* to a law, without the intervention of other influences on my sense. The immediate determination of the will by the law, and the consciousness of this, is called *respect*, so that this is regarded as an *effect* of the law on the subject, and not as the *cause* of it. Respect is properly the conception of a worth which thwarts my self-love. Accordingly it is something which is considered neither as an object of inclination nor of fear, although it has something analogous to both. The *object* of respect is the *law* only, and that, the law which we impose on *ourselves*, and yet recognize as necessary in itself. As a law, we are subjected to it without consulting self-love; as imposed by us on ourselves, it is a result of our will. In the former aspect it has an analogy to fear, in the latter to inclination. Respect for a person is properly only respect for the law (of honesty, etc.) of which he gives us an example. Since we also look on the improvement of our talents as a duty, we consider that we see in a person of talents, as it were, the *example of a law* (viz. to become like him in this by exercise), and this constitutes our respect. All so-called moral *interest* consists simply in *respect* for the law.

4 The dependence of the desires on sensations is called inclination, and this accordingly always indicates a *want*. The dependence of a contingently determinable will on principles of reason is called an *interest*. This, therefore, is found only in the case of a dependent will which does not always of itself conform to reason; in the Divine will we cannot conceive any interest. But the human will can also *take an interest* in a thing without therefore acting *from interest*. The former signifies the *practical* interest in the action, the latter the *pathological* in the object of the action. The former indicates only dependence of the will on principles of reason in themselves; the second, dependence on principles of reason for the sake of inclination, reason supplying only the practical rules how the requirement of the inclination may be satisfied. In the first case the action interests me; in the second the object of the action (because it is pleasant to me). We have seen in the first section that in an action done from duty we must look not

to the interest in the object, but only to that in the action itself, and in its rational principle (viz. the law).

5   The word *prudence* is taken in two senses: in the one it may bear the name of knowledge of the world, in the other that of private prudence. The former is a man's ability to influence others so as to use them for his own purposes. The latter is the sagacity to combine all these purposes for his own lasting benefit. This latter is properly that to which the value even of the former is reduced, and when a man is prudent in the former sense, but not in the latter, we might better say of him that he is clever and cunning, but, on the whole, imprudent.

6   It seems to me that the proper signification of the word *pragmatic* may be most accurately defined in this way. For *sanctions* are called pragmatic which flow properly, not from the law of the states as necessary enactments, but from precaution for the general welfare. A history is composed pragmatically when it teaches prudence, i.e. instructs the world how it can provide for its interests better, or at least as well as the men of former time.

7   I connect the act with the will without presupposing any condition resulting from any inclination, but a priori, and therefore necessarily (though only objectively, i.e. assuming the idea of a reason possessing full power over all subjective motives). This is accordingly a practical proposition which does not deduce the willing of an action by mere analysis from another already presupposed (for we have not such a perfect will), but connects it immediately with the conception of the will of a rational being, as something not contained in it.

8   A maxim is a subjective principle of action, and must be distinguished from the *objective principle*, namely, practical law. The former contains the practical rule set by reason according to the conditions of the subject (often its ignorance or its inclinations), so that it is the principle on which the subject *acts*; but the law is the objective principle valid for every rational being, and is the principle on which it *ought to act* that is an imperative.

9   It must be noted here that I reserve the division of duties for a future *metaphysic of morals*, so that I give it here only as an arbitrary one (in order to arrange my examples). For the rest, I understand by a perfect duty one that admits no exception in favor of inclination, and then I have not merely external but also internal perfect duties. This is contrary to the use of the word adopted in the schools; but I do not intend to justify it here, as it is all one for my purpose whether it is admitted or not. [*Perfect* duties are usually understood to be those which can be enforced by external law; *imperfect*, those which cannot be enforced. They are also called respectively *determinate* and *indeterminate*, *officio juris* and *officio virtutis*.]

---

41   From *Two Treatises of Government**

John Locke

Chapter II
Of the State of Nature

4.   To understand Political Power right, and derive it from its Original, we must consider what State all Men are naturally in, and that is, a *State of perfect Freedom* to order

---

* From *Two Treatises of Government*, Part II (first published 1690), sections 4, 6, 7, 10, 25–38, and 51. Public domain.

---

their Actions, and dispose of their Possessions, and Persons as they think fit, within the bounds of the Law of Nature, without asking leave, or depending upon the Will of any other Man.

A *State* also *of Equality*, wherein all the Power and Jurisdiction is reciprocal, no one having more than another: there being nothing more evident, than that Creatures of the same species and rank promiscuously born to all the same advantages of Nature, and the use of the same faculties, should also be equal one amongst another without Subordination or Subjection, unless the Lord and Master of them all, should by any manifest Declaration of his Will set one above another, and confer on him by an evident and clear appointment and undoubted Right to Dominion and Sovereignty. . . .

6. But though this be a *State of Liberty*, yet it is *not a State of Licence*, though Man in that State have an uncontroleable Liberty, to dispose of his Person or Possessions, yet he has not Liberty to destroy himself, or so much as any Creature in his Possession, but where some nobler use, that its bare Preservation calls for it. The *State of Nature* has a Law of Nature to govern it, which obliges every one: And Reason, which is that Law, teaches all Mankind, who will but consult it, that being all equal and independent, no one ought to harm another in his Life, Health, Liberty, or Possessions. For Men being all the Workmanship of one Omnipotent, and infinitely wise Maker; All the Servants of one Sovereign Master, sent into the World by his order and about his business, they are his Property, whose Workmanship they are, made to last during his, not one anothers Pleasure. And being furnished with like Faculties, sharing all in one Community of Nature, there cannot be supposed any such *Subordination* among us, that may Authorize us to destroy one another, as if we were made for one anothers uses, as the inferior ranks of Creatures are for ours. Every one as he is *bound to preserve himself*, and not to quit his Station wilfully; so by the like reason when his own Preservation comes not in competition, ought he, as much as he can, *to preserve the rest of Mankind*, and may not unless it be to do Justice on an Offender, take away, or impair the life, or what tends to the Preservation of the Life, the Liberty, Health, Limb or Goods of another.

7. And that all Men may be restrained from invading others Rights, and from doing hurt to one another, and the Law of Nature be observed, which willeth the Peace and *Preservation of all Mankind*, the *Execution* of the Law of Nature is in that State, put into every Mans hands, whereby every one has a right to punish the transgressors of that Law to such a Degree, as may hinder its Violation. For the *Law of Nature* would, as all other Laws that concern Men in this World, be in vain, if there were no body that in the State of Nature, had a *Power to Execute* that Law, and thereby preserve the innocent and restrain offenders, and if any one in the State of Nature may punish another, for any evil he has done, every one may do so. For in that *State of perfect Equality*, where naturally there is no superiority or jurisdiction of one, over another, what any may do in Prosecution of that Law, every one must needs have a Right to do. . . .

10. Besides the Crime which consists in violating the Law, and varying from the right Rule of Reason, whereby a Man so far becomes degenerate, and declares himself to quit the Principles of Human Nature, and to be a noxious Creature, there is commonly *injury* done to some Person or other, and some other Man receives damage by his Transgression, in which Case he who had received any damage, has besides the right of punishment common to him with other Men, a particular Right to seek *Reparation* from him that has done it. And any other Person who finds it just, may also joyn with him that is

injur'd, and assist him in recovering from the Offender, so much as may make satisfaction for the harm he has suffer'd. . . .

Chapter V
Of Property

25.   Whether we consider natural *Reason*, which tells us, that Men, being once born, have a right to their Preservation, and consequently to Meat and Drink, and such other things, as Nature affords for their Subsistence: Or *Revelation*, which gives us an account of those Grants God made of the World to *Adam*, and to *Noah*, and his Sons, 'tis very clear, that God, as King *David* says, *Psal.* CXV. xvj. *has given the Earth to the Children of Men*, given it to Mankind in common. But this being supposed, it seems to some a very great difficulty, how any one should ever come to have a *Property* in any thing: I will not content my self to answer, That if it be difficult to make out *Property*, upon a supposition, that God gave the World to *Adam* and his Posterity in common; it is impossible that any Man, but one universal Monarch, should have any *Property*, upon a supposition, that God gave the World to *Adam*, and his Heirs in Succession, exclusive of all the rest of his Posterity. But I shall endeavour to shew, how Men might come to have a *property* in several parts of that which God gave to Mankind in common, and that without any express Compact of all the Commoners.

26.   God, who hath given the World to Men in common, hath also given them reason to make use of it to the best advantage of Life, and convenience. The Earth, and all that is therein, is given to Men for the Support and Comfort of their being. And though all the Fruits it naturally produces, and Beasts it feeds, belong to Mankind in common, as they are produced by the spontaneous hand of Nature; and no body has originally a private Dominion, exclusive of the rest of Mankind, in any of them, as they are thus in their natural state: yet being given for the use of Men, there must of necessity be a means *to appropriate* them some way or other before they can be of any use, or at all beneficial to any particular Man. The Fruit, or Venison, which nourishes the wild *Indian*, who knows no Inclosure, and is still a Tenant in common, must be his, and so his, *i.e.* a part of him, that another can no longer have any right to it, before it can do him any good for the support of his Life.

27.   Though the Earth, and all inferior Creatures be common to all Men, yet every Man has a *Property* in his own *Person*. This no Body has any Right to but himself. The *Labour* of his Body, and the *Work* of his Hands, we may say, are properly his. Whatsoever then he removes out of the State that Nature hath provided, and left it in, he hath mixed his *Labour* with, and joyned to it something that is his own, and thereby makes it his *Property*. It being by him removed from the common state Nature placed it in, it hath by this *labour* something annexed to it, that excludes the common right of other Men. For this *Labour* being the unquestionable Property of the Labourer, no Man but he can have a right to what that is once joyned to, at least where there is enough, and as good left in common for others.

28.   He that is nourished by the Acorns he pickt up under an Oak, or the Apples he gathered from the Trees in the Wood, has certainly appropriated them to himself. No Body can deny but the nourishment is his. I ask then, When did they begin to be his? When he digested? Or when he eat? Or when he boiled? Or when he brought them home? Or when he pickt them up? And 'tis plain, if the first gathering made them not his, nothing else could. That *labour* put a distinction between them and common. That added some-

thing to them more than Nature, the common Mother of all, had done; and so they became his private right. And will any one say he had no right to those Acorns or Apples he thus appropriated, because he had not the consent of all Mankind to make them his? Was it a Robbery thus to assume to himself what belonged to all in Common? If such a consent as that was necessary, Man had starved, notwithstanding the Plenty God had given him. We see in *Commons*, which remain so by Compact, that 'tis the taking any part of what is common, and removing it out of the state Nature leaves it in, which *begins the Property*; without which the Common is of no use. And the taking of this or that part, does not depend on the express consent of all the Commoners. Thus the Grass my Horse has bit; the Turfs my Servant has cut; and the Ore I have digg'd in any place where I have a right to them in common with others, become my *Property*, without the assignation or consent of any body. The *labour* that was mine, removing them out of that common state they were in, hath *fixed* my *Property* in them.

29.   By making an explicit consent of every Commoner, necessary to any ones appropriating to himself any part of what is given in common, Children or Servants could not cut the Meat which their Father or Master had provided for them in common, without assigning to every one his peculiar part. Though the Water running in the Fountain be every ones, yet who can doubt, but that in the Pitcher is his only who drew it out? His *labour* hath taken it out of the hands of Nature, where it was common, and belong'd equally to all her Children, and *hath* thereby *appropriated* it to himself.

30.   Thus this Law of reason makes the Deer, that *Indian's* who hath killed it; 'tis allowed to be his goods who hath bestowed his labour upon it, though before, it was the common right of every one. And amongst those who are counted the Civiliz'd part of Mankind, who have made and multiplied positive Laws to determine Property, this original Law of Nature for the *beginning of Property*, in what was before common, still takes place; and by vertue thereof, what Fish any one catches in the Ocean, that great and still remaining Common of Mankind; or what Ambergriese any one takes up here, is *by* the *Labour* that removes it out of that common state Nature left it in, *made* his *Property* who takes that pains about it. And even amongst us the Hare that any one is Hunting, is thought his who pursues her during the Chase. For being a Beast that is still looked upon as common, and no Man's private Possession; whoever has imploy'd so much *labour* about any of that kind, as to find and pursue her, has thereby removed her from the state of Nature, wherein she was common, and hath *begun a Property*.

31.   It will perhaps be objected to this, That if gathering the Acorns, or other Fruits of the Earth, *&c* makes a right to them, then any one may *ingross* as much as he will. To which I Answer, Not so. The same Law of Nature, that does by this means give us Property, does also *bound* that *Property* too. *God has given us all things richly*, 1 Tim. vi. 17. is the Voice of Reason confirmed by Inspiration. But how far has he given it us? *To enjoy.* As much as any one can make use of to any advantage of life before it spoils; so much he may by his labour fix a Property in. Whatever is beyond this, is more than his share, and belongs to others. Nothing was made by God for Man to spoil or destroy. And thus considering the plenty of natural Provisions there was a long time in the World, and the few spenders, and to how small a part of that provision the industry of one Man could extend it self, and ingross it to the prejudice of others; especially keeping within the *bounds*, set by reason of what might serve for his *use*; there could be then little room for Quarrels or Contentions about Property so establish'd.

32.   But the *chief matter of Property* being now not the Fruits of the Earth, and the Beasts that subsist on it, but the *Earth it self*, as that which takes in and carries with it all

the rest: I think it is plain, that *Property* in that too is acquired as the former. *As much Land* as a Man Tills, Plants, Improves, Cultivates, and can use the Product of, so much is his *Property*. He by his Labour does, as it were, inclose it from the Common. Nor will it invalidate his right to say, Every body else has an equal Title to it; and therefore he cannot appropriate, he cannot inclose, without the Consent of all his Fellow-Commoners, all Mankind. God, when he gave the World in common to all Mankind, commanded Man also to labour, and the penury of his Condition required it of him. God and his Reason commanded him to subdue the Earth, *i.e.* improve it for the benefit of Life, and therein lay out something upon it that was his own, his labour. He that in Obedience to this Command of God, subdued, tilled and sowed any part of it, thereby annexed to it something that was his *Property*, which another had no Title to, nor could without injury take from him.

33. Nor was this *appropriation* of any parcel of *Land*, by improving it, any prejudice to any other Man, since there was still enough, and as good left; and more than the yet unprovided could use. So that in effect, there was never the less left for others because of his inclosure for himself. For he that leaves as much as another can make use of, does as good as take nothing at all. No Body could think himself injur'd by the drinking of another Man, though he took a good Draught, who had a whole River of the same Water left him to quench his thirst. And the Case of Land and Water, where there is enough of both, is perfectly the same.

34. God gave the World to Men in Common; but since he gave it them for their benefit, and the greatest Conveniencies of Life they were capable to draw from it, it cannot be supposed he meant it should always remain common and uncultivated. He gave it to the use of the Industrious and Rational, (and *Labour* was to be *his Title* to it;) not to the Fancy or Covetousness of the Quarrelsom and Contentious. He that had as good left for his Improvement, as was already taken up, needed not complain, ought not to meddle with what was already improved by another's Labour: If he did, 'tis plain he desired the benefit of another's Pains, which he had no right to, and not the Ground which God had given him in common with others to labour on, and whereof there was as good left, as that already possessed, and more than he knew what to do with, or his Industry could reach to.

35. 'Tis true, in *Land* that is *common* in *England*, or any other Country, where there is Plenty of People under Government, who have Money and Commerce, no one can inclose or appropriate any part, without the consent of all his Fellow-Commoners: Because this is left common by Compact, *i.e.* by the Law of the Land, which is not to be violated. And though it be Common, in respect of some Men, it is not so to all Mankind; but is the joint property of this Country, or this Parish. Besides, the remainder, after such inclosure, would not be as good to the rest of the Commoners as the whole was, when they could all make use of the whole: whereas in the beginning and first peopling of the great Common of the World, it was quite otherwise. The Law Man was under, was rather for *appropriating*. God Commanded, and his Wants forced him to *labour*. That was his *Property* which could not be taken from him where-ever he had fixed it. And hence subduing or cultivating the Earth, and having Dominion, we see are joyned together. The one gave Title to the other. So that God, by commanding to subdue, gave Authority so far to *appropriate*. And the Condition of Humane Life, which requires Labour and Materials to work on, necessarily introduces *private Possessions*.

36. The measure of Property, Nature has well set, by the Extent of Mens *Labour, and the Conveniency of Life*: No Mans Labour could subdue, or appropriate all: nor could his Enjoyment consume more than a small part; so that it was impossible for any Man, this way, to intrench upon the right of another, or acquire, to himself, a Property, to the Prejudice of his Neighbour, who would still have room, for as good, and as large a Possession (after the other had taken out his) as before it was appropriated. This *measure* did confine every Man's *Possession*, to a very moderate Proportion, and such as he might appropriate to himself, without Injury to any Body in the first Ages of the World, when Men were more in danger to be lost, by wandering from their Company, in the then vast Wilderness of the Earth, than to be straitned for want of room to plant in. And the same *measure* may be allowed still, without prejudice to any Body, as full as the World seems. For supporting a Man, or Family, in the state they were, at first peopling of the World by the Children of *Adam*, or *Noah*; let him plant in some in-land, vacant places of *America*, we shall find that the *Possessions* he could make himself upon the *measures* we have given, would not be very large, nor, even to this day, prejudice the rest of Mankind, or give them reason to complain, or think themselves injured by this Man's Incroachment, though the Race of Men have now spread themselves to all the corners of the World, and do infinitely exceed the small number [which] was at the beginning. Nay, the extent of *Ground* is of so little value, *without labour*, that I have heard it affirmed, that in *Spain* it self, a Man may be permitted to plough, sow, and reap, without being disturbed, upon Land he has no other Title to, but only his making use of it. But, on the contrary, the Inhabitants think themselves beholden to him, who, by his Industry on neglected, and consequently waste Land, has increased the stock of Corn, which they wanted. But be this as it will, which I lay no stress on; This I dare boldly affirm, That the same *Rule of Propriety*, (*viz.*) that every Man should have as much as he could make use of, would hold still in the World, without straitning any body, since there is Land enough in the World to suffice double the inhabitants had not the *Invention of Money*, and the tacit Agreement of Men to put a value on it, introduced (by Consent) larger Possessions, and a Right to them; which, how it has done, I shall, by and by, shew more at large.

37. This is certain, That in the beginning, before the desire of having more than Men needed, had altered the intrinsick value of things, which depends only on their usefulness to the Life of Man; or [Men] had *agreed, that a little piece of yellow Metal*, which would keep without wasting or decay, should be worth a great piece of Flesh, or a whole heap of Corn; though Men had a Right to appropriate, by their Labour, each one to himself, as much of the things of Nature, as he could use: Yet this could not be much, nor to the Prejudice of others, where the same plenty was still left, to those who would use the same Industry. To which let me add, that he who appropriates land to himself by his labour, does not lessen but increase the common stock of mankind. For the provisions serving to the support of humane life, produced by one acre of inclosed and cultivated land, are (to speak much within compasse) ten times more, than those, which are yeilded by an acre of Land, of an equal richnesse, lyeing wast in common. And therefor he, that incloses Land and has a greater plenty of the conveniencys of life from ten acres, than he could have from an hundred left to Nature, may truly be said, to give ninety acres to Mankind. For his labour now supplys him with pro-visions out of ten acres, which were but the product of an hundred lying in common. I have here rated the improved land very low in making its product but as ten to one,

when it is much nearer an hundred to one. For I aske whether in the wild woods and uncultivated wast of America left to Nature, without any improvement, tillage or husbandry, a thousand acres will yield the needy and wretched inhabitants as many conveniencies of life as ten acres of equally fertile land doe in Dovonshire where they are well cultivated?

Before the Appropriation of Land, he who gathered as much of the wild Fruit, killed, caught, or tamed, as many of the Beasts as he could; he that so employed his Pains about any of the spontaneous Products of Nature, as any way to alter them, from the state which Nature put them in, *by* placing any of his *Labour* on them, did thereby *acquire a Propriety in them*: But if they perished, in his Possession, without their due use; if the Fruits rotted, or the Venison putrified, before he could spend it, he offended against the common Law of Nature, and was liable to be punished; he invaded his Neighbour's share, for he had *no Right, farther than his Use* called for any of them, and they might serve to afford him Conveniencies of Life.

38.   The same *measures* governed the *Possession of Land* too: Whatsoever he tilled and reaped, laid up and made use of, before it spoiled, that was his peculiar Right; whatsoever he enclosed, and could feed, and make use of, the Cattle and Product was also his. But if either the Grass of his Inclosure rotted on the Ground, or the Fruit of his planting perished without gathering, and laying up, this part of the Earth, notwithstanding his Inclosure, was still to be looked on as Waste, and might be the Possession of any other. Thus, at the beginning, *Cain* might take as much Ground as he could till, and make it his own Land, and yet leave enough to *Abel's* Sheep to feed on; a few Acres would serve for both their Possessions. But as Families increased, and Industry inlarged their Stocks, their *Possessions inlarged* with the need of them; but yet it was commonly *without any fixed property in the ground* they made use of, till they incorporated, settled themselves together, and built Cities, and then, by consent, they came in time, to set out the *bounds of their distinct Territories*, and agree on limits between them and their Neighbours, and by Laws within themselves, settled the *Properties* of those of the same Society. For we see, that in that part of the World which was first inhabited, and therefore like to be best peopled, even as low down as *Abraham's* time, they wandred with their Flocks, and their Herds, which was their substance, freely up and down; and this *Abraham* did, in a Country where he was a Stranger. Whence it is plain, that at least, a great part of the *Land lay in common*; that the Inhabitants valued it not, nor claimed Property in any more than they made use of. But when there was not room enough in the same place, for their Herds to feed together, they, by consent, as *Abraham* and *Lot* did, *Gen.* xiii. 5. separated and inlarged their pasture, where it best liked them. And for the same Reason *Esau* went from his Father, and his Brother, and planted in *Mount Seir*, Gen. xxxvi. 6. . . .

51.   And thus, I think, it is very easie to conceive without any difficulty, *how Labour could at first begin a title of Property* in the common things of Nature, and how the spending it upon our uses bounded it. So that there could then be no reason of quarrelling about Title, nor any doubt about the largeness of Possession it gave. Right and conveniency went together; for as a Man had a Right to all he could imploy his Labour upon, so he had no temptation to labour for more than he could make use of. This left no room for Controversie about the Title, nor for Incroachment on the Right of others; what Portion a Man carved to himself, was easily seen; and it was useless as well as dishonest to carve himself too much, or take more than he needed.

42   From *A Theory of Justice**

John Rawls

Justice as Fairness

In this introductory chapter I sketch some of the main ideas of the theory of justice
I wish to develop. The exposition is informal and intended to prepare the way for the
more detailed arguments that follow. Unavoidably there is some overlap between this and
later discussions. I begin by describing the role of justice in social cooperation and with
a brief account of the primary subject of justice, the basic structure of society. I then
present the main idea of justice as fairness, a theory of justice that generalizes and carries
to a higher level of abstraction the traditional conception of the social contract. The
compact of society is replaced by an initial situation that incorporates certain procedural
constraints on arguments designed to lead to an original agreement on principles of
justice. I also take up, for purposes of clarification and contrast, the classical utilitarian
and intuitionist conceptions of justice and consider some of the differences between
these views and justice as fairness. My guiding aim is to work out a theory of justice
that is a viable alternative to these doctrines which have long dominated our philosophical tradition.

1.   *The role of justice*

Justice is the first virtue of social institutions, as truth is of systems of thought. A theory
however elegant and economical must be rejected or revised if it is untrue; likewise laws
and institutions no matter how efficient and well-arranged must be reformed or abolished
if they are unjust. Each person possesses an inviolability founded on justice that even the
welfare of society as a whole cannot override. For this reason justice denies that the loss
of freedom for some is made right by a greater good shared by others. It does not allow
that the sacrifices imposed on a few are outweighed by the larger sum of advantages
enjoyed by many. Therefore in a just society the liberties of equal citizenship are taken as
settled; the rights secured by justice are not subject to political bargaining or to the cal-
culus of social interests. The only thing that permits us to acquiesce in an erroneous theory
is the lack of a better one; analogously, an injustice is tolerable only when it is necessary
to avoid an even greater injustice. Being first virtues of human activities, truth and justice
are uncompromising.

These propositions seem to express our intuitive conviction of the primacy of justice.
No doubt they are expressed too strongly. In any event I wish to inquire whether these
contentions or others similar to them are sound, and if so how they can be accounted
for. To this end it is necessary to work out a theory of justice in the light of which these

* From *A Theory of Justice* (Cambridge, MA: The Belknap Press of Harvard University Press, 1971),
pp. 3–22, 60–5, 150–6, 251–7, and 302–3. © 1971, 1999 by the President and Fellows of Harvard
College. Reprinted by permission of the publisher.

assertions can be interpreted and assessed. I shall begin by considering the role of the principles of justice. Let us assume, to fix ideas, that a society is a more or less self-sufficient association of persons who in their relations to one another recognize certain rules of conduct as binding and who for the most part act in accordance with them. Suppose further that these rules specify a system of cooperation designed to advance the good of those taking part in it. Then, although a society is a cooperative venture for mutual advantage, it is typically marked by a conflict as well as by an identity of interests. There is an identity of interests since social cooperation makes possible a better life for all than any would have if each were to live solely by his own efforts. There is a conflict of interests since persons are not indifferent as to how the greater benefits produced by their collaboration are distributed, for in order to pursue their ends they each prefer a larger to a lesser share. A set of principles is required for choosing among the various social arrangements which determine this division of advantages and for underwriting an agreement on the proper distributive shares. These principles are the principles of social justice: they provide a way of assigning rights and duties in the basic institutions of society and they define the appropriate distribution of the benefits and burdens of social cooperation.

Now let us say that a society is well-ordered when it is not only designed to advance the good of its members but when it is also effectively regulated by a public conception of justice. That is, it is a society in which (1) everyone accepts and knows that the others accept the same principles of justice, and (2) the basic social institutions generally satisfy and are generally known to satisfy these principles. In this case while men may put forth excessive demands on one another, they nevertheless acknowledge a common point of view from which their claims may be adjudicated. If men's inclination to self-interest makes their vigilance against one another necessary, their public sense of justice makes their secure association together possible. Among individuals with disparate aims and purposes a shared conception of justice establishes the bonds of civic friendship; the general desire for justice limits the pursuit of other ends. One may think of a public conception of justice as constituting the fundamental charter of a well-ordered human association.

Existing societies are of course seldom well-ordered in this sense, for what is just and unjust is usually in dispute. Men disagree about which principles should define the basic terms of their association. Yet we may still say, despite this disagreement, that they each have a conception of justice. That is, they understand the need for, and they are prepared to affirm, a characteristic set of principles for assigning basic rights and duties and for determining what they take to be the proper distribution of the benefits and burdens of social cooperation. Thus it seems natural to think of the concept of justice as distinct from the various conceptions of justice and as being specified by the role which these different sets of principles, these different conceptions, have in common.[1] Those who hold different conceptions of justice can, then, still agree that institutions are just when no arbitrary distinctions are made between persons in the assigning of basic rights and duties and when the rules determine a proper balance between competing claims to the advantages of social life. Men can agree to this description of just institutions since the notions of an arbitrary distinction and of a proper balance, which are included in the concept of justice, are left open for each to interpret according to the principles of justice that he accepts. These principles single out which similarities and differences among persons are relevant in determining rights and duties and they specify which division of advantages is appropriate. Clearly this distinction between the concept and the various conceptions of justice settles no important questions. It simply helps to identify the role of the principles of social justice.

Some measure of agreement in conceptions of justice is, however, not the only prerequisite for a viable human community. There are other fundamental social problems, in particular those of coordination, efficiency, and stability. Thus the plans of individuals need to be fitted together so that their activities are compatible with one another and they can all be carried through without anyone's legitimate expectations being severely disappointed. Moreover, the execution of these plans should lead to the achievement of social ends in ways that are efficient and consistent with justice. And finally, the scheme of social cooperation must be stable: it must be more or less regularly complied with and its basic rules willingly acted upon; and when infractions occur, stabilizing forces should exist that prevent further violations and tend to restore the arrangement. Now it is evident that these three problems are connected with that of justice. In the absence of a certain measure of agreement on what is just and unjust, it is clearly more difficult for individuals to coordinate their plans efficiently in order to insure that mutually beneficial arrangements are maintained. Distrust and resentment corrode the ties of civility, and suspicion and hostility tempt men to act in ways they would otherwise avoid. So while the distinctive role of conceptions of justice is to specify basic rights and duties and to determine the appropriate distributive shares, the way in which a conception does this is bound to affect the problems of efficiency, coordination, and stability. We cannot, in general, assess a conception of justice by its distributive role alone, however useful this role may be in identifying the concept of justice. We must take into account its wider connections; for even though justice has a certain priority, being the most important virtue of institutions, it is still true that, other things equal, one conception of justice is preferable to another when its broader consequences are more desirable.

2. *The subject of justice*

Many different kinds of things are said to be just and unjust: not only laws, institutions, and social systems, but also particular actions of many kinds, including decisions, judgments, and imputations. We also call the attitudes and dispositions of persons, and persons themselves, just and unjust. Our topic, however, is that of social justice. For us the primary subject of justice is the basic structure of society, or more exactly, the way in which the major social institutions distribute fundamental rights and duties and determine the division of advantages from social cooperation. By major institutions I understand the political constitution and the principal economic and social arrangements. Thus the legal protection of freedom of thought and liberty of conscience, competitive markets, private property in the means of production, and the monogamous family are examples of major social institutions. Taken together as one scheme, the major institutions define men's rights and duties and influence their life-prospects, what they can expect to be and how well they can hope to do. The basic structure is the primary subject of justice because its effects are so profound and present from the start. The intuitive notion here is that this structure contains various social positions and that men born into different positions have different expectations of life determined, in part, by the political system as well as by economic and social circumstances. In this way the institutions of society favor certain starting places over others. These are especially deep inequalities. Not only are they pervasive, but they affect men's initial chances in life; yet they cannot possibly be justified by an appeal to the notions of merit or desert. It is these inequalities, presumably inevitable in the basic structure of any society, to which the principles of social justice must in the first instance apply. These principles, then, regulate the choice of a political constitution and the main elements of the economic and social system. The justice of a social scheme depends essentially on how fundamental rights and duties are assigned and on the economic opportunities and social conditions in the various sectors of society.

The scope of our inquiry is limited in two ways. First of all, I am concerned with a special case of the problem of justice. I shall not consider the justice of institutions and social practices generally, nor except in passing the justice of the law of nations and of relations between states. Therefore, if one supposes that the concept of justice applies whenever there is an allotment of something rationally regarded as advantageous or disadvantageous, then we are interested in only one instance of its application. There is no reason to suppose ahead of time that the principles satisfactory for the basic structure hold for all cases. These principles may not work for the rules and practices of private associations or for those of less comprehensive social groups. They may be irrelevant for the various informal conventions and customs of everyday life; they may not elucidate the justice, or perhaps better, the fairness of voluntary cooperative arrangements or procedures for making contractual agreements. The conditions for the law of nations may require different principles arrived at in a somewhat different way. I shall be satisfied if it is possible to formulate a reasonable conception of justice for the basic structure of society conceived for the time being as a closed system isolated from other societies. The significance of this special case is obvious and needs no explanation. It is natural to conjecture that once we have a sound theory for this case, the remaining problems of justice will prove more tractable in the light of it. With suitable modifications such a theory should provide the key for some of these other questions.

The other limitation on our discussion is that for the most part I examine the principles of justice that would regulate a well-ordered society. Everyone is presumed to act justly and to do his part in upholding just institutions. Though justice may be, as Hume remarked, the cautious, jealous virtue, we can still ask what a perfectly just society would be like.[2] Thus I consider primarily what I call strict compliance as opposed to partial compliance theory. The latter studies the principles that govern how we are to deal with injustice. It comprises such topics as the theory of punishment, the doctrine of just war, and the justification of the various ways of opposing unjust regimes, ranging from civil disobedience and militant resistance to revolution and rebellion. Also included here are questions of compensatory justice and of weighing one form of institutional injustice against another. Obviously the problems of partial compliance theory are the pressing and urgent matters. These are the things that we are faced with in everyday life. The reason for beginning with ideal theory is that it provides, I believe, the only basis for the systematic grasp of these more pressing problems. The discussion of civil disobedience, for example, depends upon it. At least, I shall assume that a deeper understanding can be gained in no other way, and that the nature and aims of a perfectly just society is the fundamental part of the theory of justice.

Now admittedly the concept of the basic structure is somewhat vague. It is not always clear which institutions or features thereof should be included. But it would be premature to worry about this matter here. I shall proceed by discussing principles which do apply to what is certainly a part of the basic structure as intuitively understood; I shall then try to extend the application of these principles so that they cover what would appear to be the main elements of this structure. Perhaps these principles will turn out to be perfectly general, although this is unlikely. It is sufficient that they apply to the most important cases of social justice. The point to keep in mind is that a conception of justice for the basic structure is worth having for its own sake. It should not be dismissed because its principles are not everywhere satisfactory.

A conception of social justice, then, is to be regarded as providing in the first instance a standard whereby the distributive aspects of the basic structure of society are to be assessed. This standard, however, is not to be confused with the principles defining the other virtues, for the basic structure, and social arrangements generally, may be efficient or inefficient, liberal or illiberal, and many other things, as well as just or unjust. A complete conception defining principles for all the virtues of the basic structure, together with their respective weights when they conflict, is more than a conception of justice; it is a social ideal. The principles of justice are but a part, although perhaps the most important part, of such a conception. A social ideal in turn is connected with a conception of society, a vision of the way in which the aims and purposes of social cooperation are to be understood. The various conceptions of justice are the outgrowth of different notions of society against the background of opposing views of the natural necessities and opportunities of human life. Fully to understand a conception of justice we must make explicit the conception of social cooperation from which it derives. But in doing this we should not lose sight of the special role of the principles of justice or of the primary subject to which they apply.

In these preliminary remarks I have distinguished the concept of justice as meaning a proper balance between competing claims from a conception of justice as a set of related principles for identifying the relevant considerations which determine this balance. I have also characterized justice as but one part of a social ideal, although the theory I shall propose no doubt extends its everyday sense. This theory is not offered as a description of ordinary meanings but as an account of certain distributive principles for the basic structure of society. I assume that any reasonably complete ethical theory must include principles for this fundamental problem and that these principles, whatever they are, constitute its doctrine of justice. The concept of justice I take to be defined, then, by the role of its principles in assigning rights and duties and in defining the appropriate division of social advantages. A conception of justice is an interpretation of this role.

Now this approach may not seem to tally with tradition. I believe, though, that it does. The more specific sense that Aristotle gives to justice, and from which the most familiar formulations derive, is that of refraining from *pleonexia*, that is, from gaining some advantage for oneself by seizing what belongs to another, his property, his reward, his office, and the like, or by denying a person that which is due to him, the fulfillment of a promise, the repayment of a debt, the showing of proper respect, and so on.[3] It is evident that this definition is framed to apply to actions, and persons are thought to be just insofar as they have, as one of the permanent elements of their character, a steady and effective desire to act justly. Aristotle's definition clearly presupposes, however, an account of what properly belongs to a person and of what is due to him. Now such entitlements are, I believe, very often derived from social institutions and the legitimate expectations to which they give rise. There is no reason to think that Aristotle would disagree with this, and certainly he has a conception of social justice to account for these claims. The definition I adopt is designed to apply directly to the most important case, the justice of the basic structure. There is no conflict with the traditional notion.

3. The main idea of the theory of justice

My aim is to present a conception of justice which generalizes and carries to a higher level of abstraction the familiar theory of the social contract as found, say, in Locke, Rousseau, and Kant.[4] In order to do this we are not to think of the original contract as one to enter a particular society or to set up a particular form of government. Rather, the guiding idea is that the principles of justice for the basic structure of society are the object of the original agreement. They are the principles that free and rational persons concerned to further their own interests would accept in an initial position of equality as defining the fundamental terms of their association. These principles are to regulate all further agreements; they specify the kinds of social cooperation that can be entered into and the forms of government that can be established. This way of regarding the principles of justice I shall call justice as fairness.

Thus we are to imagine that those who engage in social cooperation choose together, in one joint act, the principles which are to assign basic rights and duties and to determine the division of social benefits. Men are to decide in advance how they are to regulate their claims against one another and what is to be the foundation charter of their society. Just as each person must decide by rational reflection what constitutes his good, that is, the system of ends which it is rational for him to pursue, so a group of persons must decide once and for all what is to count among them as just and unjust. The choice which rational men would make in this hypothetical situation of equal liberty, assuming for the present that this choice problem has a solution, determines the principles of justice.

In justice as fairness the original position of equality corresponds to the state of nature in the traditional theory of the social contract. This original position is not, of course, thought of as an actual historical state of affairs, much less as a primitive condition of culture. It is understood as a purely hypothetical situation characterized so as to lead to a certain conception of justice.[5] Among the essential features of this situation is that no one knows his place in society, his class position or social status, nor does any one know his fortune in the distribution of natural assets and abilities, his intelligence, strength, and the like. I shall even assume that the parties do not know their conceptions of the good or their special psychological propensities. The principles of justice are chosen behind a veil of ignorance. This ensures that no one is advantaged or disadvantaged in the choice of principles by the outcome of natural chance or the contingency of social circumstances. Since all are similarly situated and no one is able to design principles to favor his particular condition, the principles of justice are the result of a fair agreement or bargain. For given the circumstances of the original position, the symmetry of everyone's relations to each other, this initial situation is fair between individuals as moral persons, that is, as rational beings with their own ends and capable, I shall assume, of a sense of justice. The original position is, one might say, the appropriate initial status quo, and thus the fundamental agreements reached in it are fair. This explains the propriety of the name "justice as fairness": it conveys the idea that the principles of justice are agreed to in an initial situation that is fair. The name does not mean that the concepts of justice and fairness are the same, any more than the phrase "poetry as metaphor" means that the concepts of poetry and metaphor are the same.

Justice as fairness begins, as I have said, with one of the most general of all choices which persons might make together, namely, with the choice of the first principles of a conception of justice which is to regulate all subsequent criticism and reform of institutions. Then, having chosen a conception of justice, we can suppose that they are to choose a constitution and a legislature to enact laws, and so on, all in accordance with the principles of justice initially agreed upon. Our social situation is just if it is such that by this sequence of hypothetical agreements we would have contracted into the general system of rules which defines it. Moreover, assuming that the original position does determine a set of principles (that is, that a particular conception of justice would be chosen), it will then be true that whenever social institutions satisfy these principles those engaged in them can say to one another that they are cooperating on terms to which they would agree if they were free and equal persons whose relations with respect to one another were fair. They could all view their arrangements as meeting the stipulations which they would acknowledge in an initial situation that embodies widely accepted and reasonable constraints on the choice of principles. The general recognition of this fact would provide the basis for a public acceptance of the corresponding principles of justice. No society can, of course, be a scheme of cooperation which men enter voluntarily in a literal sense; each person finds himself placed at birth in some particular position in some particular society, and the nature of this position materially affects his life prospects. Yet a society satisfying the principles of justice as fairness comes as close as a society can to being a voluntary scheme, for it meets the principles which free and equal persons would assent to under circumstances that are fair. In this sense its members are autonomous and the obligations they recognize self-imposed.

One feature of justice as fairness is to think of the parties in the initial situation as rational and mutually disinterested. This does not mean that the parties are egoists, that is, individuals with only certain kinds of interests, say in wealth, prestige, and domination. But they are conceived as not taking an interest in one another's interests. They are to presume that even their spiritual aims may be opposed, in the way that the aims of those of different religions may be opposed. Moreover, the concept of rationality must be interpreted as far as possible in the narrow sense, standard in economic theory, of taking the most effective means to given ends. I shall modify this concept to some extent, as explained later, but one must try to avoid introducing into it any controversial ethical elements. The initial situation must be characterized by stipulations that are widely accepted.

In working out the conception of justice as fairness one main task clearly is to determine which principles of justice would be chosen in the original position. To do this we must describe this situation in some detail and formulate with care the problem of choice which it presents. These matters I shall take up in the immediately succeeding chapters. It may be observed, however, that once the principles of justice are thought of as arising from an original agreement in a situation of equality, it is an open question whether the principle of utility would be acknowledged. Offhand it hardly seems likely that persons who view themselves as equals, entitled to press their claims upon one another, would agree to a principle which may require lesser life prospects for some simply for the sake of a greater sum of advantages enjoyed by others. Since each desires to protect his interests, his capacity to advance his conception of the good, no one has a reason to acquiesce in an enduring loss for himself in order to bring about a greater net balance of satisfaction. In the absence of strong and lasting benevolent impulses, a rational man would not accept a basic structure merely because it maximized the algebraic sum of advantages irrespective of its permanent effects on his own basic rights and interests. Thus it seems that the principle of utility is incompatible with the conception of social cooperation among equals for mutual advantage. It appears to be inconsistent with the idea of reciprocity implicit in the notion of a well-ordered society. Or, at any rate, so I shall argue.

I shall maintain instead that the persons in the initial situation would choose two rather different principles: the first requires equality in the assignment of basic rights and duties, while the second holds that social and economic inequalities, for example inequalities of wealth and authority, are just only if they result in compensating benefits for everyone, and in particular for the least advantaged members of society. These principles rule out justifying institutions on the grounds that the hardships of some are offset by a greater good in the aggregate. It may be expedient but it is not just that some should have less in order that others may prosper. But there is no injustice in the greater benefits earned by a few provided that the situation of persons not so fortunate is thereby improved. The intuitive idea is that since everyone's well-being depends upon a scheme of cooperation without which no one could have a satisfactory life, the division of advantages should be such as to draw forth the willing cooperation of everyone taking part in it, including those less well situated. Yet this can be expected only if reasonable terms are proposed. The two principles mentioned seem to be a fair agreement on the basis of which those better endowed, or more fortunate in their social position, neither of which we can be said to deserve, could expect the willing cooperation of others when some workable scheme is a necessary condition of the welfare of all.[6] Once we decide to look for a conception of justice that nullifies the accidents of natural endowment and the contingencies of social circumstance as counters in quest for political and economic advantage, we are led to these principles. They express the result of leaving aside those aspects of the social world that seem arbitrary from a moral point of view.

The problem of the choice of principles, however, is extremely difficult. I do not expect the answer I shall suggest to be convincing to everyone. It is, therefore, worth noting from the outset that justice as fairness, like other contract views, consists of two parts: (1) an interpretation of the initial situation and of the problem of choice posed there, and (2) a set of principles which, it is argued, would be agreed to. One may accept the first part of the theory (or some variant thereof), but not the other, and conversely. The concept of the initial contractual situation may seem reasonable although the particular principles proposed are rejected. To be sure, I want to maintain that the most appropriate conception of this situation does lead to principles of justice contrary to utilitarianism and perfectionism, and therefore that the contract doctrine provides an alternative to these views. Still, one may dispute this contention even though one grants that the contractarian method is a useful way of studying ethical theories and of setting forth their underlying assumptions.

Justice as fairness is an example of what I have called a contract theory. Now there may be an objection to the term "contract" and related expressions, but I think it will serve reasonably well. Many words have misleading connotations which at first are likely to confuse. The terms "utility" and "utilitarianism" are surely no exception. They too have unfortunate suggestions which hostile critics have been willing to exploit; yet they are clear enough for those prepared to study utilitarian doctrine. The same should be true of the term "contract" applied to moral theories. As I have mentioned, to understand it one has to keep in mind that it implies a certain level of abstraction. In particular, the content of the relevant agreement is not to enter a given society or to adopt a given form of government, but to accept certain moral principles. Moreover, the undertakings referred to are purely hypothetical: a contract view holds that certain principles would be accepted in a well-defined initial situation.

The merit of the contract terminology is that it conveys the idea that principles of justice may be conceived as principles that would be chosen by rational persons, and that in this way conceptions of justice may be explained and justified. The theory of justice is a part, perhaps the most significant part, of the theory of rational choice. Furthermore, principles of justice deal with conflicting claims upon the advantages won by social cooperation; they apply to the relations among several persons or groups. The word "contract" suggests this plurality as well as the condition that the appropriate division of advantages must be in accordance with principles acceptable to all parties. The condition of publicity for principles of justice is also connoted by the contract phraseology. Thus, if these principles are the outcome of an agreement, citizens have a knowledge of the principles that others follow. It is characteristic of contract theories to stress the public nature of political principles. Finally there is the long tradition of the contract doctrine. Expressing the tie with this line of thought helps to define ideas and accords with natural piety. There are then several advantages in the use of the term "contract." With due precautions taken, it should not be misleading.

A final remark. Justice as fairness is not a complete contract theory. For it is clear that the contractarian idea can be extended to the choice of more or less an entire ethical system, that is, to a system including principles for all the virtues and not only for justice. Now for the most part I shall consider only principles of justice and others closely related to them; I make no attempt to discuss the virtues in a systematic way. Obviously if justice as fairness succeeds reasonably well, a next step would be to study the more general view suggested by the name "rightness as fairness." But even this wider theory fails to embrace all moral relationships, since it would seem to include only our relations with other persons and to leave out of account how we are to conduct ourselves toward animals and the rest of nature. I do not contend that the contract notion offers a way to approach these questions which are certainly of the first importance; and I shall have to put them aside. We must recognize the limited scope of justice as fairness and of the general type of view that it exemplifies. How far its conclusions must be revised once these other matters are understood cannot be decided in advance.

4. *The original position and justification*

I have said that the original position is the appropriate initial status quo which insures that the fundamental agreements reached in it are fair. This fact yields the name "justice as fairness." It is clear, then, that I want to say that one conception of justice is more reasonable than another, or justifiable with respect to it, if rational persons in the initial situation would choose its principles over those of the other for the role of justice. Conceptions of justice are to be ranked by their acceptability to persons so circumstanced. Understood in this way the question of justification is settled by working out a problem of deliberation: we have to ascertain which principles it would be rational to adopt given the contractual situation. This connects the theory of justice with the theory of rational choice.

If this view of the problem of justification is to succeed, we must, of course, describe in some detail the nature of this choice problem. A problem of rational decision has a definite answer only if we know the beliefs and interests of the parties, their relations with respect to one another, the alternatives between which they are to choose, the procedure whereby they make up their minds, and so on. As the circumstances are presented in different ways, correspondingly different principles are accepted. The concept of the original position, as I shall refer to it, is that of the most philosophically favored interpretation of this initial choice situation for the purposes of a theory of justice.

But how are we to decide what is the most favored interpretation? I assume, for one thing, that there is a broad measure of agreement that principles of justice should be chosen under certain conditions. To justify a particular description of the initial situation one shows that it incorporates these commonly shared presumptions. One argues from widely accepted but weak premises to more specific conclusions. Each of the presumptions should by itself be natural and plausible; some of them may seem innocuous or even trivial. The aim of the contract approach is to establish that taken together they impose significant bounds on acceptable principles of justice. The ideal outcome would be that these conditions determine a unique set of principles; but I shall be satisfied if they suffice to rank the main traditional conceptions of social justice.

One should not be misled, then, by the somewhat unusual conditions which characterize the original position. The idea here is simply to make vivid to ourselves the restrictions that it seems reasonable to impose on arguments for principles of justice, and therefore on these principles themselves. Thus it seems reasonable and generally acceptable that no one should be advantaged or disadvantaged by natural fortune or social circumstances in the choice of principles. It also seems widely agreed that it should be impossible to tailor principles to the circumstances of one's own case. We should insure further that particular inclinations and aspirations, and persons' conceptions of their good do not affect the principles adopted. The aim is to rule out those principles that it would be rational to propose for acceptance, however little the chance of success, only if one knew certain things that are irrelevant from the standpoint of justice. For example, if a man knew that he was wealthy, he might find it rational to advance the principle that various taxes for welfare measures be counted unjust; if he knew that he was poor, he would most likely propose the contrary principle. To represent the desired restrictions one imagines a situation in which everyone is deprived of this sort of information. One excludes the knowledge of those contingencies which sets men at odds and allows them to be guided by their prejudices. In this manner the veil of ignorance is arrived at in a natural way. This concept should cause no difficulty if we keep in mind the constraints on arguments that it is meant to express. At any time we can enter the original position, so to speak, simply by following a certain procedure, namely, by arguing for principles of justice in accordance with these restrictions.

It seems reasonable to suppose that the parties in the original position are equal. That is, all have the same rights in the procedure for choosing principles; each can make proposals, submit reasons for their acceptance, and so on. Obviously the purpose of these conditions is to represent equality between human beings as moral persons, as creatures having a conception of their good and capable of a sense of justice. The basis of equality is taken to be similarity in these two respects. Systems of ends are not ranked in value; and each man is presumed to have the requisite ability to understand and to act upon whatever principles are adopted. Together with the veil of ignorance, these conditions define the principles of justice as those which rational persons concerned to advance their interests would consent to as equals when none are known to be advantaged or disadvantaged by social and natural contingencies.

There is, however, another side to justifying a particular description of the original position. This is to see if the principles which would be chosen match our considered convictions of justice or extend them in an acceptable way. We can note whether applying these principles would lead us to make the same judgments about the basic structure of society which we now make intuitively and in which we have the greatest confidence; or whether, in cases where our present judgments are in doubt and given with hesitation, these principles offer a resolution which we can affirm on reflection. There are questions which we feel sure must be answered in a certain way. For example, we are confident that religious intolerance and racial discrimination are unjust. We think that we have examined these things with care and have reached what we believe is an impartial judgment not likely to be distorted by an excessive attention to our own interests. These convictions are provisional fixed points which we presume any conception of justice must fit. But we have much less assurance as to what is the correct distribution of wealth and authority. Here we may be looking for a way to remove our doubts. We can check an interpretation of the initial situation, then, by the capacity of its principles to accommodate our firmest convictions and to provide guidance where guidance is needed.

In searching for the most favored description of this situation we work from both ends. We begin by describing it so that it represents generally shared and preferably weak conditions. We then see if these conditions are strong enough to yield a significant set of principles. If not, we look for further premises equally reasonable. But if so, and these principles match our considered convictions of justice, then so far well and good. But presumably there will be discrepancies. In this case we have a choice. We can either modify the account of the initial situation or we can revise our existing judgments, for even the judgments we take provisionally as fixed points are liable to revision. By going back and forth, sometimes altering the conditions of the contractual circumstances, at others withdrawing our judgments and conforming them to principle, I assume that eventually we shall find a description of the initial situation that both expresses reasonable conditions and yields principles which match our considered judgments duly pruned and adjusted. This state of affairs I refer to as reflective equilibrium.[7] It is an equilibrium because at last our principles and judgments coincide; and it is reflective since we know to what principles our judgments conform and the premises of their derivation. At the moment everything is in order. But this equilibrium is not necessarily stable. It is liable to be upset by further examination of the conditions which should be imposed on the contractual situation and by particular cases which may lead us to revise our judgments. Yet for the time being we have done what we can to render coherent and to justify our convictions of social justice. We have reached a conception of the original position.

I shall not, of course, actually work through this process. Still, we may think of the interpretation of the original position that I shall present as the result of such a hypothetical course of reflection. It represents the attempt to accommodate within one scheme both reasonable philosophical conditions on principles as well as our considered judgments of justice. In arriving at the favored interpretation of the initial situation there is no point at which an appeal is made to self-evidence in the traditional sense either of general conceptions or particular convictions. I do not claim for the principles of justice proposed that they are necessary truths or derivable from such truths. A conception of justice cannot be deduced from self-evident premises or conditions on principles; instead, its justification is a matter of the mutual support of many considerations, of everything fitting together into one coherent view.

A final comment. We shall want to say that certain principles of justice are justified because they would be agreed to in an initial situation of equality. I have emphasized that this original position is purely hypothetical. It is natural to ask why, if this agreement is never actually entered into, we should take any interest in these principles, moral or otherwise. The answer is that the conditions embodied in the description of the original position are ones that we do in fact accept. Or if we do not, then perhaps we can be persuaded to do so by philosophical reflection. Each aspect of the contractual situation can be given supporting grounds. Thus what we shall do is to collect together into one conception a number of conditions on principles that we are ready upon due consideration to recognize as reasonable. These constraints express what we are prepared to regard as limits on fair terms of social cooperation. One way to look at the idea of the original position, therefore, is to see it as an expository device which sums up the meaning of these conditions and helps us to extract their consequences. On the other hand, this conception is also an intuitive notion that suggests its own elaboration, so that led on by it we are drawn to define more clearly the standpoint from which we can best interpret moral relationships. We need a conception that enables us to envision our objective from afar: the intuitive notion of the original position is to do this for us.[8] . . .

The Principles of Justice

[. . .]

11. Two principles of justice

I shall now state in a provisional form the two principles of justice that I believe would be chosen in the original position. In this section I wish to make only the most general comments, and therefore the first formulation of these principles is tentative. As we go on I shall run through several formulations and approximate step by step the final statement to be given much later. I believe that doing this allows the exposition to proceed in a natural way.

The first statement of the two principles reads as follows.

First: each person is to have an equal right to the most extensive basic liberty compatible with a similar liberty for others.

Second: social and economic inequalities are to be arranged so that they are both (a) reasonably expected to be to everyone's advantage, and (b) attached to positions and offices open to all. There are two ambiguous phrases in the second principle, namely "everyone's advantage" and "open to all." . . .

By way of general comment, these principles primarily apply, as I have said, to the basic structure of society. They are to govern the assignment of rights and duties and to regulate the distribution of social and economic advantages. As their formulation suggests, these principles presuppose that the social structure can be divided into two more or less distinct parts, the first principle applying to the one, the second to the other. They distinguish between those aspects of the social system that define and secure the equal liberties of citizenship and those that specify and establish social and economic inequalities. The basic liberties of citizens are, roughly speaking, political liberty (the right to vote and to be eligible for public office) together with freedom of speech and assembly; liberty of conscience and freedom of thought; freedom of the person along with the right to hold (personal) property; and freedom from arbitrary arrest and seizure as defined by the concept of the rule of law. These liberties are all required to be equal by the first principle, since citizens of a just society are to have the same basic rights.

The second principle applies, in the first approximation, to the distribution of income and wealth and to the design of organizations that make use of differences in authority and responsibility, or chains of command. While the distribution of wealth and income need not be equal, it must be to everyone's advantage, and at the same time, positions of authority and offices of command must be accessible to all. One applies the second principle by holding positions open, and then, subject to this constraint, arranges social and economic inequalities so that everyone benefits.

These principles are to be arranged in a serial order with the first principle prior to the second. This ordering means that a departure from the institutions of equal liberty required by the first principle cannot be justified by, or compensated for, by greater social and economic advantages. The distribution of wealth and income, and the hierarchies of authority, must be consistent with both the liberties of equal citizenship and equality of opportunity.

It is clear that these principles are rather specific in their content, and their acceptance rests on certain assumptions that I must eventually try to explain and justify. A theory of justice depends upon a theory of society in ways that will become evident as we proceed. For the present, it should be observed that the two principles (and this holds for all formulations) are a special case of a more general conception of justice that can be expressed as follows.

> All social values – liberty and opportunity, income and wealth, and the bases of self-respect – are to be distributed equally unless an unequal distribution of any, or all, of these values is to everyone's advantage.

Injustice, then, is simply inequalities that are not to the benefit of all. Of course, this conception is extremely vague and requires interpretation.

As a first step, suppose that the basic structure of society distributes certain primary goods, that is, things that every rational man is presumed to want. These goods normally have a use whatever a person's rational plan of life. For simplicity, assume that the chief primary goods at the disposition of society are rights and liberties, powers and opportunities, income and wealth. . . . These are the social primary goods. Other primary goods such as health and vigor, intelligence and imagination, are natural goods; although their possession is influenced by the basic structure, they are not so directly under its control. Imagine, then, a hypothetical initial arrangement in which all the social primary goods are equally distributed: everyone has similar rights and duties, and income and wealth are evenly shared. This state of affairs provides a benchmark for judging improvements. If certain inequalities of wealth and organizational powers would make everyone better off than in this hypothetical starting situation, then they accord with the general conception.

Now it is possible, at least theoretically, that by giving up some of their fundamental liberties men are sufficiently compensated by the resulting social and economic gains. The general conception of justice imposes no restrictions on what sort of inequalities are permissible; it only requires that everyone's position be improved. We need not suppose anything so drastic as consenting to a condition of slavery. Imagine instead that men forego certain political rights when the economic returns are significant and their capacity to influence the course of policy by the exercise of these rights would be marginal in any case. It is this kind of exchange which the two principles as stated rule out; being arranged in serial order they do not permit exchanges between basic liberties and economic and social gains. The serial ordering of principles expresses an underlying preference among primary social goods. When this preference is rational so likewise is the choice of these principles in this order.

In developing justice as fairness I shall, for the most part, leave aside the general conception of justice and examine instead the special case of the two principles in serial order. The advantage of this procedure is that from the first the matter of priorities is recognized and an effort made to find principles to deal with it. One is led to attend throughout to the conditions under which the acknowledgment of the absolute weight of liberty with respect to social and economic advantages, as defined by the lexical order of the two principles, would be reasonable. Offhand, this ranking appears extreme and too special a case to be of much interest; but there is more justification for it than would appear at first sight. Or at any rate, so I shall maintain. Furthermore, the distinction between fundamental rights and liberties and economic and social benefits marks a difference among primary social goods that one should try to exploit. It suggests an important division in the social system. Of course, the distinctions drawn and the ordering proposed are bound to be at best only approximations. There are surely circumstances in which they fail. But it is essential to depict clearly the main lines of a reasonable conception of justice; and under many conditions anyway, the two principles in serial order may serve well enough. When necessary we can fall back on the more general conception.

The fact that the two principles apply to institutions has certain consequences. Several points illustrate this. First of all, the rights and liberties referred to by these principles are those which are defined by the public rules of the basic structure. Whether men are free is determined by the rights and duties established by the major institutions of society. Liberty is a certain pattern of social forms. The first principle simply requires that certain sorts of rules, those defining basic liberties, apply to everyone equally and that they allow the most extensive liberty compatible with a like liberty for all. The only reason for circumscribing the rights defining liberty and making men's freedom less extensive than it might otherwise be is that these equal rights as institutionally defined would interfere with one another.

Another thing to bear in mind is that when principles mention persons, or require that everyone gain from an inequality, the reference is to representative persons holding the various social positions, or offices, or whatever, established by the basic structure. Thus in applying the second principle I assume that it is possible to assign an expectation of well-being to representative individuals holding these positions. This expectation indicates their life prospects as viewed from their social station. In general, the expectations of representative persons depend upon the distribution of rights and duties throughout the basic structure. When this changes, expectations change. I assume, then, that expectations are connected: by raising the prospects of the representative man in one position we presumably increase or decrease the prospects of representative men in other positions. Since it applies to institutional forms, the second principle (or rather the first part of it) refers to the expectations of representative individuals. As I shall discuss below, neither principle applies to distributions of particular goods to particular individuals who may be identified by their proper names. The situation where someone is considering how to allocate certain commodities to needy persons who are known to him is not within the scope of the principles. They are meant to regulate basic institutional arrangements. We must not assume that there is much similarity from the standpoint of justice between an administrative allotment of goods to specific persons and the appropriate design of society. Our common sense intuitions for the former may be a poor guide to the latter.

Now the second principle insists that each person benefit from permissible inequalities in the basic structure. This means that it must be reasonable for each relevant representative man defined by this structure, when he views it as a going concern, to prefer his prospects with the inequality to his prospects without it. One is not allowed to justify differences in income or organizational powers on the ground that the disadvantages of those in one position are outweighed by the greater advantages of those in another. Much less can infringements of liberty be counterbalanced in this way. Applied to the basic structure, the principle of utility would have us maximize the sum of expectations of representative men (weighted by the number of persons they represent, on the classical view); and this would permit us to compensate for the losses of some by the gains of others. Instead, the two principles require that everyone benefit from economic and social inequalities. It is obvious, however, that there are indefinitely many ways in which all may be advantaged when the initial arrangement of equality is taken as a benchmark. How then are we to choose among these possibilities? The principles must be specified so that they yield a determinate conclusion. I now turn to this problem. . . .

The Original Position

[. . .]

26.   *The reasoning leading to the two principles of justice*

In this and the next two sections I take up the choice between the two principles of justice and the principle of average utility. Determining the rational preference between these two options is perhaps the central problem in developing the conception of justice as fairness as a viable alternative to the utilitarian tradition. I shall begin in this section by presenting some intuitive remarks favoring the two principles. I shall also discuss briefly the qualitative structure of the argument that needs to be made if the case for these principles is to be conclusive.

It will be recalled that the general conception of justice as fairness requires that all primary social goods be distributed equally unless an unequal distribution would be to everyone's advantage. No restrictions are placed on exchanges of these goods and therefore a lesser liberty can be compensated for by greater social and economic benefits. Now looking at the situation from the standpoint of one person selected arbitrarily, there is no way for him to win special advantages for himself. Nor, on the other hand, are there grounds for his acquiescing in special disadvantages. Since it is not reasonable for him to expect more than an equal share in the division of social goods, and since it is not rational for him to agree to less, the sensible thing for him to do is to acknowledge as the first principle of justice one requiring an equal distribution. Indeed, this principle is so obvious that we would expect it to occur to anyone immediately.

Thus, the parties start with a principle establishing equal liberty for all, including equality of opportunity, as well as an equal distribution of income and wealth. But there is no reason why this acknowledgment should be final. If there are inequalities in the basic structure that work to make everyone better off in comparison with the benchmark of initial equality, why not permit them? The immediate gain which a greater equality might allow can be regarded as intelligently invested in view of its future return. If, for example, these inequalities set up various incentives which succeed in eliciting more productive efforts, a person in the original position may look upon them as necessary to cover the costs of training and to encourage effective performance. One might think that ideally individuals should want to serve one another. But since the parties are assumed not to take an interest in one another's interests, their acceptance of these inequalities is only the acceptance of the relations in which men stand in the circumstances of justice. They have no grounds for complaining of one another's motives. A person in the original position would, therefore, concede the justice of these inequalities. Indeed, it would be short-sighted of him not to do so. He would hesitate to agree to these regularities only if he would be dejected by the bare knowledge or perception that others were better situated; and I have assumed that the parties decide as if they are not moved by envy. In order to make the principle regulating inequalities determinate, one looks at the system from the standpoint of the least advantaged representative man. Inequalities are permissible when they maximize, or at least all contribute to, the long-term expectations of the least fortunate group in society.

Now this general conception imposes no constraints on what sorts of inequalities are allowed, whereas the special conception, by putting the two principles in serial order (with the necessary adjustments in meaning), forbids exchanges between basic liberties and economic and social benefits. I shall not try to justify this ordering here. From time to time in later chapters this problem will be considered. But roughly, the idea underlying this ordering is that if the parties assume that their basic liberties can be effectively exercised, they will not exchange a lesser liberty for an improvement in economic well-being. It is only when social conditions do not allow the effective establishment of these rights that one can concede their limitation; and these restrictions can be granted only to the extent that they are necessary to prepare the way for a free society. The denial of equal liberty can be defended only if it is necessary to raise the level of civilization so that in due course these freedoms can be enjoyed. Thus in adopting a serial order we are in effect making a special assumption in the original position, namely, that the parties know that the conditions of their society, whatever they are, admit the effective realization of the equal liberties. The serial ordering of the two principles of justice eventually comes to be reasonable if the general conception is consistently followed. This lexical ranking is the long-run tendency of the general view. For the most part I shall assume that the requisite circumstances for the serial order obtain.

It seems clear from these remarks that the two principles are at least a plausible conception of justice. The question, though, is how one is to argue for them more systematically. Now there are several things to do. One can work out their consequences for institutions and note their implications for fundamental social policy. In this way they are tested by a comparison with our considered judgments of justice. Part II is devoted to this. But one can also try to find arguments in their favor that are decisive from the standpoint of the original position. In order to see how this might be done, it is useful as a heuristic device to think of the two principles as the maximin solution to the problem of social justice. There is an analogy between the two principles and the maximin rule for choice under uncertainty.[9] This is evident from the fact that the two principles are those a person would choose for the design of a society in which his enemy is to assign him his place. The maximin rule tells us to rank alternatives by their worst possible outcomes: we are to adopt the alternative the worst outcome of which is superior to the worst outcomes of the others. The persons in the original position do not, of course, assume that their initial place in society is decided by a malevolent opponent. As I note below, they should not reason from false premises. The veil of ignorance does not violate this idea, since an absence of information is not misinformation. But that the two principles of justice would be chosen if the parties were forced to protect themselves against such a contingency explains the sense in which this conception is the maximin solution. And this analogy suggests that if the original position has been described so that it is rational for the parties to adopt the conservative attitude expressed by this rule, a conclusive argument can indeed be constructed for these principles. Clearly the maximin rule is not, in general, a suitable guide for choices under uncertainty. But it is attractive in situations marked by certain special features. My aim, then, is to show that a good case can be made for the two principles based on the fact that the original position manifests these features to the fullest possible degree, carrying them to the limit, so to speak.

Consider the gain-and-loss table below. It represents the gains and losses for a situation which is not a game of strategy. There is no one playing against the person making the decision; instead he is faced with several possible circumstances which may or may not obtain. Which circumstances happen to exist does not depend upon what the person choosing decides or whether he announces his moves in advance. The numbers in the table are monetary values (in hundreds of dollars) in comparison with some initial situation. The gain (g) depends upon the individual's decision (d) and the circumstances (c). The $g = f(d, c)$. Assuming that there are three possible decisions and three possible circumstances, we might have the gain-and-loss table shown here.

Decisions	Circumstances		
	c_1	c_2	c_3
d_1	−7	8	12
d_2	−8	7	14
d_3	5	6	8

The maximin rule requires that we make the third decision. For in this case the worst that can happen is that one gains five hundred dollars, which is better than the worst for the other actions. If we adopt one of these we may lose either eight or seven hundred dollars. Thus, the choice of d_3 maximizes $f(d,c)$ for that value of c, which for a given d, minimizes f. The term "maximin" means the *maximum minimorum*; and the rule directs our attention to the worst that can happen under any proposed course of action, and to decide in the light of that.

Now there appear to be three chief features of situations that give plausibility to this unusual rule.[10] First, since the rule takes no account of the likelihoods of the possible circumstances, there must be some reason for sharply discounting estimates of these probabilities. Offhand, the most natural rule of choice would seem to be to compute the expectation of monetary gain for each decision and then to adopt the course of action with the highest prospect. (This expectation is defined as follows: let us suppose that g_{ij} represent the numbers in the gain-and-loss table, where i is the row index and j is the column index; and let p_j, $j = 1, 2, 3$, be the likelihoods of the circumstances, with $\Sigma p_j = 1$. Then the expectation for the ith decision is equal to $\Sigma p_j g_{ij}$.) Thus it must be, for example, that the situation is one in which a knowledge of likelihoods is impossible, or at best extremely insecure. In this case it is unreasonable not to be skeptical of probabilistic calculations unless there is no other way out, particularly if the decision is a fundamental one that needs to be justified to others.

The second feature that suggests the maximin rule is the following: the person choosing has a conception of the good such that he cares very little, if anything, for what he might gain above the minimum stipend that he can, in fact, be sure of by following the maximin rule. It is not worthwhile for him to take a chance for the sake of a further advantage, especially when it may turn out that he loses much that is important to him. This last provision brings in the third feature, namely, that the rejected alternatives have outcomes that one can hardly accept. The situation involves grave risks. Of course these features work most effectively in combination. The paradigm situation for following the maximin rule is when all three features are realized to the highest degree. This rule does not, then, generally apply, nor of course is it self-evident. Rather, it is a maxim, a rule of thumb, that comes into its own in special circumstances. Its application depends upon the qualitative structure of the possible gains and losses in relation to one's conception of the good, all this against a background in which it is reasonable to discount conjectural estimates of likelihoods.

It should be noted, as the comments on the gain-and-loss table say, that the entries in the table represent monetary values and not utilities. This difference is significant since for one thing computing expectations on the basis of such objective values is not the same thing as computing expected utility and may lead to different results. The essential point though is that in justice as fairness the parties do not know their conception of the good and cannot estimate their utility in the ordinary sense. In any case, we want to go behind de facto preferences generated by given conditions. Therefore expectations are based upon an index of primary goods and the parties make their choice accordingly. The entries in the example are in terms of money and not utility to indicate this aspect of the contract doctrine.

Now, as I have suggested, the original position has been defined so that it is a situation in which the maximin rule applies. In order to see this, let us review briefly the nature of this situation with these three special features in mind. To begin with, the veil of ignorance excludes all but the vaguest knowledge of likelihoods. The parties have no basis for determining the probable nature of their society, or their place in it. Thus they have strong reasons for being wary of probability calculations if any other course is open to them. They must also take into account the fact that their choice of principles should seem reasonable to others, in particular their descendants, whose rights will be deeply affected by it. There are further grounds for discounting that I shall mention as we go along. For the present it suffices to note that these considerations are strengthened by the fact that the parties know very little about the gain-and-loss table. Not only are they unable to conjecture the likelihoods of the various possible circumstances, they cannot say much about what the possible circumstances are, much less enumerate them and foresee the outcome of each alternative available. Those deciding are much more in the dark than the illustration by a numerical table suggests. It is for this reason that I have spoken of an analogy with the maximin rule.

Several kinds of arguments for the two principles of justice illustrate the second feature. Thus, if we can maintain that these principles provide a workable theory of social justice, and that they are compatible with reasonable demands of efficiency, then this conception guarantees a satisfactory minimum. There may be, on reflection, little reason for trying to do better. Thus much of the argument . . . is to show, by their application to the main questions of social justice, that the two principles are a satisfactory conception. These details have a philosophical purpose. Moreover, this line of thought is practically decisive if we can establish the priority of liberty, the lexical ordering of the two principles. For this priority implies that the persons in the original position have no desire to try for greater gains at the expense of the equal liberties. The minimum assured by the two principles in lexical order is not one that the parties wish to jeopardize for the sake of greater economic and social advantages. . . .

Finally, the third feature holds if we can assume that other conceptions of justice may lead to institutions that the parties would find intolerable. For example, it has sometimes been held that under some conditions the utility principle (in either form) justifies, if not slavery or serfdom, at any rate serious infractions of liberty for the sake of greater social benefits. We need not consider here the truth of this claim, or the likelihood that the requisite conditions obtain. For the moment, this contention is only to illustrate the way in which conceptions of justice may allow for outcomes which the parties may not be able to accept. And having the ready alternative of the two principles of justice which secure a satisfactory minimum, it seems unwise, if not irrational, for them to take a chance that these outcomes are not realized. . . .

Equal Liberty

[. . .]

40. *The Kantian interpretation of justice as fairness*

For the most part I have considered the content of the principle of equal liberty and the meaning of the priority of the rights that it defines. It seems appropriate at this point to note that there is a Kantian interpretation of the conception of justice from which this principle derives. This interpretation is based upon Kant's notion of autonomy. It is a mistake, I believe, to emphasize the place of generality and universality in Kant's ethics. That moral principles are general and universal is hardly new with him; and as we have seen these conditions do not in any case take us very far. It is impossible to construct a moral theory on so slender a basis, and therefore to limit the discussion of Kant's doctrine to these notions is to reduce it to triviality. The real force of his view lies elsewhere.[11]

For one thing, he begins with the idea that moral principles are the object of rational choice. They define the moral law that men can rationally will to govern their conduct in an ethical commonwealth. Moral philosophy becomes the study of the conception and outcome of a suitably defined rational decision. This idea has immediate consequences. For once we think of moral principles as legislation for a kingdom of ends, it is clear that these principles must not only be acceptable to all but public as well. Finally Kant supposes that this moral legislation is to be agreed to under conditions that characterize men as free and equal rational beings. The description of the original position is an attempt to interpret this conception. I do not wish to argue here for this interpretation on the basis of Kant's text. Certainly some will want to read him differently. Perhaps the remarks to follow are best taken as suggestions for relating justice as fairness to the high point of the contractarian tradition in Kant and Rousseau.

Kant held, I believe, that a person is acting autonomously when the principles of his action are chosen by him as the most adequate possible expression of his nature as a free and equal rational being. The principles he acts upon are not adopted because of his social position or natural endowments, or in view of the particular kind of society in which he lives or the specific things that he happens to want. To act on such principles is to act heteronomously. Now the veil of ignorance deprives the persons in the original position of the knowledge that would enable them to choose heteronomous principles. The parties arrive at their choice together as free and equal rational persons knowing only that those circumstances obtain which give rise to the need for principles of justice.

To be sure, the argument for these principles does add in various ways to Kant's conception. For example, it adds the feature that the principles chosen are to apply to the basic structure of society; and premises characterizing this structure are used in deriving the principles of justice. But I believe that this and other additions are natural enough and remain fairly close to Kant's doctrine, at least when all of his ethical writings are viewed together. Assuming, then, that the reasoning in favor of the principles of justice is correct, we can say that when persons act on these principles they are acting in accordance with principles that they would choose as rational and independent persons in an original position of equality. The principles of their actions do not depend upon social or natural contingencies, nor do they reflect the bias of the particulars of their plan of life or the aspirations that motivate them. By acting from these principles persons express their nature as free and equal rational beings subject to the general conditions of human life. For to express one's nature as a being of a particular kind is to act on the principles that would be chosen if this nature were the decisive determining element. Of course, the choice of the parties in the original position is subject to the restrictions of that situation. But when we knowingly act on the principles of justice in the ordinary course of events, we deliberately assume the limitations of the original position. One reason for doing this, for persons who can do so and want to, is to give expression to one's nature.

The principles of justice are also categorical imperatives in Kant's sense. For by a categorical imperative Kant understands a principle of conduct that applies to a person in virtue of his nature as a free and equal rational being. The validity of the principle does not presuppose that one has a particular desire or aim. Whereas a hypothetical imperative by contrast does assume this: it directs us to take certain steps as effective means to achieve a specific end. Whether the desire is for a particular thing, or whether it is for something more general, such as certain kinds of agreeable feelings or pleasures, the corresponding imperative is hypothetical. Its applicability depends upon one's having an aim which one need not have as a condition of being a rational human individual. The argument for the two principles of justice does not assume that the parties have particular ends, but only that they desire certain primary goods. These are things that it is rational to want whatever else one wants. Thus given human nature, wanting them is part of being rational; and while each is presumed to have some conception of the good, nothing is known about his final ends. The preference for primary goods is derived, then, from only the most general assumptions about rationality and the conditions of human life. To act from the principles of justice is to act from categorical imperatives in the sense that they apply to us whatever in particular our aims are. This simply reflects the fact that no such contingencies appear as premises in their derivation.

We may note also that the motivational assumption of mutual disinterest accords with Kant's notion of autonomy, and gives another reason for this condition. So far this assumption has been used to characterize the circumstances of justice and to provide a clear conception to guide the reasoning of the parties. We have also seen that the concept of benevolence, being a second-order notion, would not work out well. Now we can add that the assumption of mutual disinterest is to allow for freedom in the choice of a system of final ends.[12] Liberty in adopting a conception of the good is limited only by principles that are deduced from a doctrine which imposes no prior constraints on these conceptions. Presuming mutual disinterest in the original position carries out this idea. We postulate that the parties have opposing claims in a suitably general sense. If their ends were restricted in some specific way, this would appear at the outset as an arbitrary restriction on freedom. Moreover, if the parties were conceived as altruists, or as pursuing certain kinds of pleasures, then the principles chosen would apply, as far as the argument would have shown, only to persons whose freedom was restricted to choices compatible with altruism or hedonism. As the argument now runs, the principles of justice cover all persons with rational plans of life, whatever their content, and these principles represent the appropriate restrictions on freedom. Thus it is possible to say that the constraints on conceptions of the good are the result of an interpretation of the contractual situation that puts no prior limitations on what men may desire. There are a variety of reasons, then, for the motivational premise of mutual disinterest. This premise is not only a matter of realism about the circumstances of justice or a way to make the theory manageable. It also connects up with the Kantian idea of autonomy.

There is, however, a difficulty that should be clarified. It is well expressed by Sidgwick.[13] He remarks that nothing in Kant's ethics is more striking than the idea that a man realizes his true self when he acts from the moral law, whereas if he permits his actions to be determined by sensuous desires or contingent aims, he becomes subject to the law of nature. Yet in Sidgwick's opinion this idea comes to naught. It seems to him that on Kant's view the lives of the saint and the scoundrel are equally the outcome of a free choice (on the part of the noumenal self) and equally the subject of causal laws (as a phenomenal self). Kant never explains why the scoundrel does not express in a bad life his characteristic and freely chosen selfhood in the same way that a saint expresses his characteristic and freely chosen selfhood in a good one. Sidgwick's objection is decisive, I think, as long as one assumes, as Kant's exposition may seem to allow, both that the noumenal self can choose any consistent set of principles and that acting from such principles, whatever they are, is sufficient to express one's choice as that of a free and equal rational being. Kant's reply must be that though acting on any consistent set of principles could be the outcome of a decision on the part of the noumenal self, not all such action by the phenomenal self expresses this decision as that of a free and equal rational being. Thus if a person realizes his true self by expressing it in his actions, and if he desires above all else to realize this self, then he will choose to act from principles that manifest his nature as a free and equal rational being. The missing part of the argument concerns the concept of expression. Kant did not show that acting from the moral law expresses our nature in identifiable ways that acting from contrary principles does not.

This defect is made good, I believe, by the conception of the original position. The essential point is that we need an argument showing which principles, if any, free and equal rational persons would choose and these principles must be applicable in practice. A definite answer to this question is required to meet Sidgwick's objection. My suggestion is that we think of the original position as the point of view from which noumenal selves see the world. The parties qua noumenal selves have complete freedom to choose whatever principles they wish; but they also have a desire to express their nature as rational and equal members of the intelligible realm with precisely this liberty to choose, that is, as beings who can look at the world in this way and express this perspective in their life as members of society. They must decide, then, which principles when consciously followed and acted upon in everyday life will best manifest this freedom in their community, most fully reveal their independence from natural contingencies and social accident.

Now if the argument of the contract doctrine is correct, these principles are indeed those defining the moral law, or more exactly, the principles of justice for institutions and individuals. The description of the original position interprets the point of view of noumenal selves, of what it means to be a free and equal rational being. Our nature as such beings is displayed when we act from the principles we would choose when this nature is reflected in the conditions determining the choice. Thus men exhibit their freedom, their independence from the contingencies of nature and society, by acting in ways they would acknowledge in the original position.

Properly understood, then, the desire to act justly derives in part from the desire to express most fully what we are or can be, namely free and equal rational beings with a liberty to choose. It is for this reason, I believe, that Kant speaks of the failure to act on the moral law as giving rise to shame and not to feelings of guilt. And this is appropriate, since for him acting unjustly is acting in a manner that fails to express our nature as a free and equal rational being. Such actions therefore strike at our self-respect, our sense of our own worth, and the experience of this loss is shame. We have acted as though we belonged to a lower order, as though we were a creature whose first principles are decided by natural contingencies. Those who think of Kant's moral doctrine as one of law and guilt badly misunderstand him. Kant's main aim is to deepen and to justify Rousseau's idea that liberty is acting in accordance with a law that we give to ourselves. And this leads not to a morality of austere command but to an ethic of mutual respect and self-esteem.[14]

The original position may be viewed, then, as a procedural interpretation of Kant's conception of autonomy and the categorical imperative. The principles regulative of the kingdom of ends are those that would be chosen in this position, and the description of this situation enables us to explain the sense in which acting from these principles expresses our nature as free and equal rational persons. No longer are these notions purely transcendent and lacking explicable connections with human conduct, for the procedural conception of the original position allows us to make these ties. It is true that I have departed from Kant's views in several respects. I shall not discuss these matters here; but two points should be noted. The person's choice as a noumenal self I have assumed to be a collective one. The force of the self's being equal is that the principles chosen must be acceptable to other selves. Since all are similarly free and rational, each must have an equal say in adopting the public principles of the ethical commonwealth. This means that as noumenal selves, everyone is to consent to these principles. Unless the scoundrel's principles would be chosen, they cannot express this free choice, however much a single self might be of a mind to opt for them. Later I shall try to define a clear sense in which this unanimous agreement is best expressive of the nature of even a single self. It in no way overrides a person's interests as the collective nature of the choice might seem to imply. But I leave this aside for the present.

Secondly, I have assumed all along that the parties know that they are subject to the conditions of human life. Being in the circumstances of justice, they are situated in the world with other men who likewise face limitations of moderate scarcity and competing claims. Human freedom is to be regulated by principles chosen in the light of these natural restrictions. Thus justice as fairness is a theory of human justice and among its premises are the elementary facts about persons and their place in nature. The freedom of pure intelligences not subject to these constraints, and the freedom of God, are outside the scope of the theory. It might appear that Kant meant his doctrine to apply to all rational beings as such and therefore to God and the angels as well. Men's social situation in the world may seem to have no role in his theory in determining the first principles of justice. I do not believe that Kant held this view, but I cannot discuss this question here. It suffices to say that if I am mistaken, the Kantian interpretation of justice as fairness is less faithful to Kant's intentions than I am presently inclined to suppose. . . .

. . . I now wish to give the final statement of the two principles of justice for institutions. For the sake of completeness, I shall give a full statement including earlier formulations.

First Principle

Each person is to have an equal right to the most extensive total system of equal basic liberties compatible with a similar system of liberty for all.

Second Principle

Social and economic inequalities are to be arranged so that they are both:

(a) to the greatest benefit of the least advantaged, consistent with the just savings principle, and

(b) attached to offices and positions open to all under conditions of fair equality of opportunity.

First Priority Rule (The Priority of Liberty)

The principles of justice are to be ranked in lexical order and therefore liberty can be restricted only for the sake of liberty. There are two cases:

(a) a less extensive liberty must strengthen the total system of liberty shared by all;

(b) a less than equal liberty must be acceptable to those with the lesser liberty.

Second Priority Rule (The Priority of Justice over Efficiency and Welfare)

The second principle of justice is lexically prior to the principle of efficiency and to that of maximizing the sum of advantages; and fair opportunity is prior to the difference principle. There are two cases:

(a) an inequality of opportunity must enhance the opportunities of those with the lesser opportunity;

(b) an excessive rate of saving must on balance mitigate the burden of those bearing this hardship.

General Conception

All social primary goods – liberty and opportunity, income and wealth, and the bases of self-respect – are to be distributed equally unless an unequal distribution of any or all of these goods is to the advantage of the least favored.

By way of comment, these principles and priority rules are no doubt incomplete. Other modifications will surely have to be made, but I shall not further complicate the statement of the principles. It suffices to observe that when we come to nonideal theory, we do not fall back straightway upon the general conception of justice. The lexical ordering of the two principles, and the valuations that this ordering implies, suggest priority rules which seem to be reasonable enough in many cases. By various examples I have tried to illustrate how these rules can be used and to indicate their plausibility. Thus the ranking of the principles of justice in ideal theory reflects back and guides the application of these principles to nonideal situations. It identifies which limitations need to be dealt with first. The drawback of the general conception of justice is that it lacks the definite structure of the two principles in serial order. In more extreme and tangled instances of nonideal theory there may be no alternative to it. At some point the priority of rules for nonideal cases will fail; and indeed, we may be able to find no satisfactory answer at all. But we must try to postpone the day of reckoning as long as possible, and try to arrange society so that it never comes.

Notes

1 Here I follow H. L. A. Hart, *The Concept of Law* (Oxford: The Clarendon Press, 1961), pp. 155–9.

2 *An Enquiry Concerning the Principles of Morals*, sec. III, pt. I, par. 3, ed. L. A. Selby-Bigge, 2nd edition (Oxford, 1902), p. 184.

3 *Nicomachean Ethics*, 1129b–1130b5. I have followed the interpretation of Gregory Vlastos, "Justice and Happiness in *The Republic*," in *Plato: A Collection of Critical Essays*, edited by Vlastos (Garden City, N.Y.: Doubleday and Company, 1971), vol. 2, pp. 70f. For a discussion of Aristotle on justice, see W. F. R. Hardie, *Aristotle's Ethical Theory* (Oxford, The Clarendon Press, 1968), ch. X.

4 As the text suggests, I shall regard Locke's *Second Treatise of Government*, Rousseau's *The Social Contract*, and Kant's ethical works beginning with *The Foundations of the Metaphysics of Morals* as definitive of the contract tradition. For all of its greatness, Hobbes's *Leviathan* raises special problems. A general historical survey is provided by J. W. Gough, *The Social Contract*, 2nd edn. (Oxford: The Clarendon Press, 1957), and Otto Gierke, *Natural Law and the Theory of Society*, trans. with an introduction by Ernest Barker (Cambridge: The University Press, 1934). A presentation of the contract view as primarily an ethical theory is to be found in G. R. Grice, *The Grounds of Moral Judgment* (Cambridge: The University Press, 1967).

5 Kant is clear that the original agreement is hypothetical. See *The Metaphysics of Morals*, pt. I (*Rechtslehre*), especially §§47, 52; and pt. II of the essay "Concerning the Common Saying: This May Be True in Theory but It Does Not Apply in Practice," in *Kant's Political Writings*, ed. Hans Reiss and trans. by H. B. Nisbet (Cambridge: The University Press, 1970), pp. 73–87. See Georges Vlachos, *La Pensée politique de Kant* (Paris: Presses Universitaires de France, 1962), pp. 326–35; and J. G. Murphy, *Kant: The Philosophy of Right* (London: Macmillan, 1970), pp. 109–12, 133–6, for a further discussion.

6 For the formulation of this intuitive idea I am indebted to Allan Gibbard.

7 The process of mutual adjustment of principles and considered judgments is not peculiar to moral philosophy. See Nelson Goodman, *Fact, Fiction, and Forecast* (Cambridge, Mass.: Harvard University Press, 1955), pp. 65–8, for parallel remarks concerning the justification of the principles of deductive and inductive inference.

8 Henri Poincaré remarks: "Il nous faut une faculté qui nous fasse voir le but de loin, et, cette faculté, c'est l'intuition." *La Valeur de la science* (Paris: Flammarion, 1909), p. 27.

9 An accessible discussion of this and other rules of choice under uncertainty can be found in W. J. Baumol, *Economic Theory and Operations Analysis*, 2nd edn. (Englewood Cliffs, N.J.: Prentice-Hall Inc., 1965), ch. 24. Baumol gives a geometric interpretation of these rules . . . to illustrate the difference principle. See pp. 558–62. See also R. D. Luce and Howard Raiffa, *Games and Decisions* (New York: John Wiley & Sons, Inc., 1957), ch. XIII, for a fuller account.

10 Here I borrow from William Fellner, *Probability and Profit* (Homewood, Ill., R. D. Irwin, Inc., 1965), pp. 140–2, where these features are noted.

11 To be avoided at all costs is the idea that Kant's doctrine simply provides the general, or formal, elements for a utilitarian (or indeed for any other) theory. See, for example, R. M. Hare, *Freedom and Reason* (Oxford: The Clarendon Press, 1963), pp. 123f. One must not lose sight of the full scope of his view, one must take the later works into consideration. Unfortunately, there is no commentary on Kant's moral theory as a whole; perhaps it would prove impossible to write. But the standard works of H. J. Paton, *The Categorical Imperative* (Chicago: University of Chicago Press, 1948), and L. W. Beck, *A Commentary on Kant's Critique of Practical Reason* (Chicago: University of Chicago Press, 1960), and others need to be further

complemented by studies of the other writings. See here M. J. Gregor's *Laws of Freedom* (Oxford: Basil Blackwell, 1963), an account of *The Metaphysics of Morals*, and J. G. Murphy's brief *Kant: The Philosophy of Right* (London: Macmillan, 1970). Beyond this, *The Critique of Judgment, Religion within the Limits of Reason*, and the political writings cannot be neglected without distorting his doctrine. For the last, see *Kant's Political Writings*, ed. Hans Reiss and trans. H. B. Nisbet (Cambridge: The University Press, 1970).

12   For this point I am indebted to Charles Fried.

13   See *The Methods of Ethics*, 7th ed. (London, Macmillan, 1907), Appendix, "The Kantian Conception of Free Will" (reprinted from *Mind*, vol. 13, 1888), pp. 511–16, esp. p. 516.

14   See B. A. O. Williams, "The Idea of Equality," in *Philosophy, Politics and Society*, Second Series, ed. Peter Laslett and W. G. Runciman (Oxford: Basil Blackwell, 1962), pp. 115f. For confirmation of this interpretation, see Kant's remarks on moral education in *The Critique of Practical Reason*, pt. II. See also Beck, *A Commentary on Kant's Critique of Practical Reason*, pp. 233–6.

43   Distributive Justice*

Robert Nozick

The minimal state is the most extensive state that can be justified. Any state more extensive violates people's rights. Yet many persons have put forth reasons purporting to justify a more extensive state. It is impossible within the compass of this book to examine all the reasons that have been put forth. Therefore, I shall focus upon those generally acknowledged to be most weighty and influential, to see precisely wherein they fail. In this chapter we consider the claim that a more extensive state is justified, because necessary (or the best instrument) to achieve distributive justice; in the next chapter we shall take up diverse other claims.

The term "distributive justice" is not a neutral one. Hearing the term "distribution," most people presume that some thing or mechanism uses some principle or criterion to give out a supply of things. Into this process of distributing shares some error may have crept. So it is an open question, at least, whether *re*distribution should take place; whether we should do again what has already been done once, though poorly. However, we are not in the position of children who have been given portions of pie by someone who now makes last minute adjustments to rectify careless cutting. There is no *central* distribution, no person or group entitled to control all the resources, jointly deciding how they are to be doled out. What each person gets, he gets from others who give to him in exchange for something, or as a gift. In a free society, diverse persons control different resources, and new holdings arise out of the voluntary exchanges and actions of persons. There is no more a distributing or distribution of shares than there is a distributing of mates in a society in which persons choose whom they shall marry. The total result is the product of many individual decisions which the different individuals involved are entitled to make. Some uses of the term "distribution," it is true, do not imply a

* From Robert Nozick, *Anarchy, State, and Utopia* (New York: Basic Books, 1974), pp. 149–64. © 1974 by Basic Books Inc. Reprinted by permission of Basic Books, a member of Perseus Books, L.L.C.

previous distributing appropriately judged by some criterion (for example, "probability distribution"); nevertheless, despite the title of this chapter, it would be best to use a terminology that clearly is neutral. We shall speak of people's holdings; a principle of justice in holdings describes (part of) what justice tells us (requires) about holdings. I shall state first what I take to be the correct view about justice in holdings, and then turn to the discussion of alternate views.

Section I
The Entitlement Theory

The subject of justice in holdings consists of three major topics. The first is the *original acquisition of holdings*, the appropriation of unheld things. This includes the issues of how unheld things may come to be held, the process, or processes, by which unheld things may come to be held, the things that may come to be held by these processes, the extent of what comes to be held by a particular process, and so on. We shall refer to the complicated truth about this topic, which we shall not formulate here, as the principle of justice in acquisition. The second topic concerns the *transfer of holdings* from one person to another. By what processes may a person transfer holdings to another? How may a person acquire a holding from another who holds it? Under this topic come general descriptions of voluntary exchange, and gift and (on the other hand) fraud, as well as reference to particular conventional details fixed upon in a given society. The complicated truth about this subject (with placeholders for conventional details) we shall call the principle of justice in transfer. (And we shall suppose it also includes principles governing how a person may divest himself of a holding, passing it into an unheld state.)

If the world were wholly just, the following inductive definition would exhaustively cover the subject of justice in holdings.

1. A person who acquires a holding in accordance with the principle of justice in acquisition is entitled to that holding.
2. A person who acquires a holding in accordance with the principle of justice in transfer, from someone else entitled to the holding, is entitled to the holding.
3. No one is entitled to a holding except by (repeated) applications of 1 and 2.

The complete principle of distributive justice would say simply that a distribution is just if everyone is entitled to the holdings they possess under the distribution.

A distribution is just if it arises from another just distribution by legitimate means. The legitimate means of moving from one distribution to another are specified by the principle of justice in transfer. The legitimate first "moves" are specified by the principle of justice in acquisition.[1] Whatever arises from a just situation by just steps is itself just. The means of change specified by the principle of justice in transfer preserve justice. As correct rules of inference are truth-preserving, and any conclusion deduced via repeated application of such rules from only true premises is itself true, so the means of transition from one situation to another specified by the principle of justice in transfer are justice-preserving, and any situation actually arising from repeated transitions in accordance with the principle from a just situation is itself just. The parallel between justice-preserving transformations and truth-preserving transformations illuminates where it fails as well as where it holds. That a conclusion could have been deduced by truth-preserving means from premises that are true suffices to show its truth. That from a just situation a situation *could* have arisen via justice-preserving means does *not* suffice to show its justice. The fact that a thief's victims voluntarily *could* have presented him with gifts does not entitle the thief to his ill-gotten gains. Justice in holdings is historical; it depends upon what actually has happened. We shall return to this point later.

Not all actual situations are generated in accordance with the two principles of justice in holdings: the principle of justice in acquisition and the principle of justice in transfer. Some people steal from others, or defraud them, or enslave them, seizing their product and preventing them from living as they choose, or forcibly exclude others from competing in exchanges. None of these are permissible modes of transition from one situation to another. And some persons acquire holdings by means not sanctioned by the principle of justice in acquisition. The existence of past injustice (previous violations of the first two principles of justice in holdings) raises the third major topic under justice in holdings: the rectification of injustice in holdings. If past injustice has shaped present holdings in various ways, some identifiable and some not, what now, if anything, ought to be done to rectify these injustices? What obligations do the performers of injustice have toward those whose position is worse than it would have been had the injustice not been done? Or, than it would have been had compensation been paid promptly? How, if at all, do things change if the beneficiaries and those made worse off are not the direct parties in the act of injustice, but, for example, their descendants? Is an injustice done to someone whose holding was itself based upon an unrectified injustice? How far back must one go in wiping clean the historical slate of injustices? What may victims of injustice permissibly do in order to rectify the injustices being done to them, including the many injustices done by persons acting through their government? I do not know of a thorough or theoretically sophisticated treatment of such issues. Idealizing greatly, let us suppose theoretical investigation will produce a principle of rectification. This principle uses historical information about previous situations and injustices done in them (as defined by the first two principles of justice and rights against interference), and information about the actual course of events that flowed from these injustices, until the present, and it yields a description (or descriptions) of holdings in the society. The principle of rectification presumably will make use of its best estimate of subjunctive information about what would have occurred (or a probability distribution over what might have occurred, using the expected value) if the injustice had not taken place. If the actual description of holdings turns out not to be one of the descriptions yielded by the principle, then one of the descriptions yielded must be realized.[2]

The general outlines of the theory of justice in holdings are that the holdings of a person are just if he is entitled to them by the principles of justice in acquisition and transfer, or by the principle of rectification of injustice (as specified by the first two principles). If each person's holdings are just, then the total set (distribution) of holdings is just. To turn these general outlines into a specific theory we would have to specify the details of each of the three principles of justice in holdings: the principle of acquisition of holdings, the principle of transfer of holdings, and the principle of rectification of violations of the first two principles. I shall not attempt that task here. (Locke's principle of justice in acquisition is discussed below.)

Historical principles and end-result principles

The general outlines of the entitlement theory illuminate the nature and defects of other conceptions of distributive justice. The entitlement theory of justice in distribution is *historical*; whether a distribution is just depends upon how it came about. In contrast, *current time-slice principles* of justice hold that the justice of a distribution is determined by how things are distributed (who has what) as judged by some *structural* principle(s) of just distribution. A utilitarian who judges between any two distributions by seeing which has the greater sum of utility and, if the sums tie, applies some fixed equality criterion to choose the more equal distribution, would hold a current time-slice principle of justice. As would someone who had a fixed schedule of trade-offs between the sum of happiness and equality. According to a current time-slice principle, all that needs to be looked at, in judging the justice of a distribution, is who ends up with what; in comparing any two distributions one need look only at the matrix presenting the distributions. No further information need be fed into a principle of justice. It is a consequence of such principles of justice that any two structurally identical distributions are equally just. (Two distributions are structurally identical if they present the same profile, but perhaps have different persons occupying the particular slots. My having ten and your having five, and my having five and your having ten are structurally identical distributions.) Welfare economics is the theory of current time-slice principles of justice. The subject is conceived as operating on matrices representing only current information about distribution. This, as well as some of the usual conditions (for example, the choice of distribution is invariant under relabeling of columns), guarantees that welfare economics will be a current time-slice theory, with all of its inadequacies.

Most persons do not accept current time-slice principles as constituting the whole story about distributive shares. They think it relevant in assessing the justice of a situation to consider not only the distribution it embodies, but also how that distribution came about. If some persons are in prison for murder or war crimes, we do not say that to assess the justice of the distribution in the society we must look only at what this person has, and that person has, and that person has, . . . at the current time. We think it relevant to ask whether someone did something so that he *deserved* to be punished, deserved to have a lower share. Most will agree to the relevance of further information with regard to punishments and penalties. Consider also desired things. One traditional socialist view is that workers are entitled to the product and full fruits of their labor; they have earned it; a distribution is unjust if it does not give the workers what they are entitled to. Such entitlements are based upon some past history. No socialist holding this view would find it comforting to be told that because the actual distribution *A* happens to coincide structurally with the one he desires *D*, *A* therefore is no less just than *D*; it differs only in that the "parasitic" owners of capital receive under *A* what the workers are entitled to under *D*, and the workers receive under *A* what the owners are entitled to under *D*, namely very little. This socialist rightly, in my view, holds onto the notions of earning, producing, entitlement, desert, and so forth, and he rejects current time-slice principles that look only to the structure of the resulting set of holdings. (The set of holdings resulting from what? Isn't it implausible that how holdings are produced and come to exist has no effect at all on who should hold what?) His mistake lies in his view of what entitlements arise out of what sorts of productive processes.

We construe the position we discuss too narrowly by speaking of *current* time-slice principles. Nothing is changed if structural principles operate upon a time sequence of current time-slice profiles and, for example, give someone more now to counterbalance the less he has had earlier. A utilitarian or an egalitarian or any mixture of the two over time will inherit the difficulties of his more myopic comrades. He is not helped by the fact that *some* of the information others consider relevant in assessing a distribution is reflected, unrecoverably, in past matrices. Henceforth, we shall refer to such unhistorical principles of distributive justice, including the current time-slice principles, as *end-result principles* or *end-state principles.*

In contrast to end-result principles of justice, *historical principles* of justice hold that past circumstance or actions of people can create differential entitlements or differential deserts to things. An injustice can be worked by moving from one distribution to another structurally identical one, for the second, in profile the same, may violate people's entitlements or deserts; it may not fit the actual history.

Patterning

The entitlement principles of justice in holdings that we have sketched are historical principles of justice. To better understand their precise character, we shall distinguish them from another subclass of the historical principles. Consider, as an example, the principle of distribution according to moral merit. This principle requires that total distributive shares vary directly with moral merit; no person should have a greater share than anyone whose moral merit is greater. (If moral merit could be not merely ordered but measured on an interval or ratio scale, stronger principles could be formulated.) Or consider the principle that results by substituting "usefulness to society" for "moral merit" in the previous principle. Or instead of "distribute according to moral merit," or "distribute according to usefulness to society," we might consider "distribute according to the weighted sum of moral merit, usefulness to society, and need," with the weights of the different dimensions equal. Let us call a principle of distribution *patterned* if it specifies that a distribution is to vary along with some natural dimension, weighted sum of natural dimensions, or lexicographic ordering of natural dimensions. And let us say a distribution is patterned if it accords with some patterned principle. (I speak of natural dimensions, admittedly without a general criterion for them, because for any set of holdings some artificial dimensions can be gimmicked up to vary along with the distribution of the set.) The principle of distribution in accordance with moral merit is a patterned historical principle, which specifies a patterned distribution. "Distribute according to I.Q." is a patterned principle that looks to information not contained in distributional matrices. It is not historical, however, in that it does not look to any past actions creating differential entitlements to evaluate a distribution; it requires only distributional matrices whose columns are labeled by I.Q. scores. The distribution in a society, however, may be composed of such simple patterned distributions, without itself being simply patterned. Different sectors may operate different patterns, or some combination of patterns may operate in different proportions across a society. A distribution composed in this manner, from a small number of patterned distributions, we also shall term "patterned." And we extend the use of "pattern" to include the overall designs put forth by combinations of end-state principles.

Almost every suggested principle of distributive justice is patterned: to each according to his moral merit, or needs, or marginal product, or how hard he tries, or the weighted sum of the foregoing, and so on. The principle of entitlement we have sketched is *not* patterned.[3] There is no one natural dimension or weighted sum or combination of a small number of natural dimensions that yields the distributions generated in accordance with the principle of entitlement. The set of holdings that results when some persons receive their marginal products, others win at gambling, others receive a share of their mate's income, others receive gifts from foundations, others receive interest on loans, others receive gifts from admirers, others receive returns on investment, others make for themselves much of what they have, others find things, and so on, will not be patterned. Heavy strands of patterns will run through it; significant portions of the variance in holdings will be accounted for by pattern-variables. If most people most of the time choose to transfer some of their entitlements to others only in exchange for something from them, then a large part of what many people hold will vary with what they held that others wanted. More details are provided by the theory of marginal productivity. But gifts to relatives, charitable donations, bequests to children, and the like, are not best conceived, in the first instance, in this manner. Ignoring the strands of pattern, let us suppose for the moment that a distribution actually arrived at by the operation of the principle of entitlement is random with respect to any pattern. Though the resulting set of holdings will be unpatterned, it will not be incomprehensible, for it can be seen as arising from the operation of a small number of principles. These principles specify how an initial distribution may arise (the principle of acquisition of holdings) and how distributions may be transformed into others (the principle of transfer of holdings). The process whereby the set of holdings is generated will be intelligible, though the set of holdings itself that results from this process will be unpatterned.

The writings of F. A. Hayek focus less than is usually done upon what patterning distributive justice requires. Hayek argues that we cannot know enough about each person's situation to distribute to each according to his moral merit (but would justice demand we do so if we did have this knowledge?); and he goes on to say, "our objection is against all attempts to impress upon society a deliberately chosen pattern of distribution, whether it be an order of equality or of inequality." However, Hayek concludes that in a free society there will be distribution in accordance with value rather than moral merit; that is, in accordance with the perceived value of a person's actions and services to others. Despite his rejection of a patterned conception of distributive justice, Hayek himself suggests a pattern he thinks justifiable: distribution in accordance with the perceived benefits given to others, leaving room for the complaint that a free society does not realize exactly this pattern. Stating this patterned strand of a free capitalist society more precisely, we get "To each according to how much he benefits others who have the resources for benefiting those who benefit them." This will seem arbitrary unless some acceptable initial set of holdings is specified, or unless it is held that the operation of the system over time washes out any significant effects from the initial set of holdings. As an example of the latter, if almost anyone would have bought a car from Henry Ford, the supposition that it was an arbitrary matter who held the money then (and so bought) would not place Henry Ford's earnings under a cloud. In any event, *his* coming to hold it is not arbitrary. Distribution according to benefits to others *is* a major patterned strand in a free capitalist society, as Hayek correctly points out, but it is only a strand and does not constitute the whole pattern of a system of entitlements (namely, inheritance, gifts for arbitrary reasons, charity, and so on) or a standard that one should insist a society fit. Will people tolerate for long a system yielding distributions that they believe are unpatterned? No doubt people will not long accept a distribution they believe is *unjust*. People want their society to be and to look just. But must the look of justice reside in a resulting pattern rather than in the underlying generating principles? We are in no position to conclude that the inhabitants of a society embodying an entitlement conception of justice in holdings will find it unacceptable. Still, it must be granted that were people's reasons for transferring some of their holdings to others always irrational or arbitrary, we would find this disturbing. (Suppose people always determined what holdings they would transfer, and to whom, by using a random device.) We feel more comfortable upholding the justice of an entitlement system if most of the transfers under it are done for reasons. This does not mean necessarily that all deserve what holdings they receive. It means only that there is a purpose or point to someone's transferring a holding to one person rather than to another; that usually we can see what the transferrer thinks he's gaining, what cause he thinks he's serving, what goals he thinks he's helping to achieve, and so forth. Since in a capitalist society people often transfer holdings to others in accordance with how much they perceive these others benefiting them, the fabric constituted by the individual transactions and transfers is largely reasonable and intelligible.[4] (Gifts to loved ones, bequests to children, charity to the needy also are nonarbitrary components of the fabric.) In stressing the large strand of distribution in accordance with benefit to others, Hayek shows the point of many transfers, and so shows that the system of transfer of entitlements is not just spinning its gears aimlessly. The system of entitlements is defensible when constituted by the individual aims of individual transactions. No overarching aim is needed, no distributional pattern is required.

To think that the task of a theory of distributive justice is to fill in the blank in "to each according to his ___" is to be predisposed to search for a pattern; and the separate treatment of "from each according to his ___" treats production and distribution as two separate and independent issues. On an entitlement view these are *not* two separate questions. Whoever makes something, having bought or contracted for all other held resources used in the process (transferring some of his holdings for these cooperating factors), is entitled to it. The situation is *not* one of something's getting made, and there being an open question of who is to get it. Things come into the world already attached to people having entitlements over them. From the point of view of the historical entitlement conception of justice in holdings, those who start afresh to complete "to each according to his ___" treat objects as if they appeared from nowhere, out of nothing. A complete theory of justice might cover this limit case as well; perhaps here is a use for the usual conceptions of distributive justice.

So entrenched are maxims of the usual form that perhaps we should present the entitlement conception as a competitor. Ignoring acquisition and rectification, we might say:

> From each according to what he chooses to do, to each according to what he makes for himself (perhaps with the contracted aid of others) and what others choose to do for him and choose to give him of what they've been given previously (under this maxim) and haven't yet expended or transferred.

This, the discerning reader will have noticed, has its defects as a slogan. So as a summary and great simplification (and not as a maxim with any independent meaning) we have:

> *From each as they choose, to each as they are chosen.*

How liberty upsets patterns

It is not clear how those holding alternative conceptions of distributive justice can reject the entitlement conception of justice in holdings. For suppose a distribution favored by one of these non-entitlement conceptions is realized. Let us suppose it is your favorite one and let us call this distribution D_1; perhaps everyone has an equal share, perhaps shares vary in accordance with some dimension you treasure. Now suppose that Wilt Chamberlain is greatly in demand by basketball teams, being a great gate attraction. (Also suppose contracts run only for a year, with players being free agents.) He signs the following sort of contract with a team: In each home game, twenty-five cents from the price of each ticket of admission goes to him. (We ignore the question of whether he is "gouging" the owners, letting them look out for themselves.) The season starts, and people cheerfully attend his team's games; they buy their tickets, each time dropping a separate twenty-five cents of their admission price into a special box with Chamberlain's name on it. They are excited about seeing him play; it is worth the total admission price to them. Let us suppose that in one season one million persons attend his home games, and Wilt Chamberlain winds up with $250,000, a much larger sum than the average income and larger even than anyone else has. Is he entitled to this income? Is this new distribution D_2, unjust? If so, why? There is *no* question about whether each of the people was entitled to the control over the resources they held in D_1; because that was the distribution (your favorite) that (for the purposes of argument) we assumed was acceptable. Each of these persons *chose* to give twenty-five cents of their money to Chamberlain. They could have spent it on going to the movies, or on candy bars, or on copies of *Dissent* magazine, or of *Monthly Review*. But they all, at least one million of them, converged on giving it to Wilt Chamberlain in exchange for watching him play basketball. If D_1 was a just distribution, and people voluntarily moved from it to D_2, transferring parts of their shares they were given under D_1 (what was it for if not to do something with?), isn't D_2 also just? If the people were entitled to dispose of the resources to which they were entitled (under D_1), didn't this include their being entitled to give it to, or exchange it with, Wilt Chamberlain? Can anyone else complain on grounds of justice? Each other person already has his legitimate share under D_1. Under D_1, there is nothing that anyone has that anyone else has a claim of justice against. After someone transfers something to Wilt Chamberlain, third parties *still* have their legitimate shares; *their* shares are not changed. By what process could such a transfer among two persons give rise to a legitimate claim of distributive justice on a portion of what was transferred, by a third party who had no claim of justice on any holding of the others *before* the transfer?[5] To cut off objections irrelevant here, we might imagine the exchanges occurring in a socialist society, after hours. After playing whatever basketball he does in his daily work, or doing whatever other daily work he does, Wilt Chamberlain decides to put in *overtime* to earn additional money. (First his work quota is set; he works time over that.) Or imagine it is a skilled juggler people like to see, who puts on shows after hours.

Why might someone work overtime in a society in which it is assumed their needs are satisfied? Perhaps because they care about things other than needs. I like to write in books that I read, and to have easy access to books for browsing at odd hours. It would be very pleasant and convenient to have the resources of Widener Library in my back yard. No society, I assume, will provide such resources close to each person who would like them as part of his regular allotment (under D_1). Thus, persons either must do without some extra things that they want, or be allowed to do something extra to get some of these things. On what basis could the inequalities that would eventuate be forbidden? Notice also that small factories would spring up in a socialist society, unless forbidden. I melt down some of my personal possessions (under D_1) and build a machine out of the material. I offer you, and others, a philosophy lecture once a week in exchange for your cranking the handle on my machine, whose products I exchange for yet other things, and so on. (The raw materials used by the machine are given to me by others who possess them under D_1, in exchange for hearing lectures.) Each person might participate to gain things over and above their allotment under D_1. Some persons even might want to leave their job in socialist industry and work full time in this private sector. I shall say something more about these issues in the next chapter. Here I wish merely to note how private property even in means of production would occur in a socialist society that did not forbid people to use as they wished some of the resources they are given under the socialist distribution D_1. The socialist society would have to forbid capitalist acts between consenting adults.

The general point illustrated by the Wilt Chamberlain example and the example of the entrepreneur in a socialist society is that no end-state principle or distributional patterned principle of justice can be continuously realized without continuous interference with people's lives. Any favored pattern would be transformed into one unfavored by the principle, by people choosing to act in various ways; for example, by people exchanging goods and services with other people, or giving things to other people, things the transferrers are entitled to under the favored distributional pattern. To maintain a pattern one must either continually interfere to stop people from transferring resources as they wish to, or continually (or periodically) interfere to take from some persons resources that others for some reason chose to transfer to them. (But if some time limit is to be set on how long people may keep resources others voluntarily transfer to them, why let them keep these resources for *any* period of time? Why not have immediate confiscation?) It might be objected that all persons voluntarily will choose to refrain from actions which would upset the pattern. This presupposes unrealistically (1) that all will most want to maintain the pattern (are those who don't, to be "reeducated" or forced to undergo "self-criticism"?), (2) that each can gather enough information about his own actions and the ongoing activities of others to discover which of his actions will upset the pattern, and (3) that diverse and far-flung persons can coordinate their actions to dovetail into the pattern. Compare the manner in which the market is neutral among persons' desires, as it reflects and transmits widely scattered information via prices, and coordinates persons' activities.

It puts things perhaps a bit too strongly to say that every patterned (or end-state) principle is liable to be thwarted by the voluntary actions of the individual parties transferring some of their shares they receive under the principle. For perhaps some *very* weak patterns are not so thwarted.[6] Any distributional pattern with any egalitarian component is overturnable by the voluntary actions of individual persons over time; as is every patterned condition with sufficient content so as actually to have been proposed as presenting the central core of distributive justice. Still, given the possibility that some weak conditions or patterns may not be unstable in this way, it would be better to formulate an explicit description of the kind of interesting and contentful patterns under discussion, and to prove a theorem about their instability. Since the weaker the patterning, the more likely it is that the entitlement system itself satisfies it, a plausible conjecture is that any patterning either is unstable or is satisfied by the entitlement system.

Notes

1 Applications of the principle of justice in acquisition may also occur as part of the move from one distribution to another. You may find an unheld thing now and appropriate it. Acquisitions also are to be understood as included when, to simplify, I speak only of transitions by transfers.
2 If the principle of rectification of violations of the first two principles yields more than one

description of holdings, then some choice must be made as to which of these is to be realized. Perhaps the sort of considerations about distributive justice and equality that I argue against play a legitimate role in *this* subsidiary choice. Similarly, there may be room for such considerations in deciding which otherwise arbitrary features a statute will embody, when such features are unavoidable because other considerations do not specify a precise line; yet a line must be drawn.

3   One might try to squeeze a patterned conception of distributive justice into the framework of the entitlement conception, by formulating a gimmicky obligatory "principle of transfer" that would lead to the pattern. For example, the principle that if one has more than the mean income one must transfer everything one holds above the mean to persons below the mean so as to bring them up to (but not over) the mean. We can formulate a criterion for a "principle of transfer" to rule out such obligatory transfers, or we can say that no correct principle of transfer, no principle of transfer in a free society will be like this. The former is probably the better course, though the latter also is true.

Alternatively, one might think to make the entitlement conception instantiate a pattern, by using matrix entries that express the relative strength of a person's entitlements as measured by some real-valued function. But even if the limitation to natural dimensions failed to exclude this function, the resulting edifice would *not* capture out system of entitlements to *particular* things.

4   We certainly benefit because great economic incentives operate to get others to spend much time and energy to figure out how to serve us by providing things we will want to pay for. It is not mere paradox mongering to wonder whether capitalism should be criticized for most rewarding and hence encouraging, not individualists like Thoreau who go about their own lives, but people who are occupied with serving others and winning them as customers. But to defend capitalism one need not think businessmen are the finest human types. (I do not mean to join here the general maligning of businessmen, either.) Those who think the finest should acquire the most can try to convince their fellows to transfer resources in accordance with *that* principle.

5   Might not a transfer have instrumental effects on a third party, changing his feasible options? (But what if the two parties to the transfer independently had used their holdings in this fashion?) I discuss this question below, but note here that this question concedes the point for distribution of ultimate intrinsic noninstrumental goods (pure utility experiences, so to speak) that are transferrable. It also might be objected that the transfer might make a third party more envious because it worsens his position relative to someone else. I find it incomprehensible how this can be thought to involve a claim of justice. . . .

Here and elsewhere in this chapter, a theory which incorporates elements of pure procedural justice might find what I say acceptable, *if* kept in its proper place; that is, if background institutions exist to ensure the satisfaction of certain conditions on distributive shares. But if these institutions are not themselves the sum or invisible-hand result of people's voluntary (nonaggressive) actions, the constraints they impose require justification. At no point does *our* argument assume any background institutions more extensive than those of the minimal night-watchman state, a state limited to protecting persons against murder, assault, theft, fraud, and so forth.

6   Is the patterned principle stable that requires merely that a distribution be Pareto-optimal? One person might give another a gift or bequest that the second could exchange with a third to their mutual benefit. Before the second makes this exchange, there is not Pareto-optimality. Is a stable pattern presented by a principle choosing that among the Pareto-optimal positions that satisfies some further condition C? It may seem that there cannot be a counterexample, for won't any voluntary exchange made away from a situation show that the first situation wasn't Pareto-optimal? (Ignore the implausibility of this last claim for the case of bequests.) But principles are to be satisfied over time, during which new possibilities arise. A distribution that at one time satisfies the criterion of Pareto-optimality might not do so when some new possibilities arise

(Wilt Chamberlain grows up and starts playing basketball); and though people's activities will tend to move then to a new Pareto-optimal position, *this* new one need not satisfy the contentful condition C. Continual interference will be needed to insure the continual satisfaction of C. (The theoretical possibility of a pattern's being maintained by some invisible-hand process that brings it back to an equilibrium that fits the pattern when deviations occur should be investigated.)

44   Gender Inequality and Cultural Difference*

Susan Moller Okin

Theories of justice are undergoing something of an identity crisis. How can they be universal, principled, founded on good reasons that all can accept, and yet take account of the many differences there are among persons and social groups? Feminists have been among the first to point out that large numbers of persons have typically been excluded from consideration in purportedly universalist theories. And some feminists have gone on to point out that many feminist theories, while taking account of sexist bias or omission, have neglected racist, heterosexist, class, religious, and other biases. Yet, joining our voices with those of others, some of us discern problems with going in the direction of formulating a theory of justice entirely by listening to every concrete individual's or group's point of view and expression of its needs. Is it possible, by taking this route, to come up with any principles at all? Is it a reliable route, given the possibility of "false consciousness"? Doesn't stressing differences, especially cultural differences, lead to a slide toward relativism? The problem that is being grappled with is an important one. There can no longer be any doubt that many voices have not been heard when most theories of justice were being shaped. But how can all the different voices express themselves and be heard and still yield a coherent and workable theory of justice? This question is one I shall (eventually) return to in this essay.

Feminism, Difference, and Essentialism

Feminists have recently had much to say about difference. One aspect of the debate has been a continuation of an old argument – about how different women are from men, what such differences may be due to, and whether they require that laws and other aspects of public policy should treat women any differently from men.[1] Another, newer, aspect of the debate is about differences among women. It is "essentialist," some say, to talk about women, the problems of women, and especially the problems of women "as such."[2] White middle- and upper-class feminists, it is alleged, have excluded or been insensitive to not only the problems of women of other races, cultures, and religions but even those of women of other classes than their own. "Gender" is therefore a problematic category,

* From *Political Theory*, 22/1 (February 1994), pp. 5–24. Reprinted by permission of Sage Publications.

those opposed to such essentialism say, unless always qualified by and seen in the context of race, class, ethnicity, religion, and other such differences (Childers and hooks 1990; Harris 1990; hooks 1984; Lorde 1984; Minow and Spelman 1990; Spelman 1988).

The general allegation of feminist essentialism certainly has validity when applied to some work. Feminists with such pedigrees as Harriet Taylor, Charlotte Perkins Gilman, Virginia Woolf, Simone de Beauvoir, and Betty Friedan (in *The Feminine Mystique*) all seem to have assumed, for example, that the women they were liberating would have recourse to servants. With the partial exception of Woolf, who remarks briefly on the difficult lot of maids, they did not pay attention to the servants, the vast majority of whom were also, of course, women. The tendency of many white middle- and upper-class feminists in the mid-nineteenth century to think only of women of their own class and race (some were explicitly racist) is what makes so poignant and compelling Sojourner Truth's words in her famous "Ain't I a woman?" speech.[3] However, I think, and will argue, that this problem is far less present in the works of most recent feminists. But the charges of "essentialism" seem to grow ever louder. They are summed up in Elizabeth Spelman's (1988) recent claim that "the focus on women 'as women' has addressed only one group of women – namely, white middle-class women of Western industrialized countries" (p. 4). This has come to be accepted in some circles as virtually a truism.

The claim that much recent feminist theory is essentialist comes primarily from three (to some extent, overlapping) sources – European-influenced postmodernist thought; the work of African-American and other minority feminist women in the United States and Britain; and, in particular, Spelman's recent book, *Inessential Woman* (hereafter *IW*). Postmodernism is skeptical of all universal or generalizable claims, including those of feminism. It finds concepts central to feminist thinking, such as "gender" and "woman," as illegitimate as any other category or generalization that does not stop to take account of every difference. As Julia Kristeva, for example, says,

> The belief that "one is a woman" is almost as absurd and obscurantist as the belief that "one is a man". . . . [W]e must use "we are women" as an advertisement or slogan for our demands. On a deeper level, however, a woman cannot "be"; it is something which does not even belong in the order of *being*. (quoted in Marks and de Courtivron 1981: 137)

In the same interview, she also says that, because of the very different history of Chinese women, "it is absurd to question their lack of 'sexual liberation'" (in Marks and de Courtivron 1981: 140). Clearly, she thinks we could have no cross-cultural explanations of or objections to gender inequality.

Spelman argues that "the phrase 'as a woman' is the Trojan horse of feminist ethnocentrism" (*IW*: 13). The great mistakes of white middle-class feminists have been to exclude women different from themselves from their critiques or, even when they are included, to assume that, whatever their differences, their experience of sexism is the same. At best, she says, what is presented is "[a]n additive analysis [which] treats the oppression of a black woman in a society that is racist as well as sexist as if it were a further burden when in fact it is a *different burden*" (*IW*: 123; emphasis added).

These anti-essentialist arguments, however, are often long on theory and very short on empirical evidence. A large proportion of Spelman's examples of how women's experiences of oppression are different are taken from periods of slavery in ancient Greece and, especially, in the pre-Civil War South. It is not clear, though, how relevant is the obvious contrast between the experience of white slaveholders' wives and black female slaves to most issues involving the sameness or difference of forms of gender oppression today.

Apart from the paucity of relevant evidence (which I shall return to), there seem to me to be two other related problems with Spelman's general anti-essentialist argument. One is the claim that unless a feminist theorist perceives gender identity as intrinsically bound up with class, race, or other aspects of identity she ignores the effects of these other differences altogether. Spelman writes, "If gender were isolatable from other forms of identity, if sexism were isolatable from other forms of oppression, then what would be true about the relation between any man and any woman would be true about the relation between any other man and any other woman" (*IW*: 81). But this does not follow at all. One can argue that sexism is an identifiable form of oppression, many of whose effects are felt by women regardless of race or class, without at all subscribing to the view that race and class oppression are insignificant. One can still insist, for example, on the significant difference between the relation of a poor black woman to a wealthy white man and that of a wealthy white woman to a poor black man.

The second problem is that Spelman misplaces the burden of proof, which presumably affects her perception of the need for her to produce evidence for her claims. She says, "Precisely insofar as a discussion of gender and gender relations is really, even if obscurely, about a particular group of women and their relation to a particular group of men, it is unlikely to be applicable to any other group of women" (*IW*: 114). But why? Surely the burden of proof is on the critic. To be convincing, she needs to show that and how the theory accused of essentialism omits or distorts the experience of persons other than those few the theorist allegedly does take account of. This, after all, is the burden that many of the feminists Spelman considers "essentialist" have themselves taken on in critiquing "malestream" theories. One of the problems of anti-essentialist feminism (shared, I think, with much of postmodernist critique) is that it tends to substitute the cry "We're all different" for both argument and evidence.

There are, however, exceptions, and they tend to come from feminists who belong to racial minorities. One of the best critiques of feminist essentialism that I know of is that by Angela Harris (1990), in which she shows how ignorance of the specifics of a culture mars even thoroughly well-intentioned feminist analyses of women's experiences of oppression within that culture. She argues, for example, that in some respects, black women in the United States have had a qualitatively rather than simply quantitatively different experience of rape than that of white women (see esp. 1990: 594, 598–601). Even here, though, I think the anti-essentialist critique is only partly convincing. Although more concerned with evidence for the salience of differences than most anti-essentialists seem to be, Harris raises far more empirical questions than she provides answers. She provides just one example to support her assertion that black women's experience of rape is, even now, radically different from that of white women – that it is "an experience as deeply rooted in color as in gender" (p. 598).[4] Yet she, like Spelman, is as much disturbed by white feminists' saying that black women are "just like us only more so" as she is by their marginalizing black women or ignoring them altogether. As I shall argue, this "insult[ing]" conclusion – that the problems of other women are "similar to ours but more so" – is exactly the one I reach when I apply some Western feminist ideas about justice to the situations of poor women in many poor countries.

In this essay, I put anti-essentialist feminism to what I think is a reasonably tough test. In doing this, I am taking up the gauntlet that Spelman throws down. She says, referring to the body of new work about women that has appeared in many fields,

> Rather than assuming that women have something in common as women, these researchers should help us look to see whether they do. . . . Rather than first finding out what is true of some women as women and then inferring that this is true of all women . . . , we have to investigate different women's lives and see what they have in common. (*IW*: 137)

Trained as a philosopher, she does not seem to consider it appropriate to take up the challenge of actually looking at some of this empirical evidence. Having said the above, she turns back to discussing Plato. Trained as a political scientist, I shall attempt to look at some comparative evidence. I'll put some Western feminist ideas about justice and inequality to the test (drawing on my recent book and the many feminist sources I use to support some of its arguments) by seeing how well these theories – developed in the context of women in well-off Western industrialized countries – work when used to look at the very different situations of some of the poorest women in poor countries. How do our accounts and our explanations of gender inequality stand up in the face of considerable cultural and socioeconomic difference?

Differences and Similarities in Gender Oppression: Poor Women in Poor Countries

Does the assumption "that there is a generalizable, identifiable and collectively shared experience of womanhood" (Benhabib and Cornell 1987: 13) *have* any validity, or is it indeed an essentialist myth, rightly challenged by Third World women and their spokesfeminists? Do the theories devised by First World feminists, particularly our critiques of non-feminist theories of justice, have anything to say, in particular, to the poorest women in poor countries, or to those policymakers with the potential to affect their lives for better or for worse?

In trying to answer these questions, I shall address, in turn, four sets of issues, which have been addressed both by recent feminist critics of Anglo-American social and political theory and by those development scholars who have in recent years concerned themselves with the neglect or distortion of the situation of women in the countries they study. First, why and how has the issue of the inequality between the sexes been ignored or obscured for so long and addressed only so recently? Second, why is it so important that it be addressed? Third, what do we find, when we subject households or families to standards of justice – when we look at the largely hidden inequalities between the sexes? And finally, what are the policy implications of these findings?

Why attention to gender is comparatively new

In both development studies and theories of justice there has, until recently, been a marked lack of attention to gender – and in particular to systematic inequalities between the sexes. This point has been made about theories of justice throughout the 1980s (e.g Kearns 1983; Okin 1989b; Crosswaite 1989). In the development literature, it was first made earlier, in pioneering work by Ester Boserup, but has lately been heard loud and strong from a number of other prominent development theorists (Chen 1983; Dasgupta 1993; Sen 1990a, 1990b; Jelin 1990). In both contexts, the neglect of women and gender seems to be due primarily to two factors. The first is the assumption that the household (usually assumed to be male-headed) is the appropriate unit of analysis. The dichotomy between the public (political and economic) and the private (domestic and personal) is assumed valid, and only the former has been taken to be the appropriate sphere for development studies and theories of justice, respectively, to attend to. In ethical and political theories, the family is often regarded as an inappropriate context for justice, since love, altruism, or shared interests are assumed to hold sway within it. Alternatively, it is sometimes taken for granted that it is a realm of hierarchy and injustice. (Occasional theorists, like Rousseau, have said both!) In economics, development and other, households until recently have simply been taken for granted as the appropriate unit of analysis on such questions as income distribution. The public/private dichotomy and the assumption of the male-headed household have many serious implications for women as well as for children that are discussed below (Dasgupta 1993; Jaquette 1982: 283; Okin 1989b: 10–14, 124–33; Olsen 1983; Pateman 1983).

The second factor is the closely related failure to disaggregate data or arguments by sex. In the development literature, it seems to appear simply in this form (Chen et al. 1981: 68; Jaquette 1982: 283–4). In the justice literature, this used to be obscured by the use of male pronouns and other referents. Of late, the (rather more insidious) practice that I have called "false gender neutrality" has appeared. This consists in the use of gender-neutral terms ("he or she," "persons," and so on), when the point being made is simply invalid or otherwise false if one actually applies it to women (Okin 1989b; esp. 10–13, 45). But the effect is the same in both literatures; women are not taken into account, so the inequalities between the sexes are obscured.

The public/domestic dichotomy has serious implications for women. It not only obscures intrahousehold inequalities of resources and power, as I discuss below, but it also results in the failure to count a great deal of the work done by women as work, since all that is considered "work" is what is done for pay in the "public" sphere. All of the work that women do in bearing and rearing children, cleaning and maintaining households, caring for the old and sick, and contributing in various ways to men's work does not count as work. This is clearly one of those instances in which the situation of poor women in poor countries is not qualitatively *different* from that of most women in rich countries but, rather, "similar but worse," for even more, in some cases far more, of the work done by women (and children) in poor countries is rendered invisible, not counted, or "subsumed under men's work." The work of subsistence farming, tending to animals, domestic crafts (if not for the market), and the often arduous fetching of water and fuel are all added to the category of unrecognized work of women that already exists in richer countries.[5] Chen notes that women who do all these things "are listed [by policymakers] as housewives," even though "their tasks are as critical to the well-being of their families and to national production as are the men's" (Chen 1983: 220; see also Dasgupta 1993; Drèze and Sen 1989: ch. 4; Jaquette 1982, citing Bourgue and Warren 1979; Waring 1989).

Why does it matter?

This may seem like a silly question. Indeed, I hope it will soon be unnecessary, but it isn't – yet. I therefore argue, at the outset of *Justice, Gender, and the Family*, that the omission from theories of justice of gender, and of much of women's lives, is significant for three major reasons. Each of these reasons applies at least as much to the neglect of gender in theories of development. The first is obvious: women matter (at least they do to feminists), and their well-being matters at least as much as that of men. As scholars of development have recently been making clear, the inequalities between the sexes in a number of poor countries have not only highly detrimental but *fatal* consequences for millions of women. Sen (1990a) has recently argued that as many as one hundred million fewer women exist than might normally be expected on the basis of male/female mortality rates in societies less devaluing of women – not only the Western industrialized world but much of sub-Saharan Africa, too (see also Dasgupta 1993; Drèze and Sen 1989: ch. 4; Drèze and Sen 1990: Introduction, 11–14; but cf. Harriss 1990; Wheeler and Abdullah 1988). So here too we can reasonably say that the issue of the neglect of women is "similar but *much* worse."

The second reason I have raised (in the US context) for the necessity for feminist critique of theories of social justice is that equality of opportunity – for women and girls but also for increasing numbers of boys – is much affected by the failure of theories of justice to address gender inequality. This is in part due to the greater extent of economic distress in female-headed households. In the United States, nearly 25 percent of children are being raised in single female-headed households, and three-fifths of all chronically poor households with children are among those supported by single women. It has been recently estimated that throughout the world one-third of households are headed by single females, with the percentage much higher in regions with significant male out-migration (Chen 1983: 221; Jaquette 1982: 271). Many millions of children are affected by the higher rate of poverty among such families.[6] Theories of justice or of economic development that fail to pay attention to gender ignore this, too.

In addition, the gendered division of labor has a serious and direct impact on the opportunities of girls and women, which crosses the lines of economic class. The opportunities of females are significantly affected by the structures and practices of family life, particularly by the fact that women are almost invariably primary caretakers, which has much impact on their availability for full-time wage work. It also results in their frequently being *over*worked, and renders them less likely than men to be considered economically valuable. This factor, too, operates "similarly but more so" within poor families in many poor countries. There, too, adult women suffer – often more severely – many of the same effects of the division of labor as do women in richer countries. But, in addition, their daughters are likely to be put to work for the household at a very young age, are much less likely to be educated and to attain literacy than are sons of the same households and, worst of all – less valued than their brothers – they have less chance of staying alive because they are more likely to be deprived of food or of health care (Dasgupta 1993; Drèze and Sen 1990: ch. 4; Sen 1990a; Papanek 1990).

Third, I have argued that the failure to address the issue of just distribution within households is significant because the family is the first, and arguably the most influential, school of moral development (Okin 1989b: esp. 17–23). It is the first environment in which we experience how persons treat each other, in which we have the potential to learn how to be just or unjust. If children see that sex difference is the occasion for obviously differential treatment, they are surely likely to be affected in their personal and moral development. They are likely to learn injustice by absorbing the messages, if male, that they have some kind of "natural" enhanced entitlement and, if female, that they are *not* equals and had better get used to being subordinated if not actually abused. So far as I know, this point was first made in the Western context by John Stuart Mill, who wrote of the "perverting influence" of the typical English family of his time – which he termed "a school of despotism" (Mill [1869] 1988: 88). I have argued that the still remaining unequal distribution of benefits and burdens between most parents in two-parent heterosexual families is likely to affect their children's developing sense of justice (Okin 1989b: e.g. 21–3, 97–101). In the context of poor countries, as Papanek (1990) notes, "Domestic groups in which age and gender difference confer power on some over others are poor environments in which to unlearn the norms of inequality" (1990: 163–5). She also notes that "given the persistence of gender-based inequalities in power, authority, and access to resources, one must conclude that socialization for gender inequality is by and large very successful" (1990: 170). When such basic goods as food and health care are unequally distributed to young children according to sex, a very strong signal about the acceptability of injustice is surely conferred. The comparison of most families in rich countries with poor families in poor countries – where distinctions between the sexes often start earlier and are much more blatant and more harmful to girls – yields, here too, the conclusion that, in the latter case, things are not so much different as "similar but more so." Many Third World families, it seems, are even worse schools of justice and more successful inculcators of the inequality of the sexes as natural and appropriate than are their developed world equivalents. Thus there is even more need for attention to be paid to gender inequality in the former context than in the latter.

Justice in the family

What do we find when we compare some of Anglo-American feminists' findings about justice within households in their societies with recent discoveries about distributions of benefits and burdens in poor households in poor countries? Again, in many respects, the injustices of gender are quite similar.

In both situations, women's access to paid work is constrained both by discrimination and sex segregation in the workplace and by the assumption that women are "naturally" responsible for all or most of the unpaid work of the household (Bergmann 1986; Fuchs 1988; Gerson 1985; Okin 1989b; 147–52, 155–6; Sanday 1974). In both situations, women typically work longer total hours than men:

> Time-use statistics considering all work (paid and unpaid economic activity and unpaid house-work) reveal that women spend more of their time working than men in all developed and developing regions except northern America and Australia, where the hours are almost equal. (United Nations Report 1991: 81 and ch. 6 passim; see also Bergmann 1986; Hochschild 1989)

In both situations, developed and less developed, vastly more of women's work is not paid and is not considered "productive."[7] Thus there is a wide gap between men's and women's *recorded* economic participation. The perception that women's work is of less worth (despite the fact that in most places they do more, and it is crucial to the survival of household members) contributes to women's being devalued and having less power both within the family and outside the household (Blumstein and Schwartz 1983; Dasgupta 1993; Drèze and Sen 1990: ch. 4; Okin 1989b: ch. 7; Sanday 1974; Sen 1990a, 1990b). This in turn adversely affects their capacity to become economically less dependent on men. Thus they become involved in "a cycle of socially caused and distinctly asymmetric vulnerability" (Okin 1989b: 138; Drèze and Sen 1989; 56–9). The devaluation of women's work, as well as their lesser physical strength and economic dependence on men, allows them to be subject to physical, sexual, and/or psychological abuse by men they live with (Gordon 1988; United Nations Report 1991: 19–20). However, in many poor countries, as I have mentioned, this power differential extends beyond the abuse and overwork of women to deprivation in terms of the feeding, health care, and education of female children – and even to their being born or not: "of 8,000 abortions in Bombay after parents learned the sex of the foetus through amniocentesis, only one would have been a boy" (United Nations Report 1991; see also Dasgupta 1993; Drèze and Sen 1989; ch. 4; Sen 1990a).

In cross-regional analyses, both Sen and Dasgupta have found correlations between the life expectancies of females relative to males and the extent to which women's work is perceived as having economic value. Thus in both rich and poor countries, women's participation in work outside the household can improve their status within the family, but this is not necessarily assured. It is interesting to compare Barbara Bergmann's (1986) analysis of the situation of "drudge wives" in the United States, who work fulltime for pay and who also perform virtually all of the household's unpaid labor, with Peggy Sanday's earlier finding that, in some Third World contexts, women who do little of the work that is considered "productive" have low status, whereas many who do a great deal of it become "virtual slaves" (Sanday 1974: 201; Bergmann 1986: 260–73).[8]

This leads us to the issue of women's economic dependence (actual and perceived). Although most poor women in poor countries work long hours each day, throughout the world they are often economically dependent on men. This, too, is "similar to but worse than" the situation of many women in richer countries. It results from so much of their work being unpaid work, so much of their paid work being poorly paid work, and, in some cases, from men's laying claim to the wages their wives and daughters earn. Feminist critics since Ester Boserup (1970) have argued that women's economic dependency on men was in many cases exacerbated by changes that development theory and development policymakers saw only as "progressive." All too ready to perceive women as dependants, mainstream theorists did not notice that technology, geographical mobility, and the conversion from subsistence to market economies were not, from the female point of view, "unalloyed benefits, but . . . processes that cut women out from their traditional economic and social roles and thrust them into the modern sector where they are discriminated against and exploited, often receiving cash incomes below the subsistence level, . . . in turn increas(ing) female dependency" (Jaquette 1982; see also Boserup 1970; Rogers, in Jaquette).[9]

In both rich and poor countries, women who are the sole economic support of families often face particular hardship. However, whereas some are, not all of the reasons for this are the same. Discrimination against women in access to jobs, pay, retention, and promotion are common to most countries, with obviously deleterious effects on female-supported families. In the United States, the average full-time working woman earns a little more than two-thirds of the pay of a full-time male worker, and three-fifths of the families with children who live in chronic poverty are single female-parent families. Many such women in both rich and poor countries also suffer from severe "time poverty."

But the situation of some poor women in poor countries is different from – as well as distinctly worse than – that of most Western women today. It is more like the situation of the latter in the nineteenth century: even when they have no other means of support, they are actually *prohibited* (by religiously based laws or oppressive cultural norms) from engaging in paid labor. Martha Chen (1996) has studied closely the situation of such women in the Indian subcontinent. Deprived of the traditional economic support of a male, they are prevented from taking paid employment by rules of caste, or *purdah*. For such women, it can indeed be liberating to be helped (as they have been by outsiders like Chen) to resist the sanctions invoked against them by family elders, neighbors, or powerful social leaders. Although many forms of wage work, especially those available to women, are hardly "liberating," except in the most basic sense, women are surely distinctly less free if they are *not* allowed to engage in it, especially if they have no other means of support. Many employed women in Western industrialized countries still face quite serious disapproval if they are mothers of young children or if the family's need for their wages is not perceived as great. But at least, except in the most oppressive of families or subcultures, they are *allowed* to go out to work. By contrast, as Chen's work makes clear, the basic right to be allowed to make a much needed living for themselves and their children is still one that many women in the poorest of situations in other cultures are denied.

Here, then, is a real difference – an oppressive situation that most Western women no longer face. But to return to similarities: another that I discovered, while comparing some of our Western feminist ideas about justice with work on poor women in poor countries, has to do with the dynamics of power within the family. The differential exit potential theory that I adopt from Albert Hirschman's work to explain power within the family has recently been applied to the situation of women in poor countries (cf. Okin 1989b: ch. 7 with Dasgupta 1993 and Sen 1990b). Partha Dasgupta (1993) also uses exit theory in explaining the "not uncommon" desertion by men of their families during famines. He writes, "The man deserts [his wife] because *his* outside option in these circumstances emerges higher in his ranking than any feasible allocation within the household" (1993: 329). He regards the "hardware" he employs – John Nash's game-theoretic program – as "needed if we are to make any progress in what is a profoundly complex matter, the understanding of household decisions" (p. 329). But the conclusion he reaches is very similar to the one that I reach, drawing on Hirschman's theory of power and the effects of persons' differential exit potential: any factor that improves the husband's exit option or detracts from the wife's exit option thereby gives him additional voice, or bargaining power in the relationship. Likewise, anything that improves the wife's exit option – her acquisition of human or physical capital, for example – will increase her autonomy and place her in a better bargaining position in the relationship (Dasgupta 1993: 331–3; Okin 1989b: ch. 7).[10]

In the United States, recent research has shown that women's and children's economic status (taking need into account) typically deteriorates after separation or divorce, whereas the average divorcing man's economic status actually improves (McLindon 1987; Weitzman 1985; Wishik 1986). This, taken in conjunction with the exit/voice theory, implies less bargaining power for wives within marriage. In poor countries, where circumstances of severe poverty combine with a lack of paid employment opportunities for women, increasing women's dependency on men, men's power within the family – already in most cases legitimized by highly patriarchal cultural norms – seems very likely to be enhanced. Although, as Dasgupta (1993) points out, Nash's formula was not intended as a normative theory, employed in this context, the theory not only *explains* (much as does my employment of Hirschman's theory) the cyclical nature of women's lack of power within the family. It also points to the injustice of a situation in which the assumption of women's responsibility for children, their disadvantaged position in the paid workforce, and their physical vulnerability to male violence all contribute to giving them little bargaining room when their (or their children's) interests conflict with those of the men they live with, thereby in turn worsening their position relative to that of men. The whole theory, then, whether in its more or its less mathematical form, seems just as applicable to the situations of very poor women in poor countries as it is to women in quite well-off households in rich countries. Indeed, one must surely say, in this case, too, "similar but *much* worse," for the stakes are undeniably higher – no less than life or death for more than a hundred million women, as has recently been shown (Drèze and Sen 1990: ch. 4; Sen 1990a).

Policy implications

Some of the *solutions* to all these problems, which have been suggested recently by scholars addressing the situation of poor women in poor countries, closely resemble solutions proposed by Western feminists primarily concentrating on their own societies. (By "solutions to problems" I mean to refer to both what theorists and social scientists need to do to rectify their analyses and what policymakers need to do to solve the social problems themselves.) First, the dichotomization of public and domestic spheres must be strongly challenged. As Chen (1983) writes, in the context of poor rural regions, "So long as policymakers make the artificial distinction between the farm and the household, between paid work and unpaid work, between productive and domestic work, women will continue to be overlooked" (p. 220). Challenging the dichotomy will also point attention to the inequities that occur within households – various forms of abuse, including the inequitable distribution of food and health care. As Papanek (1990) argues, "Given a focus on socialization for inequality, power relations within the household – as a central theme in examining the dynamics of households – deserve special attention" (1990: 170).

Second, and following from the above, the unit of analysis both for studies and for much policymaking must be the individual, not the household.[11] Noting that, given the greater political voice of men, public decisions affecting the poor in poor countries are often "guided by male preferences, not [frequently conflicting] female needs," Dasgupta (1993) concludes that

> the maximization of well-being as a model for explaining household behaviour must be rejected. . . . Even though it is often difficult to design and effect it, the target of public policy should be persons, not households. . . . Governments need to be conscious of the household as a resource allocation mechanism. (1993: 335–6)

Especially as women are even more likely in poor countries than in richer ones to be providing the sole or principal support for their households, as Chen (1983) points out, they require as much access as men to credit, skills training, labor markets, and technologies (and, I would add, equal pay for their work) (1983: 221). Policies prompting women's full economic participation and productivity are needed increasingly for the survival of their households, for women's overall socio-economic status, and for their bargaining position within their families. As Drèze and Sen (1989) say, "important policy implications" follow from the "considerable evidence that greater involvement with outside work and paid employment does tend to go with less anti-female bias in intra-family distribution" (1989: 58). Because of the quite pervasive unequal treatment of female children in some poor countries, the need for equal treatment of women by policymakers is often far more urgent than the need of most women in richer countries – but again, the issue is not so much different as "similar but more so."

Implications for Thinking about Justice

Finally, I shall speculate briefly about two different ways of thinking about justice between the sexes, in cultures very different from ours. I have tried to show that, for feminists thinking about justice, John Rawls's theory, if revised so as to include women and the family, has a great deal to be said for it, and the veil of ignorance is particularly important (Rawls 1971; Okin 1989a, 1989b). If everyone were to speak only from his or her own point of view, it is unclear that we would come up with any principles at all. But the very presence of the veil, which hides from those in the original position any particular knowledge of the personal characteristics or social position they will have in the society for which they are designing principles of justice, forces them to take into account as many voices as possible and especially to be concerned with those of the least well-off. It enables us to reconcile the requirement that a theory of justice be universalizable with the seemingly conflicting requirement that it take account of the multiple differences among human beings.

In a recent paper, Ruth Anna Putnam (1996), arguing a strongly anti-essentialist line, and accusing Rawls and myself of varying degrees of exclusionary essentialism, considers instead an "interactive" (some might call it "dialogic") feminism: "that we listen to the voices of women of color and women of a different class, and that we appropriate what we hear" (p. 21).[12] Listening and discussing have much to recommend them; they are fundamental to democracy in the best sense of the word. And *sometimes* when especially oppressed women are heard, their cry for justice is clear – as in the case of the women Martha Chen worked with, who became quite clear that being allowed to leave the domestic sphere in order to earn wages would help to liberate them. But we are not always enlightened about what is just by asking persons who seem to be suffering injustices what they want. Oppressed people have often internalized their oppression so well that they *have* no sense of what they are justly entitled to as human beings. This is certainly the case with gender inequalities. As Papanek (1990) writes, "The clear perception of disadvantages . . . requires conscious rejection of the social norms and cultural ideal that perpetuate inequalities and the use of different criteria – perhaps from another actual or idealized society – in order to assess inequality as a prelude for action" (1990: 164–5). People in seriously deprived conditions are sometimes not only accepting of them but relatively cheerful – the "small mercies" situation. Deprivations sometimes become gagged and muffled for reasons of deeply rooted ideology, among others. But it would surely be ethically deeply mistaken to attach a correspondingly small value to the loss of well-being of such people because of their survival strategy.

Coming to terms with very little is no recipe for social justice. Thus it is, I believe, quite justifiable for those not thoroughly imbued with the inegalitarian norms of a culture to come forth as its constructive critics. Critical distance, after all, does not have to bring with it detachment: *committed* outsiders can often be better analysts and critics of social injustice than those who live within the relevant culture. This is why a concept such as the original position, which aims to approximate an Archimedean point, is so valuable, at least in addition to some form of dialogue. Let us think for a moment about some of the cruelest or most oppressive institutions and practices that are or have been used to "brand" women – foot binding, clitoridectomy, and purdah. As Papanek shows, "well socialized" women in cultures with such practices internalize them as necessary to successful female development. Even though, in the case of the former two practices, these women may retain vivid memories of their own intense pain, they perpetuate the cruelties, inflicting them or at least allowing them to be inflicted on their own daughters.

Now, clearly, a theory of human flourishing, such as Nussbaum and Sen have been developing, would have no trouble delegitimizing such practices (Nussbaum 1992). But given the choice between a revised Rawlsian outlook or an "interactive feminist" one, as defined by Putnam, I'd choose the former any day, for in the latter, well-socialized members of the oppressed group are all too likely to rationalize the cruelties, whereas the men who perceive themselves as benefiting from them are unlikely to object. But behind the veil of ignorance, is it not much more likely that both the oppressors and the oppressed would have second thoughts? What Moslem man is likely to take the chance of spending his life in seclusion and dependency, sweltering in head-to-toe solid black clothing? What prerevolutionary Chinese man would cast his vote for the breaking of toes and hobbling through life, if he well might be the one with the toes and the crippled life? What man would endorse gross genital mutilation, not knowing *whose* genitals? And the women in these cultures, required to think of such practices from a male as well as a female per- spective, might thereby, with a little distance, gain more notion of just how, rather than perfecting femininity, they perpetuate the subordination of women to men.

Martha Nussbaum (1992) has recently written of what happens when outsiders, instead of trying to maintain some critical distance, turn to what amounts to the worship of dif- ference. Citing some examples of sophisticated Western scholars who, in their reverence for the integrity of cultures, defend such practices as the isolation of menstruating women and criticize Western "intrusions" into other cultures, such as the provision of typhoid vaccine, Nussbaum finds a strange and disturbing phenomenon:

> Highly intelligent people, people deeply committed to the good of women and men in devel- oping countries, people who think of themselves as progressive and feminist and antiracist, . . . are taking up positions that converge . . . with the positions of reaction, oppression, and sexism. Under the banner of their radically and politically correct "anti-essentialism" march ancient religious taboos, the luxury of the pampered husband, ill health, ignorance, and death. (1992: 204)

As Nussbaum later concludes, "Identification need not ignore concrete local differences: in fact, at its best, it demands a searching analysis of differences, in order that the general good be appropriately realized in the concrete case. But the learning about and from the other is motivated . . . by the conviction that the other is one of us" (1992: 241).

As the work of some feminist scholars of development shows, using the concept of gender and refusing to let differences gag us or fragment our analyses does not mean that we should overgeneralize or try to apply "standardized" solutions to the problems of women in different circumstances. Chen argues for the value of a situation-by-situation analysis of women's roles and constraints before plans can be made and programs designed. And Papanek, too, shows how helping to educate women to awareness of their oppression requires quite deep and specific knowledge of the relevant culture.

Thus I conclude that gender itself is an extremely important category of analysis and that we ought not be paralyzed by the fact that there are differences among women. So long as we are careful and develop our judgments in the light of empirical evidence, it is possible to generalize about many aspects of inequality between the sexes. Theories developed in Western contexts can clearly apply, at least in large part, to women in very different cultural contexts. From place to place, from class to class, from race to race, and from culture to culture, we find similarities in the specifics of these inequalities, in their causes and their effects, although often not in their extent or severity.

Notes

1 This debate has been conducted mostly among feminist legal and political theorists. The legal literature is already so vast that it is difficult to summarize, and it is not relevant to this essay. For some references, see Okin (1991), ns. 1–3.
2 "Essentialism," employed in the context of feminist theory, seems to have two principal meanings. The other refers to the tendency to regard certain characteristics or capacities as "essentially" female, in the sense that they are unalterably associated with being female. Used in this second way, essentialism is very close to, if not always identical with, biological determinism. I am not concerned with this aspect of the term here.
3 In 1851, at an almost entirely white women's rights convention, Truth said,

> That man over there says women need to be helped into carriages, and lifted over ditches, and to have the best place everywhere. Nobody ever helps me into carriages, or over mud puddles, or gives me any best place! And ain't I a woman? Look at me! Look at my arm! I have ploughed, and planted, and gathered into barns, and no man could head me! And ain't I a woman? I could work as much and eat as much as a man – when I could get it – and bear the lash as well! And ain't I a woman? I have borne thirteen children, and seen most all sold off to slavery, and when I cried out with my mother's grief, none but Jesus heard me! And ain't I a woman?

4 The example is that of the many black women (and few white women) who answered Joann Little's appeal on behalf of Delbert Tibbs, a black man who had been falsely accused of raping a white woman and sentenced to death. I do not think the example clearly supports Harris's assertion that black women have "a unique ambivalence" about rape, any more than it supports the assertion she claims to refute – that their experience is similar, but different in magnitude. Black women's present experience of rape is surely similar to that of white women in several important respects: many are raped (by acquaintances as well as by strangers), they fear being raped, they sometimes modify their behavior because of this fear, and they are victimized as witnesses at the trials of their rapists. But their experience is probably also worse because, in addition to all of this, they have to live with the knowledge and experience of black men's being victimized by false accusations, harsher sentences, and, at worst, lynchings. Only empirical research that involved asking them could show more certainly whether the oppression of black men as alleged rapists (or the history of master/slave rape, which Harris also discusses) makes black women's entire contemporary experience of rape different from that of white women.
5 However, the detailed division of labor between the sexes varies considerably from culture to culture. As Jane Mansbridge (1993) has recently written, in a discussion of "gratuitous gendering":

> Among the Aleut of North America, for example, only women are allowed to butcher animals. But among the Ingalik of North America, only men are allowed to butcher animals. Among the Suku of Africa, only the women can plant crops and only the men can make baskets. But among the Kaffa of the Circum-Mediterranean, only the men can plant crops and only the women can make baskets. (1993: 345)

Her analysis is derived from data in George P. Murdoch and Caterina Provost, "Factors in the Division of Labor by Sex: A Cross-Cultural Analysis," *Ethnology* 12 (1973): 203–25. However, the work done by women is less likely to be "outside" work and to be paid or valued.

6   Poverty is both a relative and an absolute term. The poorest households in poor countries are absolutely as well as relatively poor and can be easily pushed below subsistence by any number of natural, social, or personal catastrophes. Poverty in rich countries is more often relative poverty (although there is serious malnutrition currently in the United States for example, and drug abuse, with all its related ills, is highly correlated with poverty). Relative poverty, although not directly life-threatening, can however be very painful, especially for children living in societies that are not only highly consumer oriented but in which many opportunities – for good health care, decent education, the development of talents, pursuit of interests, and so on – are seriously limited for those from poor families. Single parents also often experience severe "time poverty," which can have a serious impact on their children's well-being.

7   See Dasgupta (1993) on members' perceived "usefulness" affecting the allocation of goods within poor households in poor families. Western studies as well as non-Western ones show us that women's work is already likely to be regarded as less useful – even when it is just as necessary to family well-being. So when women are really made less useful (by convention or lack of employment opportunities), this problem is compounded. Dasgupta questions simple measures of usefulness, such as paid employment, in the case of girls (1993). Where young poor women are not entitled to parental assets and their outside employment opportunities are severely restricted, the only significant "employment" for them is as childbearers and housekeepers – so marriage becomes especially valued (even though its conditions may be highly oppressive).

8   There seems to be some conflicting evidence on this matter. See Papanek (1990: 166–8).

9   This seems similar to changes in the work and socioeconomic status of women in Western Europe in the sixteenth to eighteenth centuries.

10 I do not mean to imply here that most women, whether in developed or less developed societies, think about improving their exit options when making decisions about wage work and related issues. Indeed, in some cultures, women relinquish wage work as soon as their families' financial situation enables them to do so. But their exit option is nevertheless reduced, and their partner's enhanced, thereby in all likelihood altering the distribution of power within the family.

11 This point seems to have been first explicitly made in the context of policy by George Bernard Shaw, who argues in *The Intelligent Woman's Guide to Socialism and Capitalism* (New Brunswick, NJ: Transaction Books, 1984) that the state should require all adults to work and should allocate an equal portion of income to each – man, woman, and child.

12 As Joan Tronto has pointed out to me, the use of "appropriate" here is noteworthy, given Putnam's professed desire to treat these other women as her equals.

References

Benhabib, Seyla, and Drucilla Cornell (1987), Introduction: Beyond the politics of gender. In *Feminism as critique*. Minneapolis: University of Minnesota Press.

Bergmann, Barbara R. (1986), *The economic emergence of women*. New York: Basic Books.

Blumstein, Philip, and Pepper Schwartz (1983), *American couples*. New York: Morrow.

Boserup, Ester (1970), *Women's role in economic development*. London: Allen & Unwin.

Chen, Lincoln C., Emdadul Huq, and Stan D'Souza (1981), Sex bias in the family allocation of food and health care in rural Bangladesh. *Population and Development Review* 7: 55–70.

Chen, Martha Alter (1983), *A quiet revolution: Women in transition in rural Bangladesh*. Cambridge, MA: Schenkman.

——(1996), A matter of survival: Women's right to work in India and Bangladesh. In *Women, culture, and development: A study of human capabilities*, edited by Martha Nussbaum and Jonathan Glover. Oxford: Oxford University Press.

Childers, Marry, and bell hooks (1990), A conversation about race and class. In *Conflicts in feminism*, edited by Marianne Hirsch and Evelyn Fox Keller. New York: Routledge, Chapman & Hall.

Crosswaite, Jan (1989), Sex in the original position. Unpublished manuscript, Department of Philosophy, University of Auckland.

Dasgupta, Partha (1993), *An inquiry into well-being and destitution*. Oxford: Clarendon Press.

Drèze, Jean, and Amartya Sen (1989), *Hunger and public action*. Oxford: Clarendon Press.

——eds (1990), *The political economy of hunger: Vol. 1. Entitlement and well-being*. Oxford: Clarendon Press.

Fuchs, Victor (1988), *Women's quest for economic equality*. Cambridge, MA: Harvard University Press.

Gerson, Kathleen (1985), *Hard choices: How women decide about work, career, and motherhood*. Berkeley: University of California Press.

Gordon, Linda (1988), *Heroes of their own lives*. New York: Viking.

Harris, Angela P. (1990), Race and essentialism in feminist legal theory. *Stanford Law Review* 42: 581–616.

Harriss, Barbara (1990), The intrafamilial distribution of hunger in South Asia. In *The political economy of hunger: Vol. 1. Entitlement and well-being*, edited by Jean Drèze and Amartya Sen. Oxford: Clarendon Press.

Hochschild, Arlie (1989), *The second shift: Working parents and the revolution at home*. New York: Viking.

hooks, bell (1984), *Feminist theory: From margin to center*. Boston: South End Press.

Jaquette, Jane S. (1982), Women and modernization theory: A decade of feminist criticism. *World Politics*. 34: 267–84.

Jelin, Elizabeth, ed. (1990), *Women and social change in Latin America*. London: Zed Books.

Kearns, Deborah (1983), A theory of justice and love – Rawls on the family. *Politics (Journal of the Australasian Political Studies Association)* 18(2): 36–42.

Lorde, Audre (1984), An open letter to Mary Daly. In *Sister outsider*, edited by Audre Lorde. Trumansburg, NY: Crossing Press.

Mansbridge, Jane (1993), Feminism and democratic community. In *Democratic community*, ed. John Chapman and Ian Shapiro. New York: New York University Press.

Marks, Elaine, and Isabelle de Courtivron, eds (1981), *New French feminisms: An anthology*. New York: Schocken.

McLindon, James B. (1987), Separate but unequal: The economic disaster of divorce for women and children. *Family Law Quarterly* 12: 3.

Mill, John Stuart [1869] (1988), *The subjection of women*. Reprint. Indianapolis: Hackett.

Minow, Martha, and Elizabeth V. Spelman (1990), In context. *Southern California Law Review* 63(6): 1597–652.

Nussbaum, Martha (1992), Human functioning and social justice: In defense of Aristotelian essentialism. *Political Theory* 20: 202–46. (A version is printed in *Women, culture, and development: A study of human capabilities*, edited by Martha Nussbaum and Jonathan Glover. Oxford: Oxford University Press, 1996.)

Okin, Susan Moller (1989a), Reason and feeling in thinking about justice. *Ethics* 99(2): 229–49.

——(1989b), *Justice, gender, and the family*. New York: Basic Books.

——(1991), Sexual difference, feminism and the law. *Law and Social Inquiry*.

Olsen, Frances (1983), The family and the market: A study of ideology and legal reform. *Harvard Law Review* 96 (7).

Papanek, Hanna (1990), To each less than she needs, from each more than she can do: Allocations, entitlements, and value. In Irene Tinker, ed., *Persistent inequalities: Women and world development*. New York: Oxford University Press.

Pateman, Carole (1983), Feminist critiques of the public/private dichotomy. In *Public and private in social life*, ed., Stanley Benn and Gerald Gaus. London: Croom Helm. Also in Pateman, *The disorder of women*. Stanford, CA: Stanford University Press (1989).

Putnam, Ruth Anna (1996), Why not a feminist theory of justice? In *Women, culture, and development: A study of human capabilities*, edited by Martha Nussbaum and Jonathan Glover. Oxford: Oxford University Press.

Rawls, John (1971), *A theory of justice*. Cambridge, MA: Harvard University Press.

Sanday, Peggy R. (1974), Female status in the public domain. In Michelle Zimbalist Rosaldo and Louise Lamphere eds, *Woman, culture, and society*. Stanford. CA: Stanford University Press.

Sen, Amartya (1990a), More than 100 million women are missing. *New York Review of Books*, December 20.

——(1990b), Gender and co-operative conflicts. In Irene Tinker, ed., *Women and world develop-ment*. New York and London: Oxford University Press.

Spelman, Elizabeth V. (1988), *Inessential woman: Problems of exclusion in feminist thought*. Boston: Beacon Press.

United Nations Report (1991), *The world's women: Trends and statistics, 1970–1990*. New York: United Nations Publication.

Waring, Marilyn (1989), *If women counted: A new feminist economics*. San Francisco: Harper & Row.

Weitzman, Lenore (1985), *The Divorce Revolution: The unexpected social and economic consequences for women and children*. New York: Free Press.

Wheeler, E. F., and M. Abdullah (1988) Food allocation within the family: Response to fluctuat-ing food supply and food needs. In I. de Garine and G. A. Harrison, *Coping with uncertainty in food supply*. Oxford: Clarendon Press.

Wishik, Heather Ruth (1986), Economics of divorce: An exploratory study. *Family Law Quarterly* 20: 1.

45   Race/Gender and the Ethics of Difference*

Jane Flax

Susan Moller Okin has recently attacked the emphasis some feminists place on differences among women. She discerns "problems with going in the direction of formulating a theory of justice entirely by listening to every concrete individual's or group's point of view."[1] Okin doubts that it is "possible, by taking this route, to come up with any prin-ciples at all. . . . Doesn't stressing differences, especially cultural differences, lead to a slide toward relativism?"[2]

Okin claims that within some circles a belief that a focus on "women" necessarily reflects only middle-class White women's experience is now accepted as a "truism." In contrast, she defends an internally undifferentiated and conflict-free concept of gender. Gender is constituted through what women share, especially their differences from, and domination by, men. Women are defined by the similarities of their inequalities across race, class, and geography. Okin claims: "One can argue that sexism is an identifiable form of oppression, many of whose effects are felt by women regardless of race or class, without at all subscribing to the view that race and class oppression are insignificant."[3]

Both claims are mistaken. Okin misunderstands the genealogy, content, and ethical consequences of discourses of differences. Discourses of difference cannot be understood outside their specific historical contexts and purposes. They represent attempts to theo-rize and undo relations of domination. The participants in these debates are socially situated subjects who both resist and are constructed by context-specific social relations.

---

* From *Political Theory*, 23/3 (August 1995), pp. 500–10. Reprinted by permission of Sage Publications.

Without attention to difference, each person's multiple locations as authority, resister, and determined subject who articulates and is spoken by specific social vocabularies disappear. Attaining a "critical distance" may alert us to aspects of these multiple locations and their effects. However, it cannot render our judgments free of them. There is no Archimedean point available from which principles or practices of justice can be articulated or defended. Cross-cultural theorizing about justice requires attention to the particularity and partiality of conceptual vocabularies and practices and acknowledgment of the simultaneously determined and resisting qualities of each contributor.

Okin is also wrong to assume that race is extrinsic to gender. No "women" exist who have experience of oppression (or dominance) unmarked by race and class. Within contemporary social relations, no woman or feminist theorizing can be situated "regardless of race and class." To make such claims is to misconstrue the meaning and to miscalculate the significance of race for all women and theorizing practices. Adequate theorizing about gender and justice requires attention to inequalities among women. A homogeneous dominance/oppression model cannot account for the complicated and contradictory constitution of gender.

Difference Discourses and their Contexts

Okin traces the concern with differences to three sources: postmodernist thought, writings by African American and other minority women, and "particularly" Elizabeth Spelman's recent book *Inessential Women* (Boston: Beacon Press, 1988). Okin very briefly mentions only one article by an African American.[4] Her primary purpose is to attack Spelman's claim that race is intrinsic, not additive, to gender. A major consequence of this claim is that "women" cannot be treated as a homogeneous category. One cannot assume that "other" (e.g. non-White) women have experiences "just like ours" (White women) only more so. Gender cannot be understood as a simple binary opposition composed of two categories: man and woman.

For Okin, the stakes are clear: can "we" say that "sexism" is a type of oppression that affects all women, irrespective of their race, sexuality, and so forth? Her implicit assumption seems to be that sexism must affect a homogeneous category in relatively uniform ways to be taken seriously as a form of injustice. Why uniform oppression of a homogeneous group is necessary for it to count as injustice is not made clear. I assume it has something to do with Okin's (Rawlsian) background assumptions about universalizability. Evidently, generalizable principles require general, unitary subjects. These subjects can be either homogeneous victims of oppression or reflective practitioners in the original position. However, it cannot be difference *per se* that blocks "our" ability to articulate just principles. Okin claims that inattention to differences between men and women causes or perpetuates injustice. Why should attention to differences among women undermine or weaken our claims to gender justice? One does not have to occupy a position of pure oppression to articulate principles or engage in practices intended to end relations of domination.

Okin argues that a central claim of difference discourses – gender is constituted and experienced differently according to race and other social positions – "lacks empirical evidence."[5] She intends to provide proof that there is a collectively shared, definitive experience of womanhood. Okin also wants to demonstrate that there are generalizable theories, especially feminist critiques of non-feminist theories of justice. These can both identify uniformities in women's experience and point toward common policies to over-come our shared oppression.

She takes as her test case "the poorest women in poor countries."[6] Presumably, if they are just like "us" (White women in rich countries) only more so, we can conclude that there is collectively shared oppression. The category "woman" will be meaningful beyond whatever differences there might be. She looks at the conditions of poor Third World women in relation to four categories – inattention to gender injustice, gender-based lack of equality of opportunity, injustice in the family, and policy implications. Her conclusion is that the conditions of poor women in poor countries are generally like those of women in the First World, only more so. Policies informed by attention to gender justice, similar to those she advocates for women in the First World, could provide solutions to these conditions.

Okin does not acknowledge or confront the dangers of enlisting poor women from other countries as evidence in a dispute among women in the First World. This ap-propriation replicates the objectification and asymmetries that often typify relations between women in the First and Third World. "Western feminists alone become the true 'subjects' of this counterhistory. Third World women, on the other hand, never rise above the debilitating generality of their 'object' status."[7] Okin does not seriously address the voluminous writings of racialized women in this country. To do this would require situ-ating these debates in their specific political contexts. Even more, it requires an appreci-ation of the agency and authority that marginalized women assert in and through these debates.

Her analysis excludes both a primary purpose and the political genealogy of difference discourses in this country. Many participants were trying to compel White (and straight) women to pay attention to the actual, ongoing relations of domination among women in the United States and elsewhere.[8] These writings provide extensive evidence of the complicity of White women in racial domination and the empirical differences in women's lives. They also detail the complex interweaving and inseparability of race and gender in the lives of women and men throughout American history.[9] The disproportionate atten-tion paid to Spelman and the rapid movement of Okin's analysis to the "Third World" reflect and permit an elision of the social relations that produce discourses of difference and continue to potentiate them.

Okin does not adequately interrogate her own desire to emphasize the commonalities of women's experience and to insist that much of the shared content arises from domi-nation by a unitary other (men). Why are such claims desirable or necessary? Who gains from these beliefs and what is obscured by them? Her exclusive focus on shared oppres-sion obscures the equally important relations of domination between women. All women are not situated identically in relation to men, nor are men situated equally in relation to each other or to women. Such moves enable White women to ignore their complicity in, and privileges obtained from, their situatedness within relations of race, sexuality (if straight), and geographic location.

Despite Okin's emphasis on similarities among women, the structure of her text implic-itly reveals one way women in the First World and "others" are not similar. She splits agency and determination so that the agency exercised by racialized and "Third World women" and the determined aspects of First World women theorists are invisible. This implies that a group of objective intellectuals exists who can locate and speak for the inter-ests of others. This speech and analysis are not distorted by their own experiences or wishes. Location on this Archimedean point permits us to be objective, but "committed," outsiders. Accurate analysis of gender injustice requires this capacity for detach-ment. (Poor) women in the Third World exercise very little critical judgment. They appear all too ready to "settle for very little,"[10] while some women in the First World, despite their shared domination by men, can exercise detachment and undetermined critical judg-ment. Such objectivity enables us to be more accurate and insightful critics of other women's (and our own) societies than they can be.

Okin's argument relies on the assumption that First World women *are* outside the social relations that produce poor ones. This mistaken belief functions as a defense against acknowledging the social practices that constitute the Western observer and relations between observer and observed. It obscures "the complex interconnection between first and third world economies and the profound effect of this on the lives of women in all countries."[11] It also ignores the many indigenous forms of resistance and the many cri-tiques of this sort of lumping together of women from diverse cultures.[12] Constructing "Third World" women as an unresisting and homogeneous category positions them exclu-sively as objects of the discourses and practices of others.

Furthermore, such positioning denies the possibility that women in the First World have much to learn about themselves and others by seeing through their eyes. Taking the diversity of practices, locations, and meanings seriously entails placing Western, White women as the objects, not just subjects, of discourse.[13] This approach is also more con-gruent with a commitment to justice; it treats others as persons deserving of respect and capable of exercising authority in their own lives and those of others. It does not presume in advance whose judgments ought to prevail when differences arise.

The Inescapability of Race/Gender

Okin fails to recognize the constituting effects of race/gender on all Americans. This is obvious in her remarks about the salience of slavery to modern social relations. She says that the relevance of "the obvious contrast between the experience of white slaveholders' wives and black female slaves to most issues involving the sameness or difference of forms of gender oppression today"[14] is not clear to her. This view contrasts strongly with recent writings by Black women, for whom slavery reverberates in their history. It is a primal tragedy that lives on in one's sense of self, as the Holocaust does for me as a Jew. For example, Nellie Y. McKay writes:

> Speaking specifically of the experiences of Black and white women in the USA, for Black women there is a long and painful history embedded in the difference that separate them from white women. This history begins with the first African slave woman who encountered a white woman on this continent . . . the "often *violent* connection pitting black female will against white female racism" is a condition that penetrates all of American cultural and literary consciousness.[15]

Slavery is intrinsic to the genealogy of modern Euro-American subjects. The "modern subject may be located in historically specific and unavoidably complex configurations of individualization and embodiment – black and white, male and female, lord and bonds-man.[16] How can Whites not be affected in their thinking of themselves and Blacks by the knowledge (tacit or overt) that a little more than a hundred years ago many Black people were property, not persons?"

While for all women, "issues of gender are always connected to race,"[17] racially unmarked women can avoid recognizing this. Most discourse concerning racism focuses on its horrifying effects on its objects. While this is absolutely necessary, another aspect of racism has been almost completely avoided – "the impact of racism on those who perpetuate it."[18] We must analyze what racial ideology does to "the mind, imagination and behavior of masters."[19] Such analysis requires resistance to the denial by Whites of the constituting effects of race/gender on our subjectivities.

In this ability to ignore the effects of racism, we differ radically from racialized women. "Under no circumstances can Black women forget that. And although Black feminists, even radical black feminists have been trying to impress the significance of this truth on white feminists for more than twenty years, some still do not understand."[20] Neither White nor Black women can find some racially neutral space of gender identity or unity outside "the anguish of racial differences inscribed in the complexities of race, sex, rage and power in Black and white women's relationships."[21] Perhaps we could construct one, but that could only be the consequence of a long struggle that has hardly begun.

The Inseparability of Race and Gender

In contemporary America we never encounter an ungendered but raced person or a gendered but unraced one.[22] Race and gender intertwine and are inextricably, mutually constituting. Gender is always raced, and race is always gendered. Race and gender are not identical, or one thing, but mutually constituting, unstable, conflicting, constantly mutating, interdependent, and inseparable processes. Investment in one privilege can obscure these interwoven operations. Whatever separate lines of development they may have had in the past, each so blurs and bleeds into the other that only interwoven, processural concepts can begin to capture current complexities. Therefore, theorizing must employ metaphors of "creolization, mestizaje and hybridity, pollution and impurity . . . cultural mutation and restless (dis)continuity that exceed racial discourse and avoid capture by its agents."[23]

Discourses of race/gender are pervasive, intrinsic to, and necessary for social reproduction, systemic order, political legitimacy, and subjective stability and identity. Race/gender is intrinsic to the practice of contemporary American political institutions, and the state is an inevitable and central terrain on and over which race/gender struggles occur. While public law and legitimated race/gender beliefs have changed since the 1950s, the salience of race/gender in individual and collective identity construction and distributions of power has not. Race/gender is deployed to refer to and disguise "forces, events, classes, and expression of social decay and economic division far more threatening to the body politic than 'race' ever was."[24]

Whiteness, especially in its masculine forms, remains the unproblematized universal. Therefore, it is not seen as constituting a racialized or genderized subjectivity; being White is not a delimited (and limiting) identity. Whiteness is not seen as implicated in the production of the racialized other; nor is its dependence on raced/gendered others for its own sense of identity and social locations acknowledged. One who lacks difference can attain a more universal and objective (undetermined) moral and political standpoint.

Racialized women are necessarily produced and doubly erased within this discourse. The implicit modal person is a (White) man; therefore, qua (lesser) man, racialized men have some claims to acknowledgment and power. The modal universal racialized person is masculine. Women remain the particularized, lesser but implicitly White others. Early feminist theorizing tended to replicate this double erasure, and discourses of difference articulate attempts to resist and undo it.

Ethics of Difference

Okin's argument does nothing to reduce my suspicion of internally undifferentiated concepts of gender that define "woman" in terms of shared oppression. Structurally, such views foreclose acknowledgment of many of our conflicting positions in contemporary networks of power. They also obscure what Wendy Brown calls our "wounded attachments" and the passions that often motivate them – guilt, hate, envy, fear, and resentment.[25] Privileged people's need for abstract positions is partially driven by an unconscious guilty recognition of the determining role of domination in the formation of subjectivities (our own and the oppressed). We also fear the revenge of the oppressed on whose subordination their identities and positions depend. The dependence on the other for one's own identity is denied through the construction of a subjectivity free from any empirical context or determinant. The marks and burdens of race/gender are projected on to the other, and these become the content of the other's difference. The projection of all historical material outward allows the individual to be "free" or to acquire objectivity behind a Rawlsian veil of ignorance. This freedom includes an absence of complicity in the production of others, "their" history and their oppression.

Rather than argue it is time to "move on" from a focus on differences, I claim we have hardly begun to recognize them. White women have only begun to learn to listen to the points of view of many groups and individuals. Fearful about what they might teach us about ourselves, we are often tone-deaf to the voices of others and blind to the constituting effects of "difference" in our own subjectivities and politics. Okin evidently does not hear how offensive statements like "*committed* outsiders can often be better analysts and critics of social injustice than those who live within the relevant culture"[26] might sound to those within it.

Learning to listen is a complex process in which one must rethink one's own position and try to see oneself through the eyes of others. This mode of listening is quite different from the one adopting a Rawlsian veil of ignorance supposedly makes possible. Behind the veil of ignorance one impartially takes up one point of view after the other; one imagines a variety of circumstances, relationships, or rules as binding on the self. The requisite attitude is impartiality. One isolated rule or point of view after another is taken up and investigated. None of these positions are constitutive of the self, nor is the self implicated in their existence. They come from the outside, are subjected to rational scrutiny, and are adopted or rejected depending on whether they meet the condition of universalizability. The dialogue is between reason and an external position, experience, or rule presented to it.

The mode of listening I have in mind is quite different. It requires an uncomfortable, double vision. Those who are the marked bearers of "cultural differences" have long experience with this. One must see oneself as others do. The other's view cannot be totally alien or external, since it has constituting effects. One must struggle with and against it, and the struggle becomes part of one's self. Like the effects of the unconscious, one can never fully be aware of the effects of the other's view and the relations of power that potentiate this view and render it salient. Even ideas or aspects of subjectivity that seem exempt from the other's determination remain suspect. One can never be fully at home with, or trusting of, oneself. Decentered, partially estranged, multiple, overdetermined subjectivity is not a postmodernist conceit. Colonized and culturally, racially, or sexually defined "others" have long been familiar with it.

Persons of relative privilege do not have to adopt the double vision of subject/subjected others. Adopting such a position requires empathy and a willingness to see oneself as a contextual, situationally determined subject. One cannot be outside the relations that constitute the other; one's own identity is dependent on being in relation to her. Contrary to Okin's view, the search for, or claim of, an Archimedean point, whether via the original position or another approach, impedes rather than fosters the pursuit of justice. Attention to one's determinations, not detachment from them, alleviates the problem of "false consciousness." We need respectful engagement with others to improve our perspective.

Constructive debate about moral principles and standards of judgment requires the prior development of trust. Trust cannot develop unless each participant gives as full an account as possible of her particular commitments and acknowledges their potential for partiality, error, or harm. That each person's locations necessarily shape and limit our view must be acknowledged. Without open acknowledgment of this and its potential problems, the others have every right to remain suspicious. Unless the critic takes responsibility for the complexity of her own motives and locations, she is not approaching others from a position of respect and equality. Denial of difference renders claims of solidarity suspect. This is especially likely for those who rightfully cannot trust people who see themselves as outside out own relations of injustice. Commonality must be a result of open, mutual struggle; it cannot be assumed.

The possibility of just practices depends on fuller recognition of our differences and their often tangled and bloody histories. Until there are honest acknowledgments of our differences, hatreds, and divisions, and the multiplicity of positions as oppressor and oppressed, the call for unity can only be read as a wish to control others and a willful act of denial of the past and current conflicts that pervade the contemporary United States. Until there are fundamental redistributions of power among races, genders, and sexualities, the cry of "too much difference" must remain suspect. Justice is undermined by domination, not difference. To have mutual futures, we must cultivate new, unplatonic loves: of diversity, conflict, and that which is not shared in common.

Notes

1 Susan Moller Okin, "Gender Inequality and Cultural Differences," *Political Theory* 22, no. 1 (1994): 5.
2 Ibid., 5.
3 Ibid., 7.
4 Okin's concentration on Spelman's book rather than on writings by racialized women repeats the erasure of racial differences within feminist discourses. For extensive critiques of such erasures within feminist discourses and practices, see Maxine Baca Zinn, Lynn Weber Cannon, Elizabeth Higginbotham, and Bonnie Thornton Dill, "The Costs of Exclusionary Practices in Women's Studies," *Signs* 11, no. 2 (1986): 290–303; Maivan Clech Lam, "Feeling Foreign in Feminism," *Signs* 19, no. 4 (1994): 865–93; Ann duCille, "The Occult of True Womanhood: Critical Demeanor and Black Feminist Studies," *Signs* 19, no. 3 (1994): 561–629.
5 Okin, "Gender Inequality," 8.
6 Ibid., 9.

7   Chandra Talpade Mohanty, "Cartographies of Struggle: Third World Women and the Politics of Feminism," *Third World Women and the Politics of Feminism*, eds. Chandra Talpade Mohanty, Ann Russo, and Lourdes Torres (Bloomington: Indiana University Press, 1991), 71–2.

8   There are far too many works on the tangled histories of relations among White women, Black women, and feminism to cite. Examples include the following: Iris Berger, Elsa Brown, and Nancy A. Hewitt, "Intersections and Collision Courses: Women, Blacks, and Workers Confront Gender, Race, and Class," *Feminist Studies* 18, no. 2 (1992): 283–327; Micheline R. Malson, Elisabeth Mudimbe-Boyi, Jean F. O'Barr, and Mary Wyer, eds, *Black Women in America: Social Science Perspectives* (Chicago: University of Chicago Press, 1988); Paula Giddings, *When and Where I Enter: The Impact of Black Women on Race and Sex in America* (New York: Bantam, 1984); Angela Y. Davis, *Women, Race & Class* (New York: Random House, 1981); Patricia Hill Collins, *Black Feminist Thought* (New York: Routledge, 1990); Hazel V. Carby, *Reconstructing Womanhood: The Emergence of the Afro-American Novelist* (New York: Oxford University Press, 1987); Barbara Smith, ed., *Home Girls: A Black Feminist Anthology* (New York: Kitchen Table Press, 1983); Biddy Martin and Chandra Talpade Mohanty, "Feminist Politics: What's Home Got to Do with It?" *Feminist Studies/Critical Studies*, ed. Teresa de Lauretis (Bloomington: Indiana University Press, 1986); bell hooks, *Yearning: Race, Gender, and Cultural Politics* (Boston: South End Press, 1990); Nellie Y. McKay, "Acknowledging Differences: Can Women Find Unity Through Diversity" *Theorizing Black Feminisms: The Visionary Pragmatism of Black Women*, ed. Stanlie M. James and Abena P. A. Busa (New York: Routledge, 1993).

9   Patricia J. Williams, *The Alchemy of Race and Rights: Diary of a Law Professor* (Cambridge: Harvard University Press, 1991); and Toni Morrison, ed., *Race-ing Justice, En-gendering Power* (New York: Pantheon, 1992).

10 Okin, "Gender Inequality," 17.

11 Mohanty, "Cartographies of Struggle," 54.

12 See the essays in Mohanty, Russo, and Torres, *Third World Women*; in James and Busia, *Theorizing Black Feminisms*; Gayatri Chakravorty Spivak, "Subaltern Studies: Deconstructing Historiography," *In Other Worlds* (New York: Routledge, 1988), 197–221; Gita Sen and Lourdes Beneria, "Accumulation, Reproduction, and Women's Role in Economic Development: Boserup Revisited," *Signs* 7, no. 2 (1981): 279–98; and Aihwa Ong, *Spirits of Resistance and Capitalist Discipline: Factory Women in Malaysia* (Albany: SUNY Press, 1987).

13 Chandra Talpade Mohanty, "Under Western Eyes: Feminist Scholarship and Colonial Discourses," *Third World Women*, ed. Mohanty, Russo, and Torres; Mervat Hatem, "The Politics of Sexuality and Gender in Segregated Patriarchal Systems: The Case of 18th and 19th Century Egypt," *Feminist Studies* 12, no. 2 (1986): 251–74; and Trinh T. Minh-ha, *Woman/Native/Other* (Bloomington: Indiana University Press, 1989).

14 Okin, "Gender Inequality," 7.

15 McKay, "Acknowledging Differences," 273. See also Williams, *The Alchemy of Race and Rights*; and Toni Morrison, *Beloved* (New York: Signet, 1991).

16 Paul Gilroy, *The Black Atlantic: Modernity and Double Consciousness* (Cambridge, MA: Harvard University Press, 1993), 46.

17 McKay, "Acknowledging Differences," 276.

18 Toni Morrison, *Playing in the Dark: Whiteness and the Literary Imagination* (New York: Vintage, 1992), 10.

19 Ibid., 12.

20 McKay, "Acknowledging Differences," 276.

21 Ibid., 273.

22 On the meaning and uses of "raced," see Jane Flax, "Minerva's Owl," *Disputed Subjects* (New York: Routledge, 1993), 3–33. Contemporary American practices mark only some persons as "racialized," that is, as defined and determined by "race." All of us are, in fact, "raced"; no one exists outside socially constructed race/gender relations.

23   Gilroy, *Black Atlantic*, 2. See also Maria Lugones, "Purity, Impurity, and Separation," *Signs* 19, no. 3 (1994): 458–79; and Evelyn Brooks Higgenbotham, "African-American Women's History and the Metalanguage of Race," *Signs* 17, no. 2 (1992): 281–74.

24   Morrison, *Playing in the Dark*, 63; and Michael Omi and Howard Winat, *Racial Formations in the United States: From the 1960's to the 1980's* (New York: Routledge, 1986).

25   Wendy Brown, "Wounded Attachments," *Political Theory* 21, no. 3 (1993): 390–410.

26   Okin, "Gender Inequality," 19.

---

46   A Response to Jane Flax*

Susan Moller Okin

It is difficult to respond to Jane Flax's critique. She finds me at fault, partly for not doing what I did not set out to do – that is, for not focusing on questions of race and gender in the United States. She also criticizes me for doing what I tried to do – that is, for pointing out that there appear to be many similarities between the oppression of poor women in poor countries and that of many women in well-off Western industrialized countries. Flax says that my argument "does nothing to reduce [her] suspicion of internally undifferentiated concepts of gender that define 'woman' in terms of shared oppression." This is not surprising, for two reasons. First, I am not claiming what she thinks I am. Second, she pays no attention to the specifics of my argument, either philosophical or empirical.

In critiquing the anti-essentialist position, I do not say anything about what "defines 'woman.'" I do not claim that women in the First World "share" the oppression of Third World women (I do not know what this means); rather, I argue that in certain important respects their oppression is similar. Neither do I, as Flax claims, put forward "an internally undifferentiated and conflict-free concept of gender." I do not think that all aspects of gender oppression are similar in different contexts (see, e.g., my "Gender and Inequality and Cultural Difference," *Political Theory* 22, no. 1 [1994], 15–16), and I am clearly aware that race and class, as well as gender, are important factors in women's (and men's) lives (ibid., 7). I try to do two main things in the essay. I argue that those who charge "essentialism" at every turn should take on some of the burden of proof – should provide evidence that the differences among the situations of women are so much greater than the similarities that no meaningful generalizations can be made. And I provide at least some preliminary evidence that there are some important aspects of oppression that are cross-culturally experienced by many women. Thus Flax misrepresents the claims made in my essay.[1]

Second, it is unlikely that my argument will persuade Flax of anything unless she pays some attention to it. She does not address the two philosophical objections I raise regarding E. V. Spelman's critique of essentialism ("Gender Inequality," 7). Nor does she

* From *Political Theory*, 23/3 (August 1995), pp. 511–16. Reprinted by permission of Sage Publications.

mention any of the points I make or evidence I refer to about similarities in forms of women's oppression, whether to reject them or to concede them. Her focus, rather, is on my presumptuousness in even attempting to address the subject of such similarities. This is interesting given that, as I explained ("Gender Inequality," 8–9), I was responding to the suggestion made by Spelman – a leading anti-essentialist – that "we have to investigate different women's lives and see what they have in common." However, Flax claims that my attention to Third World women amounts to my "enlisting," "appropriat[ing]," and "objectif[ying]" them [see p. 472]. Rather than evaluating what I say, she asserts that the very structure of my text undermines my claim about similarities, for I "split agency and determination so that the agency exercised by racialized and 'Third World women' and the determined aspects of First World women theorists are invisible" [see p. 472].

I would like to respond to this point, in so far as I can understand what it means. If the first part of it means that I have not listened directly to the speech of Third World women, but have relied on writings of others about them, I acknowledge this. Both my lack of the many relevant languages and the lack of opportunity of many such women to express themselves in writing made it difficult for me to gain more direct access. Nevertheless, I thought (and still think) it worthwhile to present some of what I had learned from a sampling of the development literature most focused on women to an audience of theorists probably unfamiliar with much of it, in an attempt to evaluate that claim of anti-essentialists that differences among different groupings of women preclude the making of any generalizations about gender oppression.

As for the second part of Flax's assertion, I am not sure what I am supposed to do about my own "determined aspects" as a First World woman theorist, but I thought that trying to educate myself about the very different situations of some other women (even if only second-hand) might help. Should I instead reveal the aspects of my constituted self that Flax thinks are likely to have "determined" my beliefs? Not knowing me at all, she attempts to do this for me. But her attempt to psychoanalyze me *in absentia*, so as to derepress the unconscious guilt and other passions that apparently underlie the need of those like me to "project . . . the marks and burdens of race/gender . . . onto the other [see p. 475 above]," reveals some of the difficulties of such an enterprise. While she appears to think of me as a racially unmarked American, who must therefore harbor unconscious guilt about Black slavery, she neglects to mention the Maori wars, for which I am surely much more responsible, by her criteria, and which must presumably have played a larger determining role in the constitution of my psyche. While my racial and ethnic background may well be relevant to what I think about, as well as to what I think, I doubt that attempts to analyze me from a distance will help most readers to assess the merits of my argument.

While I am not only open to, but ready to, respond to criticism on the grounds that I am wrong, I am unsure of how to respond to criticism on the grounds that what I have done is offensive because of who I am. With the first kind of criticism, one can either try to argue against the points made, offering clarification or perhaps new evidence, or concede after reconsideration of them that the critic is right. But Flax's objection is not to any of the specific points that make up my argument, but that I have made it at all. "[E]vidently," she chides, I do not "hear how offensive" some of my statements might sound.[2] I could respond by apologizing. However, that would be hypocritical, for I knew even before I wrote the essay that it might offend some people. Angela Harris, for example, had already said that any finding by White women that the problems of women of other races were "similar to ours but more so" was insulting (quoted in "Gender Inequality," 8). I do not usually set out to risk insulting people, but in this case I thought it sufficiently important to try to further rational discussion among feminists about similarities and differences in women's lives that I was willing to take the chance of being considered offensive.

I am fundamentally at odds with Flax over two things. The first is her extreme subjectivism – her apparent underlying conviction that each person's situatedness renders her incapable of saying, and somehow reprehensible for trying to say, anything about anyone in a situation different from her own. Does this mean that what Alexis de Tocqueville had to say about democracy in the United States, what Gunnar Myrdal had to say about race relations, and what John Stuart Mill had to say about women are not only worthless but offensive pieces of argument that had been better not made? The far-reaching implications of this position undermine the possibility of any kind of social science or social theory – indeed, the possibility of any writing at all that is not autobiographical narrative (and maybe of that, too). According to Flax, my mistakes stem from my failure to grasp that "discourses of difference," which "represent attempts to theorize and undo relations of domination," "cannot be understood outside their specific historical contexts and purposes" [see p. 470 above]. And indeed, I *am* completely at a loss to understand how any discourse so socially situated that it cannot be understood outside its specific historical context and purposes could possibly have the critical force necessary for theorizing [about], much less undoing, any relations of domination. It would be helpful to have an example of one such discourse – even if no one but those from whose particular context it emanated would be able to understand it. Unfortunately, Flax is not apt to cite examples to clarify such general statements, nor evidence to back them up. Taken as a whole, the response reinforces one of the points I made in the paper – that there is a tendency on the part of postmodernist scholars to eschew the necessity of empirical evidence for their assertions. This makes arguing with them similar to disputing the Trinity with a devout Catholic. Until there is some agreement about whether evidence is necessary, about whether it should be gathered and discussed even at the risk of offending people, and about who can presume to write about what, it will be difficult to carry on a dialogue.

The second major cause of Flax's and my disagreement is due to our different prioritizing of trust (in contexts of difference), the redistribution of power, and justice. I think that considerations of justice – which should recognize differences as well as similarities – need to undergird efforts to redistribute power, and that trust is likely to be achieved in the process. Flax thinks that trust, achieved through acts of linguistic contrition and self-revelation, must come first; every person must completely acknowledge her situatedness, her consequent potential for error, and her guilt for any privilege in which she might be implicated. Only then can just practices emerge. But it is not at all clear how justice is supposed to emerge. If justice is "undermined by domination," as Flax suggests [p. 476 above], then it cannot be used to overthrow the relations of domination. Will this be done by "the new, unplatonic loves" of difference, and if so, how?

While this debate continues, women are being beaten by their husbands and are dying needlessly from botched illegal abortions, girls go undernourished and uneducated, and development policy is decided and executed. This is a critical juncture for feminist issues in a global context. The past few years have brought about a renewed focus on women's basic rights – routinely violated in many societies – as an essential part of "human rights."

There has also been widespread recognition, on the international stage, that women's and girls' welfare in many regions of the world lags seriously behind that of males, and that the well-being, the education, and the empowerment of women, important as they are to women themselves, are also crucial to the well-being of children and to the success of attempts to enable communities to become self-sustaining and to control population growth. This is a time when feminist scholars can contribute valuably to the efforts being made by international and non-governmental organizations to understand and to improve women's position in many parts of the world. It is important not to forget that many of women's concerns and needs vary from one social and cultural context to another and that the best ways of resisting oppression are also likely to be context-specific. But it is surely not the best of times to retreat into self-analysis or abstruse theorizing, on the grounds that differences among women make it impossible for us to speak about anyone but ourselves.

Notes

I would like to thank Brooke Ackerly and Elisabeth Hansot for their invaluable help in thinking about these issues. Neither, of course, should be considered responsible for anything I say.

1 Flax also says that my "argument relies on the assumption that First World women *are* outside the social relations that produce poor ones" [see p. 473 above, emphasis in original]. However, nothing in my paper rests on this assumption. I do not directly address relations between First World women and poor Third World women, which are in many cases very complex, but this does not mean that I assume there are no such relations. I would venture to suggest that some of the most oppressive and constraining practices inflicted on poor women in Third World countries have a lot more to do with their fathers' or their husbands' perceived needs and desires than with mine or Flax's. I am, nevertheless, aware that many of the clothes, toys, and other goods that she and I both buy are probably produced by the extremely low-paid labor of Third World women. My recognition of the connections between First World consumerism and Third World exploitation, however, does not undermine the evidence that there are some important similarities in the sexism practiced in both places. Why, after all, do so many of our consumer goods depend on the poorly paid labor of Third World *women*, who probably, like many women in our own society, go home from their low-paid jobs to do virtually all of the unpaid family work?

2 The statement Flax finds so offensive is the following: "*committed* outsiders can often be better analysts and critics of social injustice than those who live within the relevant culture." Is the statement offensive because of its content, or because of my status as an outsider? I raise the question because I have noticed, recently, statements similarly implying the presence of false consciousness in women made by feminists who have the benefit of being partly inside and partly outside of the cultural contexts they describe. Rosemary Ofeibea Ofei-Aboagye, a Ghanaian studying in Canada, was inspired by a Canadian court case to do something about wife beating in Ghana. Her study revealed that, although the abused wives perceived the beatings as "serious enough to warrant some outsider action," they had never thought about taking such action because "things could be worse . . . They had little or no information as to what to do, or, indeed, whether they had the 'right' to do anything at all." Pointing out how the physical punishment of disobedient wives is imbibed as a norm by small Ghanaians in their bedtime stories, Ofei-Aboagye says, "Attempts to eliminate domestic violence must deal with the bigger problem of *how to free someone from bondage who does not necessarily experience herself as being in bondage*," "Altering the Strands of the Fabric: A Preliminary Look at Domestic Violence in Ghana" *Signs* 19, no. 4 (1994): 924–38; quotations from 929, 936 (emphasis added). Farida Shaheed, a Pakistani sociologist, explaining the work done by Women Living under Muslim Laws, writes that the organization believes:

that the seeming helplessness of a majority of women in the Muslim world in effectively mobilizing against and overcoming adverse laws and customs stems not only from their being economically and politically less powerful but also from *their* erroneous belief that the only existence possible for a Muslim woman that allows her to maintain her identity – however that may be defined – is the one delineated for her in her own national context.

By contacts that inform these women of "the multiplicity of women's realities within the Muslim context . . . [and] the diversity of existing laws within the Muslim world," the group "gives material shape to alternatives . . . [and] encourage[s] women to dream of different realities – the first step in changing the present one." "Controlled or Autonomous: Identity and the Experience of the Network, Women Living under Muslim Laws," *Signs* 19, no. 4 (1994), 997–1019; quotations from 1006–7 (emphasis added). While both these women come from the cultures which they are now, in part, critiquing, they perceive their role as bringing information from outside the narrower cultural context, to help those within to envisage a different kind of life for themselves. I realize as I cite these articles that Flax may find me culpable of enlisting and exploiting their authors. Sorry, Drs Ofei-Aboagye and Shaheed; I hope you do not feel the same way.

---

47 Equality, Discrimination and Preferential Treatment*

Bernard R. Boxill

Introduction

Looking back on the United States Supreme Court's 1954 decision against segregated schools, and the civil rights revolution it started, many people in the late twentieth century began to hope that America's sense of fair play had finally gained the upper hand over prejudice and racism. They were therefore bitterly disappointed when, more than thirty years after that historic decision, a wave of racial incidents swept major American universities. They were aware, of course, that racism persisted; they would have been saddened, but not surprised, to hear of comparable or even worse incidents in some rural backwater in the deep South. But these incidents had happened in the North, and in traditional bastions of enlightenment and liberalism like the universities of Massachussetts, Michigan, Wisconsin, as well as Dartmouth, Stanford and Yale. What had caused the setback?

According to some pundits, the blame should be placed on preferential treatment. Writing in *Commentary*, for example, Charles Murray maintained that preferential treatment promotes racism because it maximizes the likelihood that blacks hired for a job, or admitted to a university, will be less capable than the whites besides them; and, he warned ominously that the recent racial incidents were only a 'thin leading edge of what we may expect in the coming years'.

* From *A Companion to Ethics*, edited by Peter Singer (Oxford: Blackwell, 1991), pp. 333–42. Reprinted with permission.

The advocates of preferential treatment reply that although preferential treatment may provoke immediate animosity it will in the long run lead to a racially and sexually harmonious society. Many also maintain that it is justified because it helps to compensate those who have been wrongly harmed by racist and sexist practices and attitudes. This essay is an attempt to evaluate these claims.

As the preceding paragraph suggests, there are two main kinds of argument for preferential treatment. The first, forward-looking argument, justifies preferential treatment because of its supposed good consequences. The second, backward-looking argument, justifies preferential treatment as compensation for past wrongful injuries. In this section I will briefly describe these arguments and the egalitarian principles they rely on. Let us begin with the backward-looking argument.

The most plausible version of the backward-looking argument relies on the principle of equal opportunity. The controlling idea of this principle is that the positions in a society should be distributed on the basis of a fair competition among individuals. It has two parts, both necessary to capture that idea. The first is that positions should be awarded to individuals with the qualities and abilities enabling them best to perform the functions expected of those filling the positions. Thus it requires that individuals be evaluated for positions strictly on the basis of their qualifications for those positions. The second is that individuals should have the same chances to acquire the qualifications for desirable positions. At a minimum this requires that elementary and secondary schools provide everyone with the same advantages whether they are rich or poor, black or white, male or female, handicapped or whole.

Most societies routinely violate both parts of the equal opportunity principle. In most societies, for example, people are frequently ruled out of consideration for positions simply because they are handicapped, or aged, or female, or members of a racial minority. And in most societies these violations of the first part of the equal opportunity principle are compounded by violations of the second part of the equal opportunity principle. Schools for the rich are usually better than schools for the poor; schools for whites are usually better than schools for blacks; talented girls are steered away from careers in engineering, architecture and the physical sciences; and the handicapped are more or less generally ignored.

Advocates of the backward-looking argument for preferential treatment maintain that violations of the equal opportunity principle are seriously unjust, and that those who have been harmed by these violations normally deserve compensation. In particular, they argue that preferential treatment is justified as a convenient means of compensating people who have been systematically denied equal opportunities on the basis of highly visible characteristics like being female or black.

Let us now consider the forward-looking argument. Advocates of this argument believe that preferential treatment will not only help to equalize opportunities by breaking down racial and sexual stereotypes, but will also have deeper and more important egalitarian consequences. To understand what these consequences are it is necessary to see that the equal opportunity principle has limitations as an egalitarian principle.

If we relied exclusively on the equal opportunity principle to distribute positions, we would tend to put the more talented in the more desirable positions. Since these positions usually involve work which is intrinsically more satisfying than the work other positions involve, our practice would tend to do more to satisfy the interests of the more talented in having satisfying work than to satisfy the like interests of the less talented. Further, because the more desirable positions generally pay better than the less desirable positions, use of the equal opportunity principle to distribute positions would also enable the more talented more fully to satisfy their other interests than the less talented, insofar at least as satisfying these other interests costs money.

In general then, exclusive reliance on the equal opportunity principle to distribute positions would tend to give greater weight to satisfying the interests of the more talented than to satisfying the like interest of the less talented. This violates the principle of equal consideration of interests which forbids giving any person's interests greater or lesser weight than the like interests of any other person. This principle does not presuppose any factual equality among individuals, for example, that they are equal in intelligence or rationality or moral personality. Consequently it is not contradicted by the fact that some people are more talented than others, and it does not have to be withdrawn because of that fact. It is a fundamental moral principle. It says that whatever the differences between people are, equal weight ought to be given to their like interests.

The principle of equal consideration of interests is the moral basis of the principle of equal opportunity. That principle has a limited place in egalitarian theories because it helps to implement the principle of equal consideration of interests. For, although it tends to give greater weight to the interests of the more talented in having satisfying work, it also tends to get talent into positions where it can better serve everyone's interests. This defence of the equal opportunity principle is, however, only partial. Although it justifies some reliance on the equal opportunity principle to match talent and occupational position, it does not justify the higher incomes which normally go with the more desirable positions. Admirers of the market often argue, of course, that such incomes are necessary to encourage the talented to acquire the qualifications required for the more desirable positions; but this is not very compelling given that these positions are already usually the most intrinsically satisfying in the society.

Advocates of the forward-looking argument for preferential treatment believe that it will help implement the principle of equal consideration of interests in addition to helping to equalize opportunities. Most societies don't come close to implementing either principle. They deny equal opportunities to certain individuals and give far less weight to satisfying the interests of those individuals than to satisfying the exactly similar interests of other individuals. For example, the interests of the aged in finding rewarding employment are routinely treated as being intrinsically less important than the similar interests of younger people, and for this reason they are often denied rewarding employment, even when they are the best qualified. The interests of the handicapped are more often downgraded in violation of the second part of the equal opportunity principle, as are the interests of women and the members of racial minorities. Such individuals are normally not given the same chance to acquire qualifications for desirable positions as men or those in the dominant racial group. If those favouring the forward-looking argument are right, preferential treatment will gradually abolish these violations of the equal opportunity principle, and help to usher in a society in which equal consideration is given to the like interests of all.

We have now sketched the two main arguments for preferential treatment and the egalitarian principles which are supposed to justify them. We must now see how these arguments are worked out in detail, and whether they can stand up to criticism. I will examine them mainly as they apply to preferential treatment for women and black people, but they can be applied to other cases where preferential treatment seems justified. In section (ii) I will examine the backward-looking argument, in section (iii) the forward-looking argument.

The Backward-Looking Argument

Perhaps the most common objection made against preferential treatment is that distinctions based on race or sex are invidious. Especially in America, critics tend to brandish Justice Harlan's dictum, 'Our Constitution is colour-blind . . .'.

Justice Harlan's point was that the American Constitution forbids denying a citizen any of the rights and privileges normally accorded to other citizens on account of his or her colour or race. The critics argue that the colour-blind principle Justice Harlan's dictum appeals to, and the similar sex-blind principle follow from the equal opportunity principle if we assume that citizens have rights to be evaluated for desirable positions solely on the basis of their qualifications for these positions, and that neither colour, nor sex is normally a qualification for a position. If they are right, preferential treatment violates the equal opportunity principle because it violates the colour-blind and sex-blind principles.

Preferential treatment certainly seems to violate the first part of the equal opportunity principle. It may, for example, require that a law school refuse admission to a white male and admit instead a woman or black who on most standards seems less qualified. But we must not forget the second part of the equal opportunity principle that everyone must have an equal chance to acquire qualifications. Unless it is satisfied, the competition for places will not be fair. And in the case under discussion the second part of the equal opportunity principle may very well not be satisfied. Whites generally go to better schools than blacks, and society supports a complex system of expectations and stereotyping which benefits white males at the expense of blacks and women. So preferential treatment need not make the competition for desirable places and positions unfair. On the contrary, by compensating women and blacks for being denied equal chances to acquire qualifications, it may make that competition more fair.

In America the objection is often made that if blacks deserve compensation for being unjustly discriminated against, so also do Italians, Jews, Irish, Serbo-Croatians, Asians, and practically every ethnic group in America, since these groups too have been unjustly discriminated against. The implication is that since the society obviously cannot meet all these claims for compensation, it has no good reason to meet black claims for compensation.

I find no merit in this objection. In America, at least, discrimination against blacks has historically been far more severe than discrimination against other racial and ethnic groups. Further, while various European ethnic groups were certainly discriminated against, they also profited from the severer discrimination against blacks since they immigrated to America to take the jobs native blacks were denied because of their race. So, the claim that many other ethnic groups besides blacks have been discriminated against falls short of its goal. If society can only meet some claims for compensation, it should meet the most pressing claims, and blacks appear to have the most pressing claims.

This argument is compelling if we focus our attention on certain segments of the black population, especially the black underclass. The black underclass is characterized by alarming and unprecedented rates of joblessness, welfare dependence, teenage pregnancies, out-of-wedlock births, female-headed families, drug abuse and violent crime. But most blacks are not in the underclass. In particular, many if not most of the blacks who benefit from preferential treatment have middle-class origins. To be preferentially admitted to law school or medical school, a black or woman must usually have attended a good college, and earned good grades, and this gives those from the middle and upper classes a decided advantage over those from the lower socio-economic classes. This fact has raised many eyebrows.

Some critics complained that it showed that the typical beneficiaries of preferential treatment have no valid claim for compensation. They evidently assumed that middle and upper-class blacks and women are unscathed by racist or sexist attitudes. This assumption is unjustified. Because of the civil rights victories, most forms of racial and sexual discrimination are illegal, and potential discriminators are likely to be wary of indulging their prejudices against blacks and women who have the money and education to make them pay for their illegality. But it does not follow that middle-class blacks and women are unscathed by racist and sexist attitudes. These attitudes do not support only discrimination. As I noted earlier, they support an elaborate system of expectations and stereotyping which subtly but definitely reduces the chances of women and blacks to acquire qualifications for desirable positions.

A somewhat more serious objection, stemming from the facts about the middle-class origins of the beneficiaries of preferential treatment, is that preferential treatment does not compensate those who most deserve compensation. The objection itself can be easily dismissed. As long as preferential treatment compensates those who deserve compensation, the fact that it does not compensate those who most deserve compensation is hardly an argument against it. The objection does, however, raise a serious difficulty since the society may not be able to compensate all those who deserve compensation. In that case present programmes of preferential treatment which benefit mainly middle-class blacks and women may have to be scrapped to make way for other programmes which compensate those who more deserve it. Besides the underclass, the main candidate is the 'working poor'.

Recent commentators have complained that in the hullabaloo about the underclass, society has forgotten the 'working poor'. The schools their children attend may be only slightly better than the schools black children in the underclass attend. If so, present programmes of preferential treatment may be particularly unfair. Because they compensate for the disadvantages of race and sex, but tend to ignore the disadvantages of class, they are apt to discriminate against white males from the 'working poor' and in favour of middle or even upper-class blacks or women whose opportunities are already much better.

Fortunately, blacks, women and the 'working poor' need not quarrel among themselves over who most deserves compensation. Although each of these groups has probably profited from discrimination against the other two, preferential treatment need not compensate one of them at the expense of the others. Conceivably, it can compensate all of them at the expense of white middle-class males. The members of this group have profited from discrimination against the members of the other groups, but have escaped all systematic discrimination, as well as the disadvantages of a lower-class education.

There is, however, a serious difficulty with viewing preferential treatment as compensation. Insofar as its beneficiaries have been denied equal opportunities, they deserve compensation; but it is not clear what compensation they deserve. Perhaps this will be clear for specific violations of the first part of the equal opportunity principle. If a firm denies a woman a job because of her sex, she deserves that job as compensation whenever it becomes available, even if others are at that time better qualified. In violations of the second part of the equal opportunity principle, it will be more difficult to determine what compensation those who have been wronged deserve. In particular it is far from clear that the compensation they deserve is desirable places and positions.

Let us consider this difficulty as it applies to the middle class beneficiaries of preferential treatment. In that case the stock answer to the difficulty is that, were it not for racial and sexual discrimination and stereotyping, the middle-class blacks and women who receive preferential treatment for desirable places and positions would have been the best qualified candidates for these places and positions. Unfortunately, however, it must contend with the equally stock objection that were it not for the past history of racial and sexual discrimination and stereotyping, the middle-class blacks and women who receive preferential treatment for desirable places and positions would probably not even exist, let alone be best qualified for any places and positions.

The point this objection makes cannot be gainsaid. Racial and sexual discrimination and stereotyping have radically changed the face of society. Had they never existed, the ancestors of middle-class blacks and women receiving preferential treatment would almost certainly never have met, which implies that the middle-class blacks and women receiving preferential treatment would almost certainly never have existed. But the objection may be irrelevant. The proposal is not to imagine a world without a history of racial and sexual discrimination and stereotyping; it is to imagine a world without racial and sexual discrimination and stereotyping in the present generation. In such a world, most of the middle-class blacks and women receiving preferential treatment would certainly exist; and the argument is that they would be the most qualified for the places and positions they receive in the present world because of preferential treatment.

Unfortunately, this won't quite do. In the alternative world we are asked to imagine, most of the middle-class blacks and women who receive preferential treatment would probably be much better qualified than they are in our present world, for they would not have to contend with any racial or sexual discrimination and stereotyping. It does not follow, however, that they would be the *most* qualified for the places and positions they receive because of preferential treatment. Present programmes of preferential treatment have forward-looking aims. They try to break down racial and sexual stereotypes by hastening the day when the races and sexes are represented in desirable positions in proportion to their numbers. This aim may not be consistent with a policy of benefiting only those who would be the most qualified for the places and positions they receive were there no racial or sexual discrimination and stereotyping.

It may seem that this difficulty can be met if we assume that the races and sexes are equally talented. Given this assumption it may seem to follow that in a world without racial or sexual discrimination, the races and sexes will be represented in desirable positions in proportion to their numbers, and accordingly that the blacks and women who receive preferential treatment for desirable places and positions would be the most qualified for these places and positions were there no racial or sexual discrimination. Both inferences, however, forget the complication of class.

Take first this complication as it applies to race. The black middle class is much smaller relative to the total black population than is the white middle class relative to the total white population. Those who compete for the desirable positions in society are drawn overwhelmingly from the middle classes; many in the lower socio-economic classes are excluded by their relatively poor education. Consequently, even if the races are equally talented, and there were no racial discrimination, the numbers of blacks in desirable positions would still be disproportionately small, and less than the number benefited by programmes of preferential treatment.

A weaker, but still significant version of this difficulty affects the argument for women. Since women are half the middle class, and half the population, perhaps we can argue that preferential treatment benefits women who would have been the most qualified for the positions it awards them, were there no sexual discrimination. It does not follow, however, that they deserve preferential treatment. The force of the appeal to a world without sexual discrimination and stereotyping is that, as far as possible, compensation should give people what they would have received in a world without injustice. Sexual discrimination is not, however, the only injustice. It is also an injustice that poor children are badly educated compared to rich children. In the absence of that injustice it is far from clear that were there no sexual discrimination and stereotyping the middle-class white women receiving preferential treatment would have been the most qualified for the positions it awards them.

I conclude that the forward-looking aims of preferential treatment outstrip its backward-looking justification. Present programmes of preferential treatment with their forward-looking aims cannot be justified solely on the backward-looking ground that they are compensation for violations of the equal opportunity principle.

The Forward-Looking Argument

As we saw earlier, the forward-looking aims of preferential treatment are to help make opportunities more equal, and ultimately, to enable society to give more equal consideration to the like interests of its members. A plausible case can be made for the claim that preferential treatment can help to make opportunities more equal. Suppose, for example, that the culture and traditions of a society lead its members to the firm conviction that women cannot be engineers. Since engineering is a rewarding and well-paid profession, and many women have the talent to excel at it, preferential treatment to encourage more women to become engineers may help to break the stereotype and equalize opportunities.

These possible consequences of preferential treatment may not be enough to justify it if, as some critics object, it violates the rights of white males to be evaluated for positions solely on the basis of their qualifications. This objection follows from the colour-blind and sex-blind principles, which in turn follow from the equal opportunity principle if we assume that the qualifications for positions can never include colour or sex, but must be things like scores on aptitude tests, and grades and university diplomas. I will argue, however, that this assumption is false, and consequently that the colour-blind and sex-blind principles must sometimes be relaxed. The crucial premise in my argument is the point made earlier that applications of the equal opportunity principle must be framed so as to serve the principle of equal consideration of interests.

Suppose that a state establishes a medical school, but most of the school's graduates practise in cities, so that people in rural areas do not get adequate medical care. And suppose it was found that applicants for medical school from rural areas are more likely upon graduation to practise in these areas than applicants from urban areas. If the state gave equal weight to the interests of rural and urban people in receiving medical treatment, it seems that it could justifiably require the medical school to begin considering rural origins as one of the qualifications for admission. This could cause some applicants from urban areas to be denied admission to medical school who would otherwise have been admitted; but I do not see how they could validly complain that this violated their rights; after all, the medical school was not established in order to make them doctors, but in order to provide medical services for the community.

A similar example shows how race could conceivably be among the qualifications for admission to medical school. Thus suppose that people in the black ghettos do not get adequate medical care because not enough doctors choose to practise there; and suppose it was found that black doctors are more likely than white doctors to practise in black ghettos; as in the previous case, if the state gave equal weight to the interests of black and white people in receiving medical treatment, it could easily be justified in requiring medical schools to begin considering being black as a qualification for admission.

Critics sometimes object that some white doctors are more likely to practise in black ghettos than some black doctors. Although what they say is undeniable, it does not invalidate the case for considering race a qualification for admission to medical school. Practically all policies awarding places and positions must rely on generalizations which everyone knows are not true in every case. For example, no reasonable person suggests that universities should abandon their policy of awarding places partly on the basis of test scores, although these scores do not, of course, infallibly predict success and failure in university.

The implication of this discussion is that what counts as qualification for a position is ultimately determined by the principle of equal consideration of interests. In particular, the qualifications for a position are the qualities and abilities a person needs in order to perform adequately the functions expected of anyone filling the position, and thereby to enable society to give more equal weight to the like interests of all. So conceived, colour and sex may be among the qualifications for positions. Although this implies that the colour-blind and sex-blind principles are not always acceptable, it does not challenge the equal opportunity principle. It allows that people have rights to be evaluated for positions strictly on the basis of their qualifications for these positions. What it denies is that preferential treatment necessarily violates these rights of white males.

Although preferential treatment need not violate anyone's rights, the forward-looking argument may be open to other sorts of objection. In particular, it depends on factual claims about the consequences of preferential treatment. Sceptics challenge these claims. They claim, for example, that preferential treatment powerfully encourages the belief that women and blacks cannot compete against white males without special help. This was the point of Charles Murray's criticism of preferential treatment cited in the beginning of this essay. But even if the sceptics are mistaken, and preferential treatment is justifiable on purely forward-looking grounds, the backward-looking considerations favouring it remain significant. People have like interests in being acknowledged to have equal moral standing. When, as in the US, a society has systematically excluded the members of a racial minority from the moral and political community, and in word and deed denied their equal moral standing, it does not acknowledge that equality simply by awarding them benefits, even if the benefits are generous. It must admit that they are owed these benefits because of their past treatment. In such cases especially, programmes based on preferential treatment are an important means to achieving an egalitarian society.

References

Harlan: Justice Harlan's comment may be found in: Bell, D. A., Jr., ed.: *Civil Rights: Leading Cases* (Boston: Little, Brown and Co., 1980). See *Plessy v. Ferguson*, 1896.

Murray, C.: 'The coming of custodial democracy', *Commentary*, 86(1988), 20–26.

48   All Animals Are Equal . . .*

or why the ethical principle on which human equality rests requires us to extend equal consideration to animals too

Peter Singer

"Animal Liberation" may sound more like a parody of other liberation movements than a serious objective. The idea of "The Rights of Animals" actually was once used to parody the case for women's rights. When Mary Wollstonecraft, a forerunner of today's feminists, published her *Vindication of the Rights of Woman* in 1972, her views were widely regarded as absurd, and before long an anonymous publication appeared entitled *A Vindication of the Rights of Brutes*. The author of this satirical work (now known to have been Thomas Taylor, a distinguished Cambridge philosopher) tried to refute Mary Wollstonecraft's arguments by showing that they could be carried one stage further. If the argument for equality was sound when applied to women, why should it not be applied to dogs, cats, and horses? The reasoning seemed to hold for these "brutes" too; yet to hold that brutes had rights was manifestly absurd. Therefore the reasoning by which this conclusion had been reached must be unsound, and if unsound when applied to brutes, it must also be unsound when applied to women, since the very same arguments had been used in each case.

In order to explain the basis of the case for the equality of animals, it will be helpful to start with an examination of the case for the equality of women. Let us assume that we wish to defend the case for women's rights against the attack by Thomas Taylor. How should we reply?

One way in which we might reply is by saying that the case for equality between men and women cannot validly be extended to nonhuman animals. Women have a right to vote, for instance, because they are just as capable of making rational decisions about the future as men are; dogs, on the other hand, are incapable of understanding the significance of voting, so they cannot have the right to vote. There are many other obvious ways in which men and women resemble each other closely, while humans and animals differ greatly. So, it might be said, men and women are similar beings and should have similar rights, while humans and nonhumans are different and should not have equal rights.

The reasoning behind this reply to Taylor's analogy is correct up to a point, but it does not go far enough. There are obviously important differences between humans and other animals, and these differences must give rise to some differences in the rights that each have. Recognizing this evident fact, however, is no barrier to the case for extending the basic principle of equality to nonhuman animals. The differences that exist between men and women are equally undeniable, and the supporters of Women's Liberation are aware that these differences may give rise to different rights. Many feminists hold that women have the right to an abortion on request. It does not follow that since these same feminists are campaigning for equality between men and women they must support the

* From Peter Singer, *Animal Liberation*, 2nd edn (New York: New York Review, 1990), pp. 1–23. © 1990 by Peter Singer.

right of men to have abortions too. Since a man cannot have an abortion, it is meaningless to talk of his right to have one. Since dogs can't vote, it is meaningless to talk of their right to vote. There is no reason why either Women's Liberation or Animal Liberation should get involved in such nonsense. The extension of the basic principle of equality from one group to another does not imply that we must treat both groups in exactly the same way, or grant exactly the same rights to both groups. Whether we should do so will depend on the nature of the members of the two groups. The basic principle of equality does not require equal or identical *treatment*; it requires equal consideration. Equal consideration for different beings may lead to different treatment and different rights.

So there is a different way of replying to Taylor's attempt to parody the case for women's rights, a way that does not deny the obvious differences between human beings and nonhumans but goes more deeply into the question of equality and concludes by finding nothing absurd in the idea that the basic principle of equality applies to so-called brutes. At this point such a conclusion may appear odd; but if we examine more deeply the basis on which our opposition to discrimination on grounds of race or sex ultimately rests, we will see that we would be on shaky ground if we were to demand equality for blacks, women, and other groups of oppressed humans while denying equal consideration to nonhumans. To make this clear we need to see, first, exactly why racism and sexism are wrong. When we say that all human beings, whatever their race, creed, or sex, are equal, what is it that we are asserting? Those who wish to defend hierarchical, inegalitarian societies have often pointed out that by whatever test we choose it simply is not true that all humans are equal. Like it or not we must face the fact that humans come in different shapes and sizes; they come with different moral capacities, different intellectual abilities, different amounts of benevolent feeling and sensitivity to the needs of others, different abilities to communicate effectively, and different capacities to experience pleasure and pain. In short, if the demand for equality were based on the actual equality of all human beings, we would have to stop demanding equality.

Still, one might cling to the view that the demand for equality among human beings is based on the actual equality of the different races and sexes. Although, it may be said, humans differ as individuals, there are no differences between the races and sexes as such. From the mere fact that a person is black or a woman we cannot infer anything about that person's intellectual or moral capacities. This, it may be said, is why racism and sexism are wrong. The white racist claims that whites are superior to blacks, but this is false; although there are differences among individuals, some blacks are superior to some whites in all of the capacities and abilities that could conceivably be relevant. The opponent of sexism would say the same: a person's sex is no guide to his or her abilities, and this is why it is unjustifiable to discriminate on the basis of sex.

The existence of individual variations that cut across the lines of race or sex, however, provides us with no defense at all against a more sophisticated opponent of equality, one who proposes that, say, the interests of all those with IQ scores below 100 be given less consideration than the interests of those with ratings over 100. Perhaps those scoring below the mark would, in this society, be made the slaves of those scoring higher. Would a hierarchical society of this sort really be so much better than one based on race or sex? I think not. But if we tie the moral principle of equality to the factual equality of the different races or sexes, taken as a whole, our opposition to racism and sexism does not provide us with any basis for objecting to this kind of inegalitarianism.

There is a second important reason why we ought not to base our opposition to racism and sexism on any kind of factual equality, even the limited kind that asserts that variations in capacities and abilities are spread evenly among the different races and between the sexes: we can have no absolute guarantee that these capacities and abilities really are distributed evenly, without regard to race or sex, among human beings. So far as actual abilities are concerned there do seem to be certain measurable differences both among races and between sexes. These differences do not, of course, appear in every case, but only when averages are taken. More important still, we do not yet know how many of these differences are really due to the different genetic endowments of the different races and sexes, and how many are due to poor schools, poor housing, and other factors that are the result of past and continuing discrimination. Perhaps all of the important differences will eventually prove to be environmental rather than genetic. Anyone opposed to racism and sexism will certainly hope that this will be so, for it will make the task of ending discrimination a lot easier; nevertheless, it would be dangerous to rest the case against racism and sexism on the belief that all significant differences are environmental in origin. The opponent of, say, racism who takes this line will be unable to avoid conceding that if differences in ability did after all prove to have some genetic connection with race, racism would in some way be defensible.

Fortunately there is no need to pin the case for equality to one particular outcome of a scientific investigation. The appropriate response to those who claim to have found evidence of genetically based differences in ability among the races or between the sexes is not to stick to the belief that the genetic explanation must be wrong, whatever evidence to the contrary may turn up; instead we should make it quite clear that the claim to equality does not depend on intelligence, moral capacity, physical strength, or similar matters of fact. Equality is a moral idea, not an assertion of fact. There is no logically compelling reason for assuming that a factual difference in ability between two people justifies any difference in the amount of consideration we give to their needs and interests. *The principle of the equality of human beings is not a description of an alleged actual equality among humans: it is a prescription of how we should treat human beings.*

Jeremy Bentham, the founder of the reforming utilitarian school of moral philosophy, incorporated the essential basis of moral equality into his system of ethics by means of the formula: "Each to count for one and none for more than one." In other words, the interests of every being affected by an action are to be taken into account and given the same weight as the like interests of any other being. A later utilitarian, Henry Sidgwick, put the point in this way: "The good of any one individual is of no more importance, from the point of view (if I may say so) of the Universe, than the good of any other." More recently the leading figures in contemporary moral philosophy have shown a great deal of agreement in specifying as a fundamental presupposition of their moral theories some similar requirement that works to give everyone's interests equal consideration – although these writers generally cannot agree on how this requirement is best formulated.[1]

It is an implication of this principle of equality that our concern for others and our readiness to consider their interests ought not to depend on what they are like or on what abilities they may possess. Precisely what our concern or consideration requires us to do may vary according to the characteristics of those affected by what we do: concern for the well-being of children growing up in America would require that we teach them to read; concern for the well-being of pigs may require no more than that we leave them with other pigs in a place where there is adequate food and room to run freely. But the basic element – the taking into account of the interests of the being, whatever those interests may be – must, according to the principle of equality, be extended to all beings, black or white, masculine or feminine, human or nonhuman.

Thomas Jefferson, who was responsible for writing the principle of the equality of men into the American Declaration of Independence, saw this point. It led him to oppose slavery even though he was unable to free himself fully from his slaveholding background. He wrote in a letter to the author of a book that emphasized the notable intellectual achievements of Negroes in order to refute the then common view that they had limited intellectual capacities:

> Be assured that no person living wishes more sincerely than I do, to see a complete refutation of the doubts I myself have entertained and expressed on the grade of understanding allotted to them by nature, and to find that they are on a par with ourselves . . . but whatever be their degree of talent it is no measure of their rights. Because Sir Isaac Newton was superior to others in understanding, he was not therefore lord of the property or persons of others.[2]

Similarly, when in the 1850s the call for women's rights was raised in the United States, a remarkable black feminist named Sojourner Truth made the same point in more robust terms at a feminist convention:

> They talk about this thing in the head; what do they call it? ["Intellect," whispered someone nearby.] That's it. What's that got to do with women's rights or Negroes' rights? If my cup won't hold but a pint and yours holds a quart, wouldn't you be mean not to let me have my little half-measure full?[3]

It is on this basis that the case against racism and the case against sexism must both ultimately rest; and it is in accordance with this principle that the attitude that we may call "speciesism," by analogy with racism, must also be condemned. Speciesism – the word is not an attractive one, but I can think of no better term – is a prejudice or attitude of bias in favor of the interests of members of one's own species and against those of members of other species. It should be obvious that the fundamental objections to racism and sexism made by Thomas Jefferson and Sojourner Truth apply equally to speciesism. If possessing a higher degree of intelligence does not entitle one human to use another for his or her own ends, how can it entitle humans to exploit nonhumans for the same purpose?[4]

Many philosophers and other writers have proposed the principle of equal consideration of interests, in some form or other, as a basic moral principle; but not many of them have recognized that this principle applies to members of other species as well as to our own. Jeremy Bentham was one of the few who did realize this. In a forward-looking passage written at a time when black slaves had been freed by the French but in the British dominions were still being treated in the way we now treat animals, Bentham wrote:

> The day *may* come when the rest of the animal creation may acquire those rights which never could have been withholden from them but by the hand of tyranny. The French have already discovered that the blackness of the skin is no reason why a human being should be abandoned without redress to the caprice of a tormentor. It may one day come to be recognized that the number of the legs, the villosity of the skin, or the termination of the *os sacrum* are reasons equally insufficient for abandoning a sensitive being to the same fate. What else is it that should trace the insuperable line? Is it the faculty of reason, or perhaps the faculty of discourse? But a full-grown horse or dog is beyond comparison a more rational, as well as a

more conversable animal, than an infant of a day or a week or even a month, old. But suppose they were otherwise, what would it avail? The question is not, Can they *reason*? nor Can they *talk*? but, Can they *suffer*?[5]

In this passage Bentham points to the capacity for suffering as the vital characteristic that gives a being the right to equal consideration. The capacity for suffering – or more strictly, for suffering and/or enjoyment or happiness – is not just another characteristic like the capacity for language or higher mathematics. Bentham is not saying that those who try to mark "the insuperable line" that determines whether the interests of a being should be considered happen to have chosen the wrong characteristic. By saying that we must consider the interests of all beings with the capacity for suffering or enjoyment Bentham does not arbitrarily exclude from consideration any interests at all – as those who draw the line with reference to the possession of reason or language do. The capacity for suffering and enjoyment is *a prerequisite for having interests at all,* a condition that must be satisfied before we can speak of interests in a meaningful way. It would be nonsense to say that it was not in the interests of a stone to be kicked along the road by a schoolboy. A stone does not have interests because it cannot suffer. Nothing that we can do to it could possibly make any difference to its welfare. The capacity for suffering and enjoyment is, however, not only necessary, but also sufficient for us to say that a being has interests – at an absolute minimum, an interest in not suffering. A mouse, for example, does have an interest in not being kicked along the road, because it will suffer if it is.

Although Bentham speaks of "rights" in the passage I have quoted, the argument is really about equality rather than about rights. Indeed, in a different passage, Bentham famously described "natural rights" as "nonsense" and "natural and imprescriptable rights" as "nonsense upon stilts." He talked of moral rights as a shorthand way of referring to protections that people and animals morally ought to have; but the real weight of the moral argument does not rest on the assertion of the existence of the right, for this in turn has to be justified on the basis of the possibilities for suffering and happiness. In this way we can argue for equality for animals without getting embroiled in philosophical controversies about the ultimate nature of rights.

In misguided attempts to refute the arguments of this book, some philosophers have gone to much trouble developing arguments to show that animals do not have rights.[6] They have claimed that to have rights a being must be autonomous, or must be a member of a community, or must have the ability to respect the rights of others, or must possess a sense of justice. These claims are irrelevant to the case for Animal Liberation. The language of rights is a convenient political shorthand. It is even more valuable in the era of thirty-second TV news clips than it was in Bentham's day; but in the argument for a radical change in our attitude to animals, it is in no way necessary.

If a being suffers there can be no moral justification for refusing to take that suffering into consideration. No matter what the nature of the being, the principle of equality requires that its suffering be counted equally with the like suffering – insofar as rough comparisons can be made – of any other being. If a being is not capable of suffering, or of experiencing enjoyment or happiness, there is nothing to be taken into account. So the limit of sentience (using the term as a convenient if not strictly accurate shorthand for the capacity to suffer and/or experience enjoyment) is the only defensible boundary of concern for the interests of others. To mark this boundary by some other characteristic like intelligence or rationality would be to mark it in an arbitrary manner. Why not choose some other characteristic, like skin color?

Racists violate the principle of equality by giving greater weight to the interests of members of their own race when there is a clash between their interests and the interests of those of another race. Sexists violate the principle of equality by favoring the interests of their own sex. Similarly, speciesists allow the interests of their own species to override the greater interests of members of other species. The pattern is identical in each case.

Most human beings are speciesists. The following chapters show that ordinary human beings – not a few exceptionally cruel or heartless humans, but the overwhelming majority of humans – take an active part in, acquiesce in, and allow their taxes to pay for practices that require the sacrifice of the most important interests of members of other species in order to promote the most trivial interests of our own species.

There is, however, one general defense of the practices to be described in the next two chapters that needs to be disposed of before we discuss the practices themselves. It is a defense which, if true, would allow us to do anything at all to nonhumans for the slightest reason, or for no reason at all, without incurring any justifiable reproach. This defense claims that we are never guilty of neglecting the interests of other animals for one breathtakingly simply reason: they have no interests. Nonhuman animals have no interests, according to this view, because they are not capable of suffering. By this is not meant merely that they are not capable of suffering in all the ways that human beings are – for instance, that a calf is not capable of suffering from the knowledge that it will be killed in six months time. That modest claim is, no doubt, true; but it does not clear humans of the charge of speciesism, since it allows that animals may suffer in other ways – for instance, by being given electric shocks, or being kept in small, cramped cages. The defense I am about to discuss is the much more sweeping, although correspondingly less plausible, claim that animals are incapable of suffering in any way at all; that they are, in fact, unconscious automata, possessing neither thoughts nor feelings nor a mental life of any kind.

Although, as we shall see in a later chapter, the view that animals are automata was proposed by the seventeenth-century French philosopher René Descartes, to most people, then and now, it is obvious that if, for example, we stick a sharp knife into the stomach of an unanesthetized dog, the dog will feel pain. That this is so is assumed by the laws in most civilized countries that prohibit wanton cruelty to animals. Readers whose common sense tells them that animals do suffer may prefer to skip the remainder of this section, moving straight on to page 499, since the pages in between do nothing but refute a position that they do not hold. Implausible as it is, though, for the sake of completeness this skeptical position must be discussed.

Do animals other than humans feel pain? How do we know? Well, how do we know if anyone, human or nonhuman, feels pain? We know that we ourselves can feel pain. We know this from the direct experience of pain that we have when, for instance, somebody presses a lighted cigarette against the back of our hand. But how do we know that anyone else feels pain? We cannot directly experience anyone else's pain, whether that "anyone" is our best friend or a stray dog. Pain is a state of consciousness, a "mental event," and as such it can never be observed. Behavior like writhing, screaming, or drawing one's hand away from the lighted cigarette is not pain itself; nor are the recordings a neurologist might make of activity within the brain observations of pain itself. Pain is something that we feel, and we can only infer that others are feeling it from various external indications.

In theory, we *could* always be mistaken when we assume that other human beings feel pain. It is conceivable that one of our close friends is really a cleverly constructed robot, controlled by a brilliant scientist so as to give all the signs of feeling pain, but really no more sensitive than any other machine. We can never know, with absolute certainty, that this is not the case. But while this might present a puzzle for philosophers, none of us has the slightest real doubt that our close friends feel pain just as we do. This is an inference, but a perfectly reasonable one, based on observations of their behavior in situations in which we would feel pain, and on the fact that we have every reason to assume that our friends are beings like us, with nervous systems like ours that can be assumed to function as ours do and to produce similar feelings in similar circumstances.

If it is justifiable to assume that other human beings feel pain as we do, is there any reason why a similar inference should be unjustifiable in the case of other animals?

Nearly all the external signs that lead us to infer pain in other humans can be seen in other species, especially the species most closely related to us – the species of mammals and birds. The behavioral signs include writhing, facial contortions, moaning, yelping or other forms of calling, attempts to avoid the source of pain, appearance of fear at the prospect of its repetition, and so on. In addition, we know that these animals have nervous systems very like ours, which respond physiologically as ours do when the animal is in circumstances in which we would feel pain: an initial rise of blood pressure, dilated pupils, perspiration, an increased pulse rate, and, if the stimulus continues, a fall in blood pressure. Although human beings have a more developed cerebral cortex than other animals, this part of the brain is concerned with thinking functions rather than with basic impulses, emotions, and feelings. These impulses, emotions, and feelings are located in the diencephalon, which is well developed in many other species of animals, especially mammals and birds.[7]

We also know that the nervous systems of other animals were not artificially constructed – as a robot might be artificially constructed – to mimic the pain behavior of humans. The nervous systems of animals evolved as our own did, and in fact the evolutionary history of human beings and other animals, especially mammals, did not diverge until the central features of our nervous systems were already in existence. A capacity to feel pain obviously enhances a species' prospects of survival, since it causes members of the species to avoid sources of injury. It is surely unreasonable to suppose that nervous systems that are virtually identical physiologically, have a common origin and a common evolutionary function, and result in similar forms of behavior in similar circumstances should actually operate in an entirely different manner on the level of subjective feelings.

It has long been accepted as sound policy in science to search for the simplest possible explanation of whatever it is we are trying to explain. Occasionally it has been claimed that it is for this reason "unscientific" to explain the behavior of animals by theories that refer to the animal's conscious feelings, desires, and so on – the idea being that if the behavior in question can be explained without invoking consciousness or feelings, that will be the simpler theory. Yet we can now see that such explanations, when assessed with respect to the actual behavior of both human and nonhuman animals, are actually far more complex than rival explanations. For we know from our own experience that explanations of our own behavior that did not refer to consciousness and the feeling of pain would be incomplete; and it is simpler to assume that the similar behavior of animals with similar nervous systems is to be explained in the same way than to try to invent some other explanation for the behavior of nonhuman animals as well as an explanation for the divergence between humans and nonhumans in this respect.

The overwhelming majority of scientists who have addressed themselves to this question agree. Lord Brain, one of the most eminent neurologists of our time, has said:

> I personally can see no reason for conceding mind to my fellow men and denying it to animals.
> . . . I at least cannot doubt that the interests and activities of animals are correlated with awareness and feeling in the same way as my own, and which may be, for aught I know, just as vivid.[8]

The author of a book on pain writes:

> Every particle of factual evidence supports the contention that the higher mammalian vertebrates experience pain sensations at least as acute as our own. To say that they feel less because they are lower animals is an absurdity; it can easily be shown that many of their senses are far more acute than ours – visual acuity in certain birds, hearing in most wild animals, and touch in others; these animals depend more than we do today on the sharpest possible awareness of a hostile environment. Apart from the complexity of the cerebral cortex (which does not directly perceive pain) their nervous systems are almost identical to ours and their reactions to pain remarkably similar, though lacking (so far as we know) the philosophical and moral overtones. The emotional element is all too evident, mainly in the form of fear and anger.[9]

In Britain, three separate expert government committees on matters relating to animals have accepted the conclusion that animals feel pain. After noting the obvious behavioral evidence for this view, the members of the Committee on Cruelty to Wild Animals, set up in 1951, said:

> . . . we believe that the physiological, and more particularly the anatomical, evidence fully justifies and reinforces the commonsense belief that animals feel pain.

And after discussing the evolutionary value of pain the committee's report concluded that pain is "of clear-cut biological usefulness" and this is "a third type of evidence that animals feel pain." The committee members then went on to consider forms of suffering other than mere physical pain and added that they were "satisfied that animals do suffer from acute fear and terror." Subsequent reports by British government committees on experiments on animals and on the welfare of animals under intensive farming methods agreed with this view, concluding that animals are capable of suffering both from straightforward physical injuries and from fear, anxiety, stress, and so on.[10] Finally, within the last decade, the publication of scientific studies with titles such as *Animal Thought, Animal Thinking,* and *Animal Suffering: The Science of Animal Welfare* have made it plain that conscious awareness in nonhuman animals is now generally accepted as a serious subject for investigation.[11]

That might well be thought enough to settle the matter, but one more objection needs to be considered. Human beings in pain, after all, have one behavioral sign that nonhuman animals do not have: a developed language. Other animals may communicate with each other, but not, it seems, in the complicated way we do. Some philosophers, including Descartes, have thought it important that while humans can tell each other about their experience of pain in great detail, other animals cannot. (Interestingly, this once neat dividing line between humans and other species has now been threatened by the discovery that chimpanzees can be taught a language.[12]) But as Bentham pointed out long ago, the ability to use language is not relevant to the question of how a being ought to be treated – unless that ability can be linked to the capacity to suffer, so that the absence of a language casts doubt on the existence of this capacity.

This link may be attempted in two ways. First, there is a hazy line of philosophical thought, deriving perhaps from some doctrines associated with the influential philosopher Ludwig Wittgenstein, which maintains that we cannot meaningfully attribute states of consciousness to beings without language. This position seems to me very implausible. Language may be necessary for abstract thought, at some level anyway; but states like pain are more primitive, and have nothing to do with language.

The second and more easily understood way of linking language and the existence of pain is to say that the best evidence we can have that other creatures are in pain is that they tell us that they are. This is a distinct line of argument, for it is denying not that non-language-users conceivably *could* suffer, but only that we could ever have sufficient reason to *believe* that they are suffering. Still, this line of argument fails too. As Jane Goodall has pointed out in her study of chimpanzees, *In the Shadow of Man*, when it comes to the expression of feelings and emotions language is less important than non-linguistic modes of communication such as a cheering pat on the back, an exuberant embrace, a clasp of the hands, and so on. The basic signals we use to convey pain, fear, anger, love, joy, surprise, sexual arousal, and many other emotional states are not specific to our own species.[13] The statement "I am in pain" may be one piece of evidence for the conclusion that the speaker is in pain, but it is not the only possible evidence, and since people sometimes tell lies, not even the best possible evidence.

Even if there were stronger grounds for refusing to attribute pain to those who do not have a language, the consequences of this refusal might lead us to reject the conclusion. Human infants and young children are unable to use language. Are we to deny that a year-old child can suffer? If not, language cannot be crucial. Of course, most parents understand the responses of their children better than they understand the responses of other animals; but this is just a fact about the relatively greater knowledge that we have of our own species and the greater contact we have with infants as compared to animals. Those who have studied the behavior of other animals and those who have animals as companions soon learn to understand their responses as well as we understand those of an infant, and sometimes better.

So to conclude: there are no good reasons, scientific or philosophical, for denying that animals feel pain. If we do not doubt that other humans feel pain we should not doubt that other animals do so too.

Animals can feel pain. As we saw earlier, there can be no moral justification for regarding the pain (or pleasure) that animals feel as less important than the same amount of pain (or pleasure) felt by humans. But what practical consequences follow from this conclusion? To prevent misunderstanding I shall spell out what I mean a little more fully.

If I give a horse a hard slap across its rump with my open hand, the horse may start, but it presumably feels little pain. Its skin is thick enough to protect it against a mere slap. If I slap a baby in the same way, however, the baby will cry and presumably feel pain, for its skin is more sensitive. So it is worse to slap a baby than a horse, if both slaps are administered with equal force. But there must be some kind of blow – I don't know exactly what it would be, but perhaps a blow with a heavy stick – that would cause the horse as much pain as we cause a baby by slapping it with our hand. That is what I mean by "the same amount of pain," and if we consider it wrong to inflict that much pain on a baby for no good reason then we must, unless we are speciesists, consider it equally wrong to inflict the same amount of pain on a horse for no good reason.

Other differences between humans and animals cause other complications. Normal adult human beings have mental capacities that will, in certain circumstances, lead them to suffer more than animals would in the same circumstances. If, for instance, we decided to perform extremely painful or lethal scientific experiments on normal adult humans, kidnapped at random from public parks for this purpose, adults who enjoy strolling in parks would become fearful that they would be kidnapped. The resultant terror would be a form of suffering additional to the pain of the experiment. The same experiments performed on nonhuman animals would cause less suffering since the animals would not have the anticipatory dread of being kidnapped and experimented upon. This does not mean, of course, that it would be *right* to perform the experiment on animals, but only that there is a reason, which is *not* speciesist, for preferring to use animals rather than normal adult human beings, if the experiment is to be done at all. It should be noted, however, that this same argument gives us a reason for preferring to use human infants – orphans perhaps – or severely retarded human beings for experiments, rather than adults, since infants and retarded humans would also have no idea of what was going to happen to them. So far as this argument is concerned nonhuman animals and infants and retarded humans are in the same category; and if we use this argument to justify experiments on nonhuman animals we have to ask ourselves whether we are also prepared to allow experiments on human infants and retarded adults; and if we make a distinction between animals and these humans, on what basis can we do it, other than a bare-faced – and morally indefensible – preference for members of our own species?

There are many matters in which the superior mental powers of normal adult humans make a difference: anticipation, more detailed memory, greater knowledge of what is happening, and so on. Yet these differences do not all point to greater suffering on the part of the normal human being. Sometimes animals may suffer more because of their more limited understanding. If, for instance, we are taking prisoners in wartime we can explain to them that although they must submit to capture, search, and confinement, they will not otherwise be harmed and will be set free at the conclusion of hostilities. If we capture wild animals, however, we cannot explain that we are not threatening their lives. A wild animal cannot distinguish an attempt to overpower and confine from an attempt to kill; the one causes as much terror as the other.

It may be objected that comparisons of the sufferings of different species are impossible to make and that for this reason when the interests of animals and humans clash the principle of equality gives no guidance. It is probably true that comparisons of suffering between members of different species cannot be made precisely, but precision is not essential. Even if we were to prevent the infliction of suffering on animals only when it is quite certain that the interests of humans will not be affected to anything like the extent that animals are affected, we would be forced to make radical changes in our treatment of animals that would involve our diet, the farming methods we use, experimental procedures in many fields of science, our approach to wildlife and to hunting, trapping and the wearing of furs, and areas of entertainment like circuses, rodeos, and zoos. As a result, a vast amount of suffering would be avoided.

So far I have said a lot about inflicting suffering on animals, but nothing about killing them. This omission has been deliberate. The application of the principle of equality to the infliction of suffering is, in theory at least, fairly straightforward. Pain and suffering are in themselves bad and should be prevented or minimized, irrespective of the race, sex, or species of the being that suffers. How bad a pain is depends on how intense it is and how long it lasts, but pains of the same intensity and duration are equally bad, whether felt by humans or animals.

The wrongness of killing a being is more complicated. I have kept, and shall continue to keep, the question of killing in the background because in the present state of human tyranny over other species the more simple, straightforward principle of equal consideration of pain or pleasure is a sufficient basis for identifying and protesting against all the major abuses of animals that human beings practice. Nevertheless, it is necessary to say something about killing.

Just as most human beings are speciesists in their readiness to cause pain to animals when they would not cause a similar pain to humans for the same reason, so most human beings are speciesists in their readiness to kill other animals when they would not kill human beings. We need to proceed more cautiously here, however, because people hold widely differing views about when it is legitimate to kill humans, as the continuing debates over abortion and euthanasia attest. Nor have moral philosophers been able to agree on exactly what it is that makes it wrong to kill human beings, and under what circumstances killing a human being may be justifiable.

Let us consider first the view that it is always wrong to take an innocent human life. We may call this the "sanctity of life" view. People who take this view oppose abortion and euthanasia. They do not usually, however, oppose the killing of nonhuman animals – so perhaps it would be more accurate to describe this view as the "sanctity of *human* life" view. The belief that human life, and only human life, is sacrosanct is a form of speciesism. To see this, consider the following example.

Assume that, as sometimes happens, an infant has been born with massive and irreparable brain damage. The damage is so severe that the infant can never be any more than a "human vegetable," unable to talk, recognize other people, act independently of others, or develop a sense of self-awareness. The parents of the infant, realizing that they cannot hope for any improvement in their child's condition and being in any case unwilling to spend, or ask the state to spend, the thousands of dollars that would be needed annually for proper care of the infant, ask the doctor to kill the infant painlessly.

Should the doctor do what the parents ask? Legally, the doctor should not, and in this respect the law reflects the sanctity of life view. The life of every human being is sacred. Yet people who would say this about the infant do not object to the killing of nonhuman animals. How can they justify their different judgments? Adult chimpanzees, dogs, pigs, and members of many other species far surpass the brain-damaged infant in their ability to relate to others, act independently, be self-aware, and any other capacity that could reasonably be said to give value to life. With the most intensive care possible, some severely retarded infants can never achieve the intelligence level of a dog. Nor can we appeal to the concern of the infant's parents, since they themselves, in this imaginary example (and in some actual cases), do not want the infant kept alive. The only thing that distinguishes the infant from the animal, in the eyes of those who claim it has a "right to life," is that it is, biologically, a member of the species Homo sapiens, whereas chimpanzees, dogs, and pigs are not. But to use *this* difference as the basis for granting a right to life to the infant and not to the other animals is, of course, pure speciesism.[14] It is exactly the kind of arbitrary difference that the most crude and overt kind of racist uses in attempting to justify racial discrimination.

This does not mean that to avoid speciesism we must hold that it is as wrong to kill a dog as it is to kill a human being in full possession of his or her faculties. The only position that is irredeemably speciesist is the one that tries to make the boundary of the right to life run exactly parallel to the boundary of our own species. Those who hold the sanctity of life view do this, because while distinguishing sharply between human beings and other animals they allow no distinctions to be made within our own species, objecting to the killing of the severely retarded and the hopelessly senile as strongly as they object to the killing of normal adults.

To avoid speciesism we must allow that beings who are similar in all relevant respects have a similar right to life – and mere membership in our own biological species cannot be a morally relevant criterion for this right. Within these limits we could still hold, for instance, that it is worse to kill a normal adult human, with a capacity for self-awareness and the ability to plan for the future and have meaningful relations with others, than it is to kill a mouse, which presumably does not share all of these characteristics; or we might appeal to the close family and other personal ties that humans have but mice do not have to the same degree; or we might think that it is the consequences for other humans, who will be put in fear for their own lives, that makes the crucial difference; or we might think it is some combination of these factors, or other factors altogether.

Whatever criteria we choose, however, we will have to admit that they do not follow precisely the boundary of our own species. We may legitimately hold that there are some features of certain begins that make their lives more valuable than those of other beings; but there will surely be some nonhuman animals whose lives, by any standards, are more valuable than the lives of some humans. A chimpanzee, dog, or pig, for instance, will have a higher degree of self-awareness and a greater capacity for meaningful relations with others than a severely retarded infant or someone in a state of advanced senility. So if we base the right to life on these characteristics we must grant these animals a right to life as good as, or better than, such retarded or senile humans.

This argument cuts both ways. It could be taken as showing that chimpanzees, dogs, and pigs, along with some other species, have a right to life and we commit a grave moral offense whenever we kill them, even when they are old and suffering and our intention is to put them out of their misery. Alternatively one could take the argument as showing that the severely retarded and hopelessly senile have no right to life and may be killed for quite trivial reasons, as we now kill animals.

Since the main concern of this book is with ethical questions having to do with animals and not with the morality of euthanasia I shall not attempt to settle this issue finally.[15] I think it is reasonably clear, though, that while both of the positions just described avoid speciesism, neither is satisfactory. What we need is some middle position that would avoid speciesism but would not make the lives of the retarded and senile as cheap as the lives of pigs and dogs now are, or make the lives of pigs and dogs so sacrosanct that we think it wrong to put them out of hopeless misery. What we must do is bring nonhuman animals within our sphere of moral concern and cease to treat their lives as expendable for whatever trivial purposes we may have. At the same time, once we realize that the fact that a being is a member of our own species is not in itself enough to make it always wrong to kill that being, we may come to reconsider our policy of preserving human lives at all costs, even when there is no prospect of a meaningful life or of existence without terrible pain.

I conclude, then, that a rejection of speciesism does not imply that all lives are of equal worth. While self-awareness, the capacity to think ahead and have hopes and aspirations for the future, the capacity for meaningful relations with others and so on are not relevant to the question of inflicting pain – since pain is pain, whatever other capacities, beyond the capacity to feel pain, the being may have – these capacities are relevant to the question of taking life. It is not arbitrary to hold that the life of a self-aware being, capable of abstract thought, of planning for the future, of complex acts of communication, and so on, is more valuable than the life of a being without these capacities. To see the difference between the issues of inflicting pain and taking life, consider how we would choose within our own species. If we had to choose to save the life of a normal human being or an intellectually disabled human being, we would probably choose to save the life of a normal human being; but if we had to choose between preventing pain in the normal human being or the intellectually disabled one – imagine that both have received painful but superficial injuries, and we only have enough painkiller for one of them – it is not nearly so clear how we ought to choose. The same is true when we consider other species. The evil of pain is, in itself, unaffected by the other characteristics of the being who feels the pain; the value of life is affected by these other characteristics. To give just one reason for this difference, to take the life of a being who has been hoping, planning, and working for some future goal is to deprive that being of the fulfillment of all those efforts; to take the life of a being with a mental capacity below the level needed to grasp that one is a being with a future – much less make plans for the future – cannot involve this particular kind of loss.[16]

Normally this will mean that if we have to choose between the life of a human being and the life of another animal we should choose to save the life of the human; but there may be special cases in which the reverse holds true, because the human being in question does not have the capacities of a normal human being. So this view is not speciesist, although it may appear to be at first glance. The preference, in normal cases, for saving a human life over the life of an animal when a choice *has* to be made is a preference based on the characteristics that normal humans have, and not on the mere fact that they are members of our own species. This is why when we consider members of our own species who lack the characteristics of normal humans we can no longer say that their lives are always to be preferred to those of other animals. This issue comes up in a practical way in the following chapter. In general, though, the question of when it is wrong to kill (painlessly) an animal is one to which we need give no precise answer. As long as we remember that we should give the same respect to the lives of animals as we give to the lives of those humans at a similar mental level, we shall not go far wrong.[17]

In any case, the conclusions that are argued for in this book flow from the principle of minimizing suffering alone. The idea that it is also wrong to kill animals painlessly gives some of these conclusions additional support that is welcome but strictly unnecessary. Interestingly enough, this is true even of the conclusion that we ought to become vegetarians, a conclusion that in the popular mind is generally based on some kind of absolute prohibition on killing.

The reader may already have thought of some objections to the position I have taken in this chapter. What, for instance, do I propose to do about animals who may cause harm to human beings? Should we try to stop animals from killing each other? How do we know that plants cannot feel pain, and if they can, must we starve? To avoid interrupting the flow of the main argument I have chosen to discuss these and other objections in a separate chapter, and readers who are impatient to have their objections answered may look ahead.

The next two chapters [not reproduced here] explore two examples of speciesism in practice. I have limited myself to two examples so that I would have space for a reasonably thorough discussion, although this limit means that the book contains no discussion at all of other practices that exist only because we do not take seriously the interests of other animals – practices like hunting, whether for sport or for furs; farming minks, foxes, and other animals for their fur; capturing wild animals (often after shooting their mothers) and imprisoning them in small cages for humans to stare at; tormenting animals to make them learn tricks for circuses and tormenting them to make them entertain the audiences at rodeos; slaughtering whales with explosive harpoons, under the guise of scientific research; drowning over 100,000 dolphins annually in nets set by tuna fishing boats; shooting three million kangaroos every year in the Australian outback to turn them into skins and pet food; and generally ignoring the interests of wild animals as we extend our empire of concrete and pollution over the surface of the globe.

I shall have nothing, or virtually nothing, to say about these things, because as I indicated in the preface to this edition, this book is not a compendium of all the nasty things we do to animals. Instead I have chosen two central illustrations of speciesism in practice. They are not isolated examples of sadism, but practices that involve, in one case, tens of millions of animals, and in the other, billions of animals every year. Nor can we pretend that we have nothing to do with these practices. One of them – experimentation on animals – is promoted by the government we elect and is largely paid for out of the taxes we pay. The other – rearing animals for food – is possible only because most people buy and eat the products of this practice. That is why I have chosen to discuss these particular forms of speciesism. They are at its heart. They cause more suffering to a greater number of animals than anything else that human beings do. To stop them we must change the policies of our government, and we must change our own lives, to the extent of changing our diet. If these officially promoted and almost universally accepted forms of speciesism can be abolished, abolition of the other speciesist practices cannot be far behind.

Notes

1 For Bentham's moral philosophy, see his *Introduction to the Principles of Morals and Legislation*, and for Sidgwick's see *The Methods of Ethics*, 1907 (the passage is quoted from the seventh edition; reprint, London: Macmillan, 1963), p. 382. As examples of leading contemporary moral philosophers who incorporate a requirement of equal consideration of interests, see R. M. Hare, *Freedom and Reason* (New York: Oxford University Press, 1963), and John Rawls, *A Theory of Justice* (Cambridge: Harvard University Press, Belknap Press, 1971). For a brief account of the essential agreement on this issue between these and other positions, see R. M. Hare, "Rules of War and Moral Reasoning," *Philosophy and Public Affairs*, 1(2) (1972).
2 Letter to Henry Gregoire, February 25, 1809.
3 Reminiscences by Francis D. Gage, from Susan B. Anthony, *The History of Woman Suffrage*, vol. 1; the passage is to be found in the extract in Leslie Tanner, ed., *Voices From Women's Liberation* (New York: Signet, 1970).
4 I owe the term "speciesism" to Richard Ryder. It has become accepted in general use since the first edition of this book, and now appears in *The Oxford English Dictionary*, second edition (Oxford: Clarendon Press, 1989).

5 *Introduction to the Principles of Morals and Legislation*, chapter 17.

6 See M. Levin, "Animal Rights Evaluated," *Humanist* 37 (July/August 1977), 14–15; M. A. Fox, "Animal Liberation: A Critique," *Ethics*, 88: 134–8 (1978); C. Perry and G. E. Jones, "On Animal Rights," *International Journal of Applied Philosophy*, 1 (1982) 39–57.

7 Lord Brain, "Presidential Address," in C. A. Keele and R. Smith, eds., *The Assessment of Pain in Men and Animals* (London: Universities Federation for Animal Welfare, 1962).

8 Ibid., p. 11.

9 Richard Serjeant, *The Spectrum of Pain* (London: Hart Davis, 1969), p. 72.

10 See the reports of the Committee on Cruelty to Wild Animals (Command Paper 8266, 1951), paragraphs 36–42; the Departmental Committee on Experiments on Animals (Command Paper 2641, 1965), paragraphs 179–82; and the Technical Committee to Enquire into the Welfare of Animals Kept under Intensive Livestock Husbandry Systems (Command Paper 2836, 1965), paragraphs 26–8 (London: Her Majesty's Stationery Office).

11 See Stephen Walker, *Animal Thoughts* (London: Routledge & Kegan Paul, 1983); Donald Griffin, *Animal Thinking* (Cambridge: Harvard University Press, 1984); and Marina Stamp Dawkins, *Animal Suffering: The Science of Animal Welfare* (London: Chapman & Hall, 1980).

12 See Eugene Linden, *Apes, Men and Language* (New York: Penguin, 1976); for popular accounts of some more recent work, see Erik Eckholm, "Pygmy Chimp Readily Learns Language Skill," *The New York Times*, June 24, 1985; and "The Wisdom of Animals," *Newsweek*, May 23, 1988.

13 *In the Shadow of Man* (Boston: Houghton Mifflin, 1971), p. 225. Michael Peters makes a similar point in "Nature and Culture," in Stanley and Roslind Godlovitch and John Harris, eds., *Animals, Men and Morals* (New York: Taplinger, 1972). For examples of some of the inconsistencies in denials that creatures without language can feel pain, see Bernard Rollin, *The Unheeded Cry: Animal Consciousness, Animal Pain, and Science* (Oxford: Oxford University Press, 1989).

14 I am here putting aside religious views, for example the doctrine that all and only human beings have immortal souls, or are made in the image of God. Historically these have been very important, and no doubt are partly responsible for the idea that human life has a special sanctity.... Logically, however, these religious views are unsatisfactory, since they do not offer a reasoned explanation of why it should be that all humans and no nonhumans have immortal souls. This belief too, therefore, comes under suspicion as a form of speciesism. In any case, defenders of the "sanctity of life" view are generally reluctant to base their position on purely religious doctrines, since these doctrines are no longer as widely accepted as they once were.

15 For a general discussion of these questions, see my *Practical Ethics* (Cambridge: Cambridge University Press, 1979), and for a more detailed discussion of the treatment of handicapped infants, see Helga Kuhse and Peter Singer, *Should the Baby Live?* (Oxford: Oxford University Press, 1985).

16 For a development of this theme, see my essay, "Life's Uncertain Voyage," in P. Pettit, R. Sylvan and J. Norman, eds., *Metaphysics and Morality* (Oxford: Blackwell, 1987), pp. 154–72.

17 The preceding discussion, which has been changed only slightly since the first edition, has often been overlooked by critics of the Animal Liberation movement. It is a common tactic to seek to ridicule the Animal Liberation position by maintaining that, as an animal experimenter put it recently, "Some of these people believe that every insect, every mouse, has as much right to life as a human." (Dr. Irving Weissman, as quoted in Katherine Bishop, "From Shop to Lab to Farm, Animal Rights Battle is Felt," *The New York Times*, January 14, 1989.) It would be interesting to see Dr. Weissman name some prominent Animal Liberationists who hold this view. Certainly (assuming only that he was referring to the right to life of a human being with mental capacities very different from those of the insect and the mouse) the position described is not mine. I doubt that it is held by many – if any – in the Animal Liberation movement.

49   The Ethics of Respect for Nature*

Paul W. Taylor

Human-Centered and Life-Centered Systems of Environmental Ethics

In this paper I show how the taking of a certain ultimate moral attitude toward nature, which I call "respect for nature," has a central place in the foundations of a life-centered system of environmental ethics. I hold that a set of moral norms (both standards of character and rules of conduct) governing human treatment of the natural world is a rationally grounded set if and only if, first, commitment to those norms is a practical entailment of adopting the attitude of respect for nature as an ultimate moral attitude, and second, the adopting of that attitude on the part of all rational agents can itself be justified. When the basic characteristics of the attitude of respect for nature are made clear, it will be seen that a life-centered system of environmental ethics need not be holistic or organicist in its conception of the kinds of entities that are deemed the appropriate objects of moral concern and consideration. Nor does such a system require that the concepts of ecological homeostasis, equilibrium, and integrity provide us with normative principles from which could be derived (with the addition of factual knowledge) our obligations with regard to natural ecosystems. The "balance of nature" is not itself a moral norm, however important may be the role it plays in our general outlook on the natural world that underlies the attitude of respect for nature. I argue that finally it is the good (well-being, welfare) of individual organisms considered as entities having inherent worth, that determines our moral relations with the Earth's wild communities of life.

In designating the theory to be set forth as life-centered, I intend to contrast it with all anthropocentric views. According to the latter, human actions affecting the natural environment and its non-human inhabitants are right (or wrong) by either of two criteria: they have consequences which are favorable (or unfavorable) to human well-being, or they are consistent (or inconsistent) with the system of norms that protect and implement human rights. From this human-centered standpoint it is to humans and only to humans that all duties are ultimately owed. We may have responsibilities *with regard* to the natural ecosystems and biotic communities of our planet, but these responsibilities are in every case based on the contingent fact that our treatment of those ecosystems and communities of life can further the realization of human values and/or human rights. We have no obligation to promote or protect the good of non-human living things, independently of this contingent fact.

A life-centered system of environmental ethics is opposed to human-centered ones precisely on this point. From the perspective of a life-centered theory, we have prima facie moral obligations that are owed to wild plants and animals themselves as members of the Earth's biotic community. We are morally bound (other things being equal) to protect or promote their good for *their* sake. Our duties to respect the integrity of natural

* From *Environmental Ethics*, 3/3 (1981), pp. 197–218

ecosystems, to preserve endangered species, and to avoid environmental pollution stem from the fact that these are ways in which we can make it possible for wild species populations to achieve and maintain a healthy existence in natural state. Such obligations are due those living things out of recognition of their inherent worth. They are entirely additional to and independent of the obligations we owe to our fellow humans. Although many of the actions that fulfill one set of obligations will also fulfill the other, two different grounds of obligation are involved. Their well-being, as well as human well-being, is something to be realized *as an end in itself.*

If we were to accept a life-centered theory of environmental ethics, a profound reordering of our moral universe would take place. We would begin to look at the whole of the Earth's biosphere in a new light. Our duties with respect to the "world" of nature would be seen as making prima facie claims upon us to be balanced against our duties with respect to the "world" of human civilization. We could no longer simply take the human point of view and consider the effects of our actions exclusively from the perspective of our own good.

The Good of a Being and the Concept of Inherent Worth

What would justify acceptance of a life-centered system of ethical principles? In order to answer this it is first necessary to make clear the fundamental moral attitude that underlies and makes intelligible the commitment to live by such a system. It is then necessary to examine the considerations that would justify any rational agent's adopting that moral attitude.

Two concepts are essential to the taking of a moral attitude of the sort in question. A being which does not "have" these concepts, that is, which is unable to grasp their meaning and conditions of applicability, cannot be said to have the attitude as part of its moral outlook. These concepts are, first, that of the good (well-being, welfare) of a living thing, and second, the idea of an entity possessing inherent worth. I examine each concept in turn.

(1) Every organism, species population, and community of life has a good of its own which moral agents can intentionally further or damage by their actions. To say that an entity has a good of its own is simply to say that, without reference to any *other* entity, it can be benefited or harmed. One can act in its overall interest or contrary to its overall interest, and environmental conditions can be good for it (advantageous to it) or bad for it (disadvantageous to it). What is good for an entity is what "does it good" in the sense of enhancing or preserving its life and well-being. What is bad for an entity is something that is detrimental to its life and well-being.[1]

We can think of the good of an individual nonhuman organism as consisting in the full development of its biological powers. Its good is realized to the extent that it is strong and healthy. It possesses whatever capacities it needs for successfully coping with its environment and so preserving its existence throughout the various stages of the normal life cycle of its species. The good of a population or community of such individuals consists in the population or community maintaining itself from generation to generation as a coherent system of generically and ecologically related organisms whose average good is at an optimum level for the given environment. (Here *average good* means that the degree of realization of the good of *individual organisms* in the population or community is, on average, greater than would be the case under any other ecologically functioning order of interrelations among those species populations in the given ecosystem.)

The idea of a being having a good of its own, as I understand it, does not entail that the being must have interests or take an interest in what affects its life for better or for worse. We can act in a being's interest or contrary to its interest without its being interested in what we are doing to it in the sense of wanting or not wanting us to do it. It may, indeed, be wholly unaware that favorable and unfavorable events are taking place in its life. I take it that trees, for example, have no knowledge or desires or feelings. Yet it is undoubtedly the case that trees can be harmed or benefited by our actions. We can crush their roots by running a bulldozer too close to them. We can see to it that they get adequate nourishment and moisture by fertilizing and watering the soil around them. Thus we can help or hinder them in the realization of their good. It is the good of trees themselves that is thereby affected. We can similarly act so as to further the good of an entire tree population of a certain species (say, all the redwood trees in a California valley) or the good of a whole community of plant life in a given wilderness area, just as we can do harm to such a population or community.

When construed in this way, the concept of a being's good is not coextensive with sentience or the capacity for feeling pain. William Frankena has argued for a general theory of environmental ethics in which the ground of a creature's being worthy of moral consideration is its sentience. I have offered some criticisms of this view elsewhere, but the full refutation of such a position, it seems to me, finally depends on the positive reasons for accepting a life-centered theory of the kind I am defending in this essay.[2]

It should be noted further that I am leaving open the question of whether machines – in particular, those which are not only goal-directed, but also self-regulating – can properly be said to have a good of their own.[3] Since I am concerned only with human treatment of wild organisms, species populations, and communities of life as they occur in our planet's natural ecosystems, it is to those entities alone that the concept "having a good of its own" will here be applied. I am not denying that other living things, whose genetic origin and environmental conditions have been produced, controlled, and manipulated by humans for human ends, do have a good of their own in the same sense as do wild plants and animals. It is not my purpose in this essay, however, to set out or defend the principles that should guide our conduct with regard to their good. It is only in so far as their production and use by humans have good or ill effects upon natural ecosystems and their wild inhabitants that the ethics of respect for nature comes into play.

(2)   The second concept essential to the moral attitude of respect for nature is the idea of inherent worth. We take that attitude toward wild living things (individuals, species populations, or whole biotic communities) when and only when we regard them as entities possessing inherent worth. Indeed, it is only because they are conceived in this way that moral agents can think of themselves as having validly binding duties, obligations, and responsibilities that are *owed* to them as their *due*. I am not at this juncture arguing why they *should* be so regarded; I consider it at length below. But so regarding them is a presupposition of our taking the attitude of respect toward them and accordingly understanding ourselves as bearing certain moral relations to them. This can be shown as follows:

What does it mean to regard an entity that has a good of its own as possessing inherent worth? Two general principles are involved: the principle of moral consideration and the principle of intrinsic value.

According to the principle of moral consideration, wild living things are deserving of the concern and consideration of all moral agents simply in virtue of their being members of the Earth's community of life. From the moral point of view their good must be taken into account whenever it is affected for better or worse by the conduct of rational agents. This holds no matter what species the creature belongs to. The good of each is to be accorded some value and so acknowledged as having some weight in the deliberations of all rational agents. Of course, it may be necessary for such agents to act in ways contrary to the good of this or that particular organism or group of organisms in order to further the good of others, including the good of humans. But the principle of moral consideration prescribes that, with respect to each being an entity having its own good, every individual is deserving of consideration.

The principle of intrinsic value states that, regardless of what kind of entity it is in other respects, if it is a member of the Earth's community of life, the realization of its good is something *intrinsically* valuable. This means that its good is prima facie worthy of being preserved or promoted as an end in itself and for the sake of the entity whose good it is. In so far as we regard any organism, species population, or life community as an entity having inherent worth, we believe that it must never be treated as if it were a mere object or thing whose entire value lies in being instrumental to the good of some other entity. The well-being of each is judged to have value in and of itself.

Combining these two principles, we can now define what it means for a living thing or group of living things to possess inherent worth. To say that it possesses inherent worth is to say that its good is deserving of the concern and consideration of all moral agents, and that the realization of its good has intrinsic value, to be pursued as an end in itself and for the sake of the entity whose good it is.

The duties owed to wild organisms, species populations, and communities of life in the Earth's natural ecosystems are grounded on their inherent worth. When rational, autonomous agents regard such entities as possessing inherent worth, they place intrinsic value on the realization of their good and so hold themselves responsible for performing actions that will have this effect and for refraining from actions having the contrary effect.

The Attitude of Respect for Nature

Why should moral agents regard wild living things in the natural world as possessing inherent worth? To answer this question we must first take into account the fact that, when rational, autonomous agents subscribe to the principles of moral consideration and intrinsic value and so conceive of wild living things as having that kind of worth, such agents are *adopting a certain ultimate moral attitude toward the natural world*. This is the attitude I call "respect for nature." It parallels the attitude of respect for persons in human ethics. When we adopt the attitude of respect for persons as the proper (fitting, appropriate) attitude to take toward all persons as persons, we consider the fulfillment of the basic interests of each individual to have intrinsic value. We thereby make a moral commitment to live a certain kind of life in relation to other persons. We place ourselves under the direction of a system of standards and rules that we consider validly binding on all moral agents as such.[4]

Similarly, when we adopt the attitude of respect for nature as an ultimate moral attitude we make a commitment to live by certain normative principles. These principles constitute the rules of conduct and standards of character that are to govern our treatment of the natural world. This is, first, an *ultimate* commitment because it is not derived from any higher norm. The attitude of respect for nature is not grounded on some other, more general, or more fundamental attitude. It sets the total framework for our responsibilities toward the natural world. It can be justified, as I show below, but its justification cannot consist in referring to a more general attitude or a more basic normative principle.

Second, the commitment is a *moral* one because it is understood to be a disinterested matter of principle. It is this feature that distinguishes the attitude of respect for nature from the set of feelings and dispositions that comprise the love of nature. The latter stems from one's personal interest in and response to the natural world. Like the affectionate feelings we have toward certain individual human beings, one's love of nature is nothing more than the particular way one feels about the natural environment and its wild inhabitants. And just as our love for an individual person differs from our respect for all persons as such (whether we happen to love them or not), so love of nature differs from respect for nature. Respect for nature is an attitude we believe all moral agents ought to have simply as moral agents, regardless of whether or not they also love nature. Indeed, we have not truly taken the attitude of respect for nature ourselves unless we believe this. To put it in a Kantian way, to adopt the attitude of respect for nature is to take a stance that one wills it to be a universal law for all rational beings. It is to hold that stance categorically, as being validly applicable to every moral agent without exception, irrespective of whatever personal feelings toward nature such an agent might have or might lack.

Although the attitude of respect for nature is in this sense a disinterested and universalizable attitude, anyone who does adopt it has certain steady, more or less permanent dispositions. These dispositions, which are themselves to be considered disinterested and universalizable, comprise three interlocking sets: dispositions to seek certain ends, dispositions to carry on one's practical reasoning and deliberation in a certain way, and dispositions to have certain feelings. We may accordingly analyze the attitude of respect for nature into the following components. (a) The disposition to aim at, and to take steps to bring about, as final and disinterested ends, the promoting and protecting of the good of organisms, species populations, and life communities in natural ecosystems. (These ends are "final" in not being pursued as means to further ends. They are "disinterested" in being independent of the self-interest of the agent.) (b) The disposition to consider actions that tend to realize those ends to be prima facie obligatory *because* they have that tendency. (c) The disposition to experience positive and negative feelings toward states of affairs in the world *because* they are favorable or unfavorable to the good of organisms, species populations, and life communities in natural ecosystems.

The logical connection between the attitude of respect for nature and the duties of a life-centered system of environmental ethics can now be made clear. In so far as one sincerely takes that attitude and so has the three sets of dispositions, one will at the same time be disposed to comply with certain rules of duty (such as nonmaleficence and non-interference) and with standards of character (such as fairness and benevolence) that determine the obligations and virtues of moral agents with regard to the Earth's wild living things. We can say that the actions one performs and the character traits one develops in fulfilling these moral requirements are the way one *expresses* or *embodies* the attitude in one's conduct and character. In his famous essay, "Justice as Fairness," John Rawls describes the rules of the duties of human morality (such as fidelity, gratitude, honesty, and justice) as "forms of conduct in which recognition of others as persons is manifested."[5] I hold that the rules of duty governing our treatment of the natural world and its inhabitants are forms of conduct in which the attitude of respect for nature is manifested.

The Justifiability of the Attitude of Respect for Nature

I return to the question posed earlier, which has not yet been answered: why *should* moral agents regard wild living things as possessing inherent worth? I now argue that the only way we can answer this question is by showing how adopting the attitude of respect for nature is justified for all moral agents. Let us suppose that we were able to establish that there are good reasons for adopting the attitude, reasons which are intersubjectively valid for every rational agent. If there are such reasons, they would justify anyone's having the three sets of dispositions mentioned above as constituting what it means to have the attitude. Since these include the disposition to promote or protect the good of wild living things as a disinterested and ultimate end, as well as the disposition to perform actions for the reason that they tend to realize that end, we see that such dispositions commit a person to the principles of moral consideration and intrinsic value. To be disposed to further, as an end in itself, the good of any entity in nature just because it is that kind of entity, is to be disposed to give consideration to *every* such entity and to place intrinsic value on the realization of its good. In so far as we subscribe to these two principles we regard living things as possessing inherent worth. Subscribing to the principles is what it *means* to so regard them. To justify the attitude of respect for nature, then, is to justify commitment to these principles and thereby to justify regarding wild creatures as possessing inherent worth.

We must keep in mind that inherent worth is not some mysterious sort of objective property belonging to living things that can be discovered by empirical observation or scientific investigation. To ascribe inherent worth to an entity is not to describe it by citing some feature discernible by sense perception or inferable by inductive reasoning. Nor is there a logically necessary connection between the concept of a being having a good of its own and the concept of inherent worth. We do not contradict ourselves by asserting that an entity that has a good of its own lacks inherent worth. In order to show that such an entity "has" inherent worth we must give good reasons for ascribing that kind of value to it (placing that kind of value upon it, conceiving of it to be valuable in that way). Although it is humans (persons, valuers) who must do the valuing, for the ethics of respect for nature, the value so ascribed is not a human value. That is to say, it is not a value derived from considerations regarding human well-being or human rights. It is a value that is ascribed to non-human animals and plants themselves, independently of their relationship to what humans judge to be conducive to their own good.

Whatever reasons, then, justify our taking the attitude of respect for nature as defined above are also reasons that show why we *should* regard the living things of the natural world as possessing inherent worth. We saw earlier that, since the attitude is an ultimate one, it cannot be derived from a more fundamental attitude nor shown to be a special case of a more general one. On what sort of grounds, then, can it be established?

The attitude we take toward living things in the natural world depends on the way we look at them, on what kind of beings we conceive them to be, and on how we understand the relations we bear to them. Underlying and supporting our attitude is a certain *belief system* that constitutes a particular world view or outlook on nature and the place of human life in it. To give good reasons for adopting the attitude of respect for nature, then, we must first articulate the belief system which underlies and supports that attitude. If it appears that the belief system is internally coherent and well-ordered, and if, as far as we can now tell, it is consistent with all known scientific truths relevant to our knowledge of the object of the attitude (which in this case includes the whole set of the Earth's natural ecosystems and their communities of life), then there remains the task of indicating why scientifically informed and rational thinkers with a developed capacity of reality awareness can find it acceptable as a way of conceiving of the natural world and our place in it. To the extent we can do this we provide at least a reasonable argument for accepting the belief system and the ultimate moral attitude it supports.

I do not hold that such a belief system can be *proven* to be true, either inductively or deductively. As we shall see, not all of its components can be stated in the form of empirically verifiable propositions. Nor is its internal order governed by purely logical relationships. But the system as a whole, I contend, constitutes a coherent, unified, and rationally acceptable "picture" or "map" of a total world. By examining each of its main components and seeing how they fit together, we obtain a scientifically informed and well-ordered conception of nature and the place of humans in it.

This belief system underlying the attitude of respect for nature I call (for want of a better name) "the biocentric outlook on nature." Since it is not wholly analyzable into empirically confirmable assertions, it should not be thought of as simply a compendium of the biological sciences concerning our planet's ecosystems. It might best be described as a philosophical world view, to distinguish it from a scientific theory or explanatory system. However, one of its major tenets is the great lesson we have learned from the science of ecology: the interdependence of all living things in an organically unified order whose balance and stability are necessary conditions for the realization of the good of its constituent biotic communities.

Before turning to an account of the main components of the biocentric outlook, it is convenient here to set forth the overall structure of my theory of environmental ethics as it has now emerged. The ethics of respect for nature is made up of three basic elements: a belief system, an ultimate moral attitude, and a set of rules of duty and standards of character. These elements are connected with each other in the following manner. The belief system provides a certain outlook on nature which supports and makes intelligible an autonomous agent's adopting, as an ultimate moral attitude, the attitude of respect for nature. It supports and makes intelligible the attitude in the sense that, when an autonomous agent understands its moral relations to the natural world in terms of this outlook, it recognizes the attitude of respect to be the only *suitable* or *fitting* attitude to take toward all wild forms of life in the Earth's biosphere. Living things are now viewed as *the appropriate objects of the attitude of respect* and are accordingly regarded as entities possessing inherent worth. One then places intrinsic value on the promotion and protection of their good. As a consequence of this, one makes a moral commitment to abide by a set of rules of duty and to fulfill (as far as one can by one's own efforts) certain standards of good character. Given one's adoption of the attitude of respect, one makes that moral commitment because one considers those rules and standards to be validly binding on all moral agents. They are seen as embodying forms of conduct and character structures in which the attitude of respect for nature is manifested.

This three-part complex which internally orders the ethics of respect for nature is symmetrical with a theory of human ethics grounded on respect for persons. Such a theory includes, first, a conception of oneself and others as persons, that is, as centers of autonomous choice. Second, there is the attitude of respect for persons as persons. When this is adopted as an ultimate moral attitude it involves the disposition to treat every person as having inherent worth or "human dignity." Every human being, just in virtue of her or his humanity, is understood to be worthy of moral consideration, and intrinsic value is placed on the autonomy and well-being of each. This is what Kant meant by conceiving of persons as ends in themselves. Third, there is an ethical system of duties which are acknowledged to be owed by everyone to everyone. These duties are forms of conduct in which public recognition is given to each individual's inherent worth as a person.

This structural framework for a theory of human ethics is meant to leave open the issue of consequentialism (utilitarianism) versus nonconsequentialism (deontology). That issue concerns the particular kind of system of rules defining the duties of moral agents toward persons. Similarly, I am leaving open in this paper the question of what particular kind of system of rules defines our duties with respect to the natural world.

The Biocentric Outlook on Nature

The biocentric outlook on nature has four main components. (1) Humans are thought of as members of Earth's community of life, holding that membership on the same terms as apply to all the non-human members. (2) The Earth's natural ecosystems as a totality are seen as a complex web of interconnected elements, with the sound biological functioning of each being dependent on the sound biological functioning of the others. (This is the component referred to above as the great lesson that the science of ecology has taught us.) (3) Each individual organism is conceived of as a teleological center of life, pursuing its own good in its own way. (4) Whether we are concerned with standards of merit or with the concept of inherent worth, the claim that humans by their very nature are superior to other species is a groundless claim and, in the light of elements (1, (2), and (3) above, must be rejected as nothing more than an irrational bias in our own favor. . . .

The Denial of Human Superiority

This fourth component of the biocentric outlook on nature is the single most important idea in establishing the justifiability of the attitude of respect for nature. Its central role is due to the special relationship it bears to the first three components of the outlook. This relationship will be brought out after the concept of human superiority is examined and analyzed.[6]

In what sense are humans alleged to be superior to other animals? We are different from them in having certain capacities that they lack. But why should these capacities be a mark of superiority? From what point of view are they judged to be signs of superiority and what sense of superiority is meant? After all, various non-human species have capacities that humans lack. There is the speed of a cheetah, the vision of an eagle, the agility of a monkey. Why should not these be taken as signs of *their* superiority over humans?

One answer that comes immediately to mind is that these capacities are not as *valuable* as the human capacities that are claimed to make us superior. Such uniquely human characteristics as rational thought, aesthetic creativity, autonomy and self-determination, and moral freedom, it might be held, have a higher value than the capacities found in other species. Yet we must ask: valuable to whom, and on what grounds?

The human characteristics mentioned are all valuable to humans. They are essential to the preservation and enrichment of our civilization and culture. Clearly it is from the human standpoint that they are being judged to be desirable and good. It is not difficult here to recognize a begging of the question. Humans are claiming human superiority from a strictly human point of view, that is, from a point of view in which the good of humans is taken as the standard of judgment. All we need to do is to look at the capacities of non-human animals (or plants, for that matter) from the standpoint of *their* good to find a contrary judgment of superiority. The speed of the cheetah, for example, is a sign of its superiority to humans when considered from the standpoint of the good of its species. If it were as slow a runner as a human, it would not be able to survive. And so for all the other abilities of non-humans which further their good but which are lacking in humans. In each case the claim to human superiority would be rejected from a non-human standpoint.

When superiority assertions are interpreted in this way, they are based on judgments of *merit*. To judge the merits of a person or an organism one must apply grading or ranking standards to it. (As I show below, this distinguishes judgments of merit from judgments of inherent worth.) Empirical investigation then determines whether it has the "good-making properties" (merits) in virtue of which it fulfills the standards being applied. In the case of humans, merits may be either moral or non-moral. We can judge one person to be better than (superior to) another from the moral point of view by applying certain standards to their character and conduct. Similarly, we can appeal to non-moral criteria in judging someone to be an excellent piano player, a fair cook, a poor tennis player, and so on. Different social purposes and roles are implicit in the making of such judgments, providing the frame of reference for the choice of standards by which the non-moral merits of people are determined. Ultimately such purposes and roles stem from a society's way of life as a whole. Now a society's way of life may be thought of as the cultural form given to the realization of human values. Whether moral or non-moral standards are being applied, then, all judgments of people's merits finally depend on human values. All are made from an exclusively human standpoint.

The question that naturally arises at this juncture is: why should standards that are based on human values be assumed to be the only valid criteria of merit and hence the only true signs of superiority? This question is especially pressing when humans are being judged superior in merit to non-humans. It is true that a human being may be a better mathematician than a monkey, but the monkey may be a better tree climber than a human being. If we humans value mathematics more than tree climbing, that is because our conception of civilized life makes the development of mathematical ability more desirable than the ability to climb trees. But is it not unreasonable to judge non-humans by the values of human civilization, rather than by values connected with what it is for a member of *that* species to live a good life? If all living things have a good of their own, it at least makes sense to judge the merits of non-humans by standards derived from *their* good. To use only standards based on human values is already to commit oneself to holding that humans are superior to non-humans, which is the point in question.

A further logical flaw arises in connection with the widely held conviction that humans are *morally* superior beings because they possess, while others lack, the capacities of a moral agent (free will, accountability, deliberation, judgment, practical reason). This view rests on a conceptual confusion. As far as moral standards are concerned, only beings that have the capacities of a moral agent can properly be judged to be either moral (morally good) or immoral (morally deficient). Moral standards are simply not applicable to beings that lack such capacities. Animals and plants cannot therefore be said to be morally inferior in merit to humans. Since the only beings that can have moral merits *or be deficient in such merits* are moral agents, it is conceptually incoherent to judge humans as superior to non-humans on the ground that humans have moral capacities while non-humans don't.

Up to this point I have been interpreting the claim that humans are superior to other living things as a grading or ranking judgment regarding their comparative merits. There is, however, another way of understanding the idea of human superiority. According to this interpretation, humans are superior to non-humans not as regards their merits but as regards their inherent worth. Thus the claim of human superiority is to be understood as asserting that all humans, simply in virtue of their humanity, have *a greater inherent worth* than other living things.

The inherent worth of an entity does not depend on its merits.[7] To consider something as possessing inherent worth, we have seen, is to place intrinsic value on the realization of its good. This is done regardless of whatever particular merits it might have or might lack, as judged by a set of grading or ranking standards. In human affairs, we are all familiar with the principle that one's worth as a person does not vary with one's merits or lack of merits. The same can hold true of animals and plants. To regard such entities as possessing inherent worth entails disregarding their merits and deficiencies, whether they are being judged from a human standpoint or from the standpoint of their own species.

The idea of one entity having more merit than another, and so being superior to it in merit, makes perfectly good sense. Merit is a grading or ranking concept, and judgments of comparative merit are based on the different degrees to which things satisfy a given standard. But what can it mean to talk about one thing being superior to another in inherent worth? In order to get at what is being asserted in such a claim it is helpful first to look at the social origin of the concept of degrees of inherent worth.

The idea that humans can possess different degrees of inherent worth originated in societies having rigid class structures. Before the rise of modern democracies with their egalitarian outlook, one's membership in a hereditary class determined one's social status. People in the upper classes were looked up to, while those in the lower classes were looked down upon. In such a society one's social superiors and social inferiors were clearly defined and easily recognized.

Two aspects of these class-structured societies are especially relevant to the idea of degrees of inherent worth. First, those born into the upper classes were deemed more worthy of respect than those born into the lower orders. Second, the superior worth of upper class people had nothing to do with their merits nor did the inferior worth of those in the lower classes rest on their lack of merits. One's superiority or inferiority entirely derived from a social position one was born into. The modern concept of a meritocracy simply did not apply. One could not advance into a higher class by any sort of moral or non-moral achievement. Similarly, an aristocrat held his title and all the privileges that went with it just because he was the eldest son of a titled nobleman. Unlike the bestowing of knighthood in contemporary Great Britain, one did not earn membership in the nobility by meritorious conduct.

We who live in modern democracies no longer believe in such hereditary social distinctions. Indeed, we would wholeheartedly condemn them on moral grounds as being fundamentally unjust. We have come to think of class systems as a paradigm of social injustice, it being a central principle of the democratic way of life that among humans there are no superiors and no inferiors. Thus we have rejected the whole conceptual framework in which people are judged to have different degrees of inherent worth. That idea is incompatible with our notion of human equality based on the doctrine that all humans, simply in virtue of their humanity, have the same inherent worth. (The belief in universal human rights is one form that this egalitarianism takes.)

The vast majority of people in modern democracies, however, do not maintain an egalitarian outlook when it comes to comparing human beings with other living things. Most people consider our own species to be superior to all other species and this superiority is understood to be a matter of inherent worth, not merit. There may exist thoroughly vicious and depraved humans who lack all merit. Yet because they are human they are thought to belong to a higher class of entities than any plant or animal. That one is born into the species *Homo sapiens* entitles one to have lordship over those who are one's inferiors, namely, those born into other species. The parallel with hereditary social classes is very close. Implicit in this view is a hierarchical conception of nature according to which an organism has a position of superiority or inferiority in the Earth's community of life simply on the basis of its genetic background. The "lower" orders of life are looked down upon and it is considered perfectly proper that they serve the interests of those belonging to the highest order, namely humans. The intrinsic value we place on the well-being of our fellow humans reflects our recognition of their rightful position as our equals. No such intrinsic value is to be placed on the good of other animals, unless we choose to do so out of fondness or affection for them. But their well-being imposes no moral requirement on us. In this respect there is an absolute difference in moral status between ourselves and them.

This is the structure of concepts and beliefs that people are committed to in so far as they regard humans to be superior in inherent worth to all other species. I now wish to argue that this structure of concepts and beliefs is completely groundless. If we accept the first three components of the biocentric outlook and from that perspective look at the major philosophical traditions which have supported that structure, we find it to be at bottom nothing more than the expression of an irrational bias in our own favor. The philosophical traditions themselves rest on very questionable assumptions or else simply beg the question. I briefly consider three of the main traditions to substantiate the point. These are classical Greek humanism, Cartesian dualism, and the Judeo-Christian concept of the Great Chain of Being.

The inherent superiority of humans over other species was implicit in the Greek definition of man as a rational animal. Our animal nature was identified with "brute" desires that need the order and restraint of reason to rule them (just as reason is the special virtue of those who rule in the ideal state). Rationality was then seen to be the key to our superiority over animals. It enables us to live on a higher plane and endows us with a nobility and worth that other creatures lack. This familiar way of comparing humans with other species is deeply ingrained in our Western philosophical outlook. The point to consider here is that this view does not actually provide an argument *for* human superiority but rather makes explicit the framework of thought that is implicitly used by those who think of humans as inherently superior to non-humans. The Greeks who held that humans, in virtue of their rational capacities, have a kind of worth greater than that of any non-rational being, never looked at rationality as but one capacity of living things among many others. But when we consider rationality from the standpoint of the first three elements of the ecological outlook, we see that its value lies in its importance for *human* life. Other creatures achieve their species-specific good without the need of rationality, although they often make use of capacities that humans lack. So the humanistic outlook of classical Greek thought does not give us a neutral (non-question-begging) ground on which to construct a scale of degrees of inherent worth possessed by different species of living things.

The second tradition, centering on the Cartesian dualism of soul and body, also fails to justify the claim to human superiority. That superiority is supposed to derive from the fact that we have souls while animals do not. Animals are mere automata and lack the divine element that makes us spiritual beings. I won't go into the now familiar criticisms of this two-substance view. I only add the point that, even if humans are composed of an immaterial, unextended soul and a material, extended body, this in itself is not a reason to deem them of greater worth than entities that are only bodies. Why is a soul substance a thing that adds value to its possessor? Unless some theological reasoning is offered here (which many, including myself, would find unacceptable on epistemological grounds), no logical connection is evident. An immaterial something which thinks is better than a material something which does not think only if thinking itself has value, either intrinsically or instrumentally. Now it is intrinsically valuable to humans alone, who value it as an end in itself, and it is instrumentally valuable to those who benefit from it, namely humans.

For animals that neither enjoy thinking for its own sake nor need it for living the kind of life for which they are best adapted, it has no value. Even if "thinking" is broadened to include all forms of consciousness, there are still many living things that can do without it and yet live what is for their species a good life. The anthropocentricity underlying the claim to human superiority runs throughout Cartesian dualism.

A third major source of the idea of human superiority is the Judeo-Christian concept of the Great Chain of Being. Humans are superior to animals and plants because their Creator has given them a higher place on the chain. It begins with God at the top, and then moves to the angels, who are lower than God but higher than humans, then to humans, positioned between the angels and the beasts (partaking of the nature of both), and then on down to the lower levels occupied by non-human animals, plants, and finally inanimate objects. Humans, being "made in God's image," are inherently superior to animals and plants by virtue of their being closer (in their essential nature) to God.

The metaphysical and epistemological difficulties with this conception of a hierarchy of entities are, in my mind, insuperable. Without entering into this matter here, I only point out that if we are unwilling to accept the metaphysics of traditional Judaism and Christianity, we are again left without good reasons for holding to the claim of inherent human superiority.

The foregoing considerations (and others like them) leave us with but one ground for the assertion that a human being, regardless of merit, is a higher kind of entity than any other living thing. This is the mere fact of the genetic makeup of the species *Homo sapiens*. But this is surely irrational and arbitrary. Why should the arrangement of genes of a certain type be a mark of superior value, especially when this fact about an organism is taken by itself, unrelated to any other aspect of its life? We might just as well refer to any other genetic makeup as a ground of superior value. Clearly we are confronted here with a wholly arbitrary claim that can only be explained as an irrational bias in our own favor.

That the claim is nothing more than a deep-seated prejudice is brought home to us when we look at our relation to other species in the light of the first three elements of the biocentric outlook. Those elements taken conjointly give us a certain overall view of the natural world and of the place of humans in it. When we take this view we come to understand other living things, their environmental conditions, and their ecological relationships in such a way as to awake in us a deep sense of our kinship with them as fellow members of the Earth's community of life. Humans and non-humans alike are viewed together as integral parts of one unified whole in which all living things are functionally interrelated. Finally, when our awareness focuses on the individual lives of plants and animals, each is seen to share with us the characteristic of being a teleological center of life striving to realize its own good in its own unique way.

As this entire belief system becomes part of the conceptual framework through which we understand and perceive the world, we come to see ourselves as bearing a certain moral relation to non-human forms of life. Our ethical role in nature takes on a new significance. We begin to look at other species as we look at ourselves, seeing them as beings which have a good they are striving to realize just as we have a good we are striving to realize. We accordingly develop the disposition to view the world from the standpoint of their good as well as from the standpoint of our own good. Now if the groundlessness of the claim that humans are inherently superior to other species were brought clearly before our minds, we would not remain intellectually neutral toward that claim but would reject it as being fundamentally at variance with our total world outlook. In the absence of any good reasons for holding it, the assertion of human superiority would then appear simply as the expression of an irrational and self-serving prejudice that favors one particular species over several million others.

Rejecting the notion of human superiority entails its positive counterpart: the doctrine of species impartiality. One who accepts that doctrine regards all living things as possessing inherent worth – the *same* inherent worth, since no one species has been shown to be either "higher" or "lower" than any other. Now we saw earlier that, in so far as one thinks of a living thing as possessing inherent worth, one considers it to be the appropriate object of the attitude of respect and believes that attitude to be the only fitting or suitable one for all moral agents to take toward it.

Here, then, is the key to understanding how the attitude of respect is rooted in the biocentric outlook on nature. The basic connection is made through the denial of human superiority. Once we reject the claim that humans are superior either in merit or in worth to other living things, we are ready to adopt the attitude of respect. The denial of human superiority is itself the result of taking the perspective on nature built into the first three elements of the biocentric outlook.

Now the first three elements of the biocentric outlook, it seems clear, would be found acceptable to any rational and scientifically informed thinker who is fully "open" to the reality of the lives of non-human organisms. Without denying our distinctively human characteristics, such a thinker can acknowledge the fundamental respects in which we are members of the Earth's community of life and in which the biological conditions necessary for the realization of our human values are inextricably linked with the whole system of nature. In addition, the conception of individual living things as teleological centers of life simply articulates how a scientifically informed thinker comes to understand them as the result of increasingly careful and detailed observations. Thus, the biocentric outlook recommends itself as an acceptable system of concepts and beliefs to anyone who is clear-minded, unbiased, and factually enlightened, and who has a developed capacity of reality awareness with regard to the lives of individual organisms. This, I submit, is as good a reason for making the moral commitment involved in adopting the attitude of respect for nature as any theory of environmental ethics could possibly have.

Moral Rights and the Matter of Competing Claims

I have not asserted anywhere in the foregoing account that animals or plants have moral rights. This omission was deliberate. I do not think that the reference class of the concept, bearer of moral rights, should be extended to include non-human living things. My reasons for taking this position, however, go beyond the scope of this paper. I believe I have been able to accomplish many of the same ends which those who ascribe rights to animals or plants wish to accomplish. There is no reason, moreover, why plants and animals, including whole species populations and life communities, cannot be accorded *legal* rights under my theory. To grant them legal protection could be interpreted as giving them legal entitlement to be protected, and this, in fact, would be a means by which a society that subscribed to the ethics of respect for nature could give public recognition to their inherent worth.

There remains the problem of competing claims, even when wild plants and animals are not thought of as bearers of moral rights. If we accept the biocentric outlook and accordingly adopt the attitude of respect for nature as our ultimate moral attitude, how do we resolve conflicts that arise from our respect for persons in the domain of human ethics and our respect for nature in the domain of environmental ethics? This is a question that cannot adequately be dealt with here. My main purpose in this paper has been to try to establish a base point from which we can start working toward a solution to the problem. I have shown why we cannot just begin with an initial presumption in favor of the interests of our own species. It is after all within our power as moral beings to place limits on human population and technology with the deliberate intention of sharing the Earth's bounty with other species. That such sharing is an ideal difficult to realize even in an approximate way does not take away its claim to our deepest moral commitment.

Notes

1 The conceptual links between an entity *having* a good, something being good *for* it, and events doing good *to* it are examined by G. H. Von Wright in *The Varieties of Goodness* (New York: Humanities Press, 1963), chs 3 and 5.

2 See W. K. Frankena, "Ethics and the Environment," In K. E. Goodpaster and K. M. Sayre, eds, *Ethics and Problems of the 21st Century* (Notre Dame: University of Notre Dame Press, 1979), 3–20. I critically examine Frankena's views in "Frankena on Environmental Ethics," *Monist*, 64: 3 (July 1981,) 313–24.

3 In the light of considerations set forth in Daniel Dennett's *Brainstorms: Philosophical Essays on Mind and Psychology* (Montgomery, VT: Bradford Books, 1978), it is advisable to leave this question unsettled at this time. When machines are developed that function in the way our brains do, we may well come to deem them proper subjects of moral consideration.

4 I have analyzed the nature of this commitment of human ethics in "On Taking the Moral Point of View," *Midwest Studies in Philosophy*, vol. 3, *Studies in Ethical Theory* (1978), 35–61.

5 John Rawls, "Justice as Fairness," *Philosophical Review*, 67 (1958), 183.

6 My criticisms of the dogma of human superiority gain independent support from a carefully reasoned essay by R. and V. Routley showing the many logical weaknesses in arguments for human-
centered theories of environmental ethics. R. and V. Routley, "Against the Inevitability of
Human Chauvinism," in K. E. Goodpaster and K. M. Sayre, eds, *Ethics and Problems of the 21st
Century* (Notre Dame: University of Notre Dame Press, 1979), 36–59.

7 For this way of distinguishing between merit and inherent worth, I am indebted to Gregory
Vlastos, "Justice and Equality," in R. Brandt ed., *Social Justice* (Englewood Cliffs, NJ: Prentice-
Hall, 1962), 31–72.

Ethics: Suggestions for Further Reading

Virginia Held, ed., *Justice and Care: Essential Readings in Feminist Ethics* (Boulder, CO: Westview,
1995).

Thomas E. Hill, Jr., *Dignity and Practical Reason in Kant's Moral Theory* (Ithaca, NY: Cornell
University Press, 1992).

Eva Feder Kittay, and Diana T. Meyers, eds., *Women and Moral Theory* (Totowa, NJ: Rowman &
Littlefield, 1987).

Tibor Machan, ed., *The Libertarian Alternative* (Chicago, IL: Nelson-Hall, 1974).

Alasdair MacIntyre, *After Virtue* (Notre Dame, IN: University of Notre Dame Press, 1981).

Onora O'Neill, *Acting on Principle: An Essay on Kantian Ethics* (New York: Columbia University
Press, 1975).

Tom Regan, *The Case for Animal Rights* (Berkeley, CA: University of California Press, 1984).

Amartya Sen and Bernard Williams, eds., *Utilitarianism and Beyond* (Cambridge: Cambridge University Press, 1982).

J. J. C. Smart and Bernard Williams, *Utilitarianism: For and Against.* (Cambridge: Cambridge University Press, 1973).

James P. Sterba, *Justice for Here and Now* (New York: Cambridge University Press, 1998).

INDEX

absurdity of life,
  in Camus, 279, 291, 294–5,
    305–12, 326
  in Craig, 279, 288–302
  in Nagel, 280, 322–9, 340–1
  in Sartre, 291
  and suicide, 306–10, 311–12,
    329
  in Tolstoy, 356
acquisition, justice in, 446–7
action, affirmative, as moral, 76,
  366, 482–9
Alston, William P., 123 n. 8
altruism, and egoism, 377,
  378–82
analogy, and argument from
  design, 140, 142, 145–50
Anderson, Bernhard, 207
anger, and incompatibilism,
  265–6
anguish, and Sartre, 316–17,
  320
animals,
  in Descartes, 495, 498, 516
  and free will, 189–90 n. 24
  and human superiority, 512
  and interests, 495
  moral status, 366, 429,
    490–503, 518
  right to life, 500–2
  and suffering, 189–90 n. 24,
    494–500, 502–3
Anscombe, G. E. M., 359, 360
Anselm of Canterbury, St.,
  and cosmological argument,
    111
  and free will, 181, 238
  and ontological argument,
    104, 106–7, 111–22, 126
anthropocentrism, and respect
  for nature, 505, 512–18
anxiety, in Camus, 308
Aquinas, St. Thomas,

and cosmological argument,
  124, 143–4, 232
as male chauvinist, 200 n. 6
Aristotle,
  and causation, 231, 234, 235
  and cosmological argument,
    124
  and justice, 425
  and male domination, 73
  and purpose of life, 279, 332
association of ideas, in Hume,
  36–7, 47–9
atheism,
  and existentialism, 104, 280,
    314–21
  and humanism, 295
  and philosophes, 315
  practical impossibility, 279,
    294–9, 300
Auden, W. H., Spain, 357
Augustine of Hippo, St., 181,
  200 n. 6
Austin, J. L., 248
autonomy,
  and moral worth, 512, 514
  and rights, 494
  of science, 73, 74
  of the will, 410, 412–13,
    439–42
Ayer, A. J.,
  and compatibilist
    determinism, 216, 225–31
  and metaethical subjectivism,
    267–8, 273

Baier, Kurt, 269
Barnes, Barry, 75–6
Barth, Karl, 200 n. 6
Beauvoir, Simone de, 79, 456
Beckett, Samuel, Waiting for
  Godot, 291
behavior,
  and belief, 156, 157–8

and causal laws, 225–6, 230
and character, 205–7, 227
and motives, 205–7, 219–23,
  237–8, 241–2, 249–52,
  400
behaviorism, sociological, and
  purpose of life, 298
being,
  dependent, 125–6, 127–8,
    129–32
  self-existent, 125–6, 130–1
belief,
  as causative, 232, 237
  and evidence, 4–5, 73–4,
    83–98, 159, 326–7
  and experience, 48, 64
  explanatory role, 65–6
  in Hume, 47–50
  and knowledge, 3
  and meaning of life, 287–8,
    341–5, 347–8, 350
  and Pascal's wager, 104,
    151–3, 155–66, 279
  philosophical, 89–90, 92, 94,
    96–8
  political, 90–2, 94, 96–8
  and practice, 157–8
  and probability, 51–3,
    158–65
  and reason, 167, 178
  religious, 92–8, 103, 279,
    281–302
  and respect for nature,
    510–12, 517
  scientific, 95–6
beneficence,
  in Kant, 400–1
  in Rawls, 440
benevolence of God, 103, 211,
  335
  and argument from design,
    166
  in Descartes, 10, 29–31

and divine racism, 203–5, 206–7
and male chauvinism, 199
and Pascal's wager, 164–5
and problem of evil, 105, 167–9, 172–4, 176, 183–4, 185–7
and utilitarianism, 392
Benhabib, Seyla, and Cornell, Drucilla, 458
Bennett, Jonathan, 70 n. 2
Bentham, Jeremy, 384, 386, 398 n. 2, 492, 493–4, 498
Bergman, Barbara, 462
biocentrism, 511–18
blame, *see* responsibility, moral
Bloch, Ernst, 297
Bloor, David, 75–6
Boer, Steven, 177
Bonhoeffer, Dietrich, 200 n. 6
boredom, and Schopenhauer, 304
Boserup, Ester, 458, 462
Bowker, John, 210
Boxill, Bernard, 366, 482–9
brain,
  in Descartes, 30–1
  and free will, 219, 222, 234–5
Brain, Russell, Lord, 497
Braithwaite, R. B., 360, 361 n. 16
Brink, David O., 269
Brown, Wendy, 475
Browne, Malcolm W., 95
Buddhism, and misogyny, 200 n. 7
Bunyan, John, *Pilgrim's Progress*, 360

Cain and Abel story, 185–7
Camus, Albert,
  and meaning of life, 279–80, 291, 294–5, 305–12, 326, 343
  and suffering, 203–5
causation,
  and arguments for existence of God, 7, 18–23, 124, 135–7, 138–9, 147–8
  and association of ideas, 37, 49–50
  and belief, 49–51
  and constraint, 216, 222, 228–30
  and dependent beings, 125–6, 127–8, 129–31
  and experience, 39–41, 42–4, 45–6, 54–6, 60, 66–8, 134–8

and free will, *see* determinism
  in Hume, 4, 49–61, 236, 354
  immanent/agent, 216, 231–8, 257–8, 333, 405
  and incompatibilism, 257–8
  and matters of fact, 38–41, 42, 60, 146
  and necessary connexion, 54–5, 56–7, 59–61
  and omnipotence of God, 171
  transeunt/event, 234–6
Chain of Being, 516
chance,
  and free will, 224, 227, 230, 247
  and meaning of life, 293, 297
  and order, 149–50
  and probability, 51–2, 53
character,
  and behavior, 205–7, 227
  formation, 261
  and will, 399–402
chauvinism, male, in religion, 104, 190–9
Chen, Martha Alter, 459, 462–3, 464, 465, 466
children, and suffering, 182–4, 185
Chisholm, Roderick,
  and compatibilism, 247–50
  and ethics of belief, 93
  and indeterminism, 216, 231–8
choice,
  and maximin rule, 436–8
  rational, 144–5, 374–82, 427, 429–30, 439–42
Christianity,
  and divine racism, 203–11
  and eschatology, 206–7, 209–10
  and existentialism, 313, 321
  and Great Chain of Being, 516
  as male chauvinist, 191–5, 197, 198, 199
  and meaning of life, 279, 287, 288, 299–300, 360–1
  and problem of evil, 179–87
  and utilitarianism, 392
citizenship, in Rawls, 432–3
Clarke, Samuel, 63–4 n. 15, 125, 126
Clarke, Thompson, 329 n. 2
class,
  and inherent worth, 514–15
  and preferential treatment, 486–7
  and race, 478

Clifford, W. K., and evidence for belief, 4–5, 83–7, 88–90, 92–8
clitoridectomy, 465–6
Cocteau, Jean, 321
coercion, and moral responsibility, 217, 228–9, 240–4, 252–3, 255
Coleridge, S. T., 87
commands, *see* law
Committee on Cruelty to Wild Animals (UK), 497
compatibilism, 215, 271–2
  and Ayer, 216, 225–31
  and Hume, 247
  and Sterba and Kourany, 216–17, 246–56
compensation, preferential treatment as, 483, 485–8
compliance, strict/partial, 424
compulsion, and freedom of the will, 216, 229, 231, 240, 252–3
computer skeptical hypothesis (CSH), 67, 68–9
Comte, Auguste, 321
Cone, James, 204
connexion, necessary, 53–61
consciousness,
  in Camus, 308
  in Flanagan, 336
  in Kekes, 342
  and language, 497–8
  in Nagel, 328–9
consciousness, false, 455, 476, 481 n. 2
consent,
  in Locke, 365, 417–20
  in Nozick, 365
  and property rights, 417–18
  in Rawls, 365–6
consequentialism, 267, 512; *see also* utilitarianism
consideration, moral, 484, 489, 491–5, 507–8
constraint, and causality, 216, 222, 228–30
constructivism, and moral objectivity, 269–70
contiguity, and association of ideas, 37, 49–50
cooperation, social, 422–3, 426, 427–9, 432
copresence, and spatial order, 142–3, 145, 147–9
Cornman, James, 70 n. 2
cosmological argument,
  in Anselm, 111
  in Aquinas, 124, 143–4, 232
  in Samuel Clarke, 125, 126

cosmological argument (*cont'd*)
first premise, 125–6, 132
in Hume, 7, 18–28, 125,
128, 129
in Leibniz, 125, 126
and order, 137, 141–50
as a posteriori argument, 111,
124, 135–6
and principle of sufficient
reason, 126, 127–8, 129,
131–3
responses to criticism,
129–31
in Rowe, 104, 122–33
second premise, 127–9,
131–3
counsels, and imperatives, 404,
405–6
Cox, D., 360, 361 n. 15
Craig, William Lane, 279,
288–302
Crick, Francis, 293, 297, 298
crime and punishment, and
incompatibilism, 258–60
CSH (computer skeptical
hypothesis), 67, 68–9
Cudworth, Ralph, 63–4 n. 15
custom, *see* habit
cynicism, in Kekes, 338
Cyprian of Carthage, St., 200
n. 6

Daly, Mary, 199
Dante Alighieri, 184
Darwall, Stephen, 269
Darwin, Charles, 143
Dasgupta, Partha, 462, 463,
464, 468 n. 7
Davies, J. Llewelyn, 398 n. 2
Davis, Lawrence H., 248
Dawkins, Richard, 75
death,
in Camus, 309
in Craig, 289–90, 297
in Flanagan, 332, 336
in Sartre, 289
in Tolstoy, 282, 287–8, 355,
356–7
see also suicide
deceit, and knowledge, 3–4,
9–10, 11–13, 16, 27, 65–
6
defiance, and the absurd, 312,
329
Democritus, 164
Dennett, Dan, 94
deontology, 267, 512
dependence, economic, 461–2,
463, 466
Descartes, René,
and animals, 495, 498, 516

and existence of God, 4, 7,
15–23, 103
and existence of material
things, 23–4
and gender, 4
and Hume, 63–4 n. 15
and immortality of the soul,
6–7
and intellect and imagination,
7, 13, 23–32
*Meditations on First
Philosophy*, 3, 6–32
and mind/body distinction,
6–7, 23–32, 516
and skepticism, 3, 6, 8–10,
286
and the will, 320
design, argument from, *see*
teleological argument
desires,
and happiness, 394–7
and will, 232, 236–8, 253,
397–8, 413 n. 4, 441
despair,
in Craig, 293
in Kekes, 338
in Nagel, 329
in Russell, 294
in Sartre, 320, 321
in Tolstoy, 282–3
determinism,
biological, 195–6, 298
hard (incompatibilist),
215–17, 218–24, 239,
245, 257–66
and human freedom, 8, 215,
218, 333
and life-hopes, 260–1
priority of existence over
essence, 318
and Skinner, 298
soft (compatibilist), 215, 216,
225–31, 246–56
theological, 173, 174
development studies, and
gender, 457–9, 460, 462,
466, 479
Diderot, Denis, 315
difference,
and biology, 73
and equal consideration of
interests, 484, 489, 491–
5
and feminism, 455–67
and meaning of life, 350,
351–2
and post-modernism, 456,
471
and race and gender, 73,
79–81, 470–6, 478–81
and rights, 490–2

Difference Thesis, 92, 94–7
discrimination,
and affirmative action, 366,
482–9
and gender, 79, 461–2
see also racism; sexism
distance, critical, 465–6, 470
DNA, recombinant, 73, 154–5
domination,
between women, 472, 475
and race and gender, 73, 79,
192–5, 455–67, 470–3,
480
and science, 76
Donne, John, 181
Dostoevsky, Fyodor, 183, 291,
295, 317, 334, 360
Double, Richard, 217, 267–74
doubt, *see* skepticism
Drèze, Jean, and Sen, Amartya,
464
dualism, mind/body, 6–7,
23–32, 516
Duff, Anthony, 165
Durkheim, Émile, 76
duty,
in Kant, 400–2, 407–8,
409–10, 413, 413–14 n. 4
in Mill, 391
and respect for nature,
511–12

Edwards, Jonathan, 232, 236
egoism, ethical, 365
individual, 374–5
as irrational, 377–82
universal, 375–7
Eiseley, Loren, 288
empiricism,
and Hume, 5
and principle of sufficient
reason, 162–3
environmental ethics, 366,
505–18
and attitude of respect for
nature, 505, 508–10
and denial of human
superiority, 510–18
and good of a being, 506–7,
510
and inherent worth, 506–8,
510–18
and justifiability of respect for
nature, 510–12
life-centered, 505–6
Epicureanism, 285, 287, 356,
359, 386–7
epistemology,
and commonsense hypothesis,
4, 14–15, 64–8
and skepticism, 3, 326–8, 329

see also Descartes, René;
    Hume, David; standpoint
    theory; Vogel, Jonathan
equality,
    and affirmative action, 76,
        366, 482–9
    and animals, 490–503
equilibrium, reflective, 431
Erasmus, Desiderius, and free
    will, 188–90 n. 17
eschatology, and suffering,
    206–7, 209–10
essence, and existence, 280,
    314–16, 318
essentialism, and gender,
    455–7, 465, 478–9
ethics,
    and animal rights, 366, 429,
        490–503
    of difference, 475–6
    and the environment, 366,
        505–18
    inductive, 384
    Kantian, 79, 365, 399–413
    in Mill, 365, 383–98
    in Plato, 365
    in Sterba, 374–82
    as transcendental, 341, 342,
        345–6
    utilitarian, 365, 383–98, 492
ethnicity, and suffering, 210–11
evidence,
    and belief, 4–5, 73–4, 83–98,
        159, 326–7
    and underdetermination of
        theory, 4, 64–5
evil, problem of, 105, 203
    adequate solutions, 167–8
    and Cain and Abel story,
        185–7
    evil as contribution to good
        of the whole, 171–2,
        182–5
    evil as counterpart to good,
        169–70
    evil as necessary means to
        good, 170–1
    evil as privation of good,
        168, 170
    fallacious solutions, 168–75
    and human free will, 172–5,
        177–87
    in Hume, 104, 150, 171, 176
    as illusory, 168
    in Mackie, 104, 167–75, 176
    moral evil, 172–5, 177, 182
    natural evil, 171, 177, 179,
        182
    in Stump, 104, 176–87
existence,
    and essence, 280, 314–16, 318

    as predicate, 117–18, 119
existence of God, 103
    and argument from causation,
        see cosmological argument
    in Descartes, 4, 7, 15–23,
        103
    and existentialism, 317–18,
        321
    and Pascal's wager, 104,
        151–3, 154–66, 279
    a priori/a posteriori
        arguments, 111, 124,
        135–6
    and problem of evil, 104,
        105, 150, 167–75, 176–87
    see also cosmological
        argument; ontological
        argument; teleological
        argument
existentialism, 279
    and anguish, 316–17, 320
    atheistic, 104, 280, 314–21
    Christian, 314
    definition, 314–16
    and forlornness, 317–21
    as humanism, 296, 313–21
    see also Camus, Albert; Sartre,
        Jean-Paul
exit theory, 463
experience,
    and belief, 48, 64
    and cause and effect, 39–41,
        42–4, 45–6, 54–7, 60,
        66–8, 134–8
    and deceit, 65–6
    and existence of God, 123,
        134–8, 139
    and habit, 46–7, 48, 50–1, 52
    and morality, 384
explanation,
    ad hoc, 65, 66
    scientific, 72, 143, 145–6,
        150 n. 2
    and simplicity, 65, 67, 69,
        72, 162, 163–4, 496–7
    skeptical, 67–70

fairness, justice as, 426–9, 435,
        438, 439–44
faith,
    and meaning of life, 279,
        285–302, 359–61
    and reason, 152, 285–6,
        358
family, and justice, 459, 460,
        461–4, 472
feeling, and action, 319, 398
femininity, and rationality,
        79–82
feminism,
    black, 474, 493

    and difference, 455–8,
        465–6, 470–6, 478–81
    and essentialism, 455–7, 465,
        478–9
    "interactive," 465, 466
    and multiculturalism, 366
    and philosophy, 81–2
    and science and social values,
        76, 77
    and social contract theory,
        366
    and theology, 193
Flanagan, Owen, 280, 330–6
Flax, Jane, 366, 470–6, 478–81
Flew, Antony, 280, 353–61
foot binding, 465–6
forgiveness, and
    incompatibilism, 263
forlornness, and Sartre, 317–21
Frankena, William K., 507
Frankfurt, Harry G., 217,
        239–46, 255–6, 258,
        273
free will,
    and alternate possibilities
        thesis, 217, 239–46, 257–8
    and compatibilism, 215, 216,
        225–31, 246–56
    as consciousness of necessity,
        227–8
    and different effort and
        attention, 250–1, 253
    and different knowledge and
        ability, 251–2, 253
    and different reasons and
        values, 252, 253
    as essence of human nature,
        205, 215–17
    as illusory, 144–5, 215–16,
        218–24, 293
    and incompatibilism, 88,
        215–17, 218–24, 239,
        257–66
    and libertarian indeterminism,
        215, 216, 231–8
    as moral term, 269–70, 411
    and problem of evil, 172–5,
        177–87
    in Sartre, 315, 318, 320
    and subjectivism, 217,
        267–74
    see also responsibility, moral
Freud, Sigmund, 195, 200 n. 9,
        293
Friedan, Betty, 456

Gale, Richard, 158–60
Galt, John, 398 n. 1
Gaunilo (monk), 104, 107–11,
        116–17
Gauthier, David, 269

gender,
  and cultural difference,
    455–67, 470
  and division of labor, 190–1,
    459, 460, 467 n. 5
  and epistemology, 3, 4,
    78–82
  false neutrality, 459
  and policy issues, 464, 472
  and race, 470–6, 478–81
  and religion, 104, 191–8
  and social construction,
    195–6
  see also domination
Gide, André, 319
Gilder, George, 73
Gilman, Charlotte Perkins, 456
Gilroy, Paul, 474, 478 n. 23
Glashow, Sheldon, 96
God,
  benevolence, *see* benevolence
    of God
  and causal laws, 171
  existence, *see* existence of God
  and maleness, 192–5, 196–7,
    198
  and meaning of life, 290–4,
    295, 298, 299–302, 334–5
  omnipotence, 166, 167–75,
    176–80, 183, 194
  omniscience, 166, 174, 176,
    178, 183, 194, 334
  perfection, 21–2, 104, 134,
    139
  and racism, 201–3
  as sum of his acts, 205–7
  and utilitarianism, 392
  will of God, 57–8, 392, 403,
    413 n. 4
  see also providence
Goldman, Alan, 70 n. 2, 71 n. 7
good,
  and good will, 399–402,
    404–13
  happiness as, 394
  of a living being, 506–8, 510,
    513, 515
  primary social, 433–4, 435,
    438, 440–3
Goodall, Jane, 498
goodness of God, *see*
    benevolence of God
Gossett, Thomas, 201
government,
  in Locke, 365, 414–20
  minimal, 365, 445
  in Nozick, 365, 445–53
  in Rawls, 365–6, 421–44
gratitude, and incompatibilism,
  263–4

greed, and Pascal's wager,
    156–7
guilt,
  and incompatibilism, 263,
    265
  in Kant, 442
habit,
  and cause and effect, 46–7,
    48, 50–1, 52, 60, 218, 220
  and desire, 397–8
  and meaning of life, 292,
    306, 324–5
Halevi, Judah, 158
happiness,
  in Flanagan, 331
  and immorality, 371–2
  in Kant, 399, 401, 402, 404,
    410, 412
  in Mill, 339–40, 365,
    384–93, 394
  and money, 395
  in Schopenhauer, 303
  in Tolstoy, 282–3, 288
  and virtue, 394–5
Haraway, Donna, 76
Harlan, Justice John Marshall,
  485
Harris, Angela, 457, 479–80
Hayek, F. A., 450–1
Hegel, G. W. F.,
  and reason, 81–2
  and sexual difference, 80
Heidegger, Martin,
  and anxiety, 308
  and existentialism, 314, 315
  and forlornness, 317
Hesiod, 370, 371
Hesse, Hermann, *Steppenwolf*,
  291
Hick, John, 178
Hillel, Rabbi, 157–8
Hirschman, Albert, 463
Hobart, R. E., 273
Hobbes, Thomas, and moral
  responsibility, 237, 269
Hocking, W. E., 293, 302 n. 5
Holbach, Paul, and
  incompatibilism, 216,
  218–24
holdings,
  historical/end-result
    principles, 447–9, 451, 453
  original acquisition, 446–7
  and patterning, 449–51, 453
  and rectification of injustice,
    447
  transfer, 446–7, 450–3
Homer, 370–1
Honderich, Ted, 257, 260

Hoyle, Fred, 297
human nature,
  dignity, 388, 412–13, 512
  as end in itself, 409–10, 412,
    512
  superiority, 512–18
  and utilitarianism, 393, 396–7
humanism,
  atheistic, 295
  existentialism as, 296,
    313–21
  Greek, 515–16
Hume, David,
  and association of ideas,
    36–7, 47–9
  and causation, 4, 134, 236,
    354
  and compatibilism, 247
  and cosmological argument,
    7, 18–28, 125, 128, 129
  Dialogues, 104, 125, 133–41,
    142, 147–50, 176
  *An Enquiry Concerning
    Human Understanding*,
    34–61, 146–7, 150, 354
  and evidence for belief, 159
  and justice, 424
  and metaethical subjectivism,
    268
  and necessary connexion,
    53–61
  and origin of ideas, 34–6
  and probability, 51–3, 135
  and problem of evil, 104,
    150, 171, 176
  and skepticism, 4, 37–51,
    134, 329–30 n. 3
  and teleological argument,
    104, 133–50, 166

ideas,
  association, 36–7, 47–9
  and belief, 47–8
  in Descartes, 16–23, 25–7
  in Hume, 34–7, 47–8, 52,
    54, 61
  as innate, 17–18, 61 n. 1
  origin, 34–6, 218
identity,
  gender, 455–8
  as illusory, 333
  racial/ethnic, 202, 474
  and self-expression, 331–2,
    333, 336
ideology, and science, 74–6
images, religious, 197–9
imagination,
  and belief, 48–9
  in Descartes, 7, 13–15, 23,
    25–6

in Hume, 34–6, 37, 47, 48, 60
and intellect, 7, 15, 23–32
immortality, 6–7
and meaning of life, 290–4, 296, 297, 299–300, 334, 356
imperative,
 Categorical: in Kant, 365, 385, 403–4, 406–9, 411–12; in Rawls, 440, 442
 conditional, 410
 hypothetical, 403–6, 440
 in Taylor, 509
impressions, in Hume, 34–6, 50, 54–5, 60–1
inclination, and duty, 400–2, 404, 408–9, 413 & n. 4
incompatibilism, 88, 215–17, 239, 245, 271–2
 benefits, 265–6
 and causal history, 257–8
 and crime and punishment, 258–60
 and free will subjectivism, 268
 and Holbach, 216, 218–24
 and meaning in life, 260–2
 and Pereboom, 217, 257–66
 and personal relationships, 262–5, 266
indeterminism, 271, 273
 libertarian, 215; and Chisholm, 216, 231–8
indifference principle, 162
indignation, and incompatibilism, 262, 265
individual,
 and ethical egoism, 374–5
 and justice, 421
 and utilitarianism, 389
inequality,
 gender, 73, 455–67, 470–1
 race, 73
 social, 423–4, 428, 432–6, 443
inference,
 in Descartes, 28
 in Double, 269
 in Hume, 4, 5, 38, 41–4, 46–7, 50–1, 52, 53, 60, 135, 147
 in Nozick, 446
 in Swinburne, 145
 in Vogel, 5, 65
insight, and evidence, 97–8
instinct, and morality, 384
institutions, social, and justice, 422–5, 427–8, 436, 443

instrumentalism, scientific, 270
integrity of science, 73–4, 75–6
intellect,
 female, 79
 and imagination, 7, 15, 23–32
intelligence, and moral status, 366
intention, and motive, 398 n. 2
interest,
 conflict of interests, 422, 499
 equal consideration of interests, 484, 489, 491–5, 507–8
 and justice, 421, 426, 427, 431, 436
 and mutual disinterest, 440–1
 and will, 410, 413–14 n. 4
intuition,
 and inference, 43
 and morality, 270–1, 384
 and principle of sufficient reason, 132
irony, and absurdity, 329
Islam, as male chauvinist, 191–5, 197, 199

Jackson, Frank, 70 n. 2
James, William, 133, 269, 335
Jaquette, Jane S., 462
Jaspers, Karl, 314
Jefferson, Thomas, 493
Jeffreys, H., 162
Jerome, St., 200 n. 6
John Paul II, Pope, 201 n. 16
Johnson, Samuel, 225
Jones, William R., 104–5, 201–11
Judaism,
 and divine racism, 203
 as male chauvinist, 191–5, 197, 199
judgements, false, in Descartes, 25–6, 29
justice,
 compensatory, 424
 and difference, 465
 distributive, 365, 423, 425, 431, 433, 435, 445–53; and acquisition of holdings, 446–7; entitlement theory, 446–53; as fairness, 426–9, 435, 438, 439–44; historical/end-result principles, 447–9, 451, 453; and patterning, 449–51, 453; and transfer of holdings, 446–7, 450–3
 and the family, 459, 460, 461–4, 472

and gender, 455, 458–61, 463, 465–7, 480
 in Hume, 424
 in Nozick, 445–53
 and original position, 426–8, 429–32, 435–9, 440–2, 465, 476
 principles, 432–9
 in Rawls, 365–6, 421–44, 465–6
 role, 421–3
 subject of, 423–5
 and veil of ignorance, 426, 430, 436–7, 438, 440, 465–6, 475

Kalin, Jesse, 376
Kane, Robert, 257, 264, 273
Kant, Immanuel,
 and Categorical Imperative, 365, 385, 403–9, 411–12, 440, 442
 and ethics, 237, 365, 399–413, 512
 and existence and essence, 314
 and good will, 399–402, 404–13
 and justice as fairness, 439–44
 and kingdom of ends, 410–12, 439, 442
 Metaphysics of Ethics, 384–5
 and moral objectivism, 270, 303, 402–3
 and ontological argument, 117
 and skepticism, 71 n. 9
 and social contract, 426, 439, 444 n. 5
 and temptation, 238
Kekes, John, 280, 337–52
Keller, Evelyn Fox, 76
Kierkegaard, Søren, and anguish, 316
kingdom of ends, in Kant, 410–12, 439, 442
knowledge,
 and belief, 3
 and deceit, 3–4, 9–10, 11–13, 16, 27, 65–6
 irrational, 358–9, 360
 and meaning of life, 284–6
 scientific, 4, 71–7
 and skepticism, 3, 326–8, 329
 social construction, 74
Kourany, Janet A., *see* Sterba, James P.

Kristeva, Julia, 456
Kuhn, Thomas, 76
Kurtz, Paul, 292, 302 n. 2

labor, and property rights,
    416–20
labor division, and gender,
    190–1, 459, 460, 467
    n. 5
language, and consciousness,
    497–8
Larson, L. C., 164
law, moral, 368, 384, 402–4,
    406–7, 409–13
law, natural,
    and cosmological argument,
        142–6, 149
    and free will, 218–19, 224–5,
        230, 247
    and order, 143–6
    and reason, 402, 415, 439,
        441–2
    and state of nature, 415
Lawrence, D. H., 358
Leibniz, Gottfried, 69, 125,
    126, 164, 237–8
Levin, Michael, 73
Lewis, David, 88–9, 91
liberation theology, 209
libertarianism,
    and indeterminism, 215, 216,
        231–8
    and Nozick, 365
liberty,
    and equality, 439–44
    and justice, 432, 434–5, 436,
        438–9
life,
    absurdity, see absurdity of
        life
    meaning, see meaning of life
    purpose, 297–9
    sanctity, 500–1
    value, 295–7
literalism, and religious images,
    197–9
Lloyd, Genevieve, and gender
    and knowledge, 4, 78–82
Locke, John,
    and freedom, 236
    and ideas, 61 n. 1
    and necessary connexion, 63
        n. 11, 63–4 n. 15
    and probability, 63 n. 9
    and property rights, 365,
        414–20
    and social contract, 426
    and state of nature, 414–16
    Two Treatises of Government,
        414–20

logical positivism, and
    metaethical subjectivism,
    271
Longino, Helen, and scientific
    knowledge, 4, 71–7
love,
    and duty, 401
    and incompatibilism, 264–5
Luther, Martin, and free will,
    188–90 n. 17
Luzatto, M. H., 161

Mackie, J. L.
    and metaethical subjectivism,
        267–8, 269, 271
    and Pascal's wager, 159
    and principle of sufficient
        reason, 162
    and problem of evil, 104,
        167–75, 176
    and skepticism, 70 n. 2
Maimonides, Moses, 157, 159
Malebranche, Nicolas, 63–4
    n. 15, 134
maleness,
    and dominance, 73, 79,
        192–5, 473
    and rationality, 78–9, 82
    and religion, 104, 190–9
Mansbridge, Jane, 467 n. 5
Mansel, Henry Longueville, 176
Marcel, Gabriel, 314
Marx, Karl, and task of
    philosophy, 269
Marxism,
    and construction of
        knowledge, 77
    and meaning of life, 294
Mathieu, Deborah, 104, 190–9
matters of fact, in Hume,
    37–41, 42–3, 45–7, 48, 60
maximin rule, 436–8
maxims, 402, 406–9, 410–13,
    413 n. 2, 414 n. 8, 438
Mazzocchi, Anthony, 155 n. 1
McCloskey, H. J., 176
McKay, Nellie Y., 473, 474
meaning of life,
    in Camus, 279–80, 291,
        294–5, 305–12, 326
    in Craig, 279, 288–302
    in Flanagan, 330–6
    in Flew, 280, 353–61
    and immortality, 290–4,
        296, 297, 299–300, 334,
        356
    in Kekes, 280, 337–52
    in Nagel, 322–9
    in Sartre, 279–80, 291, 292,
        294–5, 296, 313–21

in Schopenhauer, 279, 286,
    302–5, 307, 356
in Tolstoy, 279, 280, 281–8,
    353–9
Melden, A. I., 234, 237
Mele, Alfred, 272
memory,
    in Descartes, 24, 31–2
    in Holbach, 219
    in Hume, 34, 36, 38, 47,
        48–51
merit,
    and distributive justice, 449–
        51
    and inherent worth, 513–15,
        517
metacompatibilism, 271
metaphilosophy, and free will,
    269–70
Mill, J. S.,
    and compatibilism, 247
    and meaning of life, 339–41,
        349
    and problem of evil, 176
    and utilitarian ethics, 365,
        383–98
    and women and the family,
        460, 480
Milton, John, 87, 140
mind,
    in Descartes, 11–15, 30–1
    in Hume, 45
    as indivisible, 30
    and necessary connexion,
        55–8, 59
    and pain, 30–1
    and principle of order, 137
mind and body,
    in Descartes, 6–7, 11–15,
        23–32, 516
    in Holbach, 218
    in Hume, 55, 58, 59
misogyny, in monotheistic
    religions, 191–2, 195–9
Mohanty, Chandra Talpade,
    472, 473, 477 n. 7
money,
    and happiness, 395
    and property, 419
Monod, Jacques, 291
monotheism, and misogyny,
    191–2, 195–9
Moore, G. E., 232, 248
morality,
    and affirmative action, 76,
        366, 482–9
    and Categorical Imperative,
        365, 385, 403–9, 411–12,
        440, 442, 509
    and commands, 404

as compromise, 377–82
and duty, 391, 400–2, 407,
  413, 511–12
as good in itself, 348–9, 365,
  367–73
and instinct, 384
intuitive, 270–1, 384
and meaning of life, 345–52
as necessity, 367–8, 369
origin, 367–8
as rational, 365, 374–82, 384
and reason, 365, 374–82,
  384, 402, 439–41
and reward, 367, 369–73
and satisfaction, 348–9, 350,
  351–2, 354, 401
Morrison, Toni, 474, 477 n. 18
Morton, Nelle, 197, 198
motives,
  and alternate possibilities,
    241–2
  and behavior, 205–7, 400
  and determinism, 219–23,
    237–8, 249–52
  and habits, 324–5, 397
  and intention, 398 n. 2
  and meaning, 339–41, 344
multiculturalism, and feminism,
  366
Murray, Charles, 482, 489

Nagel, Thomas,
  and absurdity of life, 280,
    322–9, 340–1
  and moral objectivism, 270
Nash, John, 463
nature,
  balance, 505
  moral status, 366, 429,
    505–18
  universal laws, 407–8
necessity, see determinism
Newby, I. A., 201–2
Newman, J. H., 296
Newton, Isaac, 63 n. 15, 142
Niebuhr, Reinhold, 200 n. 6
Nielsen, Kai, 291
Nietzsche, Friedrich,
  and anti-Semitism, 296
  and meaning of life, 334–5,
    336 n. 1
  and nihilism, 293–4, 301
  and suicide, 305, 307
nihilism, and Nietzsche, 293–4,
  301
Nozick, Robert,
  and alternate possibilities
    thesis, 246 n. 2
  and distributive justice, 365,
    445–53

and meaning of life, 335, 336
  n. 2
Nussbaum, Martha, 466
Nygren, Anders, 203

objectivism,
  in Descartes, 18–19
  metaethical, 267, 268–9, 273
  moral, 268–71, 291–2, 295,
    298, 300, 402–9
objectivity,
  and meaning of life, 346–8,
    350
  scientific, 74, 75
  and social standpoint, 4, 77
obligation,
  in Kant, 402–4, 408, 410,
    413
  in Rawls, 427
  in Taylor, 505–6
Ofei-Aboagye, Rosemary
  Ofeibea, 481 n. 2
Okin, Susan Moller, 366,
  455–67, 470–3, 475–6,
  478–81
omnipotence,
  and free will, 173–4, 178,
    179–80, 183
  and goodness, 167–75, 176
  and logical impossibility, 169,
    179–80
  and maleness, 194
  Paradox of Omnipotence,
    169, 174–5
ontological argument,
  as a priori argument, 111,
    124
  in Anselm, 104, 106–7,
    111–22, 126
  and existence as predicate,
    117–18, 119
  and Gaunilo, 104, 107–11,
    116–17
  and God as possible being,
    118–19, 120–2
  in Rowe, 111–22
opportunity, equality, 433, 435,
  443, 460, 472
  and preferential treatment,
    483–4, 485, 486, 488–9
order,
  and cosmological argument,
    137, 141–50
  and free will, 224
  and meaning of life, 342–3,
    344–5, 348, 350–1

pain,
  and animals, 495–500, 502
  in Descartes, 25–6, 27, 30–1

and language, 497–8
and problem of evil, 171
and utility principle, 386, 389
Paley, William, Natural
  Theology, 142
Papanek, Hanna, 461, 464,
  465, 466
Paradox of Omnipotence, 169,
  174–5
Paradox of Sovereignty, 174–5
Pascal, Blaise, and wager of
  faith, 104, 151–3, 154–66,
  279
Payne, Buchner, 202
Pelagius, and free will, 181
perception, sensory,
  in Descartes, 13–15, 24–32
  in Hume, 34–6
  and impressions, 34–6, 50
  as thoughts, 34
Pereboom, Derk, and hard
  incompatibilism, 217,
  257–66, 272
perfectionism, and justice, 428
philosophy,
  as continuous with science,
    269
  as conversation, 275 n. 14
  and necessary connexion,
    53–9
  as praxis, 269–70
  as selfishness, 44–5
  and sexual difference, 78–
    82
  skeptical, 45–7, 89–90, 92,
    94, 96–8, 327
  as underpinnings, 275 n. 14
  as worldview construction,
    269–70, 274
Pindar, 372
Plantinga, Alvin, 177–8
Plato,
  and cosmological argument,
    124
  Euthyphro, 345
  Republic, 365, 367–73
pleasure,
  and the good, 403
  and utility, 386–9, 395–8
pluralism, and meaning of life,
  280, 351–2
Poincaré, Henri, 444 n. 8
politics, see government; justice;
  property
Ponge, 318
Pope, Alexander, 168
post-modernism,
  and death of the subject,
    332–3
  and difference, 456, 471

post-modernism (*cont'd*)
  and gender, 196, 456, 480
  and meaning of life, 298
  and philosophy of religion,
    104–5
poststructuralism, and death of
  the subject, 333
poverty,
  and gender, 460–4, 472
  and the working poor, 486
power, in families, 460–3, 464
praxis metaphilosophy, 269–70
principle of sufficient reason
  (PSR),
  and cosmological argument,
    126, 127–8, 129, 131–3
  and problem of evil, 176,
    177, 187
  and wager of faith, 162–5,
    359
probability,
  and Hume, 51–3, 135
  and Pascal's wager, 151–2,
    155–6, 158–65
  and problem of evil, 177–8
projectionism, 270
property, private,
  in Locke, 416–20
  in Nozick, 365, 453
providence, divine, and free
  will, 232–3
prudence, in Kant, 404, 405–6
PSR, *see* principle of sufficient
  reason
psychology, and purpose of life,
  297–8
punishment,
  and atheism, 296
  deterrence theories, 259
  and distributive justice, 448
  moral education theory,
    258–9
  quarantine model, 259–60
  as retribution, 259
  and state of nature, 415–16
  suffering as, 207–8
purdah, 465–6
Putnam, Ruth Anna, 465, 466

quietism, and existentialism,
  313, 317, 320–1

racism,
  and equality, 73, 491–3, 495
  and gender, 456–7, 470,
    471–6, 478–81
  and imbalance of suffering,
    201–2, 203–5
  and preferential treatment,
    482–9
  and religion, 104–5, 201–11

and science, 73, 76–7
and sociobiology, 74, 76
Rand, Ayn, 291
Rawls, John,
  and justice, 365–6, 421–44,
    465–6, 509–10
  and liberty, 432, 434–5, 436,
    438–44
  and moral objectivism, 270
real-world hypothesis (RWH),
  65–9
reality,
  in Descartes, 18–20, 27
  and matters of fact, 37–41,
    42, 60
reason,
  and experience, 39–41, 42–4,
    45–6, 54, 62–3 n. 7
  and faith, 152, 167, 178,
    258, 285–6
  and inference, 41–4, 46–7,
    51, 53, 496
  and justice, 427, 429, 431–2
  and matters of fact, 37–41,
    42–3, 45–7, 60, 394
  and moral superiority,
    515–16
  and morality, 365, 374–82,
    384, 402, 439–41
  seen as male, 4, 78–82
  see also law, natural
reason, practical,
  and moral objectivity, 269–70
  and will, 402–3, 408–9
reasoning,
  demonstrative, 42
  moral, 42, 269–70, 291
reciprocity, and justice, 428
Reid, Thomas, 232, 236, 237
relativism,
  and cultural difference, 455,
    470
  and gender, 82
  moral, 298–9, 300–1
religion,
  evidence for religious belief, 5
  and meaning of life, 279,
    281–8, 341–5, 348,
    350–2, 359–61
  and philosophy, 103–4
  and skepticism, 92–8
repentance, and
  incompatibilism, 265
resemblance, and association of
  ideas, 37, 49–50
respect,
  for nature, 366, 505–18
  for persons, 511–12, 518
responsibility, moral,
  alternate possibilities thesis,
    217, 239–46, 257–8

and compatibilism, 215–17,
  225–9, 247–56
and free will subjectivism,
  267–74
and incompatibilism, 215–17,
  239, 257–66
and libertarian indeterminism,
  216, 231–8
for natural world, 508–10
in Plato, 373
and utilitarianism, 394
retributivism, and
  incompatibilism, 259
revolt, and the absurd, 312
Richardson, Robert, 74–5
rights,
  of animals, 366, 490–503, 518
  and competing claims, 518
  and preferential treatment,
    482–9
  to property, 365, 414–20
  of women, 480, 490–1, 493
Roberts, J. Deotis, 204
Rorty, Richard, 275 n. 14, 336
  n. 1
Rousseau, Jean-Jacques, 79,
  426, 439, 442, 459
Rowe, William,
  and cosmological argument,
    104, 122–33
  and ontological argument,
    111–22
  and problem of evil, 178
Rubenstein, Richard, 211
Rue, Loyal D., 298–9
Russell, Bertrand,
  and cosmological argument,
    125, 128
  and meaning of life, 294, 295
RWH, *see* real-world hypothesis
Ryder, Richard, 503 n. 4
Ryle, G., 358

Sagan, Carl, 297
Sanday, Peggy, 462
Sartre, Jean-Paul,
  and death, 289
  and despair, 320, 321
  and existentialism as
    humanism, 296, 312–21
  and forlornness, 317–21
  and human nature, 205
  and meaning of existence,
    279–80, 291, 292, 294–5,
    296
satisfaction, and the good life,
  348–9, 350, 351–2, 354,
  401, 427
Schaeffer, Francis, 294
Schlesinger, George, 104,
  155–66

Schlick, Moritz, 247, 345
Schoeman, Ferdinand, 259
Schopenhauer, Arthur, 279,
    286, 302–5, 307, 356
science,
    and autonomy, 73, 74
    and beliefs, 95–6
    and instrumentalism, 270
    integrity, 73–4, 75–6
    and meaning of life, 284,
        286, 334–5, 342, 356, 359
    and philosophy, 269
    principles, 383
    and social constructionism,
        74, 75–6, 77
    and social values, 74–7
    as value-free, 3, 71–2, 73–4,
        75
Searle, John, 94
self,
    and causation, 216, 231–8
    as embodied, 473
    and meaning of life, 331–4
    noumenal/phenomenal, 441–
        2
self-consciousness,
    in Kekes, 342
    in Mill, 389–90, 397
    in Nagel, 328
self-expression, 331–2, 333,
    336, 441
self-interest,
    and absurdity of life, 291,
        299
    and duty, 400, 402
    and justice, 422, 427, 431
    and morality, 367–8, 374–82
    and Pascal's wager, 156–7
self-knowledge, in Descartes,
    11–14, 15–16, 20, 26
self-respect,
    and incompatibilism, 261
    and meaning of life, 336
    as primary good, 433, 442,
        443
self-sacrifice, 389–90
Sellars, Wilfrid, 248
Sen, Amartya, 460, 462, 466
senses,
    in Descartes, 7, 8, 13–15,
        24–31
    and error, 7, 8, 25–6, 31–2
sentience, and moral worth,
    366, 494–500, 502,
    507–12
seriousness, and absurdity, 324,
    326–8
Serjeant, Richard, 497, 504 n.
    9
sexism,
    and equality, 73, 491–3, 495

and preferential treatment,
    483
and racism, 456–7, 470, 471
and religion, 190–9
and science, 74, 76–7
and sociobiology, 74, 76
Shaheed, Farida, 481–2 n. 2
shame, in Kant, 442
Shaw, George Bernard, 468 n.
    11
Sidgwick, Henry, 441, 492
Simon, Pierre-Henri, 356–7,
    361 n. 7
simplicity, explanatory, 65, 67,
    69, 72, 162, 163–4, 496–7
Singer, Peter, 366, 490–503
skepticism,
    and absurdity, 324–8
    Cartesian, 64–70
    and Clifford, 83–7, 88–90,
        92–8
    and Descartes, 3, 6, 8–10,
        286
    epistemological, 3, 326–8,
        329
    and Hume, 4, 37–51, 60,
        134, 329–30 n. 3
    moral, 272
    philosophical, 89–90, 92, 94,
        96–8, 327
    political, 90–2, 94, 96–8
    religious, 92–8
    and van Inwagen, 87–98
    and Vogel, 4, 64–70
skill, and rules, 404–5
Skinner, B. F., 293, 298
Sklar, Lawrence, 71 n. 13
slavery, 473, 493
Slote, Michael, 70 n. 2
Smilansky, Saul, 261
Smith, John Maynard, 75
social constructionism,
    and scientific knowledge, 74,
        75–6, 77
    and self-identity, 332, 333
social contract theory,
    and feminism, 366
    and justice, 421, 426–9,
        430–2, 439, 441–2
society,
    and justice as fairness, 426–8
    and principles of justice, 433,
        438
    and role of justice, 422–5,
        426
sociobiology,
    and gender, 196
    and social values, 72, 73,
        74–5, 292
Socrates, 96, 181, 222–3, 356
    and morality, 365, 367–73

soul,
    and animals, 516
    immateriality, 218, 516
    immortality, 6–7
    see also mind
Sovereignty Paradox, 174–5
speciesism, 493, 495, 499–503,
    515, 527
Spelman, Elizabeth, 456–8,
    471, 472, 478–9
standpoint theory, 4, 77
state,
    minimal, 445
    and race and gender, 474
state of nature,
    in Locke, 414–16
    in Rawls, 426
Sterba, James P., and morality,
    365, 374–82
Sterba, James P. and Kourany,
    Janet A., and
    compatibilism, 216–17,
    246–56
Stich, Stephen, 104, 154–5
Stoics,
    and cosmic order, 342
    and Hume, 45
    and utilitarianism, 387–8,
        390
Strawson, G., 267, 274 n. 2
Strawson, P. F., 262, 271, 272
Stump, Eleonore, 104, 176–87
Suarez, Francisco de, 235
subjectivism,
    and death of the subject,
        332–3
    and existentialism, 312, 314,
        315–16, 321
    and feminism, 480
    free will, 217, 267–74
    and meaning of life, 346–8,
        350, 351
    metaethical, 217, 267–70,
        271, 273–4
succession, and temporal order,
    142–6, 148–9
suffering,
    and animals, 189–90 n. 24,
        494–500, 502–3
    biblical view, 207–10
    and children, 182–4, 185
    divine, 203–4
    ethnic, 210–11
    as evidence of divine favor,
        208
    and exaltation-liberation
        event, 209–10
    and God as sum of his acts,
        205–7
    as multievidential, 203–5,
        207–10

suffering (*cont'd*)
  as negative/positive, 209, 210
  as punishment, 207–8
  and racism, 201–2, 203–5
  as testing, 209, 211
  in Tolstoy, 283, 287–8, 355, 356–7
suicide,
  in Camus, 279, 305–10, 311–12, 329
  in Flanagan, 331
  in Kant, 407, 409–10
  in Locke, 415
  in Nagel, 329
  in Tolstoy, 282, 285, 286, 355–6, 357
Swinburne, Richard G.,
  and problem of evil, 178, 179
  and teleological argument, 104, 141–50

Taylor, Harriet, 456
Taylor, Paul W., 366, 505–18
Taylor, Richard, 292, 302 n. 3, 343, 346, 348
Taylor, Thomas, 490–1
teleological argument,
  as a posteriori argument, 124
  in Hume, 104, 133–50, 166
  in Swinburne, 104, 141–50
Tennyson, Alfred Lord, 190
Tertullian, 200 n. 6
theology,
  black, 204, 205–11
  feminist, 193
  of liberation, 209
  natural/revealed, 103
Thomson, James, 335
thought,
  in Descartes, 1, 12–15, 16–18, 24–7
  in Hume, 34–5
  and ideas, 16–21, 27, 34
  and matters of fact, 37
  and relations of ideas, 37
  and sensory perception, 13–15, 24–32, 34–6
Tillich, Paul, 289
Tolstoy, Leo,
  Anna Karenina, 354, 355, 356, 360
  My Confession, 279, 280, 281–8, 353–61
  War and Peace, 355, 360
transcendence,
  in Camus, 279
  in Flanagan, 280, 331, 336
  in Nagel, 328–9
  naturalistic, 280

in Sartre, 321
treatment, preferential, 482–9
  as compensation, 366, 483, 485–8
  consequences, 366, 483–4, 488–9
Trinkhaus, Erik, and Shipman, Pat, 95
Tronto, Joan, 468 n. 12
trust, 476, 480
truth,
  correspondence theory, 270
  in Descartes, 7, 16, 27–8, 31
  intuitive, 132
  in Nozick, 446–7
Truth, Sojourner, 456, 493

uncertainty, and choice, 436–8
underclass, black, 485–6
understanding,
  and Hume's skepticism, 37–44, 45–6, 60
  and imagination, 23–4, 26
  and inference, 51
  and ontological argument, 106–10, 112–15
utilitarianism,
  and justice, 428, 448
  and Mill, 365, 383–98
  proofs of, 394–8
  and religious belief, 392
utility principle,
  in Mill, 385–9, 392–4, 395
  in Rawls, 427–8, 435, 438–9

value, intrinsic, 508, 510, 512, 514–16
values,
  and belief, 291–2
  constitutive, 4, 72, 74–5
  contextual, 4, 72–3, 74
  social, 74–7
Van Inwagen, Peter, and evidence for belief, 5, 87–98
virtue,
  epistemic, 4–5, 67
  and utilitarianism, 394–5, 396, 397–8
Vogel, Jonathan, and skepticism, 4, 64–70
volition, *see* will, human
Voltaire, 315

Wager, Richard, 296
wager of faith,
  and criterion for betting, 160–1
  and greed, 156–7
  and "many gods" objection, 158–60, 161, 162–5, 166

and Pascal, 104, 151–3, 154–66, 279
  and principle of sufficient reason, 162–5
  and Schlesinger, 155–66
  and Stich, 154–5
Waller, Bruce, 258, 268, 271, 272
Washington, Joseph, 204
Weinberg, Steven, 96
Weissman, Irving, 504 n. 17
welfare state, in Rawls, 365–6
Wells, H. G., *The Time Machine*, 292
Wiggins, David, 348
will, human,
  autonomy, 410, 412–13, 439–42
  and causation, 144–5, 215–16, 218–24, 225–8
  as character, 399–402
  in Descartes, 320
  and desire, 397–8, 413 n. 4
  freedom, *see* free will
  in Hume, 55–9
  in Kant, 399–402, 404–13
  as practical reason, 402–3, 408–9
  in Sartre, 315, 320
  in Swinburne, 144–5, 179
Witten, Edward, 96
Wittgenstein, Ludwig,
  and ethics as transcendental, 341, 345–6
  and language and consciousness, 498
  and religious belief, 361
  and skepticism, 70 n. 1
  and Tolstoy, 359–60, 361
Wollstonecraft, Mary, 490
women, and private sphere, 80, 190–2, 195, 459, 464; *see also* femininity; gender; sexism
Woolf, Virginia, 456
worth, inherent, 399–401, 413, 506–12, 513–18
wrongdoing, and incompatibilism, 258–60, 266
Wurmbrand, Richard, 296
Wykstra, Steven, 178

Yette, Samuel, 204

Zeldovich, and Novikov, 297

Index compiled by Meg Davies (Registered Indexer, Society of Indexers)